Linda Berg-Cross, PhD

Basic Concepts in Family Therapy
An Introductory Text

Second Edition

*Pre-publication
REVIEWS,
COMMENTARIES,
EVALUATIONS . . .*

"**D**r. Berg-Cross has written a text that clearly explains even the most complex concepts of family therapy. Her smoothly flowing, conversational style of writing makes this a text that is easy to read and hard to put down. The exercises are effective in shifting what could remain an intellectual grasp of theoretical concepts into the realm of experiential understanding. Both the novice therapist and the seasoned practitioner will find *Basic Concepts in Family Therapy* an indispensable reference in the work of exploring the nuances of a family's experience."

Jacqueline Jackson, PhD
Clinical Administrator,
DC Commission on Mental
Health Services,
Washington, DC

"**L**inda Berg-Cross does an excellent job of incorporating major theoretical approaches to treating families into one source. *Basic Concepts in Family Therapy* is a comprehensive experiential resource text that no clinical student or practicing clinician should be without. The self-exploration exercises allow the reader to put theory into practice, while gaining greater insight into the influence of one's family of origin with a heightened appreciation for the impact of the social, emotional, and cultural climate that shapes one's life.

This book is an invaluable resource that should be read by all who wish to be challenged by insight that can be gained through introspection combined with theory. A deeper understanding of self and others is definitely the catalyst for change, change that can be brought about through the reading and application of this book."

Muriel Kennedy, PhD
Clinical Psychologist,
Government of the District
of Columbia,
Department of Human Services,
Commission on Mental Health Services

"**T**his is a lucid and illuminating book on family concepts that captures and engages one's own personal experience to use in the learning process. It has many unique prisms and lenses through which one can examine different kinds of family experiences, such as illnesses, rituals, and sibling relationships."

Thomas R. Kraft, PhD
Director of Psychology,
Psychiatric Institute of Washington,
Washington, DC

The Haworth Press, Inc.

Basic Concepts
in Family Therapy
An Introductory Text

Second Edition

Basic Concepts
in Family Therapy
An Introductory Text

Second Edition

Linda Berg-Cross, PhD

The Haworth Press
New York • London • Oxford

The Haworth Press, Inc., 10 Alice Street, Binghamton, NY 13904-1580

Cover design by Marylouise E. Doyle.

Library of Congress Cataloging-in-Publication Data

Berg-Cross, Linda.
    Basic concepts in family therapy : an introductory text / Linda Berg-Cross.—2nd ed.
        p.   cm.
Includes bibliographical references and index.
ISBN 0-7890-0646-4 (alk. paper).—ISBN 0-7890-0941-2 (pbk. : alk. paper).
    1. Family psychotherapy. I. Title.

RC488.5.B46 2000
616.89′156—dc21   99-054668
                                                                                      CIP

To my father,
Udel Berg

CONTENTS

ABOUT THE AUTHOR

Linda Berg-Cross, PhD, ABPP, is Professor of Psychology and former Director of the Clinical Psychology Program at Howard University in Washington, DC. She also has a private psychological practice where she works with groups, families, and individuals. Dr. Berg-Cross has published two textbooks, *Couples Therapy: A Cornerstone Approach* and *Basic Concepts in Family Therapy* (The Haworth Press, Inc.), as well as over forty articles in scholarly journals. Dr. Berg-Cross is certified in clinical psychology by the American Board of Professional Psychology and is a Fellow of the American Psychological Association Division of Family Psychology. She has worked as a consultant for numerous organizations including the Institute of Mental Health Initiatives in Washington, DC. Dr. Berg-Cross is a nationwide lecturer and trainer on brief treatment models for adolescents and their families.

Contributors

Amy Boscov, PhD, is a consultant in Wayne, New Jersey.

M. Seren Cohen, PhD, is in private practice in Madison, Wisconsin.

Sherry Molock, PhD, is Professor of Psychology at George Washington University, Washington, DC.

Dominicus So, PhD, is Assistant Professor of Psychology at Howard University, Washington, DC.

Carla Williams, MA, is currently a doctoral student in the Clinical Psychology Program of Howard University, Washington, DC.

Preface

Basic Concepts in Family Therapy: An Introductory Text presents twenty-two basic psychological concepts that you may use in understanding your family or, if you are a member of the helping professions, your clients' families. Each chapter focuses on a single concept using material from three sources:

- Family therapy literature
- Basic psychological and clinical research studies
- Cross-cultural research studies

By combining the findings of family therapy practitioners with the empirical findings of basic psychological researchers and cross-cultural researchers, we can deepen our understanding of the usefulness of each of these constructs, as well as their limitations.

Traditionally, family theorists have tried to develop broad, multiconceptual models of family functioning such as those of Minuchin, Bowen, Satir, Ackerman, and Zuk. Consequently, most books on the family have attempted to present each theory in toto and to examine its overall utility. *Basic Concepts in Family Therapy,* on the other hand, focuses on *concepts,* interrelating them with the relevant ideas of individual theorists. The intention is to present an integrated statement about each concept in the hope that this conceptual approach will further your understanding and enhance your analytical skills.

To help you apply the concepts in this book to ongoing family relationships, each chapter contains several "diaries" written by former students, clients, and friends as they analyzed their own families in terms of the concept being discussed. (Names and other identifying information have been changed.) These comments and insights from "real people" complement the formal presentation. In addition, each chapter guides you in exploring your own family of origin or nuclear family. You may use these "do-it-yourself" explorations to gain personal insight, as a springboard for group discussion, or as a catalyst for a deeper exploration of self and family with the assistance of a psychotherapist or counselor.

This book is *not* intended to present therapeutic strategies for treating dysfunctional families. I have made an effort to present only those few therapy techniques whose development is critical to the understanding of a given concept.

Readers who are interested in furthering their knowledge about specific concepts may refer to books and articles listed as Suggested Readings and to the books on family therapy listed at the end of this text. Some of this literature presents strategies for families whose dysfunction relates to the particular dimension discussed in the chapter. Purely theoretical works are also included, and I have appended to each chapter a list of films and works of fiction that illuminate specific concepts.

CAUTIONARY NOTES

Although I have tried to provide a broad range of theoretical concepts, these are not meant to be all-inclusive. The importance of the concepts presented has been demonstrated by clinical and empirical research, but it is quite possible that concepts not included in this book are equally important for understanding family dynamics—or even more important. I chose the topics covered because I personally prefer them, believe in them, and use them in my teaching and practice.

Wherever possible, I have tried to incorporate research findings both to support and to challenge the concepts presented. However, some of the studies cited are lacking methodological rigor and very, very few of them have been replicated at this time. In my judgment, providing examples of research helps pin down many of these seemingly elusive concepts, but I realize that in so doing, I run the risk of overstating the evidence presented. I urge readers to consider all the research presented here as fairly speculative.

Basic Concepts in Family Therapy is not intended to help therapists, students, or clients to deal with problems in their own families. Rather, it is intended to help these groups broaden their understanding of family functioning in general.

When doing the family exploration exercises, please do not look for a scoring or analysis key; none is included. There is no definitive way to determine the degree of adjustment within a family by doing the exercises. Their purpose is to help you apply your general understanding of each concept to your own family experience. The knowledge you gain may be very satisfying—or quite disturbing. If you become distressed by the family explorations, it is important to discuss these concerns with your teacher, your therapist, or a friend. Severe anger, depression, or distress is best handled by a professional therapist.

Acknowledgments

Many people have contributed to making this book possible. I would like to thank the editorial staff at Haworth, who demonstrated such high standards of professionalism, and a caring expertise. I most especially would like to thank Andy Roy, Melissa Devendorf, Bill Palmer, Trish Brown, Dawn Krisko, Peg Marr, Karen Fisher, Yvonne Kester, and Karen Sweredoski for their careful input and commitment to the project. The five contributing authors, Amy Boscov, Seren Cohen, Sherry Molock, Dominicus So, and Carla Williams, are part of my intellectual family, but all have been treasured students or personal friends for many years. They have added the needed breadth and depth to this second edition. It was a great privilege to work with them, and they have made this edition a much more relevant and comprehensive text. I would also like to thank the reviewers of the manuscript for their careful reading and comments, including Muriel Kennedy, Keith Erickson, Jaqueline Jackson, and Brenda Fawcett. For the fullness and contentment in my life, which nurtured my focus for this work, I need to thank my husband Gary; my son, Sage; my daughter, Gypsyamber; and my new son-in-law, Warren D'Souza. Finally, I have an ever-growing appreciation for the many students and clients who have daily enriched my understanding about the resiliency and healing power of families.

Introduction

The second edition of *Basic Concepts in Family Therapy: An Introductory Text* tries to build on the strengths of the first edition and introduces four modifications and/or additions.

First, each chapter includes new research where appropriate. An overwhelming proportion of the new material refers to ideas and articles that have become popular or worthy of investigation since 1990.

Second, the text has taken a slant designed to be particularly useful to therapists working in a family context with child or adolescent referred problems. The first edition was much more generic, but it had a slight leaning, I believe in retrospect, toward adults examining their families-of-origin and couples problems. This material still exists in the current text but has been expanded to more adequately include the child-with-a-problem perspective.

Third, five new chapters have been included. These five chapters deal with resiliency and poverty, adoption, chronic illness, spirituality and religion, and popular culture and parenting strategies. The new chapters make the book far more relevant for students and clinicians trying to bridge family theory and technique with the problems they see every day in their communities. These chapters follow the same general format as the original chapters, but each was written by an expert in that particular area.

Fourth, we have tried to add some relevant Web addresses and update all the videotherapy recommendations.

Although the book is still centered on therapeutic concepts and interventions rather than specific DSM-IV problem categories, the reader should be able to quickly discern how to implement the concepts when working with a particular diagnostic group. In general, it is suggested that family therapy should be conducted in five phases when the child has a DSM-IV disorder.

In phase I, the entire family is given psychoeducation about the problem. This includes (1) its prevalence and typical life course, (2) evidence about different proposed etiologies, (3) the types of interventions that are effective in treating the problem, and (4) the expected length of the proposed treatment.

1

In phase II, the therapist assesses the impact of the disorder both on the child and on the rest of the family, as well as how the family dynamics might have shaped or exacerbated the problems. To make a thorough assessment, each of the twenty-two relevant concepts is evaluated by the therapist (e.g., What are the resilient resources being used by the family to deal with this situation? Are the issues of separation and/or individuation affecting the expression or maintenance of the problem behavior? Are any family secrets hindering the family from creating a better solution to their problems?). In this phase, therapists are doing a two-sided assessment. First, they are assessing in what ways the problem is negatively and positively impacting on the family, as a whole, and every family member, in particular. Second, they are assessing how the family functioning is maintaining and/or exacerbating the problem.

In phase III, the family and therapist decide what therapeutic goals (i.e., family changes) will help them to resolve the current problem or make it more manageable.

In phase IV, the therapist designs a set of interventions to help the family achieve their goals. Many of the interventions described in this book could be used with individual families. However, it is hope that the concepts are vibrant enough that each therapist can custom design innovative interventions based on the concepts that are in line with the family's cultural values, thereby avoiding unnecessary resistance.

In phase V, the effects of the intervention are evaluated and a new strategy employed if needed.

We hope that this text will make new therapists feel more confident and seasoned therapists more creative.

UNIT I:
GETTING ACQUAINTED
WITH THE FAMILY

Studying this section will give you a deeper understanding of the contemporary family in its various forms, the psychological bonds that shape all families, and the developmental stages of the family life cycle. At first, the variety and complexity of family types may seem overwhelming. You may find it difficult to imagine conceptual prisms through which you can focus on such disparate social groups. The picture becomes still more confusing as you realize that any given family goes through a series of dramatic changes over time.

You can bring coherence to this baffling array of information simply by creating a genealogical diagram of the family and by identifying the most pressing issues likely to confront a family at each stage in its life cycle. In every family, certain vital statistics severely restrict the type and range of its interactions. For example, the number and ages of children, geographical dispersion of the family, physical illness, separations, and financial crises impose a certain reality upon family members, highlighting their strengths and weaknesses. You may crystallize individual roles, obligations, and conflicts by examining these facts.

This section demonstrates how the family's demography and stage in the life cycle affect family functions. It lays the foundation from which all the other concepts in this book can be explored.

Chapter 1

Exploring the Family Structure

During the first ten years of life, a child usually assumes that its family is normal and healthy—the prototype of what every family should be. This assumption need not imply that the child is totally satisfied with how his or her family functions. Most children yearn to change specific aspects of the family—to have a mom who bakes chocolate chip cookies every Friday, or a dad who can build a tree house, or parents who never fight. But such wishes do not change the inherent feeling that the current family structure is the "right" one. Children expect the outside world to mirror their own experiences. Normality consists of those experiences, and everything else is seen as abnormal. Except under extremely disruptive circumstances (divorce, abuse, chronic illness), children see the life they experience as the appropriate and desirable kind of family life.

As preadolescence approaches, and with it the dawn of mature reasoning, children begin to view their families more objectively and critically. Children develop an ideal of how families should function. Throughout their lives, children will use that ideal to judge—often harshly—how their families do in fact function.

Throughout adult life, the need to understand one's family becomes part of the need to understand oneself. The lifelong quest for self is in part a journey to discover the richness and meaning of ties with one's own clan.

WHAT IS A FAMILY?

The first step toward understanding the family is to realize that the parameters defining "family" are extremely elastic. *Webster's Third New International Dictionary* includes (among many others) the following five definitions:

- A group of persons in the service of the individual
- A group of people bound together by philosophical, religious, or other convictions

- A group of persons of common ancestry
- A group of individuals living under one roof
- The basic biosocial unit in society having at its nucleus two or more adults living together and cooperating in the care and rearing of their own or adopted children

From these varied definitions you can see that some people define a family as sharing a genetic heritage; to others, families are formed by occupying the same physical dwelling; for still others, a commonality in purpose or philosophy is the cardinal feature. In today's world, all these definitions are valid and give insight into the different notions we each have of family.

In actuality, the definition of a "basic biosocial unit" as two or more adults living together with their children now describes less than 75 percent of U.S. families (46.5 million children). The other 25 percent (15.6 million children) are living as single-parent families, stepfamilies, and foster families (U.S. Bureau of the Census, 1984a). Moreover, a staggering number of children will experience these alternative family forms in the future; current estimates are that 50 percent of all children born in 1985 will live part of their childhood in a single-parent family (U.S. Bureau of the Census, 1984b). Since a large proportion of divorced persons remarry, most children who live in single-parent situations because of divorce will also experience stepfamilies (Jacobson, 1983).

For the growing number of adults who are choosing not to marry or have children, nontraditional families are assuming increasing importance. A nonbiological "psychological family" may include:

- The honorary relative—a lifelong friend who is viewed psychologically as a sibling, aunt, or uncle, depending on age
- The workplace family
- The chosen family—people an adult designates as "part of the family." No apparent ties connect this kind of family but rather a curious mixture of fate and choice (Lindsey, 1981)

The Real versus the Ideal Family

Whatever its nature and composition, the ideal family is always pictured as a happy, contented, and conflict-free group. But has the family ever really existed in such an idyllic state? Most people envision a Golden Age of the happy family, although the specific period chosen varies greatly.

Some people fervently believe that Norman Rockwell's *Saturday Evening Post* covers are authentic portrayals—that apple pies filling the house with the mouth-watering fragrance of cinnamon, and grandmas sitting happily in rocking chairs were nearly universal life experiences of the 1930s and 1940s. Others view the feudal era or the Renaissance as times of family cohesiveness and strength. In reality, each family form that has evolved has suffered from a multitude of weaknesses even though it may have been the best possible social structure available in its time.

Weighing Costs and Benefits

Instead of searching for ideal family forms helpful to all people at all times, we need to subject family forms to an intensive analysis of their cost/benefit ratio. Do today's family structures benefit individuals and their families as a whole? Is the ratio of costs to benefits (that is, the cost of necessary trade-offs) a reasonable one for the individual? For the family? For society? Can society increase the benefits or lower the costs (economic, physiological, psychosocial) of various family structures? Can any given family do so for itself?

Psychological Characteristics of the Family

Although it is difficult if not impossible to develop a simple definition of the physical features that constitute a family, the psychological characteristics that define a family are surprisingly easy to specify. At least six characteristics define the most important psychological dimensions inherent in the term "family": (1) a sense of mutual commitment, (2) a sense of history and continuity, (3) the potential for and expectation of long-lasting relationships that are (4) extensive and (5) intense, and (6) social responsibility of the adults for the welfare and development of any children in the group (Schaefer, 1972; Lindsey, 1981).

Commitment and Continuity

A sense of commitment and a sense of continuity and history are probably the most critical psychological dimensions. Lindsey (1981) studied how these two factors work to create a family among friends. Throughout her interviews she found that two major criteria were repeatedly expressed for inclusion in the "friend family": accessibility in emergencies and history. The first appeared to be the more important (p. 54):

> "If I got arrested I could call them up and they'd bring me a lawyer," says Kathy. "In an emergency they'd be there without question,"

says Barb. "Anyone I consider family, I'd always give them money if they needed it, no questions asked." "You might bring it down to who I know would come to my funeral," says Jane.

Nevertheless, history is important, too. It is defined not only as knowing one another for some time but also as having been involved in important parts of one another's lives. Lindsey quotes Jane Howard (1978): "The best chosen clans . . . endure by accumulating a history solid enough to suggest a future." To Lindsey (1981:101):

> . . . this sense of continuity, of history, solidifies kinship more deeply even than the sense of availability in emergency. We grow and change; we move from town to town; we become involved in new enterprises. One of the most positive things the biological family gives us is a sense of stability in the midst of this change—a stability that at its best, encourages change and growth, since we are not threatened with utter rootlessness if we dare to grow in different directions from those we love. The sense of a deep and permanent connection with people who have grown in different directions is essential for maintaining continuity: I exist in this moment and this place, but I am part of my own past and part of my own future, part of others' pasts and others' futures. We are thus bonded to those we grew up with—parents, siblings, relatives, and honorary relatives who were regular parts of our childhood lives. As we grow older, we create other histories: Just as my parents and brothers have shared a time in my life on a level no one else has, so have a few key friends shared times that my parents and brothers, and other friends, have not. Such friends become a part of the fabric of one's existence: as the cliche goes, they are "in one's blood." It is lovely when one continues to share interests and enthusiasms with such friends, or with one's parents and siblings, and it allows the relationship to grow and deepen, but it is not essential to the continuation of the bonding. At some point the bonding becomes permanent—the absence, even the death of the other person doesn't eliminate it.

Love, commitment, continuity—these create deep and indelible bondings. Whatever the structure they exist in, they are the material of which kinship is made.

Potential for Endurance

Most relationships among family members begin at birth (as in the case of children) or at a major adult developmental milestone (as in the case of spouses) and are expected to continue until death or disaster. Family members help one another mark the progress of their own development as their life plans unfold over the years. Although the nature and intensity of relationships between family members vary with age and personality, it is rare to forget one's family completely for years on end. Continuity is part of what one seeks and gains from a family.

Multiple Interactions and High Intensity

Usually, family relationships are quite extensive. That is, the parents and children or other members interact in many different situations and share many different experiences. Moreover, family relationships are generally intense. Feelings of love coexist with feelings of hatred, and admiration is often mixed with jealousy.

Adult Responsibility for Children

The final characteristic that defines a family is social recognition that the adults in the structure are responsible for the welfare and development of the children.

It is the responsibility of the parents to care for the children when they are ill, support them when they feel defeated, and help them when they are in trouble. Most of the anxiety and despair involved with parenting comes from the fear that one has not successfully carried out these responsibilities. Thus, when a child is ill or in a fight or disobeys, the parent's pain of watching a loved one suffer is compounded by the self-doubting pain of unfulfilled responsibilities.

THE FAMILY LIFE CYCLES

Life cycles distinct to each type of family doubtless exist, but only the traditional family life cycle has been extensively studied. The traditional family consists of an adult male and female with one or more children. Marriage, in the legal sense, is not needed to create a traditional family.

Table 1.1 outlines the six major stages of this traditional cycle. At each stage a person must learn to let go of some family members or develop different degrees of autonomy from and interdependence with them. The important relationship shifts that are characteristic of each stage are described on the right side of Table 1.1. The detailed discussion of each stage that follows draws heavily on the discussion of family life cycles presented by Carter and McGoldrick (1980), Colarusso and Nemiroff (1981), and Karpel and Strauss (1983).

TABLE 1.1. Stages of the Family Life Cycle

Stage of Life Cycle	**Second-Order Changes in Family Status Required to Proceed Developmentally**
1. Between Families: The Unattached Young Adult	a. Differentiation of self in relation to family of origin b. Development of intimate peer relationships c. Establishment of self in work
2. The Joining of Families Through Marriage: The Newly Married Couple	a. Formation of marital system b. Realignment of relationships with external families and friends to include spouse
3. The Family with Young Children	a. Adjusting marital system to make space for children b. Taking on parenting roles c. Realignment of relationships with extended family to include parenting and grandparenting roles
4. The Family with Adolescents	a. Shifting of parent/child relationships permit adolescent to move in and out of system b. Refocus on midlife marital and career issues c. Beginning shift toward concerns for older generation
5. Launching Children and Moving On	a. Renegotiation of marital system as a dyad b. Development of adult-to-adult relationships between grown children and their parents c. Realignment of relationships to include in-laws and grandchildren d. Realignment related to disabilities and death of parents (grandparents)
6. The Family in Later Life	a. Maintaining own and/or couple functioning and interests in face of physiological decline; exploration of new familial and social role options b. Support for a more central role for middle generation

TABLE 1.1 *(continued)*

c. Making room in the system for the wisdom and experience of the elderly, supporting the older generation without overfunctioning for them

d. Dealing with loss of spouse, siblings, and other peers and preparation for own death; life review and integration

Source: Adapted from Carter, E. A. and McGoldrick, M., 1980, *The Family Life Cycle and Family Therapy: An Overview.* New York: Gardner Press, p. 19.

Stage 1: The Unattached Young Adult

The first stage of each family's life cycle begins with an unattached young adult. It is important for the young adult to create an identity at least partially independent of the family of origin before marrying or entering some other long-term commitment to a partner. Young adults have to be able to think and act autonomously. They need to develop mature values and attitudes that lead to self-fulfillment; parental approval, though valuable, is secondary. Young adults who cannot achieve psychological independence from their families will be ill-equipped for marriage. A work identity is also a prerequisite to establishing independent selfhood. Work identities help link young individuals to the adult society, give them a sense of purposefulness, and develop a capacity for self-reliance.

In his essay "The Eight Stages of Man," Erikson (1963) stresses the importance of developing a strong personal identity before attempting to develop an intimate relationship. He describes how the successful development of an intimate relationship requires that two people know what they feel, think, and stand for in order to share their sense of being with each other. Without a strong sense of identity this type of sharing is impossible, and deep, lasting, intimate relationships will remain elusive.

Thus, becoming an autonomous adult requires that individuals take risks to discover, explore, and generate alternative options that expand their horizons and help them discover their potentials. At the same time, they must create an initial adult life structure that has stability and continuity.

Stage 2: Marriage

The major task for any newly married couple is adjusting to the demands inherent in the marital situation. Each spouse must learn how to deal with the everyday moods and problems of another person. Household tasks must be organized and a division of labor decided upon. Methods of arguing and making up need to be instituted. Relationships with relatives and the need for privacy must also be worked out. McGoldrick (1980:108) believes that this period of marital adjustment will be more difficult if any of the following are true:

1. The couple meets or marries shortly after a significant loss.
2. The wish to distance from one's family of origin is a factor in the marriage.
3. The family backgrounds of the spouses are significantly different (religion, education, social class, ethnicity, the age of the partners, and the like).
4. The couple has incompatible sibling constellations.
5. The couple resides either extremely close to or at a great distance from either family of origin.
6. The couple is dependent on either extended family financially, physically, or emotionally.
7. The couple marries before age twenty or after age thirty.
8. The couple marries after an acquaintanceship of less than six months or after more than three years of engagement.
9. The wedding occurs without family or friends present.
10. The wife becomes pregnant before or within the first year of marriage.
11. Either spouse has a poor relationship with his or her siblings or parents.
12. Either spouse considers his or her childhood or adolescence as an unhappy time.
13. Marital patterns in either extended family were unstable.

Stage 3: The Family with Young Children

For most couples, the birth of a baby signifies that they are indeed a legitimate, socially sanctioned family. Each child strengthens the bonds between husband and wife as well as the bonds between the couple and their parents. The joy and excitement attending the birth of each child coexist with anxieties over one's ability to be responsible for caring for the new life. New parents worry about repeating the mistakes of previous generations and are unsure how to avoid those pitfalls.

Spouses find that instead of relating directly to each other with their full attention and interest, they are now relating to each other through the children. Most of their conversations, as well as many of their plans and frustrations, center on the children. Typically, parents miss the intimacy and communication they had before and yet are so overwhelmed and depressed by the stresses of parenthood that they find it difficult to focus on their relationship and to satisfy each other's needs.

The third stage of the family life cycle also heralds a new relationship with one's family of origin as the elder and middle generations concurrently experience the role of parenting. The elder generation finds it necessary to develop grandparent roles. Although the importance of the grandparent is currently diminishing, significant numbers of grandparents find considerable satisfaction in the role of "spoiler," "advice giver," or "gift giver."

Stage 4: The Family with Adolescents

As soon as adolescents begin socializing outside the home with their peers and other adults, both the adolescent and his or her family must balance the adolescent's need for autonomy with the need to "belong" and to be loyal to the family. Adolescents want and need to venture out into the world. Parents need to learn how to guide these explorations while managing their own fears about their teenagers' safety outside the home and the influences to which they will be exposed. Parents can err by holding adolescents too close to the family for too long or by pushing them too far from the family too fast. Even when the adolescent is home, this stage involves ever-increasing expectations of autonomy. Parental care is slowly replaced by self-care as adolescents learn to buy their own clothes, organize their own schoolwork, clean the house, earn money, and hold a job.

As adolescents face career choices and sexual confusions, many parents are facing similar crises of their own. During midlife crises, parents are also asking themselves: "What have I done with my life?" "What do I want to make out of it?" "Should I choose a new career?" "Should I have an affair?" When this self-searching reveals a flawed life structure, parents go through a period of considerable developmental crisis and turmoil as they attempt changes. Often, this tumultuous life review is coupled with a new concern for one's own parents, who are becoming less self-sufficient. Thus, three generations of the family may be facing developmental crises within the same period.

Stage 5: Launching Children and Moving On

The basic task of the fifth stage is to separate without breaking family ties. To accomplish this task successfully, parents and children need to develop compatible expectations about the nature of their relationship.

They must resolve such questions as: "How often should I write or call?" "How often should I visit?" "What kind of help can I expect to give? To receive?" Both generations face the challenge of creating a busy, meaningful, independent lifestyle while finding time to maintain their investment in one another's well-being. Later, as children marry and begin their own families, these issues will need to be renegotiated.

Once the children leave home, the couple is left with the proverbial "empty nest." They can reestablish their relationship, focusing on each other once again. For fortunate couples, increased leisure time and relatively good health can make this period one of the most satisfying in the entire life cycle.

Unfortunately, near the end of this stage, parents invariably lose a variety of important relationships. As their own parents die they find they are "next in line"; they have to face the unknown without the "backup" they once had. Retirement brings loss of earnings and a reduced sense of purposefulness. Friends relocate, neighborhoods change, and priorities are rearranged.

Stage 6: The Family in Later Life

The individual entering life's final stage needs to maintain interest in the world and a sense of humor while facing physiological decline and reduced lifestyle options. Children and grandchildren are busy with their own lives. It becomes increasingly difficult to develop a meaningful and important family role in which experience and wisdom are needed and valued. Relationship losses continue to mount as spouse, siblings, and dear friends begin to die. One begins to prepare for one's own death by trying to understand the meaning and purpose of his or her own unique family life cycle.

TECHNIQUES FOR FOCUSING ON THE FAMILY

The First Interview

The first interview usually begins with the initial phone contact or referral from the physician or parent. The pertinent information to get at the initial contact (beyond where and when the meeting will take place) includes:

1. Sex, age, grade, and school of the identified child client
2. The nature of the presenting problem and when it first began

3. Family members who would be available for the initial session
4. Sending summaries, medical records, academic records, or other documented reports on the identified child client
5. Requesting that each person in the family make a list of what they think the therapist should know and understand about the problem

Whenever possible, it is good to give some appropriate self-report instruments to the family members before the first session (either in the office prior to the interview or, better yet, through the mail, so that the therapist has a chance to review the information before he or she sees the family).

Self-Report Instruments

Self-report instruments are the most widely used empirical assessment device for diagnosing and evaluating family problems. But the use of self-report among family members is still controversial since the reliability among different family members is exceedingly low. Indeed, the more dysfunctional the family, the less they may agree on what the problems are or how the family has dealt with them. Most family scholars, though, applaud the ability of the tests to separate the individual realities of each family member. Also, when mother, father, and child cannot agree on whether affection is shared easily within the family, the therapist had better be cautious about his or her own observations and judgments in that area. Indeed, self-reports from different family members prevent therapists' initial biases and "take" on the family problem from going unchecked and unchallenged.

A number of powerful tools have been developed in the last decade to help family psychologists understand the type of events most stressful to family systems and the systemic changes that can occur when a family faces a life crisis. Most notably, McCubbin, Patterson, and Wilson (1996) have developed the Family Inventory of Life Events and Changes (FILE, which is available in English, Spanish, and Hebrew and for which there are separate Adolescent and Adult versions) and the Family Crisis Oriented Personal Evaluation Scales (F-COPES, available in four languages including French and for which there is an adolescent version and a young adult version, McCubbin, Olsen, and Larsen, 1996).

The FILE is a self-report instrument that asks family members to note which of seventy-one life changes and events their family has experienced over the past twelve months. The items cluster into nine stressor categories that have been shown to create disequilibrium in a family and force changes in interaction styles, roles, and boundaries. The nine areas include intrafamily strains, marital strains, pregnancy/childbearing strains, finance and business strains, work-family transitions, illness and family care strains, losses, transitions in and out of the family, and family legal violations.

When used as a simple screening instrument, noting all the "yes" responses ensures an appropriately broad intake interview. However, the scale can be scored using a weighted item method in which the intensity of each change is noted and the sum of all the weighted items can be compared to a table of normative scores based on the life cycle stage of the family (Gerson, 1995). Using this more sophisticated method, the therapist can see if a family that is intensely stressed is coping fairly well or if a family experiencing a relatively modest intensity of stress is unduly taxed. Is the new baby being experienced as more or less stressful than the average family finds such an event? The weighted scoring system of the FILE also allows the clinician to see how different family members are experiencing the same events. The new baby may be an overwhelmingly intense stressor to Dad but only a moderately intense stressor for Mom. Any instruments that help the family members and therapists see the different family realities will help create understanding and more realistic solutions for the family.

The F-COPES (McCubbin, Olson, and Larsen, 1996) is a thirty-item instrument that asks each family member to report how often the family uses the following five coping styles to deal with stress and changes in the family: acquiring social support, reframing, seeking spiritual support, mobilizing the family to acquire and accept help, and passive appraisal. The assumption is that the more flexible and adaptive the family, the wider the range of coping styles at their disposal. Although certain crises tend to "pull" for certain coping styles (e.g., the care of a family member after major surgery may "pull" for coping skills centered on acquiring social support, and the failure of a child to be chosen for a gifted and talented program may "pull" for a reframing of the child's talents or the school's effectiveness in identifying talented children), the current thinking is that the ability to use all five coping styles is most effective in protecting the family against disorganization and inefficiencies. The FILE and F-COPES are both available without charge and are found in *Family Assessment: Resiliency, Coping, and Adaptation—Inventories for Research and Practice* (McCubbin, Thompson, and McCubbin, 1996).

The most widely used family functioning self-report in research and practice settings may be the Family Adaptability and Cohesion Evaluation Scale III (FACES-III). FACES is a twenty-item, five-point Likert scale, used to measure two critical dimensions in family structure: cohesion and adaptability. Cohesion within the family is defined as an emotional, intellectual, and physical oneness among family members. It is a way of assessing how bonded they are with one another. Adaptability is defined as the family's ability to shift its power structure, roles, and rules of relationship in unfamiliar, stressful, or transitional situations. It is a measure of how flexible the family is in sharing roles and approaching multiple solution paths to a problem. The cohesion subscale has been shown to be a highly valid measure of family closeness, but the adaptability scale has had some validity problems as a measure of problem-solving effectiveness (Franklin and Streeter, 1993). Means and standard deviations are provided for a variety of population groups.

FACES was developed to test the circumplex model of family functioning, which assumed that moderate degrees of cohesion and adaptability would be related to the greatest satisfaction and the most robust psychological functioning among family members. The model posited that the more extreme families were on these two dimensions, the greater the risk of individual pathology and dissatisfaction within the family. The idea was that moderation in family functioning was most adaptive. However, therapists knew that for many culture groups there cannot be "too much closeness"—it simply is the closer, the better. For others, autonomy is highly valued and you just cannot be too independent to meet the family's ideal state of functioning. Indeed, Perosa and Perosa (1990), along with many others, found that high scores on cohesion and adaptability (as opposed to central range scores) correspond to healthy family functioning.

As more and more data mounted, Olson (1991) revised his theory so that healthy family functioning was related to increasing amounts of cohesion and adaptability, but only when looking at how any one family rated themselves within their family "niche." He still maintained that the ability to dramatically change the type of family you have is curvilinearly related to adaptability and cohesion. That is, within any particular family type, there is a curvilinear relationship between adaptability and cohesion. "Extreme" families have more difficulty changing their type of interactions and "balanced" families are better able to transform the type of interactions they have based on need and stage of development.

In the circumplex model, families are categorized as balanced, mid range, or extreme based on the combination of their adaptability and cohesion scores. Within the balanced, mid range, and extreme family types, the more cohesion and adaptability, the better they function. However, in order to change from one family type to another (from a balanced family into a mid range or extreme family), moderate levels of cohesion and adaptability are needed. Great extremes in cohesion (high or low) and/or adaptability (high or low) are limiting and make the transition difficult. It is when the family needs to make a second-order change and alter "how" they interact that moderation gives the needed wiggle room.

Thus, Olson postulates that within the extreme family types, those with more cohesion and adaptability will function better than those with lower levels of cohesion and adaptability. However, extreme families become that way because, at a conceptual level, their overall levels of adaptability and cohesion are too extreme. They are unable to create a second-order change and create new types of interactions. They are limited to increasing or decreasing the intensity of the interactions that history has dictated they use. Finding a way to assess this second-order curvilinear relationship is currently a major thrust.

Despite the theoretical issues surrounding these dimensions and their limited ability to accurately predict dysfunction among groups of families, I have found that family members grasp the psychological importance of these dimensions and can understand how different realities of family life are reflected in the different categories.

Usually, family members complete the instrument twice, once indicating their current perceptions of how the family is operating and once indicating how they would like the family to operate. For example, a cohesion item might read "We like to spend time with one another" and a ten-year-old might respond that this sentence describes his family "almost never" (a 1 rating) but on the second time through he might say that he would like his family to be that way "almost always" (a 5 rating). The disparity between the ideal and the current ratings gives a good indication of how unhappy someone is with the family's actual mode of relating.

The easiest and quickest of the self-report items is the Family APGAR (Smilkstein, 1978). Available for free and taking only a minute of time, a family member is asked to rate his or her family on five dimensions. Each dimension is scored with a 0, 1, or 2, giving a total score range of 0 to 10. Just like the Infant APGAR that all American babies receive within a minute of birth (yes, our testing starts that early), the 0-10 score is a quick screening guide as to whether the infant needs immediate medical intervention, should be monitored closely, or is robust and without any apparent problem (see Table 1.2).

Projective Instruments

The Kvebaek Family Sculpture Technique (KFST) assesses family members' self-report of the emotional distance between all the various members using spatial placement of symbolic figures. Each individual in the family gets to place the figures separately, indicating how emotionally

TABLE 1.2. Family APGAR Questionnaire

1. I am satisfied that I can turn to my family for help when something is troubling me.

   Almost always (2 points)
   Some of the time (1 point)
   Hardly ever (0 points)

2. I am satisfied with the way that my family talks over things with me and shares problems with me.

   Almost always (2 points)
   Some of the time (1 point)
   Hardly ever (0 points)

3. I am satisfied that my family expresses affection and responds to my emotions such as anger, sorrow, and love.

   Almost always (2 points)
   Some of the time (1 point)
   Hardly ever (0 points)

4. I am satisfied with the way my family and I share time together.

   Almost always (2 points)
   Some of the time (1 point)
   Hardly ever (0 points)

5. I am satisfied with the way my family accepts and supports my wishes to take on new activities and directions.

   Almost always (2 points)
   Some of the time (1 point)
   Hardly ever (0 points)

Source: Smilkstein (1978, p. 1238).

distant they experience each family member from one another. Then the family as a whole tries to place the figures by consensus. Validity studies of the KFST suggest that it is a useful clinical tool (Cromwell, Fournier, and Kvebaek, 1981).

The studies and clinical procedures typically require every family member to pick a different piece of wood to represent each family member. Then each is told to place the pieces on a square grid according to how close he or she thinks each family member feels toward the others. Each individual does this three separate times, away from the other members of the family. The first time, the client does the "perceived real sculpture," which requires placing the figures according to the "reality." The second time, the client does a "tension sculpture," which describes how the family members feel about one another when there is a conflict. The third time, each individual creates the "ideal sculpture," which represents how the family would be if things were perfect. In the joint session, the family is usually told to reach a consensus through discussion of each scenario, with no more than ten minutes being allotted to any one scenario.

To record the answers, the therapist places the markings on his or her own grid paper. For research purposes, the test can be scored three ways. The first score, the mean dyad distance score, is calculated by getting the mean of all the dyad distance scores for that particular member's sculptures. The second score, the mean family distance score, is the group mean of all family members' individual mean dyad distance scores. The third score, the conjoining family distance score, is the mean of the dyad distance scores on the conjoining family sculpture (Cromwell, Fournier, and Kvebaek, 1981).

Usually, it is best to administer the entire test and then process it with the family or individually, as needed.

The Family Life Space

Mostwin (1981) has developed a multidimensional genogram called a *family life space* (see Figure 1.1). This device helps people understand the tensions and lines of communication between family members. The family life space is represented by an inner circle, and the environment is represented by an outer circle. Constructing the family life space is a three-step process:

1. The individual symbolizes all the significant others in his or her life by circles (○) or squares (□) and places them within the biopsycho social territory. Significant others may include persons who are dead but in whom the individual still has a strong emotional investment. Pets and neighbors may be included, as well as work settings and institutions. Also, by locating themselves first in the life space, individuals can place significant others at appropriate distances from the respondent and from one another. Significant persons and situations may also be placed outside as well as inside the life space.
2. Psychological facts, represented by triangles (△), represent events that are emotionally significant for the individual at the time the genogram is drawn. Psychological facts can include such things as illness, hospitalization, divorce, death, pregnancy, school problems, or psychiatric problems.
3. The third step in the dynamic genogram is to represent the quality of communication between oneself and the significant others in one's life. A solid line (→) indicates good communication. Dotted lines (- -►) indicate that although one communicates with that

person, the quality of the communication is often guarded, deceptive, indirect, hostile, or in some other way dysfunctional. Finally, a crossed-out line (╫►) indicates very poor communication or none.

Mostwin (1981:84) suggests that certain positions within the family life space may have special symbolic meaning:

> The upper part of the circle symbolizes power and authority. The higher the symbolic representation of a person, the more possessive he or she is of the authoritarian role in the family. The inner zone symbolizes emotional involvement and responsibility, while the outer, lower part of the circle often indicates submissiveness and/or dependency.

Clinical Assessment Tools Helpful in the First Few Sessions

The Family Assessment Wheel is a good visual model to help guide an intake interview (see Figure 1.2) (Mailick and Vigilante, 1997). At the core of the session is the need to understand how each person in the family (even the youngest ones) views the presenting problems.

The five spokes indicate five family factors that greatly impact each person's perception of the problem. These include relevant family events that have preceded the current crisis (e.g., the other times that Joey has been suspended from school), family organization (e.g., who is responsible for making sure Joey is dressed properly for school), communication patterns (e.g., what behavioral and linguistic routines are used to resolve such a crisis?), specific aspects of culture and values (e.g., how important is educational success to this family?), and access to institutional resources (e.g., does the family relate well to the guidance counselor, are they comfortable with the idea of therapy, can they afford to send Joey to an alternative school?).

The concentric circles truly should surround and wrap the issues discussed in each of the preceding spokes and hub. Does the family have other needs or looming crisis situations that they are not aware of? Are they dealing with issues that are developmentally expected, or is this an issue that should have been resolved long ago? Are they dealing with these problems in a manner comparable to other families whose cultural and demographic profiles are similar to theirs? What are the risk factors that may make it more difficult for them to mobilize corrective actions (e.g., unemployment, drug use, social organization, etc.)? Given the cultural niche of the family, what innovative solutions may be open to them in resolving this crisis?

One can give a variety of therapeutic tasks to a family to assess their interactions. Most often used is the Family Menu Task. Here, the entire family is asked to plan a special meal with an unlimited budget. Their

FIGURE 1.1. Family Life Space

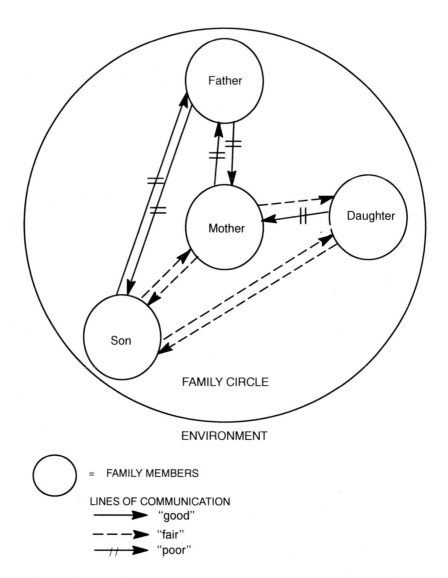

Source: Mostwin, D., 1981, Life space ecological model of family treatment, *International Journal of Family Psychiatry, 2*(1 Sup.2), p. 90. Used by permission.

FIGURE 1.2. The Family Assessment Wheel

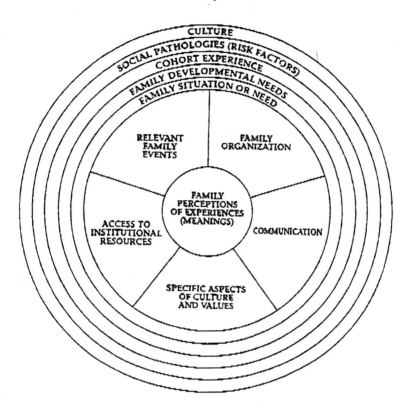

interactions are observed or tape recorded and then analyzed by a number of different possible scoring systems. Copeland and White (1991) treat the tasks as an opportunity to hear the unique musicality of the family and discern three basic themes: (a) What is the "tune" (interpersonal process used by this family? What is the characteristic tempo and style that people are using to interact with one another, regardless of what they are saying? Is it slow and deliberate or quick paced and filled with irrelevancies? (b) What are the "lyrics" (content of verbalizations) used by the family? What is the actual information they exchange with one another? Do they focus on the cost of the items, the nutritional value, or the time it will take to prepare each suggested dish? (c) What are the "sentiments" (affective displays) being expressed by the family? Are they humoring one another, depressed, resentful, or exhausted? By understanding these critical dimensions of the family, the therapist can get many insights into how the problems evolved and the type of strategies that would work to resolve the problem.

It is also useful to do a guided genogram based on the historical information that would be most relevant for that particular family.

The Genogram

The most common assessment technique family therapists use is the *genogram* (see Figure 1.3). This tree diagram provides a visual representation of the three generations in a family (grandparents, parents, and children). After the skeletal structure of the family has been charted, divorces, deaths, and other major life-cycle events are added. This technique was originally developed by anthropologists, but Bowen (1976) was the first psychiatrist to show its clinical utility. Because of its usefulness in helping therapists and families visualize some of the more potent multigenerational influences in the family, the genogram has become the most basic starting point for defining the family. Table 1.3 depicts the codes most commonly used in constructing a genogram.

Examining the information depicted in the genogram may provide limited insights. Yet, once one tries to understand the motivating forces and guiding philosophies of each person in the family tree, patterns of multigenerational influence inevitably emerge. To varying degrees, the important facets of any individual's lifestyle or personality will affect not only him or her but also parents and siblings. Six major generational influences are generally worth searching for:

1. Who were the underachievers in the family and how did that affect each of the others? Who were the overachievers in the family and how did that affect each of the others?
2. What problems do succeeding generations share and seem to be plagued with again and again?
3. What strengths do the generations share and seem to be blessed with again and again?
4. What is the geographical dispersion of the family?
5. Is there a relationship between the physical closeness of family members and their feelings of cohesiveness? Sometimes, when all members of the family stay close to their original location, the support bonds are very strong—but this is not always the case. Perhaps, just as often, the constant presence of family is suffocating and works to erode feelings of support and caring.
6. What are the economic differences within and between the generations? Which people have been upwardly mobile socially and which

have not? Economics affect extended families by influencing the frequency and nature of contacts between family members. For example, when various members of one generation are relatively affluent they are able to plan vacations and excursions together on an equal footing. With unequal incomes, there is less likelihood that their leisure patterns or work life can be shared in any meaningful and equitable way. Within families, jealousies and self-judgments make inequality in economics particularly difficult to ignore.

Genograms can be used to trace the multigenerational issues surrounding the presenting problem, whether it be sexual abuse or career decisions. For example, when an adolescent is exploring work and educational issues, a targeted genogram could help therapist and client explore such questions as: How do people in this family feel about college? About working with one's hands? About starting out as an entrepreneur? What careers and work values does the adolescent have as a model in the family? Have parents, grandparents, aunts, or uncles had to abort their education and career dreams, and how does this legacy affect the adolescent? What are the achievement expectations for your client compared to those experienced by siblings and cousins (Moon et al., 1993)?

Placement genograms are particularly important in the care and treatment of foster children. As the child moves around, the placement genogram can help a therapist deal with multiple separation issues. It can give insights into stress associated with the various roles the child has played in different types of families. It can highlight the type of problems that are family specific and those which follow the child through multiple placements (McMillen and Groze, 1994).

Genograms are also an indispensable tool for any family therapist wishing to understand the "real" (operative) culture in which a client grew up. Looking at a genogram, one can explore values and attitudes of critical family members throughout the life cycle. How individuals react to the entrances and exits of family members, as well as family crises, lets a therapist in on what resources the family has and what limitations prevent effective problem solving.

In the past, the genogram was used to gain an intellectual understanding of the family's concerns and structure. Many contemporary family therapists, however, use it to explore more dynamic family issues such as the ones mentioned above (Guerin and Pendagast, 1976; Pendagast and Sherman, 1977; Wachtel, 1982). Sometimes, by examining a genogram and talking

FIGURE 1.3. Typical Genogram of a Three-Generation Family

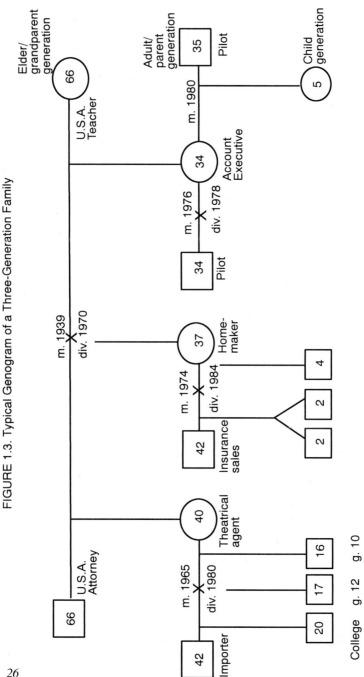

TABLE 1.3. Guidelines for the Three-Generation Genogram

1. Divide paper horizontally into three levels.
2. Males are in squares (□), females are in circles (o).
3. Begin diagramming in the middle with husband on the left.
4. Aborted fetuses, too early to determine sex, are triangles (△).
5. Twins have lines originating from the same point on the parental line.

Twin Girls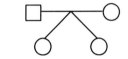

6. First child is put on the left, and subsequent children are listed in sequence.

First Child 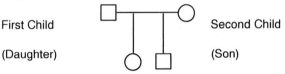 Second Child

(Daughter) (Son)

7. A miscarriage is noted with a large X with the date noted beneath the X.
8. Place adoption date below symbol, prefaced by an "a.".
   Broken vertical line indicates adoption.
9. Place death dates below symbol, prefaced by "d."—mark an X through identity symbol.
10. Place marriage date, preceded by "m." on the paired solid line.
11. Place an X through the line connecting husbands and wives if they are divorced, with date of the divorce under the X.
12. Couples living together are joined by a dotted line.
13. Couples who are separated have a single slash on their solid line, with the date of the separation under the slash.
14. Place birthdates below symbol, prefaced by "b.".
15. Indicate occupation and ethnicity of first generation alongside symbols.
16. Indicate occupation of middle generation.
17. Indicate school year or occupation of third generation (children of major couple).

Source: Adapted from Starkey, P., 1981, Genograms: A guide to understanding one's own family system, *Perspectives in Psychiatric Care* 19(5-6):164-173.

about various issues in the family tree, people become aware of their own unexpressed longings about how they would like to be and how others in the family could help them achieve those changes.

The genogram and family life space are used by most family therapists who believe that the family of origin can have a deep and pervasive effect on an adult's current behavior. Such therapists see people as being influenced and controlled by the unachieved goals and unresolved problems of the parental and grandparental generations. Healthy personality development depends on the ability to separate oneself from these irrational, intense, emotional attachments to parents while retaining the capacity for warm, expressive, and positive interactions within the family of origin.

Genograms and family life spaces can help in this process by highlighting areas where growth is being hampered. For example, if the family life space indicates that family members are not allowed to speak for themselves, are not receptive to one another, and are not able to deal openly with separations and losses, the children's quest for individual autonomy is almost surely being hampered. Likewise, if the family sees human nature as basically evil and family members are not allowed to express a wide range of feelings without undue stress, family members will be impeded in developing the intimate sides of their personalities.

It may be difficult to discern these critical family patterns of intimacy and autonomy solely by looking at the genogram and life space. Some global measure of family well-being is needed to help put the problems of any one family into a meaningful perspective.

Hovestadt and associates (1985) have developed a family-of-origin scale that measures self-perceived levels of health in one's family of origin by measuring how well the family fosters intimacy and autonomy. Families that build intimacy are characterized as responding positively to statements such as:

- In my family, it was normal to show both positive and negative feelings.
- Mealtimes in my home usually were friendly and pleasant.
- Sometimes in my family, I did not have to say anything, but I felt understood.

Autonomy-building families respond positively to statements such as:

- My parents openly admitted it when they were wrong.
- My family was receptive to the different way various family members viewed life.
- In my family people took responsibility for what they did.

The potential norms provided by the family-of-origin scale are particularly useful to therapists who wish to ascertain whether the dynamics exposed by the genogram or life space are clearly related to pathological family functioning or are occurring in an otherwise healthy family.

LORNA (lawyer, age 40)

I was unfamiliar with the genogram and the family life space until doing these exercises. Doing both of them, I learned a lot about my family, how I perceived them, and how others might perceive us.

Most startling, looking at my genogram (see Figure 1.4), is how many men there are in my three-generation family at this time: my father, my husband, my brother-in-law, two nephews, and a son! Six out of the twelve of us. Fifty percent! What's so strange about this is that my family of origin was all female except for my father and I've continued to think of us as a female-ridden family, which we obviously are not. The fact that all of the men have been outsiders to the emotional family of origin is sad and very accurate. Lately, my brother-in-law, after twenty years of marriage, is beginning to break that barrier. The one indication of this is that his Christmas gifts have become expensive and thought about, similar to the way the girls' gifts are. Another indication is that he has begun trying to do things for my mother, a helping initiative exclusively limited to her daughters in the past.

While I must admit that the genogram was interesting, I don't think it told enough about me. The family life space shows in a second where the sore spots in my family are (see Figure 1.5). As can be seen in the family life space, I have the most trouble communicating with my father and my mother-in-law. My father leads a very alien life from the rest of us. He's lived with the same woman for the past thirteen years, and we don't know anything about their life together, which is kept very secret. He visits only one time a year, and while I certainly feel he'd be available in an emergency, he's not available on a daily basis to be a father to me or a grandfather to my children.

The conflict with my mother-in-law is similar to that of my father. Her life does not involve my family except for the obligatory holidays. Although she lives only two miles away, she never asks us over and is always too busy or tired to do outings with our family. She spends a lot of time over at her daughter's house, even though she lives over twenty miles away! In a way, I should be thankful that she is not interfering or demanding. Unfortunately, I yearn for an uplifting close relationship with an older woman, and mothers-in-law are ideally suited for that role.

FIGURE 1.4. Lorna's Genogram

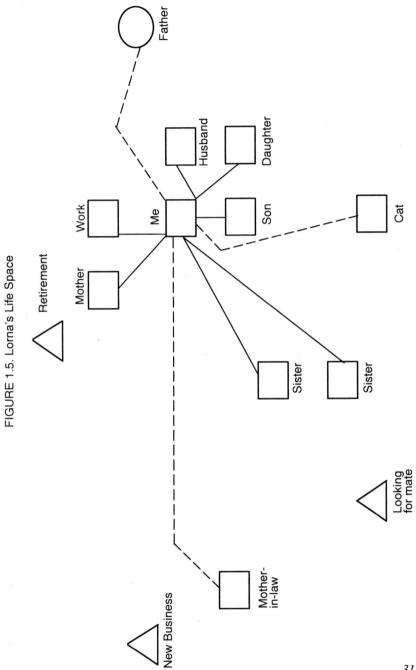

FIGURE 1.5. Lorna's Life Space

CHRISTINA (graduate student, age 24)

The genogram struck me by pointing out the large number of women versus men comprising my immediate family, including my father's siblings. I immediately began trying to understand my father's attitudes and behaviors, as a nearly lone male (since he didn't have much male support in the family, except brothers who were physically distant). (See Figure 1.6.)

Upon reviewing the marriages and divorces, I also noticed that the sisters on my father's side tended either to have never married or to be divorced from their first husbands, except one sister, Vicky, who has been married for about thirty-five years. The other sisters either remain "man-less" or, like Alice, have settled with a second husband.

I began to notice that the offspring of my father's siblings had a two-to-one ratio of females to males. I also see a tendency for the women to outlive the men in my family. My mother is an only child whose mother (age ninety-one) lives with her now, returning to her own home for only a couple of weeks during the year.

My communication with Mom is very open and honest. Sharing deep aspects of my thoughts, feelings, and actions with her has given me a deep confidence in her empathy and true feedback that she shares with me. I can really share just about anything with Mom and feel that I am sharing with a true friend. I sometimes feel burdened slightly, though, when Mom confides in me about her marital concerns as well as her sometimes trying experiences with Lynn, Val, and Grandma. (see Figure 1.7).

Dad's communication with any of his daughters, granddaughter, mother-in-law, wife, and brothers and sisters often leaves a lot to be desired because of the irrationality and lack of self-respect that accompanies his alcoholism. He impulsively communicates his anger and then spends most of the time thereafter apologizing. He and I are presently sharing what I would call a cordial type of communication, but a superficial one. I have never been able to express deep concerns with him during my development. Since I have moved out of the house, we've become more concerned about each other but more relaxed around each other, too.

Lynn and Val have become more distant, seemingly within the past few months, as they both have come to certain conclusions about each other and their personalities when under stress. My role is somewhat the go-between with these sisters, encouraging each to give the other the benefit of the doubt, but also sharing my own, sometimes negative, experiences with each. We are very close, but this availability to one another has suffered since we all live in different areas.

As mentioned, we are closer to one aunt and uncle, Vicky and Willie, probably because of their proximity, their retired status, and Vicky's self-appointed role as the family contact person. I believe my role could become comparable to her role in my generation of relatives. She and I are close superficially, but our communication is somewhat guarded on my part in an effort to resist falling into a trap set up according to her rules and expectations of me rather than my own desires and expectations.

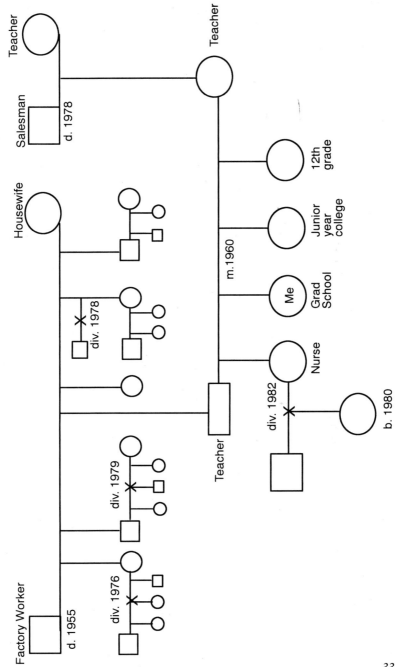

FIGURE 1.6. Christina's Genogram

FIGURE 1.7. Christina's Life Space

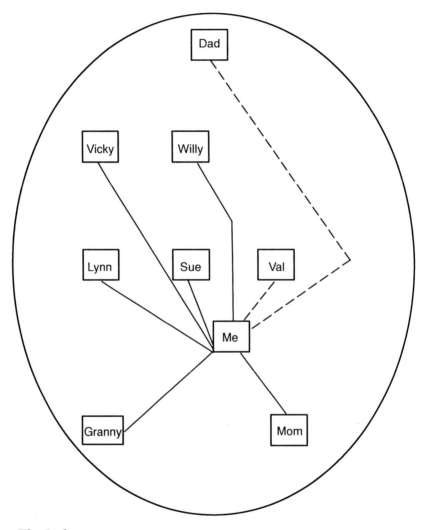

The Jack

The *Jack technique* was developed by Bradt (1978) at the Groome Center in Washington, DC. This simple graphic model provides a multi-axled mirror of the self in relation to significant others. Figure 1.8 shows the Jack as having three axes with a pole at each end.

Axis I constitutes the biological family, with one pole representing the old generation (parents and grandparents), and one pole representing the new generation (children, nieces, nephews, second cousins). For individuals without children, it may be useful to have the A pole of Axis I designate the mother and the B pole designate the father. *Axis II* represents the early-developed peer relationships. On one pole are siblings and cousins who are close in age; on the other pole are those friends with whom one grew up, played, and shared experiences. *Axis III* represents the peer relationships developed as an adult. On one pole is spouse or mate; on the other pole are friendships. Bradt suggests two ways of using the Jack to understand the importance people assign to their various relationships.

The first method of analysis involves comparing the two poles on each axis; that is, difficulties or problems with the people on one end of an axis

FIGURE 1.8. The Jack

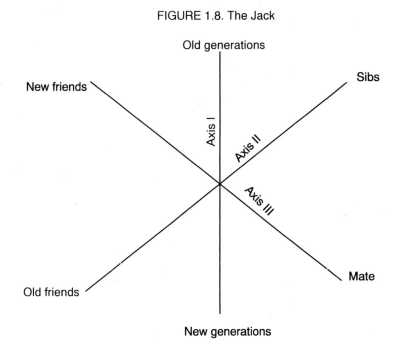

Source: From Bradt, J. O., 1980, The family with young children (Chapter 6). In: Carter, E. and McGoldrick, M. (Eds.) *The Family Life Cycle: A Framework for Family Therapy.* New York: Gardner Press.

strive for resolution or compensation with the people on the corresponding pole. Take, for example, what happens when someone gets divorced (Axis III). Suddenly, the "A" pole of the axis is empty and there is a great surge of energy and concern for the "B" pole as one increases interaction with adult friends. Activities that one routinely engaged in as part of a married couple now are altered to include a friend. When people decide not to overinvest in the "B" pole they often become highly motivated to find a new mate and so restore balance to the axis.

Besides allowing us to visualize how balanced our polar relationships are, the Jack helps us inspect how stable our whole social structure is. The iconic model of the Jack is very helpful in this second analysis. Look again at the Jack in Figure 1.8. A Jack always rests on three poles. With three strong poles it is secure. We feel intuitively that our social world is stable when we have three strong legs (poles) to lean on. People who have good relationships on only one or two poles are socially vulnerable. They are not as socially secure as the others.

HENRY (school psychologist, age 35)

Although certain poles of my Jack are stable, like a tripod with a broken leg, my entire social interpersonal structure needs more support. On Axis IIA and IIIA, specifically, the entirety of the problem presents itself, for my old friends greatly exceed my new friends in number, intensity, and quality (see Figure 1.9).

A short description should give some clarity. When someone says (Atlanta, the South, Roslyn Street, the Braves, Roosevelt High), or just "those teenage years," a smile widens across my face. For me, such nouns freely associate themselves to twenty members of a still-extant social club by the name of the Les Robes. My old friends constitute not only this club but also two sister clubs, the Foxy Forty and another by some French name I now find difficult to spell. These old friends I see twice a year, when I find myself surrounded by the streets I still call home. Together, these significant others represent my primary social interactions from high school through college. In broad contrast, Albany seems much like a stranger who just can't remember your name. I long for the camaraderie and warmth of my old Southern friends.

If Bradt's theoretical formulations are correct, the tenuousness of my new social relationships should cause a surge of concern on the other end of the pole on Axis III. This appears to have occurred, since I am presently making marital plans.

FIGURE 1.9. Henry's Jack

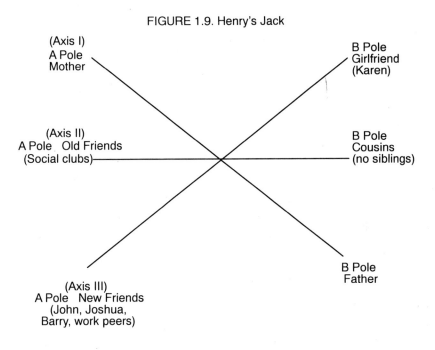

(Axis I)
A Pole
Mother

B Pole
Girlfriend
(Karen)

(Axis II)
A Pole Old Friends
(Social clubs)

B Pole
Cousins
(no siblings)

B Pole
Father

(Axis III)
A Pole New Friends
(John, Joshua,
Barry, work peers)

ROSE (graduate student, age 30)

The most unbalanced leg on my Jack is the "old friends-siblings" leg (see Figure 1.10). I am in touch with only one old friend from as far back as the high school era. We keep in touch mostly via occasional letters and infrequent phone calls but have only seen each other once in the past eight years, as he is living in Idaho. Although we have continued to share intimately with each other through the mail, this is not a very fulfilling "relationship," and although Harry is in some ways my only link with "the old days," I don't really think of him as a "close" friend any more. Because I am still living in the area where I grew up, I do regularly "bump into" friends or acquaintances from high school. (As you know, most people who grew up here seem, somehow, to never quite leave, so most of the "high school crowd" are still in the area.) In some ways, I think this makes the lack of contact even more unusual.

At the same time, although I live within ten miles of both of my sisters, I am not at all close to either of them. When we were growing up together, our relationships were very stormy and, while we stopped fighting long ago, I really don't like either of them very much. I think perhaps they, as

(continued)

(continued)

well as my old high school friends, may remind me of a past that I don't feel very good about. (I'm guessing about this, but it seems to fit the data.) We talk on the phone about every one or two weeks and nearly always to exchange some sort of information, rather than just to talk to each other. I tend to see them only out of "family duty" or guilt because they have both expressed a desire to be closer. This is especially the case with my older sister, who has told my mother "in confidence" that she feels like I don't like her very much. I had until recently been closer with my younger sister and we would sometimes get together for coffee or lunch (always on her initiative, however), but this has stopped now, too.

I have been trying during the past year to improve my relationship with my father, which was nearly nonexistent after my parents' divorce. I have noticed at the same time a compensatory (and healthy!) shift in my relationship with my mother. While I see this as a positive shift in what had been an overinvolved relationship with my mother, I feel very guilty about this—as if I'm being disloyal and sometimes catch myself "doing equal time," as it were.

I have no mate at the present time, and my "new friends" are very important to me. I have very strong attachments to them and felt the loss acutely when one of them moved out of the area recently. My closest friend is another single woman, and while this is not a sexual relationship, I think that our friendship has come to substitute for some of the emotional intimacy which we would share with mates if we had them. I am close friends with five or six single or divorced women, all of whom I came to know in the past two years. I also have two or three close male friends (established in the last year or so), but I am definitely more invested in my friendships with women right now. Somewhere, and I'm not sure where to put them, are four or five women with whom I have remained friends dating from undergraduate school. We are all scattered about now (California, Iowa, Tennessee, Maine, and Vermont), but we keep in touch regularly and visit several times a year.

SELF-EXPLORATION:
DISCOVERING YOUR FAMILY LIFE SPACE

The first step in understanding a family is to know who are the people making up the family. Your first self-exploration, then, is to develop both a genogram and a multidimensional family life space. Include all the members in the three or four generations of your extended family (grandparents, parents, your generation, and your children). As you make your dynamic genogram, be sure to note all the deaths, traumas,

FIGURE 1.10. Rose's Jack

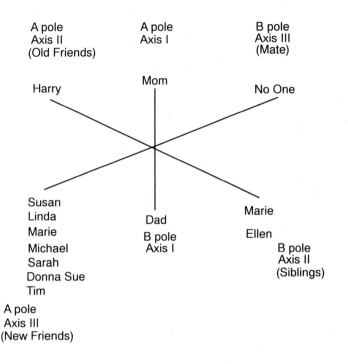

separations, and divorces that have taken place. Once you capture a historical sense of the major crises and changes in your family tree, you will begin to understand the forces that helped form you. After you have drawn your family life space, ask yourself the following questions:

1. How many significant others are you close to?
2. How many family members are outside your life space?
3. In what ways would the family life space of your mate, parents, or children be different than your family life space? What does this tell you about the different life spaces different family members live in?
4. On the basis of the family life cycles described in this chapter, what stage is your family in and what issues do they need to resolve? Would your family life space have looked any different if your family were in the previous stage? If yes, how has it changed and why?

SELF-EXPLORATION: USING THE JACK

Using Figure 1.8 as a guide, draw a large Jack and list the significant people on each pole of the Jack.

1. Are the poles of each axis equally balanced, or is one pole holding an undue burden?
2. How could you constructively work to make your Jack more balanced?
3. How many sturdy poles do you have to lean on? You may want to make a Jack for some other members of your family. Answer the three questions from their points of view to see whether you gain any new insights into their life situations.

UNIT II:
FAMILY CONCEPTS—
A SYSTEMS PERSPECTIVE

Systems theory views the family through interactive prisms that focus on the rules of the family game instead of the movements of any one player. Systems concepts show us how the parts of the family are interrelated and how a change in one person will produce changes throughout the whole family. For example, when most of us hear about someone getting a job advancement, we focus on the increased self-esteem, financial resources, and status that the individual will achieve. A systems perspective, however, would focus on how this advancement will affect the power structure within the family and the fulfillment of family roles and legacies.

According to systems theory, the members of a family are elements of an interacting group in which the behavior of one member inevitably influences all the others. Systems theory does not usually view the family en masse, however; instead it examines how the various components or subsystems of the family interact. In particular, the systems approach is an attempt to understand how the different subgroups in the family regulate information, access, and activity to include and exclude different members.

Thus, the rules and strategies governing subparts of the system are integral to understanding the whole. What sets systems theory apart from other theories is that within systems theory, the personalities and pathologies of individual family members give little insight into why the family functions as it does. Looking at the relationships between members becomes far more important than analyzing individuals. Discovering new ways of analyzing relationships becomes the key to deeper understanding of the individual.

Some of the concepts in this section describe the struggle of individuals to go beyond the family system and form their own individual characteristics and psychological boundaries. Other concepts describe the relational structures that govern family interactions over long periods. Still other concepts describe how multigenerational influences can affect the family system.

Chapter 2

Individuation

Independence is the privilege of the strong.

L. W. Nutzcha

PARENTS' SOCIOEMOTIONAL INVESTMENT IN CHILDREN: PRECURSORS TO SUCCESSFUL INDIVIDUATION AND SEPARATION

Psychologists universally acknowledge that the child's ability to bond successfully with the parent lays the foundation for successfully exploring and affecting their environment. It is ironic that the safer children feel, the freer they are to explore and separate from the parent. Children with a secure attachment are able to separate from the parent and find ways of satisfying their own needs. What creates a secure attachment between parent and child? We now know that the parent's ability to bond successfully with the child may directly affect the attachment experience of the child. The child appears to be responsive to cues of caring, attention, touch, responsiveness, and reciprocity from caretakers.

The therapist must assess a number of dimensions to see if a parent is giving a child what he or she needs to bond successfully. Bradley et al. (1997) found four distinct factors that contribute to the parent's socioemotional investment in their children. Most important was parents' acceptance of the parenting role. Acceptance involves a commitment to put the child's needs before one's own. It involves daily responsibilities to protect and nurture the child. Feeding, clothing, and entertaining a child are all part of the parental role. The ability to show delight and joy around a child appears to be a second vital cue. Next is the parent's intellectual and intuitive awareness of what an infant or child can do at various developmental stages. Simple knowledge about what a child likes (e.g., offering the child a favorite toy) builds a sense of security in the child, a knowing that others are looking out for him or her. Continually giving cues of understanding responsiveness leads children to learn that they can expect others to help them and bring them joy. The last factor is the experience of separation anxiety in the parent. Parents who are bonded to their children want to be near them and with them, much the same way that the children exhibit their bonding behaviors.

Of course, if a parent does not appear to be bonded or to like being a parent, what is the intervention? It is difficult to teach a parent to worry about a child or desire to be with the child. But it is possible to teach parents about the ages and stages of development, what to expect from children, and what children at different ages like. It is also possible to help parents gain insight into what types of parenting they experienced and how that has affected their parenting style. It is possible and exciting to teach parents more rewarding ways of interacting with their child so that they may begin to feel joy in the child's presence. Virtually all programs that are successful in saving high-risk children from dysfunction, or healing children who are already suffering developmental problems, use three specific intervention strategies: (1) teaching the ages and stages, (2) family-of-origin work about the type of parenting the child's parent received, and (3) guided play or interactive exercises with the child. The guided play exercises stimulate reinforcing, joyful interactions that create affective bonds and a memory bank of positive family interactions.

We start off in the world dependent and helpless; we need care and nurture from our parents and family to survive. Throughout history, the development of children into independent, self-sufficient adults has been a nearly universal goal of families. But the desire for children's independence is tempered by an expectation that they will continue an interdependent, caring relationship with the parents once they are adults. Unlike other animal species whose young leave the family at maturity, never to return home, human beings are torn between a yearning to stay with the family of origin and a yearning to venture beyond the home.

Successful differentiation from the family of origin involves knowing, at a deep level, that you are emotionally connected to family members while retaining a zesty freedom of personal expression. It is getting to the point where "they love you as you are." A few simple questions can help the therapist assess the degree of differentiation experienced by any one family member. First, ask the identified patient, for each person in the family, "Do you enjoy talking and spending time with _____?" (assesses emotional connectedness). Second, ask the identified patient, for each person in the family, "Does _____ respect your viewpoints even when they differ from your own?" (assesses freedom of personal expression). If the patient spends time with various family members and feels respected by most of them, individuation is unlikely to be a big issue.

THEORIES OF INDIVIDUATION

Each subculture has developed rituals and norms that help the young and their parents determine how much independence is appropriate and how much interdependence is appropriate. Within these subcultural prescriptions, each family customizes its own set of expected interactions for each stage of the family life cycle.

Many families have problems letting the children become as independent as their subculture dictates. Families that have great difficulties in developing autonomy among the family members are described as "emotionally fused" by Bowen (1978) and "enmeshed" by Minuchin (1974). A brief discussion of these two theorists will lead us to a broader understanding of how families balance keeping children close and emotionally bonded while at the same time equipping them to make their way independent of the family.

Murray Bowen's Theory of Differentiation of Self

When all think alike, no one thinks very much.

Walter Lippmann

Murray Bowen (1971, 1972, 1976) calls the process of becoming independent of the family's authority and expectations the *differentiation of self.* This concept is the cornerstone of Bowen's theory of family functioning (Hall, 1981). Differentiation of self provides both a qualitative and a quantitative measure of the extent to which people differentiate between their emotional bonding to the family and their personal, intellectual judgments. Bowen considers that the goal of development is the ability to use one's intellectual capacity as fully as possible, unimpeded by the conflicting pressures of family sanctioning mechanisms.

Family therapists often feel that two major goals of therapy are (1) to help children move away from their emotional overinvolvements with the parents and (2) to help parents with their struggle to let their children develop into autonomous adults. Individuals achieve these goals with varying degrees of success.

At one extreme are *highly fused* individuals whose intellects are overwhelmed by their emotional systems. They do not trust their own intellectual judgments. Their thinking is directed by the important others whom they feel they must keep happy. These individuals are driven to behave in ways that please and appease others. They behave very compliantly, trying to shield themselves from guilt and ridicule. Highly fused individuals tend to be highly dependent on other people. They also tend to develop many psychological problems. A low level of differentiation binds the individual to the family so rigidly that he or she is incapable of genuinely entering any other relationships.

At the other extreme is the *highly differentiated* person who has achieved a high degree of autonomy between personal intellectual functioning and emotional bonding to the family. Highly differentiated individuals may *choose* to behave in a fashion that pleases others, but they are not *driven* to act that way. Often they choose behavior that is primarily task oriented, goal oriented, rational, or expedient, annoying family members in the process. Their decisions are guided by facts and personal beliefs. Obviously, being differentiated helps thwart psychological problems.

Bowen found it useful to conceptualize differentiation as existing on a scale from 0-100. Individuals in the lowest quartile (0-25, the least differentiated) are overwhelmingly controlled by their emotions. Their dependency forces them to spend most of their energy maintaining personal relationships, sometimes to the extent of being unable to function in society.

People between the levels of 25 and 49 have somewhat more flexibility of lifestyle. Hanson and L'Abate (1982) find three distinguishing characteristics of individuals in this range:

1. Their self-images are extremely shaky, depending almost entirely upon the approval of others.
2. Their thinking ability is solid enough to enable them to do well academically, but they are not capable of using this ability in their personal lives.
3. Close relationships and approval are life goals. Ironically, even though these individuals are sensitive, emotionally expressive, and dependent, they find that when someone is willing to get close, they cannot maintain such a relationship emotionally.

Individuals in the third quartile (50-74) are quite well differentiated. They have been successful in developing into independent adults. Although these people may feel frequent emotional pulls to behave impulsively, they can usually control it. They have personal beliefs and values that they are able to act upon and express even when they know that their families and important others will not approve of them.

Very few people ever reach the fourth quartile (75-100). It is a rarely achieved state of healthy differentiation and great personal development. In reality, the process of differentiation is continual, and the dialectic between independence and interdependence nags at most people throughout the life span. Individuals able to function at the fourth quartile of differentiation have a deep understanding of the relationship between separation and bonding and live their lives with more personal freedom and self-direction.

Minuchin's Theory of Enmeshment/Disengagement

Independence is an achievement, not a bequest.

The Roycroft Dictionary

Minuchin, Rosman, and Baker (1978) believe that individuation develops best in a family context in which there are rules defining who participates in each family role and how that participation takes place. When the rules are unclear, absent, or overly rigid, two pathological extremes are possible: a "disengaged" family or an "enmeshed" family.

The Disengaged Family

In disengaged families, structure, order, and authority are lacking, and family members move in isolated orbits for long periods. Because they are not meaningfully and reliably interconnected, individuation is a futile goal. In these families, the children have been prematurely pushed into independence, most often without the necessary skills or security.

The extremely disengaged family forces each individual to develop autonomy. Because there is no effective bonding between the family members, however, the autonomy is often felt as a frightening experience of suspended animation instead of a secure push into an area of desired personal fulfillment.

Communication in the disengaged family is extremely difficult; the lack of shared experiences makes self-disclosure awkward or threatening. Often, when individuals in a disengaged family get into trouble, no one in the family will know about it. The family member muddles through without the necessary social supports. Episodes of lying, cheating, and delinquency reported by school authorities are often ignored or trivialized in the disengaged family. The family members do not feel responsibility for one another, and disengaged parents do not participate in intense socialization programs with their children. The unfortunate result is that most often behavior problems will continue to escalate until outside authorities become involved in disciplining and socializing the child.

The devastating effects of disengaged families are most visible to the community during the school years when the amount of parental involvement is most open to the public. Severely disengaged parents never attend school events or help arrange extracurricular activities for their children; they are unaware of many of their children's friends or pastimes and are not involved in helping their children master the day-to-day difficulties they encounter.

NORMAN (engineer, age 42)

My family of origin was a mess. There were nine kids in the back hills of Kentucky with a mother who only knew how to watch the soaps and game shows and keep the kids out of the kitchen. My dad knew how to drink and sell used cars. Our house was always in an uproar. Everyone did their own thing on their own schedule and fought tooth and nail with anyone who stood in their way. We never had any rituals except putting up a Christmas tree and getting one new shirt on Christmas morning. There were only three rules in the house: (1) stay out of the kitchen, (2) no boys upstairs when the girls were showering, and (3) no one was good enough to be our friend. This last point might not seem like a rule but it was. You *had* to downgrade everyone you came in contact with. It was crazy since we were undoubtedly the joke of the town! Nevertheless, if any of us ever went on a date, the rest would cut the person up so bad you'd never dream of letting anyone in the family know if there was a second date. All of us kids got real secretive, real quick. Us boys would always be sneaking out the window late at night. I had three brothers and if we ever happened to be coming or going out the window at the same time, we just stood in line like total strangers, never asking where the other was going or anything.

My childhood was never secure or happy. I was always ashamed of who I was and the family I came from. I spent my adolescence in a fog of meaningless activity, drinking, finding loose girls, and getting into trouble. Fortunately, school always came real easy to me, especially math and science. In the back of my mind I always knew that was the only handle I had to define myself in some positive light. I recently read a book, *Sins of the Family,* which captured my own feelings during childhood even though the main character was a woman. She lived the first half of her life feeling guilty for the ineptitude and lifestyle of her parents. Then she married a psychiatrist and worked it all out. I've lived over forty years with the guilt and there's no psychiatrist-wife in sight!

Some therapists have told me I have no sense of self; others say I'm denying my need for love. They all agree I'm screwed up. I've been

(continued)

> *(continued)*
>
> engaged four different times. At the last minute, I realize it just isn't right for me or the lady involved. The past seven years, I lived sort of like a hermit or a workaholic. I went to work seven days a week, was always willing to take on difficult problems, and have prospered at my firm. I get along well with my team and the rest of the staff. I haven't dated anyone except a married woman whom I get together with once a month. In therapy this time, I've been pushed to join a bowling league and I like doing it. I've also bought a condo and moved out of a dingy rented basement I've had for three years.
>
> Compared to my brothers and sisters I'm doing OK. Actually, the girls got married and moved all over the country, and it's been over five years since I've heard from any of them. Among the boys, I'm the only one who made it through college and has a professional job. Two of my brothers are manual laborers, and our oldest brother has been in and out of mental hospitals all his life. He never goes home. I hate going home and try to go only every few years, but I do help out every once in a while. My dad's car was a pile of junk last time I was down, so I just left him mine, which I was planning on getting rid of anyway.
>
> I blame my family for a lot of my current problems—I find it hard to believe that the hollowness in me is genetic. I think we lacked any of the closeness discussed in this chapter except personal space. With nine kids, the four boys shared one bedroom with two beds; the girls had a similar setup. Other than sleeping we spent as little time as possible together. We never sat around talking, joking, or discussing problems. The unspoken rule of the family was to avoid these types of encounters. In terms of generational boundaries there was a division between the kids and my parents. They did talk and brawl with each other in a different way than they did with us kids. We all knew they wanted to be in control but were too weak and disorganized to carry through on anything.

The Enmeshed Family

By contrast, in enmeshed families a tight interlocking exists between family members. The enmeshed families described by Minuchin are very similar to the families that Bowen (1978) categorizes as "fused" or "low in differentiation."

Fused families are too close, too inclusive, and too intense. The more enmeshed the family members are, the harder it is for them to relate to one another as individuals. Everyone is relating to some monolithic icon representing "the family." For example, if two family members are having a conversation and a third family member walks in, that member inevitably gets involved. It is as though acknowledging a private, two-person conversation were equivalent to fragmenting the family.

If a fight erupts between two members, a chain reaction may occur as the whole family experiences a contagious itch and gets involved. Daughters and sons are compelled to cushion the impact of the mother against the father or, less often, the father against the mother. Fighting is very threatening to enmeshed families because even if one chooses a side, the very existence of a fight makes it clear that differing views exist within the family. While arguments, disagreements, and tensions are often found in enmeshed families, such families are distinguished by their ability to let the problems continually fester without being able to resolve them.

Members of enmeshed families are very dependent upon one another. They try to present a united front and do so by engaging in excessive togetherness. Privacy is not respected in enmeshed families. The bedroom doors may have no locks; in fact, many enmeshed families have a rule that members must keep the bedroom door open at all times. Letters may be opened no matter to whom they were sent, and keeping a private diary may approach an act of treason.

Developing an independent, autonomous identity is particularly difficult in an enmeshed family. A family member who devotes time to learning a new skill or developing a variety of friendships threatens the insular togetherness that reassures the enmeshed family. It is very difficult to develop the skills for self-sufficiency in these families.

Because open conflict is so threatening, highly enmeshed families risk their members developing a myriad of psychosomatic problems. Tension that cannot be expressed outwardly is turned inward. Headaches, stomach pains, colitis, anorexia, and asthma are just a few of the potential problems. These problems often serve as a focal point for family togetherness (talking about them, worrying about them), but they also allow the symptom-bearer some way of obtaining privacy, separateness, and individuality. Of course, the problems also provide an excuse for not developing oneself outside the family circle. In extreme cases, they can even momentarily halt the individual's strong biological thrust toward social and cognitive maturation. If one is beset by physical problems, the desire to talk with friends wanes, and the attention and alertness needed for academic pursuits are overwhelmed by anxiety, pain, and apprehension.

The Overprotective Family

One of the defining anthropological features of a family is that there is usually a high degree of concern among the family members for one another's welfare (see Chapter 1). In the overprotective family, however, this concern is constant and often unwarranted. Minuchin, Rosman, and Baker (1978:31) write that "family members are hypersensitive to signs of

---

JO ELLEN (nutritionist, age 36)

Emotionally, I am still very dependent on my mother's and father's approval. What's crazy is that I am chained to my *ideas* of what they approve or disapprove of, even though it often doesn't match what they tell me! A perfect example is taking vacations. My mom and dad go to St. Paul every year to visit relatives and do it as economically as possible. Both say they would not enjoy it any more if they spent $2,000, so why spend it? On the other hand, they are always telling me that I work hard and should go to the Islands, or Europe, or especially Club Med because I deserve it and maybe I'll meet someone. I'd love to take these holidays. I have the money but I'm very insecure. I'm afraid that my parents wouldn't approve and would think I'm just squandering hard-earned dollars. Regardless of what they say, I think they admire the fact that I take a lot of long weekends with friends that end up costing next to nothing because we share travel expenses and are usually put up by people we know. But why should I care whether or not they approve? Because I feel that my survival depends on them. Not literally, of course, but figuratively. I'm unmarried, without a steady guy, in a ho-hum job. Basically, I'm happy with my life just because I feel my parents are proud of me and that lets me be proud of what I accomplish on a day-to-day basis.

I would like to be able to function on a more rational level and take a lot of the risks that I'm afraid to take now. I know that a lot of my conservatism is tied to my attitudes toward pleasing my parents, because I often have fantasies of all the things I'd be free to do if they died. I'd travel, buy an expensive condo, risk my secure job for something totally different, and develop some strong political interests. I'm very ashamed of these "happy orphan" fantasies, because when I speak to my parents I'm sure they would verbally support all those moves if only it would make me happy. The reality of my family doesn't exist on the word level, though. It's the level of family values and traditions. Regardless of the freedoms that my parents verbally bequeath to me, I am chained to the values and realities they taught me as being correct.

---

distress, cueing the approach of dangerous levels of tension or conflict. In such families, the parents' overprotectiveness retards the children's development of autonomy, competence, and interests or activities outside the safety of the family."

The child, in turn, feels great responsibility to protect the rest of the family. While overprotectiveness is a powerful explanatory concept in its own right, its relationship to the broader concept of enmeshment is obvious. Overprotectiveness is a major strategy for maintaining an enmeshed family status. Indeed, a large degree of overprotection can be found in nearly every enmeshed family.

When fights do occur, it is because the biological thrust toward maturation is forcing changes in the status quo. The rigidly held rules of the parents are being challenged by the social, mental, and physical changes unrelentingly pushing for expression in the children. For example, one family rule or ritual might be that everyone watches television together after dinner. Both the preadolescent who yearns for extended phone conversations with friends at this time and the youngster who retreats into homework too intensively are disrupting the family status and hence are the subject of arguments.

GENERATIONAL BOUNDARIES, CLOSENESS, AND ROLE BEHAVIORS

Each family system can be divided into *subsystems*. The two major divisions are the adult subsystem and the child subsystem. Both the family and its subsystems have implicit sets of rules or "boundaries" that determine who can be in the subsystem and how to behave while in it.

Boundaries

Family boundaries can be rigid, diffuse, or clear. In families with *rigid* boundaries, the subsystems are highly impermeable. For example, a child would never attempt to enter the adult subsystem. The adults would neither want nor attempt to enter the child subsystem. The generational hierarchy is as distinct as black and white. Identities are easily developed in rigid families, but they tend to be truncated and stereotyped. The rigid distinctions make it difficult for children to evolve to adulthood. These children have learned to exist within a very narrowly acceptable range of behavior. When they are outside the family and expected to adopt a mature and independent adult role, they are often woefully unprepared, unpracticed, and panic stricken.

In families with *diffuse* boundaries, the subsystems are very permeable; the children can enter the adult subsystem, and the adults can enter the child subsystem. With diffuse boundaries, there is no clear generational hierarchy. When this happens, an unwieldy range of behavior is acceptable in each of the subsystems. In this unstructured free-for-all, individual identities may be difficult to develop. It may become impossible to distinguish between "them" and "me." Family members may take shelter under the emotional umbrella of a broad family identity based on the individual or the subsystem.

Boundaries, Adolescence, and the Separation Experience

Adolescence is the start of the great process of differentiation. To learn who you are and who you want to become, a person must navigate between two thin tightropes, skipping between continuing and deepening ties with the family, while at the same time separating and distancing from them. Great interpersonal competence is required to pull this off successfully. Negotiating when and how to express closeness and intimacy as well as when and how to express independence and autonomy is a complicated art.

Adolescents who can share their fears and dreams with their parents are able to maintain a feeling of closeness. Learning to relate to a parent on a more open, adult level requires the confidence to self-disclose. This is risky and anxiety provoking. Sharing private information is dangerous because it opens the door for parental criticism and censorship. It also blurs the boundary between the private life of the adolescent and his or her more public family life. Emotional support from the parents allows the child to feel safety in this situation (Theriault, 1997).

While competent adolescents are busy creating large areas of emotional closeness, fences are being built, at the same time, to demark zones of privacy. For the autonomy building to go successfully, adolescents have to learn how to manage conflict and how to assert themselves in a nontoxic manner. If a friend is having a boy-girl sleepover party, the need for closeness may prompt an adolescent to share this information with Mother. When Mother wants to know what went on at the party, the adolescent may adamantly refuse to share any of the details (Theriault, 1997).

The rule for contemporary families with good communication patterns seems to be: share news of the upcoming happening, then leave out all the nitty-gritty details afterward. Preapproval of the activity comes with the assumption of privacy about the actual event. Tell Mother you are about to lose your virginity, but don't give a replay of the evening. Inform Father that you are sleeping at your friend's because there will be drinking, but don't share how wasted everyone got. Parents who feel they need to know all trap their offspring in a psychological never-never land, where independent action is anxiety provoking.

It is thought that diffusion in generational boundaries creates a highly fused, enmeshed family. The reasoning goes that if one does not know what is appropriate or inappropriate adult behavior, how can one risk having an adult role in the community independent of the family? Similarly, overly rigid boundaries might make it difficult to acknowledge or allow for the social and psychological growth of each person. Ideally, families should develop clear generational boundaries. The roles of the children should be clearly differentiated from the roles of the parents. However,

BENJAMIN (physician, age 68)

My father was a businessman. As a young man he was in the Medical Corps of the Bulgarian Army (from 1910 to 1918). During my first eight years he would always tell me stories about the war and helping people and I idolized him. During my later childhood and adolescence he was always very rough and rejecting toward me, but that early attachment made me want to be like him and win his approval. I felt if I helped people, like he did, I would gain his approval. By the time I was eight, I was going to be a doctor. Of course, my father would have preferred me to become a businessperson like him. I didn't like anything about business or the current Dad. I had an idealistic vision to save mankind and be like my father of my earliest memories. He had a vision of me being a wealthy businessman. The entire family, including myself, was invested in me being a big success and getting a lot of public acclaim.

During most of my adult life my father felt that it was sad what had happened to me. I was an alcoholic, straggling from one hospital post to the next and one wife to the next. My father felt it was his fault. When I was forty-five he was blaming himself and I was telling him I was happy with how I was. Really, I was screaming inside that he was right—I had grown into the mess he always told me I would become. Because I was infertile due to a terrible illness that I had as a child, I could not put my failures on to my child or hope his successes could pick me up.

I was always close to my mother because my father was so hard on her and I felt she needed a protector. I thought he had a terrible attitude toward women. For him, there was men's work and women's work, and so I consciously rejected it and became a very early feminist.

Especially in this regard, I leaned over backward to be different from my father. Now I know I was protesting too much. To strive so hard to be different from him showed I was still caught up with childish notions of proving myself to him. While my behavior was always very liberal, emotionally I have come to believe that I am like my father and I want women to be traditionally subservient despite all my hoopla.

I've come to realize also that I really do like to control people. But I like to control them by being nice to them. My father was very controlling and directive in an argumentative, negative way. At sixty-eight, I still want to be like him without adopting his noxious traits.

My ability to let go of these infantile needs started to develop with my fifth wife when I was in my late forties. By being accepted by the person that I love and being given constant approval, I began to have confidence in who I was for the first time. During this period I even changed my name from B.J. (my nickname) to Benjamin (my birth name). I really was giving birth to a self that was free of my father's nagging criticisms and disappointments.

there should be flexibility within the family so that the roles can evolve and change as the family matures or when a crisis calls for some innovative problem solving. To help families develop clear generational boundaries, we need to define the concept very precisely. As a global concept it is too vague to guide a general understanding of normal family functioning. Exactly what is it that we want families to understand about adult roles and children's roles?

Wood and Talmon (1983) have made a major contribution toward specifying the behavioral and interactional components of generational boundaries. They suggest that the concept of generational boundaries is composed of two independent dimensions: closeness and role behaviors. Both closeness and role behaviors can be defined in such a way that they can be observed and measured to determine the permeability or rigidity of the boundaries in any family.

Closeness

Wood and Talmon (1983) conceptualize *closeness* as consisting of six types of physical and psychological space that family members may share to varying degrees. The more sharing there is, the closer the family. It becomes apparent that each family has its own unique profile, being close in some of the areas, and more distant in some of the others.

The six types of physical and psychological space included in the concept of closeness are (1) contact time, (2) personal space, (3) emotional space, (4) information space, (5) conversation space, and (6) decision space.

Contact Time

Closeness can be measured by the sheer amount of time the family spends together. Watching television, eating meals, vacationing, housework, gardening, and shopping can be done routinely by individuals, by subsystems, or by the entire nuclear family. The more time that is spent together, the more family history there is to share and the closer the family is perceived to be.

Personal Space

Ethnic groups vary in the extent of personal space that can be shared. To give just two examples, Italians are noted for sharing personal space; the British are noted for avoiding close contact. Within these cultural norms, there remain wide interfamilial differences in the amount of touching, hugging, cuddling, and body contact observed. Within the cultural code, the degree of physical contact among family members is a measure of the closeness the family members feel toward one another. Watching television together in bed, eating from each other's plates, sharing clothes, being in the bathroom at the same time, or even walking holding hands are all indications of families who show closeness by sharing personal space.

Emotional Space

The quality and quantity of shared feelings determine the degree of shared emotional space. In some families, the giggles or laughter of one person sets up an irresistibly contagious effect in the others. As soon as one starts joking, the others can easily join in and play along. Families without emotional closeness have little empathy for one another. The emotional meters of each person are individually calibrated and monitored. If someone comes home feeling dejected and depressed, the emotionally distant family might recognize these emotions but remain personally unaffected. Conversely, an emotionally close family may find the dejection and depression disseminating to everyone who is in the house, radically altering everyone's mood.

Information Space

The term *information space* refers to "the set of facts about the individual including his thoughts, feelings, opinions, biographical facts and behavior" (Wood and Talmon, 1983:349). Close families know exactly what is going on at each person's work or school environment. They know the hopes and disappointments each person is coping with. Distant families may know none of this information. The self-disclosure of personal feelings and thoughts has been considered critical to intimacy between mates. So far, the importance of children's sharing this information remains unexplored. It is possible that ethnic, social, and cultural considerations help determine what is considered the appropriate level of sharing for children as well as for adults.

Conversation Space

The term *conversation space* refers to the ease and frequency with which different dyads (two-person groups) in the family share private conversations. Suppose Mom and Sis *can* sit and have long, intimate conversations when no one else is around. Then Sis can hole up with her brother and have a conversation. Later in the week, Sis and Dad can have a meaningful I/thou encounter. Each of these pairs is sharing conversation space—a time-consuming but rewarding way for the family to achieve closeness. In estranged (distant) or enmeshed families, parents and children may yearn for such conversational sharing and closeness, yet it is very difficult to achieve. Estranged families know too little about one another for relaxed conversational camaraderie. Enmeshed families share so much that honest conversations tend to reveal previously unacknowledged differences and disagreements that these families find threatening. In healthy families, relating intimately one-on-one occurs most frequently within subsystems or between allies, fortifying the special links between these family members.

Decision Space

Closeness can be measured by the extent to which decisions are made by the whole family, by subsystems, or by individuals. In close families, decisions such as where to eat Sunday dinner are arrived at by consensus. In distant families, one person may have the decision-making role. In between is the "breathing relationship" which family members take turns making such decisions.

Role Behaviors

The second independent dimension composing the concept of generational boundaries is role behaviors. Role distinctions between the children and the adults are normally made on four dimensions: (1) nurturance, (2) control, (3) alliance and coalitions, and (4) peers. In our society, generational hierarchies depend on the parents' maintaining dominance in these four critical areas and excluding the children from them, but allowing children occasional dominance in these areas fosters closeness.

Nurturance

The norms of our society maintain that throughout childhood, parents have an obligation to protect, love, and be responsible for their children. When the children feel obligated to provide these services for the parents, the hierarchy has been reversed.

Control

The parents' role is to control the children. Parents set limits, issue ultimatums, and enforce policy. When the children begin to control the parents, the generational hierarchy has been reversed.

JANICE (graduate student, age 24)

I think it is particularly easy for me to analyze my own family in structural terms because in many ways it is very much a psychosomatic family. The four characteristics (enmeshment, overprotectiveness, rigidity, and lack of conflict resolution) Minuchin describes as "encouraging somatization" were very much present in my family as I was growing up, and still representative in many cases of how my family operates. Not surprisingly, I am one in a long line of females who suffer from migraine headaches, and as a child I suffered from eczema which also required frequent medical attention. (I have been trying to recall whether my bouts with eczema corresponded to periods of stress in my parents' marriage, and while I can't specifically remember, I would bet all the cortisone cream in Delaware that they did!) The same pattern characterizes my extended family as well, and in addition to an array of migraine sufferers, there is also my bulimic cousin.

In general, I think of the relationships in my family as having been extremely enmeshed. "Privacy" in our house was equated with disloyalty or, at the very least, with rejection. We were essentially ONE—everything was community property, so to speak. Doors, for example, were never closed in our house. If you closed a door, one could assume that you were doing something WRONG. Although I may present this in an exaggerated form because I don't have much objectivity on this issue at the moment, I think this enmeshment or intrusiveness extended well beyond healthy togetherness. For example, our ONENESS extended to the use of the bathroom. Oneness in the bathroom may be OK with very young children, but when you are a sixteen-year-old girl and your father continues to come into the bathroom to use the toilet while you are in the bathtub—that's enmeshed. Furthermore, to *not* tell our parents about something was equivalent to lying about it, and as you might guess, we confided the details of our lives to our parents almost compulsively. Separations or leaving of any kind have been difficult in my family as well. No one can imagine how anyone could possibly survive if they left—that's how enmeshed (close, they call it) my family has been. The degree of enmeshment in my family has left me with very little autonomy and has left me struggling with a desire to lose myself in a relationship, but at the same time fighting very hard *not* to lose what is at times a rather precarious sense of self.

The subsystem boundaries were, of course, very poorly defined. If we as children had no privacy, the same could be said for my parents. Symbolic of their lack of privacy was the fact that their bedroom door was never closed. Everyone talked at once, and I can remember very clearly thinking that I had a perfect right to be involved in whatever my parents were discussing. This has been something which I have had to work out for myself in working with families. I have had to learn along with them that there are some things which do not concern the children, and that it is OK

(continued)

> *(continued)*
>
> as a parent to have "private" business. I have also had to overcome some strong resistance in myself to be able to say (and believe) that parents don't have to explain and justify their every move to their children.
>
> I think I was often in the role of parental child (my sisters would both certainly agree), and in fact my younger sister jokingly referred to me as her third parent.
>
> The major subsystems in my family were, I think, cross-generational. There was a very strong and rigid alliance between my older sister and my father, and an equally rigid one between my mother and my younger sister and me. I think for most of my life the family divided up into these two factions, and even today the loyalties continue to fall out along these lines. My older sister has very close contact with my father, whom I seldom see, while I remain much closer to my mother. Although I was still in high school when my parents got divorced, I became at that time an equal partner with my mother, and my involvement in the "spousal" subsystem was so great that I truly felt that my father had divorced *me* as much as my mother. My loyalty to the alliance with my mother was so great that I considered seriously at the same time changing my name to my mother's maiden name. I thought of myself as her child, not as his.

Alliances and Coalitions

Parents are supposed to have a primary alliance with each other. When the mother gets in a jam with the kids, the father's expected response is to support the mother. When the father needs an ally, the mother is usually there. When a parent consistently sides with the child instead of the spouse, the hierarchy has been reversed. Researchers have long appreciated the importance of a strong parental alliance. For example, Teyber (1983b) found that male college freshmen who perceived their parents' marital relationship as the "primary dyadic alliance" in the family adjusted better than those who did not. Conversely, those who perceived that cross-generational coalitions had primacy were likely to have academic difficulties. In another study, Teyber (1983a) found a marginally significant relationship between emotional adjustment and female students' perceptions of the marital dyad as the primary alliance in the family.

Peers

Parents are usually peers to each other; the children are peers to one another. When parent and child become peers, the generational hierarchy has been reversed.

Again, it is important to emphasize that occasional role reversals can make family members feel closer to one another, but consistent role reversals lead to an enmeshed, fused family.

Treatment of Adolescents with Individuation Issues

When a family comes in with an adolescent who is estranged and acting out, the therapeutic goal is to increase the quality and/or quantity of time that the family is spending together in each of these domains while still promoting steps toward autonomy. For example, if the family is spending all of their time together arguing and in conflict, the goal would be to spend more time in positive interactions (contact time). Dyads in the family who never spend any time in a one-on-one conversation may be instructed to take evening walks together (conversation space).

Mackey (1996:496) proposed that parents have trouble helping their children navigate adolescent developmental passages because of the dominant western Caucasian cultural context in the United States. She states:

> This cultural emphasis on individuation may lead to the acceptance and popularization of the adolescent's need for space, rejection of parental values, and attachment to peers. As a consequence, some parents abdicate parental control to outside influences early in the adolescent's development, assuming that this is normative. . . . In addition, as the adolescent begins to develop sexually, parents may respond to some of the adolescent's increasing awkwardness as a signal to refrain from physical contact. The adolescent may well associate the parental withdrawal with his or her sexual development and begin to associate physical contact with sexual contact. The danger is that the adolescent may turn to peer sexual involvement to meet the need for physical affection.

Unfortunately, when parents come to therapy for help with these problems, the emphasis is often on strengthening the parent's control over the adolescent (to decrease separation) without providing increased nurturance (to increase bonding). Consider the structural/organizational approach, which focuses on limit setting and drawing a boundary around the parental subsystem. Structural therapists identify who is the "bad-cop-parent" (the enforcer of the rules) and who is the "good-cop-parent" (the provider of nurturance). The therapeutic goal becomes to build a strong parental alliance where the "good-cop-parent" aligns with the disciplinarian so that his or her efforts are not undermined. This has the effect, all too often, of making the child feel cut off from the one source of safety and connection in the family.

Many behavioral approaches to adolescent rebellion also rely on short-ening the reins to reduce attempts at separation. Structured point systems and limit setting all take autonomy out of the hands of the adolescents and put it in the hands of the parents. Contracting is more successful with adolescents precisely because this technique allows the children to gain some valued freedoms.

In the tough-love approach, parents often resort to simply laying down the rules and evicting the child if he or she is unwilling to be controlled. Thus, there is no mastery of the separation/interdependence seesaw. The either-or proposals push adolescents into a regressive mode, forestalling their developmental tasks, or cutting them off from a family whose guid-ance and love they desperately need (Mackey, 1996). Strict contingencies only work if the reward program greatly outweighs any aversive contin-gency program. With tough-love programs, that means the emphasis needs to be on the loving end—instead of the toughness end.

Contextual therapy, on the other hand, zeroes in on creating a balance between earned individual freedoms and mandatory family obligations. Boszormenyi-Nagy and Ulrich (1981) see successful differentiation as occurring as a result of satisfying levels of connectedness. It is a much more appropriate model for conceptualizing how to successfully treat adolescent Sturm und Drang. If a teenaged boy knows that his father is proud of how he maintains his grades while still working a part-time job, he will be more likely to be assertive and successful getting permission to take a two-week road trip with friends. The connectedness lays the foundation for a safe separation.

Therapists using the contextual approach work with family members to delineate the necessary behavioral and emotional commitments that each person needs to fulfill to be part of the family. The first round of negoti-ations focuses on whether or not the commitments are reasonable and doable. The second round of negotiations has a dual focus. The family needs to learn how to create the conditions necessary for each person to fulfill the agreed-upon reasonable and doable commitments. Once the commitments are fulfilled, each family member has a host of entitlements. For adolescents, the biggest entitlements involve increasing zones of inde-pendence, autonomy, privacy, and differentness from the family ways. The third round of negotiations is to ensure that the parents respect and pro-mote the earned entitlements.

In many ways, parents are seeking permission to get stricter while in therapy. Rarely are they trying to be more giving and loving. They have been disappointed in the identified patient and have usually gone through a lot of grief on his or her behalf. Often, they are defensive about mistakes they have made in parenting. Mackey (1996) suggests that the key to moving parents to offer nurturance and survive rejection from their child is to recognize and work with the parents on their own childhood traumas and injustices. Through a personal historical analysis, parents can come to understand how they may be unwittingly hurting their own children. "Parents can then be encouraged to be the true healers not only of their child, but of future generations as they break the chain of dysfunctional interactions. They can then be coached to listen to their adolescent's pain and apologize without defending themselves. If the adolescent is able to accept the parental shift as genuine, the adolescent can be coached to listen to the parent's story" (Mackey, 1996:502).

Special Problems of the Single-Parent Family

Generational boundaries are most difficult to maintain in a single-parent family. Nurturance is often compromised since the parent does not have enough time or energy to be as loving and responsible as the emotional needs of children dictate. Control is not always possible, because the children are sometimes home without an adult. Also, the single parent lacks the emotional support he or she needs in order to stand firm and be consistent. In the single-parent family, coalitions and alliances are always intergenerational. The parent is forced to function as a peer in many family events. Then, when the parent pulls back into the one-parent subsystem, the children are confused. Why is the parent "pulling rank" all of a sudden?

Compounding these problems is the overriding need for children and parents in one-parent families to act cohesively and not to show anger or frustration. The children sense that the parent is overworked and overstressed. Having been abandoned once by one parent, they feel in danger of losing the one that remains. The parent also feels that the children are the last vestiges of the family, and fears alienating the children or hurting them further. These conflicts lead to a loss of separateness. Fusion and lack of individuation are bound to become sensitive issues in such situations.

How Much Is Too Much?

How much closeness is healthy and energizing to the family? How much differentiation? When does closeness become too close, stifling autonomy and individual development? Different ethnic and cultural groups have different answers to these questions. The Japanese traditionally emphasize a much closer relationship between generations than West-

> ## JACKIE (office manager, age 46)
>
> I was separated from my first husband when my daughter was three and my son five. For the next five years I was a single parent, and I found it very easy to maintain generational boundaries. I was the parent: the protector, the wise one, the unselfish one, the tireless one. They were the children: vulnerable, naive, selfish, cranky, and indulged. If I had to cry, I went into the garage and sat in my car so they couldn't hear me. If they had a bad day at school, I let them snuggle in my bed at night even if I was tired and wanted to just collapse.
>
> When I was dating my second husband it was clear from the start that he was dating all of us and marrying into a family first and foremost. I stayed married to my second husband for nearly five years. For the past three years I've again been on my own—this time with two teenagers, fifteen and thirteen years old. Boy, it is different! My son is 5'10" and puts on the spouse role whenever work needs to be done around the house and whenever I want to do major shopping tasks (at Christmas, we bought a new TV and I *needed* him there to help me choose it). Sometimes he's put in the spouse role when I need companionship: someone to tell how my day went or (I'm ashamed to admit it) cry with about a disappointment. My daughter is often put into the sister/sib role. Sometimes I'm shocked to find us giggling in bed after I've been out on a date. She's grilling me on the date and I'm answering her and we both get very silly.
>
> We all talk about relationships a lot. Paul (my son) discusses his girlfriends, sex, and marijuana very candidly with me. He expects a friend's understanding and not a parent's censoring. Most always, my first response is to be a friend. He knows I've smoked pot and although we wouldn't do it together (there are still some generational boundaries), he speaks easily about it in front of me. While my relationship with both my children is a far cry from the traditional family, I feel that what we have is very strong and wonderful. We have a friendship and respect for one another that will allow us to stay emotionally close to each other for years to come. They know me as a person.
>
> My strengths and weaknesses are known to them. In turn, I feel they are more open to showing me who they really are instead of just showing me the parts of them I can approve of and applaud. In the long run, I'm optimistic that they will have a much better and more helping relationship than I have with either of my two parents.

erners; for example, several generations of Japanese often sleep together in a common room even when other bedrooms are available.

A good way to determine whether closeness with parents is too close is to ask, What is the goal or end point of all the closeness? Is the main goal to learn and to get ideas and information from the guiding parents? In such a case, the outcome is likely to be a rational, independent adult whose close relationship with the parents produces personal growth. Is the main goal parental approval and emotional refueling? In adulthood such a child may remain dependent rather than interdependent. The closeness with the parents has become an impediment to maturity.

Parental closeness risks the negative connotation of "fusion" if the adult child exclusively cultivates attitudes, behaviors, and lifestyles that are directly linked to parental approval. Even then, parental closeness can have beneficial effects on the human spirit. Walter Cronkite (1983:153), for example, describes the positive impact of being close with his mother:

> At every moment of crisis . . . I have felt her hand on my shoulder . . . it was her approval that was more important to me than any of the millions who might have been out there. She has been my guide. . . .

Perhaps the quotation somewhat overstates the case. But there is no reason to think that such closeness is inherently negative or pathological. In the case of Walter Cronkite, it seems to have been a very positive force.

Gender Differences in Role Behavior and Individuation

> *A son's a son till he gets him a wife; but a daughter's a daughter all her life.*

Folk saying

Females are much more likely than males to experience difficulty differentiating themselves within the family. Even today, girls are differentially socialized by parents who encourage their dependency upon the family and shelter them from learning about the "big cold world." In learning the domestic role, girls inadvertently absorb the idea that their interactions and nurturance are crucial to the well-being of their parents and, by extension, to their families as adults.

In most cultural groups, women are designated "kinskeepers." Thus they feel morally obligated to interact continually with their family of origin. Countless observations of adult daughter/parent relations reflect this attitude (Komarovsky, 1962; Fischer and Fischer, 1963; Sweetser, 1964; Cohler and Grunebaum, 1981). Cohler and Geyer (1982) cite the following seven research findings as illustrating the commitment of women to their kinskeeper role:

1. Couples characteristically choose to spend holidays with the wife's parental family.
2. Couples often live with the wife's parents' family for a period in their early years. One study looking at immigrant Jewish families in

New York found that 93 percent of the first-generation American women in the study had lived with their own mothers at some time since marriage (Leichter and Mitchell, 1967).

3. The typical wife is more attached to her parental family than the husband is to his.

4. Among young couples who live some distance from their families, the wife is more homesick for her family than the husband is for his.

5. Couples usually settle near the wife's parents. When a couple is forced to move to a distant spot for job opportunities, very often the couple move back to be near the wife's family as soon as this can be arranged.

6. Studies in England and the United States concur that more than 40 percent of married women have some daily contact with their parents (Young and Wilmott, 1957; Wilmott and Young, 1960; Young and Geertz, 1961). Primarily, they talk to the mother or see her in person. Less than 25 percent of the women surveyed reported having contact with their parents less than once a month. Bayen (1991) found that the frequency and length of phone contact predicted how close elderly parents felt toward their children. Greater closeness was associated with frequent, long phone calls.

7. Women from lower socioeconomic levels have more contact with their parents than women from upper socioeconomic levels.

Ironically, researchers have identified little relationship between reported feelings toward parents and amount of physical contact with them. Lack of such findings suggests that the frequency of contact may be related to other factors such as feelings of filial obligation, the immediate reinforcing value of visiting (e.g., getting a meal, babysitting, advice), and for some, an inability to separate from the dependent parent/child relationship.

An interesting study on the cross-cultural pervasiveness of female kin orientation was done by McDermott and associates (1983). The study is based on a questionnaire on family attitudes administered to 158 Caucasian and Japanese-American families. Few differences were found between the ethnic groups, but striking differences in values were found between the adolescent boys and girls. In both groups, adolescent girls were more likely to agree with a host of statements that confirm strong family cohesion. Adolescent girls were more likely than boys to agree with each of the following statements:

- A family should do something together regularly.
- Every member of the family should help one another.

- Family members should openly acknowledge their affection for one another.
- All family members should share in doing the household chores.
- It is all right for a member of the family to cry openly when sad or upset.
- A family should eat together at least once a day.
- Children should be open and honest with their parents.

The finding that young women value family affiliation, closeness, and emotional expression more than young men implies that they may have different preferred routes for becoming mature adults. When socialization or temperament has created a person who values the closeness of family life and the survival of those relationships, perhaps interdependence rather than independence could be the optimum goal. People who do not value family closeness might have a more independently oriented goal.

Conflicts may develop between individual desires for closeness or differentiation and the family's overall level of closeness. Differentiation of the self may be furthered or impeded in the process. Consider the following two cases. In the first instance, the family as a whole values closeness but an adolescent son values it less. In the second instance, it is the adolescent daughter in a distant family who values closeness.

Case 1

The Davis family has always been a tightly knit group. The three children have sought one another out for play, and the parents have developed strong one-on-one relationships with each child. For years, the family have gone to church together on Sunday and then participated in some kind of family activity. Wednesday evenings the family always had a family game or project, as well. When the first son, John, entered high school, he got a part-time job and tried out for the wrestling team. He had practice on Sundays and refused to play games or fix up the house according to the family's schedule. "What's gotten into John?" the others wondered. No one understood, and conflicts started to erupt.

Case 2

The Browns have always been a loving but distant family. In this active group, the parents have each had their own civic activities. The children have had a large peer group and after-school lessons to engage their interests. Everyone made his or her own breakfast, and dinners were catch-as-catch-can. On weekends, the refrigerator was plastered with notes communicating the different schedules. Helen, the oldest daughter, began to feel lonely and depressed. She daydreamed of having a mother she could have long talks with, someone who would always come to watch her swim meets and go shopping in the mall with her. Helen often suggested family trips, but everyone's schedule was always too busy.

Both John and Helen are experiencing trouble differentiating themselves. One feels suffocated and one feels neglected, but neither feels able to relate to the family successfully without compromising his or her developing value system. If Helen and John magically switched families, each would find it easier to separate from their emotional childhood.

INDIVIDUATION AS A LIFELONG PROCESS

Formerly, it was feared that the need of grown children for autonomy and individuation would lead them, in midlife, to desert their elderly parents. It now appears that these fears are generally unwarranted. Family researchers have documented that children maintain invisible loyalties to their parents throughout life (Boszormenyi-Nagy and Spark, 1973).

Nevertheless, maintaining a meaningful relationship with elderly parents requires some changes in role, for as parents age, they become more dependent on their grown children. If an elderly parent is without a spouse or if the level of financial or emotional support provided by the spouse is inadequate, children—adult daughters in particular—are especially likely to end up "parenting their parents." Stoller (1983) found that elderly parents who required help maintaining their households received, on the average, fifteen hours per month of help from their sons and thirty hours per month from their daughters! The assistance provided ranged from food preparation to shopping to laundry to managing finances. For both sexes, married children helped much fewer hours per month than the average, and unmarried children helped many hours per month more than the average. In fact, Stoller (1983) found that married children provided twenty hours less help per month than those who were not married. This finding suggests (1) that, as folk wisdom suggests, marital responsibilities do reduce the time available for giving care to parents and (2) that the task of caring for aged parents falls disproportionately on those children who are not married.

Whereas the demands of marriage significantly reduced helping behavior, the effect of employment was very gender specific. Being employed decreased the average level of sons' assistance by over twenty hours per month, but it had no significant effect on the level of assistance offered by daughters. Similarly, the number of children in the daughters' families did not affect the level of aid that they gave to their mothers. The additional role obligation of parenting parents can produce considerable stress and guilt among adult women as they try to juggle an increasingly complex array of time-allocation decisions.

The need to change roles with one's parents may occur with tragic suddenness if serious illness strikes a parent. More often, it develops gradually over a period of years. Even the most independent parent looks to children for advice and support as the physical and emotional costs of aging mount. Most parents have a "pecking order" of the children they feel most comfortable asking for help. A child who is asked to help or advise is likely to feel an overwhelming need to be helpful, even if he or she is not really in any position to help. Bloomfield (1983:162) summarizes the dilemma:

> Whether you were the "favorite" or the "black sheep," whether you have the time, energy, funds or desire to help, and whether you feel competent to deal with the challenges your parent faces, the problems nonetheless fall into your lap. Instead of being the child who looks to your parent for help and guidance you are now expected to answer questions like "I have a pain in my side . . . do you think it's serious?" "Should I sell the house and move into a retirement home?" "Should I get rid of the housekeeper?" "Should I take the medication even though I'm feeling better?" "Should I stay with you until I find another place?" And, "Should I buy a new television set or do you think this one can be fixed?"

Ironically, now that filial dedication seems to be alive and well, experts are suggesting that many healthy, able elderly persons may need to retreat from their familial ties and obligations. The healthy aging person may require an additional developmental period of individuation in which independence and psychological autonomy from family obligations may be as important as they were to a twenty-year-old.

Cohler (1983:38) describes a typical predicament involving an older mother in an ethnic community on the East Coast. She and her husband occupy the same apartment where, as immigrants, they began raising their family half a century ago. Her middle-aged daughter enjoys bringing her retired husband and grown children to the old neighborhood for shopping and a home-cooked lunch at Mom's. She calls her mother often for advice on cooking and housekeeping.

The mother was much less enthusiastic than her daughter about these weekend visits or even about the frequent phone calls. She complained that her daughter's frequent bids for assistance jeopardized her own use of her free time. Since she still worked as a seamstress at the same job she had held for nearly half a century and since she was also very active in the parish, she had very little time for herself. She was annoyed that her only free day each weekend should be spent caring for other family members. Although she had tried to tell her daughter and other family members of her feelings, her children and grandchildren were unable to understand her perspective.

As elderly people are retaining their health and physical mobility for more and more years, the number of grandparents suffering from "too much family" will increase. Morgan (1983) discusses how some individuals approaching retirement age are already overwhelmed by financially helping out three generations of kin while trying to scrape together some time and resources for themselves. These people are supporting very elderly parents, their own children, and their adolescent and college-bound grandchildren! Here they are expecting to relax a little and find new and unexplored areas for themselves; instead their financial obligations and dependents have multiplied. While many people will feel fulfilled by their critical role in the family, others will feel angry and cheated. Some will be able to go on developing and further individuate themselves while others will unfortunately stagnate.

The burden on older parents should not be underestimated. Currently, 4.7 million grandparents are living with their grandchildren. In three-quarters of these families, it is the grandparent who is maintaining the home for the grandchildren and often the child-parents (Bryson and Casper, 1999). The

---

DEBORAH (researcher, age 43)

I am acutely aware of how I have had a lifelong struggle to become an autonomous person. For years, I was merged with my mother and her matriarchal clan, and now I am struggling over my merger with my own children, particularly my oldest.

My father died of cancer when I was seven and I was left an only child with just my mother and me in the home. Because my father was very ill the last three years of his life, by the time of his death my role as the family peacemaker was firmly established. I would do anything so people wouldn't fight and feelings wouldn't be hurt. In fact, my struggle for individuation is really the struggle of learning not to worry if I upset the applecart.

Looking back, I can recall two major events that helped me grow emotionally independent of my mother. The first was that at age fourteen I was sent away to boarding school because my mother felt I would get a superior education. Although I initially agreed to go in order to please her, it was very important for my own growth. No sooner had I arrived than I was elected class president. As a newcomer, I was elected because no one else wanted to deal with our housemother, who was a real drill sergeant. The school was

(continued)

(continued)

full of rules and restrictions, but she tightened them and added to them whenever possible. One time she was suspicious that some girls were smoking on the fire escape and called on me to sit on the fire escape all that evening and catch the culprits in the act for her. Had my mother been nearby I would have asked her advice and listened to her. Thrown on my own resources, I independently refused this frightening authority and won my first badge of mature judgment. Another time the headmaster found my friends and me eating double dip cones in town instead of attending a church service. We giggled and told him the truth and he laughed along with us. At home I would have never thought of being this rebellious and would not have learned that I don't have to lie all the time. My mother would have severely punished me for thinking of such an act and the idea that an adult could appreciate our fun was a real liberating experience.

I became even more independent when I got married. My mother disapproved, and for the first time in my life I told her I would defy her no matter what and get married. Choosing whom to marry and when was my first act of defiance in my relationship with my mother. She came around but after that I reverted back to peacemaker and always tried to please her. My husband used to hate to visit because he said that I became a daughter instead of a wife as soon as I stepped in the door. Over the years I have slowly become more and more able to be my own person with my mom but difficulties still crop up.

My individuation from my own children has likewise been a difficult and laborious task. If I take my daughter for a haircut, the whole next day I go around feeling different. This is much stronger with my older daughter, and I am constantly mixing up her failures with my failures; her successes with my successes. One positive sign of individuating from the children is that this year is the first time in fifteen years that I've bought clothes just for work—even though I've worked for six years. Before this my identity as mother was so strong everything I bought had to be rugged and mother-wearable. Now, I feel different about myself. There is a part of me that is not a mother and wife and I'm willing to acknowledge and nourish this independent part of me. I believe that for me, independence is a lifelong task and I'll just have to wait till the end of the road to see if there is a "true" me and what that woman is really like.

bond of maternal caring appears to support the older parent's individuation path in many cases. It is fulfilling to help the next generation. In other cases, though, the grandparents feel trapped, unappreciated, and angry.

SELF-EXPLORATION: INDIVIDUATION

The purpose of this exercise is to let you examine how dependent and interdependent you were with your family of origin during your teenage years (thirteen to nineteen years old).

1. Fill out the questionnaire "Assessing Generational Closeness and Role Differentiation" below to get focused on the issues. While determining your ratings, refer back to the text discussion of each item if you are unsure of what you are being asked to rate.
2. Next, discuss how close or distant your family was in each of the following areas: contact time, personal space, emotional space, information space, conversation space, and decision space.
3. Now try to examine how rigid or flexible the family's distinctions were in the following four areas: nurturance, control, alliance, and peers. Were the role distinctions overall too blurred or too rigid for you?
4. Given the nature of the generational hierarchies of your family, do you find your family to be healthy, enmeshed, or estranged?

Assessing Generational Closeness and Role Differentiation

A. Rate your family on how much closeness they showed in each of the six areas during your adolescence:

	1 2 3 Very little closeness	4 5 Moderate closeness	6 7 Great amount of closeness
1. Contact time	— — —	— —	— —
2. Personal space	— — —	— —	— —
3. Emotional space	— — —	— —	— —
4. Information space	— — —	— —	— —
5. Conversation space	— — —	— —	— —

B. Rate your family on how much role differentiation there was between parents and children in each of the four areas during your adolescence:

	1 2 3 Very rigid distinctions	4 5 Moderate role distinctions	6 7 Almost no distinctions
1. Nurturance	— — —	— —	— —
2. Control	— — —	— —	— —
3. Alliances and coalitions	— — —	— —	— —
4. Peers	— — —	— —	— —

Chapter 3

Separation

Home was a quiet place when people stayed there.

E. B. White

Fond as we are of loved ones, there comes at times during their absence an unexplainable peace.

Anne Shaw

Chapter 2, "Individuation," focused on the metamorphosis of children from dependency and emotional vulnerability into independent, autonomous adults and some of the problems encountered in this process. This chapter examines how physical separations can help or hinder individuation. Personal growth as well as the quality of family interactions can be enhanced or diminished by physical separation.

With appropriate preparation, physical separation can foster the psychological separation of children from parents. For the individual, successful physical separations validate competency and maturity, thereby constituting a rite of passage. Physical separations also make the old patterns of communicating easier to break. Thus, if communication has been following an unhealthy pattern, separation provides space for new, hopefully healthier, patterns to emerge.

Many paradoxes exist in the area of parent-child separation. Some parents can be thousands of miles away from their child, yet be in constant verbal contact (via telephone) or visual contact (via video cameras) with them. Some children can be living in the same physical structure as their parents and literally not see them for days on end because the nanny or relative does the maintenance chores and the child has personal designated entertainment systems (television, videos, games).

Many families evolve such that some of the family members experience the unit as too close or involved in one another's business. These families may contact one another at any point in the day, in any location, and for any reason. Marked separateness characterizes families at the other extreme. Nonparental child rearing allows parents to remain symbolically connected to their children while going for years without any meaningful contact.

The families who are too close for comfort are having problems separating successfully from one another as are the families that are too distant from one another. Different separations occur at each developmental stage, posing new challenges and pitfalls for the family.

INFANCY AND EARLY CHILDHOOD

Both parents and children experience separation anxiety throughout the life cycle. The external focus of concern changes at each age and stage, but the gut emotional issues of letting go of well-learned and predictable routines continue to create tension and stress. The developmental need for ever-increasing independence between parents and child conflicts with the anxiety of separation.

The Need for Attachment

Long-term or permanent parent/child separations have long been known to have potentially devastating effects on infants. These effects were established by Bowlby's studies on homeless children, summarized in his now well-known monograph *Maternal Care and Mental Health* (Bowlby, 1952). Bowlby believed that the major developmental task of the first three years of life is forming an attachment to at least one other human being. He outlined a series of distinct developmental phases by which infants come to focus with increasing intensity on one principal caretaker (usually the mother). Bowlby believed that a child who is separated from this caretaker before the attachment process runs its course will experience serious lifelong problems in relating to others. According to this theory, a child's attachment to its initial principal caretaker becomes a prototype for human attachments throughout life. (For the sake of simplicity, this caretaker is referred to as the mother in the following discussion.)

Subsequent researchers have found that infants are far more complex and interactive than Bowlby imagined and that a number of variables determine the impact of maternal separation. For example, the age of the child, the quality of its relationship with the mother prior to separation, the character of maternal care subsequent to the initial separation, and the duration of the separation experience all affect the child's experience.

Thus, mother/child separations have a more intense and negative outcome if the infant is older than six months; if there is an ongoing, close mother/child relationship; if the care subsequent to the separation is poor; or if there are relatively long separations. In addition, personality and temperament also greatly affect how children react to maternal separation (Yarrow, 1964). Even if a mother figure is continually present, infants experience a series of separation crises as they become more independent of their caretakers.

Separation Anxiety in the Infant

As infants are exposed to more people and spend more time discovering their own separateness and aloneness, they go through various stages of separation anxiety. For most children, classic separation anxiety begins at about eight months. Even by six months of age, a baby will cry when held by a stranger, indicating that it can reliably distinguish between mother, father, and other. By eight months, the child not only can distinguish among people but shows a real preference for one or two. When the mother leaves the room, the child cries and tries to follow. It seems that the child has learned in eight short months that to be in mother's physical presence is to feel safe. Despite this feeling of safety, children are ambivalent. As toddlers, they want to run and explore on their own. Consequently, toddlers are always balancing their need for autonomy against their need for a secure base. Within this dichotomy, so long as they can wander when they feel brave and cuddle when they feel afraid, things are fine.

Separation Anxiety in the Mother

For mothers, the initial strong experience of separation anxiety often occurs when their infants are weaned from the breast. After all, nursing makes a baby nearly as dependent upon the mother as it was in the womb. To let go of this dependency is more difficult for many women than it is for their toddlers. A study involving mothers who were in the midst of weaning their children revealed a large degree of openly felt ambivalence over this delayed separation (Berg-Cross, Berg-Cross, and McGeehan, 1979). While bottle-feeding mothers were overwhelmingly pleased to wean their children to a cup, none of the nursing mothers studied showed such unequivocally positive feelings. The sentiments of Jane and Alison were typical. Alison summed up her ambivalence by saying, "I felt great that I had been able to nurse successfully and glad we're both more independent. But, gee, it's sad she's no longer a baby, and I hope she doesn't feel rejected." Jane also experienced conflicts over the dependency aroused by nursing. She said (p. 354):

> I was resentful of the demands he made. I felt he was telling me I wasn't mothering him enough. But really, he only came to me when he was bored. One part of me said, "I'm a person, not a thing," and the other part said "I'm not mothering him enough." After Christmas, he didn't ask to nurse again. I felt crushed. That's not how I wanted it to end.

Not every nursing mother struggles with separation anxiety, but enough do to make weaning toe first testing experience for how mothers approach the separation process.

The Use of Transitional Objects

The child's struggle for independence from the parents continues throughout life. Many children try to resolve early separation anxieties by using a *transitional object* such as a teddy bear or blanket. The objects serve as substitute parents, providing the security and comfort associated with the family's physical presence. Initially, transitional objects are used when the child has to go to bed alone or is worried or upset during the day and seeking comfort independent of the parent. Later, children use transitional objects when they have their first sleepover, camp, or even college experience. One study found that half of the children who had a transitional object were still actively attached to it at age nine (Sherman et al., 1981). How many readers took their pillow or blanket to college with them or even to their new home after getting married? Unfortunately, parents usually do not have any analogous object and so suffer silently.

It is interesting to speculate about possible personality differences between children who have transitional objects and those who do not. Does having a transitional object influence your personality? Cohen and Clark (1984) found that college students who reported having transitional objects as children scored higher on the personality factor "tension." Scoring high on this factor indicated that those students had difficulty calming down, had a low tolerance for criticism, were easily angered, and showed an inability to hold back negative remarks.

By contrast, those college students who reported never having a transitional object scored higher on the "reserved" factor. This factor is indicative of aloofness and detachment as well as the tendency to be rather rigid, precise, and objective. Thus, it could be that children with tense personalities seek out transitional objects because they experience frustration over being independent and need the tension-reducing comfort afforded by a transitional object. Similarly, the more reserved students would seem to be less likely to experience frustrations over being independent and hence less likely to seek comfort via external transitional objects. If this finding is replicated, it may help provide an important insight into the expression of infant personality characteristics.

MIDDLE CHILDHOOD AND EARLY ADOLESCENCE

In middle childhood, the child's psychological separation from the parent seems gradual. Children still come home from school to eat, play, and sleep every night and usually are eager to partake in family outings. But the separation process remains slowly and imperceptibly still underway.

Shifts in the Parent/Child Relationship

During adolescence, children begin to spend more and more time away from home. Both parents and children feel the strain as adolescents begin to transfer the emotional ties of dependency from parents to peers and express more independence toward parental rules and values. While feeling the strain, most parents really are eager for their children to become independent. They want to help in the process, to be supportive.

All too often, though, this is a paradoxical situation for adolescents. They are supposed to maintain their affection for and communication with their parents, while avoiding parental pressures to conform. A contemporary analogy would be asking a computer to play a newly invented game without changing the programming. It just will not happen. As the adolescent struggles for individuality, he or she will increasingly feel a need to push away from the parents. This shift in parent-child relationships is the main theme of many a parenting book. In *Between Parent and Teenager,* Ginott (1969:11) states: "Letting go is the key to a peaceful and meaningful coexistence between parent and teenager; as parents, our need is to be needed; as teenagers their need is not to need us. To let go when we want to hold on requires the utmost generosity and love."

Gender Differences

Nancy Friday (1978:68) describes the particular problems women have separating from their daughters:

It is hard for women to let go. We are born collectors. We live in the treasured bits and pieces of past life. Mothers collect the memorabilia of their children's past, shoes from the time they possessed baby most totally. Grown women collect match covers and menus from nights when a man held us close, when we felt most possessed, and we count the hours dead until he calls and brings us back to life. A woman and a man exchange Valentine cards; he opens his, smiles, kisses her and then throws the card away. "You're not going to keep it?" she cries. She's saved every card since she was thirteen.

But men don't need our collections; their future may be uncertain, but they feel they have a hand in its creation. They are not dependent on the past. When we cut our hair, mother cries, "You've changed!" It is not a compliment to growth but a fear of disloyalty and separation: "You're leaving me!"

Parents and the "Empty Nest"

Despite its pervasiveness, the so-called empty nest syndrome affects each couple differently. One important factor influencing how much difficulty parents experience with the separations of young adulthood is the spacing between their children. Daniels and Weingarten (1980:229) explores the difficult challenge parents face when their closely spaced children suddenly are ready to leave home within a few years of each other.

One day we may be better able to help parents make the transition of which Daniels writes. For now, the separation experience is so difficult in our society for children and parents that it often becomes a lifelong task.

The Empty Nest Experience

The emptying of the nest—which also means letting go of our children and our power over them, letting go of child-rearing responsibility—is as essential to the process of parenthood as deciding to have a child in the first place. And it can evoke strong feelings in both mothers and fathers.

Ellie Egan, who had been "back out in the world"! for several years when her last child moved away from home, described this phenomenon: "I was all set for the last one leaving. I had had my job for quite a while, and I loved it. But Ed and I did have some trouble then, and Ed would say—because he read it somewhere, I'm sure—"You're upset because the kids are growing up and leaving." And I'd say to him, "I'm upset because you're growing up and leaving." Which was actually true. As much as he enjoyed all the things he'd done with the kids, he was like a man turned loose. All of a

(continued)

(continued)

sudden, in his forties now, he had to do everything, all at once. Now that was my empty nest.

Other couples who have fewer children, spaced closer together, do not have this extended rehearsal time in which to project themselves gradually into a post-child-rearing future. The first launch in the Franklin family occurred early, took Faye utterly by surprise, and precipitated a reaction of profound grief. For with two closely spaced children, the Franklins knew the empty nest would follow all too soon.

Faye was shocked when her older daughter decided to go to boarding school at sixteen. Five years later, when we met, her feelings about that time were as vivid as if it had happened yesterday. "It was too soon for her to go away. I had the children late in life, and then to lose the first at sixteen! I don't think I've ever truly recovered from the sense of loss."

Her husband, Fritz, felt the emptiness too, but he also recognized in himself a readiness to let go. "There is a side," he said, "that is ready for them to go off. As much as we may miss them and be sad about it, we were ready to find each other and not be so involved with the children. To have a bit more time for ourselves, and a bit less of the plans and projects of teenagers. We're glad to have them home on vacations, and we miss them when they go back to school, but you're a bit more willing to see them go at our age."

Although there is no financial necessity for it, Fritz wonders whether taking up outside work once again might make a difference in Faye's feelings. Faye says no: "There are times when the house seems like a morgue to me. It has nothing to do with whether I work or not during the day, because when I come home I see those two tidy rooms. What does what you do during the day have to do with that? I'd have to shut my heart to the loss not to feel it."

Source: From *Sooner or Later: The Timing of Parenthood in Adult Lives,* (p. 124) by Pamela Daniels and Kathy Weingarten. Copyright ©1982 by Pamela Daniels and Kathy Weingarten. Reprinted by permission of W. W. Norton & Company, Inc.

MIKE (biological researcher, age 45)

I'm glad to have a chance to collect my thoughts on this topic since I'm in the midst of the most major separation experiences of my life. Next week, I am retiring from the Army after twenty years of active service. I owe a lot to the Army: my education, my career as a research scientist, and the lifestyle I've enjoyed over the past twenty years. I've met many wonderful people and have had, by and large, the personal and administrative support of a variety of very bright and hard-working leaders. Still, I am very eager to begin my new life as a civilian working in the private sector. I'm

(continued)

(continued)

leaving in a state of exhilaration and high expectations. I feel like I've done an excellent job in the Army but that it's time to move on. Everyone around me has been very supportive of the move, and the fact that I'll be close to doubling my salary hasn't hurt me one bit!

My new job is in Oregon, so my family and I will be relocating. This is our first move in fifteen years and my wife and I are looking forward to it. Three years ago, our daughter was raped just two blocks from our home. Since that time, we have lost many attachments we felt toward the community and even our house. We're all breathing a sigh of relief that we won't need to live here any more. Moving across the country means leaving my daughters here on the East Coast and taking only my son with us (he'll be a senior in high school next year). The girls are both well settled at their respective colleges. One daughter is a sophomore and the other is a junior. Neither wants to transfer. They only come home on long vacations and the summer anyway, so it's not going to affect how often we see them. There was a sense of security knowing their parents were only three hours away that they are going to lose, but I think the distance might also give them an extra sense of autonomy. If not, they can always transfer closer to us at the end of next semester.

The best part of leaving is that we'll be living only two to three hours away from each of our parents. They're all getting on in age and it's good to know that we'll be around to help them out. I haven't been home since I left for college. Even though I was an only child, my parents were always proud of my independence from them and encouraged me to travel and explore. Our closeness was based on shared values and interests, not on how much distance there was between our houses. Even so, inside me there is a little boy, jumping up and down excited to be going home. I want to move through the next twenty years talking about how things have changed and go fishing along the banks where I first learned how to fish.

In a year and a half, when my son leaves and my wife and I are empty nesters, the impact of all these separations might seem sadder and less exciting than they do now. For now though, I'm caught up watching the growth and maturity of my adult children and enjoying the chance to be a child and grow some more myself!

LATE ADOLESCENCE AND LEAVING HOME

The two most common pivotal separations in our society occur (1) when an adolescent first leaves home for college or a job and (2) when parents divorce and children are separated from one or both adults. Both these separation experiences are discussed in the light of research findings.

The College Experience

Separation is always aided by support and nurturance. The father who promises to write every day is more likely to have a child try sleep-away camp. A mother who sits in the playground is more likely to have her toddler run off and play with the other children. Even at the college level, students who report that they feel strong support from their parents, in terms of being listened to, feeling understood, and being able to count on them to help out, are better adjusted, psychologically, than students who are low on parental support (Holahan, Valentiner, and Moos, 1994).

The separation experienced when a child goes off to college can be critical in the development of autonomy and the achievement of ego identity. Kenneth and Anna Sullivan (Sullivan and Sullivan, 1980) studied the separation experience of 242 male college freshmen by testing them before and after they left for college. Roughly half the students were living at home and commuting to college and half were living on campus. Three major findings emerged.

First, in comparison with commuters, males who moved out of the house and lived on campus reported feeling more affectionate toward both Mother and Father and felt that the parents in turn were more affectionate toward them. The parents did not get on their nerves so much, and the sons enjoyed talking to them more. As could be expected, the mothers of these boys could perceive their sons' increased affection.

JOHN (speechwriter, age 36)

I would consider my relations with Mom and Dad to be "normal." That is, I love them and feel an extra measure of security and warmth when I am around them. Yet, I have no overwhelming dependence on them nor any great emotional need to visit them often. (I am now in my mid-thirties, married, and living about ten miles from my parents.)

My life story is probably a very typical case study of the salutary effects of separation and—on the other hand—the stunting, frustrating effects of being obliged to live at home as a young adult.

When I was in tenth and eleventh grade, I was sent to a boarding school several hundred miles from home. Of course, I was still relatively immature, and I missed my parents and family enormously. Nonetheless, this premature separation motivated me to develop an independent emotional life; to make adolescent and adult friends I otherwise would not. Those two years at boarding school were a time of rapid and impressive emotional growth for me. I came into my own.

Moreover, my trips home on holidays were warm and jubilant occasions. Absence had bred fondness—just as it is supposed to do.

(continued)

(continued)

All this stands in stark contrast to my first two years of college. Without giving much thought to the emotional consequences, I decided to attend a college near home; to save money, I chose to be a commuting student and live at home.

As a result, my freshman through junior years at college were a disaster for me. On the one hand, I failed to forge friendships and ties at the university, living an extremely spartan social life. And compounding this problem, my relationship with my parents turned extremely sour.

I came to resent my ties to home; and I vocally rejected even relatively subtle assertions of authority by my parents. I gradually and nearly irreversibly retreated into my shell, became noncommunicative, and at one point even turned to alcohol as a form of escape.

By the end of my junior year, I realized this couldn't go on. I got a part-time job and made arrangements to live with a roommate near the school. It's a shame I didn't resolve to do this years earlier.

My initial feelings upon moving out of my parents' house were of escape and liberation. I didn't want to look back. Because of these feelings, and because of my lingering bitterness, I made almost no attempt to communicate with home—no letters, no phone calls, no visits (though my parents were only ten miles away) for several months at a time. Meanwhile, I tried to make up for lost time by forging friendships and getting involved with campus activities.

Gradually the pendulum began to shift in my relations with my parents. My lingering resentment subsided. I communicated with home more frequently. I even began going home for an occasional weekend visit. Ironically, home began to become a place of momentary escape from the rigors of school and dormitory-style living.

Eventually, my parental relations returned to full equilibrium. I enjoyed being away from them, just as I enjoyed being with them for short, occasional periods. More natural adult patterns of separation and reunion made for a much healthier relationship with my parents—a healthy relationship that has continued to this day.

Second, when compared with commuters, the boarders felt that their parents were communicating with them better. They also felt better about the overall communication between themselves and their parents. This is undoubtedly related to a combination of factors. For example, telephone communications are more easily controlled. Distance makes conversation more of a special event not to be ruined by probing or arguing. Also, parents know less about the day-to-day events of the child's life and thus become less upset with the child's activities and decisions.

Third, the boarding group felt more independent from their parents than commuters did. Eating and sleeping habits and social life were entirely under their own control, and this apparently had meaning for them.

Thus, leaving home to begin college seems to be beneficial in assisting the adolescent boy to become functionally independent of his parents while strengthening emotional ties to them. The Sullivans' project is a pioneering work, and comparable studies need to be done to help parents assess their own situations. For which adolescents is boarding away not a positive experience and for which is it more desirable? Are the patterns for female adolescents similar to those of male adolescents? Do social class and ethnic background influence the effect of such separation? And perhaps most important, are these *statistically* significant findings of any *practical* value?

Of course, even among college students who do leave home, a large minority are still plagued by feelings of rebelliousness toward parents or by homesickness. If the college rite is to be a successful separation experience, more than boarding away from home is required. Adolescents must be better prepared for the separation. Nearly twenty years ago, Weinberger and Reuter (1980) developed a twelve-week "life discussion" group to facilitate the personal growth and development of high school seniors. Although the content of the group sessions is unplanned and spontaneous, groups invariably find themselves dealing with their fears and beliefs about what life will be like after they leave their parental home. During the later sessions of the series, group members begin to explore such issues as: "Will I be capable when I'm on my own?" "I'm used to having things done for me. Will I be able to do for myself, and how will I do?" "Will new people like me?" They report excitement about new challenges and a sense that old settings have become routine and boring. But they also report ambivalence about outgrowing and leaving old friends and regret at ending a major life phase.

All of their lives they have had the status and privileges of childhood. The obligations and tasks of adulthood are poorly understood by most adolescents. They have seen a few role models; parents, teachers, and relatives. But for most, the vast gulf between where they are and where they see themselves as adults is so large that they have no idea how to draw up a reasonable life plan to get from here to there. Adolescents have intense curiosity about how various adults got to be the type of people they are, but there is a conspiracy, it seems, and few are willing to share their paths in detail. One of the challenges of high school education is to let students have more explicit opportunities to learn the roles, frustrations, limitations, and possiblities of adulthood.

Haley (1980) has worked extensively with adolescents who find it extremely difficult to separate from their parents. Haley has said that the most significant events in any family occur when new members enter and old members leave the family. In his book *Leaving Home,* Haley suggests that extreme psychopathology in adolescents is a direct expression of the inability of parents and child to separate successfully from each other (Haley, 1980:30):

> In two-parent families, the parents are faced with only each other, after many years of functioning in a many-person organization. Sometimes parents have communicated with each other primarily through a particular child and have great difficulty dealing with each other more directly. When the child leaves home, the parents become unable to function as a viable organization. Sometimes they threaten divorce or separation. The emphasis in this work is on problems in the offspring, but at this stage of family life, problems can appear in one or both parents. One way the young person can stabilize the family is to develop some incapacitating problem that makes him or her a failure so that he or she continues to need the parents. The function of the failure is to let the parents continue to communicate through and about the young person, with the organization remaining the same.

Many people (including the author) cannot accept that adolescent psychopathology is so clearly a buffer for the friction between the parents. Instead, it seems more valid to focus on the conflicts adolescents experience in breaking away when they feel a need to be independent while still yearning to have their dependency and esteem needs satisfied at home. Either way, adolescent separations are one of the most painful, exciting, and inescapable tasks of family life.

Disruption of Parental Attachment and Its Effect on Sibling Relationships

When children have failed to make an adequate attachment to a parent or parent surrogate, their relationships with their siblings are severely affected. Leavitt and her colleagues (1996) have identified four types of sibling relationships that are the consequence of severe parental neglect or trauma. In the "absent sibling relationship," the children have been so traumatized that they have not mastered even the most rudimentary skills in developing trust and an intimate relationship. They are unable to form any relationship with a sibling because they have no skills to bring to that relationship and indeed, may have a strong aversion to reaching out or relating to others because of repeated disappointment with the parent(s). Unable to bond with a sibling, they are poised for lifelong issues revolving around trust, intimacy, and healthy interdependencies with others.

In the "adult lock out" relationship, trauma results in the siblings developing an alternative bond with one another. Adults are excluded. The primary and only alliances exist among the siblings. Although some of these relationships are exceedingly nurturative and protective, others are characterized by volatility and abuse, the aggression being rationalized by the children as a necessary discipline method to keep one another in line.

Traumatized siblings who have extremely ambivalent relationships, characterized by episodes of happiness and nurturance alternating with episodes of difficulty, are called "half and half siblings." Their difficulties are projections and reenactments of difficulties they have experienced with parents or caretakers. I once saw a set of twins who could play for hours communicating in a secret code but invariably would end up playing ritually cruel games of "hide and seek" where the searching twin would be reduced to screaming and tears and the hider would not reveal himself (this was a reenactment of the parents' sudden, unexplained desertion of the children). Only after months of guided play solutions were the twins able to abandon such games.

The fourth type of sibling relationship is called the "trauma shield." In this relationship, siblings unite by adopting common or complementary defenses to protect themselves from parental trauma. For example, an older and younger sibling may regress to the same developmental level, even to the point of developing mutism at the same time. A complementary defense would occur when siblings reenact victim and aggressor roles that they learned in the original context of their abuse. By reenacting these dynamics they try to master frightening and uncontrollable events of their past. The clinical task with these children is to teach them how to use nurturant adults to soothe themselves rather than using each other.

Trauma and Sibling Separation

Until recently, the trauma of family separation was equated with separation from parents. Now, clinicians are acknowledging and beginning to learn about the trauma associated with separation from siblings. It appears that separation from a sibling can have a profound emotional impact on a person, regardless of whether the separation occurred as the result of a serious illness, hospitalization, runaway situation, or death. Of course, many sibling separations are developmentally provoked. I had a client who did not talk to her sister, six years her elder, for seven years because her sister "deserted" her by getting married at age eighteen. Other times, the developmental desertion is felt when a sibling goes to college or boarding school or gets a private apartment.

One of the most widespread and tragic separations of siblings occurs in the foster care system, where siblings are routinely separated from one another. Luckily, a plethora of federal and state policies that are now trying to promote "relative placement" so that siblings are more likely to be able to live together or see one another frequently while they are in foster care. This innovation in foster care is made possible by policies that allow the government to pay relatives the same foster care stipend that it would pay to an unrelated family member. Prior to these laws, if family members were willing to take children in, they did not qualify to be foster care parents simply because of their relationship to the children. Of course, this system can be abused and relatives will keep children while the mother or father are also secretly living in the relative's home (hence, the children really are not in foster care and the parents are getting a subsidy that the state does not intend for them). The benefits of the system, though, are apparent to virtually anyone involved in placing children in safe settings that minimize feelings of desertion and separation.

ALISON (English teacher, age 30)

Because my family is so enmeshed and overinvolved with one another, separations are few, but those few are very stressful. I am the fourth to fifth generation living in northern Illinois and my grandmother (mother's mother) and grandfather still live in *her* grandmother's house, where they moved when they first got married. My father grew up across the street from my mother, and when my parents got married, they bought a house within five miles of their parents. My older sister, when she got married, also bought a house within two miles of my mother's. In fact, to illustrate the level of differentiation in this family, when my parents got divorced, my father, at the age of fifty-six, "went home to mother."

My sisters and I have had very mixed feelings about leaving home. For example, after my parents' divorce, I as a parental child taking over a real executive position in the family felt that I could not possibly *leave* my mother alone to go to college—that I couldn't desert her like that. Fortunately, she had the good sense to insist that I not change my plans: I don't know whether she truly didn't need me there to be the spouse/parent I was obviously trying to be, or whether she really wanted me there but knew in her heart that it was in my best interest to get out. Keep in mind that this traumatic move to college was not halfway across the country but only about eight miles from the neighboring town.

Leaving home to begin graduate school in Kansas was somewhat more difficult a move to make. My sisters were able to cope with my leaving only by reminding themselves again and again that I left only for the purpose of going to graduate school, and that of course I would come back as soon as I finished and would establish myself in this area. My

(continued)

(continued)

older sister in particular would call or write to me often, never failing at some point to say something about how much she missed me, but that it was OK because I wouldn't be gone forever. It seemed to be very important to my family to somehow be able to feel that I didn't really choose to live in another city, because that would be (in their thinking) a direct rejection, a slap in the family face. On my own part, I can't pretend that it was easy for me to leave. I felt lonely and isolated, and when I began to get integrated into a network there, I felt extremely guilty. My telephone bills from that year bear witness to the fact that I remained very much connected to my family, And, in fact, I was engaged to a man who lived in Evans and didn't intend to stay gone forever. I think that this enduring connection had something to do with what made it possible for me to leave.

Returning to Illinois after canceling my wedding within weeks of the date was a very difficult thing to do. I viewed it very much as being a symbolic going home, as representing my failure to make it separated from my family. Fortunately I think I made a very constructive use of "returning home" and have used it in a sort of Bowenian sense to "leave" over again. I have during the past three years been going through a very painful process of individuating myself from my family, completing tasks that I should have been addressing during my adolescence when I was too busy trying to protect my mother to face the real work of growing up. I fully intend to leave home in a few years because there is a lot of world out there that I still want to see. This is something that continues to be difficult for my family (especially my older sister) to accept. She just cannot believe that I would choose to live away from home.

I think Haley's conceptualizations of mad young people and how best to help them is particularly germane to my younger sister's present situation. She is twenty-six years old, living at home with my mother and "failing" beautifully. She has managed to flunk out of college at least three and possibly four times, has made five suicidal gestures, has a drug problem, and is dating a young man who is facing some serious legal problems. However, the extremely functional role that this behavior seems to play in the system makes me think of her in some ways as a victim. (I also tend to feel guilty about it, because my role was always to be the protector of the family, and since I have been attempting to withdraw from this role, she has been left to fill it.) There are times when I think, "If I were doing my duty—being a 'good daughter' to my mother, my sister would not be trapped like this, and she would be able to grow up. It's not her fault that she's the last one at home, and I am the one who is supposed to be sacrificed for the good of the family." I realize how crazy that sounds, but writing also makes me aware for the first time, just how accurate are the theorists who see the child as *actively* taking on such functions in the family, rather than being the passive victim of parental conflict. Until I started writing this I had not thought of myself as actively trying to "save" the family.

In any case, my sister has been acting much more like a fourteen-year-old than a twenty-six-year-old. This in turn plays a significant role for my mother—it allows her to remain a parent. She has not, herself, worked through many of the issues around her divorce. She had to pull herself up

(continued)

(continued)

by her bootstraps as it were and has been running blindly forward, devoting all of her energy to making life as comfortable as she can for her children. Meanwhile, in almost ten years since the divorce, she has not been on a single date. And, essentially, she has no life of her own outside of her children. If my sister grows up and leaves, my mother is going to find herself suddenly very much alone, with nothing to keep her busily able to avoid facing her existential situation. I think for things to change at home now, either my mother has to demonstrate that she doesn't need to be protected, or my sister needs some real help to give it up regardless of what she may perceive as my mother's needs.

DIVORCE AND JOINT CUSTODY

Currently, about one out of every three children are affected by divorce.* Moreover, this figure does not include the permanent separations and desertions that are estimated to equal the number of legal divorces. In total, it is probable that three of every seven children in the United States experience some form of parent separation. In light of these statistics, it is not surprising that researchers are becoming very involved in assessing the effect that separation of the parents has on children.

Most researchers are concerned that separation and divorce increase a child's risk of experiencing short-term and long-term trauma affecting both social and emotional development. Yet to fully understand the effect of divorce, one needs to realize that many factors are involved and that divorce is not a single short-lived event. Rather, it is a series of stages, each stage having its own consequences. The immediate insecurity and wariness caused by divorce is only one factor that is likely to precipitate behavioral and emotional problems in children. Other factors that may be important are parental fighting after the divorce, father absence, financial difficulties, the personalities and pathologies of persons who divorce, societal expectations, and lack of emotional support for divorced parents (Berg-Cross and Shiller, 1985).

Factors Crucial to the Child's Reaction

Four factors appear most crucial to a child's reaction to parental divorce. First, and perhaps most important, is the *quality of parenting* the child receives (Wallerstein and Kelly, 1980; Pett, 1982). Children adjust more easily if the parents are able to continue providing consistent and

---

*Major portions of this section are taken from Berg-Cross and Shiller, 1985.

affectionate care while themselves coping with the difficulties of marital separation. The *extent to which hostilities between the parents decrease* after separation is the second influential factor in the child's stability (Jacobson, 1978; Wallerstein and Kelly, 1980). High levels of stress both tax the child directly and sap the parent's energy available for the task of child rearing.

A third factor is *frequency of father visitation.* So long as the father is not emotionally disturbed and does not seriously undermine the parenting efforts of the mother, frequent contact with the father benefits children (Wallerstein and Kelly, 1980; Hetherington, 1999). Contact with the father appears especially important for boys, particularly those ages nine and over.

The fourth factor is the *sex of the child.* Nearly every major research project has found that boys have a harder time adjusting to divorce than girls. Hetherington (1999) found that it took boys twice as long as girls to regain their stability after a divorce. Gender differences relating to the effect of divorce appear to persist into adulthood. As adults, men whose parents divorced during their childhood are somewhat more likely to report symptoms of psychological distress than are women from divorced backgrounds (Kulka and Weingarten, 1979).

Why boys fare worse than girls after divorce has not been determined. One theory is that this finding reflects boys' greater biological vulnerability. Boys are more vulnerable to virtually every type of stress than are girls (Rutter, 1979), so it would not be surprising if they were more sensitive to the many stresses of divorce. Alternatively, the fact that boys generally lose regular contact with the same-sex parent (who would otherwise be their role model), while girls maintain a relationship with the parent of the same sex, may provide the explanation for this gender difference.

Joint Custody

Given the fact that mothers with sole custody often experience problems with child rearing as well as the fact that fathers frequently want to maintain contact with and responsibility for their children, the idea of sharing custody seems a viable alternative. Joint custody is an arrangement that some see as ideal, because it allows both parents to remain actively involved in the upbringing of the children. There are two basic forms of joint custody. *Joint legal custody* gives the parents equal rights and decision-making responsibility on questions regarding the children; *joint physical custody* allows the spouses to share in the physical care of the children. Usually joint physical custody agreements stipulate that the children will alternate between parents' homes on a daily, weekly, or monthly basis.

Joint legal custody is the more common form of joint custody, but joint physical custody is the more controversial of the two forms. In an influential early book, Goldstein, Freud, and Solnit (1973) argue that splitting the child's placement between two homes will threaten the child's psychological relationship with both parents. They assert that children lack the capability for maintaining positive emotional ties with individuals who are hostile to each other, and they argue that children who are asked to maintain these ties will suffer from severe and crippling loyalty conflicts.

Relatively little research on joint physical custody has been done to date, but the few studies available indicate that negative consequences are less severe and positive benefits are greater than Goldstein and associates predicted (Arbabanel, 1979; Steinman, 1981). Steinman (1981) studied twenty-four families who had had joint physical custody for an average of four years. She found the children to be strongly attached and loyal to both parents as well as keenly aware of and grateful for the efforts their parents were making in working out the shared custody arrangements. Recognition of their parents' devotion to them enhanced their self-esteem. Loyalty conflicts in the children did not appear to be crippling to the extent often observed in children whose divorced parents were actively fighting over them, but evidence of loyalty concerns was manifested in approximately one-third of the group. These children were hyperalert to their parents' feelings and concerned about being fair to both to an extent that seemed overly burdensome for children of this age. For example, one ten-year-old boy felt very strongly that it was his responsibility to divide himself evenly between his parents. When he was sick or on vacation and spent more than the regular amount of time with one parent, he worked hard to arrange compensation time for the parent who had been "shortchanged."

Steinman found that most of the children in her sample appeared to handle the instability of the arrangement well and to have remarkable clarity regarding their schedules. However, 25 percent of the children did experience confusion and anxiety about their schedules and house switching; this appeared to be related to anxiety about the arrangement as well as about the parental separation. Negotiating the geographical distance between homes was an easy task for some but a stressful or even a frightening experience for others.

A study of twenty families with boys ages six to eleven in joint physical custody and twenty with boys in maternal custody suggested that a high level of anxiety about switching homes in joint custody may be more a reflection of problems with parenting than of the custody arrangements per se (Shiller, 1984). Many joint-custody parents reported that uncertainty about the schedule had been a minor problem for their children when they were four, five, or six years old. When parents recognized their children's uncertainty or fears and supported them in developing ways to cope with the demands of living in two homes, most children appeared to have experienced minimal anxiety. However, if parents were not particularly attentive or supportive, anxiety was likely to escalate.

For example, one nine-year-old boy who had been in joint custody for five years had recently begun to travel between his parents' homes by bus. He talked fearfully of his concern that murderers lurked in the shadows at dusk and might harm him while he was en route. He also worried that he would forget the schedule and make the bus trip on the wrong day and then have to repeat the frightening trip back to the original location. This child's parents seemed very involved with their own lives and problems and minimally aware of his needs. In this case it was not clear whether the child would be any better adjusted if he were in the sole custody of one of his parents.

Although the results of Shiller's study support those of Steinman's in indicating that joint custody can provide a healthy caretaking environment for some children, it should also be noted that Shiller concluded that joint custody is unlikely to become the norm. Most of the mothers and fathers in the maternal custody group were content with the arrangements; mothers generally were highly invested in the maternal role and fathers did not want the day-to-day responsibilities of child rearing. Also, the study found that results may be quite different when joint custody is imposed by courts rather than decided on by mutual agreement of the parents. Indeed, Folberg (1984) suggests that joint custody should never be imposed by the court. Further work needs to be done to determine when joint custody settlements are in the child's best interests.

Paternal Custody

A second nontraditional custody arrangement that is becoming more common is paternal custody. Relatively little research has been done on fathers with child custody, but available data indicate that single fathers can parent at least as well as single mothers (Santrock and Warshak, 1979). One advantage fathers have is that they are more likely to receive assistance from relatives and friends than are mothers with sole custody (Ambert, 1982).

One well-done study of families with children ages six to eleven in the sole custody of either father or mother reported intriguing results. Santrock and Warshak (1979) concluded that boys fared better in the custody of their fathers and girls did better in maternal custody. Boys living with their fathers, when compared with girls in paternal custody, were less demanding and more mature, sociable, and independent. Girls who lived with their mothers showed a similar pattern of more competent social behavior when compared with boys in maternal custody homes. Other more recent studies show that the gender of the custodial parent has little or no effect on adolescent measures of autonomy, school adjustment, or social adjustment (Guttman and Lazar, 1998).

To summarize, then, divorce is a difficult, emotional experience for everyone in the family. The separation of the parental dyad is a sign of failed expectations and arouses fears of abandonment in all children. Each frightened and nervous family member tries to minimize his or her losses during a divorce. Although there is no blueprint for successful custody arrangements applicable to all families, it seems that nearly all will minimize the damage if they adapt a problem-solving approach instead of an adversarial one. The family meets important needs for parents and children alike. Successful divorce requires that everyone find a way to meet these needs in a new alternative family structure.

In many localities, parents attend a divorce education class as part of the legally mandated divorce procedure. Some of these are as brief as two hours, but others meet regularly over a number of weeks. Carol Roeder-Esser (1994) developed the General Responsibilities of Separating Parents (GRASP) program, which is one of the brief two-hour courses required in several counties in Kansas. The course covers all the essential areas. It describes the various behavioral and emotional aspects of divorce, including the role of grief. It describes the various "pain games" couples play and how children are triangulated into the conflict by having to choose between two parents or becoming the only common concern in their parents' lives. It sets up examples of how to develop positive parenting partnerships and the type of conversational tools that can help them resolve differences in a civilized manner.

For children, the pain of divorce is endless. It just never stops. Children adapt, but at best it is like adapting to a prosthetic for a missing limb. It may be mighty fine and something to be grateful for, but it is not the real McCoy. Many programs have been developed to help children deal with their parents' divorce. A program called Sandcastles is being used throughout the country to help protect children from the most devastating effects of divorce. Here, the primary goal is to teach children not to take the blame or feel that somehow they could have prevented the breakup (Gregory and Aunapu, 1998).

PARENTAL DEATH AND A CHILD'S GRIEF

For a long time, psychologists have tried to help children deal with the loss associated with a parental death. It is notable, then, that only recently have therapists begun to unlock the therapeutic power of working with siblings together during the grief process. An innovative play therapy program was recently developed at the Kennedy Krieger Family Center in Baltimore, Maryland, to help children whose parent(s) had died of AIDS. The group was composed of five sibling dyads, between the ages of seven and twelve years old. The presence of a sibling appeared to make the children less defensive and more open about accepting and working through the painful losses they had experienced (Leavitt et al., 1996). The earlier clinical thinking was that children needed anonymity to open up. Anonymity was associated with safety. But when children face traumatic family situations, they are drawn closer to one another (see Chapter 17). Here, the presence of siblings allows them to feel safe and understood.

RYAN (graduate student, age 28)

I haven't been able to relate to a lot of the concepts that we've discussed, but I certainly have to consider myself something of an expert on this one. My first separation probably occurred when I was a technical embryo and my biological father found out my biological mother was pregnant. I have always assumed that my biological father didn't want anything to do with babies and left my mother holding the bag, so to speak. I imagine my biological mother didn't want anything to do with babies either but because of morals, family pressures, or stupidity was forced to stoically carry me to term and give me up for adoption. I don't have any strong emotions about my biological parents. I always knew I was adopted and just accepted the above scenario as inevitable. Whether I picked this up from TV or my adoptive parents I can't remember. I have never had any desire to find my biological parents or find out anything about them. I guess that I looked at them as the factory and I was the product that was meant to be distributed in the marketplace. I've read that it is primarily women who get hooked on finding out about their biological parents and so maybe it's just a sex difference. Maybe guys are more reality oriented and look at life as it is.

I was adopted by a couple who were unable to have children because of a fertility problem with the wife. Unfortunately, fertility problems were the least of my mother's problems. She was a very materialistic, social-climbing, driven woman. She always had a full-time job, and many of them required her to travel during the week. She was never very reliable as a mother, and I don't think she ever made it to one parent-teacher conference in my whole school career. My dad was more regular in his

(continued)

(continued)

hours, but his passion was his ham radio and he spent all his free time down in the basement with the radio. He would always help me if I asked him, but I never felt like imposing on him so I learned early to do by myself. My memories of growing up involve school and the neighborhood. Other than what I've just said, I have no other memories of my parents except "the big scene." One night when I was thirteen, my mother came into my bedroom and kissed me and hugged me and told me she had to go away but she would keep in touch. I remember feeling so sorry for her—not for having to leave but for feeling she *had* to give me a kiss and hug. It wasn't the type of relationship we had. When she left that night, I didn't see her again for four years. My dad and I quickly adjusted to her absence. I only remember discussing it with him the next morning when he told me Mom was crazy and had to go live by herself to see what living was about.

We never discussed her leaving again. The only anger I felt was over why she had felt obligated to adopt me. It was like kissing me goodbye. She wasn't really wanting to do those things. She just felt compelled to go through the motions.

After about a year, Dad started dating Lilly and a few months later she moved in. Lilly was the first person to ever be really interested in me. In the beginning, she tried to be the mother I never had. She would drive me to friends' houses and seemed to take an interest in my schoolwork. On my part, I tried hard to relate to her and please her. After a year, though, she got pregnant and emotionally she really withdrew from me. It was clear she was no longer interested in my school or my friends now that she was going to be a real mother. My dad was very peripheral to all this. He was traveling a lot at work during this time and was on the ham radio whenever he was home. I don't think I spoke one hundred words to him from the time Lilly moved in till I moved out to go to college. When I told Dad I wanted to go to State, he said he could give me $1,000 a year. That was it—one line was all the parental guidance I received. I didn't expect more but I still resent it. My mom asked where I was going and assured me she was too poor to help out.

When I left for college, I had no separation anxiety. I was filled with excitement that my long-awaited future was here. I had already been rejected by three mothers, and any ties to people were in the future to be developed. Now, I very rarely think of my family. I call home once or twice a year and last year I spent Christmas Day with my mom. I've made a lot of close friends whom I consider family. But even with them I feel I am more of a loner. Still, I have learned how to handle separations well. I try to wrap up whatever needs wrapping up in the relationship before I move on. But when I move on, I'm surprised by my own resiliency. Maybe I'm just one of the invulnerables or maybe growing up in a distant, aloof, and often rejecting family environment can have some beneficial outcomes. I feel I can survive anything and be a happy, productive person at the same time.

SELF-EXPLORATION: SEPARATIONS

On a piece of paper draw three columns and label them Childhood, Adolescence, and Adulthood. Under each column list all the separations you have experienced during that period. For each separation, answer the following questions:

1. What were the most difficult aspects of the separation?
2. Was it more difficult or less difficult for you than for other family members?
3. How did you prepare yourself for each separation?

Now look at all three columns and try to describe the developmental nature of how you have learned to deal with separations:

4. Have your first separations set the stage for how you react today, or have you changed how you deal with separations?
5. Have you had many separations during a particular phase of your life? If so, what was their impact?
6. Take a moment to look five years ahead. Are there any separations coming up that you need to prepare yourself for? How can you prepare for these separations?

Chapter 4

Cutoffs

There are no praises and no blessings for those who are ashamed of their families.

Jewish proverb

All happy families resemble one another; every unhappy family is unhappy in its own fashion.

Tolstoy, *Anna Karenina*

Murray Bowen (1978) developed the concept of the emotional cutoff to describe how people insulate themselves or cut themselves off emotionally from their families of origin in an effort to deal with unresolved fusion to their parental family.

THE CONCEPT OF CUTTING OFF

Cutoffs occur in one of three ways: (1) by emotionally isolating oneself while living close to relatives, (2) by physically distancing oneself enough to make infrequent communications acceptable, or (3) by a combination of emotional isolation and physical distance. Kerr (1981:249) sees cutoffs as a complicated coping strategy with three paradoxical features:

> At one and the same time a cutoff reflects a problem, solves a problem and creates a problem. It reflects the problem of underlying fusion between the generations. It solves a problem in that, by avoiding emotional contact, it reduces the anxiety of the moment. It creates a problem in that it isolates and alienates people from each other, people who could benefit from contact with each other if they could deal with each other better.

Thus, many consider cutoffs to be a desperate attempt to separate from the family of origin in an effort to develop a happier, more productive life in one's own nuclear family. Such a view emphasizes cutoffs as a developmental defense used in aid of individuation.

Characteristics of the Cutoff

While there are all gradations of emotional cutoffs, Bowen (1978:283) perceives that "an average family situation in our society today is one in which people maintain distance and a formal relationship with the families of origin, returning home for duty visits at infrequent intervals." Bowen contends that the more a nuclear family can avert such cutoffs and maintain some kind of viable emotional contact with the past generations, the more orderly and asymptomatic the life process of both generations will be. In extreme instances, the cutoffs are absolute; no contact is made with the prior family members, and the person's whereabouts may even be unknown to the rest of the kin. Bowen and his followers believe that cutoffs are always a counterproductive strategy, but later in this chapter we will try to summarize those situations in which cutoffs might be necessary for continued personal growth.

A distinguishing characteristic of cutoffs is denial. People tend to deny how many unresolved conflicts they still have with their parents. Through denial, they act as though they are more independent than they actually are. It is only after acknowledging the cutoff, trying to resume contact, and differentiating themselves that they realize how constrained their options have been and how dependent they have been upon the notion of proving themselves to their parents or fighting against the presumed authority of their parents.

HERMAN (plumber, age 25)

The biggest cutoff in my life occurred in connection with my parents' divorce. I was sixteen at the time. I was a very good student in the eleventh grade and on the basketball team. I had a good group of friends and from time to time I had a girlfriend. For my sixteenth birthday, my parents gave me their old car—a beautiful four-year-old Oldsmobile. I got a Shell credit card to use and felt that I was set for the best years of my life. My dad and I were pretty close; we'd watch the games on TV on Sundays together, do the lawn together, and sometimes even do my homework together. I loved my mom but at sixteen she was just a hassle to have around. I was sixteen

(continued)

(continued)

that August, and the week before Thanksgiving my mom and dad announced to me that they were getting a divorce. I couldn't believe it. I never thought of them as happy or unhappy. They were simply my parents. I remember choking back the tears and saying "That's OK" and asking when Dad would be leaving. He left in between Thanksgiving and Christmas. He moved about twenty miles away, but it was at least a year until he gave me his address.

All I remember during the next year and a half of high school was hearing my mother weep all night—night after night. She was depressed and angry during the day and took to telling me about what a terrible life she had had with my father. I used to get nausea hearing about their inadequate sex life, his infidelities, and his resentment toward me and my younger brother. I couldn't refuse to listen to her but my mind couldn't process it either. I started getting migraine headaches which I never told anyone about. I tried to go out with my friends but her words would haunt me. It was always like a sledgehammer was beating in the most recent crimes my mother had divulged. Writing this now, it sounds like I should have cut off my mother. I wanted to but I couldn't. She was so fundamentally correct that my dad could never have justified himself. He never tried to justify himself. He just left and started building a new life. That life did not include his children.

During the last one-and-a-half years I was in high school, he did take us out to dinner once a week, and he did come to almost all of my basketball games in my senior year. I remember discussing college with him once or twice but never in detail. The college support I was getting from him was set down in the divorce settlement so there was nothing to negotiate or discuss.

Actually, from the day he left there was nothing at all to discuss. I may have been sixteen, but I was the child and he was the parent. He should have assured me of his love. But he didn't. He should have assured me that he wasn't deserting me. But he didn't. He should have explained to me why he left. But he didn't. And I, who was the healthy, happy-go-lucky, high school jock would hear screams of agony in my head—real screams of a big mouth running after my father shouting "Why? Why? Why?" Still, I would never ask him. I just retreated. If he called me, I would always go in the beginning. I felt an obligation not to let Andy (my brother) down as he was always excited about seeing Dad.

Once I went to college, I started hearing from him only twice a year—on my birthday and once before Christmas when he would come up to school during finals and take me out to dinner. It's incredible but for the five years I was in college we only talked about sports, finals, and what to order for dinner.

It's been six years since I graduated from college and for the past three years my dad and I have gotten together once a year, during the Christmas

(continued)

> *(continued)*
>
> holidays for dinner. Now it seems like he's just a biological obligation. He tells me *now* to come to dinner, come spend a weekend, or call him. I can't believe his lack of insight. I guess I really hate him. Reading this chapter, I started to cry—something I haven't done since junior high school. I know I should try to make peace with him but I'm incapable of trying. I have to say I feel hatred, resentment, and have unfulfilled needs.
>
> I'm a grown man now and I'm sure I won't be like my father. I will be a better father. Meanwhile, I'm almost engaged and I can't even imagine having a wedding because only my mother would be invited and I'd feel terrible not inviting my dad.

Families Vulnerable to Cutoffs

Cutoffs occur most frequently in families with a high degree of anxiety and emotional dependency (Bowen, 1978). At first this seems counter-intuitive. We would expect those families with many anxieties and emotional dependencies to cling to one another, not to cut each other off. Bowen agrees that these people need emotional closeness but claims they act as though they are "allergic" to it. Theoretically, the sequence is as follows.

As the anxiety and emotionality in a family increase, family members try to minimize their differences and to become more cohesive. Conflicts are disguised, and differences of opinion are withheld because they seem too threatening to voice. In this situation, some family members find they are so personally distressed both by their lack of freedom and by the family dynamics that they use intrapsychic defenses such as denial to distance themselves emotionally.

For example, if they withdraw and suppress the desire to discuss emotionally charged issues in the presence of the family, they can remain relatively calm. When forced to communicate with any single family member, they rush to defuse the meeting and discuss *another* family member who is not present. This effectively prevents an I/thou encounter. One becomes afraid to be authentic because it is judged as being potentially too hurtful or rejecting. The alternative strategy is to physically distance oneself enough so that one need not cope with the family games on a regular basis. The visits become brief, infrequent, and filled with lots of rituals.

Generational Aspects

Bowen has found that when cutoffs exist between parent and grandparent generations, a cutoff between the parents and children in the next generation

NANCY (graduate student, age 27)

Cutoffs are a very important theme in my family. The earliest separation, which I was too young to remember but which was critical in my life as a child, was the divorce of my parents. When I was an infant, my father made a complete break, never returning to visit me. Although I grew up not knowing what it was like to have a father, I think that I felt rejected and unwanted in many ways. My mother married again when I was five years old, divorcing two years later. This separation did not make me unhappy, as I despised my stepfather.

Throughout at least half of my childhood, my mother and aunts did not speak to one another and so effected a kind of separation although they only lived four blocks apart. This separation was a difficult one because, being a child, I visited my aunts and yet their world and my mother's world were entirely separate. My aunts and my mother each tried to get my loyalty over to their side and tried to use me as a go-between. I always chose my mother, which my aunts never forgave me for. Later, after I finished college, my grandmother's will was disputed. The anger and bitterness generated permanently split my mother and aunts and caused them (aunts) to also cut themselves off from my brother and me, refusing to talk with us either. This split continued until my mother's death seven years later, at which time my aunts began speaking to us again. However, as I lived far away, very little interaction occurred in the four intervening years until my aunt's death a few months ago.

To compound these separations, I was sent off to boarding school in tenth grade. This event virtually ended what little family life had existed for me before. I lost contact with my old friends, became a stranger to my mother and brother, and never again lived closer than 2,000 miles from the family.

Looking back over all these cutoffs, I realize that both literally and figuratively my family has been divided and noncohesive. What little there was of family life was seemingly more a coincidence than anything else. The attitude of my mother and aunts was scornful both of the idea of a cohesive family and of the idea of loyalty and fondness for the place we were all from, Texas. When I think back, I can't help but feel cheated and sad to have missed out on what I might have remembered fondly. At present, there is physically little left of my family. My mother and aunt are dead. My brother and I do not communicate. I have no old friends that I have kept contact with. I feel as if I will always carry with me a void which can never be entirely filled.

is more likely to develop. These cutoffs occur especially frequently when the children are old enough to leave their parental home. Families with multiple grandparent/parent cutoffs also tend to create a myth about the "independence of the nuclear family." The nuclear family may take pride in being an island unto itself. But such isolation inevitably fosters overdependency and complex interdependencies that stifle the family and encourage eventual cutoffs among the children. An isolated nuclear family generally develops very proscribed ways for handling conflicts and meeting changes.

A family connected with its relatives and forced to deal with its problems is impelled to adopt a more flexible mode that invariably is more meaningful and more enjoyable. A family of five (mother, father, and three children) that has no contact with aunts, uncles, cousins, or grandparents is never challenged on its rituals and myths. Alliances are more likely to be rigid because there are fewer members to align oneself with. The family identity is truncated and dichotomized into horrible "others" and the virtuous "we." Children trying to differentiate themselves and create their own nuclear families may have very few options concerning how to relate. The horrible "others" and the virtuous "we" are so easy to perpetuate, and another generation of emotional cutoffs has been solidified.

THE PAINFUL PROCESS OF CUTTING OFF

The cutoff process is not as simple as turning off a faucet. The decision to turn off a family member is more often a heart-wrenching, gradual affair

---

NORMA (graduate student, age 28)

The two most significant cutoffs in my life have occurred between myself and my father, and myself and an older sister. I have severed all communication with my father. I do not even know where he lives, if he is in good health, etc. The initial cutoff with my father came when he moved out of our house. Because he was an alcoholic, my mother refused to allow him to live with us any longer. He then tended to drift in and out of our lives, whenever he saw fit. My communication with him was kept at a minimum and although I didn't have him physically, I still cared. However, when he did not attend the funeral services for my mother, my caring turned into resentment and maybe even hatred for a time. I could not forgive him for not showing up. Although we still have no communication, my feelings have somewhat softened and I do find myself caring at times.

The second significant cutoff is between myself and my sister. We have never been close, and we have felt little but contempt for each other. I did not grow up with my sister, and when she moved in with us at the age of fourteen, I felt she had intruded on my family and was taking love designated for me and my other siblings. She felt we did not want her around and treated us as if we were owed her the world. When we rebelled against her intrusion, she rebelled against us. This standoff only resulted in our growing more distant. Eventually, she left the family circle but always found ways to hang a cloud over our shoulders. At this point in our lives, we are cut off physically and emotionally. I still have a lot of anger in me toward her and she toward me. I am at a point where I am attempting to resolve the anger within myself. Although we will probably never be close, I need some peace within myself.

that is punctuated with landmarks of disillusionment. The reason cutoffs are so difficult to execute is that while the personal commitments to the relationship can wither relatively easily, the structural commitments to the relationship are far more difficult to escape.

Structural Commitments

The term *structural commitments* describes the hard-walled external constraints to dissolving a relationship. Johnson (1983) has analyzed the nature of structural commitments and found that the constraining conditions fall into four general types: (1) irretrievable investments, (2) social pressures, (3) available alternatives, and (4) termination procedures.

Irretrievable Investments

The time, energy, emotions, and money that have been invested in a relationship are irretrievable. Sometimes these investments appear to have been wasted on certain individuals. Yet, truly accepting the lost investment can be so catastrophic that emotional cutoffs are impossible.

The concept of irretrievable investment explains why it is so rare for parents to cut off their grown children; the children are more apt to cut off their parents. For parents who have spent a lifetime investing money, energy, time, and worry on a child, the cost can never be retrieved. But grown children may perceive their own investment to be minimal. They may have been merely receivers, takers, exploiters. When tensions reach a critical level, they have one less structural commitment restraining them.

Social Pressures

A second potent force against instigating a cutoff comes from the social pressure exerted by the network. Every personal relationship is embedded in a network such that each dyadic relationship is important to many others outside the dyad. Instigating a cutoff means affecting the lives of many of the network members. For example, if I impose a cutoff on my fraternal twin, my parents will have to choose sides each time there is a birthday or holiday gathering. Old friends will feel a need to choose sides. Those who refuse to take sides will have to assert their neutrality constantly. Everyone in the network who has related to us in the past will push for us to resume contact. Eventually, I might even put myself in jeopardy of being cut off from many network members who feel that I am being intractable.

Alternatives

The number of available alternatives greatly affects our likelihood of cutting off relatives. If I have but one mother and father, they are probably the only people I can look to for fulfillment of many of my nurturing/dependency/safety needs. If both of my parents have remarried, however, and my father has remarried twice, I have possibly five individuals to choose from. If my biological parents are not as giving as my stepparents, I may choose to cut off from one or more of my parents.

Difficulties

The difficulty of the specific steps that have to be taken to end a relationship can also affect whether a cutoff will be initiated. To end an acquaintanceship, one might only need to refrain from calling the acquaintance or to politely refuse an invitation. To end a relationship with a parent may require physically moving away, denying a future inheritance, dealing with feelings of failure and guilt, and losing the respect of family members.

RECONSTRUCTING THE RELATIONSHIP

Once a cutoff does occur, it is very trying and arduous to repair the relationship. The emotional boundaries against intimacy become thicker with each passing month. Surreptitious angry and resentful interactions, as well as the many neglected interactions, viciously breed more and more ill will. The only way to reconnect with cutoff family members is to make a determined effort not to fall into the old destructive patterns and to risk engaging in an "I/thou" relationship. Such an effort involves spending time with the person—just the two of you. It involves sincerely sharing your actions, feelings, and values with this other person. It involves direct communication that does not rely on talking about other relatives in order to make meaningful contact. Most of all, it requires perseverance until the cutoff member feels safe and can respond to your attempts.

This reconstruction process is movingly illustrated in the movie *On Golden Pond* (1981). Chelsea, an only child, symbolizes the middle-aged woman who is emotionally and physically cut off from her parents. She lives on the West Coast; her parents live in New England. She visits only every few years and writes very infrequently. When her mother begs her to make a token visit, she comes, but she is unable to manage even a moment of relaxed conversation with her father. She relates better to her mother, and much of the mother/daughter time together is spent discussing Chelsea's unresolved anger toward her father.

At the end of the movie, when the therapist/mother urges Chelsea to talk to her father, Chelsea says she is afraid and doesn't know him at all—she doesn't know where to begin. Her mother points out that the ailing father is eighty years old and if she doesn't begin now it will be too late. Chelsea then tries to have an "I/thou" conversation with her father. She says, "I want a normal relationship with you," "I want you to like me" "I want to be your friend." Initially, the father is unresponsive to these gestures, but he quickly warms up to her openness by being open about his own feelings. This cinematic tear-jerking final scene is gripping because each viewer can empathize with how difficult, how admirable, and how urgent it is to reconnect with family members one has cut off.

DEVELOPMENTAL TIMING

Most cutoffs occur in high anxiety/high fusion families, but the cutoffs can occur at any stage in the family life cycle. The age and stage of the

---

SARAH (housewife, age 30)

A cutoff was clearly present in my relationship with my mother. From the time I left for boarding school at age fourteen, I began to cut myself off from her. This was the only way I knew to free myself of her demands of me. While I was in high school and college, I still saw my relationship to her as positive, although I never looked forward to visiting her or hearing from her. After I left college and began a serious relationship with my present husband, my view of the relationship with my mother became increasingly negative. I responded to this by cutting off more and more. I don't believe that my relationship at that time was any worse than it had been earlier, but I was more aware of her demands and how upsetting they were to me. Again, my only way of coping was to shut her out.

This cutoff continued for the next several years until a visit I had with her one summer in which I became very upset about our interactions. After I left, I was determined to write her a letter about how I felt—a first for me. I did this, writing what I saw as a rather benign letter discussing how I felt. She did not see it as benign, however, and wrote an angry letter saying she knew I had always hated her. Later she called and hinted that she did not really mean what she had said. I felt that this was the beginning of our having a more open relationship (in Bowen's terms of myself becoming more differentiated from her). She died a year later, so there were no further opportunities for me to follow up on what I had begun. Having made that first step, however, made it possible for me to deal with her death with more equanimity.

family member at the time of the cutoff will have very specific effects on the person's future development. Today, three of the major developmentally timed physical/psychological cutoffs occur among: (1) runaway adolescents, (2) divorcing adults, and (3) the very elderly.

Each of these groups is in a transition period in which it must redefine its role in the family. The tension and problems of redefining one's role are often the last straw. It is easier to withdraw than to work to create a new, more comfortable niche. Yet, the effects of family cutoffs for these three critical populations are potentially devastating. Each group experiences the effects of emotional and physical desertion differently. Perhaps the most heartbreaking consequences of cutting off are found among the first group.

Runaways

> *Without a family, man, alone in the world, trembles in the cold.*

André Maurois

All runaways have an extensive history of emotional cutoffs preceding the physical cutoff. Brennan, Huizinga, and Elliott (1978) have empirically shown that emotional cutoffs from the family and school can serve as early warning indices for prerunaway identification. In addition, it has been documented that the emotional cutoffs with parents are not always initiated by the adolescent. Most often, parental attitudes and behaviors are an instigating source of distress.

Within the family, future runaways experience withdrawal or lack of love on the part of their parents. The parents are verbally rejecting, spend little time with the adolescent, and are remote or disinterested. Such discipline as they do impose consists of disorganized or ineffective punishments that are often physically abusive and create schisms between the siblings (Brennan, Huizinga, and Elliott, 1978). These parental behaviors severely frustrate the adolescent's needs for security, belonging, competence, and self-esteem. Thwarted in nearly all areas of legitimate youth needs, these adolescents cut off their parents to minimize their own distress and despair.

If the child is as alienated at school as at home, the probability of running away increases greatly. Early warning indices at school include truancy, disinterest in school, academic failure, and negative labeling by teachers. If home and school failures are countered only by an antisocial, delinquent peer group, runaway behavior becomes a highly expected outcome.

Over 80 percent of runaways display enough of these early warning signs that one can easily understand what made them run away. The remaining 20 percent do not seem obviously cut off; their motivation for running away is unclear. The absence or reduced severity of emotional cutoff in this small group of runaways helps explain why they are almost universally "one-timers."

The work of Brennan, Huizinga, and Elliott (1978) demonstrates that before adolescents physically cut off the family, most of the social bonds with the family have been eroded or destroyed. The emotional cutoff weakens the adolescent's commitment to the family and strengthens his or her need to be committed to the peer group or to "make it on my own." Although it is obvious that most adolescent runaways are failing to function adequately before they run away, there are some indications that physically cutting off family rarely helps and may easily worsen the life predicament of the runaway.

In 1980, a group sponsored by the National Institute of Mental Health (NIMH) reported a follow-up pilot study of fourteen youths who had run away from home as teenagers in the mid-1960s (Olsen et al., 1980). The follow-up study involved interviewing the runaways, their nonrunaway siblings, their parents, and other relatives. The results, while based on a very small sample, clearly showed that runaways had much greater problems adjusting than their nonrunaway siblings. Also, children who ran away more than once (repeaters) were much less adjusted than one-timers. The four most striking school-related findings were:

1. Of the fourteen runaways, six of the seven repeaters dropped out of high school and two of the seven nonrepeaters dropped out. Only one of the fourteen siblings dropped out.
2. None of the runaways went to college, but six of the fourteen siblings did.
3. Of the fourteen runaways, six of the seven repeaters had academic problems leading to D grades or lower; two of the seven nonreactors showed similar problems. Only one of the fourteen siblings had academic problems.
4. Similarly, all seven repeaters had behavior problems in school, and three of the four nonrepeaters had problems. Only one of the fourteen siblings had similar behavior problems.

The school problems were a predictable prelude to the problems they experienced in the work world. They had quit or been fired from a number of different jobs and were unable to make a serious commitment to the workplace. All but one of the siblings were currently employed, whereas all except one repeater were unemployed. The siblings who were employed were moderately or highly satisfied with their work. Also, with only one exception, the former runaways reported that they were in debt.

The repeating runaway who cannot come to grips with his or her family seems to cut off the future as well as the past. These individuals have the most menial jobs, earn the least money, and have been fired most often for misconduct or inadequacy on the job. Of course, the observed association of running away with future failures in school and work does not establish a cause-and-effect relationship between these failures and the cutting-off process. In some cases, distancing from the family was necessary for the adolescent's emotional survival. For example, all the runaways studied had been "hit or beaten" more than a few times before they ran away. Some probably felt that they were safer out on the road than at home.

The NIMH runaway research indeed underscores how desperate individuals must be before they cut off family. During adolescence the costs associated with these cutoffs might be much higher than the adolescents initially perceive them to be.

Divorce

Today, many people become cut off from kin as a result of divorce. Each ex-spouse has to find a way of cutting off from the other spouse. The legal marriage dissolves at a court-determined date, but the family unit is

---

SUZANNE (keypunch operator, age 30)

I ran away from home the first time when I was twelve. My mother and I had had a terrible fight and she had called me a whore. I slept at my friend's house for two nights. Then her mother said it was enough and I went home. During the next three years I ran away maybe ten times. My home life was hell. Our house was a mess. Both my parents were in the state government and made good money but our house was falling apart. We had old raunchy furniture and my brothers constantly kept it like a pigsty. My parents always ate out and we kids more or less grew up on canned food. If we got hungry we'd open a can. Canned peas, canned carrots, canned fruit, and soup. If we ran out of cans, we tried to get invited to our friends' houses. As soon as I was ten, I was making money babysitting and almost all the time I'd use my money on food. I'd go down to 7-Eleven and buy a lot of snack food.

When I was fifteen, my father crept into my bed one night and started to fondle my breasts. That freaked me out and I took off and went to Philadelphia. I lived out on the street for three years, and for two of those years I was either in a shelter or a foster home. When I lived out on the street, I

(continued)

(continued)

was never an actual prostitute, but I would shack up with someone for a few weeks if it meant food and a warm room. I had two wonderful foster homes but I was nutty, so wound up, all I could do was strike out at them. I'd lie, steal, and break rules and kept at it till they threw up their hands in disgust. Both times, I felt a strange victory about being sent back to the shelter. But I still cry over losing contact with these two couples who really tried for me and cared about me.

Now, I work as a keypunch operator and have my own apartment. I haven't seen or heard from my father in fifteen years. My mother is remarried and calls me when she needs a favor to watch her pets or something. Two brothers I've lost contact with, but the other lives in the Village and is basically a street beggar. My father beat him so bad the year after I left that he became deaf because my father kept boxing him in the ears. Now I'm trying to deal with my bulimia and to like myself a little more. Most of the time I feel I'm an uneducated runaway who picks guys up at bars when I'm lonely. When I'm being kind to myself I realize that if I hadn't been a runaway, I'd have gone crazy, killed myself, or killed someone else.

slow to disappear. Goldsmith (1980) found that one year after the legal divorce, relationships with the ex-spouse were a vital component of the reorganized, postdivorce family. Goldsmith found that for divorced couples, the parenting bond was the most important. A majority (55 percent) reported that they occasionally spent time with each other and the children together as a "family." These "family" times tended to be special events (such as birthdays or Christmas), periodic outings (museums, dinners, school or church functions), and visits to grandparents.

Even after couples have been divorced for many years, the degree of emotional cutoff varies. Only mild consensus exists about whether the ex-spouse should be involved in major events affecting the ex-partner. For example, divorced couples are divided roughly fifty-fifty about how appropriate it is to visit an ex-spouse in the hospital. Half are in favor of it, half are not (Goetting, 1979). Obviously, the legal cutoff has very different emotional ramifications for different individuals.

Besides cutting off from each other, ex-spouses many times find that they must cut off with the spouse's kin or radically change the nature of the relationship they have with them. This is often a surprising and devastating loss. Goldsmith (1980) found that "friendly" or "kin" contacts with the ex-spouse such as talking about family other than children are maintained by the majority of divorced couples. It is unusual for a couple not to maintain this kind of contact. The couples studied by Goldsmith, however, had been divorced only a year. It is possible that "kin gossip" decreases over time. Perhaps talk of kin is widespread because it is all that the couple has left in common, but it is also plausible that ex-spouses have a need not to be cut off from kin they are personally committed to but to whom they no longer have any structural commitments.

The emotional cutoffs are not restricted to ex-spouses and their kin. Members of the larger social family are also affected. Rands (1986) studied the effect of divorce on cutting off members of personal networks by using a retrospective network identification procedure. She interviewed twenty men and twenty women who had recently been divorced and asked them to identify people with whom they had various kinds of communication (sharing activities, discussing personal problems). Each respondent made two lists of people—one list of people with whom he or she interacted while they were still in a viable marriage; one of people with whom he or she interacted in the present postdivorce state. There were six major findings:

1. Forty-two percent of the respondent's marital network members had been dropped after separation.
2. The spouse's relatives were dropped frequently.
3. Persons known to the spouse first and those closest to the spouse were dropped.
4. Married friends were dropped.
5. Networks were on the average 14 percent smaller after separation than they were during the marriage.
6. Parents' networks were more stable than nonparents' networks. Children increased the number of people in the personal network of their parents. The structural commitments of these network members were frequently unchanged by a divorce.

In the immediate months after a divorce or spousal death, individuals maintained or increased contact with their own parents and siblings but had significantly decreased interactions with their former mate's parents and siblings. What is still unknown is how these socially demanded cutoffs affect the way individuals define themselves and their commitment to others. One obvious effect of the cutoffs is that each partner loses some human resources. Whereas most divorced people receive help from close kin, only about 25 percent get some form of assistance from the immediate family of their former spouse (Anspach, 1976).

Approximately four out of every five people who get a divorce will eventually remarry. The children of parents who remarry are most at risk for being arbitrarily cut off from a significant portion of their kindred. Since half of all younger divorced women remarry within three years, it is expected that a fourth of all children growing up today will have more than two parents during their youth. Although divorced persons with children are more than twice as likely as individuals without children to maintain contact with their in-laws, that still leaves a frighteningly large number of children cut off from grandparents and other kin. Over the past few years, many states have recognized the unique bond between grandparent and grandchild and enacted statutes that create a right for grandparents to seek court-ordered visitation. This often becomes a costly, time-consuming, complicated process; particularly when the child-parent is not visiting his or her child on a regular basis.

Adults also are often acutely aware of being cut off by in-laws who had become very central in their lives. Mothers- and fathers-in-law nearly always feel obligated to stick by the blood relative and can very quickly cut off the ex-spouse. This is especially traumatic among divorced persons who had difficulties relating to their own family of origin and looked at the spouse's kin as a preferred adopted family. Once the in-laws cut off these former spouses, they are left without any extended family with which they are comfortable. Additional pain is felt by rejected parents if they must witness their children cut off by formerly loving grandparents, aunts, uncles, and cousins.

Cutoffs Among the Elderly

Chapter 9, "Networks," discusses how fortunate most elderly persons in our society are in having continued interaction with most of their friends

---

KATHERINE (writer, age 49)

Learning about cutoffs was both depressing and cheering—depressing because of painful memories and cheering because I had thought this phenomenon was nearly unique to my "crazy family." Finding that it is an identified family pattern—and therefore possibly amenable to change—makes it easier to cope with somehow.

Looking back, I can see that my family of origin had a typical "us/them" fused pattern. To my mother, everyone else was "they"—and inferior, often on racial or cultural grounds. When I married, my (former) husband and I promptly began to dig in and reject all those "them's"—increasingly on moral grounds. Sadly, I see this pattern persisting in the next generation; all three of my grown-and-gone children struggle with it, as I do. Some of us are winning a good deal of the time, but my former husband and one of my daughters currently remain enmeshed in the cutoff pattern. The family runs to "irrevocable repudiations"—angry closings out. We all find it difficult to confront our differences; it's easier to bow out with accusations of treason, dishonesty, insensitivity, or whatever.

(continued)

(continued)

Really, the thing has its absurd aspects ("we have met the enemy and 'they' is 'us' "—to paraphrase Pogo). Holiday plans take on the aspects of the Vietnam peace talks as we try to "shape the table" according to which warring factions are or aren't associating with which others at a given time. Can Mother be invited to Thanksgiving dinner with Grandma and Grandpa—her former in-laws? What of the two sisters who seem unable to get along—each on the qui vive for real and imagined slights. Dad, at least, is out of it.

My former husband has "repudiated" two of his children (all live near him), attending neither of their weddings and ignoring his only grandchild. The ostensible "sins" were having church weddings—he is an atheist. But if it weren't that it would be something else. Having run into me at a restaurant where I was wearing a dashiki and makeup, he informed me by phone that I had so "violated everything we had believed in" that he would have me run off his place by the police if I set foot there.

All this might seem ludicrous—and often does—but real pain is involved, too. Four years ago our younger daughter (in her twenties) was diagnosed as having a potentially fatal disease. While she was in the hospital for biopsy she had to worry about juggling visitors, since her father had threatened awful consequences if he ran into me. Although it is ten years since the divorce, I feel that as parents of this threatened child we could gain strength and solace from each other regardless of our former differences; instead, she has the additional stress of conflicting loyalties imposed on top of her illness. (As of the moment she has chosen to deal with this by "repudiating" me.)

The loss of kindred is also painful. Both my own parents are dead. My former father-in-law, whom I loved dearly, was cut off from me by the divorce (as is not uncommon, I became the villain of the piece in my mother-in-law's eyes—the adventuress who made off with her son's mythical money). This lovely, gentle man is quite old and ill; were I to attend his funeral in tribute, however, there would likely be a painful scene.

It is sad to see these patterns disrupting the family structure. How can my son explain to *his* son a grandfather who lives ten miles away but never sees him? When will Christmas cease to be the season of the "chosen" and the "unchosen"—some included, some excluded? Seeing the patterns clearly is the first step toward change for the better. Changes are occurring. There is hope.

---

and family throughout their later years. However, the small percentage of elderly people who have no one and who live a hermitlike existence (inside or outside a nursing home) suffer immeasurably. Sometimes it is the aged individual who has initiated a cutoff—perhaps dating back many years. More frequently, it is the grown children who cut off their elderly parents. Many of the elderly in nursing homes are described as "kin wrecked."

An interesting way of assessing cutoffs initiated or maintained by the elderly is by examining their wills. It is nearly universal for people to leave their estates to the next of kin. Rosenfeld (1979, 1980) has found that more of the elderly are cutting their children out of their wills. The view offered in the best-selling book *Mommy Dearest* portrays Joan Crawford as irrationally disinheriting her two daughters and son. Contrary to this impression, Rosenfeld found that most parents who disinherit their children give quite cogent reasons for their behavior. For example, thirty-five of the wills probated in Nassau County, New York, between 1973 and 1978 involved parent/child disinheritance. In 31 percent of the cases the testators were motivated by the feeling that other people needed the money more than their children did.

Many of these elderly people were living in retirement communities and left their estates to close friends and neighbors in the same community. Most felt that their kin were financially self-sufficient and would not be angry about being disinherited. Thus, it is unlikely that many in this group were cut off from their children. The remaining two groups had obvious cutoffs from their children. Twenty-two percent of the disinheritances occurred because the parent had not seen or heard from the child in many years. The remaining 47 percent were in fact "vengeance bent" against their children. The wills not only disinherited the children but also unleashed emotionally charged accusations about their unworthiness and ingratitude.

It seems that the older the parents, the more likely they were to experience alienation. Sixty-three percent of the disinheriting parents were seventy-five years of age or older. Although the total number of disinheritances is proportionately very small, the absolute number of elderly who have no positive family ties is very discomforting.

WHEN ARE CUTOFFS BENEFICIAL?

Once in every half century, at longest, a family should be merged into the great obscure mass of humanity, and forget all about its ancestors.

Nathaniel Hawthorne, *The House of the Seven Gables*

A child asked a man to pick a flower for her. That was simple enough. But when she said, "Now put it back," the man experienced a baffling helplessness he never knew before. "How can you explain that it cannot be done?" he asked. "How can one make clear to young people that there are some things which when once broken, once mutilated, can never be replaced or mended?"

Marcia Borowsky, "Education for the New World Order"

Although most cutoffs thwart an individual's ability to be productive and creative in the nuclear family there do seem to be at least two situations in which cutoffs are vital for a new, healthier generation.

First, in some instances of physical or sexual abuse, the psychic trauma is so deep that children need to not relate. They need to look forward, not back. Often, what the abusing parent or sibling offers is too little, too late. Although abuse programs have been successful in getting parental abusers to accept more responsibility for their actions, reconstituting the family has been far more difficult. Many times such a goal would be inappropriate, so the reported failures are easily understood.

Second, when psychological exploitation occurs and one member of a family continually sabotages or blackmails another in such a way that one's basic legal, moral, or spiritual values are undermined, a cutoff may be necessary. For example, a twenty-eight-year-old woman in psychotherapy was very distressed because her older brother sold large quantities of cocaine and would use her apartment to stash the drugs for a day or week at a time. The sister's repeated protests and refusals to have anything to do with the drugs were ignored. The brother would visit continually and would leave some drugs hidden in her apartment without telling her until it was time to pick them up.

Eventually, the woman told the brother she would have nothing to do with him until he straightened out. The brother was genuinely hurt by her refusal to see him. Nevertheless, the woman cut off her brother, and at last report it had been two years since she had heard from him. She had heard that he had been busted but still had made no effort to contact him. She missed the brother of her childhood but felt that he had disappeared; the brother of her adulthood she was relieved to be rid of. How else could this woman have dealt with this problem? It could be argued that she should have turned her brother over to the police instead of cutting him off. Her legacy of family loyalty did not permit that alternative. Whether such a decision would have been preferable is questionable.

SELF-EXPLORATION: FAMILY CUTOFFS

Make a chart similar to that in Figure 4.1. In Column A make a list of all the living members of your family of origin and all the living aunts, uncles, and grandparents who were very much a part of your growing-up years.

FIGURE 4.1. Chart for Exploring Cutoffs

A	B	C	D	E	F	G	H
Family member	Frequency of visits	Frequency of phone calls and letters	Frequency of I/thou encounters	Difficulty of I/thou encounters			
	Score	Score Subtotal I	Score	Score	Subtotal II	Total

(For some readers, this list will be quite lengthy; if there are more than ten people on the list, you may choose to do this exercise in stages.)

In Column B, list how frequently you visit with each of your relatives (your home or theirs). Rate the frequency according to the following formula:

- Once a week or more   1
- Monthly   2
- Every other month   3
- Major holidays   4
- Once a year   5
- Less than once a year   6

In Column C, list how frequently you speak on the phone and/or write letters to each of your relatives. Rate the frequency according to the following formula:

- Every day   1
- Once a week   2
- Every other week   3
- Once a month   4
- Every other month   5
- Major holidays   6
- Once a year   7
- Less than once a year   8

In Column D, rate the overall frequency of "I/thou" conversations. An "I/thou" conversation is one in which nearly all of your comments are accurate and sincere statements of what you personally are doing, thinking, or feeling. Use the following formula:

- If nearly all of your conversations with this person are of the "I/thou" type, rate a 1.
- If many of your conversations with this person are of the "I/thou" type, rate a 2.
- If some of your conversations with this person are of the "I/thou" type, rate a 3.
- If none of your conversations with this person are of the "I/thou" type, rate a 4.

In Column E, imagine having an I/thou conversation with each of your relatives. Take your time and spend at least two or three minutes imagining the precise "I/thou" conversation you would have with each person today. Then, right after imagining a specific relative, rate how anxious or uncomfortable you would be in that situation using the following scale:

- Very relaxed   1
- Moderately relaxed   2
- A little anxious   3
- Moderately anxious   4
- Very anxious   5

After you have completed the table, add scale scores B and C together for subtotal I; add scale scores D and E together for subtotal II; and add both subtotals together to get the total score. Relatives with the highest subtotal I scores are most likely physically cut off from you. Those with the highest subtotal II scores are probably psychologically cut off from you. Those with the highest total scores have been undoubtedly both physically and psychologically cut off by you. Keep in mind that many physical separations have nothing to do with cutoffs. If the "If/thou" subtotal II is low, the physical separation is most likely due to other factors. How have the cutoffs evolved in your family? What could you do to "reconnect" with cutoff family members? What do you have to gain from reconnecting with them? What are you risking by reconnecting with them?

Chapter 5

Triangles

When the cat and the mouse agree, the grocer is ruined.

Persian proverb

Social psychologists and family theorists have found that family interactions often involve a "triad" or "triangle." A *triad* is a relationship pattern among three people in a family. It forms a framework within which the particulars of the family problems are enacted. Usually, triangles involve two parents and a child; the other family members are more peripherally involved. To understand the important function of triangles in family life it is vital to appreciate the strains of intimately interacting with family members over long periods.

VULNERABILITY AND SELF-PROTECTION

When we have to relate to another person over a long period of time, it is hard to maintain a social facade. The other person comes to know all our weaknesses, our points of vulnerability. Our histories of failure, faux pas, and forgotten dreams seldom can be hidden. The other person's knowledge of us makes us vulnerable. Since family members are privy to nearly all our shortcomings and are aware of so many of our hopes, they cause a special vulnerability. If they want to deflate us or lower our delicate self-esteem, they usually have all the technical know-how.

What makes these intimate others especially threatening is our knowledge that at times they might be justified in seeking retribution. We recognize that many times we have slighted, ignored, or insidiously undermined them. For example, a mother realizes that her desire to get the kids in bed is in large part due to her own need for some private time. The kids protest, Mom becomes threatening, and finally they blurt out, "I hate you!" Mother is hurt and crushed. She is continually torn between her altruistic desire to fulfill others' needs and egotistical desires of her own. Mother knows she'll repeat this sequence and so offend her children. This expectation of conflict and consequent rejection and hurt makes people defensive.

The Importance of Family Triangles

Conflict between members of the family, however, is often related to the many alliances and coalitions that inevitably develop whenever there are more than two people in a group. When the brothers Joe and Stan are together, each relates to the other's "person." It's a one-on-one relationship. When Joe, Stan, and Mom are together, suddenly there are three dyadic relationships to worry about: Joe and Stan, Joe and Mom, Stan and Mom. When Dad is included there are six dyadic relationships: Joe and Stan, Joe and Mom, Stan and Mom, Dad and Stan, Dad and Joe, Dad and Mom. When baby is included there are ten dyadic relationships going on in the household: Joe and Stan, Joe and Mom, Stan and Mom, Baby and Joe, Dad and Stan, Dad and Joe, Dad and Mom, Stan and Baby, Baby and Dad, Baby and Mom. Thus, a family of five has ten different ongoing dyadic relationships around the dinner table. No wonder it's not as pleasant as dinner for two! In actuality much more is going on besides the ten dyadic relationships. Each of these five individuals exists in six triangular relationships with a total of ten different possible triangles in the family:

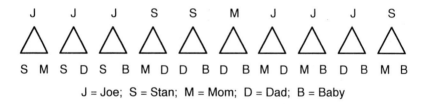

J = Joe; S = Stan; M = Mom; D = Dad; B = Baby

Triangular relationships are so important because, despite being a natural part of family life that often allows the family to function more effectively, they occasionally cause destructive family problems to stagnate. They may prevent healthy resolution of crises.

Family Stresses Lead to Triangles

Triangles are called into play whenever tension between two members of a family reaches some critical level. The most obvious example is that of two siblings having a fight. Left to resolve the argument by themselves, the dyad will have to reach agreement over the disputed issue even if it is to agree to disagree. When the argument reaches a critical intensity or critical time span, a parent may intervene and side with one child. Then we have a triangle. Triangles polarize two individuals into an alliance against a third.

Any twosome can survive without others in happy times, but when stress and strife surface, dyads invariably start to involve other people in their interactions. For example, the siblings continue to disagree with each other, but they do not have to deal with it any more once their time is occupied with worrying about or supporting the third person. Sometimes, they will use a third person as a confidante or ally, and the coalition thus formed makes it less imperative to deal directly with the person with whom they are in disagreement.

This all boils down to the observation that whenever a dyad gets into troubled water it becomes a triad. The process of triangulation is universal. Triangulation reduces two people's discomfort with each other by allowing them to focus on peripheral or even irrelevant issues. The major conflict within the dyad remains unresolved and continues to breed dissatisfaction. Often, the continuing anxiety tends to stabilize this three-person emotional system known as a triangle.

THE UNIVERSAL TRIANGLE: FATHER/MOTHER/CHILD

The most common triangle in families is the father/mother/child triangle. Here, the parents have disagreements and angry feelings toward each other. The parents either do not know how to discuss the problems or feel too vulnerable to discuss them. One way they may triangulate their child into the conflict is by both becoming very concerned about his or her misbehavior at school, or about the child's physical health. Focusing on the child gives the couple an opportunity to come together on a mutual concern.

Adaptive Value and Cultural Differences

Most chronic triangles are seen as dysfunctional. When a child is consistently triangulated, many family therapists become alarmed over the lack of generational boundaries and push the parents to deal directly with their marital conflicts or disagreements. Not all therapists see triangulation as inevitably being a problem (Hsu, 1971). Triangulation seems most dangerous in the traditional middle-class, white, nuclear family in which the mother and father are the central dyad, the heart of the family. In these families the parent dyad has to be the most important and dominant relationship, for the continuing strength of the parental dyad is the only viable way to continue that family culture. In extended families, the dominant value is more likely to be placed on an intergenerational dyad, and the marital dyad is intentionally underplayed and less valued. For example, in traditional Chinese families the dominant dyad is father/son, in some African societies it is brother/brother, and in Hindu society it is mother/son. When the married spouses triangulate a third individual in these families, the marital dyad is not additionally stressed. Indeed, it may be helped by momentarily reducing the pressure of conflict felt by the couple.

Indeed, generational coalitions (husband and wife against a parent or children against a parent) have dangerous implications for systems based on intergenerational centrality. Falicov and Brudner-White (1983:60) found that:

> these [generational] coalitions arise from marriages in which the husband supports the wife to disengage from her overbearing mother or the wife wins the husband over from his attachment to his mother. These are functional processes from the vantage point of the marital dyad, but may be very disturbing for families based on intergenerational ties. [For example] in an Italian family where the husband is a fisherman at sea for several months a year, the benefits of the wife's ties to her mother outweigh the adjustment costs when he returns. Mother and daughter function as allies to keep daughter's marriage together. Mother helps daughter with certain tasks, thus relieving pressure on the daughter's spouse. Among other things, the mother-daughter interactions may include venting complaints about the absent spouse. The cultural background of the family and the husband's occupation may work together to facilitate the continuation of the mother-daughter tree. Circumstances do not permit the strengthening of the parental or marital alliance nor may it be desirable to do so.

DYSFUNCTIONAL TRIANGLES

Triangles can involve different relationship patterns. Three common dysfunctional patterns are the detouring triangle, the parent/child coalition, and the split loyalties triangle (Minuchin, Rosman, and Baker, 1978).

The Detouring Triangle

The *detouring* pattern is the most discussed triangle relationship. This pattern occurs when the parents inadvertently reinforce or exacerbate problem behavior in one of their children because dealing with him or her allows them to detour from or avoid their own marital problems. Sometimes detouring parents focus on the child's frailties and vulnerabilities. One parent may notice a slight lisp or stutter and begin to correct the child frequently. The spouse becomes involved either by joining in the concern or by battling with the other spouse about the insignificance of the problem. Another pattern involves focusing on the child's misbehavior. Usually one parent notices that the child is engaging in a forbidden activity (lying, refusing to do tasks, socializing with censored friends) and begins to battle emotionally with the child.

In detouring, both parents may be unaware of their own problem or conflict. Both partners unconsciously begin to take their antagonistic feelings and play them out over some other issue concerning the children. A classic example is a couple who harass their adolescent daughter about her alleged promiscuity instead of dealing with their own sexual problems and frustrations. Another common example is when parents focus too intensely on their children's achievement, which is often an easy distraction from parental job frustrations and boredom.

Sometimes the expressions of conflict in the family become focused on religious or traditional issues. Nowhere is this more dramatically illustrated than in the situation surrounding young adults who decide to intermarry with someone of a different race or religion. When a historically triangulated child decides to intermarry, the parents may become very adamant that the child not intermarry even if they have never before been particularly strong adherents to their faith or traditions. After working with hundreds of Christian-Jewish intermarriages, Friedman (1971) found that it was impossible to predict how parents might react based on information such as their section of the United States, their degree of Jewish education or synagogue attendance, the amounts they gave to the United Jewish Appeal or the frequency of their trips to Israel. A history of cultural commitment simply was not sufficient to create the reaction.

When the child who has traditionally been the focus of the excess emotion in the parents' relationship is ready to leave home, the separation is likely to be more difficult for him or her than it was for the other siblings. Feelings about family become confused with feelings about heritage, and the striving child rejects the heritage. This rejection seems to be a definitive way of showing individuality and separateness from parents. The parents become distressed over losing the child who has balanced their relationship for so long, and they focus on the religious or racial issue rather than on their own personal feelings of loss.

This pattern helps explain why various children in the family who intermarry can expect different reactions from their parents. Friedman believes the child who acts like the firstborn is often the one who gets triangulated. Sometimes the siblings can intuitively understand and predict the differential reactions of the parents when they say things such as, "My brother could get away with this and it wouldn't mean anything" or "My sister could never intermarry without being kicked out of the family. With me it is different."

The most dramatic illustration of how detouring triangles function has been furnished by Minuchin, Rosman, and Baker (1978). They studied diabetic children whose medical condition was worsened by family stress and tension. Originally, the researchers were trying to understand why some children with diabetes mellitus would repeatedly succumb to episodes of ketoacidosis (diabetic coma). The presenting symptoms of ketoacidosis vary widely but can include abdominal pains, nausea, vomiting, and respiratory distress. If severe and untreated, this condition can lead to coma and ultimately death. For ketoacidosis to develop, there must be a huge increase in the concentration of free fatty acids (FFAs) in the blood. The liver metabolizes the FFAs to produce ketone bodies; excess blood levels of ketones (ketoacidosis) that eventually lead to severe symptoms.

Ketoacidosis and psychological factors are related because when one is under stress or emotionally aroused the production of FFAs is also greatly increased. Minuchin noticed that many diabetic children with recurring ketoacidosis had symptoms that would subside after the child's admittance to the hospital but would reemerge soon after the child returned home. Very rarely were medical explanations for the ketoacidosis found. Careful study of over 200 cases showed that the attacks of ketoacidosis were related to family conflict!

The parents of these children found it difficult to express conflict openly. Whenever possible they would detour their own disagreements by getting mutually involved in protecting and worrying about their child. The child became the focus of arguments and anxiety. This intense child focus was emotionally overwhelming to the children, who responded with the physical distress of ketoacidosis. In the lab, this phenomenon was illustrated by comparing the families of children with psychosomatic ketoacidosis with families with a diabetic child having a behavior problem and families with healthy children.

When the mother/father/child triangle was initially presented with the task of discussing a problem together, families with a psychosomatic child tried to avoid discussing the conflict. When these children were physically separated from their parents behind a two-way mirror and the parents were prodded into discussing the conflict area, the physiological stress of the psychosomatic diabetic child was raised just by watching the parents openly disagree. When the family was reunited and encouraged to continue discussing the topic, the parents reverted to detouring and focusing on the child instead of the conflict topic they were supposed to discuss. With the child present and available as the focus, the physiological stress indicators of the parents began to subside. The child's stress responses continued to grow, with higher and higher levels of physiological arousal. It seemed as though the child were almost literally absorbing the stress between the parents. Children from the other two types of families (families with a diabetic child having a behavior problem and families with a healthy child) did not show this pattern of absorbing the family stress.

Parent/Child Coalitions

The patterns known as *parent/child coalitions* occur when one child and one parent form a close, rigid alliance against the remaining parent. Stable coalitions can point to quite serious problems in the parents' relationships, since the primary dyad in a triangle most often "should" be between the parents.

Sometimes, in an effort to avoid parental conflict, one of the children will openly side with one parent against the other or will try to ally himself or herself so that the conflict between the parents is less obvious. For example, the author once had a client who could not understand his wife's interest in window shopping and comparison shopping. Often fights would erupt because the wife wanted to shop on an evening out and the husband wanted to do anything but shop. Suddenly, the fighting subsided when one of the daughters developed a coalition with the mother. She wanted to accompany her mother on weekends and after-school shopping trips and would often have her mother promise her a week ahead to spend at least two nights of the next week looking for a particular object. She would also get together with her mother to tease her father on his lack of consumer savvy.

In some ways, the parent/child coalition was useful in this case. Parental fights decreased; good times increased. The problematical part of parent/child coalitions, this one included, is that they prevent the adults from resolving their problems.

Gilbert, Christensen, and Margolin (1984) provided an elegant empirical investigation of differences in the patterns of alliance between distressed and nondistressed families. They were interested in determining whether distressed families had weaker marital alliances, had more of the hypothesized dominant mother/child alliances, or had more rigid alliances that could not change across a variety of situations.

The twelve distressed families in the study were tested as part of their pretreatment assessment at a mental health clinic. They all had evidenced concurrent problems in both the marital and parent/child subsystems. The twelve nondistressed families were recruited through local clinics and media announcements. To be included in the nondistressed sample, the families had to achieve normative scores on four different parent-report measures of marital and child behavior. All families had two parents in the home and at least one school-aged child (five to thirteen years old) living at home.

All the families took part in two ten-minute structured interaction tasks. In the first task, family members selected and discussed a salient problem from a standard list of family problems (problems involving chores, bed-times, etc.). In the second task, family members negotiated a mutually agreeable family menu. Verbatim transcripts were made of each of the interactions. The content of each speech act was coded to assess whether the communication was indicative of a positive alliance or a negative alliance. In addition, the affect of each speech act was also coded as indicative of positive or negative overall affect. A consensual rating system was devised so that the strength of any alliance statement could be judged from plus ten (strong positive alliance statement) to minus ten (strong negative alliance statement).

The methodology of this study is quite complex, but the results shed light on a number of important theoretical assumptions about triadic inter-action in families. First, the researchers found that the marital alliance was weaker in distressed families than in nondistressed families. That is, there were more supportive interactions between the parents and the children than between the two parents in distressed families. This finding supports the structural view that a strong marital alliance helps create a healthy family environment. Gilbert, Christensen, and Margolin (1984:83) con-cluded that:

> To the extent that the marital alliance is weak, the family no longer
> has its most experienced, knowledgeable, and resourceful subsys-
> tems fully contributing to regulatory matters (e.g., child-rearing,
> household tasks, financial responsibilities) and adaptive needs (e.g.,
> problem solving, conflict resolution, etc.).

Second, the data indicated that in two-thirds of the distressed families, the mother and the target child had considerably more negative interaction than the father and the target child. The tense mother/child relationship seen in this study contradicts the theories of most family therapists that mothers in distressed families seek out a strong positive relationship with the child as a substitute for some emotional gratification they are not getting from their spouses. Indeed, it seems that the poorer the husband/wife alliance, the more likely the mother is to project her frustrations and anger onto the child.

The third important finding of this study was that the problem-solving situation promoted less supportive interactions and more conflict in the distressed families than in the nondistressed families. Under the more neutral situation of planning a menu, members of the distressed families were able to be much more supportive of one another. Faced with a problem, distress-prone families are apparently not able to maintain their usual level of support for one another and exacerbate the existing difficulties by attacking, rejecting, and ignoring one another more than ever.

Studies have shown that college students from families with strong cross-generational coalitions experience distress and disorganization in both academic and social realms. Held and Winey (1984) found significant positive correlations between feelings of helplessness, anxiety, and confusion and the degree to which college students reported that their mothers discussed their father's faults with them or their fathers discussed their mothers' faults with them. In addition, only the women students became more distressed as they were called upon to give advice to their mothers or fathers or discuss their fathers with their mothers.

Successful differentiation of children from their family is a positive developmental step. However, it is difficult for the parent who has been in a long-standing coalition with a child to lose the support and esprit de corps that has developed between them. For the child, the rewards of independence and self-sufficiency usually outweigh the rewards available within the family structure. For the parents, the rewards within the family structure are often greater, and so they feel bewildered and rejected as their children pull away physically and psychologically.

When the child is successful in differentiating, the parents are often thrown into a panic about what is left for them to do with their lives. The so-called empty nest syndrome to which women are particularly vulnerable is part of this search for a new meaning system when the old one has fallen apart. Helpless to resist the change and ambivalent over the maturity exhibited in the child, the parents are channeled into redefining who they are. Middle-aged couples who have been happily married for twenty-five to thirty years may find themselves bickering or depressed, projecting all their fears and disappointments onto the spouse now that there are no children left at home to triangulate.

JERRY (engineer, age 46)

In my family of origin, I was the child chosen to be in the parental triangle. At age forty-six, I don't think I'm as tightly triangulated as during my youth, but the effects of my parents' shenanigans are still with me.

My parents were really very ill suited for one another from the beginning. My mother came from a large Italian family where the daughters were considered unimportant and the sons were glorified. I think that was the beginning of my mother's resentful attitude toward men. My mother is a very simple person who relies solely on her own common sense despite its obvious limitations. When her retarded brother needed a place to live, everyone said he should move in with Diane (my mom) even though she had just been married six months. Telly moved in, all right, and he's still there today. Telly is harmless enough; he's helped out at a local diner for the past eighteen years and has his own pocket money. His presence though must have caused a lot of conflict between my parents since we could never go away without him and couldn't leave him by himself. I've never heard my father speak badly of Telly but then I've never heard my father complain about any of the things that really bother him.

My father came from a matriarchal household and has always had a lot of insecurities about his capabilities. He couldn't go to college because he had to help out at home and feels very unknowledgeable.

When he got married, I think all he hoped for was someone who would cook and clean and not be too hard on him. He got two of the three. My mom has always found fault with my father. He's worked sixteen hours daily, six days a week, at his dry-cleaning store. On Sundays he puts in eight to ten hours doing paperwork. Although my father had three sons, we were never expected to put a lot of time in at the store. We each worked four hours a day in the summer and two Saturdays a month. My mom was and is always complaining about how little time he spends at home and how tired he is at home. It's been that way my whole life. She also complains that he drinks too much (he does), eats like an animal (he does), and doesn't like to do anything relaxing (he doesn't). My parents have not had any sex life for many years, and while my father's life is the store, my mother's is her house and the cat.

As the firstborn, I became the focus of a lot of my parents' attention. Even after the arrival of my two brothers, I was continually singled out to be the object of concern. A lot of my mother's concerns were just off the wall, irrational. Typical of this was one day when I was twelve or so and there was a solar eclipse. Me and my friends were going to watch it on TV but my mother became hysterical that I would go blind if I watched it on TV! I tried to explain it to her but she was beside herself. She called my father and made him come home from work. As always, my father sided with my mother on how bullheaded I was. Detouring, par excellence! Whenever I played in the band in high school, they would spend hours

(continued)

(continued)

discussing how I could do that given how shy I "really" was. Both of my parents focused a lot on what I looked like and how I dressed. My two brothers seemed to escape all this.

Now there is less detouring and more of a parent/child coalition between me and my mother. I hate my father's work schedule, eating habits, and drinking as much as she does. We'll spend a lot of phone time discussing all his problems. Basically though, I'm still there to help them avoid confronting one another. While my mother is still irrational (her new thing is that I'm going bald because I don't wear a shower cap and every week she begs me to wear one each and every time I shower), I have more sympathy for her.

Both of my brothers are married with children and involved with aggressive career ladders. I'm working day and night like my father and have a lot of insecurities and can't even find a woman to relate to and date on a regular basis. I can't help but feel that my parents' problems have created unique problems in my life. I'm trying to extricate myself from them but it isn't easy.

Split Loyalties

The concept of *split loyalties* refers to a pattern in which the child is caught between two parents, each of whom wants the child to side with him or her against the other parent. The child is in a chronic no-win situation. An expression of care or concern for one parent cannot be voiced without betraying the other. Most children become frozen when they are put into this situation. Usually, they leave the family as soon as possible.

Before a separation or divorce, children often find themselves in a split alliance. Each parent is courting the child's favor and throwing poisoned arrows at the estranged spouse. When adolescents see this pattern, they panic. They sense that their parents are becoming unable to preserve the integrity of the family unit and are on the verge of separation or divorce. Sometimes, the adolescents start acting in a way they know will outrage their parents—running away, taking drugs, or engaging in vandalism. One important consequence of these delinquent behaviors is that the mutual concern of the parents momentarily strengthens the marital dyad. Everyone is forced to mobilize around the troubled adolescent. Unfortunately, once the parents' coalition has been effective in reducing the problematic behavior, the adolescent soon finds that he or she is again in a split alliance with mother and father relating well to the adolescent but fighting bitterly with each other (Mirkin, Reskin, and Antognini, 1984).

In very distant and untrusting families, it is often difficult to find any dyad that has a truly strong alliance. Sometimes, the triangles in these families involve pets instead of family members. The function of pets in family triangles is easy to understand once we concede that all human beings need to be in a caring relationship. If two family members are very angry with each other and one or both of them are unable to positively reach out and engage another family member in a triangle, they can alternatively seek out the comfort of a pet. Sometimes the pet is the focus of a split alliance in which both parents and siblings try to turn the animal into their own intense personal ally and create a lot of distance between the pet and the rest of the family. The triangulated pet boosts their spirits, helps them solve problems, and increases their self-esteem just as a third person would (Rynearson, 1978).

TRIANGLES AND FAMILY TYPES

Triangles are a given in any family setting. Bowen (1971) has described triangles as being the molecules of any emotional system. Here, in the ebb and flow of the family life cycle, the triangles are constantly shifting; major alliances vary with how individuals perceive that their own goals and needs are being influenced by the others. For example, when a daughter wants to stay overnight at her girlfriend's, she may know that her mother would be absolutely against this but her father would be for it. If she asks her mother while her father is around, the triangular relationship would result in the father's being drawn into the discussion in support of the daughter. The relationship between the mother and daughter can shift quite dramatically when the daughter draws the mother in as an ally against younger sister for being on the phone too long. Because the mother believes in limiting phone calls, the daughter can feel confident that she can draw the mother into the sibling fight as her ally and reduce the conflict in her favor.

Triangles are an effective adaptive mechanism for dealing with the multiple alliances and conflicts that exist within any family. They become dysfunctional when the same three characters are constantly playing out the same triangular pattern.

A functional model of triangles has been developed by Karpman (1968), who uses a transactional analysis model to explain how triangles operate. On the "Karpman Triangle," each one of the three people takes on one of the following roles: persecutor, victim, or rescuer. The persecutor sets up very stringent standards for acceptable behavior. When the persecutor enforces the rules it is done in a harsh, no-guns-spared manner. The victim feels that his or her problems are externally caused (usually by the persecutor) and that he or she is helpless to prevent or change what happens. The rescuer tries to be exceedingly helpful and enjoys having others be dependent upon him or her to get out of a jam. The persecutor and victim are usually the comfortable dyad that Bowen talks about, and the rescuer is triangulated into the interaction. Of course, in most families and in most triangles, every person takes on each of these three roles in different situations.

When the family members shift roles *during* the conflict or as part of the resolution process, the emotional tension rises. Here is a hypothetical family conversation depicting the Karpman triangle:

> *Persecutor:* *Child:* Why did you cook lamb chops? You know I hate lamb chops, and these look yucky!
>
> *Victim:* *Mother:* I'm sorry, but it was all I had in the freezer that we could cook tonight.
>
> *Rescuer:* *Father:* Bobby, if you don't like dinner, be quiet about it. Your mother worked hard today so sit down and don't say another word.

If their interaction sequence could end here, the mother might feel supported and the son angry. Notice, however, the great shifts in the tension if the roles shift.

> *Persecutor:* *Father:* The lamb chops are OK but what's the matter with these vegetables? They're waterlogged and tasteless.
>
> *Victim:* *Mother:* They're the same vegetables you raved about last week. I cooked them the same way.
>
> *Rescuer:* *Child:* I like the vegetables. They taste real good.

It is generally agreed that when family members fluidly shift between triangles, the family system is more adaptive. Karpman's analysis suggests that it may be necessary to qualify that statement with the idea that within any one triangle, fixed roles are sometimes more adaptive than fluid roles. Hopefully, future research will help clarify this issue.

FEATHER (teacher, age 56)

In my family of origin, all three of the children were triangulated with my parents at different points in the family history. My older sister was considered a behavior problem from age eleven on. Both parents were very concerned that she was sexually promiscuous and physically precocious.

(continued)

(continued)

Hours of discussion were required if she wore lipstick or eye shadow. Once when she was fourteen, she was caught playing spin the bottle at a party. For months the fatal bottle spin was discussed. The conflicts between my parents were visible to everyone at that time, and despairing over my sister was one of the few cohesive activities they had. I can remember one night in particular when my sister was out with one of the "faster" boys in our already fast lower-class neighborhood. From the moment my sister left, my parents plotted how to spy on her and catch her and her boyfriend in all their wickedness. Finally, my little brother and I were whisked into the car to cruise past the party house. It was a warm summer evening, and when we found my sister outside the party house necking with one of the guys, my parents dragged her into the car and the fight went on throughout the night and into the next month. Looking back, I can't help but wonder what my parents' sex life was like at that time.

Also, in retrospect, it is no surprise that this detoured firstborn eloped at age seventeen with a long-time boyfriend. At the time everyone was shocked. Now it seems like it was inevitable.

After my sister eloped and really cut off from the rest of the family, I became involved in a parent/child coalition with my father against my mother. My father and I were both reasonable and rational. My mother was emotional. Many times after dinner we would be discussing something together and my father and I would start criticizing or putting down my mother. Sometimes, the putdowns were scathing and downright cruel. For example, one time I remember we were discussing extramarital affairs. It was the early 1960s and I was a flower child—liberated and liberal in every way. My father and I were on the side of affairs being healthy and natural. My mother was on the side of commitment and trust. By the end of the discussion, my mother was in tears, saying we were both "demented." Only years later did I realize from talks with my mother that my father was actively having affairs at that time. I don't know how I would have felt if I had known at that time, but our coalition was a strong one and while I am embarrassed to admit it now, I probably would have condoned it. I feel very guilty over the coalition I had with my father during my adolescence, and I would like to apologize to my mother. Somehow, that is such a difficult thing to do. I can't even get the beginning words out. I think it would be a real load off me if I could apologize. I don't know why it is so hard.

Anyway, after I left to go to college, I had a much more egalitarian relationship with both parents. My little brother was the last one left, and he ended up getting into a divided loyalty situation. Each of my parents wanted him to side with them against the other. My mother began to confide *everything* about my father's indiscretions. Every time my father would insult my mother, my brother knew about it. My mother also took to befriending my brother's various girlfriends. She would go shopping with them and talk with them a lot, and many stayed friends with her long after my brother was out of the picture. My father, on the other hand, started going on fishing trips with Mike and was very into selecting the right college for him. He would often tell my brother never to get married because "look at the mess" he got into. Really, my father tried to find the ally in my brother that he had once found in me. My brother's a lot more sensible though,

(continued)

(continued)

and while he listened to each parent bitch he never joined. Mike left home for college and got married in his junior year. My mother is probably closer to my sister-in-law than to either of her daughters. While my sister and I feel rejected at times, we also feel that my mother's need to triangulate people has mercifully bypassed us during this phase of our life. We all relate well to our parents now—even my older sister. My family proves, I think, that triangular relationships are not necessarily fixed or irreversible. It just seems families have different needs during different times.

RECENT RESEARCH ON TRIANGULAR EFFECTS

The early research on marital conflict and child adjustment was focused on documenting that a relationship existed between couple difficulties and child dysfunction. Although clinicians persist in seeing a strong relationship, the data shows a significant but very modest correlation between the two. Holden, Geffner, and Jouriles (1998) reviewed 481 correlations from 26 studies and found that 77 percent of the correlations were less than .30 (of course that means 23 percent of the correlations were greater than .30). In light of these minimal findings, the research focus has shifted and now more detailed studies are trying to answer the following question: "What type of parental conflicts affect specific types of children to exhibit clinical, social, and/or academic problems?" We have the most information on how the "type" of children affects marital conflict. It appears that children who have a good relationship with an adult outside the family are more likely to be protected from the trauma of marital discord (Jenkins and Smith, 1990). Also, children's coping strategies and how routine they judge the marital conflict to be can protect them (Cummings, Davies, and Simpson, 1994). Children who blame themselves for the arguments and strife are more likely to become depressed and have lowered self-esteem. Those who feel that they or their family members are in danger are likely to become anxious (Fincham, Gyrch, and Osborne, 1994). Boys are more adversely affected by parental strife if they find the conflict frightening or very destructive and don't know what to do to stop it; girls are more adversely affected if they blame themselves for the parental strife (this is typical of how boys focus on the ability to solve the problem; girls focus on their interpersonal role in the problem!) (Cummings, Davies, and Simpson, 1994). Children with more difficult temperaments react more negatively to parental fighting (Easterbrooks, Cummings, and Emde, 1994).

Some have suggested that the reason marital conflicts affect children adversely is that one's parenting abilities are compromised when angry, depressed, or frustrated in the marital relationship. Discipline is more likely to be inconsistent and impulsively delivered when marital tension is surging through the body. Parents who are emotionally drained are unable to respond to the emotional needs of their children and become desensitized to the children's overt and subtle pleas for nurturance.

Also, parents who are unhappy with each other are less willing to reconcile differences in child-rearing rules and expectations. Children are more likely to receive contradictory messages and be placed in double binds where whatever they do, one parent is going to be unhappy. Obviously, children are more distressed when the conflict and arguing are directly related to their conduct.

Other clinicians and researchers stress that when there is conflict and aggression in the parents' relationship, there is an increased chance that the child-parent relationship will also be plagued by aggression (verbal, physical, or psychological). In this sense, the disruption in the marital relationship is simply a marker of adults who are unable to successfully negotiate stressful or intimate relationships. Anyone who needs to intimately interact with them, on a day-by-day basis, will be caught in a destructive relationship.

SELF-EXPLORATION: FAMILY TRIANGLES

Family therapists agree that any two people can have a stable, close relationship when everything is going smoothly. When anxiety and tension break into the relationship, the most immediate and vulnerable "other" person in the family is enlisted to form a triangle. The best example of a triangle is the father/mother/child triangle. Look carefully at all your father/mother/child triangles as you do the following exercise:

1. Draw triangles for each of the family triads in your family of origin or current nuclear family.
2. Then examine each triangle by asking what happens to the third person when the other two folks in the triangle are having a disagreement. Remember that for *each* triangle you will ask this question three times.
3. Try to assess whether there are any persistent triangles in your family or if they are constantly changing. Look to see whether there are any detouring triangles, parent/child coalitions, or split-loyalty triangles. Can you describe the interactions that led to your getting involved in any one of these particular triangles?

Chapter 6

Rituals

We have to see, I think, that questioning the value of old rules is different from simply breaking them.

Elizabeth Janeway, *Between Myth and Morning* (1974)

Family rituals are a highly repetitive and stylized type of family productivity. Some families always eat Friday night dinner together, others always clean on Saturday morning. Some families restrict spending on each person for Christmas presents, others go camping every Fourth of July. Rituals are unspoken rules. Family rituals have been described as "symbolic behavior that develops in groups and is repeated 'for its own sake' because of the meaning and satisfaction that participants get out of it" (Klapp, 1959:212). Bell and Vogel (1963:433) add the idea that rituals "involve some degree of cooperation to promote common life and group rapport." Rituals help families remain cohesive and develop a unique identity. They make family life predictable.

A wide range exists in the number and kind of rituals that families can develop. At one extreme are the families for whom the entire day is a set of carefully prescribed rituals encompassing everything from methods of greeting one another in the morning to very specific evening rituals. A classic example in this regard involved a family who had ritualized nearly all their family interactions in a very rigid manner. Monthly lists were used to decide upon the discussion topics at dinner, to organize recreational events (which occurred every other Friday), and, of course, to delegate the household chores. Open disagreement was not allowed in this family, and holidays were so highly stylized that no one had a chance to relax or enjoy them.

At the other extreme are families whose day-to-day existence is so chaotic that only the most flimsy of rituals can be found. For example, one young man who was analyzing his family rituals in group therapy broke down in tears, realizing that the only ritual he could remember was hanging up his Christmas stocking. As he reflected on twenty years at home, this was the only predictable, regularly occurring event he could remember. He later decided to begin developing some rituals for his current nuclear family so that his one-year-old daughter could avoid his feelings of rootlessness.

TYPES OF RITUALS

Rituals serve at least five unique functions for the family (Morval and Biron, 1993):

1. Protection—The protective function of rituals begins early in life and continues until the day we die. One of the earliest protective rituals most of us learn is bedtime rituals. Whether it is getting to watch one more TV show or being read to out of a favorite book, bedtime rituals assure that children will be less likely to be afraid once the lights are out and they are alone.

2. Cohesiveness—One feature that is common to a wide array of family rituals is that they are done together. Going waterskiing, fishing, or sailing can be a solitary activity, but if it is done with other family members in a predictable way over a number of years, it becomes a ritual. It is not that "I ski" but that "My family goes skiing over the Christmas holidays." The bonding that results from shared activities is one of the strongest phenomena in social psychology.

3. Communication—Rituals are a way for one family member to communicate caring and love for the other family members. Those of us brought up in the 1950s knew that those long Sunday drives looking for land in the country were as much about saying "We want everything good for you children" as it was about how much land cost per acre.

4. Intergenerational transmission—The rituals about how to celebrate the Fourth of July or how to cook the lemon meringue pie for birthdays are important because of the way that one generation passes on its knowledge and values to the next generation. Most of us can't learn how to plant the harvest or raise the roof from our granddaddies. But survival learning was only one aspect of intergenerational transmission, even in the olden days. We can still learn from our grandparents a faith, a political orientation, a love for a certain geographical place, music preferences and food preferences. We can learn hobbies and most important, how generational ties can bind us, motivate us, and enlarge our self-definition.

5. Identity development—Children who grow up in estranged households with very few rituals often find they have a confused or empty identity. It takes lots of shared ritual to knit together a family identity that comfortably fits over our individual identities.

6. Understanding of unconscious phenomena—The rituals surrounding death help us understand the universal, multilayered symbolic and existential meanings of life and love. For example, in the Jewish faith, the mourning begins with the ritual of a speedy burial to facilitate the body's renewal process as part of the cycle of life. A piece of clothing that the mourner is wearing is ripped, symbolizing how the deceased is being torn away from the family.

POSITIVE ASPECTS OF THE RITUAL

For most of us, rituals serve a very positive function, allowing us to experience a sense of belonging and comfort in our families. Rituals that last through childhood conserve memories, helping us retain a sense of identity. Most rituals endure despite changes in jobs, homes, and family composition, albeit in various altered forms. Indeed, like Linus' blanket, rituals calm the anxieties associated with growing, changing, and taking risks.

Sometimes, though, parents use rituals to overstructure situations that provoke their anxieties. For example, in an effort to avoid family conflict, the dinner hour may become highly ritualized—so much so that only certain topics are appropriate for conversation and only certain family members can speak for any length of time. Children of such families may grow up resenting and challenging the rituals, claiming them to be vacuous and confining. Adolescents, to whom emotional separation from the family is of primary importance, are especially likely to spurn rituals. As they gain independence and become more confident, most grown children feel free to enjoy family rituals once again. But in those families fraught with an extreme degree of ritualization, the comfort gained from the ritual is overwhelmed by the smothering effect of having "a family way of behaving." In these families many rituals are best buried.

For the young child, rituals spell confidence about the right way to perform and make daily events predictable. Gesell long ago noted that by age two and a half, a child has a very strong ritualistic sense of having everything at home in its usual place and done in its usual way. Young children can become very insistent that all family members perform their ritualistic roles precisely. Lack of these vital tools and techniques for social participation seems to threaten the child's sense of security (Ilg, Ames, and Baker, 1992). Bossard and Boll (1950:58) believe that rituals provide more than security:

Although family rituals alone do not create all the subjective aspects of family life such as attitudes, values, goals, and ambitions, rituals, because they are overt behavior forms, are symptoms of these aspects, and thus convey them in a concrete manner from parent to child.

The stabilizing influence of family rituals has been affirmed in many studies. Hawkins (1997) studied the self-reports of 143 students, sixty-five outpatient depressives, and sixty-four chemically dependent clients. They were all questioned about the type of family rituals that occurred in the family of origin and what led to the disruption or discontinuation of various rituals. Indeed, disruption of rituals predicted which children from alcoholic parents would end up with pathological interpersonal styles and problem drinking. Families that were able to maintain rituals, even though there was a severe problem in the family, were often able to protect the children from repeating the fate of the distressed family members.

For rituals to endure, it is important to talk about them as well as to engage in the behaviors (Baxter and Clark, 1996). The rituals have to evoke positive memories so that thinking about them, laughing about them, and recounting the details is a sought-after pleasure. With a lively memory and discussion of past rituals comes the anticipatory pleasure of planning and looking forward to the next event.

Rituals are not the only way for families to gain a sense of cohesion and purpose. Medical problems that require the family to pull together and help out, caregiving of the young and elderly, and the homemaking efforts of family kinskeepers all work to create meaningful family contact with positive affect. Rituals, though, are by far the longest lasting and most enjoyable way to build family.

Typical Family Rituals

Rituals can often be found in a family's recurrent patterns of leisure-time activity, from photograph taking to mealtime preparations, from nicknaming to the fantasies made up by parents for their children. Rituals, by their repetitive nature, serve as a trademark or persona of the family identity. People asked to describe the type of family they came from inevitably describe rituals. One person might describe her family as the type that went on family picnics every Sunday; another describes his as the type that worked around the yard on Sunday. Over the years, the rituals come to represent what the members of the family like about themselves and what they would like to perpetuate. Rituals are the means by which people can relax and "be themselves" at home. The rituals take away the uncertainties of who will be doing what and how, and when it will get done.

A ritual is to family life as a script is to the drama. The whole aim of a ritual is that it be reenacted at precise times and in a precise manner. Acting in conformity with the classic ritual exercise is considered to be intrinsically rewarding and worthwhile. For children, it structures the complexity of the world in a way that allows them to understand and predict key events. For adults, the ritual's meaning resides in its ability to help them relive emotions, thoughts, and sentiments. An oft-repeated ritual serves as a mnemonic device that brings forward the most treasured of emotions and acts as a comfortable reminder of the ability to live through the most troubling emotions. Either way, rituals are a mark of successful collective organization and shared goals (Schvaneveldt and Lee, 1983).

Perhaps this is why the ritual of family photographs is so important. Photos capturing family celebrations and rites of passage affirm the cohesive nature of the family. Individual landmarks (birthdays, graduations) and cultural landmarks (holidays, vacations) are bounded within the nexus of the family. The family album attests to the importance of the family's social status and developmental progress. In fact, until the recent popularity of home videos, photographs were the only public record of the successful passage of the family through the varying life cycles.

Therapists who use photo albums in their work commonly observe that the most stressful years in a family's life are easily detected because no pictures are taken during such times. Pictures are a positive affirmation of family life: the fun of building snowmen, the proud smiles that accompany a new car or new bicycle, the solidarity of the extended family's presence at important life-cycle events. Rare indeed are pictures that reflect the upset that accompanies a bathroom leaking into the kitchen or a parent recovering from a serious operation in the hospital. Not only is taking pictures a family ritual, but showing the pictures often becomes a ritual as well. Looking at family albums, slides, or motion pictures (and now videos) is an established part of holiday rituals for many families.

Another cherished ritual is the bedtime story that is used by parents to ensure that the sandman comes gently and lovingly to little ones. The plot of the bedtime story is almost inconsequential. Some children hear the same story night after night, reassured rather than bored by the knowledge of the picture and words coming up on the next page. Kotkin and Zeillin (1983:85) "even met one father who put his four-year-old boy, Saul, to bed by recounting his son's own activities that day. . . . 'Once there was a little boy named Saul, and he woke up in the morning . . .'" Another father known to the author reads epic trilogies to his children night after night with a tape recorder on. Then long car trips to visit the relatives include an additional ritual of listening again to favorite stories or chapters. The bedtime story ritual has a long history; anthropologists assume that ritualistic storytelling occurred in the earliest human clans.

Orrin Klapp (1959) assessed the amounts and kinds of rituals practiced in families of college students. He then went on to test for a relationship between the importance of rituals to a family and the degree of solidarity felt among the family members. Table 6.1 summarizes the importance assigned to various rituals. Most of the rituals seemed to center on Christmas, Thanksgiving, Mother's Day, and birthdays. Ritual gifts and meals loom large in American family ceremony. Over a fifth of the students assigned considerable importance to bedtime rituals and to religious rituals such as saying grace at meals and attending church together. Regardless of which particular rituals were judged important, there was a significant relationship between the intensity of family solidarity and the number and importance of family rituals. These findings suggest that the closer knit a family is and the longer its continuous existence, the richer the ceremonials will be.

HOW FAMILY RITUALS EVOLVE AND DEVELOP

Most rituals seem to evolve by happenstance. A family may spontaneously go to a certain park one weekend in May and because the weather is perfect, the family is amiable, and the food is delicious, a May picnic at that particular park may become a ritual for many years hence. Howard (1978:271) says that "real rituals are discovered in retrospect. They emerge around constitutive moments; moments that only happen once, around whose memory meanings cluster. You don't choose these moments. They choose themselves." Of course, it takes a highly talented kinskeeper and family mythologizer who has the gift of apprehending such "once-in-a-lifetime moments" to transform these special times into nourishing family rituals.

Every time a family repeats a ritual, it develops a stronger and more enriched meaning than it had previously. The ability to deepen the family identity through cherished rituals is part of Howard's (1978:270) criteria for a good family. She says:

> Nothing welds a family more than these. Rituals are vital especially for clans without histories, because they evoke a past, imply a future, and hint at continuity. No line in the Seder service at Passover reassures more than the last: "Next year in Jerusalem!" A clan becomes more of a clan each time it gathers to observe a fixed ritual (Christmas, birthdays, Thanksgiving, and so on), grieves at a funeral (anyone may come to most funerals; those who do declare their tribalness), and devises a new rite of its own. Equinox breakfasts and all-white dinners can be at least as welding as Memorial Day pa-

rades. Several of us in the old *Life* magazine years used to meet for lunch every Pearl Harbor Day, preferably to eat some politically neutral fare like smorgasbord, to "forgive" our only ancestrally Japanese colleague, Irene Kubota Neves. For that and other reasons we became, and remain, a sort of family.

Note that rituals can be used just as effectively by nonbiological families to create a sense of "we-ness." Indeed, rituals may be even more important for these nontraditional family groups who have no common ancestry. Creating a shared emotional history through rituals develops bonds that are both primitive and strong. Such bonding can withstand the inevitable individual changes and growth that otherwise distance old friends. So long as the rituals can be repeated, the emotional security of the group's support will be available to all its members. In the movie *The Big Chill* (1983), this aspect of rituals was nicely demonstrated: the friends needed only to recount the old rituals to reawaken both the support and pressures offered by the old college clan.

SARAH (graduate student, age 26)

Rituals in my family were few and poorly defined. The major ones were Christmas and Thanksgiving. At both of these times we had dinner—just the three of us, always with a turkey and some kind of pie; other foods differed. We would eat in the dining room with my mother's best china. On Christmas morning we opened presents—no particular ritual to this; sometimes my brother and I would open them before my mother came in. Another ritual was that if we happened to be at home, we drank champagne on New Year's Eve and on New Year's Day we ate black-eyed peas for good luck. We did not usually go to church, and meals were often disorganized as my mother worked during the day and went to school at night. On Easter we usually dyed Easter eggs and sometimes had an Easter egg hunt. Birthdays we didn't have any special celebration, but sometimes my brother and I would have a party. All of these rituals were mainly in effect when we were children. All but the Christmas and New Year's rituals disappeared after I went off to school. When I finished school, I did not go back home enough even to maintain those rituals.

I don't believe that the family rituals had a lot of effect on me. I do look forward to dyeing Easter eggs, but I don't have strong feelings about Christmas or Thanksgiving. I do feel, however, that my son Michael should have some of the fun I missed out on, so I am going to try to put more ritual into our family.

TABLE 6.1. Estimate of Importance of Kinds of Ritual Practiced in Own Family

Rank		Much	Some	Little	None	Undecided
1.	Christmas dinner together	83	11	4	–	1
2.	Thanksgiving dinner together	81	16	2	1	0
3.	Opening Christmas presents together	79	13	7	1	0
4.	Gifts to family members on birthdays	60	26	12	0	0
5.	Mother's Day gifts or cards	57	28	10	4	0
6.	Celebrate birthdays with member(s) of family	52	29	14	1	1
7.	Decorating Christmas tree	47	35	4	4	1
8.	Father's Day gifts or cards	46	29	7	10	0
9.	Easter dinner together	46	29	14	8	0
10.	Dinner together on most other holidays	35	31	21	7	1
11.	Mother's Day get-together	27	34	15	10	0
12.	Saying grace at meals	24	16	19	27	2
13.	Going to church together	22	22	20	25	2
14.	Bedtime ritual (stories, drinks, kisses, etc., regularly)	22	13	11	28	5
15.	Making Easter eggs or other additional activities on Easter as a family	20	23	31	15	5
16	Visiting with relatives	17	45	29	6	
17.	Family reunions	17	28	26	10	1
18.	A special dish or refreshment served at certain meals	17	26	21	22	3
19.	Other (miscellaneous)	13	3	2	8	5
20.	New Year's get-together or party as a family	12	18	20	31	0
21.	Memorial Day visit to cemetery (or regular day for this)	12	16	14	37	2
22.	Watching or listening to a certain TV or radio program together	10	30	29	21	1
23	Family prayers (other than grace)	9	14	19	36	2
24.	A special time during the week is set apart for the family	5	18	20	31	1
25.	Halloween activities as a family	5	16	23	36	3
26.	A regular family walk or stroll	4	10	15	42	1

Source: Klapp, O. E. 1959. Ritual and family solidarity. *Social Forces, 37:*212-214.

Note: Figures are percentages of group reporting. N = 162. Subjects were asked to report either the family they grew up with or their conjugal family; the large majority reported the former (90 percent).

Not everyone believes that rituals are best nourished in an extemporaneous and unreflective manner. Consider the academic approach advocated by "Miss Manners" (Judith Martin) of *The Washington Post* (see "On the Purposeful Development of Family Rituals"). Martin believes that rituals are what gives a family its identity. She believes it is best for the family identity to be deliberately chosen and fashioned by the coheads of the family. This way spouses are aware of what rituals they are relinquishing from their own families of origin and what rituals need to be developed to meet the needs of the new nuclear family.

HELEN (graduate student, age 45)

Being more conscious of the symbolic and motivating power of ritual in our own family has sensitized me to the same possibility in other families. In the case of the H. family, the parents had adopted two sisters, six and four years of age. The mother and father saw "family time" as a kind of barometer for how they were doing in general. Family time included ritualistic leisure activity such as everyone gathering on the parents' bed watching the Muppets together. If they found/made time for this, the family was OK. Observing such rituals was a way of measuring how they were performing as parents in the task of building a family. Loss of this kind of ritual, which occurred in the multi-demanding world of Brownies, church group, speech therapy, family therapy, bridge group, and scuba class, was more threatening than it might appear to an outsider. Consequently, when they managed to reinstitute even the Muppet-type activities, the anxiety level went down. There was some truth to their perception because the "family time" became possible as the parents worked together in planning how responsibilities such as dishes and homework were going to be divided. As they functioned more effectively as a team, some of the noisy chaos, which ate up precious moments each day, began to subside, and in fact more time became available.

In our own family, I observe the ritual of knocking on the boys' doors and waiting for a response before entering. This has symbolic value as a way of defining their territory and respecting their privacy, and I expect the same from them. However, it is a myth in some ways because I have from time to time looked in their drawers or papers, which is a clear invasion! Nevertheless, I wait impatiently outside the door through which the stereo blasts and covers the sound of my knock, for the ritualistic "Come in!"

Being home every weekday by 6:00 p.m. or leaving a message or telephoning if not home is almost mandatory. It signifies respect for the family, responsibility, and concern for the feelings of worry others might endure. The same values surround being home late at night at or before the time agreed upon. The "rule" applies to adults and children alike. It is designed to avoid "wasted pain"—worry when there is no reason to do so. Several practical elements led to the development of the ritual that

(continued)

(continued)

the Bennett family is home by 6:00. First there was the problem of serving dinner to a growing and changing family. When the children were very young, I frequently fed them first, and then Bob and I had dinner whenever. That sounds better than it was, because even after they were fed the boys didn't necessarily allow us to have a pleasant dinner together. As they grew older and wanted more than pancakes or Spaghetti-O's for supper, it became a creative and difficult task to juggle several mealtimes. Finally the pressure was on Bob and me to have dinner ready and be home no later than 6:00.

Soon the boys were old enough to be off on their own in the neighborhood late in the afternoon, and it became their task to make it home. For one thing, I found myself worrying if they were not on time. For another, and more serious one, I felt rejected and unappreciated that they weren't there to eat this meal I had prepared. Food easily becomes an emotional issue. We used various logical consequences over the years. Can't make it home? Then can't leave the yard after nap. Home before we finish eating—dinner but no dessert. Home after dinner is finished—no dinner. Doling out these consequences was easier for Bob than me, and I'm sure my level of stress and discomfort did as much to get the boys to cooperate as any behavioral consequences. Plus we really tried to make meals enjoyable occasions, and had always included a bit of ceremony in them.

Everyone seemed to take the whole system for granted, so it was a shock one evening last summer when our nineteen-year-old, who rode his bike to and from his dishwashing job in Newark, failed to get home by 6:00. By 6:30 I began to wonder if he had had a flat tire. After eating, I drove to Newark along the bike route expecting to see him trudging along with a flat. No sign of him. I returned home and called the restaurant, which reported that he had left at 5:30. By 8:00 I called the police to see if accidents had been reported; none had been. When he finally walked in, he explained his boss had asked him to run some errands, which apparently the telephone person hadn't known. I was absolutely dumbfounded that he would not have called home. My face and my tears of relief told the story. For the remainder of the summer he called (tediously so, in fact) if he was going to be delayed for even a few minutes. I let it go for a while and then reassured him he needn't be that conscientious! What is almost funny to me is that the ritual makes me uncomfortable when other children are in our house at dinnertime and make no move to go home. I feel embarrassed for them if their parents have to call, even though it clearly is not an issue in their family.

On the Purposeful Development of Family Rituals

Ritual, or at least a common share of peculiar habits, is what gives a family identity. Miss Manners figures that that must be why, when so many persist in regarding the sacred subject of etiquette as one of life's frills, the highest emotions, on such basic occasions as weddings and funerals, are spent on quarreling about details of behavior.

(continued)

(continued)

Who wore what, who sat where, what was said in the receiving line and what was served to eat and drink—these are the issues of which lifetime feuds are made. That is why Miss Manners is always after you to follow the conventions on such matters. You become free from being criticized for individual choices, and can even blame Miss Manners should anyone try. She is big enough to take it.

But even she acknowledges that there are social patterns in which there is no right or wrong, but only family custom. Does father serve the family meal, or does mother? Is Sunday dinner eaten midday or in the evening? Is breakfast a time for conversation or newspaper reading?

Miss Manners advises all co-heads of families to make decisions on such questions, so as not to let them be taken over by secret judgments that one's spouse, coming from a different tradition, simply doesn't know how to behave. Couples need the strength of unity here, in order to weather such charges from the side of the family whose custom was not adopted.

Beyond that, those starting families need to develop some customs and rituals of their own. Such routines, not only pleasant in themselves, soon become so emotionally laden as to bind together the members of the family, and serve as a standard for those of flimsier background wishing to enter the family.

A married couple should develop rituals from the respective heritages and prejudices, but it is in the nature of the job that once developed, the routine must be repeated religiously.

National and religious holidays are obvious occasions for these, as are birthdays. Miss Manners believes in stating the nature of the occasion in as sentimental a fashion as possible (discussing democracy on the Fourth of July, telling baby stories about the family member whose birthday it is), although she knows she is supposed to be letting you decide these things for yourself.

She also recommends family dinners and children's bedtimes as occasions for which patterns are needed. Even the small child's last stalling tactic of a request for a drink of water is amusing if set into a ritual, so that the parent understands it cannot be skipped, and the child understands it cannot be executed twice.

Other possibilities include: Sunday afternoon tea, at which one child prepares tea or hot chocolate, another makes the bread and butter or other snack, and the family takes turns providing entertainment. Perhaps everyone has to have memorized a poem and must recite it (the parents will keep trying to appear with excuses, but the children must not let them get away with that), or a book is read aloud.

Lunch downtown, in a grown-up restaurant, between the child and one parent on a school holiday, possibly in combination with a shopping trip. A family sport, including assigned tasks for the preparation of equipment.

Sickbed luxuries, including special trays and privileges. These should be available to parents, who are not allowed to be sick but could declare temporary emotional illness on school holidays.

Opening of the season—the first picnic, nature walk, snowman building, planting.

(continued)

> *(continued)*
>
> In each of these, it must be decided what foods are appropriate, what reminiscences and what each person's task is. When you vary one of these ever so slightly, and a child screams, "No, that's not right!" you will know that you have succeeded. You will have established a tradition.
>
> *Source:* Martin, J.1984. *The Washington Post,* May 27, 1G, 7G. Miss Manners® material, copyright ©1984 by Judith Martin. Reprinted by permission.

ALTERING RITUALS AND ESTABLISHING NEW ONES

When a family crisis occurs and the family is forced to reassign roles or mourn lost members, new rituals develop to affirm the existence of a new family structure. The family in transition sculpts its identity through newly defined rituals, much like the individual who feels a need for a personal change and seeks out new hairstyles or ways of dressing to conform with the new image.

In its Folklore Archives, the Smithsonian Institution has interviews that vividly capture the importance of changing rituals when the family structure changes. One interview was with a woman whose father had abandoned her pregnant mother, her siblings, and herself when she was twelve years old (Zeitlin, Kotkin, and Baker, 1982:89):

> In the next year I don't know whether my mother did this on purpose, but we all sort of concurred in changing everything we had usually done. We had always had a certain kind of Christmas tree, a very tall Christmas tree, maybe because my father is six feet tall. But when it came time to decide what to do, it dawned on all of us at once, I think, that we should buy a short, fat Christmas tree, a Scotch pine, kind of blue. So we bought a tree that was about as wide as it was tall, and we went through all the decorations and threw about half of them out and got a lot of new ones, and we fixed the house differently. . . . It was a good Christmas. It was surprisingly good. . . . And we've done it that way ever since.

Many new rituals are being developed around the cultural passion for photos, videos, and picture taking. It is now fairly common to make a video highlighting the events in the family member's life, whether it be a bat/bar mitzvah, turning fifty, sixty, seventy, or older, having a milestone anniversary, retiring, or moving to a new location. Many young mothers are networking through the creation of the family albums, building community with other young mothers. Family albums function the same way that quilting bees did 100 years ago for young mothers. It is a weekly time, in the evening when the chores are done, for the women to get together, socialize, talk about children and family, and create cherished memories by working on their albums. Each page of the album is decorated with creative borders, balloon sayings, and annotations. The albums are sometimes organized by time (1998) or by child ("Amber's Album") or by event ("Aunt Marcie's fiftieth birthday party"). The pictures and album making are the stimulus for discussing their most cherished memories, their greatest worries, and their deepest frustrations. It is very therapeutic. On top of that, there is shared appreciation for each person's creativity and talents.

Hassia and Tova (1997) have adapted this ritual and created an in-the-office family therapy technique in which family members work together to create a collage from family pictures. This allows the family to bypass much of the self-censorship and self-consciousness that occurs within the therapy context. Watching the family work on the task is an excellent chance to observe family cohesiveness and problem solving. The resulting portrait can serve as a stimulus for discussing how the family sees itself now and how it would like to see itself.

Similarly, many people can recall Christmas rituals that had been performed by grandparents. Once the grandparents die, the rituals are relinquished, restructured, or reassigned to herald a new phase of the family life cycle.

Many couples experience the importance of creating new or slightly altered rituals as soon as they make plans for the wedding. When the marriage rituals from the groom's family differ greatly from the marriage rituals from the bride's family, there is invariably a period of tension and hurt feelings as each family tries to put its own family stamp on this critical rite of passage. This is particularly a problem in interfaith marriages, intercultural marriages, and international marriages. After the marriage ceremony there is a host of traditional family rituals that potentially can cause conflict for the new couple.

One spouse may want to go away every anniversary as his or her own parents did, while the other spouse may feel exchanging cards is most appropriate because of his or her own family rituals. Both may want to continue spending the Thanksgiving holiday or Christmas Day with their families of origin. Slowly, the couple learn how to reconcile conflicting rituals and develop new ones. Couples who cannot successfully develop mutually satisfying rituals seem most vulnerable to divorce. For when the going gets tough and major personal adjustments are required to allow a marriage to survive and grow, rituals give couples something positive to hold on to and to smooth the transition period. Without the rituals, a vital marital life support system is lost.

RITUALS AND THE FAMILY LIFE CYCLE

Do not become paralyzed and enchained by the set patterns which have been woven of old. No, build from your own youthful feelings, your own groping thought and your own flowering perception—and help to further that beauty which has grown from the roots of tradition.

Lotte Lehman, *More Than Singing* (1945)

The most elaborate rituals in any society revolve around the four major rites of passage: birth, pubescence, marriage, and death. In addition, our culture has extremely detailed rituals for certain major social events such as divorce, retirement, and geographical moves.

The family determines the emotional quality of each of these life-cycle events. The emotional significance of the rite in turn determines its success or failure in helping people mark a critical moment in the family life cycle. According to Friedman (1980), a positive emotional tone allows the family to come to the rite ready to reestablish relationships, learn about the family, and create the needed transitions. Friedman suggests that:

there seem to be certain "normal" [ritualistic] periods for change and working through of life-cycle transitions and attempts to hasten or shorten those periods unduly are always indications that there are important unresolved issues in the family relationship system. (p. 437)

Table 6.2 presents Friedman's "benchmark" periods for seven rites of passage. If people go through the rite prematurely or postmaturely, there is a strong possibility that the decisions are being made "more with their guts than with their heads, and there are important unworked-out issues still to be resolved with the family of origin" (p. 439).

Not all families are equally successful in developing rituals, and their success may also vary at different stages of the life cycle. Some parents are extraordinarily clumsy in instituting satisfactory rites for small children, yet become adept at the teenage level. Exactly the reverse is true in other families. In an effort to help families develop meaningful rituals, Susan Lieberman (1984) has written a book to stimulate families to find and

TABLE 6.2. Friedman's Benchmark Periods for Seven Rites of Passage

Rites of Passage	Extreme	Benchmark Period	Extreme
1. Age when married	Teenage elopement	No marriage or twenty-one to twenty-seven	Mid-forties
2. Length of courtship	Love at first sight to ten days	Six months to one year	Five years of going steady or living together
3. Length of engagement	Eloping right after decision	Three to six months	Many years of putting it off
4. Time to birth of first child	Pregnancy before marriage	Two to three years	Childless for whatever reason
5. Time between separation and divorce	Attempt to hasten legal limits	One to two years after legal limits	Till death do us part
6. Time between separation from one mate and going steady with future mate	Affair with future mate	Two to four years	Withdrawal, promiscuity
7. Time between divorce and remarriage	Same as examples five and six	Two to five years	Same as examples five and six

Source: Friedman, E. H. 1980. Systems and ceremonies: A family view of rites of passage. In: Carter, E. A. and McGoldrick, M. (Eds.), *The Changing Family Life Cycle: A Framework for Family Therapy*, Second Edition, p. 127. Copyright ©1980 by Allyn & Bacon. Reprinted/adapted by permission.

foster traditions that can serve as comfortable and steady markers through the years.

Although rituals vary according to each family's needs and social class, the evolution of rituals goes through distinctive stages throughout the family life cycle. Bossard and Boll (1950:152-155) arrived at seven conclusions concerning family rituals in relation to the family cycle:

1. *Early Marriage and the Expectant Family.* Here, rituals at an adult level have to be adjusted between the partners who always have some differences in ritual background. They may be assimilated, exist side by side, or one may dominate the other.
2. *The Beginning of Child bearing.* This is a period during which family ritual takes on a new meaning. Since adolescent days, the husband and wife have been tending away from traditional family procedures. Rituals now become a heritage to the future, and are frequently reestablished exactly at this time.
3. *The Preschool Family.* This period is rich in the innovation of the most elementary rituals of child rearing and household regimen. The process is very largely trial-and-error, but once culminating in a rite, the rite is strongly supported by both parent and child and is apt to endure until teenage time.
4. *The Family with Teenagers.* Ritual, at this stage, seems to multiply and to have a new function: to prepare children for adult socialization; to prevent them from complete separation from the family; and to guard them through a dangerous biological change.
5. *The Family As a Launching Center.* This part of the cycle seems the most tension-creating and disruptive of family rituals. Parents overeagerly try to perpetuate rituals, and children overzealously try to be free of them. The results are that ritualistic situations are streamlined, and that children often quit ones which they later redefine and readopt.
6. *The Aging Family.* In cases where the aging family is defined as the parent couple left alone, family ritual becomes important because: (1) older people are physically and psychologically disposed to such regimens; (2) there is an opportunity to return to loved rituals that enriched married life before children arrived; and (3) grandparent-grandchild rituals seem to be especially satisfying to both generations. Since, however, the aging family is becoming younger, there are many variations of this stage of the cycle which are worthy of further study.

Thus each new generation of parents search through their combined family histories to develop their own meaningful set of rituals. Children accept these rituals as proper and inevitable. As adolescents, they may scorn many rituals as silly, old-fashioned, or senseless. Yet as they mature and start their families, the process of reinstating and modifying family rituals begins all over again.

Some of the traditions that we cherish the most have become so commonplace that we don't even think of them as traditions anymore; instead they have become mandatory parenting practices. Bedtime stories, for example, are one of the most loved and universal of American nighttime rituals. For most children, this is one of their most vivid and warm memories of family life. From *Green Eggs and Ham* to *Willy Wonka and the Chocolate Factory* to *Clan of the Cave Bear,* children of all ages look forward to snuggling on the couch or in the bed with a parent and hearing a captivating tale. but it is not so easy to get that ritual in with the same relaxed demeanor of yesteryear. Today's parents have work schedules that have been stretched later and later due to commuting and job demands. Dinner occurs at 8 p.m. instead of 5 p.m. in many households and homework at 10 p.m. is not unusual. Where is the time for a bedtime story? Some parents scurry through one with their eyes half closed, and many others do so through clenched teeth and an aching back. But other parents are developing creative re-inventions of the old betime ritual.

One wonderful tradition discussed by Lieberman (1984) is "morning stories." She describes Maria, the mother of four-year-old Danny. She works as a reporter at a local newspaper. She is always stressed after work, trying to get to the day care center before it closes at 6 p.m. By the time she gets home, her second shift starts. The chores are the usual ones: cooking dinner, doing laundry, opening the mail, paying bills, bathing Danny, and cleaning the house. When bedtime comes, she is ready to have Danny read to her. Although she wanted to do the bedtime reading and felt obligated to do it, she knew she was in trouble when she refused to take any books longer than fifteen pages out of the library. Then, when the ritual was about to go bust, Maria and Danny invented their own special tradition. They would have "morning stories." After the evening bath, they explored the pile of available books in a relaxed manner. The chosen book was then placed on the breakfast table. As Danny ate his breakfast, he heard the story. If the story was especially long, Mom was willing to get to the day care center a few minutes late—better than paying the $1 per minute late fee they charge in the evening. Then, on the way to the day care center, they discussed what they had read. Maria found that in the morning she is a more pleasant person and that reading was a positive way for them to start the day. Danny was more eager to get dressed and be at the table, knowing story time was waiting for him. The reworked ritual succeeds for them.

Another innovation described by Lieberman (1984) is the First Day/ Last Day tradition invented by Jean Renko. Again, going back to our own childhood memories, for most of us the first day and the last day of school were events that we looked forward to with great anticipation. The Renkos made these days even more memorable for their children by adding some special family rituals. On the first day of school, the ritual involves an elaborate breakfast to fortify the children for nine long months of work. The breakfast might include fried country ham and potatoes or waffles with whipped cream and strawberries or eggs Benedict made to look like an owl on the plate. Special music is played on the CD and a festive atmosphere pervades the kitchen. Sometimes, though, they have surprised the children with breakfast in bed and bouquets of balloons. sometimes, they have breakfast on the finest china and once they even had a picnic in the backyard.

On the last day of school each child in the family receives a gift after dinner while they feast on German chocolate cake. The gifts are a reward for good performance during the year. The children that have collections can count on getting a very special addition on the Last Day.

Lieberman suggests that parents use whatever special talents they have to weave new rituals. Literary parents can write poems on special days of the year. Musical parents can compose silly songs to commemorate various accomplishments throughout the year. The events to embellish with family rituals are endless but obvious one include St. Patrick's Day, Halloween, the opening of the baseball season, Martin Luther Kings Jr.'s birthday, or the first day of spring.

In every culture, families develop rituals. They appear to be both universal and eternal. Rituals point to the human being's divergent needs for both historical continuity and creative input into the family legend.

WHITNEY (social worker, age 52)

The rituals in which my family engaged were primarily involved in the celebration of religious holidays. On Passover, Yom Kippur, and Rosh Hashana, we would gather at one of two houses, and there was very little variation in terms of the family members who attended. The Passover seder was always led by the same person, and each family member's

(continued)

(continued)

contributions remained the same, year after year. Hannukah was always celebrated at home, again with my father directing the service, and with fixed contributions made by each member of my immediate family. The foods my mother prepared for each of these occasions also remained the same, year after year. The meaning of these rituals was to emphasize the importance of family, tradition, and religious heritage. The effect on me was to make me aware of my heritage, but these rituals also imparted in me a view of religion as very solemn and rigid. We did not look upon these celebrations as occasions for amusement and sharing, and I find that I now have little desire to carry on these traditions (although I do still participate in them out of respect for my parents).

We also engaged in a somewhat less formal ritual, which involved the procedures to be followed when one of my siblings or I would become ill during the night. The procedure was as follows: First, we would quietly go downstairs to my parents' bedroom and stand next to my father's bed. We would then wait a few minutes without making any noise, hoping that he would wake up on his own (this was considered more polite, I suppose) and realize we were there. My father was a very light sleeper, and he usually would wake up as we entered the room. If he failed to wake, however, we would begin to whisper his name. He would then ask what was wrong, and we would discuss the problem. By about the middle of our discussion, my mother would invariably wake up, and we would explain the problem to her. My father would conduct a cursory examination of the problem and then decide on some appropriate course of action. In a very well-defined manner, my father would then administer the purely medical aspects of treatment (usually medication), and my mother would provide custodial care (changing our clothing, etc.) and sympathy. We would finally be put back to bed in the guest bedroom, which was across the hall from my parents' bedroom, with instructions to call, if necessary. I include this as a family ritual because I can't ever remember deviating from this pattern. And, through discussions with my siblings, I have learned that they followed this pattern, as well. I am unsure of the meaning of this ritual, except that it exemplified the significance of medical illness in my family.

The analysis of family rituals is interesting because the interaction patterns they exemplify appear to extend beyond the specific occasions for the rituals. In my family, for example, the roles taken by family members in celebration of religious holidays were consistent with the roles of these members in relation to the family in general. The recollection of rituals can be fun, and can serve as a nonthreatening way of examining common family relationships and interaction patterns.

SELF-EXPLORATION: FAMILY RITUALS

1. Make a list of all the rituals you experienced in your family of origin. Next to each ritual, rate on a scale of 0 to 100 how important that particular ritual was for you. A 0 would mean it was totally unimportant, a 50 would mean it was moderately important, and a 100 would

mean it was of the utmost importance. What made certain rituals very important to you?
2. Next, fill out the Family Solidarity Scale. Is there a relationship between the rituals in your family of origin and your feelings of cohesiveness?

Family Solidarity Scale

(Each "True" response is a sign of family solidarity.)

	True	False
1. I feel a part of this group	_____	_____
2. Members are close-knit, stick together through thick and thin	_____	_____
3. Spend lots of time together because we prefer each other's company	_____	_____
4. Private interests usually give way to common ones	_____	_____
5. When we have a job to do, everyone pitches in	_____	_____
6. We usually finish what we start	_____	_____
7. Troubles and discouragements just draw us closer	_____	_____
8. There are no serious disagreements about major purposes	_____	_____
9. We see eye-to-eye on moral matters	_____	_____

Source: Klapp, O. E. 1959. Ritual and family solidarity. *Social Forces,* 37(3):212-214.

Chapter 7

Secrets

A secret at home is like rocks under the tide.

Diana Craik, *Magnus and Morna*

Family secrets are universal. They are important because they are among the most powerful binding mechanisms within the family. Every person has knowledge of family events or traumas that must be shielded from outsiders and even at times from certain other family members. Maintaining these secrets is crucial to the family group. Betrayal of a family secret often leads to emotional cutoffs, violent and bitter arguments, and years of mistrust. Indeed the basic trust that is developed in infancy and cited as the bedrock of effective interpersonal relationships can be effectively jarred by hitting this Achilles' heel of family bonding.

Most family secrets protect the family's image in the community. It is probably still true that nearly everyone wants to be the "All-American Family"—no shoplifting, no adultery, no alcoholism, no physical abuse, nor parental disinterest. Of course, every family closet contains some sort of skeleton, and everyone knows the image is not the real story. Still, the illusion persists.

KINDS OF FAMILY SECRETS

The functional classification of family secrets has four primary categories: Secrets can be supportive, protective, manipulative, or avoidant. Any one secret could be serving more than one function, of course, and the purpose of the secret could change over the developmental life cycle of the family. Nevertheless, a functional code serves as a satisfactory starting point for discussion.

Each of these functional categories includes two basic subcategories. First, there are those family secrets that are shared by everyone in the nuclear family but are taboo topics for outsiders to hear about. For instance, the fact that mother dyes her hair may be known by everyone inside the family but intentionally kept a secret from the outside world. Second, there are subsystem secrets that a person shares with only part of the family. Most often these are taboo topics for outsiders as well. A good example of this is when a spouse gets fired from a job and the situation is kept secret from both the children and the community.

The number of secrets kept by varying types of families has not been systematically studied and is therefore unknown. It is unknown how often family secrets are revealed; also unknown is whether the consequences of revealing a secret vary with either its content or its function. We do know that the content of most secrets revolves around major life events; personal biological facts; or personal behavior, thoughts, and feelings. Grolnick's (1983) system of classifying secrets in this fashion is shown in Table 7.1.

TABLE 7.1. Classification of Secrets by Content

---

1. Events
    A. Birth-related: illegitimacy, abortion
    B. Sex-related: affair, incest, rape, homosexuality
    C. Money-related: concealed income, inheritance, family business dealings, blackmail
    D. Crime-related: past sentence, ongoing illegalities
    E. Job-related: job firings, demotions, conflicts
2. Personal Facts
    A. Biologic
        1. Physiologic (reversible): sexual dysfunction, infertility
        2. Organic (irreversible): chronic illness (diabetes, epilepsy)
        3. Genetic: inherited disorder
    B. Functional
        1. Behavior: phobic, sexual, ritualistic
        2. Thoughts and attitudes: pretense of an interest or belief whose absence is the secret; fantasies
        3. Emotions: real likes, dislikes

Source: Grolnick, L. 1983. Ibsen's truth, family secrets, and family therapy. *Family Process, 22*(3): 275-288.

Supportive Secrets

> *As scarce as truth is, the supply has always been in excess of the demand.*
>
> Henry Wheeler Shaw

Supportive secrets are those whose function is ensuring that the family presents a strong, admirable image to the subsystem, the extended family, or the community. Supportive secrets usually conceal the weaknesses, failures, or disappointments of a particular family member. Sometimes the other members of the family will join in reassuring the saddened individual that the secret will always stay "in the family" and no one else need ever know. Abortions are often found in this category. At other times the importance of keeping a secret will unconsciously and insidiously filter through the family. Getting fired from a job often becomes a secret through this slower evolutionary process. Supportive secrets occur within subsystems and within the entire family. When a sister refrains from telling the parents that her brother is smoking marijuana, the secret remains in the sibling subsystem. When the family decides that no one must ever know that the brother got arrested, the secret is shared within the entire group but may be kept from all outsiders.

Protective Secrets

Protective secrets are whose which are withheld from one family member or subsystem because the others judge it to be in the best interest of that person or subsystem to be unaware of the particular knowledge. By definition, protective secrets are never known by everyone in the family. The secret may be kept from outsiders as well. For example, for years many parents of adopted children kept the fact of the adoption secret. These parents felt that their children would grow up happier and more secure believing that their adopted parents were biological parents. The anger and guilt these grown-up children experienced when they found out that they were adopted, which many did accidentally, caused society to question the wisdom of that particular secret.

Another protective secret that is more socially condoned involves wealthy parents who keep the nature of the child's trust fund a secret throughout childhood and adolescence. The feeling that children would be "spoiled" by the knowledge that money will be available to them as adults seems reasonable to many people; this kind of secret is even applauded at times.

As seen in the issue of adoption, protective secrets can have a negative as well as a positive impact on the family system. Palazzoli-Selvini and associates (1988) describe how a protective secret contributed to an anorexic problem in a two-year-old child. In this case a woman and her husband kept secret from their two-year-old daughter the actual birth and continually worsening medical status of her seven-month-old brain-damaged sibling. Each day the mother would go visit the baby at the hospital, and each day the mother would tell the daughter she was going to see someone else's child. The secret was an awesome one, and the family tension could not be hidden. The little girl became anorexic and remained in that state until the family sought counseling. Three weeks after the family's counseling began, the baby died. Rather than perpetuate the secret, the therapists advised the father to explain to his daughter everything that had happened: the birth, the illness, and the reason these facts had not been told to her. Since the baby had already been buried, the parents were counseled to have a "phantom" burial in which the sister could help bury the baby's clothes and could place flowers at the site. After the secret had been revealed and the burial ritual performed, the girl began to eat and her symptoms never reappeared.

The negative effect of protective subsystem secrets on older children is vividly described in Bill and Vera Cleaver's book *Grover* (1970). Grover is a ten-year-old boy whose family keeps secret his mother's emergency surgery, poor postoperative recovery, and eventual suicide. Grover grieves all summer, and neither his father nor the clergyman can comfort him. Through his own personal struggle with the secret's revelation, Grover grows in his understanding of his father and himself.

Many protective secrets help families maintain important generational boundaries between subsystems. Parents generally have many secrets from their children: salaries, savings accounts, prior love affairs, and problems with in-laws are just a few examples. Keeping this information secret from the children helps set up an important boundary between the two generations. The caregiving generation does not look to the "caregetting" generation to carry the burden of its worries. Children also use secrets to maintain boundaries. The most common secrets between siblings involve sharing activities that have been explicitly proscribed or those the children fear the parents might disapprove of. Sharing such acts of disobedience allows the sibling subsystem to serve as a sanctioner of otherwise forbidden activities. It helps the children differentiate from their parents while still adhering to family norms that are represented in the sibling subsystem. It creates a new generation that is allowed to deviate from the ways and values of the older generation.

RALPH (graduate student, age 34)

It is difficult for me to come up with specific family secrets, as my family tended to be secretive about everything that happened in the family. It was seen as disloyal to talk about anything that went on even with closest friends. This put me in a conflict sometimes and made me feel very isolated because I was unable to talk about what was upsetting me. Now that I am married and separated from my family of origin, it is much easier to talk about them. However, I have adopted the same style in my present family.

This style was very difficult for me as a child because my mother and aunt did not speak to each other for much of the time. I, however, spent a lot of time with my aunt but felt bound by my loyalty to my mother not to say anything about what went on in our family. I often felt anxious, afraid that I would divulge something of importance that would hurt my mother in the mind of my aunt.

My family was very closed and secretive. Because I was never allowed to be open as a child, I find it excruciatingly difficult to be open as an adult. This causes me a lot of anguish since I still have strong needs to be open and honest with other people. For our family, keeping secrets was very tied up with loyalty, so this was one way to show loyalty. Whenever I want to be honest, I feel like I'm violating someone's trust. Thus, my loyalty has been bought at the expense of other relationships. It would have been better if there had been other ways to show loyalty, but I never learned any.

Some events are also known to everyone in the family but are treated by each subsystem as secrets to maintain generational boundaries. These "pseudosecrets" are almost always protective and help family members save face. Many fathers pretend they do not know when their daughters begin menstruating because they are embarrassed about it and feel their daughters would be embarrassed if the event were mentioned. Another common pseudosecret is when children pretend that they do not know what their parents argue about at night. Thus, pseudosecrets can also become a way of maintaining generational and sexual boundaries in the family.

Manipulative Secrets

The intent of manipulative secrets is to withhold knowledge from some subsystem or from extrafamilial others to gain a personal advantage. The young adolescent who keeps secret from her girlfriends her father's alcoholism may be protecting her father, but she also may be protecting herself from possible ridicule and rejection. Likewise, a sister may keep her brother's drug use a secret so that she can continue going out to parties with him and not because she has any particular desire to protect him from parental wrath.

Many secrets in the functional content category (see Table 7.1) are manipulative. A father may keep secret his hatred of punk rock music in order not to alienate his son and to keep open the door of parental influence. A husband or wife may keep secret what he or she feels about in-laws to keep good relations with the spouse. Such manipulative secrets arise because of an unwillingness to assert true attitudes or feelings. The manipulation may be beneficial or harmful to the family.

GINGER (college student, age 20)

I don't remember that there were very many family secrets in my family. We were typically so overinvolved with each other that everyone knew everything about each other. The biggest secret was probably my grandmother's well-guarded fifty-year secret that she was pregnant with my mother when she got married. More typical I think was the situation in which everybody "knew" the secret but pretended not to in the direct service of conflict avoidance. In this category would fall such things as my father's alcoholism and his "extramarital" entanglements. Also, I'm sure that the sexual activity of my sisters and me would fall here. I am certain that my mother knew a lot that she pretended not to know in order to avoid dealing with it. For example, all of us grew up *knowing* that if we were in the rec room with a date, my mother would not walk in on us. And she never did. When she went upstairs in the evening she would not come back down. Invariably she would call down at some point to ask us to bring her something (a drink, or whatever), but under no circumstances did she ever risk walking in on something she preferred to pretend wasn't happening.

Avoidant Secrets

Sometimes we have to change the truth in order to remember it.

George Santayana

Avoidant secrets are those whose intention is to help the subsystem or the family avoid dealing with difficult, annoying knowledge. For example, so long as a family can publicly blame a child's school absences on headaches and colds, no one has to confront the problem of school avoidance or school phobia. Although children do get involved in avoidant secrets, parents are most often initiators of secrets of this kind.

When the secret concerns how one individual is physically or psychologically abusing self or others, the family's avoidance of openly confronting the problem has the paradoxical effect of allowing the family member to continue in that destructive behavior. The person continues to rationalize episode after episode and to feel angrier and more humiliated by his or her lack of self-control. What was intended to help only hurts. Family members who are "protected" in this way often feel that if the rest of the family cannot bear to accept the truth, how can they bear to tell the family of their own self-inflicted suffering?

Thus, when adults get into serious trouble, when their problems are visibly destructive to themselves and others, a flood of shame and self-hatred overwhelms them. They are so horrified with their own behavior that they construct extensive rationalizations to enable themselves to keep their problem a secret. The rest of the family also panics, feels shame, and colludes with the troubled family member by minimizing the problem or denying it. In this way, families suffer in secret with the problems of alcoholism, child abuse, spouse abuse, incest, and attempted suicide. The problems do not go away, and the secret locks the family into a cycle of guilt and denial until a major catastrophe occurs in which some member forces an open confrontation of the problem. The extent of keeping secret ongoing problems is staggering.

Incest and Abuse

The incidence of incest is estimated at 200,000 cases a year, and at least 500,000 children are physically abused annually; 40 million American families are affected by alcohol abuse, almost 20 percent of the population. Four to 12 percent of all women are thought to have had a sexual encounter with an adult male as a child (Weissberg, 1983). Very few of these families are ever involved with child protection services or psychological treatment services. Most suffer in silence and are unable to tell the secret.

If and when a young girl does expose an incestuous parent, she risks ridicule, punishment, and rejection. By defying the father's orders to maintain secrecy, the child has in effect made him her enemy. All too often the mother is too shattered and threatened to protect the daughter and it is common for the parental couple to unite against the child and virtually drive her out of the family. In the boxed section "The Incest Secret," Weissberg (1983) describes the crisis precipitated in families when the incest secret is disclosed.

The Incest Secret

Judith Lewis Herman tells us, "All experienced workers agree that the disclosure of the incest secret initiates a profound crisis for the family." Usually, by the time the secret is revealed, the abuse has been going on for a number of years and has become an integral part of family life. Disclosure disrupts whatever fragile equilibrium has been maintained, jeopardizes the functioning of all family members, increases the likelihood of violent and desperate behavior, and places everyone, but particularly the daughter, at risk for retaliation.

The precipitant for disclosure is often a change in the terms of the incestuous relationship that makes it impossible for the daughter to endure it any longer. When the daughter reaches puberty, the father may attempt to initiate intercourse. This new intrusion, and the risk of pregnancy that it entails, may drive the daughter to attempt to end the relationship at any cost. Another common precipitant for the breaking of secrecy is the father's attempt to seclude his adolescent daughter and restrict her social life. As the father's jealous demands become more and more outrageous, she may at last decide to risk the retribution, which has been so often threatened, rather than submit. Finally, the daughter may decide to break secrecy in order to protect younger siblings even more helpless than herself.

Once the decision to break secrecy has been made, the daughter must find a person to confide in. Often the daughter is too alienated from her mother to trust her with this secret. In an effort to ensure a protective response, she frequently bypasses her mother and seeks help from someone outside the family. In a series of ninety-seven incest cases seen at the Harborview Sexual Assault Center in Seattle, for example, slightly over half (52.5 percent) of the children first reported the incest to a friend, relative, baby-sitter, neighbor, or social agency. The remainder (46.5 percent) first told their mothers.

For the mother, whether or not she suspected the incestuous relationship, disclosure of the secret is utterly shattering. First of all, she feels betrayed by her husband and her daughter. But in addition to her personal feelings of hurt and outrage, she must cope with the knowledge that her marriage and livelihood are in jeopardy. If her daughter's accusations are true, she faces the prospect of divorce, single parenthood, welfare, social ostracism, and even the possibility of criminal proceedings against her husband. These possibilities would be terrifying to any woman, even one in good health who was confident of her ability to manage alone in the world. How much more frightening, then, must such a future appear to a woman who is physically or mentally disabled, worn down by childbearing, intimidated by her husband, or cut off from social contacts and supports outside of her family. Small wonder then that many a mother, faced with the revelation of the incest secret, desperately tries to deny her daughter's accusations. If she believes the daughter, she has nothing to gain and everything to lose.

(continued)

(continued)

For the father, the disclosure is likewise a threat to his entire way of life. He stands to lose not only the sexual contact he craves, but also his wife, his family, his job, and even his liberty. Faced with this overwhelming threat, most commonly the father adopts a stance of outraged denial. He does whatever he can do to discredit his daughter and to rally his wife to his side. All too often, this strategy succeeds. Although the mother may believe the daughter initially, she soon succumbs to the barrage of entreaties, threats, and unaccustomed attentions from her husband.

Source: Weissberg, M.P. 1983. *Dangerous Secrets: Maladaptive Responses to Stress.* New York: W.W. Norton, pp. 131-133.

Many parents who physically abuse their children show a consistent pattern of being angry, disgusted, and sickened at their own behavior. As long as everyone in the family (husband or wife, grandparents) helps the parent keep the problem a secret, no one is willing to seek help. Once the outside authorities confront the family member or someone inside the family forces the member to label the behavior as troublesome, the person finds it easier to let down his or her defensive stance and talk freely of the problem.

Physical Disorders

Many physical disorders are easily made secret, especially if they lack outward manifestations. Most notable are problems such as epilepsy, diabetes, and cancer. What motivates a family to keep an illness such as epilepsy a secret? Any of the four major motivations may be involved, singly or in combination. If the illness is kept from the neighbors because the family fears the neighbors would reject the labeled family member, the secret is serving a supportive function. The family feeling is that the child or adult will get the most social support if no one is aware of the illness. If the diagnosis is kept secret from the affected family member, the secret is usually serving a protective function. Parents might fear that their child will become overwhelmed by the problem; they might want to wait until the child is older and has better developed coping mechanisms. If the condition is kept secret from the neighbors because the parents feel they personally might be rejected for having an epileptic child, the secret is serving a manipulative function. Last, the diagnosis may not be shared with the family member or neighbors because the family itself is trying to avoid accepting the diagnosis and its implications. By keeping the situation secret, everyone is spared the hardship of adjusting to it.

Parental Incarceration

Avoidant secrets can be very burdensome to children. They can cause children to socially isolate themselves from peers or adults. Some may harbor fears of accidentally telling the secret. Others may long to share the secret and keep their distance from others because they know they would not be able to withhold the secret in a warm, accepting relationship. Among children who do tell what they are not supposed to tell, secrets can generate enormous guilt and feelings of unworthiness. Often, feelings of impending punishment weigh heavily on the child. They believe God, or the parent, or the laws of the universe will punish them for their transgression. Baptiste (1995) described how a nine-year-old girl became electively mute for fear of telling anyone that her mother and "friend" were lesbians. Only after her parents released her from the imposed vow of secrecy was her mutism resolved.

An avoidant secret that is particularly burdensome for children is the secret of parental incarceration. Young children are often not told that the parent is in prison, for fear of frightening them or stigmatizing them. They are told that Daddy is working in another state or Mommy needed to go away to help a friend. When they are old enough to be aware of what is happening, most children are given some type of secrecy instructions, ranging from initiating a family "lie" as to the parent's whereabouts, to being told to confess ignorance about the parent's whereabouts, to being able to share the traumatic news with only selected family relatives and friends.

There are very few programs in the country for the children of incarcerated parents. Those that exist are mainly concerned with increasing the quality and quantity of contact between the two. For example, some programs are giving parent prisoners computers with e-mail access to their children's computers so that they can stay in touch on a daily basis. Other programs are initiating Girl Scout troops within the prisons so mother prisoners can serve as Girl Scout leaders and have a protective, happy regular meeting time with their children.

Although these are critically needed programs, as the trauma of parental separation is beyond dispute, it is equally important that the child feel comfortable with how he or she is to present the family to the outside world. Ideally, as taught in the CIP (Children of Incarcerated Parents) Program, children should have the choice to tell the truth ("thumbs up"), tell a lie ("thumbs down"), or keep it private ("hide your thumb") (Berg-

Cross and Duval, 1998). Rarely are children given the option of how they want to present this information to the world. Being able to control this aspect of the trauma is, unfortunately, one of the only issues that they potentially can control.

Children imagine that if they didn't need to keep this terrible secret, everything would be better. If only they could tell a teacher that "my mom has HIV and is in prison" or that "my dad is in jail" or that "my sister ran away and we don't know where she is," they would get all A's and be the most popular kids in the class. Adults are no less fanciful about the benefits that would come from being freed from the burden of the secret. Although the weight of the secret being lifted has a big immediate psychological benefit, it does not change the family relationships or the ongoing conflicts and problems.

ADAPTIVE VERSUS MALADAPTIVE SECRETS

The secrets of men are as different as their faces.

Adapted from the Talmud, Beratoth, 58A

When is a secret adaptive and when is it destructive? There is no simple answer to this question, particularly because the presence of a secret and its revelation will affect each member of the family differently.

It is clear that in many cases, secret keeping is necessary for healthy development. Secrets that are kept within the sibling subsystem or the adult subsystem help maintain generational boundaries and foster autonomy. For the siblings, secret keeping helps strengthen the bonds of loyalty and affection and may help prepare them for peer relationships. This privacy between siblings probably allows them to venture more easily into private relationships outside the family. Many of the secrets in the parent subsystem allow the child to avoid anxiety and feelings of helplessness.

Some secrets help the family feel close to one another and thus strengthen the entire family emotionally. Usually these binding, intimate secrets have three characteristics:

1. The secrets are known by every member in the family or they are shared within the appropriate subsystems. That is, siblings share secrets with siblings; parents share secrets with parents.
2. If subsystems are crossed and parent and child share the secret, it is a secret that shows the hidden strengths of family members instead of their weaknesses. For example, when a father and child have a secret

savings account to buy the wife a longed-for and expensive gift, the family bonds will undoubtedly be strengthened.
3. There is little pressure within the family or within the community to reveal the secret.

Conversely, secrets that are divisive and anxiety provoking have the three opposite characteristics:

1. They are secrets between parents and children that are part of longstanding, dysfunctional, triangular relationships. The secret usually binds the child to one parent against the other parent.
2. The secrets reveal weaknesses or deficiencies in character, or else they ridicule a family member.
3. There is a lot of pressure within the family or community to reveal the secret.

For instance, sisters might share the secret of their precocious sexual activities with absolute trust that their parents will never know. This type of secret puts the two sisters into an intimate and peer-related bond and usually helps strengthen the family as a whole. On the other hand, a daughter who shared with her mother the embarrassment and shame of the father's infidelity is the keeper of a divisive secret. This secret puts the child in a pseudoadult role and pits mother and daughter against the father. This type of secret rarely strengthens the family unit. Secrets become pathological when unspoken words are more powerful than spoken words in maintaining destructive family patterns.

Whenever there is a secret in the family, there is a triangle (Imber-Black, 1998). If mother and daughter keep secret the fact that the daughter is sexually active, the father is being actively excluded from that information. In this active exclusion, both mother and daughter must monitor their interactions with father. Most commonly, the person from whom the information is blocked becomes less and less able to authentically interact with the others and he or she becomes emotionally isolated. When exploring the meaning of secrets, it is always important to explore how the relationships between those who "know the secret" and those who "don't know the secret" have been constrained and altered by the secrecy.

When children are asked to keep secrets that have no emotional charge in their life, they are usually unaffected. Telling Laura that her grandmother doesn't want anyone to know she had a face lift may be an easy secret to keep and one that, if broken, would engender little guilt. Telling Laura that no one should ever know that her father was fired and is collecting unemployment may be a terribly pressing and worrisome event to Laura. It may be a problem that she feels an enormous need to talk about and to seek reassurance and solace from outside the family. In this case, all of the energy spent making sure that no one finds out the truth is taking away from the social resources that could allow her to cope with the crisis. Besides losing the advice and reassurance of friends and relatives, Laura's everyday routine may become focused on preventing the secret from slipping out. Friends may not be allowed in the house and she may have to make up additional lies about why she does not have the money to do various activities with her friends.

Most therapists would agree that it is time to "break" a secret when any of the following problems exist:

a. The child is always thinking about the secret
b. The emotional cost of the secret is depression, anxiety, or somatic problems
c. Development is arrested and the child is not meeting appropriate social and intellectual milestones (e.g., grades are dropping, they are unable to keep friends, etc.)
d. Conversations within the family have lost their spontaneity; instead, conversations are strained or focused on avoiding topics that might lead into dangerous territory
e. Intimate conversations with people outside the family are avoided for fear of divulging the hidden information
f. Individual well-being chronically takes a back seat to group fidelity

Although any one secret may be adaptive or maladaptive, the family system is stressed as the number of family secrets and subsystem secrets increases. The more topics that are taboo, the more difficult it is for the family to freely share its thoughts, ideas, opinions, feelings, experiences, and reactions. Fears about letting the secret slip out restrict the amount of honesty and candidness that can exist among the family members and their networks. Without openness between the family subsystems, trust is eroded and communication and problem solving are impaired. Without freedom to openly interact with people outside the nuclear family on truly important issues, the family becomes rigid and emotionally fused.

Although keeping family secrets is a source of stress, the discovery of family secrets can also be an especially stressful event, particularly for adolescents. On life stress scales for adolescents in psychotherapy, discovering a family secret received a mean score of 57 (out of 100), making it as stressful as being hospitalized for an illness or getting into trouble with the police (Tyerman and Humphrey, 1983). In this particular study, the one healthy adolescent in the control group who discovered a family secret gave it a distress rating of 70, indicating how vulnerable adolescents are to the trauma of unearthing painful family secrets.

Many of the great dramas about family life involve the positive and negative effects of family secrets to some degree. In Margaret Mitchell's *Gone with the Wind,* the most sustaining tension revolves around Scarlett's love for Ashley Wilkes, which is kept secret from his wife, Melanie. Even when Melanie is told of possible indiscretions she chooses to ignore them and maintain the secret, thus maintaining the tension and the love between the three characters. Both Eugene O'Neill's *The Iceman Cometh* and Ibsen's *The Wild Duck* involve characters who have a "moralistic fever" and feel compelled to help the family speak openly about its family secrets and face some truths. Unfortunately, in both cases this backfires and the families unravel and weaken.

Of course, there are some secrets that an individual has and hides from all the other members of the family. Sometimes, these secrets are common knowledge to people outside the family but are taboo topics for those inside the family. An adolescent who is sexually active may be willing to share all the exploits with the peer group but be unwilling to let anyone in the family know about them. Technically, these are not family secrets, but nonetheless, they can have an effect on family cohesiveness and family morale since they block communication on potentially important topics.

If secrets are kept over a number of years, a family myth often develops that provides a fictionalized tale of family life and helps hide the secret. Myths are easy-to-understand, larger-than-life tales that are discussed in greater detail in Chapter 8. The evolution of family myths is difficult to trace, but if we assume that every well-kept secret needs a tightly woven cover story, the myth as guard to a secret gains plausibility.

Imber-Black (1998) makes the astute observation that while, historically, cultural norms have made too many people feel shameful and secretive about too many things, today the emphasis has swung in the opposite direction. There is a sense, today, that telling secrets (or shameful events) is morally superior to keeping them private and that in the telling, one will be automatically redeemed and healed. The truth is that, for each of us, there are secrets worth keeping. While some secrets are very destructive to family life and to our own growth and well-being, others are relatively benign or the cost of telling them is too high.

How can a family member divulge a secret without hurting anyone? Imber-Black (1998) notes that the best time to share a life-altering secret is during a normal time in everyday life. Of course, usually a person comes to therapy in times of crisis or transition, and will share the secret with the therapist after a trusting therapeutic alliance has been formed. And while sharing with the therapist may provide a needed cathartic experience and room to explore the consequences of telling others, there is rarely need to rush into the "real world," purging oneself of the secret. However, after sharing the secret with the therapist and making the decision to tell the truth, the desire to immediately run off and get "the monkey off one's back" is quite strong. Clients want to rush out, sit down with the significant others, and just get it out, once and for all. Thus, while in the beginning the therapist has to encourage painful disclosures, there quickly comes a time when the sharing of those disclosures needs help in containment, until the opportune moment.

The therapist can be most helpful in assisting the client to decide when might be the best time to share the secret, and how the secret can be told in a way to minimize bewilderment, anger, and hurt feelings. Sometimes it may mean waiting a month; sometimes it may mean waiting more than a year. For example, I recently had a client who had given his brother a "loan" of $10,000 without consulting his wife for fear that she would refuse. The wife was getting ready to buy a new car. He knew he had to tell her. However, this was the week of her fiftieth birthday and her relatives were staying at the house for another six days. He had kept the secret for over a year; another week would do no harm. Better to wait and be alone to discuss the issue than to blurt it out in the five minutes they had alone and then not be able to process it for another week.

A more extreme example comes from a man who had decided in late August to leave his family and move in with his lover. His daughter was a junior in high school and needed to take the SAT and get her all-important junior year grades as high as possible. The parents decided to live together for another eight months and pretend that they were trying to resolve some problems. The daughter ended up doing very well in school and on her exams. When her parents told her about the separation, she was devastated but had the whole summer to recoup.

COCO (bookkeeper, age 50)

We had so many family secrets as I was growing up that I could probably write an entire paper in just this one area. However, I will attempt to limit my discussion to one high point. Most of our family secrets seemed to occur as a result of my parents' strong belief in the age-old adage that "what you don't know won't hurt you." Perhaps the most influential secret that was excluded from my knowledge occurred when I was hospitalized for two days at the age of eight. I was having stomach problems at the time, and it was decided that I should have a proctoscopy done while under general anesthesia. My parents recognized that this

(continued)

(continued)

would probably be a fairly traumatic event for me, since I had never even so much as been in a doctor's office before that, and they decided that it would be "best" to withhold this information from me until the night before I was to be hospitalized. Even at this time, however, I was told only that "a test" was to be performed while I was asleep. Given their reticence on the subject, I somehow felt that it would be wrong to ask for any additional information. I found out what I had undergone eight years later, from my sister, who had known all along. This experience had a rather dramatic effect on me, and to the present day, I often find myself wondering whether my doctors are being completely honest in their discussions with me.

SELF-EXPLORATION: FAMILY SECRETS

Recognition of family secrets and the role they play in your family can help you in a number of ways. By recognizing the destructive secrets, you may allow yourself to approach tarnished family members with a more open and less heavy heart. Reflecting on the productive secrets will strengthen the bonds you have with those family members and may suggest ways for sharing with the rest of your family.

1. Write down all the family secrets you are privy to. (Use the list in Table 7.1 to help you retrieve them.)
2. Which ones have been productive and which ones have been destructive?
3. Do the productive ones conform to the criteria listed above?
4. Do the destructive secrets conform to the criteria listed above? If not, what other elements of the secret do you think made it destructive?

Chapter 8

Multigenerational Effects

What a father says to his children is not heard by the world, but it will be heard by posterity.

Jean Paul Richter

Many family therapists use the concept of multigenerational transmission. Each uses a slightly different term: Lieberman (1979) calls it transgenerational analysis; for Bowen (1978), the terms are multigenerational transmission process and family projection process; Boszormenyi-Nagy and Spark (1973) uses the terms legacy and family myths. Each theorist has developed the concept with different emphasis, but all are trying to stress how important grandparents, great-grandparents, and great-great-grandparents are in influencing the values and conflicts present in the current nuclear family. All these theorists believe that the behavior and attitudes of children are shaped by their entire genealogy; to them, the influence of the multigenerational family is awesome. But is it? Is the influence of one generation on another of any lasting significance after childhood? Once out of the nuclear family, are we free to shape our own destiny? Or have the molds of destiny been preselected by our forebears?

PATTERNS OF MULTIGENERATIONAL TRANSMISSION

If multigenerational transmission is a very broad and very deep process, then children, parents, and grandparents will espouse very similar values and attitudes at equivalent times in their lives. Everyday observations on the diversity between any two known generations of kin suggest, instead, that intergenerational transmission is highly selective, greatly modified by the historical events and societal changes each generation must deal with.

Multigenerational Transmission of Family Violence

One behavioral pattern that has been documented in a plethora of studies involves the intergenerational transmission of physical aggression.

171

When children are exposed to aggression between specific family members (parent and child, husband and wife) they learn the "appropriateness" of such behavior between the inhabitants of those family roles. Thus, parents hitting children teaches the acceptability of parent/child aggression, and spouse abuse teaches the acceptability of husband/wife aggression. The modeling of aggressive family role relationships has been documented most recently by Kalmuss (1984:15) in a survey of over 2,000 adults:

> When neither form of aggression occurred (parent-child or husband-wife) in one's childhood family, the probability of the husband being physically aggressive is 1 percent. . . . When only parent-child hitting occurred, the probability is increased to 3 percent. With only husband-wife hitting, the probability doubles to 6 percent. Finally, when both types of childhood aggression occurred, the probability of severe husband aggression is 12 percent. The results are similar [for wives being physically aggressive toward their husbands]. . . . In the absence of childhood family aggression, the probability of severe wife-husband aggression is 2 percent. With parent-child hitting it is 4 percent and with spousal hitting it is 8 percent. When both types of family aggression occurred, the probability of wife-husband aggression is 17 percent. The results indicate that severe marital aggression is more likely when respondents observed hitting between their parents than when they were hit as teens by their parents. However, there also is a dramatic increase in the probability of marital aggression when respondents were exposed to both types of family aggression. (Copyright 1984 by the National Council on Family Relations, 3989 Central Avenue NE, Suite 550, Minneapolis, MN 55421. Reprinted by permission.)

Note that although there is clear-cut, unambiguous evidence for the intergenerational transmission of family aggression, the extent of that transmission is quite limited, in an absolute sense. Even when a teenager grows up being hit and sees severe physical aggression occurring between the parents, there is over an 80 percent chance that the child will not engage in any physical marital aggression. Perhaps this undesirable trait is transmitted only to those grown children who are emotionally frustrated, low in coping skills, or in a relationship that allows physical aggression. Other factors may turn out to be even more predictive of who will copy the aggressive behaviors of their parents. Other studies have confirmed that, male or female, a spouse is four to six times more likely to hit a mate if he or she grew up seeing those behaviors in the family of origin.

Multigenerational Transmission of Values

Thousands of studies have tried to determine precisely what values can be successfully transmitted across family generations. Most of the studies have such severe methodological weaknesses that it is doubtful if the reported findings are reliable or can be generalized to populations outside those studied. Ideally, researchers need to study the same family members over a long period (longitudinally) and at several different time periods in their lives (cross-sectionally). Currently, when cross-sectional data show children and their parents with very similar or dissimilar attitudes toward a particular topic, it is not known if the obtained relationship is a stable one. Perhaps very different influence patterns would emerge if we could study these same dyads again twenty years later or if we had studied them years previously. In other words, many intergenerational influences may vary dramatically over the course of development.

Troll and Bengtson (1979) reviewed over 160 of the better-designed studies that tried to assess the transmission of values across generations. Most looked at the intergenerational influence between college-age youth and their parents. A selected synopsis of their findings is presented in Table 8.1. Overall, political party affiliations, religious affiliations, achievement levels, and consumership styles were the most strongly transmitted characteristics. Sex roles, sexual behaviors, specific attitudes (political and otherwise), and lifestyle characteristics were very rarely transmitted in any predictable fashion.

As one examines the consistently transmitted values, a picture of intergenerational influence does emerge. The broader issues that define an individual and give him or her a sense of identity and purpose do seem to be transmitted from one generation to the next. It is multigenerational transmission that gives us the scripts from which we can improvise specific lines. The metastructure of a family is a given; the specifics, the fine detail, are a matter of individual choice. For example, calling oneself a Democrat or a Republican is a lifelong defining characteristic for many. Believing in the power of NATO to reduce the arms race is a more specific, variable, and transient attitude. Consider someone calling himself a Catholic or a Hindu. Such a label directs a number of life choices. Believing in birth control or the injustice of the caste system is certainly important but not as forceful as the metalabel. Similarly, levels of achievement motivation are reliably passed on from generation to generation, but the specific avenue toward which the motivation is directed is highly variable. There is a saying that in the midst of strangers and acquaintances, it is best not to talk about religion, money, or politics. The pervasiveness with which family loyalties affect these topics makes it wise advice indeed.

TABLE 8.1. The Transmission of Values Across Generations

	Range of relationships found	Range of correlations found
Political party affiliation; general political orientation (liberal, conservative, equalitarian)	High Very low to high	.55-.65 .16-.63
Specific political attitudes and opinions	Very low to high	.05-.34
Specific attitudes and lifestyle characteristics	Very low to medium	.14-.40
Religious affiliation	Medium to very high	.46-.74
Religious attitudes and behaviors	Very low to very high	.05-.67
Educational plans	Medium	.48-.50
Achievement level	Very high	.66 and up
Consumership style	Low to high	.20-.60

Source: Adapted from Troll, L. and Bengtson, V. 1979. Generations in the family. In: Burr, W. R., Hill, R., Nye, F. I., and Reiss, I.L. (Eds.), *Contemporary Theories About the Family: 1. Research-Based Theories*. New York: The Free Press, pp. 127-161.

Within the family, bitter struggles and arguments can occur when a member is unwilling or unable to carry forward some desired expression of the family values. Probably the most common example of this value category is when parents are disappointed or upset over the academic or career achievements of their children. Children and adults often judge their school or vocational success according to the family standards for achievement. When someone underachieves or overachieves at a great personal cost, the resulting stress can be very disruptive.

College students are particularly vulnerable to reacting poorly to the achievement demands of the family. An empirical study by Held and Winey (1984) found that college men became more psychologically distressed as their parents increased overt pressure on them for achievement. Parents who became upset by poor grades, disapproved of studying certain subjects, and could not bear the possibility of the son's not completing his college career were more likely to have sons who were nervous and anxious.

In addition, both women and men became psychologically distressed if the pressure to succeed was indirect, arising from a family system in which the unfulfilled aspirations from prior generations were projected onto the college student. Thus, poor college adjustment was also related to how unsuccessful the parents were in the eyes of the grandparents and how unsuccessful the mother had been in achieving her goals. That is, the more college students felt that the grandparents were critical of the parents' achievement and/or the more the mother was critical of her own achievements, the more likely the students were to show social and academic adjustment problems.

Held and Winey speculate that career success is more salient for men, who are distressed by perceived direct pressures to succeed. Yet, both men and women are sensitive to the family's social-emotional relationships and are distressed by the nuances of more subtle and indirect needs, as well as structures, within the family.

ANNA (nursing-home resident, age 80)

I've always believed that parents are the most important influence in a child's life. Everything that matters is passed down from parent to child. My father and mother came from Germany; one from the north and one from the south. My father was a specialty baker and we served the top 400 of Baltimore. With eight children everything had to be run orderly and it was. Of course, we had black and white help but we still all had our chores to do. My chore was to set the table each night. Each dinner plate had to be centered in front of its chair and the rim of the plate had to lie four inches from the table's edge. The napkin was under the forks and the folded napkins always had to be facing away from the plate. The rest of the silver and the cups had their places as well. We each had our place to hang up our coats and hats on the hallway hooks. The oldest had her hook nearest the door and the baby had its way at the end of the hall near the door into the bakery shop. As far as toys and things like that, we were taught to share and cooperate. We had only two bikes—one for the girls and one for the boys. If we disobeyed, we got a spanking from my father. He was a very gentle and loving man and sometimes he'd urge my mother not to tell him what we had done wrong because he couldn't bear to punish us that night. When we were born, he opened up a little account book for each of us and as we got older we saved all our money

(continued)

(continued)

during the year in our account book so we would have Christmas money. Throughout our childhood, our parents always taught us to be good Christians and never allowed any of us to hold malice. As teenagers, my parents were very strict. On the week nights we were never to see anyone and we were always chaperoned if we went out on a date by my mother or my father. We all worked at the bakery or one of the three retail stores until we married or got a full-time job. We were never allowed to put on the radio until after our schoolwork was done, even in high school, mind you. Even our clothes were handled efficiently. Every September the seamstress would come to our house and line us up. Each of us would have our hand-me-downs fitted and hemmed so we would look perfect at school and at church.

I tried to raise my son just like I'd been raised. The foundation was living a good Christian life. My son was brought up neat and clean with a sense of right and wrong. He had his chores to do growing up and he learned to do them so they were perfect. At twelve years old, he could mow and hedge the lawn so that it was the best looking in the neighborhood. At times, it was difficult for us to punish him but if he did something wrong, we knew it was our duty to correct him. Once he came home a half hour late from a party. He knew that if he came home late he couldn't go out for a week. Well, the week he came home late was the week of the Winter Ball at the high school. He had to miss it and I think it hurt his dad and I as much as him to see him miss it. When my son was in the Navy he was given many commendations because he was organized and efficient.

I'm happy to see that he and his wife are raising our grandchildren in the same way, also. My granddaughter comes by to see me every Wednesday and my grandson takes me to church on Sunday. My mother would have been proud of them and the strong continuity of her values and traditions. We're a line, a family, and my heirs are a hope for the human race.

We now turn to a discussion of multigenerational processes by three family therapists (Boszormenyi-Nagy and Spark, 1973; Bowen, 1978; and Lieberman, 1979). Afterward, we will examine how people can and do pay homage to multigenerational influences through family myths, treasured objects, and grandparent relationships.

Multigenerational Processes

> *Nothing has a stronger influence psychologically on their environment, and especially on their children, than the unlived life of the parents.*
>
> Carl G. Jung

When Murray Bowen (1971) uses the term "multigenerational trans-mission process" he is referring to a very specific pathogenic phenome-non: how anxiety is passed down through multiple generations of a family. An overly fused family projects problems onto children who grow up less confident than their parents; these children, in turn, project more problems onto their children, who grow up even less confident and go on to continue the cycle begun generations back.

The projection process begins when anxiety arises within a person or a relationship and the family members are so emotionally fused that the anxiety becomes a family phenomenon. Each individual has difficulty keep-ing his or her emotional and intellectual functions independent. This creates an environment where one member's failure is felt as a family failure, and the feeling of failure is translated into thinking and believing one is a failure. According to Bowen, the low self-esteem and frustrations created by this type of anxiety erupt in one of three forms: (1) marital conflict, (2) mental or physical dysfunction in one of the spouses, or (3) mental or physical dysfunction in one of the children.

Typically, families will use all three release valves in their own unique combinations. The spouses will have varying degrees of marital dissatis-faction, and the children or adults may have emotional difficulties as well as psychologically exacerbated physical problems. Bowen believes that when the anxiety is deflected onto the children, one child is picked to be the primary object of the transmission process. This child invariably be-comes less healthy and less differentiated than the other siblings. His or her physical or behavioral problems become the focus of the parent's concern. Bowen believes that over many generations, a long lineage of undifferentiated parents can produce a severely impaired family member.

Although most of us fortunately do not have a highly disturbed sibling, it seems to be universal for one sibling to be strikingly less adjusted or less socially competent than the others. This child always seems to be emotion-ally more involved with the parents. The chicken-and-egg problem is whether Bowen is correct and the parents created or exacerbated the prob-lem or whether the child's problems were so severe to start with that the parents were forced to orient toward them.

Conflicting Transgenerational Expectations

Lieberman (1979:50) describes how children can be put in the predica-ment of being torn by two different transgenerational expectations. He gives as an example:

. . . the daughter of a man whose father was a professional accountant and a woman whose mother was a tennis professional, is herself both clumsy and intellectually dull by nature. The child is encouraged by her father to be studious by giving her a desk, many books, spending time with her doing mathematics problems and entering her in a private school. The mother has taken her daughter to Wimbledon for the Lawn Tennis Tournament every year since birth and has played tennis with her from the age of three. Mother sabotages her studies through tennis lessons and subtle derision of intellectual pursuits. The father fights back by emphasizing his daughter's obvious clumsiness and lack of native ability in physical sports. His wife fights back by pointing to the daughter's poor academic record. Both husband and wife are forced to agree that their daughter is a failure at being what she should be. The daughter blames herself for her failure to fulfill either of her parents' expectations. The parents become angry that their daughter could not become what they expect her to be [what their own parents were].

As illustrated in Lieberman's example, the unconscious projection of expectations and needs from one family member onto another can be maintained for many years. Most often the projection process begins with parents projecting unresolved conflicts onto the children, but people project onto spouses with equal vigor. Spouse or child, the need to project unresolved conflict is heightened when the person who was in conflict with us dies or moves far away. Unable to cope with the unresolved anger, people look for a replacement, someone who will act and react in a manner similar to the person lost. Again, Lieberman (1979:62) provides two vignettes that are tragic illustrations of what can happen when replacement occurs.

Sarah was referred for depression and was seen with her parents. She had been born ten months after the death of her paternal grandmother. Her father, an only child, had been very close to his mother. Their only separation had been enforced by the Korean conflict. After he returned from the armed forces he continued to live in the family home even after his marriage. In desperation, his wife planned her first pregnancy with the sole purpose of forcing her husband to move from the home of her in-laws. Her husband never forgave her for this maneuver.

Shortly after the birth of their eldest daughter, the husband's mother became ill and died of that same illness two years later. Their daughter Sarah was born the year following her paternal grandmother's death. When she was born he felt she looked exactly like his mother. She grew up with him treating her as if she were his mother; he fostered the same over-close relationship with her. Sarah's mother was jealous of the over-close relationship that had developed between her daughter and husband.

During adolescence the family tension mounted as Sarah began to develop as a woman. When her body began to develop it became clear that she would take after her mother's earthy form rather than her paternal grandmother's slim figure. The growing tension at home was obvious to Sarah, but there seemed no apparent reasons for it. Her father began to withdraw from her as her development as a woman strained his ability to treat her as a replacement for his mother. Sarah became depressed.

Another example of a replacement cited by Lieberman is that of Mr. Barclay and his wife. Mr. Barclay was referred for marital therapy following the onset of acute anxiety and continuous nagging questioning of his wife. She believed that the difficulties began when she started training as a social worker. The marital quandary was the spiraling lack of trust between them. She had been a housewife whose warmth at home was matched by a fear of new relationships outside the home. He had been a dependable but unemotional man who had seemed a pillar of strength to her. When she started her course, at his insistence and with his encouragement, she became much less dependent on him for her practical needs while his emotional needs remained. Further investigation revealed that he had been strongly attached to his father's mother, who was described as a warm, caring, giving, but lonely woman whose husband died prematurely. She had a peculiar name of American Indian origin; she had lived in Mr. Barclay's family home until her death when he was eighteen. Two weeks later he met his wife. The qualities that most attracted him to her were her loneliness and her warm, giving qualities. She had an unusual name and her father was Canadian.

Lieberman's examples of multigenerational, indirect influences are depressing; they make the process seem invariably pathological. Nothing could be farther from the truth. Indirect influences are as likely to be positive as negative. Suppose the girl whose father encouraged studiousness in the first example had been intellectually gifted. The time he spent with her working on mathematics and the sacrifice involved in sending her to a private school would have been invaluable in motivating her to achieve.

THE FAMILY LEGACY

Multigenerational transmission is concerned with how anxiety gets expressed through the generations, and transgenerational analysis is concerned with how attitudes and preferences get expressed through the generations. The concept of *family legacies,* which refers to the transmission of life goals and core values, was developed by Boszormenyi-Nagy and Ulrich (1981:163). They state that it consists of

> certain basic contextual expectations (values?) that convey an intrinsic imperative stemming not from the merit of the parents, but from the universal implication of being born of parents. The roots of the individual's very existence become a source of systematic legacies that affect his or her personal entitlements and indebtedness. The origins are multigenerational; there is a chain of destiny anchored in every generative relationship.

According to these authors, the motivation to carry out the legacy is always ethical in nature. One is bound to live out the expected course because not to do so would deny the family its very existence; it is unthinkable. The legacy affirms the family; failure to do so is emotionally genocidal.

GWEN (graduate student, age 22)

Our family is constantly involved with balancing the ledgers. The most merit is given for having a respectable family, having a well-paying career, and being in the field of medicine. While my father fulfilled all three legacies and was thus merited in all three areas, my mother was demerited in the area of career obligations. She was a nurse but only worked for one year before "retiring" to have babies. My eldest sister received merit for obtaining a medical degree specializing in neonatology but was then demerited for quitting her job to raise a family. She is, however, simultaneously merited for marrying a doctor and having children. My brother is merited for his MD but demerited for not yet having married. I have been merited for getting married while simultaneously pursuing a career, but also been severely demerited for choosing a profession outside of medicine.

These legacies and the position of each of my family members in relation to them have always been, and still remain, central issues in our family system. In fact, I feel strongly that, in order to understand our family, one must be aware of these multigenerational obligations. I believe that much of our dysfunctional behavior over the years can be understood in terms of our ambivalence over fulfilling these legacies. Therefore, I must agree with those family therapists who think that defining these legacies and ledgers of merit are important in any attempt toward reconciliation within a family.

· Family legacies may be obvious—such as having a legacy of fighting for one's country or a legacy of being a pacifist. The legacy may also be subtle, such as a legacy that demands that one always save money privately and feign poverty publicly. Boszormenyi-Nagy and Spark (1973) show how even a simple legacy such as loving one's mother and father equally can have awesome psychological consequences.

Consider what happens to a child when her father deserts the family and the mother repeatedly states how horrible this is. Chained emotionally to the fairness legacy, the child will eventually resort to resenting the mother to the same extent that she resents the father. This response is fair and equal. But suppose that this child, grown to womanhood, becomes a parent herself. She may feel compelled to be harsh to her children to avoid being disloyal to her parents. It is as though she feels that being a better parent than her own parents would suggest that they could have been better parents. Such a recognition is a repudiation of the legacy and hence impossible to accept.

It is likely that many more legacies are adaptive for families than are destructive. Consider the legacies of the Chicanos and the traditions of the Hopi Indians. The philosophical system of the Hopi explains how one relates to time and space and the universe. The Chicano legacy of family includes an obligation of mutual aid to anyone in the extended kin network and has been critical in the success of the Chicano communities in the United States. Moore (1979:71) quotes Jaime Sena-Rivera, a Chicano psychologist:

> It seemed that my father's brothers, and my father in turn, would go first to one another for loans of varying sizes (not always repaid) at various times instead of banks or savings and loan associations. ("Why go to strangers?" my father said. "And besides, the Americans charge too much interest and they treat you like dirt when you don't know English so well. If you can't pay your brother back, there's no hard feelings. There are ways to make it up, always.") Also, even brothers (and uncles and cousins) would see each other, especially if the other was older, as legitimate resources for funding, work. "What is more decent," my father said, "than helping your brother or your friend to be independent, be a man, be a good husband or father or son? Besides, they put Mexicans off at the Unemployment."

Such systems take generations to develop. So long as the group remains insulated, the young continue to carry on these traditions and to pass them on to the next generation.

SANDRA (graduate student, age 32)

The major legacy which I can find in my rather scattered family is that of the importance of pursuing an intellectual or artistic career. Education was seen as very important. As far as I can tell, this legacy was consistent on both my mother's and father's sides of the family. It has been met with varying degrees of success in the three generations I am familiar with—mine, my parents, and my grandparents. My maternal grandparents started out well—grandmother a musician, grandfather an independent-businessman—but both eventually failed. My grandmother gave up her career when she married and my grandfather proceeded through a series of business failures, each one a step lower than the last. Of their two children, my aunt started out as a promising actress but gave up this career sometime in her twenties or thirties and spent the remainder of her life living with a wealthy woman who supported her. My mother got off to a bad start but got a BA degree in her forties and became a schoolteacher. My half-brother was a high-school dropout, and as far as I know has never succeeded in holding a job for any length of time. He had ambitions to be a musician and some promising talent but has so far (age twenty-nine) done nothing with this. He is extremely defensive about his lack of education.

I have less knowledge about my father's side of the family—I know little about my grandparents except that education was very important to my grandfather. My father and aunt were their only children. My father has a PhD and is a very successful chemical engineer. His sister's two daughters both have PhDs. His four children (my half sibs), so far have not shown themselves to be very academically oriented.

I was pressured a lot by my mother and aunt when I was growing up to develop an intellectual career. However, the role models I had—mother, aunt, and grandmother—were high aspirers but underachievers. This contradiction between aspirations and role models has made development of a career very difficult for both myself and my half-brother.

FAMILY MYTHS

A family tree is a tree in which the branches are so uninteresting that one is forced to brag about the roots.

Anonymous

While legacies have a direct mandate that influences and motivates the life choices of an individual, myths seem to provide more of a cohesive function, cementing one generation to another and giving the legacies a context (Byng-Hall, 1982).

Myths have been in existence as long as the spoken word. As soon as people could communicate, they tried to explain events in nature that they could not fully understand. Today much of the physical world is understood by means of scientific myths. Our social life, particularly within the family, still remains a mystery to us, calling for stories of explanation. For example, we try to understand and make up a family line on why the family decided to move to a distant state or why a favored uncle ended up as part of a fraud ring and was sent to jail. Indeed, as can be seen in Table 8.2, the events that motivated the Greeks to believe in myths, at an analogous level, still motivate family members to repeat and create myths. The typology of common family myths allows one to categorize the depth and breadth of family myths extant in any one family. If a family can run off five or six Zeus myths and can think of no others, it would be a wise guess that "power and authority" are important multigenerational issues.

The most popular myths are Prometheus myths that recount the creation of the nuclear and extended family. Many adult children know little about their parents' lives except these myths: how Mom and Dad met, the circumstances surrounding their marriage, and the birth of each child. Children enjoy hearing these stories because they provide an understandable foundation of their heritage. Their sense of identity gains roots and nourishment from these tales. When the Prometheus myths contain negative information such as a forced marriage or unwanted pregnancies, a sense of doom can hang over a person as if the tale has made a chasm in the foundation and nothing durable and admirable could be built upon it. Some people who fear this negative effect create imaginary positive myths to erase the past and build a stronger future.

Much more frivolous are the Vulcan myths that stereotype a family member's physical characteristics or personality traits. Stories about the agile acrobat grandfather who tried out for the circus, the heavy aunt who only had one dress because that was all they could find to fit her, or the uncle who graduated from MIT when he was fifteen years old make a family history unique and colorful. They provide a sense of the "in" group and the comfort of knowing "the scoop" on another person.

APPRECIATING ONE'S MULTIGENERATIONAL HERITAGE

Each of us recognizes the importance of our forebears. The ways of acknowledging it vary greatly. The importance of lineage can be found in the projected affection people have toward certain material objects that they cherish. In a society that values the new, the shiny, and the modern it is ironic that the most cherished objects for adults are often the oldest, the

TABLE 8.2. A Typology of Family Myths

Mythic Name	Nature of Related Myth	Modern Mythological term	Examples from Modern Families
Prometheus	Created man by molding a clay figure in the image of the gods and breathing life into it.	Prometheus myth (creation myths)	All stories related to the creation of the family. Stories about how spouses met, fell in love, and got married. Also includes stories about birth of children.
Zeus	King of the gods	Zeus myths (power myths)	All stories related to how authority and power have been used in the family to shape its destiny.
Pandora	The gods were angry that man had learned to use fire so Pandora was sent to earth with a box of evils. Before Pandora all men were innocent.	Pandora myths (myths of wrongdoing)	All stories related to people who were instrumental in bringing shame or misfortune into the family.
Hermes	Hermes had special charge of thieves and helped them out of their troubles.	Hermes myths (myths of luck)	All stories related to people who got away with unscrupulous or forbidden acts.
Demeter	Her story explains the seasons. She cursed the world with winter when her daughter was abducted.	Demeter myths (life-cycle myths)	Any story that tries to explain "events" that happened to a family. Stories about wars, handicapped members, old

TABLE 8.2 *(continued)*

Mythic Name	Nature of Related Myth	Modern Mythological term	Examples from Modern Families
			cars and houses, etc., are applicable here.
Atalanta	A story meant to entertain about a swift-footed girl who is outrun and wedded to the prince.	Atalanta myths (humorous myths)	Any story that is so funny or unique that it is impossible not to repeat in a local ritualistic manner.
Vulcan	He was born lame and weak and his mother Hera so disliked him she threw him down from Olympus. He returned to become a smith and the Cyclops are his workmen.	Vulcan myths (idiosyncratic myths of uniqueness)	Any stories that capture the unique physical or personality traits of family members.

simplest, and the least expensive (Csikszentmihalyi and Rochberg-Halton, 1981). When asked, "What are the things in your home most special to you?" most middle-aged adults mention some item of furniture. Invariably, the piece of furniture is prized because it belongs in the family and evokes memories of relationships with parents, spouses, and children. Among grandparents, furniture is the second most frequently named object; the most frequently selected objects are photographs. Elderly people feel these objects are irreplaceable. For them, the photo carries a freight of vivid emotions and memories.

Another set of interesting objects that are valued by one generation after the next are fragile items such as china or glass. To preserve such delicate objects, one has to care for them, guard them through moves, and protect them through the crises of day-to-day living. It has been said that "one china cup preserved over a generation is a victory of human purpose over chaos" (Csikszentmihalyi and Rochberg-Halton, 1981). As elderly people see friendships dissolve and communities transformed, it is understandable that they would greatly appreciate the deeper life meanings inherent in an unbroken dish. In nursing homes, the most dear possessions of the residents are often old, well-preserved, touch-worn photos or knickknacks.

One of the best ways to learn the multigenerational influences in a family is through the storytelling of the grandparents. Increasing alienation of grandparents from the daily lives of grandchildren often makes the oral histories and myths difficult to transmit to the next generation. Today many grandparents feel awkward telling grandchildren about what they view as a very ordinary, sad, or strife-ridden life. Sometimes, they feel as though they would bore or alienate the grandchildren with their own childhood stories. Fitzhugh Dodson (1981), author of the "how to" series of family life *(How to Father; How to Parent; How to Grandparent)* gives grandparents a topical outline of what should be covered in a family history. Various topics include discussing each member of the nuclear family of the grandparent, the places they have lived, their school and work experiences, games and sports they enjoyed, and exciting events they have witnessed. He also suggests including personality vignettes, talking about the funniest thing that ever happened, the saddest thing that ever happened, the most frightening thing that ever happened, and so on.

As the chance to leisurely soak up these stories of old is oftentimes nonexistent, some older family members are joining the electronic age and creating oral histories on audiotape or videotape recorders. Although written and electronic histories are invaluable as each generation tries to understand its roots, children also need personal interaction and a relationship with the grandparent generation. Only by knowing the family effectively with their nuances and aging presence can children get a sense of heritage that can be easily or meaningfully understood.

The book *How to Grandparent* gives a myriad of ideas on how long-distance grandparents can develop a valuable relationship with grandchildren who are seen infrequently. Heading the list are correspondence through postcards, letters, audio cassettes, phone calls, and little gifts. Visits by grandchildren without an accompanying parent can be extremely rewarding for both generations.

In summary, multigenerational analyses are important because the quality of the relationship between an individual and the members of his or her family of origin can influence an individual's subsequent marriage and the functioning of the children produced by that marriage. By understanding the primary family relationships, it becomes much easier to work on changing them and to avoid re-creating maladaptive relationships in the current nuclear family.

BARBARA (physician, age 45)

We had two very strong myths in our family; a Demeter myth that's shaped the family legacy for four generations and a Vulcan myth that has been retold and enjoyed over a dozen times a year for as long as I can remember.

The Demeter myth is about my grandfather, who was born in 1864, the year of the Emancipation Proclamation. The story goes that Grandpa was the brightest and most ambitious of the four children in the family. He graduated high school real early and went on to graduate college. He started a pharmacy ("apothecary" in the story) in the farming community he was brought up in and soon had opened a clothing store and hardware store, as well. Then at the age of thirty-five he got a terrible illness that the doctors said was terminal. There are many different versions of the type of illness he had (depending on who in the family is telling the story), but they all involve Grandpa losing weight, being very weak and in great pain. Grandpa began to pray for his life, day and night. When he was too weak to read the Bible, he had someone reading it to him. He promised that if he were allowed to live he would renounce all his worldly goods, and devote himself to spreading the Word. Grandpa was saved and did renounce his hard-won prosperity. He became a minister and took a vow of poverty. He started a church, but in five years the church had grown to over 100 families and was getting firmly established. So, he gave the church to a new minister and moved to another community to begin a new church. And so the myth of the Lasser family devoting themselves to those less fortunate than themselves was born and with it the legacy to continue the family calling. Grandpa went on to develop over 20 new churches, all over Kansas. As soon as one was on its feet he'd give it to a new minister and move on.

My father grew up hearing parts of the story from someone nearly every week. He became a lawyer but like Grandpa spent his life helping those less fortunate than himself. He would sit on the boards of endless committees and spent more time giving free legal advice than at his own practice. He was always available to donate his services to the NAACP and the Council 100. He taught Sunday school all his life and was always getting people jobs and networking for them. He always downplayed his own good deeds. He and my mother always told us Grandpa's story. In my generation, my sister became a special ed teacher and I'm a public health doctor. We both feel committed to carry out the family legacy and both have joined the family in passing the myth on to our children. My son, Gordon, has become a minister and last Christmas we told his three-year-old daughter the myth for the first time. She'll hear it many times in her life. That story is as much a part of our family as our Christmas tree ornaments or family album.

The Vulcan myths are about my grandmother and mother, who are so light-skinned that outside our community they always passed for white. There are lots of stories about Grandma and Mama "passing" in order to shop at certain stores or obtain something the family needed. Lots of other stories in the myth concern the differential treatment they received depending on what "color" they were that day.

SELF-EXPLORATION: MULTIGENERATIONAL EFFECTS

As we come to understand the previous generations in our family, we develop a self-knowledge that hopefully allows for more mature and satisfying relationships with other family members. Try to discuss the transgenerational knowledge, if any, that you have learned in the following five areas:

1. How have the previous generations responded to sexuality and what did you learn from their example? What are your children going to learn from having you and your spouse as models?
2. How independent and achievement oriented were the previous generations? What are your children learning about achievement and independence by having you and your spouse as models?
3. How have the grandparents and great-grandparents responded to the death of family members? What will your children learn from you and your spouse about death?
4. How have angry feelings been dealt with by previous generations? What rules will your children develop about the expression of anger?
5. What has been the effect of religious and political legacies in your family?
6. What are the myths in your family tree? Use Table 8.2 to help you discover these myths. How many generations back can you trace these myths?

Chapter 9

Networks and Ecosystems

*Trouble is a great sieve through which we sift our acquaintances;
those who are too big to pass through are friends.*

North Carolina Churchman

Most people find it obvious that an individual's functioning is greatly influenced by the family system, but few people realize that individual and family functioning is also greatly influenced by a wide and intricate system of friends, neighbors, relatives, intimates, and social groups. When an individual is in a crisis, the family is expected to offer emotional support, provide temporary alter egos, and help generate useful solutions to the problems. When the nuclear family has exceeded its resources, the network is often called upon to help resolve the crisis or lend support.

The term "ecosystems" includes the larger or more abstract networks that affect family life. Going beyond the immediate extended family and circle of close friends, it includes the family's ethnic and racial group, social class identification, religious community, and neighborhood. Each family member's gender and generational niche is a unique aspect of the ecosystem that affects family functioning. If it seems that the "ecosystemic" approach includes anything and everything that influences a person and his or her functioning in the family, you are right!

The implications for treatment are far reaching. Instead of asking mother and father to come to a session, all the systems that impact upon a child can be used to alleviate the problem. Bringing the parents together with the teacher and representatives of the medical, legal, religious, and social service community is seen as the most effective way to find a solution to the acting-out behavior of a child in the classroom.

Even when the representatives of each social system are not invited into a session, the ecosystemic lens requires that the therapist understand the impact of each system on the development and maintenance of the problem. It creates wider circles of inquiry and more possibilities about how to create change.

NETWORKS AND IN-LAWS

I don't believe in marriage either . . . it's really just two scapegoats sent out by two families to reproduce each other . . . the battle is which one will it be . . .

Carl Whitaker

One of the most cantankerous of network relationships involves the in-law relationship. The mother-in-law/daughter-in-law relationship is the most often cantankerous of all in-law relationships. Sometimes, the conflict is due to clashing personality styles between the two female kinskeepers. Three personality dimensions have been shown to cause possible strife: affection needs, inclusion needs, and control needs. If one in-law is a big self-discloser, telling all and seeking a deep connection with others, and the other in-law is a more private person who respects people keeping their distance, conflicts are likely. Similarly, if one in-law wants everyone to get together on vacations, weekends, and whenever time permits, and the other feels relatives should live their own lives and get together on one or two holidays, friction will ensue. Finally, the all-important power struggles that infect every dyadic relationship become major sources of irritation (Berg-Cross and Jackson, 1986; Jackson and Berg-Cross, 1988).

While decision-making authority and the privilege of opinion giving are common coin in the control currency of relationships, money is also an important factor. When the parents have substantially more financial resources than the adult children, helping out can become coupled with the power to influence decisions of the married children. Even when the children are economically self-sufficient, money can become an issue. Particularly in poor and immigrant families, the son-in-law is given enormous power in the family if he is financially successful. When the daughter-in-law is successful, the in-laws are often torn between their traditional expectations that the man should be the one to succeed and the fact that the whole family is being uplifted by the daughter-in-law. All too often, both young people suffer from strained in-law relationships when the woman earns more.

In-law problems are not always the result of style mismatches between the in-laws. Quite often, they are solutions to problems rooted in each person's family of origin or a diversion from more painful dyadic conflicts. The five most common indirect sources of conflict include the following:

1. In-law problems are a way to help an adult child avoid standing up to his or her parent and still rebel against their control or distance. By

having the son-in-law or daughter-in-law put his or her foot down and express disdain, the adult child can support his or her parents while still not having to deal directly with noxious issues.

2. In-law problems allow the parents to continue to idealize their son/ daughter while blaming all of the conflict on the child-in-law.

3. In-law problems help the older and younger generations separate from one another, as each spouse is pressured to demonstrate loyalty by being on the othe spouse's side.

4. Sometimes, deficiencies in one spouse are made up for by the complementary nature of the other spouse. A very nonassertive woman can protest that it is her husband who refuses to vacation with her parents and that she supports his decision. Alone, she would be unable to muster the courage to refuse the parents. Here, in-law problems are a vehicle for piggy-backing on desired traits in the spouse-in-law.

5. In-law problems are an easy diversion if one is simply unhappy or bored in the marriage and unable to face that reality (Carter and McGoldrick, 1988; Meyerstein, 1996).

When the conflict between the in-laws stems from these systemic problems, it is best to avoid a hostile showdown in the first meeting and meet with the subunits separately. If each group feels that they are understood and have had time to air the "righteousness" of their position, they are much more likely to be willing to enter explorations and negotiations with some calm and self-control. When the situation is being driven by some dysfunction in the parent-child dyad, the goal obviously is to get the in-law out of the line of fire. Positive lasting changes will only occur when the adult child and parent come to grips with their anger and resentments. They need to resolve to find better ways of relating to one another and solving their disagreements.

NETWORKS AND CHILDHOOD RESILIENCY

When children are "resilient" they seem to be able to bend with the strong winds of adversity. When they are "at risk," they break. Researchers have spent much time theorizing and examining the life course of resilient children to see what exactly it is that allows them to be flexible and cope with problems so successfully. Again and again, we find that resilient children are able to defocus from home stress and adversity by engaging people outside the family. Boyfriends, girlfriends, teachers, neighbors, church, dance clubs, and work create new positive trajectories that are self-reinforcing. What makes children resilient seems to be the ability to actively recruit informal support networks in the community. Katy Butler (1997:26) summarizes the activity of these children well:

> Resilient children drink up support promiscuously wherever they find it, the way a cut flower drinks water or a transplanted morning glory puts down roots and opens blindly to the sun. They were lucky that the adults they turned to supported and didn't betray them. But, they also chose well, thus helping to make their own luck.

Girls seem especially adept at creating such social supports. For example, Kurdeck and Fine (1993) found that among divorced single mother families, girls were more likely than boys to look to other adults and siblings in the house for conversation, to get help with personal problems, and to take an interest in them. This effect also successfully differentiated girls from two-parent families from girls in divorced single-mother families. It is as though the girls are aware of needing more adult support than is available from one parent and have the chutzpah to go and get it from the available alternatives.

Samuelson (1995) studied the social networks of nine- to sixteen-year-old children, all living with a single parent in Sweden, to see if the successful use of social networks differentiated those children who were being seen in the clinic from those who were adjusting more successfully. Although they only studied thirty-nine clinic children and thirty-nine controls, the results were quite clear. Children being seen in the clinic had fewer relatives and school friends whom they could turn to for companionship and help. When the clinic children had peers and relatives whom they saw frequently, they were more likely to feel alienated and misunderstood by them. What distinguished the children who were successfully meeting their developmental challenges was that they had resourceful relatives and peers available to them who were warm, accepting, and affirming. Other studies have shown that being part of a club or organization can have a protective effect on divorced men and women (Kunz and Kunz, 1995).

When we see a child having problems, we try to give the child some resiliency. As therapists, we can do this by mobilizing someone in the network to engage the child, and by helping the child accept and enjoy the activities, conversations, or advice offered by the supportive adult. Evidence suggests that it is not critical that the child initiate the activity or seek out supportive adults in order to benefit. Having an adult create the opportunity for nonstressful, enjoyable interactions seems to create a strong resiliency effect. Consider the results of the evaluation study conducted by Public/Private Ventures in Philadelphia on the effectiveness of the Big Brothers/Big Sisters program. They found that, compared to a control group, 33 percent of the participants were less likely to exhibit violent behavior, and 46 percent were less likely to ever try illegal drugs (Butler, 1997).

As to having the child enjoy or benefit from the time with the supportive adult, there has to be a good match in terms of interest and interpersonal style. However, it is not very hard to target activities that will bring excitement and happiness to a child. Ron Taffel, a family therapist in New York, uses a very simple question to start mobilizing the network. He asks the child, "What is it that you love to do?" Once you know where the child's natural energy and interests are flowing, you are far more likely to be successful in creating a workable network match. If the child loves to collect Beanie Babies, perhaps the mom can find some friends at school who share that interest and develop weekly Beanie Baby Play Days. If the child only wants to learn ice hockey, many men and women who play in adult leagues would be more than happy to take an interested young novice under their wing.

While realizing that psychologists cannot get involved in screening strangers and verifying that they are competent to deal with their child clients, therapists can and must mobilize parents, teachers, or other direct caretakers of the child to search out such people. Psychologists need to reassure parents that it take more than a village to raise a child—it takes an active, involved village. Parents are still the creators of the environment. Parents remain the monitors of the child's safety and well-being. But parents cannot be all things to all children all of the time. Wise is the parent who knows when to utilize another helpful adult and wiser still is the therapist who can guide a parent toward embracing the wider community of parent surrogates.

It is also important for therapists to assess the negative impact that networks can have on a child. I recently saw a five-year-old boy who, for the past year, had been plagued by "voices in his head" telling him that he was going to go to hell and that he should kill himself. The parents reported that the voices started when the Sunday school teacher gave the children a chilling and graphic description of hell. It was described as being in a dark room, alone and scared, and never being able to get out. Far from the beginning of a psychosis, this problem was quickly resolved by having the religious network altered and screening the potential Sunday school teachers.

The list of negative network influences is endless, including egregious teachers, peers who are intent on getting into trouble, harsh relatives, abusive friends, and so on. Much therapeutic work has gone into marshalling the positive resources of the extended social system. Therapists are more likely to ignore or tolerate disruptive or detrimental forces in the social environment out of respect for cultural or individual differences. Who am I to say that these parents should not be sending their child to a fundamentalist school? Is it biased to tell the parents to move to a different apartment or neighborhood so that the child client would have more friends to play within the immediate neighborhood? Therapists need to acknowledge that the ecosystem may have toxic effects, and when this is the case, it must be aggressively changed or altered.

The conflicts that occur in trying to change toxic networks are usually complex and not easily resolved. Consider a case I had a few years ago, in which the mother was very upset that every time she left her preschooler with her mother-in-law, he would come back with a host of curse words and some new, very obnoxious racist attitudes. The mother had pleaded repeatedly with the mother-in-law and with the husband for the mother-in-law to refrain from these practices. They laughed it off, saying the child had to get used to being around all types of people and that the mother-in-law was entitled to her opinions. This problem was not easily resolved. Although the mother used this as an opportunity to teach her son to filter and critically evaluate the behavior of elders, the behavior and the tension it provoked was an ongoing issue.

ZONES OF INTIMACY

Boissevain (1974) developed a five-zone model for use in analyzing the form and function of social networks (Figure 9.1). The uppermost zone (Zone 1) is composed of close relatives and friends. The rules distinguishing the rights and obligations of people in the uppermost zone are critical. Each innermost member has a primary relationship to the network owner with very specific obligations, debts, and entitlements. Innermost members relate to us on many levels. We might tell them our problems, participate in leisure activities with them, celebrate rituals with them, or help them with day-to-day tasks. Regardless of the specifics, our relationship with these innermost network members is both extensive and intensive.

The second zone (Zone 2) is composed of other relatives and friends. These folks lack the intimacy of those in the first zone but are still involved with us in multiple relationships. For example, a friend at work might be someone I socialize with on weekends and occasionally go shopping with. Network members in the second zone are seen on a regular basis. Zone 3 includes friends and relatives with whom the individual is not in frequent contact but who have historically been in multiple relationships with him or her. In Zone 4 are people with whom the individual has economic or political relationships; interactions are primarily in terms of

FIGURE 9.1. The Five Zones Composing a Social Network

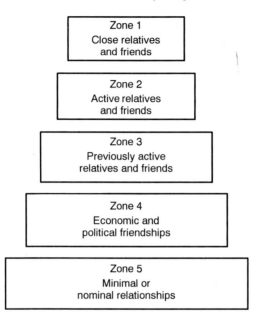

Source: Adapted from Boissevain, J. 1974. *Friends of friends: Networks, Manipulators, and Coalitions.* New York: St. Martin's Press.

their work roles. Colleagues, shopkeepers, teachers, and beauticians belong to this fourth group. The fifth zone is for the "leftovers," those people with whom we chat, have fleeting dealings, and exchange information.

Generally, most individuals can find forty individuals in the first three zones of their personal networks (Rueveni, 1979). Some people have as few as twenty in their networks. Others have upward of eighty members. In the course of daily events our social networks are vital in helping us adjust to the exigencies of living. Through our networks we often find new jobs, new friends, and companionship. This web of forty or so individuals weaves the fabric of social relations that makes life worth living.

It has been estimated that the average individual in the United States is embedded in a series of social relationships that include direct or indirect connections with 1,000 to 1,500 people. Obviously, most of these people belong to Zones 4 and 5. Still, the potential for network members being able to help us out in times of need is great indeed.

THE IMPORTANCE OF NETWORKS

Inevitably, each of us is embedded in a social network. The extent or nature of our networks affects our marital stability, our self-esteem, and even our general mental health. The importance of networks to our mental health shows up as soon as we leave the security of our family of origin. For instance, college students who have a large network of friends feel more adequate than students with minimal networks. Evidence is even accumulating that our physical well-being is related to how well our network can help absorb the stress accompanying illness. A striking example of this is a 1980 study which reported that men with heart attacks had a more successful outcome when their wives utilized a larger number of sources for help and support during the crisis (McCubbin et al., 1980).

Networking and Couple Relationships

When we have a rich and extensive network, we feel better about ourselves. We feel more important and more powerful—in fact, by participating in the wider social network we do become more powerful. Even satisfaction with the marital relationship increases when we have a strong network. For example, couples who rely only on each other for companionship invariably become insulated and stressed by the overwhelming demands of the relationship. Without friends for stimulation, boredom is very common. Such couples also become alienated from the social forces that could support their identity as a couple. Only by interacting with other couples can the husband and wife appreciate their special bonds and strengths. Also, as couples struggle with the role of parenthood, socializing and discussing problems with other parents gives new ideas and reassurances that are vital in avoiding husband/wife conflicts. In fact, it has been empirically demonstrated that married women tend to be happier with their maternal role if they belong to a strong social network (Bott, 1957). Bowen (1982) more recently found that divorced women were happier with their maternal role when they were satisfied with the relationship they had with their parents and with their network of friends.

Thus, for married couples, involvement with a social network of mutual friends has been related to healthier and more cohesive marriages. Ironically, despite the increased cohesiveness, the more involved a couple is in the family's kin network, the greater the segregation of role behaviors expected of the wife and husband (Turner, 1967; Bott, 1957). This phenomenon has been related to the fact that historically as the networks of married couples expanded, the wife was interacting with more women and more children and husbands were interacting with more and more men.

The women supported one another, helping with child care and advising on housekeeping tips and budget strategies. The wives ended up with little reason to rely on their husbands to share their role. Similarly, the husbands always had a fishing partner or someone to build a porch with; they did not need to rely on their wives for sharing their role. Since both men and women are rapidly creating more flexible and androgynous roles for themselves, sexual segregation among friendly adult couples may eventually change, although no such signs are currently on the horizon.

Networks and Family Stability

What happens when there is no network—when a family is isolated and receives no support from outsiders? When a family is cut off from relatives, has no friends, and does not take part in community affairs, it becomes brittle and rigid, lacking flexibility. Dysfunctional ways of relating begin to breed. It is as though the family were the crew on a boat whose ports of destination are continually changing. Only by keeping contact with the others outside the family who are knowledgeable about the forces shaping their mission can they function cohesively and effectively as a group.

Many situations illustrate how social networks help stabilize the family. One striking example is the hundreds of communities across the country that have formed to raise thousands of dollars needed for an organ transplant or a life-saving operation for a local citizen. Less dramatic but far more common are the churches in each community that routinely marshal their congregations to offer time and emotional support to families in crisis. Those who have been the beneficiaries of such extended networks of friends and neighbors uniformly find it a spiritually uplifting, effective way to meet the crisis—often the only way. Although networks are important to all of us, they have been imperative for the elderly, the poor, and the minorities of this nation.

RACHEL (housewife, age 50)

My mama came from a family of ten children and my daddy came from a family of ten children. Everyone just about married and had a family and lived within a half hour's drive of each other. With such a large network, we got specialized real quick. Some of the family were givers while others were takers. My mama was the leader of the givers and by extension I have taken on that role in my life as well. My mama was the one who made sure

(continued)

(continued)

that there was family around to be a nurse when needed and a handyman when needed. If my aunt needed her fence door put back on (which fell off at least once a year) my daddy would go down or Mama would find one of my uncles to do it. From ten till eighteen years old I would go with my brother every Saturday morning down to Granny's to mow her lawn. This meant putting the mower onto the truck and taking a fifteen-minute drive across town. That wouldn't have been bad hadn't there been four cousins living next door to Granny who could have done it! Every Sunday, Granny would make a chicken dinner for everyone and this was the most coopera- tive people ever got. Everyone would bring something, or help clean up.

Now, to show you how things change and things stay the same: I've lived in my current house for over six years and other than my immediate family of origin, no other relative has stepped inside. We all sort of drifted apart. Still, I am the helper. I would never ask any of my neighbors or friends for any help whatsoever. If I'm sick, I manage. If I'm short on funds, I make do. But I never say no to anyone. I get a lot of jobs helping the elderly couple who live on my block. I take them shopping once a week, take them to their doctor's appointments, plant their garden and whatever little things I can. I help out my friends whenever I can. I would be a great person to invite to one of those network sessions but no matter how des- perate things got, I can't imagine agreeing to have one.

NETWORKS AND ELDERLY PEOPLE

For elderly people, a rich support network has been empirically demon- strated to correlate with life satisfaction, absence of feelings of loneliness, and general mental health (Cohen and Sokolovsky, 1981). When an elder- ly person feels isolated or lonely, a high degree of alienation between the elderly individual and other family members invariably exists. The degree of alienation is directly related to the well-being of older people. A high degree of social participation is associated with a high degree of physical and mental health and a much lower degree of physical debilitation and senile behavior.

The stereotype of widespread ill will between elderly parents and their children has been repeatedly refuted in the literature. In 1979, Ethel Sha- nas found that 75 percent of older parents either lived with or within a half hour's distance of an adult child and that 77 percent had seen a child during the week prior to their interview. Among the very old (over eighty), 98 percent of the women and 72 percent of the men lived with a child or within ten minutes travel time of one (Shanas and Sussman, 1981).

Unfortunately, in today's mobile society, one-third of all older parents live over 500 miles from at least one of the children. However, there is evidence that while parent-child contact is reduced with increasing distance, the quality of the parent-child relationship is unrelated to the geographical distance that exists. Strong affective ties can be maintained despite considerable distances. For example, Moss, Moss, and Moles (1985) found that over one-third of all adult children who live more than 500 miles away from their parents are in phone contact more than once a month even though they see them only about once a year. When adult children live within two to ten miles of their parents, over 50 percent speak on the phone at least twice a week as well as seeing them at least once a week.

As can be seen by Table 9.1, the potential family networks of the elderly are larger than expected. Only 6 percent of the elderly individuals are without any immediate family and over 80 percent have one or more living siblings.

TABLE 9.1. Potential Family Members Available to Persons Sixty-Five Years and Older

	Percentage
Married (males)	75.0
Married (females)	41.0
Widowed (males)	14.0
Widowed (females)	48.0
Never married (males)	4.0
Never married (females)	6.0
Divorced (males)	3.0
Divorced (females)	50.0
One living child	75.0
Has a child over age sixty-five	10.0
Living grandchildren	70.0
Households have grandchildren living with them	5.0
Without any family	6.0
Great-grandchildren	40.0
Living brother or sister	80.0

Source: U.S. Bureau of the Census. 1999. *Sixty-Five Plus in the United States.* Statistical Brief. Washington, DC: U.S. Department of Commerce, U.S. Bureau of the Census.

The number of friends and neighbors one can relate to easily becomes very important in providing contact with the outside world. Older people feel most comfortable with people who are very similar to them. Sharing the same neighborhood, going to the same church, and having the same background make contacts more meaningful. This is why it is important to be familiar with a community before retiring there. Folks who suddenly decide to retire in Arizona because it is warm may find themselves very lonely and isolated. Indeed, research has shown that people who make seasonal migrations during their middle-aged years (every winter going to Florida, every summer going to Vermont) are most successful in retiring to these areas permanently when they are older, presumably because they have formed networks there (Vivrett, 1960).

Helping Behaviors and the Elderly

Fifty percent of people over age eighty-five need help performing everyday activities such as bathing, getting around inside the home, and preparing meals (U.S. Bureau of the Census, 1999). The help elderly people receive from their networks also includes considerable emotional gratification and household management. Aged men and women greatly appreciate being taken shopping, being checked on when they are ill, and being helped with home maintenance and repairs. Of course, when the elderly become disabled, family and other network members increase the time they spend helping. The greater the disability, the greater the help received. For example, data obtained from time diaries kept by married children with an elderly handicapped parent in their home indicated that the elder's care took one-and-a-half.to three hours a day, depending on the level of disability that the parent had. Overall, more than 40 percent of the wife's free time was spent caring for the parent, irrespective of the wife's employment status (Nissel, 1984).

Most elderly people do not merely take; they are active contributors to their friends and relatives. Grandparents often help out grandchildren financially in addition to helping out their own children. Only in poorer socioeconomic levels do the elderly routinely receive financial help from their kin. Indeed, the prominent picture is that of mutual aid, with most parents giving to their children as much as they can for as long as they can (Troll, 1971).

For aged people who have no family, friends are obviously far more vital. The ties between elderly friends are quite strong even when children are alive and active with the parent. This is evidenced by the phenomenon in many retirement communities where friends leave their estates or a portion of their estates to a needy friend in the community. Often these wills state that their children are self-sufficient and will understand their need to take care of this beloved friend (Rosenfeld, 1980).

The Need for Social Contact

Maintaining social contact with others is as strong a motivating need for the elderly as for any other age group. In virtually any setting, elderly people try to develop friendships and meaningful contacts. Elderly people who live in SRO hotels (single room occupancy) are considered among the most isolated in our society. Even here, the average elderly resident can name over seven people with whom she or he has regular and friendly contact (Cohen and Sokolovsky, 1981). Well over half of these contacts occur with people outside the hotel, both kin and non-kin. Of course, some residents live the stereotypical hermit existence and can name no one as a friend. Others know up to twenty-six network members. Cohen and Sokolovsky found that the elderly men and women they studied who lived in midtown tenement apartments had extensive personal networks during the day but virtually no contacts during the evening. In this respect the SRO residents were at an advantage, since two-thirds of them had evening as well as daytime contacts.

It may be very misleading to attempt to predict an elderly individual's life satisfaction merely from the number and density of his or her social network. Neither number of friends nor frequency with which kin or friends visited was predictive of loneliness in two studies (Baldassare, Rosenfield, and Rook, 1984; Ward, Sherman, and LaGory, 1984). Rather, the more satisfied the elderly felt with their social relations, the less lonely they were. Even those who were widowed, living alone, or seeing friends infrequently were unlikely to feel lonely if they were satisfied or content with the quality of their social relationships.

The work of Ward, Sherman, and LaGory (1984) is important because it suggests that simply networking for the elderly may not be enough to offset loneliness. Loneliness in later life is undoubtedly related to lifelong attitudes in forming and maintaining relationships. If this is true, then the beneficial effects of networking will in part vary with the personality type and social history of the older person.

In attempting to understand the role that children play in the support network, the older person's attitude is critical. Children nearly always play a central role in the elder's life, but access to and interaction with children has little relation to subjective well-being (Ward, Sherman, and LaGory, 1984:100). "Whether children are nearby and seen regularly is less important than whether they are seen 'enough' and whether interaction with children has the quality desired by the older individual." Although loneliness develops when people are deprived of emotional intimacy (like that offered by kin), it also develops when they are deprived of a sense of social integration.

At all ages, people need to feel part of the social fabric of society by belonging to a network of friends, a club, a civic organization, or a professional group. This explains why someone who has enormous family support might complain of loneliness, and conversely, why someone who has an extensive network of friends and civic responsibilities might also feel lonely. Since loneliness involves a complex array of emotions that includes feelings of estrangement, rejection, and being misunderstood, lonely older people often feel out of place and self-conscious about not having what they consider an appropriate social partner to accompany them to events in the community. Consequently, they miss out on many activities that could provide that vital sense of social integration. A cyclical pattern of failure is formed when the loss of intimate others hinders the promotion of meaningful social contacts, because meaningful social contacts often provide the major opportunities to develop intimate relationships.

NETWORKS AND BLACK AMERICANS

In 1965, the U.S. Department of Labor published the so-called Moynihan report, which announced that the plight of poor urban blacks was due in part to the disintegration of the family structure (Moynihan, 1965). Statistics showing the large percentage of female-headed households were used to substantiate the assertion that these families were without the needed filial and affial networks. Unfortunately, the Moynihan study never directly assessed the extent of the networks, the true family structure among this population. Nearly thirty-five years of research has repeatedly shown poor black urban Americans to have some of the most extensive and intensive kin networks in the United States.

For example, Faegen (1970) found that in a black community such as Roxbury, Massachusetts, about 20 percent of the people are involved with relatives in the giving or receipt of financial aid in any one year. Martineau (1977), studying blacks in South Bend, Indiana, found that 85 percent of the inner-city residents have relatives in the area whom they see at least once a week; 39 percent see their relatives daily; 75 percent have direct contact with friends at least once a week; 25 percent have daily contact.

The networks are not confined to the poor. McAdoo (1978) studied 178 middle-income black families with children in Washington, DC, and Columbia, Maryland. She found that these families had extensive kin networks that frequently helped with child care and provided financial and emotional support when needed. In fact, virtually every study since the Moynihan report has found that black Americans are tightly involved with relatives outside the home.

Martineau (1977) found that 75 percent of inner-city blacks knew two or more people who could and would help them out in a time of crisis. Only 4 percent said they had no one. In the Southern and rural parts of the country, the kin network appears even stronger. Ball (1983), in a survey of black families in Alachua County, Florida, found that all the participants had a close relative living nearby. Forty-five percent said they saw family members who lived outside their home "all the time." An additional 44 percent said they saw them often.

Stack (1974) found that in black communities, friends as well as relatives were involved in an elaborate exchange network of goods and services. Friends who could be called in to help at any time and who never disappointed a person in need came to be considered as kin. Fictive kin are common among black Americans. Close friends especially become cate-

---

HELEN (systems analyst, age 36)

I've always had a very supportive network of family and friends, but up until two years ago, I took this pretty much for granted. At that time, two things happened that required me to depend on this network for my survival. First, my marriage of ten years came to a sudden and, for me, surprising end. Then, seven months later I suffered a devastating illness.

At the time my marriage ended, my parents, my brother, my mother-in-law, and aunts and uncles (even those of my husband) all called me often, listened to me, shared tears, and offered me comfort in forms ranging from prayer to money. Almost without exception, they didn't pry for details or give unwanted advice. Although they were 500 miles away, they were very close. My friends, especially those who had had similar experiences, gathered around. At first they just made sure I wasn't alone; later they began to reinitiate me into the single social life. Within a couple of months, my periods of depression became fewer, and I began enjoying life again.

Seven months later, just as I was really beginning to feel that I had adjusted to being a single person again, I got sick. At first, I thought it was the flu. After ten days, however, I was so weak that a friend who had stopped by to look after me insisted that I call my parents. My mother hopped the next plane (even though she'd only flown once before, and never alone) and immediately put me in the hospital. My condition deteriorated and emergency surgery was required. My mother relied on her brother, a surgeon, to help her make decisions concerning my treatment. My ex-husband and two of my friends stayed with my mother during the surgery, and my father and brother

(continued)

(continued)

arrived the next day. I remained in critical condition for three weeks and was in the hospital for six weeks. During that time, my family lived in my house and stayed with me every day. One aunt sent money so that I could have private nursing, and flowers, cards, and telephone calls came by the boat-load. As soon as I was able to think of such things, I was given reassurance that my job would be waiting for me when I recovered. When I left the hospital, my former mother-in-law stayed with me until I was strong enough to cook and care for myself again.

The scenario doesn't end here; when I put a network to the test, I don't let it off easy! During the next year, I had five additional hospitalizations and four more operations. The support from my family, friends, and co-workers never lessened. My mother was with me during every hospitalization, even when it meant traveling twice to Rochester, Minnesota, in the dead of winter. After each "bout" my mother-in-law nursed me at home, and I was always permitted to return to my old job either part-time or full-time whenever I was able. My company provided excellent medical and disability coverage so that I did not suffer financial problems during the time.

Currently, I am back on the road to good health. I had the final round of surgery a month ago, and I will return to my work in two weeks. I am glad I've been asked to write about my network of family and friends while my experiences are so fresh. I feel that during this two-year period, the support of my network has been critical for my emotional and physical survival. I do not think I could have lived through this time, much less remained sane, without their constant help. I feel that the only way I can repay my debt is to be ready to help others whenever I can. As a result of the example set by my network, I am now much more sensitive to the problems and needs of others. I hope this means that I have grown into a better person.

gorized and described as being relatives. It is a term designating their importance in the social network.

USING—AND NOT USING—NETWORKS

I do then with my friends as I do with my books. I would have them where I can find them, but I seldom use them.

Ralph Waldo Emerson

Some studies have shown that people are as likely to request help from friends as from kin, but the nature of the help requested varies. For short-term day-to-day problems (such as a one-day illness or driving the children to a lesson), friends and neighbors are relied upon. For extensive problems such as recovery from surgery, however, help from relatives is almost always sought. In times of serious illness or death, family networks are very important. Relatives from out of town report extraordinarily low tensions when visiting during a crisis (Rosenblatt, Johnson, and Anderson, 1981). Everyone seems to value the visit and understands the unique and irreplaceable role of being available to kin at such times.

Most people feel that they have a number of people they could call on for help when faced with a major problem. Yet surprisingly few people actually do call upon network members to help them. Ball (1983) found over 75 percent of a group of women saying they had friends and relatives whom they could ask for help in resolving a problem, but only 25 percent actually asked for help from network members.

Hesitancy to call upon network members can arise from a variety of sources. First, there is the possibility that while the network members would be eager to help, realistically there might be nothing that could be done to alleviate the problem. Second, many people prefer not to become too indebted to their network members. Receiving help and favors in a time of need implies that you will be willing to return the effort at a later date. These anticipated reciprocal obligations are often too burdensome.

Third, asking for help of any kind almost always requires extensive self-disclosure of the problems present in the household. Some people find that this type of self-disclosure demeans them and lowers their self-esteem. Their broader notions of independence and respect are threatened by admitting to narrow needs of assistance.

Fourth, family are much more likely to be receptive to pitching in than other network members. Even within the family, primary kin (parents, siblings, and children) are the most likely to feel a moral obligation and responsibility to help. Most secondary kin (uncles, aunts, cousins) usually keep up on the news about one another, but the relationships tend to be shallow and to depend on hearsay delivered from primary kin. No evidence suggests widespread expectations of extensive obligations to one another among this wider kin group. Consequently, there is little potential for systematic caring. Some of the most touching relationships involve secondary kin who have become truly committed to one another: a grandfather-and-grandson team, an aunt-and-nephew match.

Fifth, in any network it has traditionally been the women who have extended care and help. Although patterns are shifting, the female members of the network probably remain far more pivotal than the men in determining whether and how much help is given (Allan, 1983). More and more women are employed; they have much less time and energy available for helping members of the network. Most people in distress are aware of the many demands on women today and are hesitant to add to the load.

Strategies to Promote Networking

Mental health professionals have long realized that governmental institutional structures have the most success when they are reaching out and helping the people who have the potential to help themselves. When a person requires constant or intense supervision or reassurance, the governmental structure often fails. The 1970s heralded a new approach to working with multidisabled and severely troubled individuals and their families. Observations of the versatility and productivity of naturally occurring networks have spurred family theorists into calling network helpers together en masse for a total supportive effort to resolve crises for families that are stalemated. By mobilizing the social network to provide the support needed to achieve some self-sufficiency in the future, outside agencies have been able to facilitate the functioning of many families that were previously "unworkable."

Externally stimulating the network to give its time, energy, and resources is done only when the family has exhausted the resources of institutional helping agencies. Families are usually very wary, since networking in a crisis initially engenders a great loss of self-respect among the family members. Once everyone is gathered together, sordid problems become known to all; their conflicts and perhaps irrational feelings are revealed to public scrutiny.

Network therapy comes in many different treatment packages, but they all involve getting network members beyond the nuclear family involved with the problem-solving efforts of the family or individual. The network is made aware of the problem and helped to find ways of contributing to the solution. The original family networking therapy was developed by Ross Speck and Carolyn Attneave and outlined in their book *Family Networks* (1973). Uri Rueveni further developed the technique in his book *Networking Families in Crisis* (1979).

Both procedures are similar. They begin with a team of therapists making a home visit to the family. The meeting is attended only by members of the nuclear family. The goal of this visit is for the therapists to understand the nature and scope of the problem—to pinpoint where the family members disagree, how each of them is dealing with the conflict, and the roles they have been assigned in the family system. After the dimensions of the crisis have been delineated and the dynamics of the family interactions understood, the therapist helps each family member develop a list of family and friends who are in the first two interpersonal zones and often in the third and fourth zones as well (see Figure 9.1).

The nuclear family members are responsible for calling the network participants and enlisting their help. The family is instructed to briefly explain the nature of the crisis to the people on the list and to tell them they are needed to participate in a network session to help the family solve its problem. When all of the network assembles, people spontaneously begin milling around, reconnecting with friends and relatives they have not seen in some time and introducing themselves to the new people. This so-called *retribalization phase* is the first of six stages in the network intervention.

Stage two, *polarization,* occurs when the leaders direct the immediate family members to take a seat in the center of the room and to take turns explaining the crisis from their particular vantage point. Each family member says what he or she expects and needs from the network. As the story unfolds, the different perceptions and feelings of the family members become crystallized. The network participants initially become polarized toward supporting some members of the family and not others. The network members are encouraged to share their concerns and their points of view. Questions are freely asked and perceptions are challenged.

After the side-taking and expressions of concern, *mobilization,* the third phase, occurs. Mobilization is a natural outgrowth of involving the network members with all facets of the problem. In a large enough network there are always those individuals who feel that they can offer assistance or help reduce the family's pain. These "activists" have the resources to help and are motivated to offer such help. The team leaders (the therapists) facilitate this process by encouraging the activists to be very specific in the type of help they can offer. The team tries to pin down who will do what, when, and with whom. For example, if someone offers to help supervise the teenager in the family, it must be made explicit when the teen will report to the network person, and what authority the network person has over the teen. In addition, the teen must agree to take part in the new arrangement. Once the network members narrow down what they can and cannot do, the members often go through a depression phase. They are frustrated at being unable to find an immediate or easy solution and are often upset that their suggested solutions were not accepted.

The fifth phase, *breakthrough,* occurs when they realize that with negotiation some workable solutions are still possible, and their contributions and efforts can pay off for the family. People realize that the crisis can be resolved or abated without permanently resolving all the problems that were expressed within the family.

The final, sixth, network phase is *exhaustion-elation.* This is a period when the glow of accomplishment and joy of giving are felt by many network members. This elation is accompanied by an extreme emotional and physical tiredness—one feels "spent."

The success of a network session depends in large part on how the network members can pool their resources in a collaborative effort to help the family. Sometimes it requires coordinating efforts to find some alternative living arrangements or a job or financial help. Often, increased social contacts and friendship need to be promised. Whatever the commitments, the network members who become activists cannot be expected to maintain high levels of involvement for very long. Experience indicates that the network of activists reports a decreasing level of involvement as the crisis abates. Usually the time span of network involvement varies from three weeks to three months.

Everyone benefits from networking. It offers help to the family when all else has failed, and it provides the network members with a transcendent tribal feeling of oneness and betterment. Speck and Attneave (1973: 96) give a wonderfully glowing description of the type of "turn on" phenomenon involved: "[After the session] attenuated relationships are

---

COLLETTE (nurse, age 60)

I am a bitter old woman in the eyes of my children and colleagues. I know that they find me self-centered and ungenerous. I am both of those things, but for the first fifty years of my life I was continually rejected or ignored by the supposed members of my network. As a child, I was born with a cleft palate. I wasn't attractive, and the neighborhood kids taunted me, called me "doody girl," and wouldn't invite me to their parties. My parents and siblings tried to ignore me; like ragweed, I was an irritant they had to put up with. My sisters were indulged with a new outfit every year; I received their hand-me-downs. My brother was encouraged to go to college and my sisters to secretarial school while I was told to look for jobs in the government. I was a real-life Cinderella, except I was unattractive and never found my prince.

I was so miserable at home and at my future prospects, I joined the Navy. Clearly, this network, while personally rejecting and often humiliating, helped to give me a career I wanted—nursing. The war years were the most meaningful years of my life. I occasionally would go out with the girls and in 1944 found my husband, Lewis. While Lewis and I had some things in common (we came from the same region of the country and were the same age), it was never a passionate love affair. He was going off to war and wanted to go to bed with me. In those days, that was a socially acceptable set of circumstances to get married. Lewis left ten days after we were married and I didn't see him for two years.

(continued)

(continued)

After the war, our life together was rough. He was verbally abusive from the start and very hesitant about getting a job. He worked with his mother in a snow cone concession in Coney Island in the summer and then would stay on unemployment all winter. When I had my first daughter, he told me to put her up for adoption because he wasn't ready for children. Of course, I couldn't. By 1952, we had two girls and a boy. He was a terrible do-nothing father, we fought often, and by now he had become physically abusive. He'd pull my hair, slap me around, and bite me if I acted "out of line." My mother said I should be thankful to have any husband and I must be provoking him. In all the years of the kids growing, she never once offered to watch them overnight. She never helped me out financially, emotionally, or physically. While the other children did not get a whole lot from my mother, they definitely got more than I did.

My father totally ignored me and my children. My brother and sisters, who had become financially much better off than me, never helped either. What hurt most in those days is that they would never come to my apartment in Brooklyn. I always had to go out to Nassau County to the new big houses where "there was enough room." Some network! In 1965, I had a gallbladder operation. No one came to the hospital. My kids fared on their own and when I came home I nursed myself.

With such a brutal relationship with Lew, nursing was a refuge. But even at work, I would get the worst assignments and hard as I tried, I never fit in. My own children began disappointing me, one by one, when they got into high school. My eldest daughter quit school in eleventh grade. She married a bus driver and they moved to Louisiana when she was eighteen. At first, I sent letters and money but I never got a "thank you" or "how are you?" I'd hear from her at Christmas and get a card on Mother's Day, sometimes. My second daughter graduated but was a hippie, took a lot of drugs, and went to live on a commune. Out of the three I think she tried to make contact with me but she hated her father and couldn't stand to be around him. Today, she's married and lives in Manhattan with her husband and son. I visit them every few weeks and am always willing to help her out. I think she feels some obligation to me, but time will tell. My son was a chronic truant and was caught for stealing repeatedly. By age twenty-six he was in prison. He'll come see me occasionally and I always wrote him in prison. Currently he's a thirty-year-old heroin addict. It disgusts me. I look for what I did wrong and I feel like if I had just gotten some help along the way, maybe I could have given more to them.

Lew left me twelve years ago for another woman. I was relieved. My old battered body didn't want to ever be touched by another person before the undertaker. In the years alone, I find I have no support network from my neighbors and/or colleagues. My arthritis is quite bad and it's very painful for me to do many household chores or go shopping. My neighbors, some I've known thirty years, never offer to help out. I fear that if I had a networking session, no one would show up. I might have ten people I would call but no one would show up. Life has been hard to me and a network definitely would have helped but what can I do now and what could I have done then?

revived, while symbiotic ties are loosened or severed. Latent interests are energized by newly appreciated talents, and newly expressed needs elicit the sharing of practical experience. Old ghosts are exorcised and locked doors are opened; zest and fun are rediscovered."

SELF-EXPLORATION: NETWORKING

1. Write down all of your network members in each of the five zones (see Figure 9.1). Do you think that you have an adequate network? Why or why not?
2. What determines whether or not you would ask a network member to help you out?
3. Has anyone from your network ever asked you for help? How did you feel and how did it work out?
4. Imagine your family having a therapeutic networking session similar to the one described by Rueveni (1979). Can you think of any family problem that therapeutic networking could help? Why or why not?

UNIT III:
FAMILY CONCEPTS—
ECOLOGICAL STRESSORS

Our understanding of the ecological component of family dynamics has grown considerably in the past decade. Psychologists appreciate that while the family is affected by individual personalities, systemic dynamics within the family, and community events, it is also greatly affected by unavoidable and unwanted environmental stressors that are part of the everyday life of the family. We have chosen to discuss three of the most pervasive ecological stressors that invade the internal life of a family: illness, poverty, and adoption and infertility. There are many other such stressors, including sexual orientation, out-of-family steprelatives, and job stress. Hopefully, our sampling will provide the reader with a model of how to assess and treat a broad spectrum of ecological stressors.

Chapter 10

Family Resiliency and Poverty

Carla Williams

According to the 1997 U.S. Census Bureau statistics, 7.5 million families (10.8 percent) lived below the official government poverty level, which represented an annual income of $15,569 for a family of four. That translates to 14.7 million (20.0 percent) American children living below the poverty level in the United States. This chapter will explore how competency-based, resilience-focused family interventions can help to address the plight of impoverished families. Examples of practical techniques that may prove effective in addressing the special needs of families living in poverty will be provided.

To be maximally effective in working with families living in poverty, it is important for family therapists to be aware of the implications of impoverished conditions for the family's productivity and well-being. Indeed, the hazards associated with poverty for children and families have received great attention from politicians, policy analysts, sociologists, and psychologists. Much research energy has been invested in investigating the risk factors associated with poverty. The effects of poverty have been investigated beginning with prenatal life and extending to old age. Many important conclusions have been drawn from this research.

POVERTY-ASSOCIATED RISKS

Risk factors are those circumstances that increase the likelihood that a child will develop adverse outcomes. In addition to early developmental delays and school failure, poor outcomes in children can be evidenced as externalizing problems such as conduct problems, delinquency, and violence. The effects of exposure to risk factors can also appear as internalizing problems such as depression and anxiety. Further, outcomes of risk exposure may be played out in the family process, resulting in out-of-home placement, family discord, marital discord and dissolution, and various forms of family deviance. It has been widely suggested that these undesirable outcomes do not result from exposure to any single risk factor. Rather, it is the combination of multiple risk factors exerting simultaneous or sequential effects that is associated with negative outcomes for children and families (Bradley et al., 1994; Parker, Greer, and Zuckerman, 1988).

Studies of the infant developmental risks associated with poverty published from the late 1980s to the late 1990s were reviewed by Zeanah, Boris, and Larrieu (1997). They found that poverty was strongly related to a number of infant developmental problems which create important challenges for those providing intervention services to economically disadvantaged families. These problems included low birth weight, increased risk of lead poisoning, failure to thrive, chronic ear infections, and anemia (Parker, Greer, and Zuckerman, 1988). Infants born into poor families have also been found to be at increased risk of death from sudden infant death syndrome (Wise and Meyers, 1988). Bradley et al. (1994) suggest that being born into impoverished conditions makes infants and young children particulary susceptible to the cumulative adverse effects of poverty. They suggest that economically disadvantaged infants may be at risk of developmental delay stemming from a series of economically linked variables. For example, malnourished infants may have poorly developed immune functioning, which may make the developing nervous system vulnerable to infection and result in developmental and cognitive delays. Indeed, Pollitt (1994) revealed that such difficulties were associated with poorer outcomes as measured by scores on developmental and cognitive functioning scales. Halpern (1993) reported that drug abuse is more common among impoverished women living in the inner city. The problems associated with maternal drug use not only exert direct toxic effects on the developing fetus, but also negatively affect maternal nutrition and hence indirectly affect the developing fetus.

Bradley and colleagues (1994) also assert that infants growing up poor may be exposed to chaotic, unstimulating, unsupportive home environments. Infants living in very crowded homes may have to compete for attention. Poverty may affect parenting by creating stressors and sources of frustration that take away from parents' contact time with young children and reduce their emotional capacity for nurturing feelings and behaviors. Feelings of powerlessness combined with lack of parenting and social supports may result in displacement of aggression and frustration onto children. Bradley suggests that the combination of lack of material goods and limitations placed on parents' emotional attachment and involvement may prevent children from learning to trust that the environment can meet their needs. This, in turn, may lead to decreased feelings of self-efficacy, which may give rise to various forms of psychopathology.

For instance, McLeod and Shanahan (1996) studied data from the Children of the National Longitudinal Survey of Youth data set. A total of 978 four- and five-year-old children of the original 1979 baseline cohort were interviewed in 1986 and followed through 1990. They found that children who had an early history of persistent poverty had higher levels of depression. When these children were reinterviewed again in 1990, they continued to have higher levels of depression than those who were more affluent. McLeod and Shanahan concluded that children whose early life experiences are impacted by poverty are at increased risk for experiencing mental health problems regardless of whether they move out of poverty over time. Thus, poverty not only affects cognitive development but general mental health and well-being as well.

The precise mechanism by which poverty negatively influences child development is unclear. Although the effects of risk exposure are thought to be cumulative, the quality of parenting is likely to exert a major impact on children's well-being. Of specific concern are the negative effects associated with child maltreatment. Drake and Pandey (1996) examined the relationship between living in impoverished neighborhoods and child maltreatment. These researchers suggest that living in poor neighborhoods creates substantial distress. In addition to lack of material wealth, living in poor neighborhoods can lead to social isolation and increased exposure to community violence. In their study, Drake and Pandey utilized data on suspected and substantiated child maltreatment cases in a Midwestern urban area. They used zip code information to identify 481,722 families living in neighborhoods they categorized as low, medium, and high poverty areas. The rates of substantiated cases of physical abuse for low, moderate, and high poverty areas were 1 to 6 to 19, respectively. Rates of neglect were 1 to 7 to 46 for low, medium, and high poverty neighborhoods. Although rates of substantiated sexual abuse were much lower than physical abuse and neglect, the same pattern emerged. For low, medium, and high poverty areas, the sexual abuse rates were 1 to 2 to 4. The authors concluded that living in high poverty urban neighborhoods creates a substantial risk to the well-being of children. Interestingly, substantiation rates were consistently higher in high poverty families (32 percent) than in low and moderate poverty families (12 percent and 20 percent, respectively). This suggests that systemic factors in the child welfare system may play an important role in fact-finding and decisions made in child abuse cases. Poor families may be stigmatized by child welfare workers who allow their prejudices about how people come to live in poverty and attributions about why they remain in poverty influence the actions they take in a child maltreatment case.

Negative appraisals of impoverished families have a detrimental impact on their interactions with social service agencies. For example, Jarrett (1996) conducted a focus group of recipients of Aid to Families with Dependent Children (AFDC) to learn how the social stigma and devaluation of aid recipients impacted on their self-appraisals and feelings of self-efficacy. This study found that women who received AFDC benefits felt stigmatized around issues related to economics and family. They felt that the media and other public images portrayed them as having a poor work ethic. They felt that their nonmarital childbearing was viewed as a way to maintain themselves on welfare and they believed that they were assumed to be inadequate parents simply because they received AFDC.

Thus, the stigma associated with being poor not only negatively affects welfare workers' interactions with poor families, but also has damaging effects on the way that impoverished children and families view themselves and their beliefs about and subsequent actions toward improving their conditions. For example, many people may think that the poor have a less favorable attitude toward work. In the face of current welfare reform, this stigmatizing belief creates a quandary for poor job seekers. Jarrett (1996) points out that the perception that welfare recipients lack a strong work ethic may influence an employer's willingness to hire them. People seeking work will undoubtedly become discouraged that their prospects for getting a job are reduced before they even walk in the door of a prospective employer's office. Poor job seekers may eventually come to believe that they are unemployable and sink further into an abyss of learned helplessness. However, research has shown that this process is based on a fallacy.

Caputo (1997) examined the attitudinal characteristics of beneficiaries of public assistance. The subjects in this study were 12,686 adults who were part of the original National Longitudinal Survey of Youth in 1979. Interviews conducted in 1993 revealed that poor people have work ethics similar to those of nonpoor individuals. The reasons for use of public assistance by study participants had less to do with personality characteristics and more to do with structurally related needs. The factors that were found to affect whether or not subjects used public assistance included working fewer hours, the number of children in the family, the length of time spent in poverty, and being unmarried.

Just as children do not escape the risk associated with poverty, neither do they escape poverty's stigmatizing effects on self-worth and self-efficacy. Weinger (1998) used projective story-telling techniques to study children's perceptions of impoverished children's career opportunities. Weinger showed twenty-six children, ages five to thirteen, pictures of homes that would clearly be associated with living in either a poor neighborhood or a middle-class neighborhood. The participants were asked to tell stories about the career opportunities of children living in each of the homes. Results revealed that children who were perceived to be from poor backgrounds were thought to have fewer career opportunities than children from middle-class neighborhoods. Although the participants, who were all from low-income families, believed that their own chances for career success were good, they consistently viewed other poor children's future opportunities as quite limited. The children explained these limitations in terms of associating present resources with the ability to obtain future resources. Although children in this study believed success could be obtained with self-determination, they also perceived societal inequities that favor the nonpoor and provide better opportunities for the affluent. These children were clearly aware that the odds are stacked against poor children.

THE RESILIENCE MODEL

Thus far, a litany of risks associated with poverty have been identified. Although it is important to be aware of how risk factors impact impoverished families, it is much more important for the family therapist to be aware of how resilience helps families move beyond the risks. Just as the detrimental effects of poverty begin even before birth, so do the effects of resilience. Bradley and colleagues (1994) studied what leads to early resilience in infants considered to be in double jeopardy from being born at low weight and being born into poor families. These researchers studied the outcomes of 243 premature infants. They found that only about 10 percent were functioning in the normal range for cognitive, social, health, and growth parameters at age three. This small minority of at-risk infants were found to show early signs of resilience due to a combination of protective factors such as having an uncrowded home environment, a stable residence, safe play areas, the presence of a male adult/partner, acceptance, adequate play and learning materials, parental responsivity, limited use of physical punishment, and a variety of types of stimulation. Just as risk factors are thought to have cumulative harmful effects, this research suggests that the benefits of protective mechanisms also seem to be cumulative. The resilient infants were found to have three or more protective factors working in their favor. Because the presence of enough protective factors does not appear to be the norm in homes with poverty risk factors, it can be concluded that one focus of family intervention should be to cultivate the protective factors that lead to resilience.

The interplay between risk and resilience certainly occurs at many levels including the level of the individual; the microsystem level, which includes the family and immediate social networks; the exosystem level, which encompasses community factors such as neighborhood and local norms; and the macrosystem level, which relates to cultural and societal factors. Until recently theoretical and empirical work on resilience has focused on how the individual responds to disruptive life events. Because outcomes are typically measured at the individual level, it makes sense to invest time and energy in trying to understand what leads to individual resilience. Although person-specific traits such as locus of control or coping style certainly have important effects on resilience, further investigation into how those traits develop invariably returns to the presence of risk and protective factors in the individual's environment (Garmezy, 1993). The familial environment has paramount importance in that it mediates contact with factors operating at the community level and the societal level. Thus, a focus in family therapy should be on developing familial resilience which, in turn, will foster individual resilience.

To help families cultivate resilience, family therapists must have a meaningful understanding of the concept that can be effectively communicated to the client. Thus, it is important to make the resilience concept relevant to each individual family's experience with poverty. The general concept of resilience refers to the ability to respond effectively to adversity. Stressful life events can be conceptualized as falling on a dual axis continuum on which experiences range from mild to severe on one axis and from brief to enduring on the other. The grid in Figure 10.1 can be used as a means of charting a family's experience with economic adversity over time. Mapping out the family's economic history allows them to realize that the experience of poverty is dynamic and is affected by an infinite combination of individual, familial, community, and sociocultural factors. This exercise provides concrete evidence that the family has survived money problems in the past, thus illustrating their ability to overcome adversity. Also, the episodes on the grid that represent times when the family had minimal financial woes demonstrate evidence of their competence. Visually representing different chapters in the family's economic history may help them to see links between the severity of economic hardship and the development or exacerbation of problems within the family. Moreover, the family can gain perspective on how their strengths are evidenced differently depending on the current financial climate.

FIGURE 10.1. Economic Adversity Grid: The Dynamics of Severity and Longevity of Stressors

Enduring

						Credit Card Debt
		Lower Pay at New Job (2/99)	7			
			6			Emergency Room Bill (11/98)
1	2	3	5	6	7	8
			4			
			8			

Mild

Severe

FIGURE 10.1 (continued)

Insurance Cancelled (9/98)	4	
	3	Laid Off (8/98)
	2 Car broke down (6/98)	
Phone Disconnected (12/98)		
Bounced Check (6/98)	1	

Brief

For example, do they tend to pull together when times are the toughest? Or does the fabric of the family begin to disintegrate during difficulties, but repair itself once the stressor has been removed? Clearly, a family can have experiences at multiple points along the continuum of the poverty experience. Thus, resilience does not only refer to rebounding after adverse life events, but also managing the minor irritants so that they do not become major sources of distress.

Resilience can be viewed, not only as the mechanism that promotes rebound from adversity, but also as the buffer that protects the family from the potentially damaging effects of stressful life experiences. Put most simply, resilience is the ability to stay afloat while riding the ebb and flow of daily life and the capacity to return to the journey once the torrents of the occasional unavoidable storm have subsided. The ability to effectively cope with difficulty bears directly on whether the family will reap the benefits of the protective factors or processes that moderate the relationship between stress and risk. Protective factors, according to Rutter (1993), are those things that change responses to environmental hazards for the better. Protective factors exist at the individual, family, community, and societal level. Examples of family-level factors include attachment, parental management (rules, expectations, consequences, supervision), parent and nonparent adult influences, and the family's support networks.

McCubbin and McCubbin (1988) suggest that three key factors are associated with familial resilience. *Regeneration* refers to hardiness and coherence of the family unit. *Regenerative resilience* is evidenced through holding a shared worldview, especially regarding feeling confident that the family can overcome distress, reframing adversities as challenges, and seeing problems as solvable puzzles. *Rhythm* is an aspect of resilience that refers to how the family uses contact time, routines, and rituals as coping tools. McCubbin and McCubbin reserve the term "resilience" to refer to the family's capacity for flexibility and how much of a buffer the family's level of bonding provides against stress.

According to Hawley and DeHaan (1996), family resilience describes the path a family follows as it adapts to adversity and prospers in the face of acute and chronic stress. Thus familial resilience can be conceptualized as the choice of paths that the family makes on their journey toward desired goals and the way in which they respond to the beauties and hazards encountered along the chosen path. Germain and Gitterman (1980) assert that the function of therapists who approach treatment from a resilience perspective is to mobilize and enhance the "personal and environmental resources needed to motivate coping with life stress, providing support to elevate self esteem, and to help manage and regulate negative feelings aroused by life stress" (p. 495). Interventions should, then, be dually focused. First, goals of family therapy should be to reduce the risk level by assisting the family in identifying attainable goals and making appropriate choices that will allow them to move along the path to those goals. Also, interventions should be aimed at modifying perceptions of and responses to obstacles and pitfalls encountered along the journey.

Economic adversity can come in a variety of forms and have a wide range of consequences for the family's functioning. Financial strains can range from relatively mild matters such as underemployment, low wages, and lack of transportation to moderate stressors such as mounting revolving debt and substandard housing to severe stressors including health and household emergencies and homelessness. Although the more severe issues such as homelessness are particularly devastating economic crises for the family, each of these situations can be detrimental to the well-being of the family by gradually tearing away or suddenly shredding the fabric of the family bond.

Two fundamental themes are relevant to working with families living in poverty: self-efficacy versus dependence and growth versus stagnation. The competency-based approach to therapy addresses these issues by combining the foci of the solution-focused and resilience-oriented approaches. Solution-focused approaches address the issue of self-efficacy versus dependence. The essential question here is, "Does the family see itself as resourceful and able to effectively engage the environment or as dependent on others to meet their needs?" Greene and colleagues (1998) posit that solution-focused therapy hinges on the assumption that clients have the capacity to meet their own needs, set and attain desired goals, and successfully adapt to and/or modify their environments to produce optimal functioning. The function of therapy is to build on the family's inherent strengths and to help the family put their own resources to use.

Resilience-oriented approaches compliment the solution-focused approach by addressing the theme of growth versus stagnation. This question is concerned with, "Does the family seek to move through and grow from difficulties or does it become easily bound by challenging experiences?" Like solution-based approaches, resilience-based approaches also focus on the family's strengths rather than its deficits. However, viewing families through a lens of resilience, according to Walsh (1996) focuses not just on becoming aware of the presence of those strengths, but also on the process through which the family's resources are garnered and developed. Walsh contends that resilience approaches are concerned with the processes that enable families to cope with challenges to their existence and emerge hardier from crises or stresses.

Application

Synthesizing these two perspectives, which move away from seeing families as damaged to seeing them as challenged, attends to the reparative potential inherent to the family. Each approach has the ultimate goal of placing the power to control life in the hands of the client. Combining the benefits of both paradigms results in a model that rests on the position that strengths are forged through adversity and are waiting to be realized and concretely displayed. Each family can be viewed as a diamond in the rough. In contrast to medical models, the solutions to problems are not conceptualized as being outside of the client and needing to be imparted by the therapist; rather, the solutions are perceived as being part of the client's current inner resources. The family is viewed as the expert on how to go about applying solutions to its problems. The function of the therapist is to assist the client in removing the veil of stressors that may hinder clearly envisioning the family unit as resourceful and capable.

Restructuring the Experience of Poverty

The first step along the road to utilizing a competency-based approach to therapy is to conceptualize the family not as "poor people," but as people living in poverty. The former label denotes that the family itself is poor which, according to *Webster's New World Dictionary,* means that the family is "without resources, having little or no means to support [itself], feeble, lacking excellence, inferior, contemptible, lacking skill, and/or worthy of pity." Such connotations associated with the way a client is referred to will no doubt affect the clinician's perspective on the reasons underlying the family's current problems. Conversely, the latter term represents a condition in which the family currently exists and reminds the therapist and the client that the family's economic conditions are separate from their identity. Later in the chapter, we will explore how to restructure the clinician's view of the impoverished family.

If clinicians become ensnared in the murky depths of the stigma associated with poverty and/or become overwhelmed by the magnitude of the risk factors related to poverty, it will be difficult, if not impossible, for the therapist to genuinely guide clients toward seeing themselves as resourceful and capable of successfully navigating their own paths. Thus it is important that clinicians deal with their own schemata regarding families living in poverty and question whether they see the client as trapped by risk or liberated through their own resilience. Both clinician and clients will have to work together to address faulty cognitions regarding impoverished families.

Azar (1996) suggests clinicians must take three key steps to restructure their beliefs about the family affected by poverty. This process is intended to replace distorted beliefs with more adaptive assumptions. The process Azar intended for clinicians can be easily adapted and integrated into the process of therapy. By working together to challenge their existing schemas, both family and clinician can become aware of how those schemas affect their behavior and beliefs.

The first step in the process of restructuring the experience of poverty is to identify sources of bias. By discovering the origins of the stigmatizing images commonly associated with poverty, both client and therapist can begin to recognize the power and influence they exert on thoughts and behaviors. Azar suggests that sources of bias include the media, professional theoretical traditions, research data, and personal experiences. Although theory and research are primarily factors that will only directly affect the therapist, exploring the influence of the media and the history of personal experiences can be an effective way to bring the therapist and client to a point of shared understanding about how they came to hold their beliefs about poverty and how those beliefs relate to the process of therapy.

Azar suggests that this task could be accomplished by cataloguing evidence of bias in various media forms. Each family member and the therapist could be asked to monitor television programs, films, and printed media for one week. Information about how people living in poverty are portrayed can be recorded on a form similar to Figure 10.2. In a subsequent session, the family and therapist could share their findings. Important points for discussion around the effects of the portrayal of poverty in the media include historical views of poverty and how those images impact upon present beliefs and future expectations. Example of questions that may prove helpful in this process include: Who lives in poverty in America? What are some of the beliefs we have about why people remain in poverty? What do people living in poverty believe about themselves? Where did the beliefs originate? What do nonpoor people believe about impoverished families? How are the portrayals inferior to other families? In what ways are the strengths of people in poverty shown? The latter two questions can be used as a starting point to open a discussion about what "good" and "bad" families are supposed to be like and, thus, begin the process of bringing awareness to the problem issues the family is contending with. For example, the therapist could ask, "Which undesirable behaviors and patterns that people commonly associate with poverty actually are present within the family?" Similarly, a question such as, "Which positive aspects of the portrayal of poverty do family members see in themselves?" could be used to ascertain how the family sees its current strengths.

FIGURE 10.2. Media Exploration of Poverty Portrayals

Type of Media	What do the people look like?	How do they behave?	How do others respond to them?	What message did you receive?	How did you feel about what you saw?
TV					
Film					
Magazines					
Internet					

CHEVONNE (age 15)

Yeah, I hear everybody telling me that I messed up my life. They don't come right out and say it like that, but they give me this look when they see me with Samuel. I always see these posters at school with a picture of a girl carrying a backpack with her baby in it and she's looking all sad and stuff, like she knows what a big mistake she made. Or the one with the boy pushing the baby in the stroller talking about "this wasn't the set of wheels he wanted" or something like that. I think it's terrible that they try to make teenagers feel bad about their children. I know it's not the best way to have your kids, being young and still being in high school and all, but it's like they try to add more regrets to what you already feel. I mean I love my baby and I want him to have it all and to grow up happy. So why are they trying to make me feel bad about myself? That's not helping me or my baby, you know. You would think the schools would be the place to try to help you. I know they want to keep kids from having kids too young, but

(continued)

(continued)

it's like they don't realize how it makes people who already have kids feel. I mean yeah, I know it will be hard, but my dad and my aunt are going to help me. But people don't focus on whatever good can come of it, it's just always the bad parts they're talking about. You won't get a job, you'll always have to struggle, your baby needs more than you can give him and all like that. Who are they to tell me that I can't give my child the best? I'm giving him the best of me and working hard and trying hard but it's like that's not enough. I see now that people get their views of what a teenager mother can do from television and the news statistics and stuff. All people who haven't been through it know is what they read or what they see on TV. I wonder, have they ever really sat down and talked to a teenage mother? If you haven't walked in my shoes then you can't judge me. I didn't really even realize how it affects a person until I really sat down and thought about it. I know it's my fault I have a child now. I could have made different choices, but I also know that I can't handle it all by myself. I know I need people to show me what to do and help me learn to be a good parent. But I also know I need to do things for myself. Like it's up to me to get my homework done every day and still make sure my child is taken care of. But if my dad can help me by giving the baby a bottle or a bath then that helps me be able to do what I need to do. And then I thought, I can ask my friends to babysit for me sometimes. That way it helps me and it helps them too. Like it gives me time to do stuff I need to do and helps give me a break like we talked about so I don't get worn out from the baby all the time. And it helps them see what having a baby is really like. I think that's much better than slapping those silly posters up all over the place. I mean, it's like a way to help everybody without making anybody feel bad or dumb. Why don't they put programs like that in school instead of just talking at you and having you carry an egg around for a week and all that? It's like they think getting pregnant is something you're going to catch, like a cold or something. I mean if people had the real information then they wouldn't look down on other people, but they probably wouldn't imitate what they do either. You see it's a choice that some people made and you can make different choices, but everybody can have a happy life. Those posters don't ever show a girl and her baby laughing or playing or how good it feels when they smile at you or how you're proud when they make sounds and talk to you. I mean there's a lot of happy stuff that never gets shown. Having Samuel has brought my family closer. I mean my dad and my aunt didn't really talk much before the baby, but now they're so proud of him and always talking about him to everybody. And my getting pregnant got us the help we needed when I was a kid. My parents didn't take any classes or read books about how to raise kids. But now we've been able to talk about the good things and the bad things about how they raised us and so we can do better by Samuel.

Genograms

The genogram may be a useful tool for helping a family explore its historical competencies and challenges by tracing patterns of maladaptive behaviors, identifying how problems may be related to social and economic adversities, and shedding light on effective and ineffective coping traditions. For example, in working with a family trying to overcome issues of child maltreatment, a genogram could be used to illustrate historical patterns of child abuse and to trace how the problem has traditionally been addressed. Which family members dealt with the issue effectively? Which family members chose ineffective means of resolving problems? How could things have been changed? What prevented them from finding and maintaining more productive behaviors? What differences do they expect in present and future generations? How will those differences be enacted? These are some of the primary questions that will help the client identify personal solutions. Further, this exercise can be used to explore how patterns of socioeconomic adversity can be overlaid onto the patterns of maladaptive behaviors and coping strategies to illustrate the relationship between economic distress and generational transmission of abuse. This process may perhaps reveal an association between an extensive history of economic adversity and inadequate coping skills.

However, the family should not leave this experience feeling as though they exist within an inescapable cycle of poverty and abuse. Another layer of the genogram should focus on the resiliencies and competencies displayed despite the difficulties experienced. How has the family survived through generations of adversity? What are the historical strengths of the family? How are they demonstrated in the present? This exercise should have the ultimate goal of instilling hope that the current problems can be resolved by recognizing patterns that need to be altered and implementing changes by building on the already present strengths.

Solution Finding

Circular questioning, an effective technique that brings about awareness and prompts exploration of problems, can be equally effective in shedding light on solutions. The process of exploring solutions allows clients to see their problems as solvable and the solutions as within their grasp. Berg (1994) suggests that a dialogue of this sort includes the exploration of exceptions, outcomes, and coping. "Exploring the exception" asks the client to focus on times when the problem was not present or was less severe. Discussions of "outcome" relate to finding solutions and envisioning the differences expected after the solutions are implemented. Considering how they and others will be able to recognize that solutions have been applied is a way for clients to begin to concretely document the process of change. Asking clients to discuss how they have been able to contend with the current problem and/or different problems in the past provides evidence of their capacity for "coping."

Greene and colleagues (1998) suggest that a useful method for entering into this type of circular dialogue is through the use of the dream question. This technique could be used with the family by asking each member to imagine that they have a dream in which their current problems are solved. Although when they wake up they are unable to remember the details of the dream, they begin to notice that things have actually changed for the better. What changes will they notice in themselves? What differences will they see in other family members? What will nonfamily members notice? When has the family previously engaged in the adaptive behaviors demonstrated in the dream? This dialogue can then be extended into application by asking the clients to begin gradually enacting behaviors revealed in the dream. Although there are an infinite number of ways to reach the same end point in therapy, this technique is especially relevant for working with families living in poverty because the client is encouraged to see that they create their own solutions by garnering their resources and using those resources to alter the world around them for their benefit.

Metaphors, Themes, and Stories

Together, the information obtained about the family's history with adversity and the solutions generated through circular dialogue can be used to help clients develop metaphors and themes that serve to describe and give meaning to their experiences. Families can become aware of their own stories that may have been previously inaccessible to them. As they become more and more clear about the history of the problem and the source and nature of the solutions, the family's story develops a clear beginning and ending where, previously, there was only a middle (i.e., the presenting problem) without origin or conclusion.

Themes, metaphors, and stories are powerful ways to attach purpose to adversity and bring hope for transformation. For example, earlier in the chapter, the competency-based model was described as a way of seeing each family as a diamond in the rough. This diamond theme can be a powerful metaphor for families who have undergone substantial economic difficulty. The beauty and value of a diamond is directly related to the amount of time spent under pressure. The family can begin to see its history as the pressure that has formed and perfected them. Extending this model further can help the family become invested in the process of therapy. Often, families living in poverty are referred for therapy through social service agencies. The family typically sees the social service system as an intrusion on their lives. They often feel they have been judged unfairly and treated with disrespect. Initially, they may be quite resistant to the prospect of family therapy because it represents just another way to emphasize their faults and weaknesses. For a family who feels disenfranchised, powerless, and vulnerable, viewing the process of therapy as a way for the gem to be refined can remove a major barrier to progress. The diamond theme can even eventually be used to help the family understand the system that brought them into therapy in the first place. For a diamond, the process of being dislodged from a place where it has existed for millions of years must be a traumatizing experience. Further, no one particularly likes diamond miners. They carve up the earth and rob it of its treasures. Nevertheless, no matter how much disdain we hold for the miners, without them the world would never know the beauty of a diamond. Metaphors such as this are not only empowering, but uplifting and liberating as well. Once the family begin to see themselves as a collective diamond, they will be invested in protecting their newly realized treasure. The journey toward this healing and renewal begins with taking small steps toward mobilizing the resources and enacting the behavior that will bring about change.

Budgets

The goal of therapy, however, is not simply to place a rose-colored veil around the clients' problems by focusing only on their positive attributes while the negative aspects of their behavior are ignored. Rather, the ultimate goal of therapy is to help clients move beyond those factors that place them at risk through actualizing their resilience and integrating and extending the family's competencies throughout all aspects of their lives. Thus, in addition to restructuring their experiences with poverty, practical application of life skills must also be a therapeutic task.

Often, families with substantial financial stressors take a piecemeal approach to money matters. Because financial resources often do not stretch beyond meeting needs for food, clothing, housing, and so on, families living in poverty may proceed without a financial plan or goals. In so doing, money becomes the proverbial carrot at the end of the stick which commands and directs, rather than a tool which serves. Thus, the family budget can be an important focus of clinical attention.

Helping the family to develop a practical budget serves a twofold purpose. First, it is a concrete way for the family to look at its financial resources and demands. Many times, people operate without a real sense of how their money is being used over time. Using a budget allows the family to see which areas are a priority for them and helps them see how environmental pressures can easily overshadow other goals. A budget is a very practical tool that will allow the family to begin to make more effective use of its financial responsibilities. Second, the family budget can be used as a way of acquiring shared goals and common priorities.

Creating a family budget can (and should) be a collaborative process involving all family members. Each person should list items that they would like to see included in the budget. Once all items are listed they should be categorized according to what type of need they meet (shelter, food, education, clothing, recreation, etc.). Then the family should work together to prioritize the list. This process helps everyone agree upon what the most pressing needs are. Often, parents emphasize the lack of monetary resources by repeatedly making a general reference to their scarcity. Phrases such as, "We can't afford it" or "Money doesn't grow on trees" clearly communicate that the family has certain financial priorities, but those messages do not help the child to understand how his or her wants and needs fit into the family's financial plan. Sharing in the development of the budget helps children better understand how the family's income is being used to meet collective needs. Also, jointly developing the family budget allows everyone to have a more accurate view of exactly how much surplus remains after basic needs are met. Together, the family can make decisions about how and where to conserve resources. They can set family goals and agree to work within a unified financial plan.

Undoubtedly, multiple and potentially conflicting views of how some of the family's financial resources should be used will arise. The job of the therapist is to guide the family through the process of framing the multiple needs. Here it is important to distinguish between priority and value. Although many items on the family's budget list may not be high priorities, it is important to discuss reasons why such items are of value to the individual. Thus, while several wishes and desires may go unmet, the process of giving attention and consideration to them provides a validation of each person's needs. It is often the validation of worth, not the actual meeting of the need, that is paramount in diffusing conflicts around money.

Further, it may be necessary to educate a family about the importance of developing a budget that is comprehensive and not only addresses basic needs, but also devotes at least a modicum of the family's resources to things that provide sources of pleasure and personal fulfillment. The therapist should help the family frame these expenditures as different types of "basic" needs. Additionally, planning for a financial future that includes goals such as a college education for the children is often not a consideration for families who struggle to maintain stable, suitable housing and meet immediate goals such as paying the phone bill or having money for transportation for the week. However, although there may not be many, or sometimes any, resources to devote to long-range economic goals, the family should still include plans for attaining them in the budget. Thinking in terms of long-range goals rather than immediate and short-term needs can help the family to develop overarching objectives that permeate how they see themselves in the present and in the future. Although plans for the children's college education may not include trust funds and stock portfolios, the idea that parents are planning for their children's college education in some fashion sends a powerful message that the children's future paths will be quite different from their parents'. The point of this exercise is not to make irreversible decisions and unbreakable rules about how the family handles their finances. On the contrary, the goal is to begin to recognize that there are many different needs within the family that are all valid in some respect. Furthermore, the family should come to appreciate the value of each member's contribution toward the family's overall productivity.

A modified accounting balance sheet format provides a very concrete way to allow the family to see what assets they possess and how they are utilized. First, the family should identify all expenditures. These can be grouped into two main categories: expenses and investments. Expenses denote assets used to meet immediate needs such as housing, transportation, food, etc. Investments refer to use of resources based on expectations of future and/or long-term gains such as bank savings accounts and retirement plans. Other examples of investments include things such as taking care of health during pregnancy by getting regular prenatal care or investing in physical health and well-being by joining a community-sponsored exercise class or spending a little more money to buy healthier foods such as fresh fruits and vegetables. The purpose or benefits of each expenditure should be listed and discussed.

The same process can be repeated for nonmonetary expenditures. Nonmonetary expenses include factors such as the time and energy expended to meet daily obligations. These include activities such as going to school or work, doing homework and household chores, and participating in extracurricular and civic activities. When the purpose or benefits of these nonmonetary expenses are listed, many of them will also be shown to be important investments in the future. For example, the immediate benefit of doing homework may be getting good grades. However, good grades may translate into a college scholarship, and therefore, time spent doing homework is also an investment in an academic future.

A similar process should be used to identify the family's resources that can be classified as financial, practical, or social/emotional. Financial resources include all sources of income as well as the value of savings and real property. Practical resources refer to the family's assets and abilities that allow them to manage daily life tasks. For example, in addition to wages, having a grandparent who provides free baby-sitting services can be listed as an asset that helps defray the survival expenses. Similarly, young children or stay-at-home parents fulfill important concrete needs essential to the family's productivity such as cooking or picking up toys. Finally, social/emotional resources includes the all-important emotional support that comes through listening, laughing together, or giving hugs and should be listed as family resources. As each resource is identified, the purpose or benefit should also be clearly stated. Thus, the process of creating a comprehensive budget allows the family to see their financial responsibilities in relation to their economic and personal resources. Figure 10.3 provides an example of what a comprehensive budget might look like.

FIGURE 10.3. Comprehensive Budget

Monetary Expenditures

Type	Description	Purpose/Benefits	Monthly Cost
Expense	Rent/Utilities	Safety, comfort, stability	$600
	Food Bills	Health, not hungry	$400
	Car Payment/Ins.	Reliable way to get to work	$385
Investment	Savings Account	Plan ahead, prepare for emergencies	$100
	Health Insurance	Health maintenance and emergency care	$120
	Braces for Liz	Self-esteem	$85
	Prenatal Care	Have a healthy baby	$25

Nonmonetary Expenditures

Type	Description	Purpose/Benefits	Time Required
Expense	Going to School	Get a good education	30 hours/week
	Going to Work	Provide for family	50 hours/week
	Doing Homework	Get good grades	10 hours/week
	Helping with Homework	Get good grades	5 hours/week

FIGURE 10.3 *(continued)*

Nonmonetary Expenditures

Type	Description	Purpose/Benefits	Monthly Cost
Investment	PTA Meetings/ Activities	Be informed/active	4 hours/month
	Piano Lessons/ Practice	Self-fulfillment	4 hours/week
	Family Night	Family Bonding	3 hours/week

Resources

Type	Description	Purpose/Benefits	Value ($ or %)*
Financial	Wages	Pay bills	$500/week
	Food Stamps	Buy healthy foods	$125/month
Practical	Food Preparation	Feed the family	100%
	Housecleaning	Clean, comfortable home	100%
	Baby-sitting by grandparents	Allow parents free time Get to know grandparents	150%
Social/Emotional	Listening	See other's point of view	100%
	Showing Understanding	Make others feel valued	100%

* Monetary value or percentage of immediate family benefiting

Resource Manuals

Another useful activity that has great practical value is to develop a manual with information about local and national resources available to help the family meet its needs. The manual should list local social services agencies with descriptions of what services they provide and the population they are intended to serve. Spaces should be provided to list contact names and data that need to be submitted in order to be considered for services. Although the therapist should begin with offering information that is relevant to current pressing issues the family presents, clients should be encouraged to actively seek out information to add to the manual. The manual need not solely consist of service providers, but it can also be a place to catalogue information about school and occupational activities. Clients should be encouraged to stay aware of community events and actively participate in various neighborhood and community organizations.

MONICA (age 15)

We can't go anywhere or do anything. Mommy's always saying that "money don't grow on trees." I wanted to be on the basketball team at school, but she said I couldn't because we couldn't afford to pay the activity. So I said, "okay." I know she is doing the best she can and money is tight so I wasn't pressured about it. Then I said I wanted to be in this community choir with a lot of other kids from my church. All the money for trips and stuff comes from fund-raisers so the parents don't have to pay anything. All I needed was a dark blue skirt and a light blue top, which I already had. But then she said "No" because we didn't have transportation for me to get to rehearsals every week. She doesn't like for me to ride the bus by myself because it's dangerous and the choir practices late into the evening sometimes. It was always something like that. My friends were always saying, "Your mom is so strict, she don't let you out of the house to do nothing." I felt bad for being mad at Mommy. I see her going to work every day and I know she wants us to have good things. She always says, "You've never been hungry and you don't wear second-hand clothes. I couldn't say that when I was coming up." And I do appreciate that she makes sure we have everything we need for school work and stuff, but it's like she thinks we don't need a social life. She'll always say, "You don't need nothing but your family." Or, "You don't need to be hanging around those kids anyway because they're not your real friends if they talk about you like that." But, dang, kids are gonna talk about you if you're the only one who never gets to do anything.

Now that we see our budget, it's getting a little better. I mean Mommy says we still can't be spending money on stuff like Jordan's or nothing. But I never really wanted no Jordan's anyway because it don't make no sense to pay that much for some sneakers that somebody comes along and steals. I was never concerned about that kind of stuff, but now at least I can be involved in school activities. The money I made from working this summer, I used to pay the fees and stuff. I made enough money to pay the activity fee to be on the basketball team and I bought my own school clothes and supplies even though Mommy said she would buy them because that was her responsibility. But I see we have to make our money work for us so she can put the money for school supplies onto other bills. Like the electric bill was real high in August and I gave her $50.00 to put toward it. It felt good 'cause I did it 'cause I wanted to, not 'cause I had to. I may try out for cheerleading too this year. Even if I can't afford to pay to get the uniforms and go to camp, I just want to see if I can make the team. Mommy said she would help me though if I really wanted to do it. I think she was kinda proud watching me play basketball.

The process of developing the manual can be empowering in itself because it is an opportunity for people to become informed consumers who are aware of their rights and responsibilities. Because parents who seek services such as AFDC often feel devalued and unfairly treated by social service workers, it is necessary that parents be prepared to respond appropriately when they feel their rights have been violated. Often service agencies stigmatize clients or only provide minimal assistance and information. Homework assignments in which they are asked to initiate contacts with people from their directory will be useful for developing the client's feelings of self-efficacy about engaging various organizations and systems. Learning how to negotiate these contacts is vital to developing and maintaining feelings of empowerment. Clients may need to rehearse contacts and practice how to get the information they need from busy case workers and staff. Using written lists of specific questions to be asked and a checklist of information to be obtained is often useful.

HERNANDO (age 24)

They call me Mr. Mom at Ariana's school now and Ariana is doing really well. I was really upset when we got a letter saying she was having problems behaving in class. Me and Elana went up there to talk to the teacher and the counselor. They said Ariana wasn't paying attention and couldn't sit still. She said we should have her tested for attention disorder. I knew she wasn't hyper. She's a really sweet child. She's always getting into things, but she always does what we tell her. Ms. Maxey said sometimes kids don't show any problems until they get into school and have to keep to the structure of the classroom and Ariana might need medicine to help her pay attention. They said health insurance might cover the testing, but we didn't have any insurance. So I called the school system and asked for information. They said because Ariana was in Head Start, she would have to wait until she was in kindergarten before the school system could do the testing. They said even if the kindergarten teacher recommended her for testing, it would probably not be until close to the end of the year before she would get tested. We didn't want her falling behind in school before she even got started, so we started making a lot of calls to see if we could get some help. That's how we found the Center for Children and Families. We got Ms. Vann as our case worker. She knew the system and found us a place that would test Ariana and let us pay according to our income and we didn't have to pay it all at once. Mr. Quarles did the evaluation. He said the results showed that Ariana was fine and she was really smart for her age. He said the problem might have been that Ariana had been at home with Elana all her life and she always got to go outside whenever she wanted to and she wasn't used to a structured situation

(continued)

(continued)

like kids who maybe went to day care or preschool. We took the report back to Head Start and they still didn't want to believe it. We had been going to the open houses and all the parent meetings and doing everything the teacher and the counselor suggested and they were still saying our child was "hyper." Then one day when I was off from work, I decided to visit her classroom. I didn't like what I saw, not one bit. The teacher didn't let the kids talk or show any energy or anything. They expected those four- and five-year-old kids to sit and pay attention like they were in college or something. I couldn't blame them for not paying her any attention. Ms. Maxey was so boring and didn't have any life to her at all. All she kept saying was, "Sit down" and "Be quiet," but she didn't give them any reason to want to behave. Even I know you have to grab a child's attention. They're not just going to sit still and listen to somebody talk. And that teacher's aide was even worse. I couldn't believe she was yelling at those kids like that. I did not send my child to school to be yelled at. Well, you better believe I was in that director's office making a big fuss. I asked them for their guidelines and standards and it said each classroom should have an evaluation done every year. I asked to see the evaluation for Ms. Maxey's class. Ms. Katz was very nice and pulled the evaluations from the year before. I felt really good when she said that the evaluators had some of the same comments I was talking about. I asked for Ariana to be moved to a different classroom and things were much better. I don't know if those teachers are still there or not, but I make sure that everybody at the school knows me and that I know what's going on. I visit her class about once a month as a helper and I worked on a PTA committee to work out a system for parents to be able to give comments to the teachers and the principal. I kept all the information I got when I was running around trying to get Ariana tested in my resource manual. We still participate in the Center for Children and Families support groups.

MULTIFAMILY GROUPS

The multifamily group offers a great advantage for working with families in poverty because it allows clients to recognize the universal nature of the experience of poverty. Just as in traditional group therapy, clients can benefit from the curative effects of seeing their problems as human experiences shared by many others. In the multifamily setting, clients can share their experiences with economic hardship, stigmatization, marginalization, and so on. Moreover, multifamily groups help reduce the social isolation that families in poverty tend to experience.

Becvar, Ray, and Becvar (1996) suggest that all families have resources which may be useful to other families. They proposed the concept of reciprocal foster families in which kin and nonkin networks function as support systems. By pooling resources and sharing tasks such as child care, home maintenance and repair, communicating information, and offering advice, families can develop their own systems of social support and build important alliances.

By interacting with other families, clients benefit from the social referencing that helps to normalize some of their experiences. Furthermore, because clients perceive that others truly understand their situation, families may be more receptive to solutions generated with the help of their peers than when those alternatives are developed with the therapist alone. Multifamily groups also provide a platform for testing the reality of individual views about living in poverty. The group setting provides an arena for challenging the stigmatizing views of impoverished parents and children that group members may hold. One technique that can be useful is an extension of the media exploration. Families can be separated into teams and given the task of providing evidence from their own knowledge and experiences that contradicts the stereotypes and debunks the negative descriptors as invalid, unsubstantiated, and/or broad overgeneralizations.

The multifamily group experience is particularly useful for exploring cross-generational issues. The Greek Chorus technique can be adapted to use in the multifamily setting such that observing group members provides feedback to clients about their perceptions of familial interactions acted out during role-play exercises. In the single-family encounter, both parents and children may be unwilling try new ways of interacting with one another. However, by taking advantage of the opportunity to create different adult-child combinations by mixing members from different families for experiential exercises, both adults and children are given a clean slate with which to practice new behaviors and patterns of interaction. Once they accept that they actually have the capacity to relate differently, more adaptive patterns can be translated to real familial interactions.

Often, providing separate group experiences for adults and children is an effective method for working through blocks that have previously prevented clients from resolving conflicts and moving ahead. Working in age-matched groups can remove some of the pressure to maintain control and allow clients the opportunity to entertain alternative viewpoints. At the same time, age-matched groups may provide validation of feelings. Group facilitators may find it useful to allow each generation to speak to the other as a group. Family members who have difficulty communicating with one another can benefit from hearing the same messages coming from nonfamily members.

The pitfall to avoid in multifamily group therapy is for participating families to begin to separate themselves from other families who live in

JANICE (age 40)

At first I felt we were being picked on when everybody was trying to say that I wasn't giving my kids love and affection. They didn't know what it was like to grow up like I did. When I was coming up, we didn't always have enough food to feed all eight of us and we didn't always have clothes that fit. I remember wearing shoes with holes in them for months before we could afford new ones. My uncle molested me and my father beat me and my mother half to death because he didn't have anybody else to take his pain out on. How could anybody say I wasn't giving my children love? Here we are working fifteen- and twenty-hour days at the shop trying to keep the business growing and reduce expenses so we can turn more and more profit which comes home for the kids to have what they need. Wendell and I were breaking our backs trying to give them everything we never had and yet they're acting up all the time, getting in trouble at school, and constantly fighting with each other. I really couldn't understand it. Why was I being blamed for doing what I thought every good parent should do? And who are they to judge me? I know now that I was being defensive about it because I thought to myself, "Yeah, they can afford to stay home with their kids and have play time all the time because half of them are on welfare and the other half work in little dead-end jobs that will never amount to anything. They don't know what it is to own your own business where you don't just pick up your paycheck every week." Sometimes we have to invest money back into the business to replace equipment or cover the insurance. Sometimes we have to use the household money to keep things in stock until we collect on some accounts. We don't have the luxury of sitting around the dinner table playing Monopoly like some family on TV. For us, time really is money. I felt like we were focusing on the important things like getting our kids out of that rough neighborhood, but that means we have to make the mortgage payment every month. I thought all they needed was food, clothing, and shelter, and protection from people who might hurt them. All we asked in return was for them to go to school, stay out of trouble, and behave around the house. Those are real simple things and I honestly was very upset that they weren't doing it. I took it as they were being disrespectful and unappreciative of what they had. I felt like, how dare my kids act like they have it so tough? They really don't know what it means to be abused. The spankings they got were nothing compared to the beatings I got from my father. And I mean beatings to the point where I had black eyes and bruises. Now that's child abuse. I was doing every-thing I possibly could to raise my kids right and now these people are telling me I'm wrong? That just didn't make any sense to me. I couldn't accept what the group was saying until I saw the kids do their skit. It didn't matter what kind of family they came from, they all had the same mes-sage. All the kids wanted their parents to connect with them, really be with them and hear them. It didn't matter if their parents didn't spend time

(continued)

(continued)

with them because they were with a boyfriend, or working, or high on drugs, or whatever—they wanted that time more than anything else. I know it was Natasha and Paul's idea to make the skit like a stockbrokers' meeting because they always hear us talking about investments. Even though my own kids said the same thing to me before, in all different ways, I really didn't hear them because I was too busy defending myself, saying that they were too young to understand that it was all for them. And in a way it was, but in a way it was me trying to make up for all the hurt I experienced as a child by giving my kids material things. I see now that I was trying to undo the past and make my family look and act like I thought a family was supposed to. I believed that giving my kids those things was showing them that I loved them. I thought I was better than those parents who weren't even trying to make a better way for their children. But now I saw my kids saying the same thing as the children of those parents I thought I was better than. I'm kind of ashamed that it took all that for me to wake up, but at least now I can start doing something about it.

impoverished conditions and take on a "we-they" attitude that continues to pigeonhole families who do not appear to be actively involved in self-improvement activities. Rather than allow families to tear down others, the job of the facilitator is to help the group identify the strengths and competencies in those families who may embody many of the stereotypes associated with poverty. The reciprocal fostering that develops within the group can be extended to offering assistance to non-group members. By helping others, the participating families can further bolster their confidence in their ability to meet their own needs by realizing that they also have resources to help meet the needs of others.

PROFESSIONAL CONSULTATION AND TRAINING

Families in treatment are not the only ones who should consider actively reaching out to others. The therapist can have far-reaching effects on the service systems that families in poverty encounter by providing consultation and training services. Kaplan et al. (1996) suggest that family therapists work with social service agencies with the goal of helping other professionals foster resilience within the families they serve. Family therapists can teach basic concepts of competency-based approaches and assist social service workers in developing a focus on the family's strengths while helping them to develop competency in areas where they are challenged.

In addition to the media exploration activity, Azar's approach to cognitive restructuring for the professional includes two additional steps. After becoming aware of how we buy into the stereotypes and myths about poverty, it is important for professionals to determine what type of paradigm influences their expectations of and responses to clients living in poverty.

Brickman et al. (1982) suggest four possible models. Under the *moral model*, individuals are viewed as being responsible for their problems and their solutions. The *enlightenment model* presupposes that while individuals are responsible for their problems, the solutions must be given to them from a source outside of themselves. Thus, they become enlightened about why they are having problems and how to go about solving them. By contrast, the *medical model* sees the problem as a disease. The individual has little power over the cause and no power over the cure. To stop the disease, clients need not understand the disease nor the treatment. All that is necessary is full compliance with the prescribed course of treatment. Finally, the *compensatory model* takes the position that although the problem may have originated from sources outside of the client, it is up to individuals to compensate for the deficits imposed upon them and overcome the barriers they encounter.

Understanding how the professional views the development and response to impoverished living conditions sets the stage for how the issues will be addressed and where intervention will be targeted. Each way of conceptualizing the problems associated with poverty has merits and drawbacks. Under the moral model, the family's behaviors and choices are viewed as the only factors that will determine their future course. While the family is seen as having the capacity to make adaptive decisions, the professional who espouses the moral model may believe that it would be futile to offer assistance to the clients beyond that which the clients specifically request, as the clients' requests are a direct indication of their goals. Thus, these professionals may limit the options they present to the clients and may not be a strong advocate on the clients' behalf. By contrast, those who fancy themselves as sources of enlightenment will see it as their responsibility to provide clients with the solutions to their problems and thus may provide a number of useful options for clients to take advantage of. However, this approach is often perceived as being highly intrusive in that social service workers may provide step-by-step instructions about how clients should live their lives. Since professionals who adhere to the medical model see the client as a victim of a disease, less blame is ascribed to the client for their circumstances. However, the level of intrusiveness of the intervention is generally equal to, if not greater than, that of workers who subscribe to the enlightenment model. Because the professional believes he or she holds the keys to changing the client's situation, they may attempt to alter the family's entire system of functioning. In so doing, many unique and valuable traits that not only define the family but have been instrumental to its survival may be lost. Similarly, in treating many illnesses (cancer, for example), healthy aspects of the individual are often jeopardized in the process of trying to eradicate the disease.

Finally, the compensatory model seeks to empower the clients to solve their own problems by making better choices, building collaborative networks, and learning about and accessing resources. The intervening professional collaborates with clients to find workable solutions. The disadvantage of this model is that clients are not asked to take ownership of the origins of their problems. Becoming aware of how their own behavior impacts upon their circumstances is an essential step in becoming empowered to take control of their lives.

It is important for the intervening professional to recognize how he or she may be preventing clients from reaping the full benefits of being involved with a service delivery agency. It is equally important that social service professionals have their own sense of self-efficacy regarding their ability to be maximally effective in their jobs. After months or years of seeing many clients flounder in their efforts to overcome obstacles, many professionals see their efforts as worthless. Family therapists can intervene to help build self-efficacy among the staff. For example, sharing success stories instills hope that the system does indeed work. These successes are also a way of further challenging the professional's schema regarding families in poverty.

SELF-EXPLORATION:
FAMILY RESILIENCY AND POVERTY

1. What did your family of origin believe about the reasons people lived in poverty? How were the messages conveyed? In what ways do the lessons you learned about poverty from your family still influence your views today?
2. Conduct a media exploration for one week. Pay special attention to the portrayal of poverty in various media forms including television, film, television news, newspapers, cartoons, music, talk radio, posters, etc. Complete the media exploration exercise in Figure 10.2. How does the portrayal of poverty affect you personally and professionally?
3. Have you ever encountered disconfirming evidence about the stereotypes associated with poverty? What were the sources of this evidence? How were your beliefs influenced by it?

Chapter 11

Chronic Illness in Children: Stressors and Family Coping Strategies

M. Seren Cohen

PREVALENCE AND NATURE OF PSYCHOLOGICAL DISORDERS

The Chronically Ill Child

Compared with healthy peers, children with ongoing health conditions experience higher rates of mental health problems. These include psychological and emotional disorders, abnormal behavioral symptoms, and school-related adjustment problems (Silver, Westbrook, and Stein, 1998). One large-scale epidemiological survey found the odds of developing a diagnosable psychiatric disorder in a child with a chronic physical illness were approximately 2.2 to 1 (Pless and Nolan, 1989). Another epidemiological study found four- to sixteen-year-olds with chronic health problems were 2.4 times more likely to have a diagnosable behavioral disorder (Cadman et al., 1987; Goldberg et al., 1997).

A meta-analysis provided by Lavigne and Faier-Routman (1993) found: (1) children with physical disorders are at greater risk of overall adjustment problems, including internalizing and externalizing symptoms; and (2) family/parent variables, child self-concept and intelligence, and life stress were more powerful predictors of child adjustment than disease severity or prognosis.

Bennett (1994) reviewed sixty empirical studies of depression among chronically ill children and adolescents. The median prevalence rate for major depressive disorder or an unspecified depressive disorder was 9 percent across eighteen studies using standardized diagnostic interviews (n = 1,063), compared to an estimated prevalence rate of 1 percent to 5 percent among community-dwelling children. Forty-two additional studies measured depressive symptoms (n = 3,002), the majority of which were based on child self-report to standardized instruments, e.g., Children's Depression Inventory. These studies found ratings of depressive symptoms among children were slightly higher, approximately one-fourth of one standard deviation, above controls. Although great variability in depressive symptoms was found among children with the same disorder, children with certain disorders (asthma, recurrent abdominal pain, and sickle-cell anemia) were at greater risk than children with others (cancer, cystic fibrosis, diabetes mellitus). Unpredictability of symptoms, pain management, and lower levels of home treatment with reduced family involvement (e.g., reduced "buffering") were suggested as potential variables contributing to differential depression risk.

Like Lavigne and Faier-Routman (1993), Bennett's 1994 meta-analysis found illness factors (type, severity, duration) relatively poor predictors of depression. He interpreted results as suggesting that variables known to predict depression among physically well children (e.g., life stress, family system factors, attributional coping styles) might also be powerful explanatory factors among youngsters coping with illness.

The Parents

Chronic illness in a child presents mental health risks to parents. A variety of illness factors and caregiving burdens increase parental stressors and strains, as well as vulnerability to depression and marital discord (Quittner, Opipari, Regoli, et al., 1992; Thompson et al., 1994; Silver, Bauman, and Ireys, 1995; Ievers and Drotar, 1996; Quittner et al., 1998).

Studies have failed to demonstrate, however, that medical indicators of disease severity or physician ratings of severity predict parents' psychological status. This suggests that factors other than illness severity influence parental adaptation (Silver, Westbrook, and Stein, 1998). Furthermore, while the specific nature of the relationship between childhood illness and parental functioning remains unclear, two working hypotheses appear accepted. First, substantial evidence indicates that childhood illness has a powerful impact on the total family system, including fathers (Drotar, 1992; Roberts and Wallander, 1992; Quittner et al., 1998). Second, recent research suggests that concrete, behavioral demands of illness, rather than its medical severity, sheds light on factors affecting the mental health of mothers and fathers (Silver, Westbrook, and Stein, 1998; Quittner et al., 1998).

Mothers, Fathers, and the Two Together

Research has neglected fathers as well as role differences between mothers and fathers. Some findings are emerging: Mothers have more involvement in treatment and interact more with health providers (Haunstein, 1990; Silver, Westbrook, and Stein 1998); mothers perform more caregiving at home (Quittner, Opipari, Regoli, et al., 1992; Silver, Westbrook and Stein, 1998); children's ongoing health conditions are associated with higher levels of distress among mothers than fathers (Engstrom, 1991; Timko, Stovel, and Moos, 1992; Silver, Westbrook, and Stein, 1998). Fathers report greater stress in relation to finances and emotional attachment to the child (Quittner, Opipari, Michel, et al., 1992; Holmbeck et al., 1997; Kazak, 1997). Findings about mother/father interactions have particular significance for family therapists. For example, Timko, Stovel, and Moos (1992) found the best predictor of maternal or paternal mental health after one year was the spouse's level of depression. These results suggest support of the marital dyad is a crucial element in family system intervention. Keep the couple dyad strong and supportive and each partner/parent will be protected.

Siblings

A growing body of research indicates childhood illness impacts the total family system, well siblings included. Parents may have less time to spend in social and recreational activities that nurture well siblings and support their development (Quittner, Opipari, Regoli, et al., 1992). Well siblings may also experience differential treatment in relation to the child with the illness (McHale and Pawletko, 1992; Quittner and Opipari, 1994). Research suggests that over one-half of well siblings exhibit psychological or behavioral symptoms. Parental distress has been associated with increased behavioral problems in well siblings, suggesting a mediating effect between parents' ability to cope with their sick child's illness and their ability to parent well siblings (Cadman, Boyle and Offord, 1988; Tritt and Esses, 1988; Wamboldt and Levin, 1995).

THE BAD NEWS ABOUT PREVALENCE

Ireys, Werthamer-Larsson, Kolodner and Gross (1994) studied the prevalence of psychiatric symptoms among young adults with a chronic condition since childhood (age, M = 21.9). The age-stratified, random sample was diversified by culture (79 percent European-American, 15 percent African-American, 4 percent Hispanic) and diagnostic group (35 percent congenital condition; 31 percent musculoskeletal; 30 percent central nervous system and/or sensory functional loss). Approximately 70 percent were never married, 60 percent were living with parents or relatives, and 30 percent were living with spouses or significant others.

Over 30 percent of this patient population exhibited severe symptoms of mental health distress, predominated by depressive disorders. Multivariate analysis showed that four factors predicted psychopathology: poor future prognosis, restricted activity days, communication problems, and unpredictability of symptoms. The significant risk among this population underscores the importance of effective assessment and intervention among younger patients and families.

THE GOOD NEWS ABOUT PREVALENCE

Families facing serious pediatric illness are essentially ordinary families facing extraordinary stressors (Kazak, 1997). The majority of families coping with chronic childhood illness are capable and the children resilient. Illness stressors, however, are associated with greater mental health risks.

The general outline emerging from prevalence indicates:

- the majority of families and children present resourceful competence;
- they also carry an increased burden of psychiatric symptoms and risk;
- fortunately, the factors most powerfully associated with child and family outcomes are those most accessible to clinical assessment and therapeutic change: *family system variables* that support the health of the *total* family.

A FAMILY SYSTEMS FRAMEWORK
FOR UNDERSTANDING CHRONIC ILLNESS

"Chronic illness happens to a family, not just an individual" (Patterson and Garwick, 1998). The Family Adjustment Adaptation Response model (FAAR) conceptualizes family adaptation to illness as a process emerging out of the total family system. The *total family system* becomes the unit of assessment and intervention. It evolves in a dynamically changing biopsychosocial landscape. It affects and is affected by the illness experience because the family and illness are viewed as sharing reciprocal, interactive relationships.

Families, like all systems, attempt to maintain balance. When faced with a stressor, such as illness, the family uses *capacities* (i.e., internal and external resources and coping skills) to meet *demands* (i.e., internal and external stressors and strains). Implicit and explicit *meanings* mediate the family's experience of "balancing" family life between stressful demands and protective resources. Indeed, recent research indicates three key findings regarding interactions between family systems and chronic illness (Campbell, 1993, 1995). First, the demands of childhood chronic illness impose severe stressors on families. Second, resources of the family system impact the course of illness and patient outcomes. Third, the most powerful factors affecting patient and family adaptation to illness are concentrated in the *family system* as a whole (this includes the implicit and explicit meanings the family constructs about the illness).

ILLNESS DEMANDS

Impact of Illness

The historic research record includes a debate regarding "which comes first," the illness or family dysfunction? Early theorists such as Minuchin, Baker, and Rossman (1975) presented interpretations regarding "psychosomatic" families. These were later viewed as attributing illness to family psychopathology in such a way that families were "blamed" for illness.

Gustafsson, Bjorksten, and Kjellman (1994) took up the challenge of examining whether family factors predicted development of a childhood disorder. Pregnant women and their partners were recruited by physicians if one or both parents and one current child had an atopic illness. The initial assessment found 20 percent of the infants "healthy," 70 percent with recurrent wheezing or eczema, and 10 percent with recurrent infections without atopy.

Family systems were evaluated first at three months and then at the times of infant clinical evaluations. Approximately 37 percent of families were found to have dysfunctional patterns at the first evaluation. The most common dysfunctional pattern was low cohesion.

The three-month family evaluation did not predict development of future illness or recurrent infections. However, families of children who developed chronic wheezing or recurrent infections were statistically more likely to be found dysfunctional at eighteen months than were families of children who were healthy or developed eczema. A comparison of family evaluations at three and eighteen months found that families whose children remained healthy or developed eczema were more likely to remain or become functional during this time period. There were no consistent relationships between type of illness and degree of dysfunction. The factor that best predicted family dysfunction was the number of stressful life events. The authors conclude that family dysfunction does not precipitate development of asthma. Instead, families coping with illness stressors are more likely to develop dysfunctional family patterns. Furthermore, the psychosocial demands of asthma present families with two stressful factors: (a) constant unpredictability and (b) recurrent threat (via infections). These demands are relatively more stressful than those found among families coping with stable, less threatening chronic illnesses such as eczema.

These results suggest that illness demands contribute substantially to associations between family systems and chronic illness. Dysfunctional family patterns appear to be associated more with the *impact* of childhood chronic illness than with its *cause* (Campbell, 1995). The impact of illness is seen clearly in the next section.

The "Plus Factors" of Illness Demands

Families dealing with chronic illness face the same stressors and strains faced by other families. Plus, they must bear added demands presented by chronic illness. These constitute an additional "plus factor." The plus factors include: (a) stressors and strains on parents ranging from financial pressures to stress interacting with providers and insurers to loss of free time for other family members and personal pursuits; (b) existential themes of grief, isolation, and threats to integrity; and (c) marital strains and role conflicts.

FAMILY SYSTEM RESOURCES
AND FAMILY SYSTEM DYNAMICS

Balanced Coping: "Putting the Illness in Its Place"

The importance of the total family system emerges throughout the literature. In a study assessing psychosocial correlates of child adjustment to chronic illness, Lavigne and Faier-Routman (1993) found family variables and life stress more powerful predictors than disease factors or SES. Drotar (1997) found adaptive family relationships and parental psychological adjustment useful predictors of child adjustment, and less adaptive family relationships consistently predicted poor child adjustment. Holden et al. (1997) studied 112 children with diabetes or asthma and found that differences in adjustment attributable to specific illnesses became insignificant once general family factors were controlled. Ireys and Silver (1996) found the mothers' perception of illness impact on *total* family life was a significant predictor of maternal mental health.

Balanced Coping: Seeing the Whole Child in the Whole Picture

An exceptionally clear portrait of the power of balanced coping comes from results reported by Perrin, Ayoub, and Willett (1993). The study included 187 children with diverse chronic conditions and a subgroup of healthy controls. The study included three "observers" who reported child adjustment: the child, the parent, and the teacher. For all children, quality of family life was the most powerful predictor of child adjustment. It had a substantial, independent, and direct effect regardless of health status or observer. This result was not caused by a differential influence of any one family variable (e.g., cohesion). It was due to the synergistic effects of the total family system.

Results indicated that "all else being equal," healthy children tended to be rated by all observers as being better adjusted than children who have a chronic illness. However, "all else is *not* equal" (Perrin, Ayoub, and Willett, 1993). Observer differences were found and these interacted with variables such as a child's health status, verbal intelligence, family environment, and maternal health locus of control. Each observer contributed distinctive perceptions that added directly and substantially to the clinical assessment.

Children with *orthopedic* conditions appeared to be as well or better adjusted than their healthy peers. Their conditions are visible, stable, and do not interfere with nonmotor brain functions. Children with *cerebral palsy* were perceived by their parents to be at special risk; the children, however, saw themselves as almost as well adjusted as their peers. The static, visible nature of the condition may again contribute to perceptions of self-control that support coping and help shape stable perceptions from others. Children with *seizure disorders* have conditions with less visible and predictable effects. Less than one-half of teachers were aware of children's seizure diagnoses, unlike the clearly visible conditions among children with cerebral palsy and orthopedic impairments. Despite verbal intelligence in the average range, these children were more likely to be rated by teachers as less well adjusted. The expression of seizure symptoms also often involves intermittent, nonvisible behaviors that may present as "daydreaming" or "inattentiveness" and may have affected the teacher's perceptions.

Factors Mediating Adjustment

Several risk and resistance factors combined to support a resilient child's self-righting tendencies or to stress another child's coping mechanisms: (1) Quality of family life had a powerful, independent, and direct effect regardless of health status or observer. (2) Maternal health locus of control and children's verbal intelligence appear to interact together with the specific nature of the illness. Mothers' beliefs about the determinants of their own health may influence their perceived control over their children's health outcomes. (3) Gender seems to be an important predictor of psychosocial adjustment regardless of illness status. All observers rate girls as better adjusted than boys. Furthermore, this finding is consistent with other research showing boys with chronic illness exhibit significantly greater levels of emotional and behavioral distress when compared to healthy boys (Gortman et al., 1990; Holden et al., 1997).

Other Significant Family System Variables

Personal Resources

Psychological resources of self-esteem, self-efficacy, and a sense of mastery have often been identified with better health outcomes for a variety of chronic conditions (Kager and Holden, 1992; Silver, Bauman, and Ireys, 1995).

Family Structure

Family organization has been identified by many studies as a factor that promotes adaptive behavior. Structural resources include clarity of rules and expectations; routines for daily family tasks; clear generation boundaries with a parental hierarchy; reliable discipline; and marital relationships characterized by mutual support, intimacy, satisfaction, and shared goals (Patterson and Garwick, 1994).

Flexibility

The ability to shift priorities, create new rules for new situations, and learn new behaviors is associated with better outcomes in chronic illness

(Watson, Henggeler, and Whelan, 1990). Families overwhelmed by demands may substitute rigid adherence to routines for authentic balance and stability.

Cohesion

Family cohesion is probably the most emphasized resource of adaptive families (Patterson and Garwick, 1994). This is consistently reported as a powerful factor mediating better outcomes for patient and family coping with chronic illness (Daniels et al., 1987; Biegel, Sales, and Schulz, 1991; Wallander and Varni, 1989; Varni, Wilcox, and Hanson, 1988; Hamlett, Pellegrini, and Katz, 1992; Patterson and Leonard, 1994).

CLINICAL ASSESSMENT OF FAMILY MEANINGS: THE MEANING OF ILLNESS EVOLVES

The Family Systems-Illness Model (Rolland, 1998) accentuates the significance of meaning in the family's illness experience. A primary developmental task for the family facing chronic illness is to create meanings that promote competence and mastery (Rolland, 1998). A primary task of the clinician is to *listen* for family meanings that underlie descriptions and images used to relate the illness experience. It is then possible to develop interventions that enable the family to develop affirmative meanings congruent with family values and cultural traditions.

Rolland suggests a basic premise: there are not good and bad beliefs. Instead, what matters is the quality of "fit" between a family's belief system, the psychosocial demands of the illness, and the belief system of providers.

One aspect of the quality of fit is the congruence of shared beliefs. Another is the pace at which families process information and create useful meanings. The family pace may not match the speed with which providers give information. Remaining attuned to a family's pace for acknowledging and processing illness demands is an important aspect of the quality of fit. Rolland (1998) emphasizes that meanings of the illness evolve over time for the family. Research regarding illness schemas suggests that the cognitive frames used to guide illness behavior develop gradually and change as experience informs perception (Crisp, Ungerer, and Goodnow, 1996; Clemmey and Nicassio, 1997; Schiaffino, Shawaryn, and Blum, 1998). This work supports Rolland's view that meaning is shaped by belief content but evolves over time.

According to Rolland, significant beliefs include: (1) early "frames" of the illness, (2) normality, (3) mind-body beliefs, (4) mastery and control; (5) causes of illness, and (6) cultural and gender-related health beliefs about illness roles and behaviors. Each of these are discussed, now, in greater detail.

Early "Frames" of the Illness

The beginning of a family's illness experience often unfolds in turmoil. Discussions with providers about the nature, cause, and prognosis of the disorder help the family form their first cognitive "frame" of the illness. This frame often forms when family members are in states of acute, reactive stress, and so vulnerable to intended as well as unintended messages. These early experiences are also crucial to forming trusting collaboration between the family, physician, and other providers. Clinicians can support the family's capacity to receive helpful information and clarify misunderstandings. Exploratory questions can help families process these framing events.

Useful questions include, "What was this time like for you? How did these first experiences shape your ideas and actions about living with the symptoms and treatments? Did these early experiences affect your relationship with physicians or other providers?" Early assessment and intervention in family experiences during the "framing" period can support the growth of trusting family-provider collaborations that optimize care.

Family Beliefs About Normality

Families often hold implicit beliefs about conformity, help seeking, and where one "should" be on a perceived continuum between normal and abnormal. These beliefs may be powerful players in adaptation to chronic illness. For example, seeking help may be associated with weakness or shame. "Normal" may be equated with "problem-free." Such beliefs restrict a family's ability to use support or communicate candidly about symptoms and concerns.

Two questions may help clinicians explore these beliefs: "How do you think other average families would deal with a similar situation?" This question may provide a good indication of what family members perceive as typical. Another question, "How would a healthy family cope with your situation?" invites the family to express what is optimal or desirable. It can also be helpful for providers to normalize a biopsychosocial frame of illness in which interactions between illness and stress, rather than being "psychosomatic," are "normal" in the interaction between thoughts, feelings, and symptoms.

Mind-Body Beliefs

Beliefs about the relationship between mind and body also influence interaction between family members and health care professionals. Tremendous diversity in mind-body beliefs emerges from culture, religion, ethnic traditions, and individual life experience. It is helpful to distinguish four distinct assumptions regarding the "mind-body" construct.

Several questions may elicit mind-body beliefs: "Does your family believe specific thoughts or feelings may hurt or help a person's health? What do you believe will cause healing? Is there anything your family could have done to prevent this sickness from occurring now? In your culture, when someone becomes ill, where does the family go for healing? Do any of the treatments we have talked about seem difficult or strange? Outside of the treatments we have talked about, will your family do other things to treat this sickness or speed healing?"

Belief in Mastery and Control

Beliefs about mastery, the ability to influence events and outcomes, may also affect a family's illness experience and relationship with providers. If the outcome of an illness is predestined or fate, families may establish only marginal relationships with providers and treatment. For example, families accustomed to high degrees of control may find it difficult to tolerate a patient's admission to hospital treatment, an event that signals loss of control. This same family may cope well when a patient with complex needs returns home. Stressors associated with increased caregiving diminish with experiences of regaining competence and control. A family who attributes control to health care professionals, on the other hand, may require more support when faced with hospital discharge. It may mean the loss of professional care, the family's perceived source of "controlling" the illness. Such families may need longer periods of assistance to develop self-directed competency.

Clinicians and families can collaborate to create adaptive meanings for success and healing. Families with flexible belief systems, in which the meaning of "control" varies in the face of changing situations, may adapt more easily to illness demands. A family that must "beat" an illness risks a double loss—lost hopes for their loved one's recovery plus the loss of mastery.

It is often more adaptive for families to link mastery to holistic life experiences. Clinicians can encourage families to interpret mastery in terms of processes rather than physical symptoms. Meaningful processes may include the family's level of involvement and participation in the total process of care, renewed family rituals, or the experienced quality of family life and relationships. Focusing on processes and the quality of family life allows the family to self-define "mastery," embracing dimensions beyond "cure."

Useful questions may include: "When you think of your family now, with the illness, what do you feel best about? When does it feel good to be together now? How do you know when you're being with the illness and when you are being together?"

Beliefs About Causes of Illness

Faced with illness, people commonly ask, "Why me, or us, or why my child?" and, "Why now?" People answer these questions. They construct explanations or stories that make the illness experience "make sense." Their answers become powerful tools for organizing their illness experience.

The answers may be informed by objective medical science. Yet many families face persistent uncertainties regarding the "real" cause of an illness, or what will happen next. Constructing explanations fills in these gaps and helps organize tumultuous, stressful experiences. The uncertainties and stressors of illness may evoke highly personalized, idiosyncratic answers. Explanations may mirror an entire family's belief system, multigenerational legacies, or powerful, one-time traumas in the life of a family member.

Wynne, Shields, and Sirkin (1992) emphasize the importance of distinguishing beliefs that attribute cause to "external" forces (e.g., society, natural disasters, viral infections) from those associated with internalized, negative myths. Blame, shame, or guilt is often embedded in negative myths about how people in the family come to experience misfortune.

Negative beliefs are toxic to family life. Examples include the belief that illness is a punishment for misdeeds (e.g., an affair); caused by a blamed family member ("You just drove him until the stroke almost killed him"); linked to inappropriate guilt (e.g., a mother's belief that her child contracted cancer because of her incompetence as a mother); or due to "defective" genetics (e.g., "The illness runs on *that* side of the family").

It is useful to ask each family member for his or her explanation of what caused the illness. Destructive beliefs associated with blame or guilt often remain hidden, causing intense, isolated suffering. Also, these beliefs often combine idiosyncratic interpretations with accurate bits of data from the "real" world. When clinicians hear how patients and family members "explain" the illness, it becomes possible to offer alternative, more accurate and adaptive narratives.

Cultural Health Beliefs About Illness Roles and Behaviors

Culture, ethnicity, and religion strongly impact family health beliefs. Clinicians need to explore cultural differences between themselves and the family. Differences may include beliefs about (a) the appropriateness of the "sick role"; (b) the nature and degree of open communication about illness; (c) who should be included in the caretaking system; (d) who should be included in shared decision making; and (e) the types of rituals and illness behaviors expected at different phases of the illness (McGoldrick, Giordano, and Pearce, 1996).

The illness experience easily disempowers patients and families. Health care systems sometimes foster dependency or threaten abandonment. Dialogue about health beliefs invites families to assert mastery by creating affirmative meanings for the illness experience. It invites family inclusion and participation. It allows clinicians to assess the strategic function of the family meanings that mediate interactions with illness, capacities, and demands (Rolland, 1998).

Summary of Research Findings That Inform Clinical Treatment

- Family system variables are more powerful predictors of adaptation and adjustment than disease factors or illness severity.
- The synergy of the total family system is more important than specific family factors.
- Family system variables and illness demands share an interactive, reciprocal relationship, offering multiple points and levels for intervention.
- Treatments can support family adaptation through interventions that reduce illness demands, increase family resources, or alter meanings.

What Makes Families Resilient?

How families explain and think about disability impacts their ability to move ahead and find stability. When they can explain the condition in a way that makes sense to them and fits their beliefs, they are more apt to find coping strategies that allow them to move ahead with their lives.

According to the Institute for Health and Disability at the University of Minnesota, there are family resilience "indicators":

- Family members emphasize positive rather than negative reasons for the chronic illness or disability.
- Families are not preoccupied with why the condition happened.
- Family members manage illness demands within the context of family life.
- Families have a coherent explanation of the cause of the condition consistent with their worldview. (*Institute for Health and Disability Newsletter,* 1998)

A TREATMENT MODEL FOR MEDICAL FAMILY THERAPY: STRATEGIES FOR CHRONIC ILLNESS

McDaniel, Hepworth, and Doherty (1992) recommend ten strategies that medical family therapists should try to utilize: (1) recognize the biological dimension of disease; (2) assess the psychosocial demands of illness; (3) reinforce what works, respect defenses, and accept the unacceptable; (4) solicit illness stories; (5) support communication and connection; (6) reinforce family structure and identity; (7) reinforce family function and adaptive coping patterns; (8) promote agency; (9) attend to developmental needs and family balance; (10) provide psychoeducation on chronic illness and coping.

Recognize the Biological Dimension of the Disease

Part of joining the family involves accepting that the patient, family, and providers are focused on the patient's sickness, treatment, and recovery. Medical family therapy begins by sharing this focus. The biological dimensions of disease forcefully shape illness demands. Understanding interactions between disease and illness experience informs family system assessment and treatment planning.

The Biological Imperative

Clinicians working in medical contexts must integrate the biological imperatives of disease with the psychosocial demands of illness. First, this includes consulting with attending physicians about the current course of illness, prognosis, and barriers to recovery or adaptation. Physicians' concerns regarding patient management, family needs, or behavioral barriers to compliance reveal crucial aspects of the family system. Physicians also hold unique perspectives on patient and family medical history. Often, physicians have shared with families the "ups and downs" of facing treatment successes and disappointments.

Multidisciplinary Collaboration

Psychologists working in health care systems often have ongoing, collaborative relationships with other health care professionals. Consultations may occur regularly in institutional medical settings. Psychologists in private settings, however, need to develop networks with providers. In the therapeutic triangle between medical system, family, and psychologist, there are benefits to communicating directly (McDaniel, Hepworth, and Doherty, 1992). It avoids unhealthy "coalitions" or "splitting." It also keeps the psychologist attuned to beliefs and meanings reverberating through the whole therapeutic system. Recommendations regarding principles of collaboration are discussed in depth by McDaniel, Campbell, and Seaburn (1995). A report regarding integration of mental health services into an HMO primary care setting is available from Fischer et al. (1997). Belar (1997) provides an excellent overview of the roles and services provided by clinical health psychologists in collaboration with other medical health professionals.

Disease-Specific Psychological Factors Affecting Physical Condition

Current research regarding the interaction between psychological factors and a specific disease is invaluable. Interactions between psychosocial factors and biological processes are sometimes disease-specific, and psychological side effects may be associated with specific medications or treatments. Individual differences between patients in the degree to which psychosocial stressors exacerbate disease symptoms or medication reactions can be striking. A psychologist who becomes informed on these disease-specific issues is an invaluable ally as patients and families interpret their illness experience.

The Body Experience and Meaning

The physical, bodily experience of illness holds profound meaning. Pain, disfigurement, distractions and discomforts of symptoms, the inability to control bodily excretions—these features suggest only a partial list of physical experiences associated with illness. Threats to bodily integrity and safety, from disease, examinations, surgery, or treatments, are often intensely threatening, isolating experiences. Feelings of shame, dread, or revulsion may become hidden, draining psychological resilience. Attending to the physical experiences of illness may validate painful realities while modeling mastery. By inviting patients and families to express thoughts, feelings, and meanings associated with body experiences, clinicians support the capacity of patients and families to gain mastery over illness demands (Klonoff and Landrine, 1993, 1994).

Assess the Psychosocial Demands of Illness

Illness intrudes. It does not ask. It demands. And the demands may cover a myriad of behavioral, cognitive, affective, and relational changes. Each illness requires a daily set of concrete, specific actions. Illness demands may change meals and family menus, sleeping patterns, room arrangements, vacations and holidays—the list goes on. The clinician must explore with each family member: What does this illness make you do every day (Rolland, 1993, 1998) and, how can we make this better?

Reinforce What Works, Respect Defenses, and Accept the Unacceptable

Families coping with chronic illness face life-changing and sometimes life-threatening stressors. The cycles of adjustment, crisis, and adaptation mean clinicians often see families when their most familiar, reliable coping patterns are disintegrating or appear as dimly seen "works in progress." Indeed, illness exposes the clinician to the child and the family at their worst.

Illness stressors routinely evoke maladaptive responses. What becomes more impressive over time is that family systems endure. In joining the family, first reinforce what works. Then approach maladaptive coping styles as priorities and resources allow. It is often unclear whether maladaptive responses reflect long-standing patterns in the family system or temporary, reactive disruptions. In any event, it can be enormously helpful for a clinician to identify and directly affirm family strengths. This creates an opportunity for a clinician to validate stressors, threats, and the illness experience. It also creates an opportunity for the family to receive much-needed support.

Four coping patterns often emerge with illness: denial, internalizing illness, blame, and shaming negative feelings (McDaniel, Hepworth, and Doherty, 1992).

Denial

Denial is a common mechanism for dealing with illness. It is also a complex affective and cognitive phenomenon. Patients, family members, subgroups, or entire systems may be perceived as refusing to acknowledge the life changes illness or treatment may demand. Denial may create conflicts with other health care providers who are anxious to speed treatment and perhaps baffled by family intransigence.

Accepting denial while providing support and positive reframing are first steps in helping the family develop a more realistic view of the illness. This dialogue also allows the clinician to assess the nature of denial. It may have an affective core associated with actual or feared losses. It often has a cognitive component. Patients and family members face a tremendously complex cognitive transition. They must reorganize their inner, relational world. They must reshape a fundamental schematic expectation for "who is who" and "who does what" in family life. This assessment informs treatment. It may also help the clinician frame family behavior to physicians or other health care providers. Framing denial as one step in a progression toward coping may reduce negative frames resulting from team frustration. Other health care professionals can be resourceful allies in helping the family replace denial with adaptive behaviors.

Internalizing Illness

Rather than denial, some patients or family systems become so focused on the illness that it dominates identity. Patient and family life become organized around the illness. The patient may become identified as a "disease X patient" (e.g., "arthritic patient," or "CF patient"). The family may become a "cancer family." When the illness dominates patient or family identity, it restricts access to psychological resources needed for adaptation, meaning, and resilience.

When a patient or family has difficulty separating the patient or themselves from the illness, it is possible to help them externalize the illness. The patient might be asked to anthropomorphize the illness: What does it look like? What does it do to the patient? Does anything work to calm it? When are family members interacting with the illness and when are they interacting with the person? Changes in language and behavior can encourage the family to differentiate the illness from the person and family.

Blame

Patients and families create personal theories regarding the cause of illness. It is common for people to cope with crisis by trying to achieve control. Sometimes, the psychological act of blaming recovers feelings of mastery. People may blame themselves, the patient, family members, or physicians. It is helpful to explore questions such as, "What might have been done to prevent this illness? Could anyone have done something different and made things better?" Exploring individual explanations allows the clinician to assess needs for removing unwarranted guilt or developing needed rituals of forgiveness. These also reinforce and make more available the family's shared resources of love, affirmation, and support.

Shaming, Negative Feelings

Negative feelings such as anger, sadness, resentment, or guilt routinely arise in the illness experience. These feelings often evoke shame or seem unacceptable. People may adaptively reframe these experiences and "keep things in perspective." However, they may also isolate to contain negative states. People may feel ashamed or afraid of the intensity of anger, fear, or despair that they experience. The content of thoughts and wishes may be distressing, such as resenting the resources in time or money that a loved one's illness demands, or wishing the patient would just "go away" and let the family get back to a normal life. Medical family therapy can normalize these experiences and frame them in the context of issues that arise when family members care deeply about one another. It also invites families to acknowledge and resolve the real sources of conflict rather than staying focused on shaming emotions.

Solicit Illness Stories and Multigenerational Legacies

The joining process in medical family therapy includes soliciting and listening to illness stories. Early joining questions provide a context for eliciting the illness story. Questions such as, "Who are family members? Who works in and out of the home? What do they do? How do they spend their couple time and family time together?" provide a view of the family independent from illness. The family's ability to answer these questions also gives some indication of the degree to which the family is organizing itself around illness.

The clinician can next begin to elicit the illness story. Table 11.1 lists a series of eighteen questions that can be used to elicit illness perceptions. Listening to family narratives, the clinician begins to enter the family's world and share their language for illness. It also provides data needed to develop hypotheses regarding ways the illness story influences the family system.

TABLE 11.1. Questions to Elicit the Family Illness Stories

1. What do you think caused the problem?
2. Why do you think it started when it did?
3. What do you think the sickness does to the patient? How does it work?
4. How severe is the sickness? Will it last a long time or just awhile?
5. What chief problems does the sickness cause for you?
6. What do you fear most about the sickness?
7. What kind of treatment(s) do you think might make things better?
8. Will there be complications or will the sickness get worse?
9. What has been the experience of extended family with the illness?
10. Does anything make it hard to get well?
11. Do you see yourself as having much to live for?
12. What changes have happened in family responsibilities because of the illness?
13. What other changes might happen?
14. Who is going to help with the patient's needs or care?
15. How will you handle the illness over the long haul?
16. What does the illness make you do every day?
17. What has the illness taken away from you?
18. What has the illness given you?

The construction of meaning about illness is ongoing. It may be a transactional series of negotiations about what constitutes sick roles and rules for caregiving (McDaniel, Hepworth, and Doherty, 1992). It may also be transgenerational. The meaning of illness may have developed across generations, embedded in family stories about disease, threats to survival, and how one survives. Fiese (1997) suggests that family stories provide coherence in relationships. Stories about illness guide behavior (Reiss, 1989). The "practicing family" is observed in the rituals that regulate and stabilize family structures and functioning. Family stories and rituals may both become evident in the process of eliciting the family's "illness story."

Two clinically based research studies highlight the powerful interaction between parental life experiences, meaning, and family adaptation. Sheeran, Marvin, and Pianta (1997) investigated mothers' resolution of their child's diagnosis of chronic illness and self-reported measures of parenting stress, marital relationships, and social support. Mothers were administered the Reaction to Diagnosis Interview and classified as resolved or unresolved with respect to diagnosis of either mild to moderate cerebral palsy or epilepsy. Receiving a diagnosis of a child's illness represents a traumatic stressor to parents, and the lack of resolution can lead to parenting difficulties and attachment distress.

Wamboldt et al. (1995) demonstrate that parental history of traumatization prior to onset of chronic childhood illness complicates parental management of the illness experience. Based on a study of sixty-two adolescents with severe, chronic asthma, the investigators found parental traumas were associated with greater probability of adolescent anxiety or depressive disorders. The trauma experience mediates parental ability to cope with anxiety and stress arising from the child's illness, compromising the ability of the family system to cope with illness.

Increase Connection and Communication

There is never just one illness story, and each is distinctive. Inviting the family to hear each member's illness story also supports connection. Family members have opportunities to share empathy, validate experiences, remove blame, and use relational resources to form accurate, adaptive conceptions of the illness.

The stories of patient, mother, father, siblings, grandparents, and godparents form the family whole. Each family member can be invited to express his or her narrative explanations. Eliciting different views reinforces that diverse perspectives are normal and expected. It becomes possible to allow a range of responses appropriate to each member's developmental stage and illness experience. The process, highlighting individual differences, supports the family's tolerance for members' individual developmental needs. Some behaviors, for example, may become framed as "taking time to take care of yourself" (and so supporting the family's whole "health"), rather than isolating or withdrawing.

Reinforce Family Structure and Identity

Families coping with chronic illness often feel the illness "takes over." Connections with the extended family network, cultural or religious communities, and friends may shrink under the weight of illness priorities. Family goals, routines, rituals, and life priorities may all seem to be "put on hold." Families may come to feel they "are" the illness.

Parental needs for nurturing marital bonds, well siblings' needs for parental guidance, and patient needs for being other than "the sick one" are examples of potential role strains and structural stressors. Families may be asked, "How did you define yourself as a family before the illness? How do you define your family now? If the illness disappeared tomorrow, what would you do differently? It is important, however, to help families differentiate between the illness and the patient. Imagining a different life may be threatening if this connotes imagining life without the loved one. Family identity and goals embrace the patient as a person, flexibly, sometimes with and sometimes without the illness.

Reinforce Family Functioning and Adaptive Coping

Medical family therapy has many tools for assessing and improving family function. Helping families mobilize their resources of cohesion, problem solving, adaptability, affective expression, and control mechanisms are all potential dimensions for intervention. Fundamentally, functional patterns and adaptive coping responses become visible in what a family does. Functional coping may result in (a) reduced number or intensity of demands, (b) increase or preservation of family resources, (c) altering the meaning of a situation to make it more manageable, or (d) managing the tension associated with unresolved strain (Patterson and Garwick, 1994).

Increase Agency

Agency is a multidimensional construct. It includes psychological reservoirs that nourish self-care, autonomy, and resilience. Family structure and identity, functioning and coping patterns, adaptive meanings, and connection all contribute to agency. Medical family therapists can strengthen family awareness and experience of agency. Interventions include helping the family distinguish between what can and cannot be controlled; reflecting to families how well, in fact, they are functioning; acknowledging multiple losses and encouraging needed grief work; increasing tolerance for uncertainty and the ability to build flexibility into planning; enhancing family self-directed competence and mastery over the illness experience; supporting the family in its effort to create "balance" and keep the illness "in its place."

Attend to Developmental Issues

Consistent with traditional family systems therapy, medical family therapy attends to developmental needs. However, in medical contexts, the scope of "development" expands. It considers normative life cycle stages and tasks in the illness context: the progression of illness phases or stages of disease; interaction between illness demands and family developmental tasks; effects of illness demands that disrupt normative "timing" of life cycle events; and developmental dynamics of the caregiving system.

Gonzalez, Steinglass, and Reiss (1989) describe the importance of "putting the illness in its place." Families need to attend to the demands of illness, yet not allow the illness experience to dominate family life or overwhelm developmental needs. Families are encouraged to maintain routines, rituals, and holiday traditions and to attend to all family members' developmental issues.

Provide Psychoeducation

Families coping with chronic illness benefit from receiving information about the illness and possible coping strategies (Sherman, Oresky, and Rountree, 1991). It is helpful when the medical family therapist reinforces family knowledge of the disease, expected difficulties, and the range of coping responses. Families may also receive this information from providers. Anxiety and stress reactions, however, often make it difficult for families to cognitively process information when it is first presented. Repetition and reinforcement support the family's ability to process and integrate illness-related information. Sherman, Oresky, and Rountree (1991) recommend that clinicians structure initial sessions as psychoeducational sessions and focus on the illness rather than family patterns around illness. Psychoeducational sessions can also include information about alternative coping strategies and problem-solving methods found effective in dealing with chronic illness.

Many of the strategic principles outlined by McDaniel, Hepworth, and Doherty (1992) are evident in the following two examples of family-system interventions.

Results of a Hospital-Based Family System Intervention

Weinstein et al. (1992) developed a family-centered hospital-based treatment program for forty-four severely asthmatic children. Three dysfunctional family patterns were the target of treatment: persistent smoking in the home, poor parental supervision of medication administration, and ineffective discipline practices.

In the intervention, children were admitted to the hospital to stabilize physical condition and medication regimens. Families participated in twice-weekly family sessions focused on behavioral coping and contracting, medication administration and supervision, and extensive education about asthma and its management. Families also received brief family therapy when this was indicated.

In the year following the interventions there was a 91 percent reduction in hospitalization for this patient group, an 81 percent reduction in emergency room visits, significant reduction in steroid use, and improvement in lung function. A comparison of pre- and postintervention scores on a battery of standardized measures of psychological functioning for patients and families also found significant gains in psychological well-being. This study does not allow researchers to identify which parts of the intervention were most effective. However, its results are nonetheless impressive, pointing to the value of intervening at the level of the family system. The focus was on the disease and the child, and the family system. The family was seen as an essential partner in treatment management (Campbell, 1993).

Results of Multiple Family Group Interventions

Steinglass (1998) and Wamboldt and Levin (1995) report results of interventions based on a Multiple Family Group intervention (MFG). This model, originally developed for use with families coping with chronic mental illness (Steinglass, 1998) offers advantages to families coping with chronic physical illness. First, the model allows providers to capitalize on family system variables believed to improve medical outcomes (Patterson and Garwick, 1994). MFG participation allows providers and families to form the collaborative relationships key to effective treatment compliance and to control of negative factors such as psychosocial stress. The model engages all family members, patents and nonpatients, in ongoing illness management.

Second, MFGs are particularly well suited to support development of family coping resources specifically needed to respond to the acute versus chronic stage of illness (Cole and Reiss, 1993; Rolland, 1994). Third, MFGs reduce the severe social isolation reported by many families coping with chronic illness. The experience of meeting other families in the same situation helps reduce stigmatization and isolation (Steinglass, 1998).

Conceptually, the model is based on an understanding of the family's developmental risks and needs. Stressors of the acute phase experience often prompt families to reorganize around the illness. Initial efforts to reorganize may turn into permanent ways of life, even after the acute phase is over. The family's life becomes "invaded" by illness demands. As a result, the family system drifts away from other priorities and life cycle needs.

One of the results of all medical crises is that families need to increase order and regularity to control resources needed to manage imminent illness demands. For most illnesses, "overregulation" of family life in service of illness management is temporary. Once the illness has stabilized, a more balanced family life can be restored. If this "rebalancing" does not occur, the family "gets stuck" around illness issues (Steinglass,

1998). The MFG model supports families' transitioning from the "stuck" phase of illness coping to a phase of renewed family adjustment and adaptation.

In brief assessments based on participant program evaluation and measures of attitude change, the programs resulted in improved family functioning and illness management. This was true in adult, child, and adolescent populations, as well as in cross-cultural populations. The Medical Family Therapy Toolbox includes an outline of a sample MFG program.

A MEDICAL FAMILY THERAPY TOOLBOX

A wide variety of intervention tools are available to support families coping with childhood chronic illness.

Assessment Tools

A Qualitative Assessment Process

Figure 11.1 provides a graphic summary of a qualitative clinical assessment process, based on the FAAR clinical model. Clinicians can discuss these dimensions (demands, resources, meanings) in culturally appropriate forms with the family. This provides an opportunity for the clinician to "normalize" demands and stressors, and also begin to affirm positive family strengths and resources.

A review of these factors with families begins a rich clinical dialogue about the family's illness experience, and simultaneously starts the psychoeducation process by alerting families to key factors in coping.

Standardized Assessment Instruments

The following measures are noted in the literature as supporting assessment of family system variables in cases involving childhood chronic illness: Application of the Impact of Illness Scale is described in Ireys and Silver (1996) and detailed references are available in Stein and Jessop (1985) and Stein and Riessman (1980). Silver, Westbrook, and Stein (1998) describe use of the Questionnaire for Identifying Children with Chronic Conditions. This measure is based on the noncategorical approach and is specifically designed to identify children with ongoing illnesses and disabilities. References detailing instrument properties include Stein, West-

FIGURE 11.1. Key Illness Demands, Family Resources, and Meanings

brook, and Bauman (1997). The Psychiatric Symptom Index (PSI) is noted as an effective predictor of maternal mental health. Maternal results on the PSI were also found to be effective predictors of behavioral psychosocial symptoms in chronically ill children under five years of age (Goldberg et al., 1997). DeVet and Ireys (1998) report psychometric properties of the Maternal Worry Scale. The scale has demonstrated acceptable psychometric properties. It held an especially strong association to child internalizing symptoms. Sheeran, Marvin, and Pianta (1997) report on use of the Parental Reaction to Diagnosis Interview. The interview structure is based upon attachment theory. It profiles the nature of parental resolution of a diagnosis of child illness as either "resolved" or "unresolved." PRDI results were found to be reliable indicators of parenting stress, marital factors, and parental coping styles (Pianta and Marvin, 1992). Patterson, Budd, Goetz, and Warwick (1993) describe use of the Coping Health Inventory for Parents (CHIP). The scale is described further in McCubbin, McCubbin, and Patterson (1983).

Intervention Tools

Exercise One: Eliciting the Family's Illness Story—
Family Storytellers and Scribes

Table 11.1 presents questions adapted from McDaniel, Hepworth, and Doherty (1992). Families can use these questions to engage in an exercise called "Telling our Illness Story." For example, questions can be written on separate sheets of paper and placed inside a brown paper "story bag." Each family member can take turns drawing out a question and then give their own answer, contributing a "mini chapter" in the family's illness story. Large sheets of poster paper allow other members to take turns as the "scribe," writing down key words and phrases. The family can create its own large "storybook" about the illness and healing.

This exercise allows each family member to share his or her illness experience and also hear the experience of others in the family. The process of self-disclosure and mutual discovery can often elicit stressful meanings and resourceful ones as well. This exercise also allows the clinician to observe family structure and processes around illness, intervening in the storytelling process to model, affirm, and reinforce adaptive coping behaviors.

Exercise Two: Drawing the Illness
with Child and Family Art Montages

Stein (1997) and Wamboldt and Levin (1995) describe the use of art and drawings in medical family therapy. Drawing often opens channels for adults and children to express their illness experiences. Stein incorporates Draw-a-Person and the Kinetic Family Drawing tests as activities in pediatric practice. Wamboldt and Levin (1995) incorporate art therapy into medical family therapy. Prompts include:

1. Most families have some problems they have already successfully solved, as well as some they are still struggling with. Draw a picture showing a problem the illness caused in your family and how you successfully solved it.

2. Draw the ways the illness has affected your family.
3. Even though you do not see any solutions to dealing with the illness right now, draw an imaginary way you would like to cope with your child's illness.
4. Draw the illness.

Exercise Three: Using the Genogram in Medical Family Therapy

Schilson, Braun, and Hudson (1993) report on the use of genograms in medical family therapy. The genogram (Wachtel, 1982) has been used to accomplish multiple therapeutic tasks. It is: (a) a medium for family members to express emotions by telling "facts"; (b) a way to join the family and lay the foundation for a therapeutic alliance; (c) a medium through which the clinician can learn key words and ideas for later use in developing directives or schema-focused interventions; (d) a glimpse into each member's idiosyncratic concerns, values, wishes, and fears; and (e) a source of "clues" that can form the basis for hypotheses about system dysfunctions and possible solutions. Schilson, Braun, and Hudson (1993) applied genogram interventions as instruments to gather patient history for family practitioners in a family practice residency program. Results of this pilot study suggest valuable uses for genograms in medical family therapy.

Exercise Four: Multifamily Psychoeducational Groups

Excellent references are available to clinicians interested in sponsoring multifamily groups for families coping with medical stressors. Resources include:

Steinglass, P. (1998). Multiple Family Discussion Groups for Patients with Chronic Medical Illness. *Families, Systems and Health, 16*(1-2), 55-70.

Steinglass includes detailed descriptions of MFG program outlines, evaluations, and results in four separate MFG pilots. The pilots reported in this article included MFGs for families coping with dialysis, one sponsored for families with diverse disorders, one for families coping with cancer, and another for families coping with diabetes. The article provides an excellent synopsis of clinical concepts and treatment outlines that could form the basis for adaptation in private and community-based practices.

Wamboldt, M. and Levin, L. (1995). Utility of Multifamily Psychoeducational Groups for Medically Ill Children and Adolescents. *Family Systems Medicine, 13*(2), 151-161.

Wamboldt and Levin (1995) report on the implementation of an MFG for families coping with childhood asthma. The article includes a specific protocol for implementation with families, including child patients, parents, and siblings. It also reports on the integration of art therapy into the MFG protocol, as well as a summary of outcomes based on a brief attitudinal measure. Both articles provide rich clinical and research references. Some key principles include:

1. The establishment of a community of families with shared experiences
2. The emphasis on family strengths and a nonpathologizing stance
3. The richness of multiple perspectives on illness issues within the family system
4. Encouraging and modeling the families' ability to take an observational stance, externalize the illness, and engage in collaborative solution processes

Sample sessions can include the following:

A. Illness Impact Component (2 Sessions)
   1. Identify illness issues and family perspectives
   2. Facilitate connections between participants and families with shared experiences
B. Family Development Component (3 Sessions)
   1. Organize shared experiences and issues into categories and metaphors, with particular emphasis on "keeping the illness in its place"
   2. Describe and clarify each family's view of the impact of illness via family constructions of art montages visually representing pre- and postillness family life
   3. A family-by-family presentation of their montages to the group followed by feedback from other group members
   4. An abstracting (reframing) of each family's story about their montages with an emphasis on core family values that have been maintained or derailed by the intrusion of illness into their lives
   5. Each family discusses specific posttreatment goals/issues and explores strategies
C. Family-Illness Integration (1 session)
   1. Have group members bring to the final session a "physical reminder" of the illness. Use reminders to clarify impact of positive and negative feelings on family structure and function and ongoing coping processes.
   2. Use discussion to "normalize" family feelings and experience of uncertainty.

3. Devise a family ritual for each family in the group that might serve symbolically to help the family find "an appropriate place" for illness experience in the family's life; support the family's transition and "off-illness" coping style.

Exercise Five: A Protocol for Ill Children
Presenting Psychosocial Symptoms

Simms (1995) reports a protocol for ill children presenting psychosocial symptoms. He acknowledges two "potential disasters." The first is exacerbating symptoms, often linked to conflicts or inadequate coordination among adults on the health care team. The child's complex medicosocial ecology may include parents, physicians, teachers, social workers, psychologists, and perhaps others. To be effective, this team must resolve conflicts and reach a consensus regarding the cause and appropriate treatment for psychosocial or behavioral symptoms. The second disaster is failing to treat. This arises when the treatment frame is too narrow. The child is viewed as the problem and the target of intervention. This approach excludes the multifactorial nature of behavior and child development. The development of shared goals and an alliance among adult providers is pivotal. Shared goals and ideas among adults become the "fiber comprising the lifeline" for the child. Several key principles are detailed below.

Symptoms signal loss of mastery. Psychosocial symptoms signal that the child's coping resources are taxed beyond critical thresholds. Loss of mastery is often at the heart of symptoms. A child strives to learn actively, approach interesting tasks, confront frustrations, and discover solutions. Illness can present impossible barriers to a child yearning for mastery over his or her body, wanting so much to "grow up" and trying so hard to be loved and protected. Opportunities to practice the small steps to mastery at school, on the playground, and in the neighborhood may be missed. This leaves the child always at a competitive disadvantage with his or her peers.

Children need motivation. Children may not change because someone else wants them to change. An ill child needs motivation before feeling a "pull" toward effective coping. They may have fewer opportunities to experience the shared behavioral guidance and reinforcement known among well children and parents. Psychosocial problems, signaling distress, may also be markers for the child's restricted learning history. Restricted by illness, this learning history likely resulted in narrower behavioral repertoires and limited rewards. Parents, other adults, and other children may all need to be enlisted to create opportunities for timely, age-appropriate interactions and supportive relationships.

Control is a myth. When children show severe distress, adults responsible for their care naturally feel compelled to minimize or eliminate the cause. When a child shows psychosocial distress, however, direct and immediate control is unlikely. Worry, anger, fear, and frustration are facets of the illness experience. These psychosocial symptoms are a "given" in illness. Rather than "controlling" these symptoms externally, these experiences can be accepted. They become a starting point for constructing a map that will guide and encourage the child to master age-appropriate strategies for experiencing and coping with difficult emotions. To be able to support the child in discovering this "map," adult team members must first learn to accept and tame their own emotional "pulls" to control the child's distress.

Relationships are key. Effective coping with a serious illness occurs within a context of safe, supportive, and enduring relationships. Children need parents, married, separated, or divorced, to stay connected and collaborate in guiding the child's development. Children also need parents and health care teams to create, nurture, and maintain collaborative relationships.

Five steps for constructing solutions:

1. Conduct a developmentally focused assessment

   - Identify concrete symptom behaviors linked to identifiable developmental phases (e.g., tantrums among two- to four-year-old children)
   - Relate problem behaviors to the child's inherent pursuit of mastery
   - View psychosocial symptoms as signals of thwarted, delayed mastery

2. Create problem definitions that include three persons

   - Psychosocial symptoms are embedded in an interpersonal context
   - A relational frame shifts focus from "diagnosis" to therapeutic action
   - Identify at least three persons as connected to the presenting symptoms
   - Symptoms "belong" to the child but adults are good-faith partners in solving problems

3. Frame psychosocial symptoms as the child's response to the illness experience

- They are signals that the patient requires "something different" from key adults
- The "something different" might include ways for the child to regain competency
- Rather than symptoms identifying a "diagnosis," they become signals for the child and others to shift relational behaviors together

4. "Join" the family and support them

- Support parent's primary role in guiding the child's mastery and coping

5. Focus on competence

- The illness experience creates a context where child and family are seen "at their worst"
- Maintain an unrelenting search for child and family strengths
- The focus on competence allows family and child to recover aspects of self currently "eclipsed" by illness

SELF-EXPLORATION: CHRONIC ILLNESS

Using Table 11.1, answer the eighteen questions in relation to a chronic health problem that has affected you, a family member, or a close friend. What new insights have you gained, if any, about how the chronic health problem is interwoven into family life? If possible, ask another family member to respond to the same set of questions and see what that adds to your understanding.

Chapter 12

Adoption and Infertility

Sherry Molock

Approximately 5 percent of all children are legally adopted by nonrelatives. Although many more children are informally adopted by relatives than nonrelatives, particularly in the African-American community, this chapter will focus on adoptions in which a couple has adopted a child who is biologically unrelated to the mother or father and where, in the majority of cases, the biological parents are unknown to the adoptees and the adoptive parents. Some research notes that adopted children are more likely to have problems with adjustment, as is suggested by the disproportionate numbers of children seen in outpatient and inpatient mental health facilities. This chapter will explore the normative processes and challenges that adoptive families face. First we will discuss the different types of adoptions that are available to families. Then we will discuss the adjustments that adoptive families make throughout the development of the child, issues that typically present themselves to the family therapist when working with an adoptive family, and how transracial adoption impacts on the adoptive family.

TYPES OF ADOPTION

Generally, there are two kinds of adoption: agency and independent. In both cases, the birth parents relinquish their parental rights to their child; in agency adoptions this right is typically relinquished to the state or local jurisdiction, while in an independent adoption the consent goes directly to the adoptive parents. There are two types of agency adoptions: public or private. They are supported by the tax dollars of the state, county, or local municipality. They are often more flexible in their criteria for becoming an adoptive parent (e.g., they may allow adoptions by single parents, low-income families, etc.). They generally have lower and sometimes no fees, but they tend to offer fewer pre- and postadoptive services. Private adoption agencies are supported by agency fees, community organizations such as the United Way and religious, fraternal, and/or family foundations. Most private agencies are nonprofit, but they still charge relatively higher fees ($5,000 to $20,000) to pay for administrative staffing, office overhead, and sometimes for the medical and counseling needs of birth mothers. A third type that is becoming more common is the "assisted adoption," which is a combination of an agency and independent adoption. The birth parents have direct contact with the adoptive parents, but they use an adoption agency for pre- and postadoption services.

Adoptions can be viewed on a continuum of openness. Confidential adoptions were the prevalent form until the 1970s. In confidential or closed adoptions, minimal information is shared between the birth and adoptive family members and the exchange of information stops after the child is placed for adoption. In the mediated or semiclosed adoption, nonidentifying information is shared through an agency or other intermediary (social worker, attorney, and adoption consultants). This sharing of information can be time-limited or ongoing. Fully disclosed or open adoptions involve the direct communication and full disclosure of identifying information, which also may be time-limited or indefinite, (Grotevant et al., 1994; Johnston, 1992).

Historically, formal, legal adoptions were sought by white, middle-class couples who experienced infertility (traditional adopters). These couples wished to adopt healthy white infants. In the 1960s, this picture began to change primarily because of the legalization of abortion, the decrease in the stigma attached to single parenting, and the increase in the use of contraceptives. With these broader societal changes, the number of healthy white infants available for adoption decreased significantly.

With this decrease in available healthy white infants, there was a simultaneous rise in the number of "preferential adopters." These families were primarily motivated to adopt for altruistic reasons; they often had biological children but wanted to provide homes for needy children. They tended to adopt children with special needs (e.g., mentally or physically disabled children) or children who were hard to place (e.g., older children, minority children) (Anderson, Piantanida, and Anderson, 1993; Brodzinsky, 1998). With the decrease in the availability of healthy white infants, traditional and preferential adopters increasingly turned to transracial and international adoptions in the 1970s.

NORMATIVE PROCESSES AND DEVELOPMENTAL ISSUES OF ADOPTIVE FAMILIES

Adoptive families generally have the same basic issues that most families have. They worry about their children's scholastic achievement and wonder if they have some hidden talent that can be developed and nurtured.

However, some issues are unique to adoptive families. These processes are not necessarily pathological; in fact, many of them are normative within the context of adoption. The family therapist who chooses to work with adoptive families needs to be aware of these normative issues. It is helpful to discuss such issues using a developmental framework based on the age of the child and on the developmental period of the family vis-à-vis the adoption.

Preplacement Issues

The Legacy of Infertility

Infertility is defined as the inability to achieve a pregnancy after one year of sexual relations without the use of contraceptives. Nearly one out of twelve couples experiences infertility. Infertility represents a violation of cultural norms to parent children, since most couples assume fertility and have the desire to have children (Brodzinsky, 1998). Because of the inability to meet this cultural expectation, individuals and couples who experience infertility often feel ostracized, isolated, and alienated. Most couples who experience infertility seek medical intervention; 50 percent of those who do get pregnant. Of those who experience infertility, 25 percent go on to adopt (Meyers et al., 1995).

Infertility creates a great deal of stress for the couple and at times represents a crisis in their marriage. Men and women tend to react differently to infertility. Women describe feeling depressed and having a sense of despair and disappointment. Men tend to use denial and isolation to deal with their feelings about infertility (Meyers et al., 1995). Infertility also affects sexual functioning, as many couples feel that all the spontaneity has gone out of their sex lives. Some couples even report feeling that there are "third parties" in their bedrooms (i.e., the physicians directing the treatment cycle).

For religious couples, infertility can represent a crisis of faith as well. Infertility places the couple in touch with mortality because children are often an important link to the future. It also impacts on their notion of God as provider and divine healer (Devor, 1994). Not only do infertile individuals feel they are being punished (e.g., for an earlier abortion, delaying childbearing for educational or career goals), but they wonder why God would torment them by not removing the desire to have a child (Molock, in press).

Sandelowski, Harris, and Holditch-Davis (1989) use the concept of "mazing" to characterize the journey that infertile couples undergo in pursuit of a child. They note that the process of mazing is "recursive, iterative, and capital-intensive, demanding vast expenditures of time, physical and psychic energy and the financial resources to direct it" (p. 222). Some couples go through a sequential process in which they completely exhaust one option (e.g., in vitro fertilization) before considering another option. Others backtrack and revisit options. It is not uncommon for couples to take a break from treatment to allow them to regroup. Unfortunately, some couples get stuck on the treatment merry-go-round. If treatment is unsuccessful, the couple may have to reframe the desire to have children: do they want fertility and the subsequent pregnancy or do they want to parent? At this juncture, some couples may decide to remain childless, while others may go on to adopt.

Adoption does not automatically cure the emotional scars left from infertility. Johnston (1992) talks about the difficulty that some waiting prospective adoptive parents have with experiencing what she terms a "psychological pregnancy." She notes that the waiting couple need to incorporate the adopted child into their emotional images. The parents need to perceive the child as a reality and begin making plans to receive the child. This psychological pregnancy often becomes difficult because the prospective parents do not know when the child will arrive and are sometimes unsure how old the child will be. Some couples are afraid to emotionally invest in the adoption process after so many disappointments with infertility treatment. Others, mindful of the few unsuccessful adoptions publicized in the media are afraid to emotionally invest lest the birth mother reclaim the child.

Psychological Issues and the Adoption Procedure

Couples who adopt because of infertility need to acknowledge and not feel guilty about the decision to adopt as a second choice. The adoption process can be stressful, and family therapists should be familiar with the different phases of the process so they can best assist parents through this journey to parenthood. Initially, prospective parents go through an explo-

---

JACK AND JUDY

Jack and Judy Smith finally got pregnant after five years of intermittent trials of in vitro fertilization. Everything was going well until the sixth month when Judy gave birth to a beautiful but tiny boy they named Damon. Damon's lungs were too immature and he died three weeks later in his parents' arms. After two years, they decided that they would try adoption and went to a small, nonprofit private adoption agency. It soon became clear to their social worker that they had not completely worked

(continued)

(continued)

through some of their grief over the loss of Damon. They had unrealistic expectations of what their adopted child would be like and made unrealistic demands on the birth mothers in the adoption agency's program. They insisted on visiting the birth mother's home, but did not want to reciprocate and allow her to visit them. They wanted an independent physician and psychologist of their choosing to evaluate the birth mother to make sure she was in excellent physical and mental health. They wanted the birth mother to be continuously monitored to ensure that the unborn baby was in good health. They wanted the birth mother to sign an affidavit guaranteeing that she would not smoke cigarettes, drink alcohol, or use drugs during the pregnancy, even though both of the Smiths smoked themselves. They were referred for short-term treatment by the adoption agency to help them resolve some of this unspoken grief over the loss of their child Damon.

For many couples, cognitive behavioral techniques are effective in helping the couple reframe their issues around the adoption process (Meyers and Wark, 1996). We began treatment by doing an assessment of the appraisals and attributions the Smiths made about their infertility and the loss of their child. Judy harbored a lot of guilt because she had smoked off and on during the pregnancy. Jack had great difficulty coming to terms with parenting a child who was not biologically related to him, for he had been raised by a maternal aunt and never knew his father. They also worked on their communication as a couple, for each was unsure of their desire to adopt but was going along to please the partner. After six weeks of treatment, the Smiths decided to postpone the adoption process until they could more thoroughly sort through the feelings about parenting an adopted child. On a follow-up call four months later, the Smiths informed me that they decided to remain child free.

ration phase in which they seek information about adoption and contact several agencies. The couple then selects an agency and is accepted as a client of that agency. Some couples have to wait three to five years before a placement, particularly if they want a healthy white infant. Prospective parents who are willing to parent children with special needs (e.g., older children, siblings, disabled children) generally have a shorter waiting period. Other prospective parents have turned to domestic transracial adoptions or to international adoptions to decrease the waiting period. These options may be particularly important for older couples who are near the cutoff age for most adoption agencies (typically forty for the mother and forty-five for the father). It is important that the family therapist affirm whatever choice the couple makes in the adoption process. Parenting is a lifelong commitment, and if the couple feels they cannot handle the challenges of raising a racially or ethnically different child or a child with physical and/or emotional disabilities, then this decision needs to be respected.

African-American adoptive parents usually have a much shorter waiting period because there tend to be more African-American infants available for adoption. Hispanic and Asian couples will have a more difficult time finding a child from their ethnic background in domestic adoption agencies. These couples will probably be more successful pursuing an international adoption.

After selecting an agency, the prospective parents undergo a home study that can take anywhere from six weeks to six months to complete. After this, the couple may wait from a few months to several years for a child. Once the child is placed, the couple then has to undergo an extensive supervisory period that usually lasts six months, in which the adjustment of all family members is evaluated. If everything works out well, the adoptive parents can then apply to finalize the adoption. The entire adoption process, from home study to finalization, usually takes a minimum of one year, and often takes longer.

Given this arduous process, it is easy to see why many prospective adoptive parents feel the decision to parent is out of their control. Unlike a nine-month pregnancy, the prospective parents are unsure of how long the adoption process will take. This may be particularly difficult for couples who have spent years trying to become pregnant via assisted reproductive techniques (ARTS). Other couples resent having to "prove" to the adoption agency or the birth parents that they are fit parents when biological parents do not have to undergo such scrutiny. Some couples find the home-study process demeaning and intrusive.

Brodzinsky (1990) suggests that the adoption process involves loss for all three members of the adoption triad: the birth parents, the adoptive parents, and the adopted child. The couple or single parent has to grapple with the fact that they are not raising a child that is biologically related to them and need to mourn the loss of the idealized biological infant that they thought they would have. The adoptive parents also have to decide if they can bond with a child that is not biologically related to them. Adoptive parents often not only feel deprived of the biological child, but also of the "perfect" fantasized adopted baby, for adoption agencies often warn prospective parents to be realistic when they say they want a healthy infant. Although it may be unrealistic to expect a perfectly healthy infant, it is quite normal to fantasize about one. All prospective parents, adoptive and nonadoptive, fantasize about a perfect baby.

Many adoptive parents have very little information on the genetic background of the child, which heightens their sense of anxiety during the adoption process. Will some unforeseen medical condition or mental health problem surface down the road? Adoptive parents have to consider how extended family members will react to the adopted child. Sometimes prospective parents for the first time become aware of hidden prejudices and stereotypes that extended family members have toward disabled persons or toward people of another racial or ethnic group.

Unlike nonadoptive families, adoptive families have to decide whom to tell that the child is adopted. This issue has become easier with the generally more accepting attitude toward adoption and with the availability of adoption announcement cards and adoption baby books. Adoptive parents also have to decide when and how to tell their child about his or her adoptive status. The parents have to answer difficult questions about birth parents and may have to decide when and how to share painful background information (e.g., child abandonment).

Adoptive parents also have to confront the stigma associated with adoption: that somehow these children are "bad seeds." The lingering legacy of this view can be seen in media reports of crimes in which the perpetrator's adoptive status is reported, as if there was a causal relationship between the two. Adoptive parents also have to come to terms with the perception that they are not the "real" or "natural" parents of their adopted children (van Gulden and Bartels-Rabb, 1993). Because the adopted parents are not seen as legitimate, people often feel free to ask inappropriately personal questions about the child's background. When I adopted my oldest daughter, the cashiers in my neighborhood grocery store would ask me if her "real" mother was on drugs or a prostitute.

Kirk (1964), in a landmark study, noted three approaches that adoptive families tend to take regarding the meaning of adoption in the family. Some families react to the adoption by *rejecting differences*. These families deny any differences between adoptive and nonadoptive families. Kirk notes that this only meets the needs of the adoptive parents. The parents often try to minimize the pain of the loss associated with adoption for the child or try to minimize the loss they fear will occur if the child decides to search for his or her birth parents.

Acknowledgement of differences is characteristic of families who are open to exploring and discussing issues about adoption. Many adoption agencies and advocates promote this perspective because they feel it creates a trusting relationship between parents and children: there are no secrets. An open and honest perspective on adoption helps the child integrate the missing aspects of his or her life and helps the child sort through fantasies and erroneous information from the past. An open-door policy on discussing issues pertaining to adoption also helps to build a strong foundation for positive self-esteem and a healthy sense of identity (Schooler, 1993, p. 121).

Some families *insist on differences* between adoptive and nonadoptive families. These parents overemphasize differences, which builds a schism between the adopted child and family. Schooler (1993) notes that this often occurs when the family is in crisis. Brodzinsky (1990) suggests that at different times in the family's life, they may go through all of the stages. For example, he argues that when a child is initially placed, parents may primarily reject differences in order to forge a strong sense of family unity. As family ties are strengthened, families may move more into acceptance of differences. Most adoption experts agree that insistence on differences can be divisive in the family and serve to isolate and sometimes ostracize the adopted child.

Postplacement Issues

The Early Years

The day has finally arrived and the parents are on cloud nine. They cannot believe they ever had any concerns about the baby's background or how others would react because they are absolutely, wildly, and passion-

---

LORRAINE AND BURT

Lorraine and Burt Milton had experienced four miscarriages in five years. Each time she became pregnant, Lorraine would have an uneventful pregnancy until the twentieth to twenty-fifth week, when she would go into premature labor. After a lot of soul-searching, they decided that it was more important to them to parent a child than it was to be pregnant and have a child who was biologically related to them. As Lorraine put it: "We have four birth certificates and four death certificates. We have four sets of baby footprints from the hospital and have had four funerals. We simply cannot lose another baby." The Miltons decided to work with a small nonprofit adoption agency. This particular agency promoted semi-open to open adoptions, and in their desperation to parent, the Miltons agreed to an open adoption, even though they had some concerns about meeting the birth parents. The Miltons sailed through the home study phase of their adoption and eighteen months later, they welcomed Maria Lorraine Milton into their loving family. Although they knew that the agency had a "ceremony" in which both the birth and

(continued)

(continued)

adoptive parents participated when placing the child, the Miltons kept rescheduling the ceremony. Lorraine later complained that she felt the agency had "rammed the ceremony down our throats. What should have been a joyful day for us was turned into a really sad experience that I'll never forget. Once again, I was robbed of the joyful experience of bringing my baby home for the first time." As the Miltons were undergoing their six-month home study to prepare for finalization of the adoption, the agency's social worker began to express concerns about the way the Miltons were handling exchanging information with the birth parents. The Miltons constantly had to be reminded to send in information and pictures about the baby's progress so they could be shared with the birth parents. When the Miltons were confronted with their reticence to share information, Burt blurted out: "Well, I'm not comfortable with all this sharing. We are constantly reminded every day by this agency that Maria is adopted. I think the agency cares more about the needs of the birth mother than they do about Maria or us. Every time I have to send *that woman* a picture of Maria I think she is just going to take one look at Maria, see what she is missing, and change her mind. Everything is 'adoption, adoption, adoption!' We don't think of her that way at all. She is just our little girl. Why should we focus so much on the adoption? When she grows up, she is going to feel different and ostracized. She'll have a hard enough time coping with racism and prejudice as a black woman. To be honest, we're having second thoughts about why we have to tell her about the adoption anyway. What good can come of it?"

The Miltons were still affected by the legacy of their multiple miscarriages. They never allowed themselves to really mourn and process what it meant to lose four children; in fact, they acknowledged that they had never really talked about it. This couple was not a good candidate for an open adoption because contact with the birth mother, albeit mediated contact, was too threatening for this family. The contact with the birth mother represented a potential loss to the couple. Similarly, the concern they had about overemphasizing Maria's adoption status was really about their fear that they would lose Maria later to her birth parents. Before this couple's adoption was finalized, they received intensive work on processing their grief over the loss of their other four children. We also had them work in an adoption parent support group for several months. Their work in the support group was invaluable because they were able to share their feelings and concerns in a forum that was nonjudgmental and nonevaluative. They also began to see the benefits of discussing the adoption with their child as they heard stories of the importance of integrating the adoption experience into the child's sense of identity. They were surprised that many of the parents in the support group envied their open adoption. Some of the families were trying to help their adopted children begin a search for their birth parents. They relayed the importance of this search process to their children and shared the frustration of not always being able to get this information for their child.

ately in love with their baby, right? The first few weeks after the baby joins the family are not always this idyllic. Many first-time parents are surprised that they do not feel an intense immediate attachment to their baby. I remember when we adopted our second child. It was a hectic time in our lives and we did not have a "psychological pregnancy" with him. For the first two weeks after his arrival, I felt like I was baby-sitting a really nice baby. I did not realize I had bonded with him until he was in the emergency room two weeks later with pneumonia. As the physician began to discuss the possibility of transferring him to a pediatric hospital via ambulance, they asked me if I had brought my car so I could ride behind the ambulance. I looked at the physician as if he had lost his mind and told him in no uncertain terms that *my baby* would either be accompanied by me in the ambulance to the hospital or I would take him myself. There was no way I was letting *my baby* out of my sight!

Anderson, Piatanida, and Anderson (1993) states that adoptive families need to go through several normative processes in order to gel as a family. Claiming is the process by which the parent or parents make an emotional commitment to the child such that they view the child as a full-fledged member of the family. The process of claiming may be interfered with by fears of birth parents reclaiming the child. This fear is fostered by the notoriety that a few adoption cases receive in the media when birth parents have stepped forward and fought for custody of their children after the child was placed for adoption. Families can help facilitate claiming by establishing rituals within the family to commemorate the adoption.

Adoptive families often do not feel a sense of "entitlement" regarding parenting because they have to "prove" themselves to be worthy of parenting in the adoption process. Some couples may feel unworthy of parenthood, or they can accept and nurture a child but have difficulty disciplining the child because they feel so grateful for the opportunity to parent.

Adoptive families also have to work to forge a sense of family. This may be particularly difficult if the adopted child is older (over the age of two) at the time of placement. The older child may have trouble accepting his or her new family, especially if there have been multiple placements. Anderson, Piatanida, and Anderson (1993) suggest that older children be given ample preplacement preparation so that they transition into their new family slowly. The adoptive parents need to have realistic expectations and recognize that forging a sense of family with an older child may take longer. When adopting an older child, the parents are also thrust into dealing with developmental issues all at once and are not given the advantage that biological parents have of gradually confronting developmental issues (e.g., the struggle between autonomy and interdependence that is characteristic of adolescence).

Preschool Years

Preschoolers almost always have a very positive view of adoption primarily because that is the story that has been shared with them. Parents can be encouraged to develop a "life book" which they can put together with their child that describes how the child joined the family. Even if the parents do not have information or pictures of the child's birth parents, they can include pictures and information on foster parents.

Children as young as three begin to ask parents about their origins, and some children may fear they caused the loss of their birth parents. Adoptive parents need to think about and sometimes even practice what they are going to tell their young children. The family therapist may have to educate some parents about the cognitive abilities of preschoolers. Parents need to be advised to listen carefully to what the child is asking, so that the child is not overwhelmed with information. If parents are unclear about what the child is asking, they should seek to clarify the question before answering. Young children do not need to know information that is potentially psychologically scarring. One of our deepest regrets is when our then four-year-old oldest daughter inadvertently saw a scene from the movie *Losing Isaiah* in which a drug-addicted birth mother left her baby on top of a trash pile. For weeks thereafter, our daughter had to sleep with the light on and be assured that her birth mother did not leave her in a garbage dump.

Although the parents have probably recounted the adoption story numerous times, it is common for young children to mix reality and fantasy together, so the adoption story may become confused in their minds. Adoptive parents have to be careful of the language they use when discussing adoption with young children. For example, calling the birth parents the child's "real parents" may create the fear that the adoptive family is somehow temporary. Some children will insist they grew in Mommy's tummy. Adoptive parents need to check their child's mood when these kinds of incidents occur. Because the child may be trying to establish closeness to the mother, every inconsistency or inaccuracy does not have to be corrected.

During the preschool years, some children will begin to search for their birth parents. At times, this can be embarrassing. One of my clients said that she hated to go outside because her four-year-old was constantly going up to strange women on the street and asking them if they were her mother. After viewing the Disney movie *Pocahontas* for the hundredth time, my then three-year-old daughter asked me if Pocahontas was her birth mother. The search for a birth mother may be more pronounced in a child who is adopted transracially, particularly if they rarely see people from their own cultural background. Children who are placed when they are older (over the age of two) or who have had multiple placements may be afraid that their status in the family is temporary and that they are being moved to another placement. One family told the story of how their five-year-old Korean-born son became frightened of going to Chinatown. When asked what he was frightened of, he told them he was afraid "those people" would keep him. The family was advised to explain the purpose of the visit before the outing and to reassure the child that everyone would return home as a family.

Questions and concerns about their origins may be more pronounced in children whose ethnic/racial background differs from that of their parents. Children as young as three are aware of racial differences. Adoptive parents need to be aware of the messages they give their children by either overemphasizing or underemphasizing racial differences. One client recounted the story in which she was sharing a bath with her three-year-old African-American daughter. When her daughter kept looking at the differences in the colors of their arms, the mother said to her daughter: "See, your skin looks just like Mommy's!" This is not only confusing to the child, but it suggests that she is not good enough just as she is. On the other hand, if your Korean son, in an attempt to identify with his father, says, "I have eyes just like Daddy," the father does not have to insist: "Oh, no. You have nice Asian eyes. We like them just the way they are!"

Transracially adopted children may also be exposed to unkind stares, unpleasant comments, and inappropriate questions at preschool and during mundane family outings. During the preschool years, the parents should start to talk about racism to their children. Although the parents do not need to go into the entire legacy of racism in America, parents of racially different children are being naïve if they think that young children do not experience racism.

Similarly, while it is important to be an adoption advocate, adoptive parents need to realize that they do not have to explain their child's presence in their family or tell the child's entire adoption story. Parents do not want to give their child the message that they need to be explained or justified. Family therapists can encourage parents to respond in ways that affirm their child. When asked "Where did you get him?" they can give the name of the city. The frequent but inappropriate question of "How much did she cost?" can be answered by a quick "She's priceless; how much did you spend for your kids?" Comments such as, "Oh, poor thing, his real parents didn't want him" can be quieted with a simple "What ever gave you the idea we didn't want him?"

Middle Childhood

During middle childhood, children can now think more logically. They can begin to experience empathy and begin to understand the perspectives of others. The emphasis on socialization starts to shift from the family to the peers. Children between the ages of six and twelve are old enough to understand that adoption is associated with loss. It is usually during this period that you begin to see a rise in clinical referrals of adopted children.

It is unclear if adoption places children at higher risk for maladjustment. Wierzbicki (1993) did a meta-analysis of sixty-six studies that looked at the adjustment of adopted and nonadopted children. The adopted children had significantly higher levels of academic problems and externalizing disorders. It was unclear why these children were overrepresented in clinical populations. Haugaard (1998) did an exhaustive review of the literature and discovered contradictory findings. The clinically based literature suggests that adopted children are at higher risk for maladjustment, as indicated by their overrepresentation in inpatient and outpatient mental health facilities. However, research on nonclinical samples indicated no differences in the mental health of adopted and nonadopted children. Some of the longitudinal studies in Haugaard's review found maladjustment at some ages but not at others, suggesting that the problems are transitory. Haugaard's review suggests that some of the differences between adopted and nonadopted children in the maladjustment literature are due to differences in referral patterns. Delinquent adopted children are more likely than nonadopted delinquent children to be referred for treatment by teachers and law enforcement officials. Adopted children with mild to moderate problems are more likely to be referred to treatment by their parents than nonadopted children.

Brodzinsky (1990) notes that adopted children begin to deal with a lot of issues of loss at this age. The child begins to come to terms with the loss of his or her biological parents and often feels rejected by these parents. There are issues pertaining to self-esteem, as children may feel damaged or that they are somehow to blame for the adoption. My son once asked me if his birth mother "gave me away because I'm a scaredy cat." The sense of rejection may be more pronounced if the child learns that the birth mother has other children that she did decide to parent.

Brodzinsky (1990) posits that adopted children also have a loss of genealogical continuity. They are not continuing a biological line with the adoptive parents because they are not biologically related to them. This sometimes affects the child's sense of identity. The child wonders where he or she belongs, and who he or she looks like. Children at this age do not like to be different from their peers, and the fact that they had a different beginning enhances their feelings of isolation.

The loss due to adoption is different than other losses because it is reversible. Like all children, adopted children have "perfect parent fantasies." While nonadopted children can fantasize that they have another set of wonderful parents who let them do anything they want, the problem for the adopted child is that there is a grain of truth to the fantasy. Because most adopted children have no memory of their birth parents, there is a greater tendency to either negatively or positively distort them, making it harder to resolve the loss (Brodzinsky, 1990). It is not uncommon for adopted children to say they want to live with their birth parents. The family therapist can help the parents see that this is part of normal development and not necessarily a rejection of the adoptive parents. The parents have to be encouraged to keep the lines of communication open, lest the child not bring up questions about the birth parents for fear of hurting the adoptive parents' feelings.

Many parents complain that their children never want to talk about adoption during this stage. Parents have to recognize that during middle childhood, children do not want to be different from their peers. Although Robert used to grin when his father told his adoption story to his teacher, he now cringes when his father suggests he come to school and do a presentation on adoption for Robert's class. Adopted children may also have difficulty with school projects such as a family tree.

In the classic book *Making Sense of Adoption*, Melina (1989) suggests that parents ask teachers at the beginning of the school year about projects pertaining to family or personal origins. Parents and teachers can work together to modify the assignment or be more alert to signs that the child is having a hard time with the project. Melina also suggests that children can make a circular, half-wheel family tree that includes both adoptive and birth family history. If information about the birth parents is unknown, the tree could include activities or hobbies that the birth parents may have included on the agency application.

During middle childhood, parents also have to decide how to share difficult information about the child's background. Difficult information might include rape, incest, drug use, abandonment, and murder. Although it is natural for parents to try to shield their children from painful experiences, adoptive parents have to recognize that children will make their own answers to questions that their parents feel too uncomfortable to discuss. Children can often piece together scenarios that are strikingly close to the real story just by their parents' behavior and extended family members' innuendoes. Van Gulden and Bartels-Rabb (1993) suggest giving children difficult information between the ages of eight and nine. They posit that telling children at this early age allows the child to gradually process and integrate the information into their identity.

Most adoption advocates suggest that parents seek professional advice on how to tell their child about a difficult history. The family therapist can help prepare the parents for the possible reactions the child may have to this information: depression, regressed behavior, acting out, and a drop in academic performance. The family therapist can also help the family not demonize the birth parents but help the child to find a way to embrace both family heritages. The family therapist can help children reframe the history so that they can begin to separate their birth parents' behavior from their own identity. It is important to let children know that there are no "bad genes" or "bad blood"; if their own conception was the result of an act of violence, it does not mean they are destined to become violent people (Van Gulden and Bartels-Rabb, 1993).

If the child seems reluctant to discuss the issue, parents can do what I call "planting seeds." Planting a seed requires that you place the seed in the soil at the right time and that you nurture the soil so that it is prepared to facilitate the seed's growth. Parents can share a little information about the child's history (planting the seed), and if the child is unresponsive, let the child know that the parents are available at any time to discuss the issue further (nurturing the soil). This approach respects the child's need for space while at the same time giving the child permission to discuss the topic at a later point when he or she is ready.

Adolescence

Identity development is a lifelong process, but it is a critical developmental task during adolescence. Identity development becomes increasingly complex as the adolescent focuses on becoming more differentiated from the family. Although all adolescents focus on differentiation, non-adopted teens still have appearance, temperament, and talents that can be traced to family members. Adopted teens usually know very little about their birth parents, so the process of differentiation may be particularly difficult for them because they do not have the benefit of the connectedness that comes with similarities in appearance and talents. If the adolescent is ethnically or racially different from the adoptive parents, then the child has to not only sort through "Who am I?" but also sort out to what group he or she owes allegiance (Grotevant, 1997).

LARRY

Larry is an eleven-year-old boy who was adopted shortly after birth through an independent adoption. Although he has always known he was adopted, he has never received much information about his birth family. At a family barbecue, he recently overheard his grandmother and aunt talking about how much Larry looks like his father, who turned out to be his Uncle Jonathan. After confronting his parents, he found out that he is the product of an incestuous relationship between his Uncle Jonathan and Larry's second cousin Melissa. Larry wants to confront his uncle and birth mother, but he is discouraged from doing so by his parents, who just want to "let sleeping dogs lie." Larry's grades begin to plummet, and he begins to get into fights at school. The parents do not know what to do. they want to be supportive of Larry, but they want to put this painful family incident behind them. they are afraid that Larry's confrontation may result in an irreparable schism within the extended family.

Although Larry's complex situation may seem to be the stuff from which daytime talk shows are made, his situation is not as uncommon as we think. Families often harbor tremendous, painful secrets that are given a lot of destructive power because families do not openly address the issues. In this type of situation, the family therapist has to be careful not to become triangulated in the family system. It is easy to fantasize that you can "fix" the child and do a better job at handling these issues than the parents. It is important to remember that family dynamics are very complex and while they may be unhealthy, they do served a function for the family. The family therapist can first assist the family by helping all family members acknowledge how painful this incident is for Larry and to have the parents reframe what their intent was in keeping this information from him. The therapist must also help the family rebuild trust, which has been violated by keeping the true familial relationships hidden. If possible, the therapist can also set up a meeting between the birth parents and adoptive family so that the entire family system can process what happened and sort through what types of relationships they can forge from here.

In seeking to forge an identity, all adolescents need to connect their past, present, and future. Children typically learn about their identities through narratives that essentially reconstruct their identity within the context of the family (Grotevant, 1997). Adopted adolescents often feel that there is a part of their story that remains untold because of information that they do not have about their birth parents. Thus, it is common in early adolescence to see a reawakening of the loss issues that surfaced earlier in middle childhood. It is usually at this time that adoptive parents have to confront the fact that their child may want to search for his or her birth parents. What complicates this desire to search is that for many confidential adoptions, the child is not allowed to request information until the age of eighteen or twenty-one, depending on the state in which the adoption was finalized. Some states refuse to open records, even in medical emergencies. Sometimes it helps to arrange a meeting between the child and other birth parents so they can get a sense of what thought processes go into the decision to place a child for adoption. Many adoption agencies who have good postplacement programs have support groups for adopted teens and birth mothers, and they routinely get these two groups together for some cathartic and healthy exchanges.

The family therapist can also help the parents put some of the adolescent's behavior into perspective. Since they are primarily working on differentiating from their adoptive parents, some teens feel they are predestined to be like their birth parents, whom they may perceive in a negative light. Although the teen is really angry at the birth parents, he or she may take this anger out on the adoptive parents, who are readily available. Anger is also a means by which the adolescent can distance himself or herself from the parents, which is a developmental task of adolescence anyway (Van Gulden and Bartels-Rabb, 1993). In the case of difficult birth histories, the family therapist has to help both the adolescent and the adoptive parents openly discuss their fears that the child will become "just like the birth parent." Parents also may need assistance with recognizing that for some adopted teens, the separation-individuation process may take longer. Separation from the family may be very frightening

SHEILA

Sheila was a thirteen-year-old who was adopted at two months of age through a public agency. She was an excellent student and excelled athletically. When she began attending a more academically rigorous school, her grades began to drop and she became insolent with some of her teachers. When she discovered that she had the first "D" in her academic career, she hid her report card from her parents until the school called and wanted to know why the parents had not returned the signed report card to the school. Sheila had no explanation for her behavior change, but promised her parents she would do better. Her grades did improve slightly but she began to isolate herself more from the family, remaining in her room for long periods of time. After repeated attempts to get her to talk about what was troubling her, Sheila's mother went into her room and read her journal. She discovered that Sheila had made two suicide attempts in the past month; once through taking a bottle of Bayer aspirin and another time by ingesting ten to fifteen Tylenol tables. Sheila wrote very critical self-

(continued)

(continued)

statements in the journal, and ended several entries by commenting that she was unable to please anyone; it was no wonder that her birth parents gave her away. In individual therapy, Sheila revealed that she felt her parents had unrealistic expectations of her and that she was terrified that her birth parents would die before she got a chance to meet them.

As Sheila was beginning to separate from her parents, she simultaneously was dealing with the rigors of a challenging academic program in which her usual peer support system was missing. As she was struggling with integrating her adoption status into her identity, she realized that she might never have the opportunity to really know who her birth parents were. She was also concerned that she could not live up to her parents' expectations and began to internalize that this had something to do with her being adopted. Sheila was seen in short-term individual therapy to help her mourn the loss of her birth parents. She was also placed in an adoption support group for teens where she could discuss her concerns and fears in an environment where she did not feel different or ostracized. In the family sessions, we focused on helping the family communicate more openly about Sheila's fears and also encouraged the parents to learn to "plant seeds" rather than have grand "meetings" in which to discuss adoption issues.

We also encouraged the family to do more claiming and belonging during this difficult period. Although differentiation from family is one of the primary tasks of adolescence, Van Gulden and Bartels-Rabb (1993) argue that claiming and belonging become particularly important during adolescence. The family therapist can help the family navigate through this potentially difficult period by encouraging the family to be accepting of the teen's need to point out how he or she is different while simultaneously reinforcing that each unique person is an important, valued part of the family unit. Part of Sheila's struggle was that she had very little information about her birth parents, so she could not integrate characteristics from all four parents.

for the adopted adolescent who is still struggling with a sense of loss and rejection.

In late adolescence, some adopted children may decide to search for their birth parents. Adopted parents should support the child's desire to search, in spite of their many fears. Some adoptive parents feel threatened by the desire to search, for fear that the child will reject them as parents. Other parents are afraid their child might be devastated if he or she finds the birth parent, only to be told that the birth parent does not want to have any contact with the child. The search process can also be extremely frustrating for the adopted individual because it is difficult to get the information they need to conduct it.

The therapist can assist the family during a search by having family members openly acknowledge their fears and fantasies about what the search will mean. The adopted person must also have realistic expectations of what such a reunion will mean and be emotionally prepared that the fantasy of reunion and the reality of the reunion are probably two different things. For example, many adopted persons are hurt when they find out that they have older siblings whom the birth mother decided to parent. Above all, the search process should be a time for healing for the adopted person, and the adoptive parents should support him or her.

It is also important to note that not all adolescents are interested in searching for birth parents. Many adopted teens go through adolescence without having major problems in adjustment. Benson, Sharma, and Roehlkepartain (1994) did a landmark study in which they studied 715 families from the Midwest. They found that contrary to popular belief, adopted adolescents were not particularly vulnerable to maladjustment. The adopted adolescents were just as positive as the nonadopted teens in the study. Most of the teens felt very attached to their adopted parents and had a positive view of adoption. Most of these families acknowledged differences between adoptive and nonadoptive families but did not dwell on the differences. Although more of these teens had been in therapy than the nonadopted teens, the adolescents who were in therapy were still within the normal range on the Child Behavior Checklist. Thus, while parents and family therapists need to be aware of the important issues that adopted adolescents confront, they also need to recognize that most adopted adolescents make it through this developmental stage relatively healthy.

TRANSRACIAL ADOPTIONS

Although the author has attempted to address the issue of transracial adoption in earlier sections of the chapter, transracial adoption brings up particular challenges to adoptive families that warrant further discussion. As previously noted, the 1960s saw an increase in the number of transracial adoptions until 1972, when the National Association of Black Social Workers (NABSW) wrote a position paper opposing transracial adoption. They argued that transracial adoption would result in cultural genocide because white parents could not teach black children about black culture or how to survive in a racist society. Boykin (1985) says that parents have to teach African-American children to negotiate three levels of reality. The first level is mainstream culture, which represents the values and norms of white middle-class America. The second level of reality is the child's minority group status. Minority groups in the United States have different levels of status. For example, research suggests that African Americans are viewed more negatively than other ethnic minorities. Different minority groups choose to interact with mainstream culture in different ways. For example, Asian cultures tend to promote more assimilation than other cultural groups. Finally, African-American children must also learn to negotiate within their own cultural group. Boykin argues that African-American children have a triple quandary because they have to negotiate three realities that do not always have compatible goals.

The opponents of transracial adoption also argued that policy makers need to address the larger issues involved in assuring that children have access to economic resources so they do not have to be involved in the child welfare system. While efforts to recruit African-American adoptive families have increased, a 1991 survey by the North American Council of Adoptable Children (NACAC) found that 83 percent of agencies surveyed said there were still organizational barriers that prevented or discouraged families of color from adopting (Hollingsworth, 1998). Molock (1995) noted a number of barriers to adoption for African-American families. Many African-American families cannot afford the exorbitant fees associated with adoption. Even families who can afford the fees often chafe at the prospect of "buying" a baby in light of the legacy of slavery in the United States. African Americans have the highest rate of informal adoption in the United States, so they often balk at having to go through all the legal red tape involved in legal adoptions. Adoption agencies are typically located far away from the African-American community, again giving the impression that adoption is for white middle-income families.

The NABSW position paper had a powerful effect on transracial adoption, and there was a sharp decline in the number of African-American children placed in white homes until the 1980s. Proponents of transracial adoption argued that race-matching policies in adoption was due to a combination of white racism, black nationalism, and biologism (Bartholet, 1993). Bartholet coined the term "biologism" to describe the tendency of adoption agencies to imitate biological families when making decisions regarding adoption placement. Since it is "natural" for children to physically resemble their parents, adoption agencies try to place children who physically resemble their adoptive parents. Bartholet questioned the soundness of this policy given that minority children are overrepresented in the foster care system. Bartholet argues that race matching is not in the best interest of the children in foster care because 50 percent of the children in the system are children of color but most of the prospective adoptive parents are white. She further argues that race matching is out of sync with laws based on discrimination, because race becomes the central factor in placing the children. This practice would be illegal in other areas of the law. Bartholet notes that there is no evidence that transracial adoption is harmful to children of color, and that transracial adoption has many benefits. Positive aspects of transracial adoption include more positive attitudes toward a racially integrated society. These children are more likely to describe themselves as "human" rather than by a racial classification. Transracial adoption has a positive impact on the race attitudes of the white members of the family as well. White parents of black children have a heightened awareness of racial issues, and the white siblings of black children are committed to a multicultural world.

Recently, the number of transracial adoptions has increased, largely due to the passage of the Multiethnic Placement Act (MEPA) of 1994, which prohibits adoption agencies that receive federal funds from denying placement solely on the basis of race, color, or national origin of the adoptive parents.

Most studies do suggest that transracial adoption is not harmful. Alexander and Curtis (1996) did a review of the literature on the adjustment of transracial adoptees and found no empirical evidence to suggest that transracial adoption was harmful to African-American children. However, Penn and Coverdale (1996) argue that studies on the adjustment of transracial adoptees often compare the children to their white siblings, suggesting that as long as the African-American adoptees perform the same as whites, then they have good adjustment. Hollingsworth (1997) did a meta-analysis of six methodologically sound adoption studies and found that transracial adoption did not have a negative impact on self-esteem, but that it did have a negative effect on the racial and ethnic identity of African-American and Mexican-American children, particularly as the children got older.

Although transracial adoption remains a politically charged topic, families will continue to adopt transracially, so parents need assistance to help their culturally different children navigate a complex world that embraces both their family and their native culture. Even when children are adopted as infants, parenting may have culturally different nuances. Prospective parents who are considering an international adoption should note differences in the child's native diet, the way babies are generally held, the way crying infants are handled, and language barriers (Schooler, 1993). Parents need to incorporate the child's native culture into family rituals in a natural manner. Including dolls, toys, and pictures from the child's native culture gives the message that parents acknowledge and embrace the child's cultural heritage.

Parents who object to the emphasis placed on the racial/ethnic heritage may need some help from a therapist who can help the family embrace and

KAMAU

Kamau, a twenty-five-year-old African American who was adopted by a white family as an infant, still has a trace of sadness as he recounts his bittersweet adolescence. He grew up in a small town in the Midwest where he was one of the few people of color in the entire town. His parents insisted on living a "color-blind" existence, so matters of race were rarely discussed in his family. He most vividly remembers watching a documentary on slavery when he was eleven years old. This was the first time he had heard any real discussion about slavery. He was overcome with emotion as he watched the slaves being shackled and beaten. Instead of his parents discussing his feelings with him, his mother forbade him from watching any more of the series. He also remembers feeling tremendously ugly because none of the girls in his high school would date him. Although he was a straight-A student and captain of the track and football teams, he never went out on a date until he was in college. He bitterly notes: "I was good enough to win their football games, but I wasn't good enough to date their daughters." He changed his name from Kenneth to Kamau as a way of trying to more fully embrace his African heritage. Figuring out a way to embrace both of his heritages has always been a struggle. He chuckles when he says, "I'm too black for the white folks and too white for the black folks." While Kamau loves his parents, he resents them for robbing him of his heritage.

incorporate the child's heritage into the family unit. Parents are being naïve when they state that they harbor no prejudices and want to raise their child in a color-blind family. The problem with this philosophy is that part of who we are is shaped by our culture. By denying the child's cultural background, you deny part of the child's identity. At some point, the child has to interact in a racially divisive society that will treat the child as a person of color. Children need to be prepared to deal with racism and discrimination. Families should carefully consider the racial/ethnic diversity of the community in which they live. Parents have to find positive role models within the child's native culture so the child will not feel alienated and isolated from his or her surroundings.

CONCLUSION

Adoptive families are more similar than dissimilar to nonadoptive families. In working with adoptive families, it is important to keep in mind that not all therapeutic issues relate to the adoptive status of the family. At the same time, it is important to be sensitive to the unique challenges and normative processes that are characteristic of adoptive families. Family therapists who work with adoptive families should have a general understanding of the adoption process and of how infertility can have emotional sequelae for the couple and the family. Therapists have to help the family understand the context of loss that is involved in most ¦adoptions for all members of the adoption triad: the birth parents, the adoptive parents, and the adopted child.

Parents of racially/ethnically different children should be encouraged to develop a sensitivity to the child's native culture and to incorporate aspects of the child's culture into family rituals. Families must also be prepared to live in communities that have the greatest likelihood of affirming both the parents' and the child's cultural heritage.

Family therapists can also be very instrumental in helping parents tell their children about difficult birth histories. Shielding children from difficult pasts is not protective, and is sometimes more harmful as children use their vivid imaginations to fill in the blanks. Sharing difficult information before adolescence allows the child to gradually incorporate the information into his or her sense of identity. Finally, some children will want to search for their birth parents when they get older. The family therapist can help the entire family see that the search process is not one of rejection, but of healing for the child, and should be supported if at all possible.

SELF-EXPLORATION:
ARE WE READY TO ADOPT A CHILD?

The purpose of this exercise is to help the couple explore whether they are ready to adopt a child. The couple should answer each of these questions independently and see how much agreement they have on their answers. There are no right or wrong answers. This exercise is designed to facilitate discussion of the decision to adopt. Use the scale listed below to answer each question.

1. Strongly agree 2. Agree 3. Neutral 4. Disagree 5. Strongly disagree

1. I want to adopt a child so I can give a needy child a wonderful, loving home.
2. I want to adopt a child because the world is already overcrowded and there are plenty of children who are already here who need good homes.
3. I want to adopt a child because we are unable to have children of our own.

4. I think that adoptive families are just like all other families.
5. I don't think our infertility will affect our raising an adopted child.
6. I think I can love an adopted child just as much as I would love a child born to me.
7. It is important to me that I pass along my genes to my offspring.
8. I worry about my ability to bond with a child who is not related to me by blood.
9. I have more concerns about adoption than my spouse.
10. I am not as enthusiastic as my spouse about the idea of adopting.
11. I think I could parent a child who has a different racial background than myself.
12. I think I could parent a child who comes from a different country than myself but has the same racial heritage.
13. I think I could parent an older child who might have some emotional problems.
14. I think I could parent a child who has physical disabilities.
15. I think my family (e.g., parents, siblings) would be supportive of our adopting a child.
16. I think my in-laws would be supportive of our adopting a child.
17. I think my parents would be supportive of our adopting a child of a different racial/ethnic background.
18. I think my parents would be supportive of our adopting a physically disabled child.
19. If my parents could not accept my adopted child as their grandchild, I would still maintain ties with my family.
20. I would want to do an open adoption in which we had routine contact with the child's birth parents.
21. I would want to do a semiopen adoption in which we would send information to an agency about our child and they would share this information with the birth parents.
22. I do not think it's a good idea to have any contact with the birth parents during the adoption process.
23. I am worried that the birth parents may want to reclaim the child after the child is placed with us.
24. I worry that one day my adopted child may want to go and find his or her birth parents.

UNIT IV:
FAMILY CONCEPTS—
A COGNITIVE PERSPECTIVE

The cognitive approaches described in this section are the most intuitively appealing perspective from which to examine family life. At the heart of the cognitive approach is the assumption that human beings are active, information-seeking, information-using organisms. Here, the family is comprehended best by understanding the thoughts, perceptions, expectations, plans, and styles of communication inherent in the repertoire of each person. The cognitive approach stresses how any one individual influences other individuals or the entire family system. Each chapter in this section demonstrates that the rules governing individual perception and attitudes can set limits on the family as surely as any interaction pattern.

Chapter 13

Communication Styles

If I knew you and you knew me
*   as each one knows his own self, we*
Could look each other in the face,
*   and see therein a truer grace.*
Life has so many hidden woes,
So many thorns for every rose,
The "Why" of things our hearts would see
If I knew you and you knew me.

Author unknown

Almost all of us have had the uncomfortable experience of having to find our way with a new group of people. Perhaps we were moving to a new neighborhood, starting a new job, or joining a new club. We feel background anxiety about wanting to be accepted, but in addition, much of our unease stems from not yet having a comfortable repertoire of topics or an acceptable style of interacting with the new folks.

One of the reasons family life is so comforting and gives so much security is that the communication patterns are as clearly mapped out and understood as the road we take to work each day. The effortless nature of the communications makes everything seem quite spontaneous and authentic. Individuals feel they express "the real me" when at home. In actuality, families have myriad rules governing their communications, and these rules may be every bit as restrictive as those of the workplace. But these are the rules we grew up under. They are accepted as proper and "natural." Indeed, we use our family communication styles to judge how "normal" our interactions with others are.

Individuals and families each develop distinctive styles of communicating. Body language, voice intonations, and topics of conversation all become connected with the family identity. Although most families cultivate a narrow inventory of conversation topics, very little research has been done to assess whether preferred topics of conversation have any differential influence on family cohesiveness or individual development. One reason the content of family conversations has not been vigorously researched is that the pool of topics from which families can choose is limitless. By contrast, the quality of communications (emotional tone, body language, intensity, etc.) is more distinctive and consistent. Thus, many researchers have tried to develop models of family communication to describe the critical process of communication without regard to content.

Most of these approaches assume that every utterance in the family contains two messages: (1) the words, or content message, and (2) the unspoken metamessage. The latter term refers to the context in which the words are spoken and helps define the relationship between the two people communicating. The metamessage often restricts the meaning of the spoken words and always colors their interpretation. For example, if a mother scowls at her child and says "Your room looks great" in a chiding voice, everyone will understand that the mother's metamessage is that she is criticizing the child for a messy room. This metamessage is often assumed to influence and shape family dynamics more than the spoken words.

Communication styles have often been characterized by type as individual, parental, or spousal. Various studies have focused on each of these types. All three are analyzed in this chapter. You will notice some overlap among these conversational domains, and you will also notice distinct differences. The communication style each family member uses may vary according to the role relationships between the communicators and the topic they are discussing. Regardless of the communication style used, the ease and effectiveness of communication are enhanced when all concerned acknowledge and accept the behaviors, feelings, and motivations of the others.

INDIVIDUAL COMMUNICATION STYLES

Five easily recognized communication styles have been described by Satir (1967, 1991): "The placator," "the blamer," "the super-reasonable one," "the distractor," and "the congruent one." Most family members fit readily into one of these five categories. In some families, communication styles are fluid—this year's placator may be next year's blamer—but it is more common for individual communication styles to persist for years on end. The style is like a protective armor buckled on to a person early in family life. As one grows, the armor is tighter and tighter, yet the thought of removing it gets more and more threatening. Once a family member has been labeled, the outcome of interactions with other family members appears inevitable.

The Placator

The placator is fairly easy to identify. He or she is too accommodating, too polite, too apologetic, or just "too good to be true." Placators are desperately motivated to have everything run smoothly, to avoid conflict at any cost. Their anxiety tends to impel them to act like doormats. "I'm so sorry dinner is cold," a wife says breathlessly. "I had to rush Jeffrey to the emergency room. Then I got caught in traffic, and there was a hundred-car freight train at the crossing, and . . . and." The apologies go on all through dinner.

Placators are always trying to absorb blame or minimize hurt so that conflicts will not openly erupt. The verbal style of the placator is characterized by few revelations of personal needs and desires. It is very friendly, though, full of chitchat and playfulness.

The Blamer

The blamer also would like to see the family function smoothly and efficiently. But when the routine is disrupted or expectations are not met, the blamer can always find someone else in the family to hold responsible. Blamers never see themselves as at fault and rarely see circumstances outside the family as contributing to the family difficulties. Blamers are very good at pointing fingers within the family and telling others how to correct their flaws. They usually know how to shout and are apt to be clever at composing cutting reprimands. Blamers are no fun to be around, and they develop a very bad reputation in the family. The verbal style of the blamer is high in emotion and low in personal disclosure. Words such as "should," "ought," "always," and "never" are liberally distributed. This imperial voice does a lot of directing, blaming, advising, and speaking for others.

The Distractor

Like the placator, the distractor is highly motivated to have peace and harmony pervade the home front. Unlike the placator, however, the distractor finds it difficult to accept responsibility for family difficulties. Neither is he or she comfortable attributing blame to others. Instead, the distractor tries to defuse family conflicts by forcing the family to unite and face an equally pressing but less divisive concern. For example, a child hears her parents fighting over which bills to pay; the mother is blaming the father for losing too much at poker. Suddenly the daughter develops an intense intestinal cramp, a headache, or a homework problem that temporarily distracts the parents and focuses their concern on some new crisis.

In a few families, the tensions are so intense and a family member so vulnerable that "opting out" of the environment seems to be the only way to cope. The distractor turns to irrelevancies. For example, everyone in the family is violently arguing about the burial service for a suddenly deceased uncle. The irrelevant distractor, meanwhile, is wondering what type of rice is most popular among the Renji Indians. Irrelevant behavior need not be this bizarre. Just imagine a mother trying to describe her marital problems to her adolescent daughter. The daughter feels awkward, angry, and sad. She keeps interrupting her mother, asking for a definite date when they can go to the mall to buy a promised set of designer jeans. Sound closer to home? Psychotic people may be experts at irrelevance, but normal people can be quite adept at it too.

Perhaps the reader is thinking, "Yes, that happens, but why can't the girl with the complaining mother learn to tell her that she feels uncomfortable and she would rather not know the nitty-gritty details?" True, the girl can learn to express her discomfort and the mother can learn not to involve her daughter in marital spats. But confronting the need to revise one's family behavior takes insight, experience, and, often, the help of an objective outsider. Even when people want to change, they often are too anxious, too afraid, or too unskilled to know how to do it. Indeed, changing these communication styles is one of the major goals of family therapy.

The Super-Reasonable One

The super-reasonable family member is the one who always stays "cool," analyzing problems so objectively that the solutions sound extremely rational. Often they are very rational. Super-reasonable people tend to assume the upper hand in family crises and to criticize freely. They point out the blamer's role in problems. They tell the placator to be more assertive. Statements of the super-reasonable person are highly responsive to what the other person has just said. Emotion tends to be lacking; speech has a tentative, searching, highly reflective style. Words such as "probably," "maybe," "perhaps," "could," and "might," are used frequently.

What super-reasonables have trouble doing is getting in touch with feelings—their own and those of others. Consider the example of a wife who has begun to work full-time outside the home and finds she needs more help with the housework. A super-reasonable husband might quickly agree that the wife does not have the time to do everything that she did before. He might point out the contributions of each child and how the children's responsibilities could be increased. He may even acknowledge his own inability to help out more. What he does not tune into are his feelings and his wife's feelings. He is unable to get in touch with his wife's frustrations over his criticisms of the home's disarray and the precooked dinners. He is unable to get in touch with his own frightened feelings about being obligated to help out more and his angry feelings over the loss of services he has long been accustomed to receiving. His analytic detachment protects him against a number of emotional, intense issues. For the super-reasonable person the only issue is the observable, stated one; objective analysis of all pertinent (but nonemotional) factors is the only way to arrive at a workable solution. Super-reasonable people are never wrong in their own eyes. Yet they are rarely right because they only see one layer of reality.

The Congruent One

Congruent individuals have the most versatile method of communicating with family members. Therapists often try to influence clients toward

---

ANGELA (graduate student, age 32)

When my half-brother and I were children, the predominant family behavior patterns were these: my mother—placator, my brother—irrelevant, and me—super-reasonable. I don't believe that we were pure types, as our pattern of arguing tended to be that of blaming. A typical interaction would go like this: My brother would make an excessive demand on my mother, she would ignore him for a while and finally give in, and I would give her advice about how she should behave in this situation. The interaction between my mother and me was that she would ask me for advice, I would give it to her, and then she would continue to behave in a placating manner toward my brother. My brother all the while would be ignoring the interaction between the two of us and trying to get as much as possible out of my mother. I think that my super-reasonable stance in the family may have been responsible for the family reputation I had of being cold and distant. My role was to be cool and reasonable no matter what else was going on.

As my brother and I grew up, the blaming aspects of our family role became increasingly salient. I became aware of being used by my mother as a child and became more blameful of my mother, yet still maintained much of my super-reasonable stance when I was with her. My brother became extremely blameful of both my mother and me but still held on to many of his irrelevant actions. My mother, deprived of me as a confidante, became blameful of me for neglecting her, being inconsiderate, etc. She continued to placate my brother though she complained to other people about his actions. At present, I believe that my brother and I still maintain the same postures relating to each other. I am alternately blameful and super-reasonable and he is both blameful and irrelevant.

this style. Congruent individuals want to express how they feel and to provide a rationale for why they are behaving a certain way in a particular situation. Sometimes, congruent personality types get angry and upset because expressing their rage is more important than keeping peace and harmony. Sometimes they accept the blame for a crisis if they feel responsible or guilty for what has happened. Congruent individuals are the antithesis of irrelevant people. They never run away from the issue. Satir (1967:49) describes this mode of operating as follows: "Nothing is crossed out; nothing has to be eliminated. Anything can be talked about; anything can be commented on; any question can be raised; there is nothing to hold you back."

The verbal style of the congruent person is marked by intimacy—by sharing a lot of feelings and personal information. The congruent style opens a person up to sharing very vulnerable points. This person can accept responsibility and blame and is interested in conveying care and cooperation to the other person. The congruent style gives the individual the highest degree of personal freedom and gives families the greatest hope of successfully maintaining trust and support within their nuclear group.

Mix and Match

Most people adapt just a single communication style as their modus operandi. At times, however, family members change roles according to the subgroup they are interacting with. Perhaps they will adapt one communication mode when they are with their mother, another when with their father, and still another when interacting with siblings. Consequently, different family members may perceive the same person differently. Father may well be a placator toward his daughter, a blamer toward his son, and super-reasonable toward his wife. Such disparities underlie the complexity and multifaceted nature of family communications.

VERNON (businessman, age 40)

Analyzing my family in terms of Satir's four interactional patterns, I came up with the following. Dad falls into the role of the placator in most of the more intense situations. Mother has two roles she fluctuates between, blamer and irrelevant, and it's sometimes hard to predict which one she will be in. This effectively results in her getting treated with kid gloves most of the time so she won't go into one of her "spells," as she calls them. She has also developed a hearing loss to match my father's, which comes in very handy

(continued)

(continued)

at times. Cathy spends most of her time in the placator role also, but can be congruent when she needs to be. I spent most of my life in the super-reasonable role, which was a functional way of distracting people from their worries.

So when my dad and I are together, we get along fine. He always tries to boost me and goes along with most of my analyses of the family and of politics, as well. My mom and I can't stay in the same room for more than ten minutes without getting on each other's nerves. I understand that we're all supposed to have a primary bond with our mother, but this woman has always made me positively bristle. For example, last weekend I'm talking about what type of car I should buy and she starts telling me if I had become an engineer I wouldn't have to worry about fuel economy! It wasn't like she just mentioned this either. She went on and on and on about all these engineers she knew and what type of work they did. I was tired and it took me a half hour to get up from the table and leave the room. If I had sat for an hour, she would have kept on going.

My relationship with my sister is good, although sometimes it is very threatening. She's trying to live her life to the fullest, to experience the deepest and broadest range of emotions available to her. I'm busy trying to figure out what is the logical, sensible way to run my life. I envy her joie de vivre but as I said, it's also very frightening.

When we're all together, my mother always starts a scene and I get sucked into showing her the error of her ways. The other two act as referees. This pattern reappears in every family memory I can recall. While I feel an analytic superiority that I don't think I'll ever relinquish in my family of origin, if and when I get married, hopefully I'll be able to be congruent much of the time.

BELINDA (graduate student, age 25)

In the early days, my father was the super-reasonable one in the family, my mother tended to be a placator, and the three kids tended to be blamers. I spoke to my mother about this recently and she said something like, "Your father was impossible in those days. You could not win an argument with him because he would not participate in it." As young kids we all blamed everyone else for everything. I can remember one interaction with my mother when I was eight years old and I wanted her to help me with a paper for school. She wouldn't help me, and when I got mad she told me to put it away until I was in a better frame of mind. My response to this was that "I'll flunk out of school, and get married, and have twenty babies and it will be *all your fault* because you wouldn't LET me do my homework." And as my mother said, my father truly was super-reasonable in those days— there really was no way to argue with him.

(continued)

(continued)

Over the years, however, as my father stayed drunk more and more of the time, he became the blamer. During the last year that he lived with us, he and I were constantly at each other's throats, name-calling and blaming with the best of them. Interestingly, it was my mother who then became super-reasonable. Funny, because she doesn't see herself as being like my father had been. And yet, there's no arguing with her now and she has a very intellectual way of looking at every problem.

When my mother and I interact now, we are either super-reasonable to each other, or eventually I get sick of that and turn into a blamer. With my younger sister, my mother has finally lost her ability to be super-reasonable. However, instead of being congruent, she either blames (in which case a yelling match ensues, and my sister has much greater endurance), or she turns into a placator, feeling guilty and responsible for my sister's problems (my sister does blame her for them).

I think in my interactions with my sisters I learned to be a placator because they were both more effective blamers and better fighters than me. I learned that it is much safer to placate, take the blame, put yourself in a one-down position, and get it over with fast than to try to blame or even to be congruent. I learned to be submissive and to duck a lot, which was probably the only way I could have survived the assaults. I think that this has carried over to my peer relations, however, so that I also tend to take this role most of the time outside my family. When I was ten years old this was a very effective stance to take, but I don't think that it is particularly functional in my life at age twenty-five.

SPOUSAL COMMUNICATION

How often couples converse and what they say depends on age, interests, and social class. In general, researchers report that the answer to "How do you communicate with your mate?" is all too often "seldom."

The longer a marriage endures, the less opportunities seem to occur for nurturing trust, promoting feelings of closeness, and being introspective about one's own feelings. Yet most adults seem to feel that intimate conversation is vital to their self-esteem and mutual well-being. Intimate conversations strengthen the couple's mutual appreciation and understanding.

COMMUNICATING INTIMATELY

Miller (1975) has specified seven aspects of skillful intimate communications. Certainly no one can incorporate all these skills into every interchange, but on those special occasions when deeply meaningful exchanges occur, these aspects are certain to be present.

The first skill, validation, means the ability to reassure the other person that you truly understand the depth and scope of what is said. Telling a depressed spouse who feels unloved that tomorrow will be better leaves the spouse feeling flat. It is as though the partner was not listening to what the spouse said. To validate successfully requires restating in your own way what the other person has just said. This technique ensures that you are experiencing what that person intends you to experience. Overreacting to what is said can be every bit as insensitive as underreacting. For example, suppose a husband complains of a mild, nagging headache. His wife says, "Here's some Darvon to kill the pain. Take a few." She is overreacting. She is not being respectful of the quality of his headache (mild). A validating response might be, "Gee, I know how annoying that type of headache can be. Do you want to do anything for it?" Thus, when a spouse responds as an effective therapist would, he or she is probably using validation.

When a wife who attends college asks the husband to leave the door to her study area closed, she hopes that her husband will appreciate and respect her need for privacy and quiet. If the husband ridicules or patronizes the wife by suggesting that such a request is "silly," "cute," or "going overboard," the wife will retreat to other communication styles and forgo attempts at intimate communication.

Second, people take responsibility for their own feelings and thoughts. They have to be able to admit to themselves what is making them angry or depressed. Often, when people analyze why they are angry at their spouses, they realize they are really disappointed with themselves and frustrated that their mates cannot alleviate their pain. In these cases, responsibility for change rests on one's own shoulders. But if your spouse's behavior or attitude is violating a value you hold dear, you are responsible for communicating this fact.

Third, precision is important to communication. Telling a spouse that you feel the budget is too tightly controlled is too vague. Stating that you need at least 100 dollars a month for a discretionary spending allowance would be much more precise.

Fourth, intimate communication requires a rationale for what is said. For instance, you can explain how you expect to spend the discretionary money or why it is important to you to have it. (Saying "I need to feel that I have some money I need not account for" is a valid—and may be an important—rationale.) Giving reasons puts the couple on the road to a successful discussion.

Fifth, intimacy requires a good sense of humor. The ability to laugh at a situation together creates bonds between couples and makes the expression of disagreements much less threatening.

Sixth, asking questions when information is needed is a sign of objectivity. For example, the wife whose husband states a need for discretionary money might ask, "How would this affect our savings plan? What would you consider a reasonable amount of allowance?" Such questions create a climate of cooperation; the spouses become comrades instead of adversaries.

Last, effective, intimate communication requires a climate of safety. People need to know that their boundaries will be respected. The ability to be intimate seems to rely on the skill couples have to communicate a sense of friendship when they are together.

Problems of Distressed Couples

Gottman (1986) compared distressed couples in therapy with couples not in therapy. He found very specific interactions associated with the necessary spirit of friendship. All the interactions related to the seven aspects of intimate communication described above. For example, couples in therapy were consistently less positive and more negative in their interactions. They were also more likely to shuttle complaints back and forth and to be sarcastic.

When Gottman analyzed how the two groups tried to resolve marital problems, he found that the distressed couples got off to a bad start by attributing negative thoughts and feelings to one another and expressing negative feelings themselves. The nontherapy couples showed more control; they tried to get off to a good start by getting the partner to express concerns and by actively validating or agreeing with each other whenever the opportunity arose. Similarly, nondistressed couples tried to negotiate a resolution by contracting a settlement and minimizing differences; distressed couples engaged in a string of counterproposals and continually mirrored any frustration or anger seen in the partner. Thus, differences were heightened rather than minimized.

Gottman's (1998; Gottman et al., 1998) recent work finds four communication patterns that predict divorce: the husband rejecting the wife' influence attempts; a lack of physiological soothing (physical comforting) of the wife by the husband; negative, complaining openers by the wife; an an inability of eitehr husband or wife to keep calm when the spouse gets upset.

Gottman's work strongly suggests that intimacy and friendship emerge out of a specific kind of marital interaction and that couples may be helped to develop deeper and more successful marriages by participating in marital enrichment programs geared to teaching successful styles of interacting. A questionnaire for measuring intimate communication in your family is included in the self-exploration exercises at the end of this chapter.

MARIO (buyer, age 27)

I'm in the midst of separating from my wife, so this topic is going to be a difficult one to write about. I'll start by reflecting on my parents' relationship. My mom and dad had a very traditional marriage, but they were happy and had a lot of intimate conversations in front of us kids. My dad was forever starting businesses; he owned a grocery store, a gift shop, a printing shop, and even a luncheonette. Obviously, none of them was very successful, but before each venture my parents would plan and talk together for days on end and with each failure they cried together for nights on end. We kids were included, but it was always clear that as a team Mom and Dad would bear the brunt of emotions and we would always be safe and cared for. Mom and Dad would kiss and hug in front of us and they would tell off-color jokes. I always felt free to talk with them and felt I had a strong foundation to build an intimate relationship with my wife.

My wife and I met at a party and immediately we were both smitten with each other. Within eight weeks we were essentially living together and twelve months after we met, we were married. I loved being married. I loved the intimacy of going down the food aisles of the supermarket together, planning our weekends together, and sharing our workdays. I thought my wife was equally happy, but about three years ago she started complaining that we weren't intimate enough, that I wasn't relating to her. At first, I tried to spend more time with her and to be sensitive to what she wanted to talk about. She only became more disgruntled with how "superficial" I was. It got so bad we decided to go into marital counseling. Our counselor gave us a series of marital enrichment exercises like the ones presented in this chapter. I found that I really enjoyed doing them and was sharing parts of myself with Sue that I hadn't been sharing before. Sue got a lot happier at first and then became worried that without the structure of counseling, we would drift apart again. Luckily (I guess), we were able to maintain a lot of openness and sharing. We were so open with one another that when she told me she was attracted to a guy at work I told her I'd be nervous and anxious but she could feel free to go to a dinner reception with him at the office. Well, seven months later, they're madly in love, we have a painfully intimate relationship, and I'm getting a divorce. The openness I've shared with Sue lately I'd like to have in the next relationship. It's not the intimacy my parents had. It's more self-centered and introspective. Maybe it's the intimacy required by the ME generation of the 1980s. If Sue and I hadn't been more intimate, our marriage would have ended three years ago. As it is now, I'm ready for the 1980s and for a new relationship that will hopefully have a stronger foundation.

Promoting Intimate Communication

Unfortunately, intimate conversations do not occur naturally in most marriages. Many marriage therapists have therefore devised structured communication exercises to help their clients develop an intimate conversation style.

Some common topics explored in the marital enrichment programs developed by L'Abate (1976, 1981) are listed in the boxed section below:

Besides learning how to discuss intimate topics, couples need to learn how to convey their messages appropriately. If a wife overcooks the steak, her husband's jokes about resoling his shoes with the result may be intended to ease the situation by reducing it to absurdity. If she interprets the remark as ridicule of her cooking skills, however, his attempt at humor is doomed. On the other hand, if ridicule really was his intent, a fruitful—if painful—discussion is more likely to ensue than if he tried to cover actual annoyance with an insincere communication. It is important to suit one's manner to one's real message.

Understanding each other's emotional messages has long-term benefits for couples. Markman (1984) found that spouses who were able to achieve the intended emotional effects of their communications with their mates were far more likely to be happily married than those whose spouses reacted differently than they had intended.

Topics of Conversation/Communication for Learning to Know Your Mate

1. What do you see as your strong points as a person? What do you see as your weak points or things about yourself that you would like to change?
2. In what way are you two alike as people? In what ways are you two different?
3. How have your likes and dislikes changed over the past five or ten years?
4. In general, do you see yourselves becoming more similar or more dissimilar over the past five years?
5. Have you ever felt the need for more privacy or more separateness in your family? How do you deal with your need for privacy?
6. Who makes the decisions in this family? Are there any ways that decision making could be shared more fairly in the family?
7. How are the household duties distributed? Are there any ways the household duties could be distributed more fairly?
8. How are the financial burdens shared in this family? Are there any ways in which the financial burdens could be distributed more fairly?
9. Imagine you are seventy years old. You're thinking back over the course of your life. Describe what you have done. What have been your happiest times and saddest times? If you could, how would you change your life?

Source: Questions taken from L'Abate, L. 1976. *Understanding and Helping the Individual in the Family.* New York: Grune & Stratton.

TERRI (graduate student, age 43)

My first marriage really had no intimate communication. We talked about our work and our schedules and that was it. It caused me to cut off my feelings and to have low self-esteem. I didn't feel as though my thoughts or dreams were important. I pushed them away and by the end of four years I was very insecure and shy. I don't know why my ex-husband couldn't share. He did have a miserable childhood with a broken home and a lot of hostility—but so do a lot of people. Living with him was like living with a continual stranger. My whole life was a secret to him and it would have been all his for the asking!

My current husband and I love to have time together to talk and play. I really treasure those times. Some of our most intimate times would look idiotic to other people. We like to plan fantasy vacations and make plans for our dream house. We love to analyze our respective families of origin and read poetry together. After ten years of marriage, these times are less frequent but when they do come around, they're even more valuable than in our early years.

In the early years, the stepchildren were constantly interfering with any signs of intimacy between us. For example, during the first two years we were married, Gina, my stepdaughter was very threatened by our intimacy. If we sat down on the sofa together and were giggling or starting a relaxed conversation she would plop herself between us and come up with the most silly problems or questions. Once she sat down, she was there for good! Even in the car, if we began talking about anything meaningful, she'd turn up the car radio, get carsick, or want to play a travel game with her dad. In order to get some intimacy time we had to go out for dinner.

Recently, our biggest problem is that we don't communicate or share feelings because we feel that it would hurt the other person. For example, I'm very upset that Jake is so busy traveling. In between transcontinental work weeks and jet lag I often feel like a widow. I know Jake is even more stressed than I am by this arrangement, and if I express myself it will only make his blood pressure go up and his ulcer bleed. I don't want to sound too trite but sometimes the most intimate communications occur when you refrain from talking. I feel that by not discussing my frustrations, I'm communicating my love for Jake in the deepest possible way. I'm sure there are things that he refrains from discussing for similar reasons. In a way I sometimes long for the open, uninhibited soul-baring episodes of our early days together, but more often than not I accept the fact that that type of naive intimacy is reserved for the beginnings of relationships. After that, they're too taxing, too depressing, and take too much time!

PARENTAL COMMUNICATION

The most widely used typology of parenting behaviors is that developed by Baumrind (1973, 1983). She found three basic types of parenting styles: the authoritative, the authoritarian, and the permissive (see Table 13.1). These three parenting styles appeared to be associated with different characteristics in children. When parents behaved in an authoritarian manner, the children were withdrawn, discontented, and distrustful. Children of permissive parents tended to have little self-control and little self-reliance but were considerate, friendly with their peers, and high in self-esteem. Authoritative parents had the most competent children. These children were independent and achievement oriented. They were friendly and cooperative with adults and peers.

TABLE 13.1. Baumrind's Types of Parenting

Authoritarian Parents	Permissive Parents	Authoritative Parents
There is strict discipline and the child is expected to conform to the parents' standards.	There is as little discipline as possible and the child has as much freedom as is consistent with the child's physical safety.	There is strict discipline and the child is expected to conform to the parents' standards.
The parents are not interested in the child's opinion when family decisions are made. When the parents punish the child, no line of reasoning is offered.	The parents are very interested in soliciting the child's opinions and feelings when family decisions are made. When the parents punish or restrict the child, they explain why they have decided to act harshly.	The parents are very interested in soliciting the child's opinions and feelings when family decisions are made. When the parents punish or restrict the child, they explain why they have decided to act harshly.
The parents have very high standards and expect the child to perform well intellectually and socially.	The parents intentionally do not put pressure on the child to excel or perform better in any particular area. They have a laissez-faire policy to typical childhood achievement goals.	The parents have very high standards and expect the child to perform well intellectually and socially.
The parents take little pleasure in the children and their accomplishments and do not openly express a lot of warmth and affection.	The parents are very warm and nurturing with their children. The parents are concerned for the child's well-being and take a lot of pleasure in the child's accomplishments.	The parents are very warm and nurturing with their children. The parents are concerned for the child's well-being and take a lot of pleasure in the child's accomplishments.

LINDA (teacher, age 32)

I remember reading about Baumrind's three types of parenting as an undergraduate taking my child psychology course at the University of Miami. It made a lot of sense to me then, and I was certain that I would be an exemplary authoritative parent. Ten years later, I can say that it isn't that easy or that effective! Sometimes, probably most of the time, I do act in an authoritative way, but that's because most of the time things are going along fairly smoothly. When I'm happy with myself, very busy at work, and getting along with my husband, I drift into being a permissive parent. I let them go unsupervised, trusting them and the world, that no harm will come to them. This is particularly true for my young daughter who at four seems quite mature and competent to me. The other day I was busy studying for an exam and so she not only fixed her own breakfast and lunch but made herself chocolate pudding for dessert! When I'm feeling low and pressured I get to be very authoritarian. The kids have to do what I want when I want, or there will be screaming and punishments galore. My mom had these rampages and so do I. Basically, the quality of my parenting seems to vary with how I feel about me. Also, the child's personality is very important. While I am very permissive with my little one I am much more authoritarian with my older one, where my expectations are very high. Maybe as Baumrind's theory gets more refined it will ring true with parents as much as with parents-to-be.

Not all parents could be described as fitting into one of these three patterns. It is also important to note that there is no solid evidence that these parenting styles are responsible for the behavior seen in the children. More likely, certain kinds of children interact with their parents differently, helping to create the parenting styles observed.

How Age Affects Content and Style

Researchers are also investigating the effect of age on parent/child communication styles. An abundance of studies demonstrate that both the content and the style of parent/child communication changes in precise ways from infancy through the preschool years. No clearly identified stages or processes have been found in communication studies of normal school-age children and adolescents. The content of parent/adolescent communications has not received a lot of attention, though. A notable exception is the research on mother/daughter communications about sex discussed below.

Yalom, Estler, and Brewster (1982) interviewed college-aged women and their mothers about their ways of communicating about various aspects of female sexuality. Seventy percent of the mothers felt "comfortable" or "very comfortable" discussing sexuality with their college-aged daughters; only husbands or lovers rated higher. In comparison, nearly half the 1,980 daughters surveyed (46 percent) reported that they were "comfortable" or "very comfortable" in discussing sex with their mothers. In a list of ten possible communicants (including male and female friends and groups of friends, sister(s), brother(s), father, and surrogate mother), only sexual or romantic partners rated higher than mothers.

In response to another question, the majority of mothers expressed satisfaction with the current communication about sexuality between themselves and their daughters, with 65 percent responding positively, 28 percent responding neutrally, and 7 percent responding negatively. To a lesser extent, the 1,980 students expressed qualified satisfaction with the sexual communication between themselves and their mothers, with 48 percent evaluating it positively, 24 percent neutrally, and 28 percent negatively. It is noteworthy that the size of the group expressing dissatisfaction with sexual communication was 28 percent in the daughters' sample compared with 7 percent in the mothers' sample—a fourfold increase. Clearly, the daughters were identifying the problem of poor sexual communication more readily than the mothers. Daughters who rated their communication as poor frequently stated that they could not be open or honest with their mothers because mother and daughter had different ideas about acceptable behavior for an unmarried woman of college age; many indicated that they avoided discussing personal situations that might lead to conflict. For the most part, the poor communicators seemed to believe that silence was the best policy.

The respondents in both groups were asked to identify the sexual topics that had been discussed in mother/daughter conversations. Table 13.2 shows percentages of the two groups reporting discussion of each topic and ranks the topics according to frequency of discussion. Both groups reported menstruation, marriage, abortion, pregnancy, and love relationship with a male as the most frequently discussed sexual topics in mother/daughter conversations. Masturbation, orgasm, multiple sexual relations, and love relations with a female ranked as the least frequently discussed subjects for both groups.

Possible Pitfalls of Open Parent/Child Communication

Open communication between parent and child may not always have positive effects. Sometimes, parents' attempts to openly express their own insecurities and fears overwhelm children who feel vulnerable and frightened without an all-knowing, confident parent. An interesting example of this problem occurs when parents with horrifying wartime experiences openly share their grief and sadness. Lichtman (1984) studied parents who had survived the Holocaust and the effects their communications about the

TABLE 13.2. Sexual Topics Discussed by Mothers and Daughters

Topic	Mothers		Daughters	
	Percent	Rank	Percent	Rank
Menstruation	99	1	97	1
Marriage	88	2	92	2
Abortion	81	3	62*	6
Pregnancy	80	4	75	5
Love relationship with a male	78	5	77	4
Contraception	75	6	58	7
Virginity	69	7	54	8
Cohabitation	68	8	78	3
Sexual intercourse	66	9	53	9
Sexually transmitted disease	64†	10	32†	10
Masturbation	26*	11	9*	14
Orgasm	24	12	13	12
Multiple sexual relations	21	13	20	11
Love relations with a female	21	14	12	13

* Significant at .05 level
† Significant at .01 level

Source: Yalom, M., Estler, S., and Brewster, W. 1982. Changes in female sexuality: A study of mother-daughter communication and generational differences. *Psychology of Women Quarterly, 72*(2): 149.

war had on their now-adult children. She found that the gender of the parent who did the talking as well as the gender of the child involved affected the relationship between parental communication of the Holocaust experiences and second-generation personality traits.

When the mothers frequently and willingly communicated their wartime experiences, the adult female children became high in anxiety, paranoia, and hypochondriasis, and low in ego strength. It is as though the female children identified with their mothers' sense of being victimized. Male children did not show this pattern of identification with the mother.

When the fathers frequently and willingly communicated their wartime experiences, both sons and daughters experienced less depression and hypochondriasis. Fathers seemed more likely to present to their children the identity of a fighter, helping to fortify the self-images of the children. Fathers and mothers who used a lot of guilt-inducing communication ("For this I survived Hitler?") or indirect communications ("It was rainy like this the day we were deported from the ghetto") had children with high degrees of anxiety. Lichtman's findings are particularly important because they cast doubt on the popular advice that children of survivors are uniformly benefited by having parents who openly discuss their experiences. It may be that excessive talking or extreme lack of communication could adversely affect children, but this will have to be tested in future studies. The Holocaust experience is a prototype of parents communicating about their own powerlessness, fears, and losses. To the extent that one can generalize, it is prudent to keep in mind that the effects of parent/child communications are complex. At times, withholding information from children may help maintain generational boundaries and thereby protect them.

THE "KA" SOLUTION:
NEW TERMS FOR STEPFAMILIES AND THE NEW TIMES

"Dadka and Momka, I love you."

"My stepfather won't let me go to the mall." "We are spending Thanksgiving at my stepmother's mother's house." These statements are common. We all understand what is being said on a content level. Yet, the metamessage contained within these comments is that the child is not on a

---

BUTCH (student, age 22)

I'm sure that anyone who knew my parents and the relationship I have with them would agree that they are very permissive with me. Partly this is because I'm the only son (I have one sister) and partly this is because I have always been very mature and responsible. When I was nine I got my own paper route (really, my neighbor was the official carrier but I paid him two dollars a week to be my cover). I always had my own money and never got an allowance. Still, if I ever asked my parents for money they gave it to me and never would question what I wanted it for. I was always allowed to regulate my own bedtime and by seven years old I had outgrown the need for babysitters. When I was fourteen I got a job on a clamming boat and would get up at three in the morning and be out with these twenty-year-olds. My parents were proud of me but their friends thought they were crazy. All my life they let me do as I pleased, dress as I pleased, and think as I pleased. I'm sure that their willingness to give me the freedom I needed allows us to have the open and trusting relationship I have with them today.

A good example of this occurred with my girlfriend Jan last year. Whenever we go home on holidays we sleep in my bedroom together. I've always been able to do this and while in high school my friends were all astounded by my parents' permissiveness, I've gotten used to it and don't really think about it. Anyway, we got into this ridiculous fight because I picked her up

(continued)

(continued)

an hour later than planned and by the time we arrived home we were both real angry—so angry we didn't want to sleep in the same bed. This posed a problem because I couldn't very well sack out on the couch without my parents knowing something was amiss and setting up bad vibes for the visit. Instead, we sat down with my parents and talked it out with them. I felt good about it and so did Jan. It's a small example, but it says a lot about how things have worked out.

I don't think I'm lacking in self-reliance or self-control (two characteristics associated with permissive parents). In fact, I think I'm just the opposite. My parents were more authoritative with my sister. They set limits on her comparable to the limits set by her friends' parents. I don't know how this has affected her relationship with them but it definitely has made her jealous of me!

---

level playing field in terms of family. The "steps" connote how many steps away he or she is from the "ideal nuclear family." The "steps" connote an emotional distance between "real kin" and this "forced arrangement." The new blended family has been stymied by an odd lag in linguistic evolution. We have simply adopted sociological terms for alternative family forms as the everyday, colloquial language. I suggest that this sociological language has hampered the bonding between family members and made conversation about family stigmatizing and sometimes shaming.

When children enter a blended family, if they are under five years of age, they usually adopt the relational terms used in traditional families (Cherlin and Furstenberg, 1994). The children call Mom "Mom" and Dad "Dad," regardless of which is their biological relative. It is as though enough of childhood lies ahead of them that it is permissible to act as though this is the "real McCoy" of family relationships. If they are older than ten, they very rarely call the nonbiological parent by a term of endearment. Instead, the cultural habit is to use a first name when addressing the non-biological parent. Dad becomes "Harry"; Mom becomes "Marcie." To call Harry, "Dad" or Marcie "Mom" is a betrayal of the special affection and bond that the child has or dreams of having with the biological mother or father.

Calling stepparents by their first names is psychologically inappropriate for two reasons. First, it confuses the parent-child boundaries. Stepchildren are not peers of their stepparents. Indeed, most children are not allowed to call any other adults by their first names because it suggests lack of respect and unwillingness to keep a generational boundary of power and admiration between the adult and child. Second, calling a stepparent by his or her first name robs the relationship of any emotional specialness. Having a special name for parents constantly reinforces the special bond between parent and child. It is time to invent new everyday words that help validate the care and commitment inherent in the life of stepfamilies.

If we look to Hindi, the root of many Indo-European languages, we find that by adding a "ka" to the end of a word, we can denote "similarity" or "diminutiveness." Using a suffix rooted in the evolution of English will ensure that it is more likely to be adopted as natural sounding. Under this simple system, we would suggest adding the following words to our everyday lexicon:

- Stepfather would become "fatherka"
- Stepdad would become "dadka"
- Stepmother would become "motherka"
- Stepmom would become "momka"
- Stepbrother would become "brotherka"
- Stepsister would become "sisterka"
- Stepson would become "sonka"
- Stepdaughter would become "daughterka"
- Stepfather would become "grandpaka"
- Stepmother would become "grandmaka"

Whoever has the primary emotional bond with the child should be "mother" or "father." Only when the child has a preexisting emotional allegiance to a father or mother does the "ka" solution make sense. When a parent has no competing contenders, it is natural and probably best for the child to use "mom," "dad," "grandma," "grandpa," and so on. Where this is a competing claim, the "ka" solution should be presented and encouraged. Using these suffixes would encourage children to feel closeness and unique relationship with the stepparent without feeling they are betraying the primary affectively bonded parent. One could have a father or dad, and also a "fatherka" or "dadka." No, he is not the biological or original father, but a loved psychological father. These are not fighting words; they are words of affection with deep family ties inherent in the sounds.

Note that dadka and momka would be inappropriate names for children to use for fathers who had children conceived by donor sperm or mothers who had children conceived by donor eggs. In these cases, the original bond is with the two parents who welcome the child into the world.

New family titles have been successfully introduced during the past two decades. Most notably, "Ms." is a term that originally inspired hoots of laughter and derision and is now evaluated as highly as other courtesy titles that mark the female gender (Crawford, Stark, and Renner, 1998).

It is time to help families find new terms for the new times. Some families may want to look toward their own linguistic origins (e.g., Mandarin, Spanish, or one of the African dialects) to find special terms to denote the psychological parent. As a country, though, we need some positively affective terms to describe family relationships among steprelatives. I suggest the "ka" solution. I hope others will suggest other solutions and one will take hold. Our families will only be strengthened and our children normalized.

SELF-EXPLORATION: FAMILY TYPES

Look at the popular triangles in Figure 13.1. Then answer the following questions:

1. Did any of these triangles typify the relationship you most frequently had with your parents?
2. Which one typifies the triangle you have in your adult nuclear family, with your spouse and any one of your children?
3. Try to remember some recent conflicts in which these roles were apparent. Write down the vignettes as well as your feelings about the role you ended up enacting.
4. Have you ever tried to break out of your role?

SELF-EXPLORATION: PARENTING STYLE

1. Try to analyze what type of parenting style your parents had at home. Begin by answering the following four questions:
    a. How controlling were your parents? By what means did they try to control you?
    b. How effective were your parents in communicating to you why they wanted you to do certain things? Could you understand their feelings and their attitudes?
    c. Did your parents make a lot of maturity demands on you or very few? What types of behavior were important for them?
    d. Were your parents very warm or cold? How did they express their love for you?
2. Use the summary table (see Table 13.3), Parental Patterns of Child Rearing, to see if your parents fit into any of the patterns.

SELF-EXPLORATION: INTIMACY

One of the most important and difficult communication skills for anyone to develop is the ability to be intimate.

1.   Take Dyer's sharing questionnaire (Figure 13.2) to see how much intimate communication occurred in your family. If there was little intimacy, why was that?

2. How do you think the amount of intimacy communicated in your family has affected how you interact with your friends?

3. If you are married, try to assess how intimate you are with your spouse. How difficult or easy would it be to discuss the intimate topics mentioned on p. 312? Do you agree that you would feel closer to your mate after discussing these topics? Why?

FIGURE 13.1. Common Family Triangles

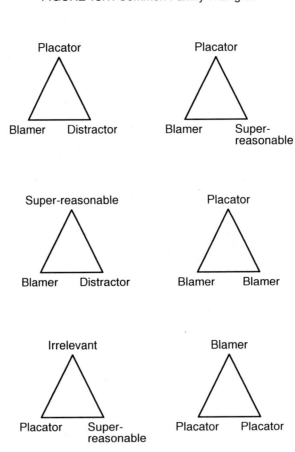

TABLE 13.3. Parental Patterns of Child Rearing

Pattern	Control		Clarity of Communication		Maturity demands (demands for independent behavior and responsibility)		Nurturance	
	High	Low	High	Low	High	Low	High	Low
Authoritarian	X			X	X			X
Authoritative	X		X		X		X	
Permissive		X	X			X	X	
Nonconformist	X		X			X	X	

Source: Damon, W. 1983. *Social and Personality Development.* New York: W.W. Norton. Based on Baumrind, D. 1967. Child care practices anteceding three patterns of preschool behavior. *Genetic Psychology Monographs, 75,* 43-88.

FIGURE 13.2. Sharing—A Family Exercise

Have each member of your family rate himself or herself in the following ways by placing an "O" in the applicable blank.

	Always	Sometimes	Never
1. As a family, we get together and make important plans and decisions.	O	—	—
2. As a child, I feel free to talk over serious concerns with my dad.	O	—	—
3. As a child, I feel free to talk over serious concerns with my mother.	O	—	—
4. As a mother or father, I feel I can talk over important issues with the children.	O	—	—
5. As a husband or wife, I feel a certain restriction or constraint in talking over important things with my spouse.	—	—	O
6. Brothers and sisters in our family really talk to each other.	O	—	—
7. We all like to sit and talk at the dinner table or in the front room.	O	—	—
8. We find time for private talks between a parent and each child.	O	—	—
9. I usually plan very carefully before I will discuss anything of real importance with anyone in the family.	—	—	O
10. I often wish that our family would share more with each other	—	—	O

Source: Dyer, W.J. 1975. *Creating Closer Families.* Provo, UT: Brigham Press.

Note: Every answer that falls in the circled category receives a score of 1. Maximum sharing score of 10.

Chapter 14

Problem Solving

Life is not having been told that the man has just waxed the floor.

Ogden Nash

Each family has to be able to find solutions to the myriad problems it faces in every area of living. Besides knowing what to do and how to do it in specific instances, it has to develop *metarules*. These overall operating guidelines involve understandings about who is to set the rules for living together, how to resolve disagreements about those rules, and what to do when enforcement of one rule conflicts with enforcement of another. Thus, the family's first problem is deciding how it will go about solving problems.

Because they delineate how each person can contribute to the problem-solving process, metarules help define family relationships. If one family's metarules dictate that only the eldest daughter can dissent from the parents' views, this daughter has been given more power than her siblings. She is more an equal with the parents.

The task of generating rules for problem solving is never completed. In healthy families, rules are always being changed or modified to fit the changing capabilities of the children and the nature of the problems they face. No one has ever attempted to document how many problems a typical U.S. family faces in even a single week. Problems arising from the family's interactions with the community are undoubtedly far fewer than the problems that arise internally. Just having young children automatically creates continual minicrises.

Fawl (1962) analyzed nonproblem preschoolers and reported an average of 3.4 disturbances per hour. Children ages two to three had the greatest number of disturbances—twice as many as children ages four to five. Thus the siblings and parents of preschoolers need to handle an average of three problems an hour, just by being in the presence of the young child.

Most family conflicts are not so loud or visible as the disruptions of the preschooler; they are more subtle, more important, more difficult to solve. Still, having a well-functioning family requires continually effective problem solving, particularly when there are adolescents in the family.

325

To ascertain the level of conflict adolescents and their mothers experience, Prinz and associates (1979) developed the Interaction Behavior Questionnaire (see Figure 14.1). The mean score on this instrument was twenty-nine for adolescents whose mothers were seeking help for the family and eight for the control group of adolescents who agreed with their mothers that they were getting along fine. This questionnaire has separate versions for parent and adolescent and can be adapted to ascertain the level of conflict with any family member or subgroup. The underlying theme throughout the conflict items is the presence of persistent unpleasantness in interacting with the target person. Whenever the level of conflict reaches an unbearable state, people try to resolve the problem, hopefully with adaptive strategies.

FIGURE 14.1. Interaction Behavior Questionnaire for Adolescents

Think back over the last four weeks at home. The statements below have to do with you and your mother only. Read the statement, and then decide if you believe that the statement is true. If it is true, then circle *true,* and if you believe the statement is not true, circle *false.* You must circle either *true* or *false,* but never both for the same item. Please answer all items.

true	false	10.	We (my mother and I) joke around often.
true	false	11.	We do a lot of things together.
true	false	12.	We almost never seem to agree.
true	false	13.	I enjoy the talks we have.
true	false	14.	At least three times a week, we get angry at each other.
true	false	15.	After an argument that turns out badly, one or both of us apologizes.
true	false	16.	We argue at the dinner table at least half the time we eat together.
true	false	17.	My mom and I compromise during arguments. ("Compromise" means we both give in a little.)
true	false	18.	At least once a day we get angry at each other.
true	false	19.	The talks we have are frustrating.
true	false	20.	My mom and I speak to each other only when we have to.
true	false	21.	In general, I don't think we get along very well.
true	false	22.	We argue at the dinner table almost every time we eat.

true	false	23.	We never have fun together.
true	false	24.	My mom and I have big arguments about little things.
true	false	25.	We have enjoyable talks at least once a day.
true	false	26.	If I am right, my mother doesn't admit it.
true	false	27.	My mom picks on me.
true	false	28.	My mom understands me.
true	false	29.	Several hours after an argument, my mom is still mad at me.
true	false	30.	My mom brings up a lot of my faults when we argue.
true	false	31.	My mom likes my friends.
true	false	32.	My mom slaps me when she gets angry.
true	false	33.	She says I have no consideration for her.
true	false	34.	She says bad things to other people about me.
true	false	35.	My mother is bossy when we talk.
true	false	36.	When I try to tell her something, she doesn't let me finish.
true	false	37.	She makes me feel that the argument is all my fault.
true	false	38.	My mom understands my point of view, even when she doesn't agree with me.
true	false	39.	My mom can tell when I have something on my mind.
true	false	40.	My mother is interested in the things I do.
true	false	41.	When my mother punishes me, she is usually being fair.
true	false	42.	My mom screams a lot.
true	false	43.	My mother never apologizes first.
true	false	44.	My mother rarely listens to me during an argument.
true	false	45.	My mom puts me down.
true	false	46.	She thinks my opinions are childish.
true	false	47.	When I am arguing with my mother, she doesn't give me the chance to state my views.
true	false	48.	My mom nags me about a little thing, and we end up in an argument.
true	false	49.	When we argue, she says I am stupid.

FIGURE 14.1 *(continued)*

true   false   50. Even when she doesn't let me do something I want to do, she still listens to me.

true   false   51. If I run into problems, my mom helps me out.

true   false   52. My mom gets angry at me whenever we have a discussion.

true   false   53. It seems like whenever I try to talk to my mother, she has something else to do.

The short form of the Interaction Behavior Questionnaire is scored in the following manner:

Adolescent's Version of IBQ
A1:   Appraisal of parent: add one point for each TRUE for items #17, 18, 20, 21, 23, 24, 25, 26, 27, 28, 33, 34, 35, 36, 37, 38, 39, 40, 43, 44, and one point for each FALSE for items #19, 22, 29, 30, 31, 32, 41, 42. (TOTAL POSSIBLE = 28)
A2:   Appraisal of dyad: add one point for each TRUE for items #3, 5, 7, 9, 10, 11, 12, 13, 14, 15, and one point for each FALSE for items #1, 2, 4, 6, 8, 16. (TOTAL POSSIBLE = 16)

Do the questionnaire a second time, this time responding to each item as though it refers to your father.

Source: Prinz, R. J., Foster, S., Kent, R. N., and O'Leary, K. D. 1979. Multivariate assessment of conflict in distressed and nondistressed mother-adolescent dyads. *Journal of Applied Behavior Analysis, 12,* 691-700.

STRATEGIES FOR REDUCING CONFLICT

Chafetz (1980) postulates that individuals usually use one of four basic strategies to resolve the conflicts arising among family members: influence, authority, control, or manipulation. *Influence* is being used when a person uses information, persuasion, and reasoning to change the other's attitudes. For example, imagine that you and your mate are buying a car with which the mate will commute to work. The car will be in both names but will be paid for by the mate. The conflict concerns what type of car to buy; you would like a VW Golf and your mate would like a Honda Civic. Pointing out the quality and good resale value of Hondas is an example of an influence attempt.

Authority strategies are used if a person feels that he or she has an indisputable and appropriate right to decide how the conflict should be resolved. If your mate believes that paying for the car and being its primary user entails authority over the decision process, he or she will forcefully and definitely push for the Honda.

Control attempts at conflict resolution occur when one person attempts to get another person to do as he or she wishes by using inducements or threats. Suppose your mate says, "If we buy the Honda, I'll go along with those weekend trips you've been talking about." Control is at work.

The *manipulator* uses calculated behavior to control the other person. Instead of promoting the purchase directly, for example, the manipulator who favors a Honda may be "too busy" to visit other manufacturers' showrooms. If pushed into buying the VW, the manipulator "can't find time" to apply for the car loan.

In the discussion that follows, we will focus primarily on the two most adaptive problem-solving strategies: influence attempts and authority attempts. In the problem-solving process, the first stage involves defining the problem and generating and evaluating possible solutions. This stage goes most smoothly when influence strategies predominate. During the second phase of problem solving, which involves implementing one of the solutions and evaluating its effectiveness, authority strategies seem to dominate naturally.

Influence Strategies and Effective Problem Solving

You can exert no influence if you are not susceptible to influence.

Carl Jung

Influence strategies rely on communication. The communication styles discussed in detail in Chapter 13 are the medium through which the strategies are expressed. No technique or strategy is universally suited to all families.

Individual abilities and temperaments must be taken into account. A communication model that functions well for a family of intelligent, complex, multifaceted adults may be poorly suited to a family composed of highly concrete, simple adults with a multitude of children. Even if we confine our attention to families with middle-of-the road abilities for information processing, the usefulness of any given strategy is greatly influenced by the composition of the individual family. For example, six group communication variables have been most consistently related to effective problem solving. But if only one member of a family displays a trait or employs a communication style, these variables may be ineffective. Klein and Hill (1979) reviewed the major theories of family problem solving and current empirical research. They concluded:

1. The more people talk, the better the solutions. However, if one person monopolizes the talk time, the quality of the solution suffers greatly.
2. The richer the language code used by the people, the more varied the vocabulary, and the more complex the thoughts expressed, the better the solution. However, if one person has a considerably more enriched language code than the rest, the effectiveness of the solutions is diminished.
3. The more creativity the people have in generating alternative and original solutions, the more effective the problem solving. However, if one person monopolizes the creativity, the quality of the problem solving is reduced.
4. The more praise, encouragement, and support there is among the family, the better the problem-solving effectiveness. However, when support is concentrated and the praise and encouragement come from one person, problem-solving effectiveness is hampered.
5. The more the family communicates nonverbally, by looking at each other and using body language, the better the problem-solving efforts will be. Yet when the nonverbal communication is dominated by one person, problem-solving effectiveness is diminished.
6. The more people express disagreements or reject one solution because of a different point of view, the more likely they will end up with a higher quality solution. If the disparagement is concentrated in one person, the quality of the solution will suffer.
7. The more power is distributed in the family according to cultural norms, the more effective will be the problem solving. The more power is allocated at variance with cultural norms, the more likely the effectiveness of the solution will decline.

A number of additional situational variables and interpersonal processes are critical to the influence process. Jacobson (1981) and other behaviorists have pinpointed procedures that help maximize the success of couples in resolving conflicts.

Procedures for Maximizing Success

First, the couple must agree on a time for negotiating differences. This time is not to be before dinner (when most people are tired and irritable), while in bed (where the connotations should be kept upbeat and positive), or en route to or from a party (the most common time for bringing up grievances). The acknowledgment of a problem should, however, occur as soon as one of the partners is aware of the problem.

During a negotiation session, the victimized partner follows a two-point rule: (1) he or she is to talk *only* about what the other person *did* and how it made him or her feel; (2) the listening partner must sit and listen, without interjecting, asking questions, or apologizing. For the first five to ten minutes the victim has an uninterrupted chance to express his or her point of view.

Giving the victimized partner a chance to vent implicitly affirms the cognitive attitude that "the victim is always right." In most behavioral programs, each partner is taught this cognitive attitude because recognizing the partner's legitimate claim to hurt feelings is a prerequisite to being open to negotiation (Jacobson, 1981). If partners get stuck debating whether one is *entitled* to feel hurt, the relevant issues are never brought to the table. Accusations will abound without any movement toward resolution.

After the victim is finished explaining his or her point of view, the listener tries to paraphrase what has been said. This restatement assures the victim that the problem has been heard and understood.

When the couple begin solving problems, insults, past wounds, and blaming are likely to creep into the conversation and turn it into an argument. One technique for preventing this phenomenon requires the couple to mark down each "zap" (verbal punishment) and to drop the subject for that day after a predetermined critical number of zaps has been reached. This strategy is designed to prevent disagreements from escalating into full-blown arguments.

During the negotiating phase, partners take turns offering solutions. The solutions should be very concrete and very specific. Every effort should be made to pinpoint specific behavior changes that each partner would like to see in the other. Often the desired changes are negotiated in a tit-for-tat format. The wife agrees to do a, b, c if the husband agrees to do x, y, z. To add more motivation, negative consequences are often contingent on violating the agreement. If the husband has promised to be home by six, he might have to give his wife ten dollars or do the laundry for her during the next week for each night he breaks his promise.

The Family Council

Basically, the same procedure is used by families who follow Driekurs, Gould, and Corsini's (1974) notion of the family council. The family council is a democratic, regularly scheduled meeting of all family members in a particular household. Every family member has the right to speak out concerning problems without interruption and without fear of consequences. A father and preschooler are given the same opportunities to state their needs or problems. When a decision must be made, the group deliberates until all members present can come to a common understanding and agree on a course of action.

The only topics inappropriate for a family council are those that a sub-group of the family wishes to keep private to maintain generational bound-aries. For example, parents may choose not to bring up marital disagree-ments, sexual conflicts, or differences of opinion on religion, politics, or relatives. Siblings may choose not to discuss skipping classes, smoking, or cheating in school. The most appropriate topics are those to which the family group is going to be allowed to propose a solution and for which it is capable of finding one. If the parents use the council as a device for forcing children to see their point of view or accept their authority on an issue, the procedure will not work.

Parents often find this idea appealing but then find that implementing such an equalizing procedure is very threatening. The power base of the parents does get chiseled at as the air gets cleared of accusations and everyone is responsible for finding bearable solutions. Many parents who implement family councils find it hard not to "pull rank." They talk too much, criticize, act bossy, skip meetings, or forget to follow through on the decisions of the council. Driekurs, Gould, and Corsini (1974:106) suggest the following four guidelines to avoid these pitfalls:

1. Parents should support and follow through on all family decisions.
2. Parents should consider all relevant topics for discussion, even when the concerned member is absent.
3. Parents should refuse to make decisions outside the family council that belong on its agenda.
4. Parents should participate as equals with other family members.

Cultural Variations

Different ethnic groups develop different communication styles and differ-ent ways of handling conflict in the family. So far in discussing problem solving, we have seen that the effective family communication style involves such features as being assertive and speaking for oneself, articulating one's own feelings rather than blaming others, and keeping the intensity of the discussion in a rational low-keyed range. This communication model has been developed and validated on families that were part of the dominant white, middle-class culture of the United States. Is it equally valid for other ethnic groups?

One good counterexample of seemingly effective family communications that do not model themselves after the white middle class comes from Win-kler and Doherty (1983). They found that among Israeli couples living in New York, marital dissatisfaction was not related to how verbally aggressive, excited, or angry the spouses got when resolving conflicts. That is, their level of marital satisfaction could not be predicted by knowing the level of aggression expressed during a conflict. For their American friends, of course, a significant negative relationship was obtained, so that the more aggressive the response styles of the American couples, the less marital satisfaction there was overall. Thus, effective models of family communication vary across cultures and undoubtedly evolve and change within any one culture over the generations.

FRANK (minister, age 52)

I tried to examine the problem-solving strategies in my family of origin by analyzing the conflicts my brother had with my parents. He died at age thirty-five, from a liver that couldn't function and a body worn by fifteen years of alcohol abuse. I often wondered what we as a family could have done to prevent his death. On one level I know that the self-destructive tendencies in a person cannot be erased or altered by a well-meaning family. On a deeper level, I feel we were responsible for helping him save his life and we failed him, particularly my parents.

Looking at the behavior questionnaire, there was a fair degree of conflict in Len's interactions with our parents. Although he drank with my dad, even as a teenager, and was very solicitous to my mother, they would get angry with each other every day, argue a lot over little things, and didn't really push him to work on his problems as a teenager. For example, in high school he was very frustrated by the demands put on him, and when he failed geometry, he refused to go to summer school and quit high school completely. When he announced he was dropping out my parents were upset but didn't use any problem-solving strategy; they didn't try to reason with him, or impose their authority, or be manipulative or controlling. They simply felt bad and abdicated all parental responsibility. Once out of school, he got a good job as a mechanic, but he was afraid to learn how to drive. He'd spend one and a half to two hours on public transportation, each way! Again, my parents accepted the problem and helped him work around it. They never helped him face the problem and try to solve it. When he went to Korea, he got engaged to a Korean woman, but for some reason she was not allowed to come back with him. Everyone accepted it! No one fought it and Len stayed heartbroken. Again and again this inability to sit down and talk and problem solve brought him down. When he was twenty-eight, I tried to teach him to drive, but he was very reluctant. I finally got him to the point where he was driving around parking lots, but then I had to go back to college and it was not followed up. He always lived at home and never felt comfortable or confident to go out on his own. No one really talked about it or

(continued)

(continued)

helped him deal with it. Tragically, as his drinking became worse and worse, it became a suicidal lifestyle. I don't think he was a responsible adult and we were not responsible kin.

    In my own nuclear family, I always tried to use reason and authority to help my children overcome problems. I'd even use manipulation if it would get them out of a glitch. They grew up with their share of problems, all right, but I think all three of them know how to confront a problem. I've always been able to discuss our differences at length (often after an initial blowup). I can't think of a skill more important for family life and just wish my brother could have experienced some of it. It could have saved his life.

HOSTILITY AND INTIMACY

People who fly into a rage always make a bad landing.

Will Rogers

    Since no family can avoid conflict, what determines whether the couple or family has been successful dealing with it? Rands, Levinger, and Mellinger (1981) have found that both the amount of hostility used to discuss the conflict and the degree of closeness felt between the couples after the discussion affect marital satisfaction.

Aggressiveness versus Intimacy

    These two dimensions yield four types of couples: nonaggressive-intimate; aggressive-intimate; nonaggressive-nonintimate; and aggressive-nonintimate. The most happily married couples are not aggressive when trying to solve a problem. Each feels the other is trying to work out a compromise and to be reasonable. Each feels the spouse is sensitive to understanding the other's point of view. After the argument, each feels closer and more loving toward the spouse. Sometimes the couple ends up agreeing that it is OK to disagree, and often they have fun making up. These happily married couples who are nonaggressive during the conflict and feel more intimate afterward composed 30 percent of Rand's couples.

    Another 30 percent of the couples represented the opposite, unhappy pole where conflict was always associated with aggression and always ended with the escalation of the problematic aspects of the situation. With these couples, discussing a conflict with the spouse inevitably involved trying to hurt the other's feelings by being sarcastic, getting mad and yelling, and even walking away in anger. As a result, they felt that talking was a waste of time and that the spouse was going to go ahead and do what he or she felt like doing. These couples felt that disagreeing about one topic always led to arguing about many things.

Twenty percent of Rand's couples were both nonaggressive and nonintimate. Although they could sit down and talk over the pros and cons of an issue, afterward they simply went on their way; neither escalations nor warm feelings occurred. These marriages were unexciting but comfortable. A last group, representing the remaining 20 percent, were very nasty fighters but afterward felt very close and loving to their spouses. These last two groups reported intermediate levels of marital happiness.

Avoidance of Confrontation

Although aggressive and compromising strategies are used by many people confronted with a problem, another very popular stance is to try to avoid any confrontation. This style involves clamming up, becoming distant and aloof. Spouses avoiding confrontation hold in their feelings. How does this avoidance style fit into the fourfold classification? It fits in a complicated manner: If an aggressive-nonintimate spouse perceives the partner as trying to avoid confrontation, marital satisfaction is increased. The spouse seems to appreciate the effort involved in avoiding all the discomfort and bad feelings that happen during a confrontation. However, with a nonaggressive-intimate spouse, avoidance in the partner is taken as a sign of rejection. Since the couple usually feel better once the issue is aired, avoidance seems to be counterproductive for this group.

In summary, the process of problem solving is greatly affected by the context in which it occurs. The emotional tone of the discussion as well as the resulting emotional state both affect the overall level of marital satisfaction. The difficulty of classifying couples into one of the four hostile/ closeness quadrants is illustrated by the finding that only 30 percent of the husbands and wives agreed on which quadrant their conflict patterns belonged to. Perhaps in the future, objective observations will lead to a greater consensus, or perhaps the importance of other variables such as avoidance will have to be integrated into the model to achieve consensus.

USING FIGHTS TO ADVANTAGE

Even with the best intentions and a highly effective communication style, families are bound to quarrel. So long as the family is effectively allowing people to mature and individuate, occasional personal animosity and anger will be part of the fabric of family life. The conflicts will arise because despite love, commitment, and maturity, individuals are infinitely complex, and the exact pattern of attitudes and desires present in any one of us can never be authentically duplicated by any other person. In an atmosphere where one is free to assert one's feelings and then argue for the implementation of one's decisions, the seeds for harmonious family relations will take root and prosper; so also will the seeds of discontent.

Some theorists are quite confident that learning how to express anger appropriately is part and parcel of learning how to express love appropriately. They point knowingly to Harlow's (1971) studies on monkeys who were deprived of the rough-and-tumble aggressive play of peers and grew up to be incapable of forming a healthy sexual relationship with a mate or a loving, nurturing relationship with their children.

Of course, with monkeys and humans the nature, intensity, frequency, and form of quarreling determine how beneficial this self-expression can be. The extremes are to be avoided. When individuals act as though they never argue and always settle their disagreements with love and understanding, they either are fooling themselves or are sacrificing the growth of each person for some sense of strength within the total group. Such strength is more illusionary than real, and always fragile.

On the other hand, some families have constant bickering and arguments. Often they are venomous and hurtful; the bitterness bristles in every room of the house. Such consistent and frightening anger can only result in very insecure and troubled children. Somewhere between these two extremes is the ability to have healthy arguments that truly promote the strength and happiness of the family.

Learning to "Fight Fair"

Many enrichment counselors find *The Intimate Enemy: How to Fight Fair in Love and Marriage* (Bach and Wyden, 1969) indispensable in helping couples and families learn to fight fairly. According to these authors, a productive fight is the composite result of (1) fighting fair, which is defined by using nine specific guidelines to structure the argument, and (2) assessing how many of twelve possible positive effects the fight has achieved. Although the book also contains suggestions on where to fight, how to start a fight, when to stop, and how to stop, the nine "fight elements" and twelve "fight effects" are its "guts."

First, the fight should be based on rationally justifiable considerations. It should be "based on reality" that objective outsiders could understand. Second, everyone must be "fair." Each person must be careful not to say things that are too hurtful or too humiliating for the other to tolerate. Third, both parties have to be "actively involved." If one person is fighting and the other is passively accepting it, the result is brutality, not argument. Fourth, all parties have to accept responsibility for their participation and for personally wanting a resolution. Fifth, being able to joke or find humor in the situation helps relieve the strain of an argument. Sixth and seventh, the individuals have to be able to express their disagreement openly and to communicate it clearly in words and body language. Eighth, the argument has to be "direct"—take place in the here and now with no references to irrelevant or old situations. Ninth, the attacks should be focused on "very specific actions, feelings, or attitudes." Screaming a generality such as "I hate your stingy personality" is not helpful. Being specific is more likely to be fruitful. "Carol is my best friend. It's important to me to buy her a nice wedding present. How can I do that for fifty dollars?"

You might object that a family who could work together enough to carry out these nine steps would have nothing left to fight over. This is probably true. Nevertheless, Bach and Wyden's nine fight elements provide an excellent prototype of the successful argument. No family or couple will be completely successful every time. But those who have tried to incorporate the nine steps find the effects of fighting are a lot more rewarding after the program. They feel less fearful, less hurt, and more in control. Their relationships feel more cohesive and the partners have more trust. They do not suffer the usual negative consequences of fighting. Desire for revenge decreases. Individuals do not feel they have lost ground or been inhibited from expressing their true feelings.

Although Bach and Wyden support their conclusions by discussing various case studies, no controlled studies have documented the claimed benefits of this training. The criteria for healthy fighting do, however, appear to hold a lot of promise. James Creighton (1998) has written a similar but more recent book on how to fight successfully *(How Loving Couples Fight: Twelve Essential Tools for Working Through the Hurt)*.

The Issue of Context

The context in which conflict situations are discussed clearly influences problem-solving style. Couples who are dissatisfied with their marriages will expose more negative feelings when a conflict topic is presented. From this negative context comes a readiness to match the distress and unhappiness seen in the partner. The most important message each spouse wants to send is "I am not happy with our marriage." If one spouse gets angry and makes an accusation, the pull to retaliate with a more hurtful accusation or a putdown is far greater among dissatisfied couples than among contented couples.

Indeed, the anger and tension between two unhappily married spouses is undoubtedly the single message that these spouses are most successful at communicating. Research suggests that the distress can be communicated physiologically. Levenson and Gottman (1983) videotaped couples with varying levels of marital satisfaction as they discussed various problems they were facing. Each couple was "wired up" to monitor heart rate, skin conductance, pulse transmission time, and somatic activity. All four of these measures are sensitive to sympathetic nervous system activity, which has an evolutionary connection with negative emotions such as fear and anger.

Using a combined overall measure of physiological arousal, Levenson and Gottman found that the more unhappy the couples were in the marriage, the more likely they were to respond to physiological arousal in their partners by getting more physiologically aroused themselves. This "physiological linkage" was not found in happily married couples. Nor was it found in the distressed couples when they were talking about nonconflictual events of the day. When presented with a conflict, couples low in marital satisfaction began to communicate viscerally. No words were needed. Upset in one was matched by upset in the other, and they both understood the futility of trying to cognitively and rationally discuss the problem. Levenson and Gottman found that they were able to account for 60 percent of the variance in marital satisfaction on the basis of physiological linkage—quite a feat, considering that questionnaire measures typically account for less than 10 percent of the variance in marital satisfaction.

PROBLEM SOLVING AND PROBLEM BEHAVIORS IN CHILDREN

Problem children—where do they come from? This question is older than psychology. The answer is becoming clearer, although it is not a simple one. There is overwhelming evidence that families that are unable to effectively solve problems and have antagonistic social climates leave children at increased risk for conduct disorders and other behavior problems. Yet, there is also overwhelming influence that siblings, peers, temperament, and genetics also influence the emotional and social development of children. The following discussion is centered on how family dynamics influence the course and nature of childhood problems. But let us not forget that they are not the only influences, or in many cases, not the most important ones.

Rutter (1994) hypothesizes that family discord is harmful to children for at least three different reasons. First, when children watch their parents argue or be mean to each other, they are traumatized by witnessing the violence. Even if they are not involved in the fights, they are victims of the emotional fallout, as surely as if they were under an atomic cloud passing overhead. Second, very often children are not left to be innocent bystanders. Rather, they are actively coerced into the family fracas, scapegoated, and used to funnel all the negative energy flowing between the couple. Often, they form destructive alliances with parents that cause them to alienate one parent in order to solidify their ties with the other parent. Third, it is very likely that simply having an unhappy mother and father who cannot get along reduces the ability of each adult to be a happy, comforting parent to the child. In this view, it is because the adult's overall adjustment is compromised by the marital problems that the child's relationship to the parent becomes compromised. Regardless of the mechanisms involved, it has been shown that child and adolescent inpatients report significant problems across all seven areas of family functioning measured by the McMaster Family Assessment Device: problem solving, communication, roles, affective responsiveness, affective involvement, behavioral control, and general functioning (Kline, 1995).

Speaking a bit more precisely, it now appears that effective family problem solving may be one of the most potent factors protecting children from behavioral and emotional disturbances in their development. Family problem solving is affected by the following three factors: natural, developmental trends in the child toward autonomy; the family environment during problem solving (hostile or supportive); and the systemic dynamics in the family that can keep children trapped under the cloud of parental conflict (as discussed by Rutter, 1994).

Children's Developmental Needs for Autonomy

Research has shown that there is a substantial decline in the quality of family problem solving between childhood and preadolescence (ages nine and one-half to eleven and one-half years old) (Vuchinich, Angelelli, and Gatherum, 1996). The decline in problem-solving effectiveness is related to the preadolescent's need to be autonomous and not go along with parental suggestions.

The research paradigm used in these studies could be usefully adapted for direct clinical work, to help families understand what they are doing wrong and the different conversational and interactional options open to them. The family starts out being presented with a list of forty to fifty parent-child issues that are often the source of difficulties in the home. Typical of such problems are computer usage, telephone time, allowance, chores, bedtime, homework, fighting with siblings, lying, stealing, bad grades, lack of obedience, disrespect, cursing, grooming, practicing instruments, parties, sleepovers, movies, dress codes, hair styles, diet, and so on. The child and the parent each get to independently pick a topic that they believe has been a problem during the past month. Then the family is videotaped as they try to solve the problem for ten minutes. In half of the families, the child-selected problem is addressed first, and the parent-selected problem is addressed first in the other half. Although the number of rating scales that can be used to assess family problem solving is vast, Vuchinich, Angelelli, and Gatherum came up with three simple, clinician-friendly scales. The first question asks, "What was the quality of the solutions proposed?" (answers range from "no solution proposed" to "excellent solution proposed"). The second question asks, "What was the degree of consensus?" (answers range from "no resolution/total disagreement" to "problem resolved"). The third question asks, "How well did family members consider one another's views and perspectives and promote group participation?" (answers range from "extremely poorly" to "extremely good"). Obviously, if these scales were used with a family in therapy, the therapist would explain his or her reasoning for each of the ratings and invite the family to rate themselves.

The researchers found that families were significantly more successful in resolving these problems when they were talking to the nine and one-half-year-olds than when they were talking to the eleven and one-half-year-olds. During those two years, the preadolescents became both less positive and more negative and participated less in parent-selected topics. Fathers, in particular, had more problems working on the parent-selected problems. They were, like their older sons and daughters, much more negative and less positive. Mothers still seem to try to be peacekeepers as their children strive for increasing autonomy. Most important, though when the child was allowed to pick the topic, problem solving was substantially better on all three scales. It is as though, when they could pick the exact play, act, and scene, they were ready to go on with the show. Feeling that they were talking about something important to them and that their parents were giving them the time and attention to deal with their self-perceived pain led to much better solutions.

The lesson for family therapists here is quite direct. Let the preadolescent or adolescent be heard—validate the importance of their lives and they will be more willing to join the family in a productive way.

Family Environment and Its Effect on Problem Solving

Regardless of the age of the child and who is judging the behavior as a "problem," research consistently indicates that a hostile interaction style is very predictive of destructive problem solving and a supportive interactive style is very predictive of constructive problem solving (Rueter and Conger, 1994).

Teaching families to acknowledge and monitor the emotional climate during family problem solving is one of the greatest clinical challenges but one with the greatest payoff. Families in conflict usually have three "deadly Ds" infecting their problem solving: disruptiveness, denial, and degrading attitudes (Rueter and Conger, 1995). If you have an audio or videotape of a problem-solving discussion it is very easy to process it with the family and let them find the three Ds, which they can hear themselves again and again.

Therapists can help people acknowledge their *disruptiveness* by pointing out on a recording of their problem-solving session how often they change the topic, ask inappropriate questions, or refuse to directly answer questions.

Degrading attitudes are a reflection of interpersonal insensitivity. Here, therapists can point out when a family member is impatient, inconsiderate, or unwilling to go along with someone else's suggestions.

Denial is the refusal is to take responsibility for your part in the problem. Denial is hard to break through, but family members can be shown ways to take some responsibility for the problem without taking total or primary responsibility. When someone in the family refuses to take any responsibility for a problem, it is sometimes useful to have a philosophical sidebar and spend a few minutes with the family discussing if it is ever possible for a family to have a problem that is solely due to one person. Quickly, the discussion will turn to how other family members' behavior can impact the original problem and make it worse or better by their actions or inactions.

Family sessions devoted to analyzing problem-solving styles are some of the most useful family sessions to have. A family that can recognize and identify the corrosive elements of their interactions are empowered to change to a more supportive stance.

Basically, when families have a supportive interaction style, each member of the family is able to do two things very frequently: first, he or she can show warmth and support by smiling, praising, or encouraging another family member (Rueter and Conger, 1995). The daughter can say, "Go on, Daddy, I know you want to talk about this" or the father can say, "Meredith, tell me how you see this situation, really see it." Second, each family member can show support by acknowledging the "truth" of what the other person is saying. If the father says, "You talk on the phone too much to Laura" and Meredith simply smiles and says, "Yes, I know I spend a lot of time on the phone with her—I love her and she's my best friend!" the daughter has shown an excellent supportive style. Similarly, if the father had said, "It's wonderful to have a best friend but it's also important to get homework done," he would have shown excellent support. Support is something that therapists have to model for client families. When they learn how to inhibit the negative, they have to learn some alternative—it does not simply jump out spontaneously as though it was hidden in some box. The list of positive skills to model and teach includes the following (Rueter and Conger, 1995):

Facilitative engagement:

1. Ask a family member to describe the problem in more detail.
2. Ask a family member to stay on task.
3. Give a summary of what you think the family member has just said.
4. Ask what other people in the family think about what the third person has just said.

Solution generation:

1. How many different solutions can I think of and offer?
2. Are the solutions I am suggesting reasonable and realistic?
3. Are the solutions that I am suggesting clear enough so that they can be implemented if everyone agrees to try them?

Interpersonal flexibility:

1. Are you patiently listening to each member of the family?
2. Are you willing to add to their ideas and tell them they have good points?
3. Can you look for a way that there are no "losers" in resolving this problem?
4. Can you compromise and make concessions?

Systemic Issues and Family Problem Solving

In Chapter 5, we discussed how complicated relationships become when children are used to contain the messy emotional arrows being slung by conflict-ridden parents. Indeed, Vuchinich, Wood, and Vuchinich (1994), using the same problem-solving paradigm discussed above, found that strong parental coalitions were linked to low levels of family problem solving in at-risk and referred families but not in control families. Strong parent-child coalitions did not differentiate problem solving styles across the three groups. It appears that in stressed parental relationships, parents who scapegoat their children are unable to let the children voice their views or participate in any meaningful way in family decisions. In these families, it is always the child who is at fault, and the only solution offered is that the child change who he or she she is or what he or she she needs or wants. There are no viable solutions for the child to offer.

Of course, it is possible that this finding is more about the nature of difficult children than the nature of scapegoating parents. These referred children may be very difficult to begin with and the parents may have been forced into an unremitting parental coalition to keep any semblance of control over family life. Still, even if a child is temperamentally impulsive or disruptive, the need for respect, understanding, and increasing areas of autonomy remain important issues.

Even if the family has a positive problem-solving style, individual characteristics of the parents and family can still conspire to create developmental problems. In a fascinating study by Barret, Rapee, Dadds, and Ryan (1996), the authors demonstrated that the behavioral tendencies of both anxious children and oppositional children are shaped and reinforced by family discussions on how to resolve issues. In this study, children were given twelve ambiguous situations that they solved independently and then again in collaboration with their parents. A typical scenario was as follows: "You see a group of students from another class playing a great game. As you (your child) walk (walks) over and want (wants) to join in, you notice that they are laughing. What do you think is happening? Which of the following explanations do you think is most likely? (a) they are telling secrets about you; (b) they will soon ask you to join in; (c) one of them is likely to jump up and push you away; or (d) one of them is likely to notice you and smile. What would you (or your child) do?" Suggested solutions were rated prosocial, aggressive, or avoidant. The researchers found that both oppositional defiant children and avoidant children, when seen individually, saw a large degree of threat in ambiguous situations. The oppositional defiant children met this threat by being aggressive; the anxious children met this threat by being avoidant. What was most interesting was that the parents of these children mirrored their response styles (parents of anxious and oppositional children saw more threat than parents of nonclinical children and differentially predicted greater avoidance and/ or aggression). Most shocking is that after parental discussion, the anxious children avoided even more and the oppositional children aggressed more often than when they were making the decisions independently. This finding that parents collude in promoting a child's nonnormative behavioral propensities is in need of much further study. As clinicians, we need to help parents work to get their children to show increased flexibility in problem solving, instead of increased comfort or confidence in their own response style.

Behavioral Approaches Toward Increasing Child Compliance

Family psychologists cannot always rely on interactional training to get the desired changes in the family. Often, when children are young, they are unable to benefit from or understand conversational directives. Particularly with young children, behavioral programs to increase child compliance are still very popular and very effective. We are learning new ways to teach parents how to manage their children behaviorally. Most parents who have difficult preschoolers have problems getting their children to listen to them about morning rituals (when to get up and what to wear), mealtime rituals (washing hands, using forks and spoons, etc.), and clean up/bedtime rituals (washing, brushing teeth, picking up toys, etc.). The three routines a therapist tries to teach a parent sound pretty simple (Powers and Roberts, 1995). The first routine is as follows:

> Step 1: Give an explicit, clear direction. ("Pick up your blocks. Put them in the toy chest.")
>
> Step 2: If the child complies, give contingent praise within five seconds. ("Gee, that's great! Let me give you a hug!")

The second routine is not much more difficult:

> Step 1: Give an explicit, clear direction. ("Pick up your blocks. Put them in the toy chest.")
>
> Step 2: If the child does not comply, give a warning. ("You have to pick up your blocks now, or I will send you to time-out.")
>
> Step 3: If the child complies, give contingent praise within five seconds. ("Gee, that's great! Let me give you a hug!")

The third routine is also direct:

> Step 1: Give an explicit, clear direction. ("Pick up your blocks. Put them in the toy chest.")
>
> Step 2: If the child does not comply, give a warning. ("You have to pick up your blocks now, or I will send you to time-out.")

Step 3: If the child still does not comply, then the parent would take the child to the time-out chair and say, "You have to sit here for one minute." (Chair time-outs can be enforced with a spank on the back-side.)

In a session, most parents say they understand how to do this. But when they get home, the routine seems to unravel. Powers and Roberts (1995) devised a clever "play therapy" for parents to teach them how to more effectively deliver behavioral contingencies. It worked this way: Parents wore a "bug" in their ears so that they could hear the coaching of a secondary therapist who was monitoring the parent's performance. The primary therapist played the child by using a doll. A small experimental room was transformed into a simulation room, complete with bedroom, bathroom, dining table, and play areas, each containing appropriate clothes, utensils, soaps, and so on. "A script defined the doll's response to each instruction on the ordered list for that simulation. The doll either complied (70 to 80 percent of the time) or did not comply (20 to 30 percent of the time) with instructions. If the doll did not comply, mothers were trained to give warnings, to which the doll complied (92 to 98 percent of the time) or did not comply (2 to 8 percent of the time)" (p. 91). For each instructional trial, the coach checked the script and transmitted the task request (e.g., "Get the toothbrush") to the parent via the bug. Using her own words, the parent then instructed the doll to do the task. The doll responded according to the script and again the parent was prompted to give the appropriate response. In this way, the parents were forced into 100 percent correct practice sessions before having to go home and try it with their own child. Needless to say, research confirms that this controlled, prompted, rehearsed method of teaching behavioral contingencies works better.

POWER AND PROBLEM SOLVING

The great secret of power is never to will to do more than you can accomplish.

Henrik Ibsen

As already mentioned, family members must be efficient problem solvers with a free-and-easy communication style if effective decision making is to occur. Once the solutions are generated, however, a centralized authority is needed to coordinate the implementation of the solution. If there is no authority, the discussions can be endless and impossible to resolve.

Most social scientists agree that the concept of "power" refers to the ability of one person to change the probability of another person's behavior. Understanding the power plays within a family involves understanding how each person tries to control the others and how everyone responds to everyone else's control attempts. All decisions and conflict resolutions involve having two or more people try to influence one another. By definition, then, all decisions and conflict resolutions involve social power.

Distributing Family Power

The exertion of power in any social group is inevitable. Properly used and distributed, power can help the group to be productive, efficient, and pleasant. Misused or too greatly concentrated in the hands of one person, power exerted in the family can be as abrasive and morally repugnant as power misused politically.

How does the family decide who is to have the most power and who the least? The answer is complex. The distribution of power can vary according to the task confronting the family and may shift with each stage of the family life cycle. A homemaker wife may have considerable power to decide when a crying infant should be soothed or when a toddler should take a nap. By the time the child is in school the father may well have some power over these decisions—and new areas for decision will have developed. The allocation of power depends upon five factors discussed below.

Areas of Expertise

When someone in the family knows a lot about a certain subject, the others agree to recognize his or her power claims in that area. Men traditionally have known more than women about car servicing, and 92 percent of the husbands in a recent survey made the decisions about where and when to service the car. Women traditionally know more about housecleaning, and wives makes over 80 percent of the decisions in that area (Stohs, 1991). Adolescents often are able to determine where the family buys pizza and which films their parents see, since they have most expertise in pizza and movies.

Cultural Norms

Every society and subculture tends to assign areas of social power based on sex and family position. In Italian families the father has stereotypically had the power to forbid his children to associate with certain neighborhood children; in Jewish families the mother has been ascribed this power. Fifty years ago, American culture gave men the power to control the frequency of sex in a marriage; today that power is more equitably distributed. Both the husband and wife are likely to feel that initiating sexual activities is within their control. Parents have always been ascribed greater power than the children in a wide spectrum of activities.

Control of Rewards and Punishments

When one person in the family is able to dispense a greater number of rewards, more important rewards, or less available rewards, that person's power base is increased. The equity discussion in Chapter 19 is solely devoted to the ins and outs of this type of power. The control strategy of Chafetz (1980) mentioned at the beginning of this chapter is another example of how the power to reward and punish family members is used to influence decision-making processes.

Intimacy

When we trust and feel very close to someone, we believe that person would base decisions only on what was in our own best interests. Since that concern for us is paramount, there is little reason to object to his or her use of power within our relationship.

Personality

Some people are so talkative and persistent that they tend to dominate the decision process. Sometimes the sheer intensity a person displays toward an issue makes the others too inhibited to object to that person's wishes.

Patterns of Allocation: The Powergram

Although the relative power each spouse has can vary across decision-making areas and influence areas, the pattern of power allocation as well as specific power areas can be a source of contention. Acknowledging the power a spouse feels in each area can open up a broad exploration of how decisions are made by the couple. The "powergram" (Stuart, 1980) can be used to visualize current and desired distribution of decision-making authority. Stuart provides a list of sixteen common decision-making areas, which are distributed as points on a graphic scale according to their importance and who makes them. Other items may be added and irrelevant items may be deleted. The couple rate these items according to their importance and then list their perceptions of who makes the decisions in each area: (1) the husband alone, (2) the husband after consulting the wife, (3) both, (4) the wife after consulting the husband, or (5) the wife alone.

Examining the powergram can be very revealing. For example, when spouses have different perceptions of who makes the decisions in a particular area, conflicts are to be expected. Suppose the wife believes that decisions about where to live are made by her after consulting the husband but the husband believes he alone makes the decision. This husband has "pseudostrength" because he believes that he exercises more authority than his wife has actually ceded.

With another couple, the wife may believe her husband makes this decision while he believes that she makes it with his concurrence. This wife has "pseudojuniority" because she believes that she has less power than her husband feels she now exercises. Both of these couples will undoubtedly run into troubles when they have to decide on a new place to live. The first wife will be trying to directly influence a decision that will not really involve her (since he feels it is his decision); the second wife will feel pressured into responsibility for a decision she believes is rightfully her husband's. A self-exploration exercise in using a modified powergram appears at the end of this chapter.

BILL (engineer, age 40)

I've decided to analyze the problem-solving abilities of my family by analyzing the most catastrophic problem that has ever been faced by the family—my "coming out" about my homosexuality. It was a multifaceted problem, but after thinking about it quite a while I have decided the way it was handled was typical of how we handled other problems as well.

My wife, according to the powergram, had a lot more power in the family than I did. I let JoAnn decide on where we'll live, what we'll buy, our social life, and a lot of other things as well. I don't begrudge her this power. I admire her organizational skills, and our values and tastes are very similar. As far as the children go, she's with them more and so has more of the day-to-day control over them. I coach the Little League team the girls are on and I help with homework and project ideas, but JoAnn often has useful comments in these areas, as well. Because JoAnn wields so much power, she thought my "coming out" was something that she could contain if not control. After the crying and shock, we had endless long night discussions. This was her attempt to influence me and my attempt to influence her. I tried to tell her how unhealthy and illogical

(continued)

(continued)

it would be to maintain the facade of a traditional marriage and continue living together. She would point out that sex has always been unimportant to her and make me cry by pointing out all the things I would miss that we do together as friends, as a couple, and as a family. After two weeks of this it became much more emotional. She'd say if I loved her and had any commitment or feeling for the girls I'd stay. I'd try to defend myself and explain how I do love her and the kids and am committed to both but cannot continue to live in the house. It was clear influence was getting us nowhere. Control and manipulation attempts then began to dominate as they always do when we reason ourselves out. She began to threaten me that she would tell the children and my parents since I was so "eager" to come out. I began to tell her that she would find herself without the funds I had promised her if she wouldn't separate in a peaceful manner. I started manipulating her by telling her I had to work late, and in the next two months I took three "business trips" that allowed me to stay at friends' houses for two or three days at a time. JoAnn began making social commitments for us in September and October (it was only July at this point!). I refused to make some furniture purchases we had planned to make over the summer until she agreed to give me a few pieces of furniture (any ones would do; I just didn't want to have to go and buy everything for the apartment). I left with us both very angry and very nervous. The first four weeks were hell. JoAnn refused to let me see the girls at all. I'd come over and she'd tell them to go upstairs and lock themselves in the bedroom. After the first week, she had all the locks changed on the doors.

I left over eighteen months ago and we are legally separated, now awaiting a final divorce. I see the girls at least twice a week and maybe once a month JoAnn and I go out for dinner. It's still the same. On a lot of issues we'll be able to reason it out because we do have basically the same approach to things. When we've passed some critical point whose detection always eludes me, it's manipulation and control by both of us. For us, the hostility during a fight wipes away any good feelings of intimacy. We both are emotionally spent for a few days.

I haven't had any real long-term relationships with another man yet and I wonder if I'll repeat the pattern I've shown with JoAnn or if I'll be able to argue with less disastrous results. After going through this unit I felt bad JoAnn and I hadn't read Bach's book on fighting fair. It might have made the past (as well as the future!) easier on us.

Using Power in Parenting

Power is equally critical in understanding the communication style and problem-solving abilities of the children in a family. Children's power needs are considerably less than the parents' since control functions are part of the adult's role. In addition to having this socially legitimate power, the parent almost always has more skill in a given area. This greater expertise gives enormous weight to the parent's power base. The child's power needs are expressed through the ability to make life easier or harder for the parents and to gain their attention and praise.

The child who feels competent to secure the parents' love and protection honestly feels very powerful. Powerless children feel inferior—undeserving of or lacking in their parents' recognition. Adler (1924) believes that when children feel powerless, they resort to misbehavior, seeking goals that an immature mind believes will lead to increased status: attention, power struggles, revenge, and inadequacy.

Dreikurs, Gould, and Corsini (1974) suggest that all types of juvenile misbehavior can be explained in terms of these goals. The child who is crying while the mother is on the telephone (attention), the child who refuses to go to bed (power), the child who gets drunk at the parents' party (revenge), and the child who is too insecure to go on sleepovers (inadequacy) all suffer from the same basic malady—a sense of powerlessness. In each case the goal of the parents is the same: to help the child find better ways to feel competent about maintaining the parents' affection.

The Adlerians have numerous strategies for handling these problems. Many of their parenting strategies are similar to Gordon's (1975) commercially popular Parent Effectiveness Training (PET). Gordon's program has three component techniques: (1) active listening, (2) sending "I-messages," and (3) "no-lose" problem solving.

With *active listening* the parent learns to send messages that help the child understand, accept, and deal with his or her feelings. For example, if a child comes home from school and says that his teacher was mean to him, the parent would decode that message to identify the underlying feeling and would respond, "You feel angry at Ms. Smith today because she made you stay after school when other children who were misbehaving didn't have to stay." This message keeps the door for communication open so that both parent and child can explore the problem. To be effective, the parent must not question or ridicule. These tactics will only increase the child's defensiveness and close doors to further exploration.

The *"I-Messages"* technique teaches the parent how to express frustrations without giving the child "you're not OK" messages. When father comes home tired from the office and finds his newspaper strewn all over the living room and the children playing noisily around his chair, he can say, "Hey, kids, I'm really wiped out right now and I need some time to relax and unwind. How about letting me have my chair and newspaper for a while and then you can come back and play in here after dinner?" That message is vastly different from telling children how inconsiderate and messy they are.

When the parent has just cleaned the kitchen floor and Johnny tracks mud through it, the parent can say, "I'm so frustrated . . . I just finished cleaning the floor and now it is all messed up again." In both of these examples, the parents are trying to communicate what they are feeling and what their needs are. They are refraining from giving the typical "you" message that blames the child for being inconsiderate, bad, or stupid (e.g., "Don't be such brats. Get out of here" or "How could you dare dirty the floor?").

In the *no-lose* method of problem solving, "when a conflict between parent and child occurs, the parent asks the child to participate in a joint search for some solution acceptable to both. Either may suggest possible solutions, which are then evaluated. A decision is eventually made on the best solution. They then decide how it is to be carried out. No coercion is required, hence no power is used" (Gordon, 1975:176). With this method no one in the family loses. The six steps in the no-lose method are as follows. A transcript showing the first four steps in action appears in the boxed section "No-lose Problem Solving in Action."

Step 1: Identifying and Defining the Conflict

During this step, the parents must get the child's attention and persuade him or her to enter into the problem-solving process. This goal is accomplished by discussing the problem when the child is relaxed and willing to listen, using a lot of "I-messages," and stressing the need to find a solution acceptable to both parents and child.

Step 2: Generating Possible Alternative Solutions

In this step it is important to generate a large choice of different types of solutions. Children should be encouraged to be creative and give their suggestions first. Parents should not judge or belittle any of the solutions offered.

Step 3: Evaluating the Alternative Solutions

Once all the solutions have been generated, both parents and children start looking to see which solutions are most acceptable for everyone involved. Any member who feels unhappy with a solution should make that point explicitly clear at this stage.

Step 4: Deciding on the Best Solution

Often, the best solution will emerge naturally out of the previous discussion. At other times, there may be more than one good solution and someone will suggest trying the easiest one first to see if it really could do the trick.

Step 5: Implementing the Decision

In this step, it is important to spell out in great detail who is to do what, by when. A dinnertime solution that involves having the children do the dishes twice a week will work only if it is known which of the children are responsible for each of the chores (washing, drying, sweeping, counters) on what days.

Step 6: Follow-Up Evaluation

Sometimes, the first solution does not work because it is far more difficult to carry out than anyone expected. Parents need to check back and find out how everyone thinks the decision is working out. If it has not worked out, the solution is modified to increase its chances of success, or a different solution that was generated in Steps 2 and 3 can be implemented.

The no-lose method of problem solving is Gordon's most distinctive contribution. He feels that problem-solving families are superior to both authoritarian and permissive families who are locked into win-lose situations when a conflict between parent and child occurs. In the authoritarian family, the parents decide what the solution must be. If the child does not agree with the solution, the parents use their power and authority to coerce the child into compliance. In these families the parents always win; the child always loses. In the permissive family, the parents may make some effort to persuade a child to accept the parents' solution, but if the child protests, the parents give in and let the child do what he or she wants. In these families the child always wins; the parent always loses. When Gordon's approach is successful, it lets both parent and child win. The no-lose method can also be used to help couples resolve their disagreements, without one spouse "winning" and the other spouse "losing."

No-Lose Problem Solving in Action

M: You remember I said at dinner that there's a problem about you and vegetables.

J: Yeah, I don't like to eat them.

M: I guess I know that by now. Now, Jay, this is a problem we need to work out together. You don't like to eat vegetables. But I'd like for you to eat them because they contain certain vitamins that your body needs. Do you have any ideas about what we should do about this problem? Do you have any suggestions for a solution?

(continued)

(continued)

J: No.

M: Well, try to think of something. Isn't there something you can think of?

J: (Sort of whining) No, I can't think of anything.

M: OK, Jay, I'm going to suggest a solution, and then you tell me what you think of it. We won't settle on anything until we both agree to it. OK?

J: (Somewhat skeptical) OK.

M: What would you think of this? Would you be willing to take at least one taste of the vegetable at each meal? If you didn't like it, then you wouldn't have to eat any more.

J: No.

M: No?

J: I don't like that idea. I'm not going to do that.

M: You don't think that's a good idea? OK. Then you think of an idea.

J: I can't.

M: Well, then . . . uh, Jay, are there any vegetables you do like?

J: Yes, I like raw carrots.

M: Anything else?

J: Celery sticks.

M: And?

J: And beans. Not beans from the garden, but beans from a can.

M: Any more?

J: Nope. That's all.

M: I see. Now I wonder what we could do.

J: Could you fix one of those vegetables for me every time?

M: (Slowly) Yes, I suppose I could. It really doesn't matter to me which vegetables you eat. I'm just concerned that you eat some vegetables. Yes, I think I could agree to that.

J: (Lightly) OK.

M: Now, there's one other thing. Sometimes you don't like to eat the main dish either.

J: Yeah, if it has onions in it.

M: Well, what could we do about that?

J: I don't know.

M: Well, would you be willing to taste the main dish?

J: But what if I don't like it?

M: What could you do if you didn't like it?

J: I could fix myself a sandwich.

M: A sandwich? Yes, I guess you could. At least you'd get something to eat that way. So you would try at least one bite, and then if you decided you didn't like it, you would make a sandwich. OK. That sounds good to me. Do you suppose we should write down our agreement?

J: Yes, let's make a sign and hang it by the table so you'll remember it.

Source: Gordon, T. 1975. *Parent Effectiveness Training: The New Tested Way to Raise Responsible Children.* New York: Plume, 228-229.

SELF-EXPLORATION: PROBLEM SOLVING

Try to reconstruct the problem-solving processes that were used in your family of origin. You may first want to fill out the Family Problem-Solving Component Checklist (see Figure 14.2).

1. How did your mother try to influence the children? By authority, control, influence, or manipulation? How did your father try to influence the children?
2. How did you perceive your parents' trying to influence each other?
3. Who had the power for important decisions? Complete the power-gram in Figure 14.3 to help guide your analysis.
4. After a problem or conflict was brought out into the open, was it usually better or worse for you than before it was brought up? Why?
5. How do you think the problem-solving strategies of your family of origin have affected your current ways of handling conflict?

FIGURE 14.2. Family Problem-Solving Component Checklist

1. Enough time is always spent discussing a problem.
   Yes   No

2. Each person gets enough time to discuss what he or she thinks ought to be done.
   Yes   No

3. In my family, most of us can suggest a lot of different solutions.
   Yes   No

4. Sometimes pretty unusual ways of handling a problem are brought up.
   Yes   No

5. When my family has a problem, I can tell just by looking at my siblings' reaction what they think of my ideas before they have a chance to speak.
   Yes   No

6. The "leader" in my family always knows how to get us to face up to a problem.
   Yes   No

7. I can tell just by looking at my parents' reactions what they think of my ideas before they have a chance to speak.
   Yes   No

8. When we have a problem, everyone tries to be very supportive.
   Yes   No

9. We usually all get along, so when a problem crops up we don't try to "get even" with each other.
   Yes   No

10. We usually can all agree on what the problem really is.
    Yes   No

11. Everyone feels free to criticize one another's suggestions if they don't make sense to us.
    Yes   No

12. My parent(s) are usually very eager to hear the children's opinion when we face a common problem.
    Yes   No

13. When no one really knows how to solve a particular problem in the family we ask friends or relatives outside the family for their help.
    Yes   No

14. Everyone in my family usually feels he or she has something to say or contribute.
    Yes   No

15. Everyone in my family respects one another.
    Yes   No

16. Our family has a shorthand so with just a few words, we know what each person's feelings on a topic are.
    Yes   No

17. We enjoy sharing ideas and information.
    Yes   No

18. My family understands that we all can't agree on every issue.
    Yes   No

19. We can find a solution pretty quickly that we all go along with when we have to make a quick decision.
    Yes   No

20. My family expects and allows disagreements with one another.
    Yes   No

21. I can think of a number of times in the past when the family has had to pull together to make difficult decisions.
    Yes   No

Source: This list was adapted from a family communications handout and the author is unknown.

FIGURE 14.3. Powergram Items

Describe who has the power to decide each item at the current time in the marriage by placing the letter corresponding to the item in one of the five sections of the powergram. Placing an A in column 1 indicates that the husband almost always makes the decision. An A in column 2 indicates that the husband almost always makes the final decision, but only after consulting with the wife. An A in column 3 indicates that the husband and wife share equally in making decisions. An A in column 4 indicates that the wife almost always makes the final decision, but only after consulting with the husband. An A in column 5 indicates that the wife almost always makes the decision. (In order not to get confused as the powergrams are compared, one spouse uses uppercase letters and the other spouse uses lowercase letters.)

Powergrams can be used to describe how the spouses would like to see decision making allocated by sorting the statements into a desired authority pattern. When there is a large discrepancy between the present and the desired future authority pattern, the couple will be in a lot of conflict.

a. Where the couple lives
b. What job husband takes
c. How many hours husband works
d. Whether wife works
e. What job wife takes
f. How many hours wife works
g. Number of children in the family
h. When to praise or punish children
i. How much time to spend with children
j. When to have social contacts with friends
k. When to have social contacts with in-laws
l. When to have social contacts with relatives

m. When to have sex
n. How to have sex
o. How to spend money
p. How and when to pursue personal interests
q. Whether to attend church, and if so, which church to attend
r. Whether to quit a current job
s. Whether to take a new job
t. Where to go for vacation
u. How to make investments
v. Which magazines to subscribe to
w. Which home improvements need to be done
x. Which furniture to buy

Present Authority Pattern

1	2	3	4	5
Husband only	Husband with wife's approval	Both	Wife with husband's approval	Wife only

Desired Authority Pattern

1	2	3	4	5
Husband only	Husband with wife's approval	Both	Wife with husband's approval	Wife only

Source: Stuart, R. B. 1973. *Scale of Marital Precounseling Inventory: Behavior Change Systems.* Champaign, IL: Research Press. Reprinted with permission of R. B. Stuart.

Chapter 15

Family Productivity

Showing up is 80 percent of life.

Woody Allen

How can you come to know yourself? Never by thinking, always by doing. Try to do your duty, and you'll know right away what you amount to. And what is your duty? Whatever the day calls for.

Goethe

In terms of the family, *productivity* means the ability to perform the roles and achieve the goals that are central to the family's successful functioning. Satir (1972:256) views family productivity as a kind of family engineering task.

It isn't too different from engineering anywhere else in that a family, like a business, has time, space, equipment and people to get its work done. With any kind of engineering, you find out what you have, match it with what you need, and figure out the best way to use it. You also find out what you don't have and figure out a way to get it.

Today, the family's productivity revolves around its ability to satisfy eight specific family needs (Nye, 1976): (1) provider needs (money for food and shelter), (2) child care needs, (3) child socialization needs, (4) housekeeping needs, (5) kinskeeping needs, (6) therapeutic needs, (7) recreational needs, and (8) sexual needs.

Satisfying these needs leads to a sense of family purpose and wellbeing. Each person feels he or she matters—that what he or she is doing is important. Thus, a very productive family is usually a well-adjusted family. Of course, the ability to satisfy each of the eight needs varies over the family's life cycle, and at any one time, some needs may conflict with others.

357

For example, in any family, stressful events may temporarily lower productivity. Somewhat surprisingly, though, studies have shown that families who are chronically low in productivity and struggling to maintain family unity do not have more stresses to deal with than families who are high in productivity (Westley and Epstein, 1969). Financial problems may beset either kind of family; so may illness. What distinguishes the two types of families is not the number of problems they face, but their success in solving their problems. Highly productive families know how to cut back in times of a financial crisis or how best to enlist the aid of friends and relatives; less productive families get paralyzed in their problem-solving strategies or try solutions with virtually no chance of success. Each of the eight areas will be discussed below with an emphasis on how American families try to be productive at each stage of the family's development.

PROVIDER NEEDS

Provider needs are most essential for the family's survival, and the person responsible for fulfilling this role is often the key influence in the family. Traditionally, both sexes have been socialized to rely on the man to contribute the major portion of provider needs. But while men have historically been the major contributors, the idea that men are the *sole* providers of the family income is a myth. The most cursory view of U.S. social and economic history reveals a continuing joint economic contribution by both men and women for a significant majority of U.S. families (Aldous, 1981).

Women As Providers

In the late 1800s and early 1900s, when nearly half of all U.S. women lived on farms, wives would continually earn money from their gardens, from homemade products, and from the sale of butter and eggs. Similarly, recent studies looking back at Atlanta, Georgia; Nashville, Tennessee; and Massachusetts in 1896 showed the proportion of employed black wives to range from 44 percent to 65 percent. During the early 1900s a fifth of the immigrant wives worked in textile mills and other factories. The American wife has also consistently opened the home to outsiders, providing room and board as a means to supplement the family income. It is estimated that in the first half of the twentieth century, 15 to 20 percent of urban households contained lodgers or boarders at any one time (Aldous, 1981). Thus, the history of American women is to a significant extent the history of American working women. What has changed dramatically over the past fifty years is the ever-increasing numbers of women employed outside the home in traditionally male-dominated hourly or salaried jobs, so that by 1985 a majority (54.4 percent) of all married couples belonged in this category. Nearly 40 percent of married women are now employed all year, full-time. In 1995, over 55 percent of married women who had given birth in the past year were employed on a full-time or part-time basis. For women thirty to forty-four years old who had their first child, 77 percent were employed. Over 10 million preschoolers are being cared for by nonparents each workday (U.S. Bureau of the Census, 1998).

The Importance of Providing Adequately

Irrespective of who brings home the weekly paycheck, someone must do so if a family is to be productive. In some families, economic productivity is so highly valued that everyone in the family is expected to help fulfill this need as soon as possible. Baby-sitting, lawn care, and newspaper routes are the traditional and still most popular methods by which children can earn money. While children from poor families do these chores because it is necessary if they want shoes, lunch money, or other necessities, many middle-class children seek out these jobs because they have been taught to value providing for themselves. In many school districts, the high schools have responded to the adolescents' need to feel economically productive by allowing them to go to school only half a day in their junior and senior years if they are employed during the other half of the day.

When families cannot earn enough money to fill their basic needs, they often have trouble being productive in other spheres as well. Feelings of low self-esteem, depression, and preoccupation with making ends meet leave little energy to be put into the other areas. Very often, part-time jobs are used to cover the additional and unexpected costs of car repairs and home repairs, so that the actual time left to devote to other productive areas is drastically reduced.

Developmental Differences in Provider Needs

A life-cycle analysis of provider needs suggests that the vast majority of American families are highly motivated to increase their income until the spouses are well into their forties. A midlife crisis tends to occur when people have to adjust to the fact that their chances for further promotions are very small and all they can look forward to is holding on to whatever rung they have already reached. Frustrated and trapped by the stagnation of doing the same type of work for years on end and realizing their decreased opportunities for advancement, many couples question their earlier materialistic values and refocus their energies on community involvement or hobbies. Others, experiencing burnout and boredom in their current occupations, decide to retrain for a different career.

Mayer (1978:210) interviewed a former policeman retrained as a professional nurse, who stressed the new satisfactions that have opened up to him since he decided to retrain:

> It took a lot to sign up for this course, knowing the reaction we had to face back at the station house. You have to have some guts to go ahead and say I'm going to change my whole conception of what I want to do, how I want to fulfill myself. At one stage of my life, money was the big thing, but I'm not interested in the cash value of life anymore.
>
> I've spent seventeen years of my life missing everything. If there was a picnic or a wedding or a christening I always had to say, "No," I was working. Now I'll have a job where I can say, "Yes!" And maybe I'll just work three or four days a week, and home will be wherever me and my wife want it to be. We'll be free!

For women, midlife often means reentry into the workforce on a fulltime basis. For them, the chance to choose a new and more interesting career path is socially very acceptable. Men are more likely to be scorned and viewed as immature if they openly decide to seek out more independent, rewarding careers.

Traditionally, couples retired from the workforce and reduced their standard of living during the later stages of the family life cycle. Currently, there is a trend for people to continue working past their eligible retirement age and to obtain part-time employment after their formal retirement. The trend of continuing to work as long as one is physically able has been bolstered by economic need and by the realization that elderly people derive self-esteem and life purpose from the provider role.

The government has begun to support older workers on a number of fronts. Nine of the fourteen recommendations of the 1981 White House Conference on Aging focused on employment-related issues such as developing part-time, flex-time, and job-sharing work strategies for older Americans. More and more state governments are passing legislation to raise the mandatory retirement age above seventy and are promoting state laws against age discrimination in employment. Most states are also trying to counsel and retrain elderly workers with funds provided by the Title V Senior Community Service Employment Program (SCSEP). Finding employment through these programs would lessen the dependency of some older people on their children and would allow other elders to give their children more financial help.

CHILD CARE AND CHILD SOCIALIZATION

The concept of *child care* encompasses all the time and activities that are required to physically care for a child and guide the child to function effectively in school and neighborhood activities.

Changing Roles in Child Care

The possible tasks in this category are limitless, but they generally include washing, toileting, dressing, undressing, nursing when sick, visits to doctors and dentists, afterschool activities and visits to friends' houses, feeding, putting to bed, getting up and ready for school, choosing day care and camps, planning birthdays and holiday events, and assisting with homework. Child care has traditionally been a female role, and some women are very hesitant to relinquish this productive task. Many working women feel very guilty when they have to ask other family members to help out with child care or when they have to hire outside help to perform these tasks. Women through the centuries have been responsible for the survival of future generations, and this responsibility is not easily shared.

Still, the times are changing, and many younger parents have made a conscious decision to share child care. Fathers in increasing numbers are changing diapers, driving car pools, and preparing meals. Currently, many single fathers with joint or sole custody of their children are providing total child care and loving it.

Whether parents are married or single, the child care functions essential to healthy survival of the children are difficult *not* to perform. It is only in extremely unproductive family situations that the children are physically neglected, starved, or left alone for days on end. Attention to child care functions that are merely socially expected (giving parties, getting the child to school on time) are more likely to fluctuate in response to family stresses. When job pressures, money worries, illness, and arguments weigh heavy on the parent's mind, socially expected child care functions are likely to decrease or become more erratic. In families with a low level of stress, productivity in this area may be very high.

Some might expect that when the burden of child care is greatly increased by a child's illness or disability, or because of a large number of children in the family, the parental relationship will be the first to suffer. Research contradicts this popular belief. Handicapped children, for example, rarely precipitate marital discord between otherwise happy partners. Korn, Chess, and Fernandez (1978) studied 162 families to whom handicapped children were born as a result of the 1964 rubella epidemic. Marital discord followed the birth of the handicapped child in only two families. In both of these cases the child was seen as the precipitator of the difficulties. Yet thirty-six of these families (22.2 percent) attributed a major disruption in the family productivity to the rubella child. Among these thirty-six families:

> . . . the most frequently cited problems involved: a) intense emotional reactions to the handicapped child, by one or both of the parents, that persisted over time and spilled over into their personal interactions; b) inability to go on vacations, visit friends or places as a family because the handicapped child was disruptive or embarrassing; c) limited social life for the parents as a couple because of the inability to find baby-sitters willing and able to care for the special needs of the handicapped child; d) neglect of other children because of the excessive demands made by the handicapped child often leading to the siblings resenting the handicapped child. Parents also complained that their friends had abandoned them and they had less time and money for their own interests. Often, they were so overwhelmed that they could not organize or else neglected their housekeeping routines and spent too much time worrying about the care of the handicapped child. On the average, each family involved in this group cited two such complaints as family problems that they attributed directly to the handicapped child. (p. 306)

Child Socialization

The concept of *child socialization* refers to the family's need to teach the children specific attitudes, values, social skills, and norms so that they will be accepted members of the social community. In our society, both parents are expected to help socialize the children. Research findings suggest that mothers and fathers agree on what skills and abilities are important for a son's socialization but disagree on what is important for a daughter's. For example, Gilbert and Hanson (1983) observed that parents agreed they were both responsible for ensuring that their sons developed reading skills, learned how to deal with disappointment, learned how to get along with others, learned right from wrong, learned how to play basic sports, and learned how to express affection toward others and to respect each parent. By contrast, mothers were alone in assuming many of the responsibilities for the daughter's socialization.

For example, mothers felt it was important for them to teach their daughters how to express anger, how to make a decision, and the importance of physical exercise and family life. The fathers did not see this as their responsibility. Mothers also took responsibility for teaching their daughters mathematical skills, to question roles and standards, and to understand their own sexuality. Fathers did not concern themselves with these issues, either. The fact that both mothers and fathers were committed to socializing a son in many different areas while fathers showed less responsibility toward socializing their daughters on 25 percent of the items covered in the study may be a positive or negative factor in the female child's development. Future research hopefully will focus on the differences between women whose fathers have been very concerned with socializing them and those whose fathers have been very uninvolved.

Social Policy Regarding Child Care

Most contemporary governments take the position that families need help in meeting their basic productivity needs. In the industrialized countries, governments range from having implicit and reluctant family policies (Canada, Britain, the United States, and Israel) to having explicit and comprehensive family policies (Sweden, Norway, and Hungary).

Family policy in France concentrates on income maintenance. Monthly family allowances are granted to the family for each child (excluding the firstborn) up to the age of sixteen and a half, up to eighteen if the child is in an apprenticeship, or up to twenty if he or she is pursuing studies or incapable of working. An allowance is given for a firstborn if he or she is handicapped, is the last child still in the care of a family that has reared several children, or has a single parent. Housing allowances and low-interest home loans for families are also available in France. There is an extensive system of government-funded education, from two-year-old children in *ecoles maternelles* to young adults in the universities. Even private schools (religious and secular) can get grants from the state to cover costs, thus allowing parents a wide range of educational choices (Questiaux and Fournier, 1978).

When government support of families exists within a broad national "family policy," the benefits may be tenuously balanced by restrictions on family life. Such is the case in China, where family size is limited by government policy. Thus, each culture must balance the desire for government support of families with the perceived danger of government intrusion.

Developmental Changes

Examining childhood care and socialization from a life-cycle perspective helps dramatize the long period of dependence for American children. Most parents continue to support and guide their children through their early twenties. Adolescents tend to consider themselves independent of their parents when they have control over making their own decisions, do most of the daily tasks of living for themselves, and are financially independent (Moore and Hotch, 1983). Comparable data for parents is not available, but most likely they have similar feelings. If so, they may begin to ask "Where does it end?" as they find themselves financing not only college educations and weddings but home down payments, home improvements, and divorces. Many adult children are even finding that they are economically forced out of the housing market and must return home to live for an indefinite period of time, prolonging parental responsibilities once again.

Added to these economic forms of care are perhaps thousands of hours of supportive conversations and problem-solving discussions, as parents continue their socialization function. Sometimes, parents continue fulfilling both the psychological and economic needs of their children until the day they die. More often, parents eventually give up this job except for occasional periods of crisis in their adult children's lives.

HOUSEWORK

Make it a point to do something every day that you don't want to do. This is the golden-rule for acquiring the habit of doing your duty without pain.

Mark Twain

The term *housework* is difficult to define precisely because each family varies in the way it classifies work and leisure. Depending on the family, housework can include any or all of the following tasks: meal preparation and cleanup, housecleaning, laundry, record keeping, and transporting family members.

Gender Differences

Housework has traditionally been defined as a female job. Despite modern conveniences, housework is still a time-consuming chore that takes well over thirty hours a week in an average family. As more and more women enter the extrafamilial work force, they are spending more hours away from the home. Everyday observation reveals that most women continue to do the overwhelming majority of the household tasks, even if they are working full-time in the traditional job market. Empirical research supports these observations, showing the typical wife averaging thirty hours per week in housework and the typical husband averaging around two hours. The husband's average is misleading, since well over 70 percent of the husbands reported doing no housework whatsoever. Those husbands who reported doing any housework contributed about seven hours a week (Nichols and Meltzen, 1982).

However, the inequality may not be as severe as it appears on the surface. If one combines paid work hours and household work hours (per week in labor market work and housework combined), husbands contribute, on the average, 46.8 hours and wives 47.2 hours per week. Thus, while women are continuing to do most of the housework, men are continuing to put in much longer traditional workdays. When women work outside the home as many hours as their mates, the average husband's contribution to housework rises quite dramatically (Fox and Nickols, 1983).

Also, year by year more men are beginning to undertake at least some housework. Interestingly, some types of housework seem to be particularly difficult to reassign because they are so strongly stereotyped as women's work. Probably the least shared task is the laundry. Dryers and washers, the receptacles where our outer shields are cleaned and purified, are strongly linked with womanhood.

If equality in housework is ever achieved, it is at least two or three generations away. In Sweden, where the national policy of flextime has tried to allow men to be equally involved in the family, women continue to do most of the housework and to be more concerned than men about family matters (Haas, 1980). Further support for the long road ahead was given by Juliette and Ronald Goldman (1983), who interviewed over 800 children five to fifteen years old in Australia, England, North America, and Sweden. They found that children continue to perceive the roles of mother and father in a stereotyped manner. Mothers are seen as predominantly concerned with domestic duties, care of children, and low-status occupations. Fathers are seen as concerned with matters external to the household including leisure, authority and leadership, and high-status occupations. What is surprising about these results is that children in Sweden, where schools have provided compulsory sex education and human education programs for over forty-five years and where parents have flexible work schedules, responded similarly to children from more traditional countries.

Children and Household Chores

While men are making at least some progress in increased participation in household tasks, how about the children? The average child seems to contribute twice as much as the average husband.

Lawrence (1984) surveyed 2,100 families in eleven states, asking in detail about the nature of children's chores around the house. He found that the average child, aged six to seventeen, averaged forty minutes a day in housework and related activities. While combining such a diverse age group together makes the results difficult to interpret, it provides some basis to begin more detailed studies. He found that children spent, on the average, fifteen minutes a day working in the yard (mowing the lawn), taking care of pets, and cleaning cars. Housecleaning averaged eleven minutes, food preparation, eight minutes; dishwashing, four minutes; and care of clothing, two minutes.

Developmental trends were found, as expected, with older children doing significantly more than younger children. Girls spent significantly more time than boys on chores inside the house; boys did more outside the home. Boys did do maintenance tasks inside the home, such as window washing and moving furniture, with the same frequency as girls.

In 1984, when this survey was conducted, there were already a significant number of women working outside the home. Yet Lawrence found an interest interaction between the mother's working status and the children's participation in two household tasks: food preparation and dishwashing. In these two tasks, if the mother was employed part-time outside the home, then the children did significantly less work in this area (after all, Mom was making time for these chores) than children whose mother did not work at all (here, moms may have felt justified in teaching children to be self-sufficient since they clearly were doing their jobs as homemakers on a full-time basis and couldn't be criticized). Children whose mothers worked full time outside the home did the most in these two areas (their moms needed them to get the family chores done in this area since there simply was no time for Mom to do them). Thus, kids whose moms worked part-time ended up doing the least housework and kids whose moms worked full time ended up doing the most.

Nearly twenty years later, I am confident that the total time children spend on housework has declined significantly, mostly because teenagers now routinely work outside the home at paid jobs, few people prepare family dinners every night, and even lawn mowing has become a service many parents outsource to professionals.

Developmental Differences

Before children, housekeeping chores are less burdensome. Women are often eager to set up house and show that they can excel in the traditional female role. Men at this time are eager to show their flexibility and are willing to share many tasks not consistent with the prevalent gender roles. It is during this honeymoon period that household chores are most likely to be equitably shared. Once children arrive, housekeeping becomes considerably more complicated and time consuming. Yet, during this period, women begin to specialize in the traditionally feminine tasks. Husbands begin concentrating more on traditionally masculine tasks.

During the child-rearing years, housework responsibilities can have a depressing and alienating effect on many women. Pogrebin (1983:160) vividly portrays the female housework dilemma in this simple farming analogy:

> Holidays and every day, that cherished thing known as "family life" is purchased with a woman's time and labor. Warm family memories rest on a network of chores she accomplished, responsibilities she remembered, get-togethers she organized, messes she cleared away, rooms she made welcoming, food she cooked to please. The rest of the family adds the conversation, games, laughter, stories—the seeds of family closeness. But seeds cannot be planted unless the earth has been plowed and cultivated. Like plowing, housework makes the ground ready for the germination of family life. The kids will not invite a teacher home if beer cans litter the living room. The family isn't likely to have breakfast together if somebody didn't remember to buy eggs, milk, or muffins. Housework maintains an orderly setting in which family life can flourish.
>
> If one person on a farm is solely responsible for all the plowing, it stands to reason that she will have a different relationship to the planting and the harvest. For one thing, she will be tired when the others are just beginning. Then too, she will feel separate and estranged for having worked alone before they got there. And, if her plowed field is taken for granted, she will be bitter.
>
> The alternatives are obvious: either everyone plows as well as plants so that the pleasures of the harvest are more fully shared, or an outside person is paid to do the plowing so that everyone in the family can start even, and together sow the seeds of family life.

While the marital roles stay sharply divided even after retirement (husbands and wives doing different chores from each other), older couples are more likely to ignore sex role definitions of what is an appropriate work division. Work assignments for older adults are often based on physical ability, energy, and current interests.

BRAD (student, age 21)

In retrospect, it seems to me that the productivity of my family was pretty poor. I cannot remember an organized family task that we tried to carry out, but one example of a family working together would be holidays. For our family, on Christmas, we opened presents and afterward had a Christmas dinner. My memories of these occasions were pretty unpleasant. The opening of presents went along more or less peacefully, but when it came time for the dinner, there was a lot of conflict. If the three of us (mother, brother, and myself) managed to all sit down at the table together, we were often not talking because of earlier fights. It seemed that usually before the end of the meal, someone would get up and leave the table in a rage (usually my brother).

We did manage to do some things together as a family. For example, we went on some trips together—usually down to the beach. These I remember to be the most enjoyable of the things the family did together—possibly because the beach was a big place and we could get away from each other. In general, though, because of my mother's difficulty in taking charge of a situation, our family productivity was pretty low. I, as the parentified child, would try to take charge, but my brother would not obey me. My brother would try to take charge in that he would try to get my mother to do something for him or take him somewhere that he liked. I would rarely go along with this and would argue with him and try to sway my mother not to listen to him. My mother was pulled back and forth between the two of us and would rarely take a stand on what she thought was right to do. Therefore, our family interactions were usually pretty chaotic.

KINSKEEPING

Keeping in touch with the extended family (kinskeeping) is an important family function that is discussed at length in Chapter 8. Most families try to be productive in this area.

Although there is a lot of visiting, both sides of the extended family are not seen equally. There is a strong tendency for husband and wife to see one side of the family much more often. While this is a general phenomenon, it becomes much more marked in particular ethnic groups. Jewish women, for example, retain particularly strong ties to their families of origin. When asked who would take custody of their children in the event of their own or their husband's death, 75 percent of the Jewish women in one study chose a maternal relative while only 31 percent of Protestants and 48 percent of Catholics did so (Sanua, 1978). This strong favoring of one's family of origin among Jewish women may derive from the filial obligation among Jewish children to provide satisfaction or pleasure to their parents. This pleasure can be given in many forms, including financial success, marriage, and grandchildren. Pleasure from female children also seems to include a large degree of physical availability that is not as much expected from the sons.

A life cycle analysis of kinskeeping reveals that kinskeeping duties are present at every stage. In a three-generational study, Hill and associates (1970) found that 70 percent of young married couples saw their parents weekly and 40 percent of their parents (the middle generation) saw their own parents weekly. Though most individuals continue to have cross-generational contact, the nature and purpose of the contact varies with the stage in the family's development. In the young family, the new parents seek out their families of origin for help with problems of child care and for economic assistance. They also want the understanding and closeness their family offered them when they were unmarried and living at home. During the middle stages of the family life cycle, adults primarily seek emotional gratification from their parents and also are in a patron status, giving more than receiving. In the final stages, the elderly must look to their own children for help with problems of illness and household management.

Today, kinskeeping responsibilities are focused on one's family of origin. While there are various distinct ethnic patterns regarding kinskeeping, most adult children in our country feel responsible only for keeping in touch with their parents and siblings. Many feel no obligations whatsoever toward aunts, uncles, cousins, or grandparents.

THERAPEUTIC NEEDS

Today, the family needs to provide its members with an emotional buffer against a very complex and demanding world. Family members often constitute our only advocates—the only people who are "for" us.

The longer a family exists under the same roof with at least mildly affable relationships, the stronger the tendency to mutual nurturing becomes. Feelings of security and well-being develop from long-standing interactions. The plans and activities that weave the family members together create a "family album" of shared experiences. This continuity of past and future provides an existential validation of our own being. In the family, one's dreams and fears are understood in context. That is why it is so difficult to find people outside the family who can understand why a certain type of house is so important to us or why the completion of a certain task at work so vital. How easily understood these concerns are at home!

Marital Intimacy and Therapeutic Needs

Some might reasonably argue that to be successful, all the therapeutic needs in the family must be mediated by a deep intimacy. Waring and Reddon (1983) have demonstrated that marital intimacy is composed of eight distinct components. According to this research, an ideally intimate couple would:

1. Be easily able to resolve differences of opinion.
2. Be equally committed to the marriage.
3. Feel emotionally close to each other.
4. Be able to work, play, and enjoy sex together.
5. Share important feelings and attitudes.
6. Be confident and have a good level of self-esteem.
7. Have both gained independence from their families of origin and their offspring.
8. Would almost always be able to respond supportively and favorably to the spouse, irrespective of the issue.

The last prerequisite may be the most important. Within such a relationship, the healing power of the family would be at its maximum. The therapeutic role involves being available to the other person and identifying with that person's history and future. It requires an empathy toward the other's disappointments, frustrations, and joys. One mate exhibits concern and tolerance for the weaknesses and vulnerabilities of the other.

Family Enrichment Programs

In the early 1970s, therapists began to develop family enrichment programs with the express goal of helping families develop communication skills in nurturing and intimate relationships. One popular type of program is the family growth group, composed of three to five families who meet regularly and frequently for mutual care and support and for the development of family potential. A meeting might begin with the families sharing a "bag" supper that is followed by some physical sport or by games. During the second part of the meeting, the group may engage in growth-producing activities developed by family educators, discuss a common concern, or hear a speaker. A typical growth exercise is one

> . . . in which all the members of a family take turns sitting opposite each other in dyads sharing positive feedback by completing a series of statements, including "I feel loved and appreciated when you . . ." and "I feel joyful when you . . ." Other exercises help family members to increase awareness of their family's unique beginnings and of their latent resources. (Anderson, 1974:10)

Churches have been instrumental in developing these types of programs. Although a family may easily find some exercises contrived and others boring over a long period, the short-term effect is very uplifting.

Family enrichment opens up new avenues of appreciation and support within the family. The short-term booster effect has led to family enrichment weekends when families mix rest and relaxation with a more intentional and systematic revitalization of the family spirit. There are even family camps that provide a holiday setting and are devoted to giving families the skills needed to be therapeutic to one another.

Productivity versus Therapeutic Needs

In healthy families, concern for maximum productivity coexists with and is modulated by this therapeutic need to attend to each individual. Yet many families are so concerned with getting things done, they show very little concern for family members' personal needs. They accomplish a lot of their goals, but often a single authority directs all the action and is insensitive to other points of view. Obviously, though very productive on a number of dimensions, these families will encounter apathy, resentment, resistance, hostility, or rebellion.

At the other extreme are families who are so concerned with therapeutic needs, with no one feeling stressed or angry and everybody having a good time, that they skirt issues concerned with achievement or results. These families are usually very low in most of the other areas of productivity. Feelings of guilt and insecurity often haunt these family members as they try to separate from their families of origin and lead independent, productive lives. The most disastrous type of family combines lack of concern for setting and achieving goals with lack of concern for how the family members feel. In these apathetic and disinterested families, everyone has given up on life and on one another. The ideal family is one in which both work and human concerns thrive. There is a team spirit, with each understanding and respecting the authority of the others (Dyer, 1975).

Currently, a great deal of attention has been focused on families with high productivity demands and little sensitivity to individual needs. In particular, these upwardly mobile families push to make children very productive in terms of adult standards. David Elkind (1981) has termed such a child as "the hurried child." He has attributed the phenomenon to the stressed parents' need to see their children as symbols instead of whole persons:

> Symbols, oversimplifications really, are energy conserving. Parents under stress see their children as symbols because it is the least demanding way to deal with them. A student, a skater and a tennis player, are clear-cut symbols, easy guides for what to think, to see, and how to behave. Symbols thus free the parent from the energy-consuming task of knowing the child [and serve] as ready-at-hand targets for projecting unfulfilled needs, feelings, and emotions. Thus, by treating children as symbols, parents conserve the energy needed for coping with stress and have ready-made screens for projecting some of the consequences of stress, fear, anxiety and frustration. (p. 29)

Children are pushed to become proficient and competitive athletes at age six. When parents feel they have been unsuccessful, they are more likely to want their children to be successful and to feel that the earlier they start the better the children will be. Early training can give an extra edge of competency in a specific area—but not always. Some studies have shown that the most avid readers as adults were those who were introduced to reading later in their elementary school careers. Many studies have shown that children who begin school as "old sixes" have distinctly more successful academic careers than the "young fives."

Outside the academic realm, children are being urged to become productive partners in housework and family decision making. With both parents often working, children are sometimes given the responsibility for doing the majority of housework. In addition, single parents often make children their confidants. All of these efforts to create "superchildren" detract from the therapeutic needs of children to feel unconditionally worthwhile and loved. Often, they also lose the freedom to explore fantasies and potentialities.

Developmental Differences

Throughout the family life cycle, sensitivity to individual needs is vitally important. Before children, the couple have only each other to emotionally nurture and support, and feeling "loved" is relatively easy. After the children, needs for attention, physical contact, and understanding must sometimes go unfulfilled as other family goals take precedence.

Although companionship is almost always a highly valued family goal, it is very difficult to achieve and to sustain. The family enrichment programs described above are helping some families; still, the need is great among a large minority of families. For example, more than three out of ten teenagers feel their fathers spend "too little time" with them, and 28 percent would like to spend more time talking to both parents (Pogrebin, 1983). Happily, it does appear that the majority of families with children are successful in providing companionship and support to one another.

During the later stages of the life cycle, adult children and their parents again strive to have a mutually reciprocal relationship, with each generation emotionally supporting and reassuring the other. Many geographically dispersed families bridge the physical distance between their homes by weekly telephone calls in which the trials and tribulations of the past week are shared and each generation receives emotional fortification for the week ahead. The phone bill may be high, but an hour on the phone with the family costs significantly less than an hour's visit to a psychologist. At less frequent intervals, sibling visits and phone calls are sometimes able to serve this therapeutic function also.

Little empirical or theoretical data indicates how well older couples satisfy each other's therapeutic needs. Some evidence suggests that older couples pass through a series of stages that affect their ability to be emotionally sensitive to each other. For example, Gilford (1984) found a distinct trend for increasing marital happiness over the early stage of old age (sixty-three to sixty-nine) and a decline over the later stage (seventy to ninety).

Couples in their sixties are often in an enjoyable honeymoon stage of retirement. Many couples at this age have lots of leisure time, good health, and an adequate income with which to negotiate marital happiness and care for each other. Depression, reduced physical abilities, and disease may lead individuals to become more self-absorbed in the final years and less able to emotionally nurture their spouses. The observed decrease in marital happiness among this eldest group of couples could be associated with giving or receiving less care.

SARA (retail store manager, age 37)

Both Abe and I are high-energy people, and our style at work and at home is to be very productive. My girlfriend JoAnn says that I better never write a Christmas letter to everyone where I review all we've done during the year because people hate hearing about so many accomplishments. That may be, but it is a great source of pride to me that as a family we do get so much done.

For example, in terms of recreation: Abe is a competitive long-distance runner and I jog and do aerobics (religiously). My two sons are on the local soccer teams and swim teams. As a family, we go out nearly every Saturday afternoon, hiking or fishing and skating in the winter. Besides our annual week at the beach, we try to get away at least four weekends a year as a family. This year we went to Lancaster, Pennsylvania, Williamsburg, Virginia, upstate New York, and to Ohio for a convention. We also visit with each set of grandparents two or three times a year.

Sexually, Abe and I are very active (I think) and we usually make love three or four times a week. After seventeen years of marriage I'm surprised we still are both so interested. Using your list of motivations, I think all those forces are operating at different times (except impregnation and procreation!).

Abe and I spend a lot of time catering to each other's emotional needs as well as to the emotional needs of the children. In fact, I think it's because we're so productive in this area and give it our number one priority that we're able to pull the rest off. I think we try to be available to one another as much as possible. Abe and I always spend the first half hour after he gets home unwinding and we each tell the other about our day. Then we have dinner together and the children get to talk about what's on their minds. Abe wants to teach them current events over dinner but I think it's more important to have a relaxed dinner hour where anything can come up. I've taken a huge pay cut so I have a job where I can be home by four. A lot of times the kids come home with a lot of emotional baggage from school, and if I'm not there I feel they sort of repress it and miss a chance to share it and grow from whatever the experience was. At night, Abe spends fifteen to thirty minutes with each child alone, talking or reading. Of course, sometimes we overextend ourselves and aren't this "perfect"—but we all get so grumpy and miserable we soon revert back to our soothing routines.

Probably the area where we are least productive is housework. Our house is what some might see as a complete mess! The stairs are often treacherous to walk up, spider webs do gather in the corner of some rooms, and my oven is ever ready for the "before" picture used in TV commercials. I don't think we've ever washed all the dirty clothes or had an empty dryer. My family feels compelled to clean when they visit but we're clean enough for me. The rooms stay fairly straightened, dishes are always washed and put away, and most of the time everyone can easily find a clean outfit for the day. I guess our standards are different than a lot of other people. Maybe productivity is best measured against a set of personal standards instead of cultural standards or objectively derived standards.

RECREATIONAL NEEDS

Play is as important to a family as work. Besides providing a change in pace, play induces relaxation and regeneration. No theory has been developed by which to judge how much leisure time is "enough" to balance a specific occupation at a specific point in life. Many studies, however, have documented how people divide their time between work and leisure.

Patterns of Family Recreation

There is every reason to believe that family recreation is as important as individually oriented and peer-oriented recreation. Vigorous family recreation, in particular, would seem to provide critical opportunities for relaxation and pleasure. Recreation has been shown to affect marital cohesion. Spouses who report enjoying the same type of recreational activities also report high marital satisfaction. For those who enjoy very different recreational activities, marital satisfaction tends to be low (Murphy, 1981).

Orthner (1976) found that the kind of recreation shared is in itself a critical variable. In this study, joint activities that require significant interaction were associated with high marital satisfaction for both husbands and wives. Solitary activities that did not directly influence the feedback mechanisms of a relationship were negatively related to marital satisfaction, especially for wives whose husbands engaged in solitary activities. Some joint leisure activities that encourage open communication and may help develop alternate role relationships among the participants are listed in the box "Joint Activities That Encourage Open Communication." These activities naturally promote interpersonal satisfaction and mutual understanding.

For example, whenever a group of people take an adventurous trip together, strong friendships and a deep intimacy develop among the participants. The Outward Bound experiences in which small groups of participants make a wilderness expedition together are often described as peak experiences causing sharp redefinitions of values and deepening the meaning in one's life. Families undergoing such adventures create bonds and gain understandings that may be impossible to achieve any other way.

Shared family recreation may well be the most effective form of therapy in a society where the family seems to be the chief victim of major socioeconomic and cultural stress. Bonds of affection are intensified and a collective identity is nourished and strengthened when family members engage in enjoyable recreational activities.

It is commonly accepted that parents have a responsibility to ensure that children have ample opportunities for play and recreation. Even thirty years ago parents executed this role primarily by allowing or encouraging children to "go outside and play." Today, children's recreation is as organized and structured as the school day and is sought primarily through the multitude of organized youth sports. There are lessons and teams in every activity imaginable including soccer, baseball, football, wrestling, basketball, swimming, diving, track, bowling, dancing, horseback riding, gymnastics, karate, ice skating, ice hockey, and roller skating. Rarely now are middle-class children told to "go outside and play." If they are not studying or performing household chores, they are being whisked away to a lesson or team.

Joint Activities That Encourage Open Communication

Going to parks or playgrounds
Visiting a zoo
Attending drive-in theaters
Spending time in taverns, night clubs, lounges
Visiting amusement parks
Attending parties
Picnicking away from home
Eating meals out
Riding in auto for pleasure
Playing billiards or pool
Playing basketball, baseball, volleyball
Playing tennis
Snow skiing
Bowling
Sailing
Playground games
Taking part in amateur dramatics, debates, discussion groups
Attending craft or adult education classes, fraternal organization meetings, community social events, church socials, church suppers, family or club reunions, other socials outside the home

Motorboating
Flying for pleasure
Playing handball
Attending organized camps
Going on hayrides
Playing badminton
Playing shuffleboard
Riding horses
Playing miniature golf
Playing golf
Camping (organized area)
Camping (backwoods)
Playing backyard or lawn water games
Dancing or attending dances
Playing football
Playing card games
Playing ping-pong
Community service groups
Parent/teacher activities
Playing informally with the children
Engaging in affectional or sexual activity
Casual conversation

Overall, the effects of organized lessons and teams are very positive. Children develop confidence, skills, and lifelong recreational interests. Of course, each child gets something different from recreational involvements. Some enjoy the winning; others enjoy the team spirit. Research suggests that parents are socializing their sons and daughters to relate to different aspects of sports.

McElroy (1983) studied 900 boys and 900 girls between the ages of ten and sixteen who were participating in the soccer portion of the National Youth Sports Program. She was interested in seeing whether the parent who encouraged the sports activity of the youngster also affected the child's value orientations to the sport. The value orientations were determined by asking the children the following question: "In playing a sports game, which one of the following is most important: (a) defeat your opponent or other team (win); (b) play as well as you can (skill); (c) play fairly (fair play); and (d) involve everyone on the team in the games (everyone wins)?" The value orientations of skill and winning are traditional competitive and competency values that men are assumed to pass down to their sons or daughters. The value orientations of fair play and egalitarian participation are traditional nurturing and tactful values that women are assumed to pass down to their daughters or sons.

CLARE (editor, age 50)

I grew up in a small East Coast town during and after the Second World War (ancient unmentionable times, my kids call them). Comparing our games and pastimes with the structured and even regimented patterns of today makes it seem like a different century. No Little League—softball was played in the nearest empty lot or field with whoever came along. Springtime brought the roller skates out—on the sidewalks or even the street, there were so few cars. No one in town had a swimming pool—not even the "Y"—and auto excursions to nearby lakes were a big treat maybe once or twice a summer week if that. No organized swimming or diving teams—just paddling about in the water as we pleased, or taking Red Cross swimming lessons. Of course, some of us went to camps that were pretty primitive compared with today's. On long summer evenings we caught "lightning bugs" and imprisoned them in jars on the bed table overnight, counting them as we released them in the morning. Treehouses were built with scavenged scrap lumber. In winter there was skating whenever the ponds froze over—no rinks or formal lessons. And after school there were games of tag or imaginary battle scenes (this was wartime) or acting out stories that we made up as we went along, often with cowboy heroes. TV existed, but until the later 1940s the house that had an antenna was a rarity. One or two of the kids would break off the afternoon play each day in time to listen to *Jack Armstrong, the All-American Boy* and *Superman* on the radio. And of course there was *The Lone Ranger* three times a week. The principal difference as I see it was that we used our imaginations more than children seem to today—even radio required imagination in a way that TV does not. We had to make our own play—it was not laid out for us; even the rules of softball tended to have wild and wooly variations so that a game with newcomers had to be preceded by "Well, we play it this way here. . . ."

(continued)

(continued)

My own kids, who grew up in a semirural area during the 1960s, were in a kind of time warp in that we didn't have TV for most of that period. When we did have it, watching was strictly limited to specific programs. Because of the nature of the area where we lived, there was little formalized recreation (a matter for many petitions to the local government). So my kids drew and painted, read books, and played an ongoing (I mean years) "soap opera" game involving imaginary characters, much digging in the dirt, and many trucks, cars, and scrap-lumber constructions in the big back yard. Meanwhile most of their contemporaries were watching TV—though not to today's extent.

Watching today's kids—even two-year-olds going to "school" with recreation and "learning play" that's planned for them—I feel something has been lost. It seems there should be a balance; some structure, some "loose" time to play and dream. All three of my children have grown up to be creative, entrepreneurial types who have accomplished a great deal, often in very original fashion, without the benefits of formal education past high school. I did, too. Without knocking planned "enrichment"—I wish it had been available—I wonder whether being thrown onto one's own recreational resources at least some of the time doesn't foster initiative and creativity to a high degree. This would make an interesting subject for study.

McElroy found that when the fathers were the chief promoters of their sports activity, boys were socialized into the "male" values of winning and skill. If the mothers were the chief promoters, they were socialized into the "female" values of fair play and equal participation. For the girls, the "feminine" ideals of fair play were predominant regardless of which parent encouraged the sports participation. Indeed, if the fathers encouraged the sports activity, the girls had an even more "feminine" orientation than if the mothers were the encouraging agents.

The most reliable predictor of whether a child gets involved with sports is whether the parents were involved with sports in their youth or adulthood. A second potent predictor is whether the parents are interested and encourage their child to participate in sports. The observation that parents have an overwhelming influence on the nature and extent of their children's sports involvement is obvious to anyone who has children. The spontaneous afternoon stickball and chase games of old have been replaced by organized after-school sports programs that nearly always require parental scheduling, parental transportation, and parental funding.

An uninterested parent is far more likely to have a child unproductive in sports. Of course, during the high school years, adolescents can arrange these activities themselves and most do so. But those who have not played in the organized sports arena for the previous nine years often feel inferior and, in fact, probably are in many instances. When children ages ten to sixteen were asked, "Who shows the most interest in your playing sports?" 80 percent named their mothers or fathers. Only 20 percent said friends, teachers, or coaches were the primary influence. This finding reinforces the general idea that sports involvement is a family affair (Greendorfer and Lewko, 1978).

Developmental Differences

A life cycle analysis suggests that recreational needs are most easily satisfied in the early stages of the family life cycle, before the arrival of children. Couples in the courting and honeymoon phase are eager to be together and usually have long periods of time free from other obligations.

During the early child-rearing years, recreational needs are often severely frustrated. The new parents feel psychologically overwhelmed, physically exhausted, financially drained, and limited in their ability to find time for recreation. What recreation there is usually involves the whole family and is limited to picnics, visits to parks, and visits to relatives. As children enter middle childhood, family recreation begins to increase, as attendance at children's sports events and school events becomes ritualized. By early adolescence, teenagers are beginning to spend a lot of their recreational time with peers. In the later teens, recreational time is virtually all oriented toward peer-group activities. Still, both older and younger teenagers have a desire to have recreation with family.

As would be expected, family recreation varies with the number of children in a family as well as their ages. Carlson (1979) reports that small families are more likely to engage in active outdoor activities, whereas larger families are more likely to engage in passive outdoor and group indoor activities.

As children begin to leave home, couples have an opportunity to return to the leisure activities of earlier years or to develop new pursuits. This is often a trying experience. People feel idle with the extra time available to them but find it difficult to develop satisfying leisure patterns after years of structured, time-constraining obligations. Increased awareness of the role of exercise in maintaining physical well-being is providing the impetus many of the middle-aged and elderly need to get involved in some physically oriented leisure activity. Success of the elder exercise movement is evident worldwide, from 60,000 older citizens regularly engaged in Switzerland's Senior Gymnastic Program (Gurewitsch, 1983) to the growing popularity of the Senior Citizen Olympics developed in the United States (Smith, 1982).

SEXUAL NEEDS

Sexual needs are complex and multifaceted. Berne (1970) has itemized over a dozen discrete motivating urges, including (1) impregnation, (2) procreation, (3) duty, (4) ritual, (5) relief, (6) physiological readjustment giving a feeling of well-being, (7) the pleasure of orgasm, (8) mutual pastime, (9) the play of seduction and retreat, (10) a medium for union and understanding, (11) intimacy and attachment, (12) expression of love, and (13) an expression of passion.

Sex is an important part of most, although by no means all, marriages. In a study by Carlson (1976), 73 percent of wives and 85 percent of husbands indicated that sex is "extremely" or "quite" important to them.

In their large-scale study of American couples, Blumstein and Schwartz (1973) made six major conclusions about the sex lives of couples. First, most married couples have sex at least once a week. Even after ten years of marriage, 63 percent of the couples reported this frequency. The 1994 sexual survey by Laumann and colleagues found that 25 percent of married couples reported having sex three to six times a week.

Second, the frequency of sex declines the longer the couple is married. Couples attribute the decline to lack of time, lack of physical energy, and simply "being accustomed" to each other. Although the frequency of sexual relations in marriage decreases with increasing age, psychological and relationship factors also influence the frequency of sexual relations. Parelman (1983) found that "androgynous" men and women had more sexually expressive marriages than men and women who were stereotypically sex-typed or cross sex-typed. That is, when people were aware of both the "masculine," assertive aspects of themselves and their "feminine," nurturative aspects, sexual activity within the marriage was high. Also, if one's parents had been emotionally close, sexual activity remained high.

Third, when the nonsexual aspects of a marriage are going badly and couples argue about things such as housekeeping and money, their sex life suffers.

Fourth, a significant number of married men (33 percent) and women (40 percent) reported that both partners in their marriages initiated sex fairly equally. Traditional male prerogatives are still prominent, though, as 51 percent of the men and 48 percent of the women reported that the male partner was more likely to initiate sex. Rarely do women initiate sex more frequently than their husbands, and when they do there is a slightly heightened likelihood of partners becoming troubled. In marriages in which the husbands initiate more, 72 percent of the husbands and wives are very satisfied with their relationship. In marriages in which the wives are the more frequent initiators, only 66 percent of the husbands and 68 percent of the wives are very satisfied with their relationship. The greatest satisfaction (80 percent for men and women) is found when there is equality of initiation.

Fifth, the less power a wife has in the marriage, the more likely that the couple's intercourse will be performed in the missionary position. And last, married men who receive oral sex or perform oral sex are happier with their sex lives and with their relationships, in general, than those who do not. Indeed, oral sex plays an interesting role in shaping intimacy patterns. Laumann et al. (1994) reported that while 30 percent of women usually perform fellatio on their male partners in short-term relationships, less than 12 percent of married women frequently use this erotic technique. Men, on the other hand, once they are married, slightly increase the frequency they routinely include cunnilingus as an erotic technique (15 percent of men usually use this technique in short-term relationships and 17 percent usually use this technique in marriages). Thus, while "playing the field" men are more likely to receive oral sex; after marriage they are more likely to perform oral sex. Since 16 percent of married women prefer reaching orgasm with oral sex and only 6 percent of men prefer this mode, it appears most married couples are trying to please their partners. The heightened frequency of fellatio among men in short-term relationships is undoubtedly also related to birth control concerns, the erotica of a new relationship, and intimacy boundaries between couples (intercourse being more intimate than oral sex).

Extramarital Affairs

Today as in yesteryear, sexual needs are sometimes satisfied in extramarital affairs. One in three married men and one in four married women have had at least one extramarital affair (Janus and Janus, 1993). Extramarital affairs occur in all types of relationships: happy marriages, unhappy marriages, with the spouse's consent, or without the spouse's consent. The extramarital affair can be based solely on the pleasurable sexual experiences that the lovers have together or on a deeper love relationship that is manifested sexually as well as in other ways.

Why do people have affairs? A number of demographic variables have been related to extramarital sexual permissiveness. A sociological profile suggests that a likely candidate has a high degree of premarital sexual permissiveness, has an unhappy marriage and low religiosity, and is age thirty-five or over, politically liberal, well-educated, and from an urban region of the country.

The psychological factors predisposing individuals to extramarital affairs have not been extensively studied. We do know that sexual dissatisfactions in the husband/wife relationship are not always the primary force behind extramarital affairs. Sometimes one partner feels that the other has generally failed to live up to expectations. Often, one mate feels that the other mate should meet his or her every need. When this does not happen, the mate looks outside the marriage to have these needs fulfilled.

Overall, most experts agree that extramarital affairs take away energy that could and should be used to enrich the marital relationship and threatens the foundation of mutual trust that is critical for a long-term successful marriage. Ables and Brandsma (1977:225) summarize these feelings well:

> It's easy to recapture romance in a brief stolen evening with wine by candlelight in front of the fire, where none of the pressing problems of everyday life intrude and where the couple can pour all of their energy into each other. Affairs are intensive; marriage extensive. Marriage, in terms of romantic charm, cannot compete with an affair. Thus, the person having the affair adds to marital discontent and drains off energy that could be directed toward improving the relationship. The predilection to turn to a lover for reassurance and nurturance at times of tension between spouses works against the spouses focusing on the problems constructively, negotiating around them, and learning to deal with pain.

An equally important hazard to marriage posed by extramarital affairs is the dissolution of trust on which most relationships are based. Once an affair has occurred, spouses struggle over and over again with the issue, "How can I ever trust you again?"

Developmental Differences

A life cycle analysis of sexual behavior in marriage shows, not surprisingly, that the honeymoon period has the greatest amount of sexual activity. The advent of children reduces the frequency of sexual relations. During the last months of pregnancy and the early months postpartum, couples become sexually limited or inhibited for a variety of reasons, including fears of infection or injury to the fetus, physical discomfort, and the pregnant wife's negative body image.

During the child care years and beyond, the frequency of sexual intercourse continually declines. A 1972 national survey found that married couples in their teens have intercourse nearly three times a week on the average. This frequency drops to about twice a week at age thirty, one and one-half times per week at age forty, once a week by age fifty, and to once every twelve days by age sixty. Of course these are median frequencies and there is a wide range of variation among the couples in each age group (Bell and Bell, 1972).

Consumers Union conducted a large-scale survey of the sexual practices of women and men ages fifty to ninety-three (Brecher, 1984). Over 4,000 individuals were studied. The researchers found that among married men in their fifties, 87 percent are having sex with their wives; in their sixties, 78 percent are having sex with wives; and in their seventies, 59 percent are having sex with their wives. Married wives report similar figures. In accordance with previous reports, they found the frequency of sex drops from 1.3 times per week in the fifties to 0.7 times per week in the seventies. Among the unmarried, 50 percent of the women and 75 percent of the men remain sexually active, although the frequency is much more variable.

Thus, sexual ability and activity can continue into the early eighties and beyond. Individuals who have maintained some steady degree of sexual activity may continue to enjoy sex throughout their lives if health permits. Masters and Johnson (1966) found the following five factors interfered most with the sexual desires and activity of older women: hormone deficiencies following menopause, lack of partner, the idea that older women should not be interested in sex, illness in the partner, and use of menopause as an excuse for abstinence. For older men, the five most detrimental influences were boredom, mental fatigue, physical fatigue, disease, and fear of poor performance. While the quality and nature of lovemaking necessarily change in old age, many feel that this new level of development can be every bit as satisfying as previous stages. Butler (1975:141) describes it quite eloquently when he says that:

> Human beings can acquire new insights and new levels of feeling during a lifetime of love-making. There is a developmental potential to sexuality. Sex is not the same in age as in youth, and love and sex vary throughout the course of life. Maurice Chevalier said, "There are ten thousand ways of loving. The main thing is to choose the one that goes best with your age." At the very end of life, there is the bittersweet sense that every moment is precious, and sometimes the sense that each encounter may be the last. . . . Those who maintain that the sexual salt loses its flavor may be expressing the great difficulty inherent in creating, imaginatively and significantly, the second language of sex. It is difficult to master, but it is a beautiful and satisfying aspect of relating that goes far beyond pure biology.

Hite's (1976) interviews with older women revealed that many felt their sexual pleasure had increased with age. Typical of her findings was the following statement from a postmenopausal woman:

> I think that sexual desire, attitudes, pleasure, etc., certainly change with age, but the change is qualitative rather than quantitative. It's a matter of growth and development, from a simplistic yes-or-no view of sex to much greater complexity, variety, subtlety, fluidity. I don't mean this so much in terms of increasing sophistication in "technique," though I suppose that's part of it. It's like the difference between a young shoot and a tree with many branches and a unique shape and structure and pattern of growth all its own. This is a natural growth process, but I believe that in our culture this process is often inhibited and retarded; we've all been told that all cats are gray in the dark, and many of us come rather late to the recognition and appreciation of her or his own unique and intricate sexual personality. I find it much easier now to know and accept and act on what I want and feel, instead of worrying about what I should want and feel. (p. 352)

Besides the sex that occurs within the spouse subsystem over the life cycle, families have the developmental task of socializing the children to become sexually responsible adults. Many parents abdicate this task because they are unknowledgeable and/or uncomfortable in this area, while many others who try to openly educate their children are shunned or ignored as the children look to their peer group or the media for sexual role models (Mancini and Mancini, 1985; Fabes and Strouse, 1985). When parents do get involved in sex education, it is primarily the mother who encourages the children to learn about sex and offers them information (Coreil and Parcel, 1985). Ethnic differences are large, though. For example, black mothers strongly encourage their children to learn about sex and contraception while Mexican-American mothers are extremely hesitant to share such information (Coreil and Parcel, 1985).

SUMMARY

Family productivity is a multifaceted concept. Yet all the facets are interrelated, and the satisfaction or frustration of any single family need will have repercussions on the ease or difficulty with which other needs are satisfied. For example, taking a second job to better fulfill the provider role reduces the time available for housework and child care. Increasing sensitivity to therapeutic needs can reduce time available for housework or additional employment. Increased kinskeeping can help or hinder satisfaction of other family needs, depending on the nature of the relationships involved.

Matters get more complicated throughout the family life cycle as different needs become highlighted and gain increased importance. A simplified overgeneralization would suggest that therapeutic, recreational, and sexual needs are paramount in the beginning stages. In the middle stages housework, child care, and provider needs dominate. In the final stages, kinskeeping becomes more salient and there is a resurgence of the importance of therapeutic and recreational needs. The family's productivity gives purpose to daily family life and becomes the visible manifestation of its history. What the family does together and accomplishes together creates memories and fuels the desire to create stronger, more meaningful families in the future.

MARTHA (salesperson, age 40)

I believe that this concept of productivity is one of the most essential components of family life. I have two teenage sons, a daughter, a husband, and a dog and we often have to struggle to accomplish all the family goals we have set for ourselves. Except for the dog, we all work. I have a sales job, my husband has a retail sporting goods store, Peter plays in a rock band, John paints houses, and Kim babysits. The task of finding family time is severely restricted by our different work schedules. Yet, we need the money and everyone gets a very satisfied feeling by being able to obtain their own spending money.

We're a very big sports family. Unfortunately, we each are involved in a different sport! I jog and compete in 10 Ks, my husband plays on an adult soccer team, Peter plays ice hockey, John is into a platform tennis league, and Kim does gymnastics and modern dance. While we certainly don't have time to watch each other practice, we keep a big bulletin board in the den with all meets posted, and everyone usually gets at least one family member to watch at least one half of any particular event. When one of us is lucky enough to get into a championship, we all come out.

Because our schedules are so varied, we always end up with a different combination of people at the dinner table. While I feel a little guilty that we can't manage a traditional family dinner hour, it does allow us to pay more attention to whoever happens to be next to us that day.

(continued)

(continued)

In order to get the chores done, I do them. I'm still the billpayer, bedmaker, clothes washer, food shopper, and chef. I get resentful at times, but the point is that the whole family functions in all the other realms so well! Also, I feel it's unfair to have to continually and singlehandedly fight ever-present cultural conditioning. It's easier to whistle while I work and just hope they don't mess things up too quickly!

The hardest areas for us to be productive in are the kinskeeping and therapeutic areas. Both our extended families are scattered all over the country. We never have time to write and phone calls, even with MCI, are so expensive. We end up seeing some relatives on Christmas and a few others during the summer. The visits are always a lot of fun but they are hectic and it's hard to get time to just relax together and catch up on who we are as people. Really, this same problem occurs in our nuclear family. While we all know what the others are doing, we often know little about what each person is feeling. Often, bad times are suffered through in isolation because no one has the time to find out what the problem is or even if we know the problem, we don't have time to help find a solution. Overall, I guess we're a pretty productive family but there certainly is room for improvement.

SELF-EXPLORATION: PRODUCTIVITY

1. Describe the productivity that existed in your family of origin in each of the eight areas:

    a. Providing
    b. Child care
    c. Child socialization
    d. Housekeeping
    e. Kinskeeping
    f. Therapeutic functions
    g. Recreation
    h. Sex

2. What made your family high or low in productivity in each area?
3. Would you have liked your family to be more or less productive in each area? Why?
4. What areas of productivity are or will be most important for your nuclear family? Why?

UNIT V: \
FAMILY CONCEPTS—
A SIBLING PERSPECTIVE

Sibling influences begin at birth and often continue until death; for those who have siblings, each stage of development coexists with a new stage of sibling influence. Direct interactions and sentiments between siblings exert an enormous influence on behavior during childhood—and sometimes in adulthood as well. Siblings also exert strong indirect influences because parents' responses to each child are influenced by the birth order of the child; the number of other children in the family; and the age, sex, and personalities of the other children. Although life cycle perspectives are discussed throughout this book, the usefulness of a developmental perspective is most vividly seen in relation to sibling influences.

Chapter 16

Birth Order

As I was growing up, I was absolutely certain that I was the favorite. I mean I just considered myself more important [than the other siblings]. I was very conscious of my role in the family. My parents made a great to-do about the fact that I was first. For instance, on Christmas, when we came in to the tree in the morning, I was always the one allowed first in line. I was older and smarter and stronger, and I think my mother also gave me an unusual amount of responsi- bility, so that I learned to think I could do a lot more things than [my younger siblings] could do. I saw myself as a surrogate mother and loved it.

Lucille Forer, *The Birth Order Factor*

Many people believe the most influential peer a person has is a sibling. Marked differences in personality, values, interests, and lifestyles can ensue from having a sibling of a certain sex and age difference. The magnitude and depth of sibling influence may be related mainly to the sheer amount of time brothers and sisters spend together. The strength and duration of influence may also be related to the intimacy of activities that siblings share—bathing, sleeping, arguing, and playing together. Bossard and Boll (1956:171) summa- rize the impact of siblings quite aptly: "Life among siblings is like living in the nude, psychologically speaking." After all, siblings know all one's strengths and weaknesses. They have witnessed all one's childhood victories and defeats. They are an inescapable part of one's future as well as one's past.

APPARENT EFFECTS OF BIRTH ORDER

It is true that our siblings powerfully influence our lives, shaping our personalities, our interests, and our coping styles. Accumulative evidence appears to support this idea. And common sense suggests that the mere existence of a sibling assures that we will be treated differently by our parents. Table 16.1 lists some commonly reported differences in children

TABLE 16.1. Summary of Commonly Cited Birth Order Effects

Oldest	Middle	Youngest	Only
High achiever	Competitive	"Laid back"	When anxious and fearful, seeks out others
When anxious and fearful, seeks out others	Good negotiator	Carefree	Conceptual thinker
Conservative	Hard, steady worker	Entertaining	Interested in heritage
Serves others	Carefree	Makes excuses; deceptive	Conscientious
Conceptual thinker	Analytical thinker	Dependent	Critical
Consistent and rigid	Friendly	May feel inferior	Independent
Leadership posi-tion	Empathetic	Affectionate	Parent-oriented
Seeks signs of appreciation	Sensitive to peers	Creative	
Interested in heritage	Realistically self-accepting		
Higher self-esteem	Self-confident		
Extrovert	Most adaptable to others		
Serious	Popular with peers		
Conscientious	Practical		
Critical	Goals are realistic		
Self-assertive	Accepts advice readily		
Parent-oriented			
Attains higher academic levels			
Scores higher on National Merit Scholarship exam			

and adults associated with birth order. For instance, researchers have found that firstborns are characterized as very ambitious, consistent, and rigid in their principles. The later-borns are more pragmatic and deceptive. In *The Promised Seed: A Comparative Study of Eminent First and Later Sons,* Irving Harris (1964) supports the pragmatism of later-borns histori-cally by pointing out that of thirty-five presidents, seven of the twenty firstborn have led the country into war (Madison, Polk, Lincoln, Wilson, Roosevelt, Truman, and Johnson) but only one of the later sons did (McKinley). This is hardly a random sample of statistical significance, but the results are interesting.

Gender Roles and Gender Differences

The impact of birth order on personality is moderated by the sex of the siblings and the spacing between them (Hoffman and Leyber, 1979). Girls seem to benefit from close spacing. When girls are closely spaced (only one or two years apart), they tend to develop comfortable and secure methods for satisfying their need for interpersonal relatedness. Having a sister four or five years older or younger seems to preclude the constant give and take needed for optimum social development. Brothers, on the other hand, seem to benefit from wider spacing. They are more outgoing and more confident in their ability to control their own fate when they are four or five years apart. Researchers theorize that closely spaced brothers are more likely to have been exposed to intense sibling competition and shows of one-upmanship and thus, may feel less competent and in control of their environment.

Apparently, wide spacing is beneficial for brothers but not for sisters because the greater the spacing between children, the greater the parental influence on both of them. Much parental influence is directed toward sex role development, and parents are better able to reinforce traditional values on widely spaced children. For boys, the traditional emphasis is on competency and independence. The more effective parents are at socializing boys in these traditional values, the more capable and confident the boys will feel when they meet up with difficult situations. Widely spaced girls, however, get an extra dose of dependency training. This emphasis on dependent "femininity" carries into their adult lives, making them feel more vulnerable in adverse or problematic situations.

Firstborn Children

As you can see from Table 16.1, firstborns appear to be characterized by extremely high levels of achievement and by a very special parent/child relationship (Sutton-Smith, 1982). The high expectations parents have for the firstborn (to be the smartest, the richest, the most responsible) were long considered the critical ingredient in explaining why firstborns are consistently overrepresented among eminent persons, national merit scholars, and PhDs. In proportion to their number in the population, there has been an excess of firstborns in *Who's Who in America* and *Who's Who in Science*. Altus (1966) believed that analysis of other achievement-oriented publications would yield similar results. While many still feel that parental expectations are critical, Zajonc (1976; Zajonc and Marcus, 1975) provided another explanation for the intellectual superiority of firstborns that is based on family size.

Zajonc's Theory of Confluence

Zajonc's "confluence theory" associates smaller family size with higher average intelligence in the family. According to this theory, the family's average intelligence is pulled down with the birth of each additional child, because, in an absolute sense, younger children are less able than older children. Thus, families with few children have a higher average intelligence than families with many children.

To some extent, intelligence is believed to be influenced by environment. Confluence theory suggests that the intellectual stimulation available in small families is superior to that available in large families, because the parental resources associated with an intellectually enriched environment include time to talk, reason, explain, and play with a child. These activities become increasingly burdensome with each additional child. Time and money must be divided again and again, so that the average resources available to each successive child decline.

A simplified quantification of Zajonc's model helps explain this phenomenon. Suppose each member of a childless couple has an intellectual rating of 100. The family intellectual environment (IE) would be expressed as:

$$100 + 100 \div 2 = 100$$

Suppose that when a child is born, its intellectual rating is 0. The family's IE quotient is now:

$$100 + 100 + 0 \div 3 = 67 \text{ (rounded figure)}$$

Suppose further that a two-year-old's intellectual rating is 40. If a new baby is born when the first child is two years old, the family IE is affected as follows:

$$100 + 100 + 40 + 0 \div 4 = 60$$

With each successive child, the family's intellectual environment will continue to depreciate on the average (despite the growth of the existing children). Zajonc's model aptly accounts for the finding that children from smaller families tend to have higher IQs. Looking at group data, within any family size, early-borns tend to have higher scores than later-borns.

Family Size

Of the birth-order effects reported in prior studies, many are also family size effects or at least can be explained in these terms. In studies comparing firstborns with later-borns, the samples of firstborns have been biased for small sibling configurations; that is, while many of the firstborns came from two-child families, many more of the later-borns came from families of more than two children. Children from small and large families do not have the same background and do not live under the same conditions. Comparisons between subjects of different birth order that disregard family size show spurious interfamilial differences.

Focusing on studies that have controlled for family size, Ernst and Angst (1983:284) conclude that "there is no evidence of any personality or intellectual differences based on birth order." Once family size had been controlled for, the IQs of firstborns were not consistently higher than those of later-borns. They showed no higher need for achievement, no higher actual levels of achievement, no higher occupational status, no greater anxiety, no lower adjustment, no lower self-esteem, and no greater authoritarianism. Firstborns tended, however, to be consistently described by their parents as more sensitive, serious, and responsible and less impulsive, happy, socially active, and outgoing. When siblings within the same family were studied, these researchers found no actual differences in personality or personality traits associated with birth order.

Although these researchers found that many birth order effects are in fact family size effects, they do not feel that family size is any more potent a socializing feature than birth order. Their results, in conjunction with a survey of world literature, indicate that:

> . . . birth order and family size do not have a strong impact on personality. The present investigation points instead to a broken home, an unfriendly educational style, and a premature disruption of relations with parents as concomitants of neuroticism, and to higher income and social class (with all assets implied) and an undisturbed home as concomitants of higher achievement. Besides these influences, details of socialization seem to shrink to insignificance. (Ernst and Angst, 1983:284)

The most recent studies continue to find no overall relationship between measures of academic success and birth order from childhood through the teenage years (Steelman and Powell, 1985). It seems clear that sibling relationships and interactions among siblings and parents have a more potent effect on academic success than simple birth order.

Still, birth order effects cannot easily be ignored. First, in real life, the family size and birth order variables are highly confounded. That is, the majority of firstborns come from small families (every family with children has a firstborn) and the majority of later-borns come from large families (the larger the family, the more later-borns there will be). Thus, research that does not specifically study and control for family size will continue to obtain academic differences attributed to birth order. Second, while family size obviously helps shape many of the experiences and interactions of children of different birth orders, there may be a number of birth order effects, particularly those pertaining to middle, youngest, and only children, that will remain independent of family size. Third, the interactions imposed by family size are not universal. As discussed in the next section, both the sex of the children and the family's social class moderate the effect of coming from a small rather than a large family. Thus, it is possible that in certain family configurations, birth order does truly exert an important influence.

ROCHELLE (nursing-home resident, age 92)

I was a firstborn and I was taught responsibility from the day I was born. I can remember as a toddler, my dad taking me out to the well, back of our house in Williamsport, Maryland, and showing me how to put the water bucket down. And he would put his hands on top of mine and help me pull up the pail. As I got older, his hands helped me less and less, and by age five was bringing the buckets on my own. Momma was always busy with the babies. She had five boys after me but only one, Scottie, lived to be past ten. As the little ones died, Mom and Dad clung to me more and more. I was given a lot—a good Lutheran upbringing, my own horse, music lessons—even in those days. But they always expected me to be the best in whatever I did and if for some reason I wasn't the best at school or so, my parents would be so disappointed; it would break my heart to look in their faces. Scottie was the baby and always protected. They worried a lot that he would be taken from them like the other boys but, thank the Lord, he lived a long life.

When I graduated, I got married to a Mr. W.F. Rector. He was an ornamentalist and did all the fanciest carpentry between New York and Richmond. He had to travel a lot but that was OK with me. I bought a small general store and brought my parents to live with me. I took care of me, my two children, and my parents just fine. I loved the store and was a good businesswoman. When Mr. Rector had a heart attack and died, I sold the store and moved into the city. I started buying big old townhouses and fixing them up and getting respectable people to move in. I was very good at this and it allowed me to bring up my boys in a proper fashion. I was always trying to better myself and push myself to do more. Most firstborns are like that—at least they were in my day.

After the children had grown and got married, I got remarried to Mr. George Saul. He was a railroad man and we could travel anywhere on our railroad passes. Over the years, I had made a number of wealthy friends and they retired in the South or out in California. With Mr. Saul's passes I was busy half the year traveling to this one or that one.   *(continued)*

(continued)

When Mr. Saul died, I decided that I needed to find my own place; a place where I would not be a burden to anyone. I came to the home seventeen years ago. When I first was interviewed by them and told them of all my business experiences they told me I could work in the snack shop. For the next thirteen years I made that snack shop into a thriving business. I even got them to add on the gift shop! My brother Scottie just never had any of the ambition and drive that I had. Mom and Dad were always protecting him and he grew up thinking that life was just getting by, making do, and staying out of trouble. I'm old now, and this is going and that is going and the connections between my memories are hard to find. But I know I had a spirited life and feel like I've been responsible for my life. I don't complain.

PROBLEMS IN IDENTIFYING BIRTH ORDER EFFECTS

Many researchers are beginning to believe that family interaction variables are much more potent than simple family configuration variables. While the confluence model can explain over 90 percent of the variance in IQs in groups of children, the explained variance is reduced to 3 percent when trying to predict any one individual's scores; the dramatic change is undoubtedly due to the overpowering effect of family interactions and other factors.

Among poor and deprived Oriental Israelis, for example, increasing family size is associated with an increased IQ (Davis, Cahan, and Bashi, 1977). As the firstborns enter the school system and become more educated than their parents, they increase the total family's intellectual environment, directly benefiting the younger children. These later-born siblings are growing up in an intellectually more invigorating environment than the firstborns, and their IQ scores reflect this.

Gender Differences

Another potent interaction effect was demonstrated by Mott and Haurin (1982), who used data from the National Longitudinal Survey of Work Experience of Young Men and Women to test how confluence theory interacts with sex of the child. They examined the differential importance of coming from a smaller rather than a larger family for males and females in terms of academic and occupational achievement. The subjects were 5,000 young men and 5,000 young women who were initially interviewed when they were fourteen to twenty-four years old. Over the next ten years they were repeatedly interviewed; by the last interview they were twenty-four to thirty-four years old. Their results show quite consistently that birth order is more important to a female child's future than a male child's. Specifically, they found that women who were the older of two children showed superiority in three distinct areas when compared with women from any other sibling configuration (including women with no siblings):

- They had statistically significant higher IQ scores.
- They were more likely to complete college.
- They were the only female group who anticipated an above-average occupational status. Also, they were more likely to anticipate employment in an occupation not traditionally held by women.

For men, the most important predictor of occupational success was coming from a small rather than a large family. In general, small families were also advantageous to the women. Yet no special advantage was found in being an only child, although in many instances being an only child was preferable to coming from a large family.

Middle Children

In generations past, large families were the norm. Thus, it is likely that there are two or more presently adult middle children available for study for each oldest child or youngest child. Yet this birth order is the least studied.

Common sense suggests that middle-borns should be artful negotiators who are easy to get along with. Since birth they have tried to compete with their ever-superior older siblings and to show off to their ever-inferior younger siblings. Learning to relate to those more and less competent than oneself is an important survival skill. Middle children are shielded from the great expectations of their parents as well as from their protectiveness. They are probably the least known by the parents. It is possible that this "fading into the background" during childhood stimulates middle-born children to strive to distinguish themselves from the group. If everyone in the family lives on the East Coast, they may move to the West; if everyone is in favor of the ERA, they may be against it. This tendency may seem negative, but it is not inherently detrimental. More often than not, the need to find a special niche will motivate a person toward excellence.

Middle children are the most heavily invested in the sibling system and the least heavily invested in the parental system. They are most involved in developing fair, honest sibling relationships. Middle children need to relate as equals because it is rare that they have any significant ability to wield power with their parents. "Have-nots" have always wanted to do away with the existing power structure. Sibling have-nots are no exception.

LARRY (graduate student, age 23)

I was a middle child with a sister three years older than me and a sister three years younger than me. Being the only boy wasn't the distinctive call to fame that it is in a lot of families. My family was very egalitarian, and the firstborn expectations went to my older sister. She was always urged to take on the most responsibilities around the house and to get the best grades.

I was profoundly affected by being in the middle. Although my sisters were six years apart, they were always fighting with each other. My little sister would want to follow my older sister around, eavesdrop on her telephone calls, and tattle about any indiscretion. One day they got into such a heated fight that my older sister, Linda, took a kitchen knife and started chasing after my little sister, Katie. They were running all over the house screaming until my dad came in and saw Linda looking like a crazy butcher. After that, Linda had her own room and I had to share my room with Katie. My parents had always given me my own room because I was the only boy, but this battle alarmed them and for a year and a half Katie and I shared a room.

I really liked both of my sisters. Linda was smart, baked me cookies, helped me with all my homework, and went to more of my baseball games than Mom or Dad. Katie was my constant slave. She would do anything that I asked her. We both liked to watch a lot of horror movies in our teens, and for a few years we did a lot of movie watching and ice skating together.

Whenever my parents got upset with Linda, I would rush to her rescue. Later, she would confide in me about things she would never tell our parents. I always valued how she trusted me and felt duty bound to protect her from any parental tyranny that I could. Whenever my parents got upset with Katie, I would try to pooh-pooh my parents for picking on an innocent little kid. Even though I hadn't taken psychology yet, one of my favorite lines was, "Can't you find anyone better to dump your frustrations on?" It nearly always worked, and then I'd sit and be a mentor to Katie, counseling her on how to live a good, clean life. When Katie and Linda were battling no one could really intervene successfully, but I could at least get them to go to their own bedrooms.

All this negotiating ability seems to be very typical of middle children. I learned early that some people got more than me and some people got less than me. If I can give and take effectively things go smoother for everyone. I hate fights and would rather negotiate and end up with a disadvantage than fight and end up with an advantage.

Being in the middle has always made me want to be different. The girls live in New York. I chose to live in California. The girls both went on to careers in the business world like my parents, and I'm going to be a psychologist. I'm living with a Mexican woman. My sisters never dared to date someone who wasn't Lutheran.

All in all, I'm happy I was a middle child. It helped shape me into a rational person, a flexible person, and a self-directed person. In fact, I think it's too bad not everyone can be a middle!

Youngest Children

Alfred Adler (1946), a pioneering theorist on birth order effects, saw the youngest child as at risk for being overprotected and babied. Having parents and older brothers and sisters who take charge when problems arise may initially lead the youngest child to breathe a large sigh of relief. But in the long run an inability to overcome adversity by oneself leads to deep-seated feelings of insecurity. The short-term relief of not having to cope is overshadowed by the long-term fear of being unable to cope if left alone. The feelings of insecurity that are sown in the life experiences of lastborns stand in stark contrast to the feelings of competency and independence that flourish among firstborns. The difference in self-confidence between first- and last-borns is nicely illustrated by the finding that among college-age youths, 25 percent of firstborns report having had nightmares during the past year, while 85 percent of the last-borns report such an experience (Brink and Matlock, 1982). Nightmares have long been associated with fear-provoking daytime experiences. The more than three-fold increase in nightmares between first- and last-borns attests to the heightened trepidation youngest children must feel as they meet the problems of day-to-day living.

SIMON (corporate attorney, age 40)

I was the youngest of two boys. My brother, who was five years older than myself, was my idol. He was a local neighborhood success story from the beginning. He was always a high achiever. He was president of the student government and team leader of the lacrosse team. He got an academic scholarship to attend Dartmouth and was valedictorian of his class. When we were very little, I would get very jealous of whatever he had. If he had something, that meant it was valuable and so I wanted it. As we got into later childhood and adolescence there wasn't any of that. I thought of us as two very different types of people and never thought of trying to out-achieve him. In fact, I probably de-identified to such a large extent that I became a remarkably unambitious adolescent. While my brother was off at college, he became an outspoken activist and was very involved in antiwar issues. I was shy, playing the guitar and making a minimal effort at school. My parents never pushed me to achieve and even when I got over 1400 on my SATs, no one heralded me as the intellectual star of the family. Perhaps my parents just expected that I would naturally do as well as my brother, so there was no need for any hoopla.

I went to Colgate but instead of having an intense academic career I was more of a beer-drinking fraternity guy. I never got any rebuffs about

(continued)

> (continued)
>
> lifestyle, not even from my brother, who has always and consistently played the older, wiser brother role.
>
> As I search through the years, I can think of three instances where my birth order affected me. One was obviously in terms of achievement. Because my brother was such a successful firstborn, I was more or less allowed to go my own way. My parents did disapprove of some of my activities. They didn't like me giving guitar lessons when I was in high school so my mother, particularly, would balk at that. But basically I was a good kid and there was very little friction. But there was very little stroking either or pushing for excellence. My parents didn't push me and I didn't push myself, at least until recently. I had one English teacher in high school who thought I was exceptionally talented and so I decided to major in English. After Vietnam, I wanted to take advantage of the GI Bill, so I decided to go to law school. It wasn't so much a need to be a professional as a good idea to be in school at the time.
>
> The second instance of birth order affecting my life is an incident that occurred when my brother got divorced from his first wife. He wrote my father a letter telling him about it, and my father told me about it. It wasn't crucial that he tell me directly. It just points out the family dynamics and the relationship of firstborns to their parents. If something of that importance happened to me, I'd be just as likely—maybe more likely— to tell my brother before my father.
>
> The third instance concerns how I react to my two daughters. Because I was the second-born with an older, competent brother I have a special sensitivity to my younger daughter. She's remarkably gifted intellectually, but shy. She looks with awe and jealousy at her older, more competent sister. Although I greatly admire many of my older daughter's personality traits and abilities, there is a special connectedness with the younger one that I attribute to our similar birth order.

Only Children

Since 1978, the Center for Population Research of the National Institute for Child Health and Human Development has funded research on the one-child family. Its overall conclusion is that there are no major differences between only children and others. They found no negative effects of being an only child. Contrary to popular belief, only children are not more maladjusted or more self-centered than children with siblings (Pines, 1981). In general, the parents of only children do not differ from other parents in terms of education or occupational status, although they do tend to be a little older than average. An exception occurs among black mothers, in whom there is a positive relationship between attaining high educational achievement levels and the likelihood of having an only child.

Nevertheless, many Americans feel that it is bad for a child to have no siblings.

Despite the prejudice against "onlies," the percentage of women eighteen to thirty-four years old choosing to have only one child rose is increasing in the United States from 18 percent in 1971 to 21 percent in 1983 to over 25 percent in 1999. This increase in only children can be explained in large part by the economic consequences of having children in today's world. The average two-child middle-income family with a part-time working wife has to plan on spending $153,660 on each child reared in 1998 dollars (not including college costs). College costs can add anywhere from $40,000 to $160,000 (Borland, 1998). Thirty-three percent of the cost is spent on housing; food, 18 percent; transportation, 15 percent; entertainment and personal care items, 11 percent; clothing, 7 percent; health care, 7 percent; and child care and education, 9 percent. Annual costs for a two-child family ranged from $8,060 to $9,170. Women must help cover these costs in most families. Since most women employed outside the home find it easier to make day care arrangements for one child than for two or more children (DeJong, Stokes, and Hanson, 1980), it is likely that the attractiveness of having one child will continue to increase. In addition, many more women are in the work field for a number of years before starting families. This trend continues to influence the number of one-child families.

Some evidence indicates that parents with only children are overanxious and overconcerned about the child. This parental overinvolvement received extensive publicity in mainland China, where a national birth control policy attempts to restrict all couples to having only one offspring. Traditionally, Chinese culture has placed heavy emphasis on intergenerational structures. If all one's expectations for future generations rest on the continued well-being of one child, parental alarm over minor incidents is almost inevitable. Most Americans with only one child are undoubtedly overinvested as well. Such overinvestment in the only child receives indirect support from Falbo (1982), who found that mothers of onlies have fewer friends and fewer close friends than mothers of two or more children. Reduced investment in people outside the family increases risk of overinvolvement within the family.

Prior studies have shown that only children do not have the intellectual advantage often found in firstborns. Given that both firstborns and onlies have a lot of parental attention and encouragement, why do firstborns seem to retain intellectual superiority?

Comparisons of firstborns and only children have generally found the firstborn to be more competent. Falbo (1978) hypothesizes that the firstborn with siblings has an extra advantage because being able to tutor younger siblings has a positive effect on the learning capabilities of the older child. Both firstborns and onlies receive a lot of adult attention and are highly motivated to master the components of the adult world. Firstborns have many opportunities to implement their knowledge and to refine it as they try to impress and pressure the younger siblings.

Teaching has always been a most effective method for consolidating knowledge, deepening understanding, and increasing self-confidence on any given topic. These advantages automatically accrue as the eldest sibling takes on the role of mentor and older, wiser sibling. To benefit from this effect, siblings probably need only minimal sharing of knowledge regarding strictly academic material. The expectation that such sharing is possible, coupled with the social comparison process during childhood, might be enough to validate the firstborn's continual intellectual superiority over younger siblings. It may also account for firstborn superiority over only children. Only children must use their peer group for social comparisons, and it is much harder to take on the leadership and mentor role with age mates than it is with developmentally less advanced siblings.

Another explanation is that since only children are more likely to come from one-parent homes, their intellectual family environment is, on the average, lower than firstborns (Falbo, 1982). If the model developed by Zajonc (1976) is correct, children with one parent should perform somewhat less well than expected, irrespective of the number of siblings, because the intellectual environment of the family will inevitably be lower with only one adult's intelligence entering into the equation instead of two:

$$100 + 100 + 60 \div 3 = 87 \text{ two parents/one child}$$
$$100 + 60 \div 2 = 80 \text{ one parent/one child}$$

Support for this explanation was provided by Falbo (1982), who found that she could account for 25 percent of the IQ score difference between first and only children by taking into account the incidence of single parents among one-child families.

THE LARGE FAMILY

Families with eight or more children have never been common, but over the past 150 years they have become increasingly rare in Western societies. Some observers consider the large family in danger of becoming extinct. Although the economic and sociological factors affecting family

---

ROSE (realtor, age 45)

This was an important occurrence in shaping my relationship with my family and with my spouse. I was the oldest child of a youngest child (my mother) who divorced right after I was born. The stage was set for me to become a parental child—to help my mother make decisions and to become a substitute spouse. This is indeed what happened. My mother treated me more as an advisor and confidante than as a child as far back as I can remember. After her second marriage and divorce, I was enlisted as an adviser in my half-brother's parenting. This already defined role was probably reinforced by the fact that he was male. Oldest sisters are commonly given responsibility for care of younger brothers. I think a large part of the anger I felt toward my mother in my twenties and even now was due to her never having allowed me to be a child and constantly using me to take responsibility for my brother.

I think in many ways, my life has been influenced by being an oldest. I have a fairly high motivation for achievement and am a pretty responsible person—often overly responsible. Probably because of the six years of being an only child, I am very desirous of having my own way in things and often find it difficult to compromise.

---

size are often cited, little attention has been given to the psychological consequences of being brought up in a large family. In the early 1950s, Bossard and Boll (1956) studied 100 large families. Among their many findings the most interesting were the following:

1. Half of the families studied considered the general tone of their family relations as very positive and described themselves as happy families. The "happy large families" were the result of a conscious effort of the parents to promote family group life and excellent administrative and managerial ability on the part of the mothers. Promoting family group life was often accomplished in the cultivation of rituals. Holidays, anniversaries, meals, and vacations were proscribed formal procedures that everyone considered very purposeful; these helped unite the group.

2. The more children there were in a family, the greater the tendency to have to lay down strict rules and a litany of standard operating procedures. For instance, in most large families, meal times were standardized. Individual tastes were not catered to.

3. Parents and children in large families developed a sense of perspective about children's problems, mishaps, and crises. Broken bones, bloody noses, poor grades, and peer rejection were just a few of the occurrences that came to be handled in an efficient, nontraumatic manner.

4. In many large families the older children became surrogate parents for the younger ones. Sometimes the older children were put in a position where they had to delay, change, or forgo their own life plans to care for the younger siblings.
5. Persons from large families tended to marry less frequently than persons from smaller families. Persons reared in large families did not in turn produce large families. Bossard and Boll (1975:281) found that of "529 married siblings, only fifteen had six or more children. The percentages which these numbers represent are strikingly lower than those found in the same category in the population at large."

In summary, most of those studied thought large families were fun, but one experience was enough for a lifetime.

BIRTH ORDER AND MARRIAGE PARTNERS

Walter Toman (1976) has suggested that the more closely the marriage relationship duplicates that of one's sibling childhood, the more successful it will be. Thus, a firstborn should marry a second-born (retaining firstborn status), and individuals who had opposite-sex siblings should, in general, be able to cope with a marriage better than individuals who had only same-sex siblings. Research has given this theory only partial support. A study done by Mendlesohn et al. (1974) found that brothers with younger sisters who married sisters with older brothers had a more satisfactory marriage relationship than brothers with older sisters who married sisters with younger brothers. According to Toman, they should have been equally happy since both had experience with appropriate birth ordered, cross-sex siblings. The data seem to show that women who experience having an "older, wiser, firstborn male" in their family of origin tend to "knuckle under" to a husband with conventional expectations of dominance.

Toman hypothesized that since only children spend the overwhelming majority of their time around caring, protective adults, they would adjust best to a spouse who was willing to be a nurturative parent figure. The theory is that male only children prefer the motherly type who is willing to subordinate her life and interests to the male's career. Of all the sibling types, male only children are thought to find it easiest to opt for a child-free marriage because it allows them to retain all the spouse's attention and love for themselves. Female only children are hypothesized to prefer the oldest brother of sisters; one who is used to providing fatherly guidance. Very little evidence exists either to confirm or to cast serious doubt on this portion of Toman's theory.

SELF-EXPLORATION: BIRTH ORDER

1. Consider the birth order effects discussed in this chapter. In your family of origin, what was the firstborn like? The middle? The youngest? How much of the behavior and attitudes of each can be explained by his or her birth order?
2. This portion of the exercise requires you and each of your siblings to answer the following four questions. Do not discuss your answers with one another until everyone has had a chance to reflect and write down impressions. Then compare notes and decide how important a factor birth order was in your family. Did the siblings have very different developmental experiences because of their birth order or was that not a factor?

    a. What were each of your responsibilities around the house? At age five? At age ten? At age fifteen? Did the firstborn have more responsibilities than the others?
    b. What were your parents' responses to your report cards and homework assignments? At age five? At age ten? At age fifteen? Did the firstborn receive more criticism and encouragement to excel?
    c. How many photos do you have of yourself? At age five? At age ten? At age fifteen? This will give some indication of the amount of leisure time each of you experienced with your parents. Did the oldest and youngest have more leisure time with your parents?
    d. What was your parent's general response when you were fighting with your siblings? At age five? At age ten? At age fifteen? Were the older children blamed?

3. Do you think your parents or siblings would have treated you differently if you had had a different birth order? How so? Do you think it might have affected the type of personality you now have?
4. If you are an only child, were you compared with cousins or friends in terms of academics, sports, personality, or responsibility? How do you think your childhood and adulthood would have changed by having a sibling?

Chapter 17

Sibling Relationships

The supreme happiness of life is the conviction that we are loved.

Victor Hugo

Sibling relationships are the most enduring relationships we have, often continuing for seventy or eighty years. They are also the most egalitarian relationships. The relationships of middle childhood that seem so strongly affected by birth order develop into myriad adult relationships that are shaped by economics, circumstance, and personality. Beyond the interactions imposed by birth order, sibling relationships may be classified as sibling solidarity, fervent sibling loyalty, and sibling rivalry. It is easy to find "pure" examples of these three types of sibling relationships, but they are not always mutually exclusive and often coexist to varying degrees.

SIBLING SOLIDARITY

Four major theories have arisen to account for the solidarity that generally exists among brothers and sisters. First of all, siblings share a genetic heritage (unless they are adopted) and usually a common home environment. On the average, siblings share 50 percent of their genetic endowment; thus they have more in common with one another than with strangers who have no common genes. This combination of shared home environment and shared genetics might allow a degree of closeness and understanding that would rarely be developed with peers outside the family.

With ever-increasing numbers of children affected by divorce, it is interesting to speculate whether sibling solidarity is affected when siblings are split up to live in different households or have different custodial parents. If siblings reared somewhat independently still evidence comparable rates of sibling solidarity, arguments for genetic similarities promoting sibling bonding will receive some support. Similarly, if adopted siblings showed less sibling solidarity than natural siblings, a genetic similarity theory would again receive some support.

A second explanation associates children's attachment to siblings with the attachment and dependency they feel for their parents. When, as children, we interact with our parents, our siblings are, literally or figuratively, always present—and vice versa. Through simple conditioning, brothers and sisters come to be associated with the security offered by the parents. In effect, they offer a second base of security.

Third, sibling solidarity may also originate in the cognitive need to have a lifelong model of meaningfulness. Siblings help us develop our identities, learn and share the appropriate filial obligations, and learn the expectations of our generation. It is easier for us to assess our success and failure, courage and cowardice when siblings are available at vital checkpoints. Siblings serve as models and as yardsticks by which we can measure our own accomplishments. This yardstick is often missed by only children.

Fourth, sharing a stressful home environment may prompt siblings to find compensatory support from one another. Kier and Lewis (1998) found that infants from separated families, regardless of gender, interacted more with each other than siblings from intact families. It appears that negative family experiences, even at the youngest ages, promote greater closeness between siblings. Perhaps this is because the parents are too busy to attend to the children's social needs.

An important distinction needs to be made between negative family experiences (e.g., trauma or disruption of desired routine) and hostile family environments (e.g., conflictual interactions). The effect on siblings seems to vary greatly with these two family stressors. When there is trauma, there appears to be a drawing together of the family. When there is a hostile family environment, sibling relationships tend to get disrupted. Many studies have found that, among intact families, tension and conflict in the parental relationship and/or the parent-child relationship are mirrored in a cantankerous relationship between the siblings (McGuire, McOale, and Updegraff, 1996). Clinical experience confirms that not all trauma uniformly sends a message to induce sibling closeness. In one family, a father's alcoholism tears apart all sibling relationships, as the parents fight with each other and with the children. In another, the calm and compensatory behaviors of the mother, older sibling, or relative promote sibling bonding.

When there is a lot of hardened sibling rivalry, the therapist needs to explore the festering issues between the parents and between each parent and child. Table 17.1 summarizes the extent of solidarity in adult sibling relationships.

TABLE 17. 1. Adult Sibling Relationships As Surveyed by Cicirelli (1982)

Attribute	Percentage
Have close or very close relationship	68
Have no closeness at all	5
Feel they get along well or very well	78
Feel they get along poorly	4
Get considerable or great satisfaction from relationship	68
Get little or no satisfaction from relationship	12
Feel siblings were very interested or moderately interested in their activities	59
Feel siblings had no interest in their activities	21
Feel free to discuss personal or intimate matters	41
Rarely or never talk about intimate matters	36
Usually or frequently talk over important decisions with a sibling	8
Rarely or never talk over important decisions with sibling	73
See closest sibling at least once a week	17
See closest sibling at least once a month	33
Turn to sibling for psychological support	7

Source: Data from Cicirelli, V. G. 1982. Sibling influence throughout the life span. In Lamb, M. and Sutton-Smith, B. (Eds.), *Sibling relationships: Their nature and significance across the life span.* Hillsdale, NJ: Lawrence Erlbaum Associates.

Changes Through the Life Span

During middle childhood, siblings often spend more time with one another than with anyone else. While rarely the preferred playmates, siblings are often the most available playmates. Siblings will almost always defend one another from the hostilities of the peer group and very early develop a sense of cohesiveness.

During the college and postcollege years, sibling relationships seem to become much stronger. The newfound adventures of living away from home, traveling, and dating are experienced in the same sociopolitical climate. These shared generational experiences during young adulthood allow siblings to share a common worldview that is often unavailable to the older and younger generations. Survey data (Cicirelli, 1980a) confirm that college students feel closer to their favored sibling and share a greater similarity of views with this sibling than with their fathers or mothers. With their siblings they are relaxed; they feel understood. Siblings represent both the interests of the peer group and the interests of the family.

As people get married and start having their own children, the ties to siblings weaken. Still, 48 percent of middle-aged people describe themselves as having a close or very close relationship with their siblings (Cicirelli, 1982). Among middle-aged adults, pairs of sisters are the closest, with 60 percent reporting a high degree of closeness. One explanation is that the common experiences of homemaking and motherhood forge a lasting bond between the sisters. Pairs of brothers are the most likely to drift apart, with only 36 percent of the middle-aged men in this study reporting a high degree of closeness with their brothers. The favored interpretation is that rivalry, often beginning in childhood, persists longer and is more intense among men. Their decreased closeness is obviously related to a persisting higher level of jealousy. Among middle-aged brother/sister pairs, 46 percent report a high degree of closeness (Adams, 1968).

Although feelings of closeness remain rather high, siblings tend to have less actual contact in their middle years. Roughly 40 percent of the siblings studied saw each other once a month, usually in the parents' home, but most siblings see each other four or five times a year (Cicirelli, 1982).

The closeness of adult siblings does not signify a high incidence of helping behaviors. Money is rarely lent, nor are troubles worked out with a sibling's help. Parents are relied on for these matters. The help of brothers and sisters may be sought, however, for crises that cannot be solved by the nuclear family or with the help of parents. Assistance takes such forms as caring for children, sharing household responsibilities, or even making funeral arrangements. The companionship and support offered by siblings is often the most soothing and reassuring contact people experience during a crisis (Troll, 1975).

In old age, sibling relationships take on a new cast as siblings try to assume the supportive and emotional roles that parents and spouses had once provided. Brother/sister pairs draw much closer as sisters take over many of the domestic chores that had traditionally been done by the now deceased mother and wife. A widowed or divorced sister will often rely on her brother to fix up the house or to serve as a traveling companion. Sister/sister pairs are more likely to live together or to interact often in old age than other sibling pairs (Cicirelli, 1980b; 1982).

Changes Related to Critical Life Events

Throughout the years, the closeness between siblings will change not only as a function of age but as a result of critical life events. Moving geographically away from siblings reduces closeness; moving nearer to them increases it. In general, marriages are more likely to pull siblings apart than to draw them together. Allegiances to the new spouse coupled with the many possible clashes in personality and values make a negative effect on the sibling relationship twice as likely as a positive effect. If the spouses-in-law get along very well, the siblings will find it easier to maintain an intimate relationship. Death and divorce of parents may momentarily bring brothers and sisters closer together, but in the long run the dissolution of the family of origin tends to diminish sibling obligations and loyalties. When divorce or death of a spouse occurs, however, the overwhelming sibling response is positive support, with increased feelings of closeness and "family."

Changes Related to Value Differences

Differences in values have the most pervasive negative effect on sibling solidarity. Differences in morals, lifestyles, and notions of family loyalty inevitably pull siblings apart. In some cases, relationships will be terminated and no attempt at contact will be made. Cutting off a sibling is very rare, but when it does occur, value differences are the most common instigator of the cutoff. When values and lifestyles are highly similar, a very close and intimate relationship can survive even long separations (Ross and Milgram, 1982).

FERVENT SIBLING LOYALTY

I was always putting myself in my sister's place, adopting her credulousness, and even her memories, I saw, could be made mine. It was Isobel I imagined as the eternal heroine—never myself. I substituted her feelings for my own and her face for any face described. Whatever the author's intentions, the heroine was my sister.

Mavis Gollent, *Its Image on the Mirror,* 1964

An advantage over a kinsman is the worst kind of disadvantage.

Apocrypha II; Maccabees 5:6

Some siblings are modern Hansels and Gretels; they are intensely loyal, offering assistance to one another like overprotective mothers. When one sibling is hurt or in need, the other siblings feel an irrationally intense need to help. Fervently loyal siblings prefer each other's company to all others' and are unhappy if they are deprived of seeing each other for too long. This phenomenon is commonly associated with twins but is by no means their exclusive domain.

Such intense overattachment tends to occur in families where the parents are physically or psychologically unavailable to their children. The children, confronted with a bleak, hostile, frightening environment, cling to one another for emotional nurturance and security. For example, Anna Freud (Freud and Dann, 1951) found that this kind of relationship developed among six unrelated children orphaned in their infancy by the Nazis. Basically deprived of adult nurturing for the next two years, the children became attached to one another to an extent unheard of in three-year-olds. After the children were found and put in a wartime nursery, detailed observations revealed that they cared greatly for one another and wished always to be together. They would pick up one another's toys, be concerned for the others' safety when out walking, and share all types of treats. This type of exemplary behavior and responsibility is rarely seen in the spontaneous behavior of loved, family-raised, preschool siblings.

Bank and Kahn (1982a, 1982b) have studied contemporary siblings whose feelings of loyalty and closeness are so intense that each feels responsible for the other's day-to-day well-being. They are extremely devoted to fulfilling each other's needs and are willing to make great personal sacrifices to ensure the other's happiness. The research presented so far suggests that such intense sibling loyalty is an uncommon phenomenon. This do-or-die loyalty, usually reserved for parent/child relationships, requires special conditions such as parental absence or neglect, so that children are forced to depend only on one another for continuing comfort and security. These researchers also found that the intensely loyal siblings all had at least one nurturing parent in their early years to act as a model of caring for the family. Moreover, none of these sibling relationships had been undermined by parents' attempts to downgrade how the siblings interacted or felt toward each other. For this special bonding to occur, it was essential that siblings be close in age and continuously reared together.

Bank and Kahn (1982a, 1982b) reported three distinguishing characteristics of fervently loyal siblings:

1. Loyal siblings actively try to be with one another and have negative reactions to being separated. They make sure that all holidays are spent together and prefer to spend their leisure time with one another whenever possible.
2. The relationships of loyal siblings are marked by cooperation, sympathy, and mutual helpfulness. They will help one another study for exams and help protect one another in their youth. As adults, they try to advance one another's careers and stand willing to help out financially.
3. Fervently loyal siblings often develop a special language not understood by anyone else. The language is very rich in codes and metaphors. The intensity of a frown can communicate exactly how disap-

proving one is of another; a single word can summarize one's feelings about an entire subject.

Loyal siblings always defend one another against serious outside threats. As children, the siblings often protect one another from neighborhood fights or assaults by parents. One middle-aged woman proudly tells the story of how, as a child, her brother would protect her from her father's strap:

> Whenever Papa took the strap down off the wall, my brother would rush and shut me in the bathroom. Standing guard at the bathroom door he would shout, "Hit me! Hit me instead of her. I will not let you near her. Hit me forever. I will not let you near her."

ELIZABETH (nursing-home resident, age 86)

My sister was my life. My identical sister. . . . We lived together for seventy-one years. Oh, I never thought of her as my "twin" even though no one could ever tell us apart. She was my best friend. My name was Elizabeth Cleo and hers was Cleo Elizabeth. She called me Liz; I called her Cleo. Our mother died of TB when we were nine but my aunt moved in and raised us. We both loved her.

Cleo and I just fit. We kept the same in school; what was hard for her was hard for me. We played the same and ate the same. We spent our lives working as dressmakers and we worked so much the same she could pick up my work and I could pick up hers and you would never tell. The one problem we did have is that what she called the bottom of the cuff, I'd always call the top and what she'd call the top, I'd call the bottom. Every once in a while this would get us into trouble since we never could agree on what to call it. But we never did fuss much at each other. We agreed on how to decorate the house and every Christmas we'd love to put the decorations in each room. . . . Neither one of us ever had a fella, I don't know why but neither she nor I had any interest or anything for men. Just never wanted to get around them too much. Cleo either. . . . Now, there were two little differences between us. She liked to get out and be with people more than I did and every once in a while she'd go downtown in Baltimore with our cousin. I'd stay home. Another thing is that she was a better thinker and a little stronger. She was the older one, born five minutes before me. And I'd let her tell me what to do. When she said we should sell the house, I agreed. When she said we should go to the home, I agreed. Poor thing, she had cancer at the time and didn't know it until we got here. On July 6, it will be fifteen years that she is dead. I miss her so much.

My friends at the home think that Cleo bossed me around too much, I don't know. Since she has gone I have had to make so many decisions formyself that she would have made. But I do better than I thought! They say twins live about the same length of time but that's not true. But I wish it was true. The greatest puzzle to me is how come I'm still here after so many years without Cleo. It never seems right to me and I don't understand it. . . .

SIBLING RIVALRY AND TENSIONS

Siblings have trying relationships for man reasons. First, the age differences between siblings create their own tensions; children at different stages have different social needs. Dealing with someone at a different psychosocial juncture involves dealing with different behavioral competencies, pleasures, and conversation. Also, when one of the children is perceived as a parent's "favorite," his or her relationship with the second-place siblings becomes strained and fraught with jealousies. Also, individual idiosyncrasies, such as being gifted or very tall, can make children feel different from their "normal" siblings. They may try to isolate and distance themselves, because having to make frequent comparisons is too painful.

Conflicts, tensions, and jealousies invariably result in the eruption of sibling arguments and fighting. Sibling fighting is the cause of much family tension. An interesting study by Martin and Ross (1995) found that among siblings between two and five years old, parents responded to less than half of the incidents of aggression between the children. The elder children seemed to set the pace for future interactions: if they were highly aggressive at the first testing, their younger siblings had higher aggression rates two years later, compared to younger siblings who had not been exposed to an aggressive older sibling. This study begs for more than group data analysis. How many of the mothers always responded to their children's aggression, and how aggressive were those particular children? Likewise, how many mothers never or rarely intervened and how did these children present themselves? Did extroverted, confident children respond differently than introverted, anxious children to having an aggressive older sibling? And what are the interactions between sibling style, the child's style, and the parent's frequency and style of intervention? Despite these unanswered questions, psychologists trying to deal with sibling fighting and rivalry are starting to study all of these factors.

A number of dimensions are important to assess in aversive sibling relationships. The most important are as follows (Graham and Cutler, 1994):

- *Empathy:* What is the degree of empathy between the siblings? Does each understand what the other one is coping with in a compassionate manner? All too often, one sibling's pain is the cause of the other sibling's scorn. Feelings of parental favoritism, rejection, and inferiority can make a sibling's pain even cause for a private celebration.
- *Boundary Maintenance:* How much to do the siblings share? A room? Friends? Secrets? Chores? Clothes? Toys? CDs? Computers?
- *Similarity:* Do the siblings have common interests, hobbies, attitudes, lifestyles, or academic skills?

Data indicate that social relationships at school, in the early elementary years, can be predicted by the quality of sibling relationships (Stormshak, Bellanti, and Bierman, 1996). Children with positive, involved sibling relationships tend to do better on a number of school adjustment measures than children who have conflicted relationships with their siblings.

Nearly three-quarters of the adults studied by Ross and Milgram (1982) reported that at some time they have felt rivalry toward their brothers and sisters. Nearly half admit those feelings are still with them. Not all the jealousies began in childhood; 33 percent first felt jealous during adolescence and 22 percent were adults when they first experienced envy.

Parent-Related Rivalry

Most sibling rivalry revolves around competition for parental approval and the feeling that parents had definite "favorites." Sometimes it was the grandparents or teachers who showed favoritism. The jealous siblings always felt they were being compared with a brother or sister and felt compelled to compete almost constantly. Parent-prompted rivalry can be overtly or covertly stimulated. Overt stimulation of jealousy occurs whenever a parent or grandparent makes a point of praising the valued traits in one sibling and urging the other to become more like the valued sibling. Covert stimulation of jealousy comes into the picture when a child or adult knows, despite the absence of verbal comparisons, that the parent has greater affection or admiration for another one of the children.

Research has shown that despite most parents' claims to the contrary, fathers and mothers do treat their children differently. Differential actions of parents are shaped by the ages and personalities of their children as well as by birth order. Bryant and Crockenberg (1980) found that when both first- and second-born girls were in a problem-solving situation with their mother, the mothers were consistently more responsive to the second-born. Other studies have shown that mothers show more warmth and protectiveness to the second-born (Lasko, 1954). As these goodies are delivered to the second-born, it is easy to imagine the firstborn yearning for the "olden days" when no rival was there to take away Mother's attention and affection. These empirical studies support the cries of first-borns all over the country who feel that their little brothers or sisters are "getting all the attention."

Rivalry Within the Sibling Group

Although rivalries are often based on competition for parental approval and rewards, just as frequently they arise within the sibling group. Each sibling tries to gain status and improve his or her self-image by comparisons with brothers and sisters. Within the sibling group, each member wants to be the most powerful and the most admired. When self-comparisons are made and a person feels inferior to one or more siblings, jealousy and rivalry are bound to ensue. Siblings are the yardstick by which one measures one's achievement of family goals. To constantly compare oneself and never be the winner is a very painful experience.

Of course, the picture is rarely so black and white, with one sibling having no merit and the other forever winning. Simple jealousies, reciprocal jealousies, and sex-linked jealousies are far more common (Ross and Milgram, 1982). With simple jealousies, the siblings are essentially of equal accomplishment except in one particular area or trait—for example, the musical genius of a sister or the outstanding athletic prowess of a brother. In large families, it is common for a person to have several concurrent simple jealousies with different brothers and sisters.

Reciprocal rivalries occur when each sibling perceives the other as having a valued trait that he or she is lacking. One brother might be valedictorian of his college class but admire his kid brother who is more socially adept at asking girls out. The girl-savvy brother, on the other hand, might be awed by his brother's intellectual achievements. Simple or reciprocal sibling rivalry revolves around five socially valued traits: achievement, physical attractiveness, intelligence, interpersonal competency, and maturity. These are the main standards by which the siblings are making comparisons.

For women, sex-linked sibling rivalries are commonly found in ethnic groups that adhere to strict sex stereotyping. In subcultures that value sons more than daughters, sisters become very jealous of the privileges and status given to the brothers and resent the restrictive conditions they have been subjected to. Overall, however, boys seem to have the most blatant attacks of sibling rivalry. The need for one brother to excel over the other comes through in simple observational studies. The brother who is the "lesser" in the social comparison feels resentment and jealousy toward the brother who outshines him. The "winning" brother often feels uncomfortable and even guilty in the presence of the other brother. Sibling rivalry can be a very destructive force in this situation.

DEIDENTIFICATION

One defense against sibling rivalry is to try to be different from one's sibling—to deidentify and thus avoid competing for mastery in the same areas as one's sibling.

The "Cain Complex"

The process of deidentification can lead to the development of what is called the Cain complex. In the Bible, Cain and Abel were two brothers with diametrically opposed personalities. Just as Cain derived a sense of superiority from disparaging Abel's traits, so do any two siblings find it easier to feel superior if each feels qualitatively different from the other. For example, two sisters may deidentify by one's developing into a belle-of-the-ball type—flirtatious, popular, and happy-go-lucky—while the other develops an intellectual and highly logical personality. The "popular" sibling feels superior in terms of telephone calls and dates, viewing the sister's lifestyle as downright dull. The "intelligent" sibling can feel superior to the other in grades and relationships with adults, viewing the other sister as a bit of a nitwit. Thus, the differences allow each sister to shine in an independent spotlight.

Such deidentification may affect the relationship positively. If it is carried to extremes, though, each sister may reject the other as "too weird"; their feelings for each other may be diminished. For most siblings, the Cain complex helps strengthen bonds of love. For "by expressing themselves in different ways and in different spheres, siblings are spared the necessity of constantly defending their turf against incursions from each other. Negative feelings abate, strengthening the bonds of love between them" (Schacter, 1982:130).

Predicting Deidentification

Schacter (1982), who developed the concept of the Cain complex, has done extensive research to see which sibling pairs were most likely to deidentify. She asked her subjects to rate each member of the family, including himself or herself, in regard to such descriptive terms as "good," "extroverted," "fast," or "delicate." Subjects who rated a sibling and themselves very similarly received high identification scores. Subjects who consistently rated themselves as different from their siblings received a high deidentification score. (Schacter's scale is shown in Figure 17.1 at the end of this chapter.)

Schacter found that over half her subjects considered themselves different from their siblings. The difference is most pronounced, however, between the firstborn and second-born siblings. In two-child families, 62 percent of the siblings say they are different. In three-child families, 75 percent of the first- and second-borns say they are different from each other while only 52 percent of the second- and third-borns say they are different from each other, and 45 percent of the first- and third-borns say they are different from each other.

These results were highlighted further when Schacter asked the mothers to rate the personalities of their children. Eighty percent of mothers with two children judged them "different." In three-child families, mothers judged 91 percent of the firstborns versus second-borns different, 66 percent of the second-borns versus third-borns different, and 58 percent of the first-borns versus third-borns different. Not only do the first two children deidentify the most strongly, but if they are of the same sex the process is significantly heightened. Thus, the first two brothers or the first two sisters are most likely to develop different personalities.

Roles Used in Deidentifying

Bossard and Bell (1960), Zuk (1972), and others have identified the distinct personality roles that children develop while deidentifying and making their position in the family a meaningful one. These include (1) the responsible sibling, (2) the popular, well-liked sibling, (3) the socially ambitious sibling, (4) the studious sibling, (5) the self-centered, isolated sibling, (6) the spoiled sibling, and (7) the peacemaker sibling. Children develop these reputations regardless of birth order, but in a large family, parental interactions are more heavily influenced by the distinctive tag of the middle children.

The benefits of deidentification vary over the course of a lifetime. The sibling who had the reputation for being caring and a responsible, hard worker may bask in that assignment for many a year. But when an elderly parent develops Alzheimer's or Parkinson's and needs assistance, the prestigious reputation becomes an annoying burden as other siblings and relatives assume "the caretaker" destiny is beyond negotiation.

Many popular children's stories and television series rely on these distinct personality styles to develop a family to whom readers or viewers can relate. In literature, Judy Blume's popular *Tales of a Fourth Grade Nothing* provides an example. The main character, Fudge, is an incompetent mess; his older, in-control brother is always rescuing him. On television, the sitcom *Family Ties* used an intellectual older brother, a socially oriented older sister, and an athletic but slightly spoiled younger sister to present different facets of contemporary sibling interactions.

Of course, sibling deidentification refers to perceived dissimilarities. It is possible that the siblings are really much more similar than they or their parents perceive. It is also possible that genuine differences are genetically derived or are related to some environmental factor other than pressure to deidentify.

ALLEN (college professor, age 37)

My brother and I were very, very jealous of each other. Ever since I could remember, we fought. I wanted to be the pride and joy of my parents' life. So did my brother. I should have had an edge because I was the eldest, but he was more handsome and bigger and more athletic. My mother always said I was the brains and he was the beauty. It objectively wasn't true. He was smart, very smart, and neither of us were beauties by any stretch of the imagination. Still, my mother believed it and for many years we believed it. Even though we were "given" different personalities, I was always jealous of how he looked and of every sign of his popularity. I can still remember how angry and depressed I was when he was elected class president in high school. I was two grades ahead of him in school, and he was always checking to see if his report cards matched up to mine when he was in the same grade.

Most of our rivalrous feelings were expressed through board games. I can remember how we used to go down in our finished basement and play the game "Gettysburg." We would build up an enormous amount of tension (more than was probably at the actual battle), and then when it was obvious that one of us had victory at the door, the other would leave the room screaming and crying. One day, it got so bad that I picked up the board and ripped it in half. Well, that ended our "Gettysburg" era, but we repeated the pattern with chess, card games, and lots of other board games. We would always end up hurt and upset, screaming that the winner had cheated. Once Danny got bigger than me, he would physically pin me down and tickle me as I tried to leave the game. When you're mad, that's the worst possible torture.

My dad seemed to promote our competition and rivalry. At the dinner table, even during our teens, we would sit around with him and play "Twenty Questions." Each of us would build up ridiculous storehouses of trivia so we could prove the other stupid. Danny knew all the presidents and their cabinets, backward and forward. I knew the Greek tragedies. Even here, two or three times a week, I'd leave the kitchen table depressed or angry or both.

Once we left for college, we had little contact. He got his law degree the same year I got a PhD in the classics. He was jealous of the depth and intensity of knowledge my degree stood for, and I was jealous of the social acceptability and financial lucrativeness of his degree. Later, I was jealous of the wife he chose and then he was jealous of mine. Then when I got divorced, he was jealous of my freedom.

This went on nonstop until my mother died eight years ago. We both rushed home to St. Louis and did the traditional Jewish shivah. We covered the mirrors and stayed in the house all week. Locked in the house together, we got into a week-long dialogue. We went over everything. We hit deep port. We talked about our families, our relationship, and our own personal plans for the future. We talked a lot about our mother and our father. I'm not sure what all happened that week, but the rivalry went away. Maybe my mother's death meant she wasn't going to be comparing us any more. Maybe it was that we were finally able to relate to one another on an adult level. Whatever it was, I'm glad it happened. I realize also that as we hit our midlife crises some of these jealousies may resurface, but I'm determined that next time we'll discuss them before we get caught acting them out.

IDENTIFICATION

But whom do siblings choose to model their personalities after, if not each other? Freudian theory postulates that each child identifies with the same-sex parent and tries to model or emulate that parent's behaviors and attitudes. Alas for Freud, research shows that children are just as likely to identify with the opposite-sex parent as with the same-sex parent (Schacter, 1982).

Identification with a Parent

As Schacter (1982) examined the consistent perceived differences between siblings who deidentified, it became obvious that they must be identifying with different parents, irrespective of sex. Assuming a firstborn child has a small natural inclination toward one parent instead of the other, the child will choose that parent to emulate. Unless the next child has a strong inclination to be like the parent chosen by the firstborn, he or she chooses the other parent. Later children might again be free to choose either parent or may choose one of their siblings. This process of younger children identifying with the parent not chosen by older siblings is called *split-parent identification.*

By asking people to rate how siblings were like their fathers and mothers, Schacter found that mothers reported a split-parent identification for 89 percent of the children in two-child families; 89 percent of the time, if one child was reported to be like the mother, the other child was reported to be like the father. Assuming that all children identify with one parent or the other, the odds according to chance would be fifty-fifty that a child would be like one or the other parent. We would expect 50 percent of siblings to have split-parent identifications. Eighty-nine percent split-parent identifications greatly exceeds what one would expect by chance. However, maternal reports may be highly biased and may not accurately reflect the proportion of split-parent identifications that actually exist. When siblings were asked which parent they were like, only 66 percent of the siblings in two-child families exhibited split-parent identifications. This is considerably below the incidence of split-parent identification reported by mothers, but it is still significantly more than would be expected by chance.

Identification with a Sibling

Everyday observation confirms that siblings do identify with one another. Younger children look to the older ones to learn how to dress, how to interact with the parents, and how to play. Sex roles are learned from our siblings as well. Research has shown that both boys and girls from same-sex families appear more sex-typed than children from cross-sex families (Koch, 1956). These findings appear to contradict the theory of deidentification, but the apparent contradiction can be explained by a developmental model of sibling relationships. During the preschool years and middle childhood, siblings tend to emulate, model, and identify with their brothers and sisters. During adolescence, three forces begin to work against identification: jealousies and rivalry increase, temperamental differences and talents become more pronounced, and cognitive abilities have developed to the point where self-definition is possible. These three forces might cause older siblings to deidentify with one another.

Both identification and deidentification are apparent to some degree throughout the life span. Future research needs to concentrate on how siblings integrate or balance these two forces throughout their lives. Adams (1981:34) hints at this process when she states, "Possibly there is a balance between the functional and dysfunctional aspects of the sibling relationship which is manifested in solidarity vs. rivalry. There may be a love-hate dialectical process throughout the life span that leads to new levels of maturity or immaturity in sibling relationships." The challenge of the future is to discover how to maximize the benefits of sibling relationships and minimize the liabilities.

Siblings As Orientational Others

Consciously or unconsciously, we use siblings to learn about ourselves throughout life. When we are little, it may be as simple as learning how to play a computer game by watching a sibling or copying his or her desire to ride horses or have a skateboard. As we get older, the idealization and modeling of siblings seems to yield to emerging differentiation and deidentification needs. Many older children use siblings more abstractly, in a point/counterpoint relationship. The siblings become a model from which a brother or sister must make unique modifications to be successful as an individual. Yet, there are times when behavioral guidelines are unclear, and if there are no strong competing influences, siblings still have a direct, positive effect on our behavioral choices. For example, Widmer (1997) found that when older brothers were sexually active at an early age, siblings were more likely to follow suit. An older sister's behavior did not have the disinhibiting effect, possibly because negative stigma continues to be associated with female sexuality.

Mental Health and Sibling Relationships

Overall adjustment of a child is affected by the degree of disturbance in the siblings. Deal and MacLean (1995) found that children (nine to fifteen years old) with a sibling aged twelve to eighteen, who had one or more psychiatric hospitalizations, were more psychologically distressed themselves and had poorer relationships with their peers. Not surprisingly, they had a more negative view of their brother or sister than the normal controls and identified less with the troubled older sibling. Also, when one sibling has a clinical psychological disorder, sibling relationships suffer. Slomkowski, Cohen, and Brook (1997) reported that adolescents who were diagnosed with a conduct disorder or an oppositional disorder reported a more negative sibling relationship than adolescents without a psychological disorder.

Important developmental trends affect how siblings interact when one has an observable psychological problem or learning disability. As mentioned above, when children are very young, under two years of age, they often try to imitate the ways of the older sibling, even when those ways are atypical or socially scorned. But rather quickly, as soon as they have mastered some language skills, they recognize the differentness of their sibling and begin imitating parents and playmates, especially picking up cues on how to interact and treat the learning disabled sibling (Hames, 1998).

Although many siblings drift apart after adolescence, in the last stage of life, a rapprochement occurs, as siblings look to one another as a source of companionship, for emotional support, and to reaffirm the importance of the family unit.

JANE (housewife, age 38)

My brother and I were only sixteen months apart and so I was never treated like "the baby" or he like "the firstborn." Instead, we were both "the big kids," and the forty or so foster children who shared our house with us throughout the years were "the little ones." Since I was eight years old when Mama got into foster care, I loved and welcomed the babies. They were better than any doll! In those days, a baby had to be six months old before it was put up for adoption, so we had a lot of newborns who stayed that long. Later it was changed to three months and so they stayed a shorter amount of time. I guess one effect of having so many baby brothers and sisters all the time was that I learned to be a very responsible person. Throughout my growing up there was always someone who needed watching over or caring for. They never grew up or became independent, they were just replaced.

(continued)

(continued)

Another enormous influence they had on me was that I learned to handle separations very well. Gee, I got so attached to so many of those babies. Mama would always cry when they left. I only did for my special kids. One very special baby was "Sissy." She was sick a lot and one day had a real high fever. Mama rushed her to the hospital but they said Mama should just take her home. That night Sissy had a convulsion and she had two more the next day. Social Services was afraid she might have gotten some brain damage, so they let Sissy stay until she was three before she was put up for adoption. When she left, I was heartbroken. Mama would always take a picture of each child when they came and when they left. When they left she always got them a new set of clothes. I still remember the outfit Sissy got without even looking at the photo.

The only times I resented the kids is when I wanted to have Mama come to the school or take me somewhere. She was always stuck to the house with the babies. Once in a while we got older kids and I had to share my bedroom, which I didn't much care for. I don't think my brother ever resented them. I also would get peeved when I would have to babysit if Mama had to go somewhere.

My brother and I are real close now. In fact, he's probably closer to me than to anyone else. Every year of my life we've gone Christmas shopping together, and we talk about our values and problems together. Sometimes he'll stop by with a book he thinks I might like to read or some small thing for the house that he knows I've been looking for. He's great with my kids and gets along well with my husband. I think one reason we're so close has to do with his temperament. He's a very quiet, shy, and sensitive person and always has been. I'm more impulsive and talkative. Also, maybe with all the young kids coming and going all the time, we developed a special bond of belonging to each other—of being there for each other.

SELF-EXPLORATION: SIBLING RELATIONSHIPS

1. Fill out the Self and Sibling Personality Scales (see Figure 17.1) and use the accompanying answer sheet (see Figure 17.2) and scoring instructions. Which siblings are you most similar to? Most dissimilar to?
2. Does the sibling most dissimilar to you get along better with a different parent from the one you get along with best? (Is there evidence of alternate parent identification?)
3. How close are your mother and father to each of their siblings?
4. What type of relationship would you like to have with each of your siblings during the next twenty years? What could you do to promote those relationships? What could jeopardize those relationships?

FIGURE 17.1. Self and Sibling Personality Scales

Please rate yourself on each of the following scales and put your rating on the answer sheet in Figure 17.2.

	A						B
1.	Good						Bad
	1	2	3	4	5	6	7
2.	Pleasant						Unpleasant
	1	2	3	4	5	6	7
3.	Cheerful						Depressed
	1	2	3	4	5	6	7
4.	Active						Passive
	1	2	3	4	5	6	7
5.	Fast						Slow
	1	2	3	4	5	6	7
6.	Hot						Cold
	1	2	3	4	5	6	7
7.	Strong						Weak
	1	2	3	4	5	6	7
8.	Rugged						Delicate
	1	2	3	4	5	6	7
9.	Deep						Shallow
	1	2	3	4	5	6	7
10.	Tense						Relaxed
	1	2	3	4	5	6	7
11.	Introverted						Extroverted
	1	2	3	4	5	6	7
12.	Conventional						Unconventional
	1	2	3	4	5	6	7
13.	Achieving						Nonachieving
	1	2	3	4	5	6	7

After you have rated yourself on all 13 traits go back and rate each of your siblings. Take your oldest sibling first and rate him or her on all 13 items. Then take the next oldest sibling and rate him or her on all 13 items. Continue with this procedure until all your siblings are accounted for.

Source: Adapted from Schacter, F. F. 1982. Sibling deidentification and split parent identification: A family triad. In Lamb, M. and Sutton-Smith, B. (Eds.), *Sibling relationships: Their nature and significance across the life span.* Hillsdale, NJ: Lawrence Erlbaum Associates.

FIGURE 17.2. Answer Sheet for Self and Sibling Personality Scales

	Self-rating	Sibling rating	Differ score (self-sibling 1)	Sibling rating	Differ score (self-sibling 2)	Sibling rating	Differ score (self-sibling 3)
1.							
2.							
3.							
4.							
5.							
6.							
7.							
8.							
9.							
10.							
11.							
12.							
13.							

Scoring Instructions

Step 1. For each personality description, subtract your sibling's score from your score. If your sibling's score is the higher, subtract your score from your sibling's. In this way all differences are positive.

Step 2. Add all 13 of the difference scores together.

Step 3. A high number (i.e., a number over 40) indicates that you do not see yourself as like your sibling. A low number (below 20) indicates that you see yourself as similar to that sibling.

For siblings 2, 3, 4, etc., repeat steps 1 and 2 above.

UNIT VI:
FAMILY CONCEPTS—A SOCIAL
PSYCHOLOGICAL PERSPECTIVE

Gordon Allport (1968:3) has defined social psychology as a discipline that "attempts to understand and explain how the thoughts, feelings, or behavior of individuals are influenced by the *actual, imagined, or implied presence of others.*" (Emphasis added.) This definition is particularly relevant for understanding family dynamics because family members not only react to the actual messages sent to one another but are equally prone to misunderstand one another and react to imagined or implied messages.

Most often, the extent of misunderstanding within a family is determined by both the personalities involved and the type of situations facing the family members. When the situation is emotionally neutral, most people can accurately ascertain another person's intentions and attitudes. Family situations, though, are almost always emotionally loaded. People find their own needs and desires coloring their interpretations of what is said or done by other family members. Hence, the social psychological concepts presented in this section are attempts to explain family relationships by understanding the unique interactions between different types of personalities and various family situations.

Besides providing an interactive perspective, explanations of family dynamics based on social psychology have considerable appeal for those who value the long scientific tradition of mainstream psychology. The social psychological concepts discussed in this section have been the subject of extensive experimentation. Persuasive statistical evidence shows that these concepts can both explain and predict how people behave and feel in a variety of situations.

425

As more and more family scholars come to appreciate the increased accuracy, scope, and fruitfulness of this approach, social psychological concepts may become as popular as systems concepts are today. But as Kuhn (1962, 1980) pointed out more than thirty years ago, human values have a real impact on which theories become popular in the scientific community. Family theorists who value structured interactions will tend to continue to see systems theory as a simpler and more fruitful approach. By contrast, family theorists who value the role of individual differences and situational social variables will be much quicker to embrace the new social psychological theories.

REFERENCES

Allport, G.W. 1968. *The person in psychology: Selected essays.* Boston: Beacon Press.

Kuhn, T.S. 1962. *The structure of revolutions.* Chicago: University of Chicago Press.

Kuhn, T.S. 1980. Theory choice. In Klemke, E.D., Hollinger, R., and Kline, A.D. (Eds.), *Introductory readings and the philosophy of science.* New York: Prometheus Books.

Chapter 18

Attribution

If you look at life one way, there is always cause for alarm.

Elizabeth Bowen

The theory of attribution tries to explain people's ways of assigning causes to their own behavior and that of others. Heider (1958) suggests that when people see someone behaving in a particular way, they first try to determine whether the person was responsible for initiating the behavior, whether circumstances necessitated it, or both. Holding others personally responsible for their behavior allows us to feel angered or hurt, flattered or joyous, in response to their actions. When we assume full responsibility for our own behavior, we attribute any failure to deficiencies inherent in ourselves (we are not smart enough, strong enough, and so on). Similarly, we attribute success in achieving our goals to our own unique assets. Conversely, if we assume that we have very little control over our lives, we see both failure and achievement as being due to the help of others—to luck or even to fate. Thus, attributions greatly affect our feelings and attitudes about ourselves and others. The concept of attribution has great importance in understanding family dynamics.

PATTERNS OF ATTRIBUTION

Anytime something unusual happens in the family, a number of different attributions must be made (Kelly, 1967). Suppose an adolescent son gets into a traffic accident. The parents need to decide:

- Was the accident due to the son's negligence or to the reckless behavior of another person? (*internal* versus *external* attribution)
- If the son was responsible, was he being a daredevil or did he misperceive some traffic situation? (*intentional* versus *accidental* attribution)
- Did weather conditions or road conditions contribute to the accident? (*circumstantial* attribution)

427

The most accurate attribution would be obtained after a period of fact-finding and questioning. Unfortunately, there is evidence that individuals may develop characteristic attributional styles for responding to particular individuals. If you have been in a situation similar to the adolescent's car accident, you can probably recall how quickly the concerned others made an attribution. One parent might have instantly blamed the son while another blamed the driver of the other car. A sibling might have attributed the accident to the bad brakes on the car or the heavy rains.

Specific Mechanisms of Attribution

Social psychologists have started to define some of the specific mechanisms affecting the attribution process. Specifically, in any family conflict, the responsibility for the family's difficulties can be attributed to (1) self, (2) other family members, (3) the relationship, (4) the external environment (either outside persons or situational factors), (5) theological causes (God), or (6) luck, chance, or fate (Doherty, 1981, 1982).

If the conflict is attributed to people or problems within the family, it becomes important to make at least three other attributions. First, did the person involved intentionally create the crisis or was it accidental? Second, will the cause of this particular crisis disappear or is it due to some stable personality dispositions in one or more of the family members? Third, if a personality characteristic is involved, is its scope limited to the particular problem at hand or could it potentially create many different types of crises? The answers to these questions will help determine how much blame and problem solving the family will get involved in.

Take the case of a couple who have gotten into a fight over what to buy the in-laws for Christmas. The husband wanted to buy both sets of in-laws microwave ovens and the wife felt that was too extravagant. The discussion escalated into an enormous argument. Suppose the husband believes that the argument took his wife by surprise (was unintentional) and assumes that she is just nervous over money since she has not yet heard about her yearly raise (temporary condition). In this situation, he is not likely to blame her. He may also recall that she is not worried about buying the new car they have been shopping for. (This means the argument had a specific attribution.) Indeed, under these circumstances the husband may be very motivated to resolve the crisis. Contrast this with the situation that would occur if the husband assumes that the wife objected to the gift because she did not like the idea of his taking charge (intentional), was generally stingy with money (stable condition), and was already highly nervous about buying the new car (general). This set of attributions is likely to lead to a lot of blame and minimal problem solving.

External versus Internal Attribution

Every day, couples run into situations that need some explanation. If a husband promised to move a desk to another room before the week was over and the desk never got moved, the wife may indeed ask herself why. The reason she generates will be either an external or an internal attribution. External attributions include such reasoning as: "The desk would not fit through the doorway" or "He tried, but it was too heavy to move alone." Internal attributions would refer to personality dispositions or traits in the husband, which might be either positive or negative. Positive attributions would include the idea that he was so busy thinking of work that he forgot his promise or that his back must have been bothering him too much to move the desk. Negative internal attributions would include accusing him of being a basically thoughtless and inconsiderate person or of purposely trying to annoy his wife by not fulfilling his promise. Obviously, the type of attribution the wife has made will greatly affect how she broaches the topic again and how willing she will be to listen to his own attribution.

Most marriages reach a crisis point when the spouses are continually making negative personality attributions to explain the behavior of the other. A husband who forgets an anniversary is labeled as "unloving and heartless," not "absent-minded, with his head in a cloud." A wife who objects to her husband's vacation plans is labeled "stingy" or "boring" instead of "helpfully frugal." A spouse in an ornery mood may label a simple action such as mowing the lawn as "avoiding being in the house" instead of "helpful." One of the most unfortunate aspects of these negative attributions is that when we make both positive and negative attributions about someone, our overall impression of that person is more negative than would be predicted by simply averaging all the positive and negative attributes (Kanouse and Hanson, 1972). For love to survive, it must be, if not blind, biased enough to see the best in a mate.

Family Attribution and Self-Awareness

Are you beginning to see why the attribution process is so important in understanding how a family functions? Once you can identify the kinds of explanations family members use to understand one another, you can assess the validity of those attributions. You can judge whether alternative explanations are just as likely to "fit the facts." Most important, your awareness of the attribution process helps broaden the range of information you consider before you make an attribution.

Besides providing insights into how personality labels develop in families, attribution theory explains when and why we hold some and not other family members responsible for their behavior. Remember that the most basic attribution involves assessing intentional versus nonintentional causation. What evidence supports the belief that a person's behavior is chosen? What evidence suggests that external constraints are involved? Suppose your mate acts aggressively, shouting at you and finding fault with a meal, an opinion, or the way you are dressed? Is he or she choosing to act that way? Or is he or she impelled to act that way by fatigue, frustration, or emotional distress? If you consistently judge your mate's actions to be intentional, you are holding that person accountable for what is done. If you consistently make external or nonintentional attributions, you are excusing that person, not holding him or her responsible. You can see that attribution of responsibility has important implications for family interactions.

Once we hold people responsible for what they are doing, we will actively reward or punish them, according to how their behavior affects us. If we do not hold them responsible, we become more pliable; we might simply accept the status quo instead of dispensing rewards or punishments. We may even assume a protective role. In the case of the angry, fault-finding mate, an intentional attribution could lead you to withhold sex or to give him or her the "silent treatment." An unintentional attribution could lead to the exactly opposite response.

Two familiar attribution phenomena often found in families are scapegoating and self-handicapping. *Scapegoating* occurs when an innocent person is blamed for one's misfortunes while the real source or responsibility resides in oneself or in other more powerful persons. For example, a mother may scapegoat her children. "Will you quiet down—you're giving me a headache!" she cries. She knows she has just been on edge all day, or she is aggravated by an argument with her boss that happened before she left work. But the children are a specific and safe target.

Scapegoats are usually chosen because they are relatively powerless to defend themselves against accusations or to retaliate against the accuser. They provide no real threat. Yet they do help downcast, frustrated individuals find reasons for their misfortunes that do not lower their already fragile self-esteem or put them into a precarious position with powerful others. In any society, scapegoating is virtually always a destructive attribution. The word "scapegoating" derives from the biblical custom of symbolically heaping the sins of the community onto a goat which was then killed, thereby relieving the people of the burden of their anxieties. These days, the scapegoats are other people and the act of loading our anxieties on them only temporarily relieves us and in the long run burdens us more.

Self-handicapping attributions occur when individuals attribute faults or limitations to themselves that preclude attempts to change or improve. For example, if a young woman believes that she has no steady boyfriend because she is dull and unattractive, she will be unable to socialize and mingle with an air of confidence. Her self-handicapping becomes a self-fulfilling prophecy. Her attributions become a leading cause for continued failure.

In any close relationship there are myriad interpretations for each person's behaviors and attitudes. Three major principles affect the development of interpersonal beliefs (attributions):

1. Individuals tend to blame their shortcomings or errors on environmental constraints or bad luck; others tend to attribute the shortcomings or errors to some characteristic or intention of the individual family member.
2. Consistency in behavior leads to internal attributions; inconsistency leads to external attributions.
3. Situational factors affect attributions. Changes occurring in complex, chronic situations promote external attributions. Changes occurring in simple, evolving situations promote internal attributions.

For the most part, these principles have been experimentally verified in nonfamily settings. Presumably they are equally valid in explaining family dynamics.

FACTORS AFFECTING
INTERNAL VERSUS EXTERNAL ATTRIBUTIONS

The great thought, the great concern, the great anxiety of men is to restrict, as much as possible, the limits of their own responsibility.

Giosue Borsi

Actor/Observer Differences

The person who violates a family standard or breaks a family rule generally tends to attribute his or her actions to some compelling situational demands—to environmental constraints or bad luck. The rest of the family is likely to attribute the trespass to a negative personality characteristic of the offender (Jones and Nisbett, 1972; Kanouse and Hanson, 1972). An adolescent who goes to a party knowing there is a midnight curfew and comes home at two in the morning is likely to recite a litany of reasons. The car ran out of gas. Or one of the girls was very upset and had to be calmed down. Or the movie started an hour later than expected. All of these external attributions are extremely valid for the adolescent. The parents are more likely to attribute the late homecoming to a lack of judgment or immaturity, an unflattering dispositional attribution that could justify more parental supervision.

Consider a wife who finds herself entertaining a recently divorced neighbor one evening while her husband is away on a two-week trip. The neighbor is very lonely. He momentarily whisks the hostess off her feet and into the bedroom. The wife may attribute her infidelity to the neighbor's extreme feelings of isolation and her need to relate to someone, however fleetingly. The husband, upon finding out about the episode, is more likely to attribute it to immorality or lack of commitment on the part of his wife.

Compas and associates (1981) investigated this actor/observer difference in attributions in the differing explanations children and parents have for the child's success and failure experiences. Their subjects were sixty-five children ages six to seventeen who had contacted a university psychoeducational clinic during a six-month period. Each child had been diagnosed by the parents or the school as having a learning problem. Each child and each parent was given a questionnaire that consisted of sixteen items describing possible causes of school performance (see Table 18.1). Eight items focused on the reasons given for the child's success in a certain area of school performance and eight focused on the reasons for the child's specific learning problems. Within each set of eight explanations, four causes were internal to the child (related to effort and ability) and four were external (related to luck and task difficulty).

Among the fifty parents, thirty-eight rated an internal cause as the most important factor explaining the learning problem and only twelve rated an external cause as most important. Thus, parents were three times more likely to see the major cause for the learning difficulty as residing in the ability or motivations of the child. By contrast, the children were evenly split; half felt that an external factor was most important in understanding their learning problem while the other half felt an internal factor was most important.

When the children and parents tried to explain why a child behaved in ways that got him or her "into trouble," the same phenomenon emerged. Parents saw the child as responsible for getting himself or herself into trouble; the children saw more external causes controlling them. By contrast, both parents and children were more than twice as likely to attribute their successes to internal causes. Perhaps teaching parents to be more empathic to the children's viewpoint would facilitate productive communication and problem solving.

A follow-up study by Compas and associates (1982) suggests that empathy and productive communication can be promoted if children and parents try to sit down together and decide what is causing the child's difficulty. This group found that parents and children differed most in the focus of their attributions when interviewed individually; parents perceived the child as responsible and children blamed the extenuating circumstances. When families were interviewed together, the children used internal attributions more often, and the parents cited a greater number of external factors, leading to a much greater consensus between the two groups.

TABLE 18.1. Child/Parent Attribution Questionnaire

A cause of my (my child's) success (in the identified area) was	A cause of my (my child's) problem (in the identified area) was
a. Being lucky enough to get good teachers or other adults who helped.	a. I (my child) was not smart enough to learn the needed skills.
b. I (my child) was naturally skilled—for example, being born with a particular talent or ability.	b. I (my child) didn't try hard enough or work hard enough to learn.
c. I (my child) tried very hard.	c. Not being interested or not caring or not working hard enough to learn.
d. Being with other kids who made it go well.	d. Not being lucky enough to get good teachers.
e. The area was an easy one for me (my child) to do well in.	e. The assignments moved too fast or were harder than they should have been.
f. My (my child's) being very interested or caring about it or wanting to do it.	f. Being in class with other students who were distracting.
g. My (my child's) learning the basic skills in this area when I (my child) was younger.	g. A problem such as not being able to sit still; or mixing up letters, words, or numbers; or getting so upset I (my child) wasn't able to do well.
h. Some other person, such as a teacher or parent, made it easy to do well in this area by not expecting too much.	h. Some other person, such as a teacher or parent, expected too much.

Source: Adapted from Compas, B. G., Adelman, H. S., Freundl, D. C., Nelson, P., and Taylor, H. 1982. Parent and child causal attributions during clinical interviews. *Journal of Abnormal Psychology, 10*(1):77-84.

Consistency in Behavior

Sometimes a family member consistently responds to a situation in the same manner, no matter how the other people in the family change their behavior. This behavior leads the rest of the family to make an attribution

---

PETER (reporter, age 38)

Approximately a year ago, my wife received a major promotion at work—a promotion that, virtually overnight, gave her a great deal of power and responsibility at the office. Of course, with the added responsibility came additional worries, pressures, and insecurities. These negative forces had a major impact on our relationship.

Cathy's attitude toward me changed from one of tolerance, tenderness, and warmth to one of intolerance, toughness, and coolness. My initial explanation for this change was very negative. As I saw it, her new status and power had gone to her head. She now saw herself as top dog at work and was determined to assert the same status in our relationship (so I persuaded myself).

Convinced of these negative, even aggressive motivations, I dug in my heels and adopted a cool, argumentative, unyielding response. The result was intense conflict and a great deal of unhappiness.

After several weeks of cold war and frustration, we finally had a heart-to-heart talk. What I learned—to my surprise and relief—was that my explanation for Cathy's behavior was way off target.

She explained that she was suffering a kind of crisis from a lack of confidence at work, that her new responsibilities were straining her nerves and abilities to the limit. Her reaction, she explained, was to hunker down into her shell, to impose a forceful, no-nonsense, cool attitude toward the outside world. She apologized for the fact that this had unintentionally spilled over into her dealings with me. She reassured me that she wasn't trying to "take over" the marriage, and that she would make a major effort not to let her workplace struggles poison our relationship.

Well, for me, this cast Cathy's behavior in an entirely different light. And my response to her sometimes trying emotional state changed accordingly. I became far more tolerant and understanding to her occasional bad moods—realizing that they were not caused by or specifically aimed at me. I became extremely supportive and sympathetic to her, doing everything possible to bolster her confidence and security—the better to fortify her for what she was experiencing at work.

Cathy recognized my change of attitude and was enormously appreciative of my understanding and support. Our bonds were reaffirmed and strengthened. Our relationship was back on track.

---

about what is motivating the person to respond in that fixed manner (Kelly, 1967). It becomes a standard method for developing stereotypes about family members. If a wife constantly says that she is too tired to make love, the husband may try a variety of strategies to make his wife more peppy. After offering to do the dinner dishes, suggesting an afternoon nap, and going to bed earlier without results, the husband will make an internal attribution: His wife is frigid, or depressed, or using sex as a weapon to punish him. Similarly, an adolescent who has previously done well in school and suddenly fails an English course may be given a tutor and after-school help. If he or she continues to fail, he or she will be attributed with "being negative" or "unmotivated" or "acting out."

Situational Factors

> *The father entered the room just as the children were starting a free-for-all. "See here, Johnny," said the father, grabbing one of the youngsters, "who started this?" "Well," said Johnny, "it's all Freddy's fault. He started it when he hit me back."*

Author Unknown

The attributional style of any person is not a static characteristic. People do not simply look for consistency and self/other distinctions when making attributions. Rather, attributional style is a composite of attribution tendencies that vary with the situation. For example, a study by Holloway and Fuller (1983) demonstrated the situational nature of internal and external attributions in a group of women judging the causes of their own parenting behaviors. The researchers interpreted internal attributions of responsibility as signifying that the mothers felt they were personally responsible for the success or failure of their attempts to influence their husbands and children. External attributions were considered indicative of feeling that other family members, fate, society, or some other outside factor was operating to create change in the family. The method involved presenting fifty-eight working women with a set of eight questions that assessed areas in which women typically try to exert some influence. Three typical series of questions were:

- Have you ever tried to change anything about the way your husband helps you with child care? Yes or no? How did it work out? Why did it work out? Why do you think you were successful or unsuccessful?
- Have you ever tried to increase or decrease the time you spend with your children? Yes or no? How did it work out? Why did it work out? Why do you think you were successful or unsuccessful?
- Have you ever tried to settle a dispute between two of your children? Yes or no? How did it work out? Why do you think you were successful or unsuccessful?

The answers were audiotaped, and judges rated each explanation of a successful or unsuccessful intervention as indicative of an internal attribution, an external attribution, or a combination of both. The results indicated that the mothers attributed their success to their own personal effectiveness if (1) they were in a situation where there were few children, (2) the child care was the sole responsibility of the mother, and (3) the mother had obtained child-rearing information through formal classes and books. External attributions were associated with women in a situation where (1) they had a lot of children, (2) some of the children were adolescents, (3) child care was shared with the husband or other relatives, and (4) they had not read child-rearing books nor gone to formal parenting classes.

When the externally attributing women successfully settled a fight between the children or got the husband to help out more with child care, they attributed the success to the kids being in a good mood or the father having extra time on his hands. External attributions apparently increased as collective interests and interdependence increased in the family structure and the women had no recognized formula or schema for effective parenting (such as that found in child-rearing books or formal classes) that they could call upon to help effect change. As expected, no significant patterns emerged when the women were unsuccessful in effecting change; everyone tended to blame the failure on outside constraints.

Another example of how situational factors can affect the development of an attributional style can be observed in the children of alcoholic parents. A child with an alcoholic parent grows up in a very unpredictable household. The drinking parent may permit some activities when sober that are highly punishable when he or she is drunk. The drinking parent's responses seem capricious; the time of day, the number of drinks, and a host of other factors make it very difficult to predict just how Mom or Dad will react. These are the precise conditions needed for developing a cognitive lifestyle of external attributions.

This assumption has been verified by Prevett, Spence, and Chaknis (1981). They gave a test measuring internal and external attributions to fifteen children whose parents had a severe drinking problem and to fifteen children who came from homes with no drinking problem. Children with an alcoholic parent were significantly more external. It was as though they had learned that life's consequences was unrelated to their behavior. Since their rewards and punishments were attributed to fate or luck, their behavior was not regulated by their desire to affect the environment.

FACTORS AFFECTING ATTRIBUTION STYLE

Reinforcing interactions and positive attitudes toward an individual lead us to make positive personality attributions; punishing interactions and negative attitudes toward an actor lead us to make negative personality

MYRNA (housewife, age 53)

Sometimes one behavior can have such different attributions associated with it, that it invariably becomes the focus of family struggles. Behaviors related to money are a prime example. Over the thirty-one years of my marriage, some of the most critical events involved money-related behaviors and the various attributions that were made about those behaviors. When I first got married, my husband's family was just getting by. My family was upper middle class and I had a small but dependable yearly stipend from a stock portfolio set up by my grandparents. To me, marriage was (and still is) a forever commitment and I wanted to adjust the portfolio to reflect the partnership I was now a part of. My family was horrified by my behavior. To me the act was a reflection of my trust, my commitment, and my interconnectedness to my husband. My family felt I was shutting them out and stupidly taking care of a new husband instead of myself and my "real" family. They attributed my behavior to immaturity; I attributed it to a mature, adult mode of operation. These different attributions led to a lot of conflicts.

Later, after the boys were born, we had the opportunity to buy my aunt's cottage in Cape May. Herb's business was still on shaky ground, so we sold all the stock and used it as a down payment on a house that we jointly owned. After five years, Herb had a chance to make his store part of a national chain, but he needed a lot of cash. We sold the house and he used the $40,000 to put into the new business. Because the new business would be owned by my husband and another partner who wanted no involvement from wives, I lost title to the money. My husband attributed his behavior to the reality demands made by the partner. I saw his cavalier attitude as a message that he was pursuing his career and that he was letting his career interfere with *our* partnership. I never told my dad that I wasn't part of the partnership because he would have attributed Herb's behavior to consciously trying to put one over on me and that I didn't need to hear! Herb never, to this day, saw my point of view.

Last year, my mother died and left me some money. Unlike my decision twenty-five years ago, I put the money in a money market certificate in my own name. Herb thought it was fine but said I was doing it "because my mother would not have wanted him to have it." I'll let him keep that attribution even though it isn't true. Truth is that I did it because I want to be equal to Herb—not just in spirit but on the bottom line of the ledger. While realistically, that is pretty unattainable, it was the motive in not putting his name on the account. At the end my mom really loved Herb and she probably would think I'm a stinker after he has been "such a good provider."

One last example will show the effects this obsession with money behavior has had on my kids. Tevia is fourteen now and ever since he was ten we have given him $50 on Chanukah to spend as he likes during the year. Tevia now has $200 (plus interest of course). I feel that he's saving it because he's afraid of spending it in a way that he'd be criticized for; it proves to me he's insecure. Herb says it proves that he's a wise kid who knows the value of a dollar. Tevia says that everything he decides to buy is too expensive so he just keeps saving.

attributions. When family members behave kindly to the others, helping and being thoughtful, there is a strong tendency to credit them with positive personality dispositions. If they hurt us or refuse to help us, we attribute negative personality dispositions to them (Walster, 1966).

Researchers have repeatedly documented that what are typically called personality traits are very situation specific. They do not invariably direct how we will respond. Within the family, personality labels are usually the result of restricting our interactions to very proscribed scenarios (Mischel, 1968, 1976). That is, if our interactions with a family member usually occur in a specific set of circumstances, we may view that person as always acting in a particular way. Each experience reinforces our previous personality attributions. We become more and more sure of being right.

Consider the following situation. A young boy's father picks him up from school whenever possible. All spring, the father serves as an assistant coach to the boy's Little League team. Dad is an avid sportsman who is almost always ready to take the boy to see a baseball game, a hockey game, or even a video game tournament. The father is an architect and would very much like to see his son follow in his footsteps. To encourage his son to like building, he buys the child an elaborate train set, works with him on high-level Lego constructions, and teaches him to use a variety of construction tools. On the basis of the son's enjoyment of these activities, the son concludes that dad is a loving, generous, unselfish man.

With his wife, however, this same man has a very different set of interactions. Although she works full-time, he earns over twice what she does, so he feels "it's only right" that he controls the family budget despite her pleas for an equal voice. She is eager to share news about their respective workdays; he says he wants to "forget about the office" when at home. These attitudes and actions provoke feelings of rejection in the wife. On the basis of her feelings, she concludes that hubby is a cold, selfish, controlling man. If the child has positive attributions about Mom as well as Dad, he will be confused and angry when and if the parents break up. How could two such wonderful people not get along?

Events, as in the previous example, that invalidate previously positive attributions nearly always result in feelings of rejection and anger. Sometimes this situation occurs when a healthy family member develops a physical or mental disability. Suddenly, a rational, competent person is seen as irrational and incompetent. Feelings of anger and frustration well up among the healthy family members, creating further difficulties in the family situation. For example, a little boy of four has a father who is dying of a brain tumor. This man had been a very caring, loving father until six months ago, when his condition became apparent. He now has no patience with his son, wants no physical contact with him, and has fits of rage when around him. The young son, whose attributions about illness are poorly developed, listens to the adults' explanations for the father's behavior. But then he asks, "But why is he mean? Why does he hate me?"

Both children and adolescents are always weighing how much to attribute to the person's intentions and personality traits. Faced with the same behavior, different people weigh the internal and external factors differently. Consider the problem facing an adolescent with an alcoholic parent who often acts inappropriately in social situations. Father may miss an appointment for a school event after promising to attend. Or Mother may forget the important school gossip that was shared with her only the day before. The adolescent who attributes these disappointments to the disease of alcoholism will be far more likely to retain positive feelings for the parent than the one who attributes the difficulties to total self-absorption.

Hence, our attitudes greatly influence how we interpret the behavior of other family members. With a positive attitude, we are willing to blame outsiders and fate for the difficulties we observe and to applaud the family member for the successes. With a negative attitude, the attributional process is reversed. Nowhere is this phenomenon more apparent than among divorced parents who decide on a joint custody arrangement for their children. Fathers who had taken no interest in nurturing their children suddenly find themselves bathing them, cooking for them, entertaining their friends, and cuddling them. Almost invariably they attribute this change to a newfound opportunity to express their "true nature." The legal demands of the custody agreements and the social expectations of others are rarely mentioned except by the ex-wife and other detractors.

Another common example of this differential attribution process occurs when typically stoical men respond emotionally, becoming visibly upset or anxious, or perhaps crying. Their supporters within the family tend to attribute such moments of vulnerability to the "true nature" of the person and to dismiss his everyday persona as a well-learned or protective facade. Detractors within the family will search long and hard for external attributions before conceding the emotional behavior is sincere.

If a family member acts "out of character" in a way that provokes embarrassment or social disapproval, people who like and support the family member are unlikely to make a dispositional attribution. Instead, they will try to find the extenuating circumstances that made the family member act that way (Kelly, 1967). Negative personal attributions are made by those who are already unhappy with the family member. A classic example is the case of a generally well-behaved, intelligent eight-year-old boy who gets into a fist fight with the class bully. Teachers, principals, and parents are very unlikely to say the usually well-behaved lad is to blame even if it is known that he threw the first punch. Everyone will try to figure out what terrible remark the bully could have made to force our lad to act in such a manner. Of course, many siblings suffer when their parents make such differential attributions according to the role each sibling has in the family. When the "less intelligent" sibling fails a course, a dispositional attribution is made: The child is stupid and lazy. When the "more intelligent" sibling is failing, extenuating circumstances are blamed: The teacher is too unreasonable or the sibling has taken up too many other responsibilities.

Focusing on the marital dyad, Fichten (1984) attempted to determine whether the quality of the husband/wife relationship would affect the type of dispositional attributions that the partners made about each other. Specifically, she assessed whether the degree of marital happiness in couples affected the perceptions or attributions about each other's behavior during a ten-minute discussion of a problematic issue in their relationship. She found that happily married partners perceived each other as equally skilled and facilitative at communicating about the problem at hand. Among the distressed couples, spouses perceived themselves as communicating far more effectively than their mates. These perceptual biases had a direct effect on the type of attributions each couple made.

Happily married couples attributed more positive than negative traits both to themselves and their spouses as they reviewed their behavior during the discussion. Distressed partners were self-serving. They attributed more negative and fewer positive traits to their spouses than to themselves. The happy spouses attributed more control to themselves for determining the atmosphere during the argument than they attributed to the spouses. Distressed couples put far more responsibility on the spouse for determining the atmosphere during the argument. The happy spouses attributed the best problem-solving efforts of their mates to their positive personality features. They were less likely to attribute personal responsibility to the spouse for ineffective problem-solving efforts. Distressed spouses showed the reverse pattern. They were most likely to attribute ineffective problem-solving efforts to the negative personality features in their spouses. They were less likely to attribute personal responsibility to the spouse for effective problem-solving efforts. The self-serving bias and cross-blaming consistently found in distressed couples confirm that the partners' attitudes toward each other are of fundamental importance in a relationship and shape the type of attributions family members make about one another.

Just as a positive attitude toward a person inclines us to explain his or her actions in the best possible light, a positive attitude toward our family guides us toward explaining the family's actions in the best possible light. As children, our identity is so merged within the family that our perception of the family's "goodness" can affect our attributions of self-worth. When a family is conflicted, divided, or noncohesive, the child's attributions of self-worth are diminished. A child who sees dissatisfaction, disruptions, or disorganization in the family asks, "What is causing this? What is making everyone so unhappy?" All too often, children attribute the unhappiness, at least in part, to some badness or defect in themselves. In part, this internal attribution is based on the child's cognitive inability to separate personal success and failure experiences from familial success and failure experiences.

Cooper, Holman, and Braithwaite (1983) investigated the relationship between attitudes toward family and attributions of self-worth. They asked nearly 500 fifth and sixth graders to determine how cohesive their families were by choosing from a series of diagrams that portrayed families as cohesive, divided, parent coalitions, or as child-isolated (see Figure 18.1). The children who picked the cohesive diagrams to describe their families had higher levels of self-esteem than the children who described their families as divided or child-isolated. Children from two-parent cohesive families had the highest reported self-esteem but were followed very closely by the children from one-parent cohesive families.

Cooper also found that the children in one-parent families, particularly where there were feelings of closeness and support, were more likely to attribute the family's prior problems to the absent parent, which in most cases was the father. Attributing prior problems to the absent father was also reported by Parish (1981), who found that undergraduates made the most positive personality attributions about their fathers when they came from intact, happy families; remarried, happy families in which the father had died; and nonremarried, unhappy families in which the father had died. The most negative attributions came when the family configuration had a divorce—that is, from divorced, nonremarried, happy families; divorced, remarried, happy families; and divorced, nonremarried, unhappy families. When these adolescents sought to identify who had brought these prior hardships upon the family, the answer was virtually always "the father."

Interestingly, the largest number of negative attributions were made by students from the currently happy but divorced families. These students felt that the current situation was without difficulty, so the past difficulties must have been related to the absent father. In unhappy divorced families, the attributions toward the father, while clearly negative, were less fre-

FIGURE 18.1. Diagrams of Family Cohesiveness

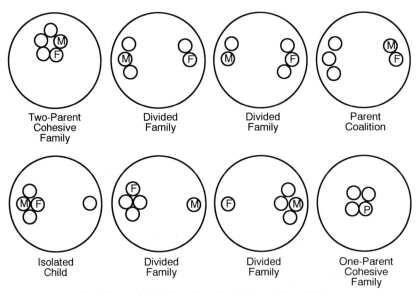

M = Mother; F = Father; P = Single Parent; O = Children

Source: Cooper, J. E., Holman, J., and Braithwaite, V. 1983. Self-esteem and family cohesion: The child's perspective and adjustment. *Journal of Marriage and the Family, 45*(1):155.

quent than those from the happy families. Adolescents in this family type found it harder to attribute all the hardships to the father because, even after he was gone, the family continued to have some distress.

COMPLEX ATTRIBUTIONS AND NARRATIVE THERAPY

Narrative therapists believe that we spontaneously make up stories about ourselves and our families to make sense of our experience. Our identity is built upon these stable, interlocked sets of explanations and attributions. We naturally create explanatory stories about how we got to be the way we are. Whereas individuals create personal stories, the family, as a whole, develops stories to explain the life history of the group.

As in all stories, personal and familial narratives have a major theme that ties all the chapters together. The constructions are endless, but popular themes include "the neglected child," "the favorite child," "the perfect family," "the loyal clan," "the overburdened workers," "the religiously committed," and "the do-it-all modern family." The themes become guides for how to interpret and record new experiences. The birth of a child in one's forties is seen as "a miracle" by the person with a religious theme and "a monumental responsibility" by the mother who is an overburdened worker. These labels then affect the type of interactions that are initiated by the parents and the mood that prevails during the interactions. Like a self-fulfilling prophecy, the labels help to shape and confirm the "reality" of our initial perceptions. This assimilation to our preferred thematic story is balanced by entertaining new perspectives.

For most of us, over time, the stories do get dramatically modified as new and interesting plots and subplots occur in our lives. The themes become more numerous and more complex as we understand more about life. Some themes that were completely absent can begin to dominate us as the result of some traumatic or wondrous event (e.g., having a child often creates new sacrifice themes).

When we stick to the simple themes of our youth (e.g., "I'm appealing to men") and refuse to add new themes or modify the old ones (e.g., "Men relate to me as though I'm their mother"), it is a sign that we are struggling and unhappy. Narrative therapists try to understand the story that the family and the individual members bring to the encounter. If it sounds as though the story is limiting opportunities for change or festering unnecessary resentments, they look for ways to help clients create new stories.

There are two main schools of narrative therapy. The first and major school is the "reauthoring" school, represented by such therapists as David Epston and Michael White (1992). The reauthoring approach asserts that it is essential to break free of oppressive stories that make people identify themselves as inferior and without agency. The most dominant confining stories in our culture identify people as identical and inseparable from their problems. So the story of "the angry child" or "the shy child" is a story in which the problem is part and parcel of the person's primary identity.

What reauthoring tries to do is to take the problem and externalize it. The angry child becomes a child who sometimes is attacked by anger; the shy child becomes a child who sometimes is haunted by shyness. Anger and shyness become external problems plaguing the child, but the child's personality and spirit remain intact under this telling of the story. Most important, the externalizing story assumes the best about the child's intentions to be well-behaved, sociable, and agreeable. It is the gravity of the problem that has befallen him or her that is causing the distress. Externalization increases hope for change and decreases self-blame.

One way of promoting externalization and helping a child or family set a goal is to ask them to rank the problem on a scale from 1 to 10. A "1" indicates that the problem is totally in charge of the client and "10" indicates that the client is totally in control of the problem. A "5" indicates that sometimes the client is in control and sometimes the problem is in charge. The first ranking concerns the current state of the problem. The second ranking concerns where the family or child would like the problem to be in the following week or month.

Once the problem is externalized, the child can be enlisted to help fight it. Therapist, parents, and child are all on the same team with the same objective. One very potent technique is to have the family role play dealing with the externalized problem. If the problem of a chaotic, disorganized family life has been reframed so that now the "family is being bulldozed by organized after-school activities," have the family act out being bulldozed. The therapist can play the part of the bulldozer and various chairs with appropriate labels can be enlisted. The visual enactment of the problem easily propels the family into a mode in which they can think of ways to stop the bulldozer and get out of its way. Thus, this type of narrative therapy has three phases: the understanding of the current story, the externalization of the problem, and the new empowerment story about how to deal with the external threat.

The second type of narrative technique is called "dialogic." Here the goal is to help the family create multiple narratives that liberate them from the stuck monologues that maintain the problem. Anderson and Goolishian (1988), who are among the leading proponents of this approach, try to listen to the perspective that the family is using to create the story—the theatrical voice they have adopted. By helping people create longer, more complex stories, they enlarge the possibilities for action.

A metaphor that I have found very useful in getting people to understand the dialogic approach is asking them to imagine life as being represented by the World Trade Center in New York City. As they know, the World Trade Center has many, many floors and, depending on the floor you go to and the elevator you ride, you get an entirely different view of the city. Life is like that. You can have multiple perspectives on any one incident. Some are so different from each other that it is hard to believe that they both can be true pictures. Some people, out of habit or choice, always take the same elevator and get out on the same floor. Every day and every year, life looks pretty much the same to them. Other people take a different elevator every few days and go to all the floors to see which views exhilarate them or make them peaceful. Solving personal problems always involves a willingness to try a new elevator and/or get out on a different floor. It is not that the old perspective has disappeared or is not true, it is simply that some new ways of looking at life are required at this point. This working metaphor is very useful in motivating people to reframe their stories and try out new themes.

Solution-Oriented Therapy and the Attribution of Personal and Familial Efficacy

In solution-oriented therapy, the focus is on the future and the power of people to come up with their own solutions to their problems. The attributional task for the therapist is to help the client find powerful internal attributes that can help them successfully reach their goals. The therapist guides the family into a method of problem solving that points the way to increasing the frequency of desired behaviors and emotional relief.

Solution-oriented therapists point out that the three most popular strategies that parents use to influence children and solve conflicts with them are notoriously unsuccessful. Those three strategies are lecturing (e.g., restating the obvious facts), setting a high moral ground (e.g., saying "If you loved me you would have called"), and self-sacrifice (e.g., "I will just wait up and make sure you don't need me to give you a ride"). What does seem to help children change, instead, is identifying times when they were behaving in a way that their parents approved of and trying to recreate the conditions that led to that behavior. It is definitely a stimulus-bound approach. Put children in the same environment that they were in when you were pleased with them, and chances are you will again find their behavior commendable. Finding that environment requires using the solution-oriented method (Metcalf, 1997).

> Parents begin by informing the child or adolescent about their feelings and why they are upset. Then they point out a time when the child acted in quite a different way and how happy the parents were with that behavior. Then, three questions are posed to the child: (1) "When was the last time you were able to do that (the desired behavior)?" (2) What did we do that helped that to happen? If there was a movie made of us that day, how would that movie be different than a movie made of us today?" (3) "What do you think we might do to make things better?"

Metcalf (1997) cites eight hints for successfully using solution-oriented therapy with children:

Step 1: Do not notice only problems—always look for the exception to the problem. If the child forgets to hand in his math homework every day, talk about how he remembers to hand in his geography maps all the time.

Step 2: Do not waste time trying to figure out "why" a child will not do something or is doing something. (This assumes the narrative is not as powerful as many believe it to be.) Rather, focus on the goal.

Step 3: Allow children to set their own goals. If a parent says, "You must get B's," reactance will force the child to think the parent is pressuring him or her for perfection and C's are just fine. Ask the child what grades he or she would like to get on the next spelling test, and a likely answer is 85 percent! Your approval of his or her goal is highly reinforcing.

Step 4: Do not think complex problems always require a complex solution.

Step 5: Try to get a child's worldview. How does he or she view the problem or conflict? Note that you cannot force people to change their perceptions. You can only offer additional perceptions that, if accepted, will complement or challenge existing values and attitudes.

Step 6: Focus on behaviors, not emotions or intentions. Telling a child that he has to love his little sister is doomed to lead to empty or negative responses. Asking what are the most fun games and activities to play with his sister leads to real behavioral choices. When a child is choosing his or her own goals, the goal should be anchored in behavior. If the child says, "I want to be smart," the parent has to figure out what behaviors the child really wants to achieve. Is the goal to work on the homework assignments until they are perfect, to get above 75 on the exam, or to be able to answer the questions that the teacher asks?

Step 7: Watch to see if changing time and place changes the child's situation. If a teenager is always sullen at the breakfast table, try having dinner together at a fast-food restaurant or taking a walk together after midnight. Is it the same old attitude or is there a more relaxed, open spirit in the new context?

Step 8: Do what works. Stop what does not.

Chapter 10, "Family Resiliency and Poverty" discusses solution-oriented approaches in more detail.

HENRY (shop owner, age 45)

Out of all the concepts we've studied so far, this one is the best at explaining the glitches my family has been plagued with ever since I can remember. Consistently, attributions have been made that, correct or incorrect, have altered the course of our family's life path. The most obvious attribution revolves around explaining the motives and behavior of my father. When my father "disappeared" with his partner's wife thirty-five years ago, my mother attributed his leaving to the conniving, unscrupulous morals of his lover and the fact that he was a "mean and crazy" man. My two older brothers and myself kept waiting for our father to explain himself. He never did. Instead, when we pushed him to discuss it, he said he could not explain it, that he could not tell us anything about the life circumstances of his lover, and that maybe if he had woken up a bit later or a bit earlier that day he would never have left. My brothers were twelve and fifteen years old at the time and although I was only ten, I was quite mature. The three of us took his lack of noble self-attributions as a sign that there were none. We felt that our mother must be correct. Our father was an irrational person who was responsible for leaving us, emotionally and financially, at a time when we needed family stability the most. We were left with the job of being substitute husbands for my mother. None of us was very good at it. We saw very little of my father after that. He would send us money for Christmas each year, but instead of attributing this gift to a desire to befriend us, we were always told by "the expert" (my mother) that he was just trying to appease his guilty conscience and it had nothing at all to do with pleasing us. I think we all believed Mom.

I got married when I was twenty-four and by age twenty-eight had two little girls. I opened a small plumbing supply store with some financial backing from my in-laws and mother. By age thirty-eight, after fourteen years of marriage, I got a divorce. The divorce was preceded by a lengthy custody battle which I lost (girls need their mother, I was told). My relationship with my girls is strained now, and I find it difficult to be the type of father I want to be. In therapy, I've learned that a lot of my avoidance of the girls is due to deep-seated insecurities and fears of rejection. I lie awake nights wondering if my wife is attributing our divorce to our mutual problems of incompatibility or to the fact that I am a "mean and lazy" man like my father. Since my divorce, I have sought out my father and have had a lot of discussions with him about why he did leave. He now explains his behaviors in terms of the pain and unhappiness he felt in the marriage. He says he always felt it would affect our masculinity adversely if he told us boys how unhappy he was in the marriage and how content he was with the new relationship. I go home from these discussions with him and my head reels. A six-pack later I'm still dealing with the anger I have toward him for not explaining his behavior to us at the time and for me not being able to explain myself to the girls. Not that his attribution would be right and my mother's wrong or my wife's attributions wrong and mine right. It just seems to me that children need to be given all the possible explanations so they can hang on to whichever ones they need. The word "attribution" may be new to me but I've lived with its consequences all my life.

SELF-EXPLORATION: ATTRIBUTION

1. For each person in your family, think of a specific behavior that bothers or irks you. Using the Attribution Grid (see Figure 18.2), write a brief description of each problem under each person's name.

2. From the following list of reasons,* record those that could explain why each person behaved the way or he or she did:
   This family member (_____) did (_____) because:

   a. He or she is a selfish person.
   b. He or she thinks it would be in my best interest.
   c. It's a pleasurable thing to do.
   d. Of the physical condition he or she is in.
   e. Some friends pressured him or her to do it.
   f. He or she doesn't care for me.
   g. Of the mood or mental state he or she is in.
   h. That's the kind of person he or she is.
   i. He or she believes it is the right thing to do.
   j. Of some unusual situation that has occurred.
   k. He or she is dumb and unthinking.
   l. He or she isn't concerned enough to be aware of what he or she is doing.
   m. It is very important in making him or her happy.
   n. It helps him or her cope with things better.
   o. It is just the accepted way of doing things for most people today.

3. In each of the following three attribution categories (negative, positive, environmental/circumstantial) there are five items that reflect that particular attribution. Each person on your grid should receive a score of 0 to 5 in each attribution category, depending on the number of reasons you checked in that category that could explain their behavior. For example, if you check b and j, that person would receive a score of 2 in the "positive" attribution category:

   • Category I—Negative personal attributions: a, f, i, l, m
   • Category II—Positive personal attributions: b, c, j, n, o
   • Category III—Environmental or circumstantial attributions: d, e, g, k, p

---

Source: Adapted in part from Passer, M. W., Kelley, H. H., and Michela, J. L. 1978. Multidimensional scaling of the causes for negative interpersonal behavior. *Journal of Personality and Social Psychology,* 36:961-962.

4. Analyze your attributions:

   a. Do you tend to use one type of attribution or does that attribution vary by person and situation?

   b. Can you imagine what attributions each person would use to describe his or her own behavior? Is it similar to or different from yours?

   c. Can you imagine in what ways your interactions with each person would change if the attributions changed but the behavior remained the same?

   d. How sure are you that your attributions are correct in each case? Have you ever tried to check them?

5. Now try to think of two or three behaviors that you have engaged in recently thht have bothered your family. How do you explain your own behavior? Was it intentional? Accidental? Were there extenuating circumstances? Did anyone in the family have a different explanation for your behavior?

FIGURE 18.2. Attribution Grid

	Person 1	Person 2	Person 3	Person 4
Name				
Problem				
Relevant attributions				
Positive personal attribution score				
Negative personal attribution score				
Environmental or circumstantial attribution score				

Chapter 19

Equity Theory

One hand washeth the other.

Old Greek saying

An eye for an eye, a tooth for a tooth

Exodus 21:24

Sociologists, anthropologists, and psychologists agree that some form of family life is necessary if human beings are to keep their sense of purpose and meaning in life. Every known society has valued the security that comes from the family's commitment to meeting the individual's physical and psychological needs. Despite its rewards, however, the costs of family life are high. Often family members must give up the freedom of pursuing individual goals. Equally often, family pressures force individuals into activities they find unattractive—even repugnant—that are valued by others. Fortunately, individual goals and family goals often coincide. When this occurs, the more one is rewarded, the more the family is rewarded. For example, when one spouse gets a sought-after salary raise the additional funds can be spent on objects and trips that are presumably a source of pleasure for everyone in the family. Obviously, activities that further the group's goals while furthering individual goals contribute to family cohesion.

THE THEORY OF FAMILY EQUITY

Not all individual goals allow the wealth to be shared, however. If one person wants to get a pilot's license, the more money and time spent pursuing this goal, the less time (and perhaps money) there is for everyone else. Or if one spouse chooses to spend a lot of free time working on the computer, less free time is available for couple activities. Activities perceived as gains for one individual but losses for the others spur resentment and conflict.

The basic premise of equity theory is that families function best when each member feels that the rewards of family membership equal or outweigh the costs (Nye, 1976; 1980). Each cultural subgroup develops its own norms about appropriate costs and appropriate rewards. In general, though, the broad categories of rewards that families strive for include social approval, security, money, confirmation of beliefs and values, and achievement of individual family goals. The specific rewards available to any one person vary endlessly. Of course, some rewards are more meaningful than others, and the task of creating equivalent reinforcement exchanges is most often quite subjective. Yet it is precisely this state of equity that each dyad tries to achieve.

When everyone in a family feels equal to the others (giving and receiving in comparatively equal amounts), the members are going to enjoy being around one another. Since each has the same amount to offer the others, the threat of rejection is greatly reduced. In families as elsewhere, equals rarely attack one another. Some family theorists, such as Boszormenyi-Nagy and Spark (1973) believe that parents and children are not capable of achieving equity in the formative years of the family life cycle. Others such as Dreikurs and Soltz (1967) believe that parent/child equity is not only possible but may be the most positive possible form of family functioning (see Chapter 14).

To begin our discussion of equity, let us focus on the husband/wife relationship. Most modern marriages are founded on explicit equity principles. Each partner is aware of what he or she is giving to the relationship and what he or she is getting out of it. Inequitable marriages breed marital instability. Osmond and Martin (1978) found that 72 percent of couples in egalitarian marriages remain married compared with 27 percent of those in which one spouse had significantly more power than the other.

An important initial dimension of equity between couples is physical attractiveness. The values of the dating "marketplace" are such that everyone wants a potential mate to be the most attractive person possible. In actual practice, however, lasting relationships are most likely to form between partners whose attractiveness (or perceived attractiveness) is approximately equal (Walster and Walster, 1969; Berscheid and Walster, 1978). When attractiveness is not equal, the less attractive partner usually becomes the "giver" in the partnership in an effort to balance out the mate's superior good looks. A large majority of these marriages end in divorce, as the more attractive partner seeks out others with more resources or the less attractive partner wearies of being exploited (Kelley, 1979).

EQUITY AND FAMILY ROLES

If you want to be equal with me, you get your own Rolls-Royce, your own house and your own million dollars.

Muhammad Ali

I married beneath me. All women do.

Nancy Astor

The family has many group-specific needs. Some are psychological, some are social, and some are physical. Someone who has the resources to supply those needs becomes a valued family member. Developing equitable roles to satisfy these needs is a major goal of all families; each marital partner must contribute in order to retain a position of importance. The fulfillment of these goals is the focus of Chapter 15. In terms of equity, however, the provider role, the child-care role, the housekeeper role, the sexual role, or the therapeutic role can have enormous impact on the family system.

Equality and the Provider Role

Providing economic support is probably the most important family role since it allows the family to satisfy its most basic needs: food, shelter, and security. Contributing to the provider role gives a man or woman considerable power in the family politic; conversely, inability to contribute to this role invariably whittles down one's authority and bargaining power. Studies done during the Great Depression of the 1930s showed that in nearly a quarter of the families, when the husband lost his job, he began to lose his authority (Komarovsky, 1940). More recent studies concur that men who become unemployed soon lose power in the family (Cavan, 1973).

Conversely, women who have a source of income independent of their husbands have more power than those who do not. Not surprisingly, women whose husbands have high earnings gain less power from working than women whose husbands have low or moderate earnings (Hoffman and Nye, 1974). When a woman from a low-income family goes to work, her earnings are very important to the family, and her power is proportionately enhanced. Women from wealthier families who work for "pin money" or "personal satisfaction" are usually adding proportionately less to the total financial resources of the family; hence their power base is not greatly enhanced. In those families where both spouses are earning high incomes, the wife seems to possess a power base equal to her husband's.

Blumstein and Schwartz (1983) selected a random sample of seventy-two married couples from Seattle, San Francisco, and New York to explore the dynamics of influence and the negotiation of control between partners. A major finding of their study was that money does indeed help establish the balance of power in marital relationships. For example, a third of the husbands wielded more power in the home if the husband's income exceeded the wife's by more than $8,000. Only 15 percent of the husbands continued to wield the greater power if the wife's income exceeded theirs by more than $8,000. Thus, as wives earned more they felt freer to spend money and less accountable for what they spent.

Blumstein and Schwartz's (1983) study also underscores that money is far from the only determinant of family power. Even when the husband's income greatly exceeded the wife's, 66 percent of the couples had equitable or female-dominated relationships. Another important finding was that partners who felt they had equal control over how their money was spent had a more tranquil relationship. Sometimes feelings of equality were achieved by couples deciding jointly on items before purchasing them. At other times, it was agreed that each spouse would be individually responsible for personal purchases. Either way, so long as both partners felt they had control over the financial arrangement, frustrations were low.

PAUL (journalist, age 36)

Mary and I have been married for several years. We are the archetypal young, upwardly mobile, 1960s-generation couple. We moved to Washington five years ago and quickly adapted to the world of professional achievement and material success.

Before coming to Washington, Mary and I were both teachers in a midsized southern city. We brought home nearly identical paychecks, had nearly identical ideals and ambitions, and shared nearly identical problems and challenges at work. Our relationship was one of exceptional mutual support and equality.

When we came to Washington and began new careers—Mary in the computer field, I in journalism—we began to develop diverging values, ambitions, and friends. Our work experiences became different, and—most important—our relationship began to change.

In the course of our first four years here, it was clear that my professional responsibilities were greater than Mary's. I was earning considerably more money than she, and my work was perceived by relatives and friends as more "prestigious."

Largely unconsciously, I began to assert myself as the dominant partner in our relationship—taking the principal role in planning our weekend activities, deciding what we would have for dinner, insisting on driving the car (all minor things, but somehow telling). On a more negative note, my dominant status manifested itself in an increasingly judgmental, critical attitude toward Mary—a subtle message that she should defer to me and "keep in her place."

(continued)

(continued)

Mary accepted all this like a good soldier and martyr—for the good of our marriage. She bore the criticism quietly, endured the temper tantrums, and swallowed her own ego and pride.

Then, about a year ago, Mary made a quantum advance in her own career. All of a sudden, she was catapulted to a position of great responsibility, pressure, and "prestige." The demands on her were enormous.

Well, this had an immediate impact on the balance of power in our marriage. She found my ascendancy increasingly grating, annoying, and—finally—unacceptable. A crisis point was reached where she told me, in no uncertain terms, "Enough!"

She told me that my attitudes were making her miserable and that she was unwilling to go on playing poodle to my top dog. Clearly, her new job responsibilities were the catalyst for this "rebellion." She was now performing work that was equal to mine in prestige, salary, and professional demandingness—and she wanted that act reflected in our relationship.

We had several bumpy weeks and a series of heart-to-heart talks. But gradually the adjustment was made. I realized that my behavior had become increasingly thoughtless and inconsiderate, and that she was entitled to a restored position of equality in our marriage. (As I saw it, she was entitled to this equality not because of her new job, but for reasons of basic human dignity and equality. Nonetheless, as I have said, the job promotion was a catalyst for her demands and for my coming back to my senses.)

Ironically, in recent months the balance has actually shifted against me in the marriage. Because Mary's job demands so much travel and overtime, I have found myself doing nearly all the chores around the house. Moreover, I am no longer the central focus of Mary's attention—she seems to have bigger fish to fry at work (she is becoming infatuated with her success and ambition). This, of course, is creating new stresses in our marriage.

All in all, our relationship has evolved back to a status of rough equality. It is much healthier than before—and, for Mary, a lot kinder to her ego and self-esteem.

Child Care, Housekeeping, and Kinskeeping

> *I do not refer to myself as a housewife for the reason that I did not marry a house.*
>
> Wilma Scott Heide

Women have traditionally been responsible for the triad of child care, kinskeeper, and housekeeper roles. As more and more women became involved with work outside the home, it was expected that their homebound roles would be lessened or more equitably shared with their husbands. By and large, this shift has not occurred. Despite increasing involvement in the working world, women have retained their primary involvement with traditionally female jobs. Consider that while over 55 percent of married couples are dual earners, only one half of these dual earners are employed all year, full-time (roughly 25 percent) (U.S. Bureau of the Census, 1998). Among married women, most continue their traditional priorities of fitting their employment schedules to their family responsibilities. Men continue doing the opposite by fitting their family responsibilities to their employment schedules. Efforts by the government to support equal involvement at home, as has been done in Sweden by granting maternity leave to both men and women and providing flextime for both parents, have met with dubious success, since women continue to be more caught up in family matters (Haas, 1980).

Even when both spouses work full-time, the overwhelming bulk of the housework continues to be done by women. Blumstein and Schwartz (1983) found that while 59 percent of full-time working women spent more than eleven hours a week on housework, only 22 percent of their husbands spent more than eleven hours a week on housework. Eighteen percent of the women spent more than twenty hours per week while only 4 percent of the men spent this much time.

Sexual Roles

Blumstein and Schwartz (1983) found that in the first two years of marriage, 45 percent of couples have sex three times a week or more. The longer the marriage, the less frequent were sexual relations, so that for couples married two to ten years, only 27 percent were having sex three times a week or more, and for couples married more than ten years, only 18 percent maintained that frequency. Regardless of the frequency, when each partner experienced equality by feeling free to both initiate and refuse sexual activity, the couple's sexual activity was more frequent and more satisfying.

When initiation/refusal was unequal, the partner who was more active in refusing sex tended to be the more powerful partner in the marriage. Blumstein and Schwartz (1983:221) hypothesize that women refuse sex more often than men because in this way they can exercise their power:

> We believe that women's right to refuse sex has evolved hand in hand with the conventional belief that women have a weaker sex drive. It may be that it has been in their best interest to suppress sexual desire in order to become less dependent on sex and, therefore, more powerful. Perhaps, then, the idea that women have fewer needs has evolved as a counterbalance to their weaker position in their relationships.

Once both partners agree to have sexual relations, the power equation affects the type of relations that occur. Blumstein and Schwartz (1983: 229) found that "the less power the wife had in the marriage, the more likely that the couple's intercourse would be performed in the missionary position." Of course, in many of the couples, women sometimes assumed the "male" position. "This happened more in couples where the man did not completely dominate the relationship and where the partners shared power more equally."

Even among unmarried couples, the partners' perceptions of how equitable a relationship is will affect their willingness to enter into a sexual relationship. Walster, Walster, and Berscheid (1978) found that couples in equitable relationships had the most frequent sexual relationships, including the most sexual intercourse. Partners who were greatly underbenefitted (gave more than they got) or overbenefitted (got more than they gave) tended to stop before "going all the way."

Among married couples, an equitable relationship is one of the strongest deterrents to extramarital affairs. Discussing data collected from a large sample of *Psychology Today* readers, Hatfield and Traupmann (1981:177) found that:

> Both overbenefitted and equitably treated men and women were very reluctant to experiment with extramarital sex (on the average, they waited 12-15 years before chancing an extramarital involvement with someone else). Deprived men and women experimented far earlier —only 9-11 years after marriage. Overbenefitted and equitably treated men and women had the fewest marital encounters (0-1); the deprived had the most extramarital liaisons (1-3). Again, it would seem that equitable relations are more likely to be stable than inequitable ones since both partners are motivated to be faithful.

A number of studies have shown that young dating and married couples are deeply concerned about the fairness or unfairness in their relationship (Traupman, Hatfield, and Wexler, 1982). One study (Hatfield et al., 1982) even found that differences in marital contentment could be predicted among newlyweds on the basis of the perceived equity of their relationship.

Yet, the one empirical study done on older women (ages fifty to eighty-two) found almost no differences in contentment between the overbenefitted, underbenefitted, and equitably treated. Because of the design of this study, it is unclear whether these older women have different attitudes about equality than today's younger women—or whether wives become less concerned about issues of fairness after many years of marriage (Traupman and Hatfield, 1983).

LANYA (part-time teacher, age 42)

While I was growing up, there was the traditional inequality within tasks, except in my family it was not tolerated well. My father was a veterinarian and by all accounts we should have grown up in a secure economic environment. But because my father has recurrent episodes of depression and has very low self-esteem, he never tried to practice his profession. Instead he worked for the government in the Agriculture department. He ordered veterinarian supplies. While it was a steady income, it was never enough for us as a family (there were five kids), and so my mother had to work part-time jobs all the time. Even though my mom virtually always worked five to six hours a day, all of the other tasks became her responsibility. She cooked, cleaned, washed, made our parties, and planned our family outings. Until I was twelve, she didn't even own a clothes washer but took all our clothes to the laundromat on Saturday. She used to work until she dropped with fatigue. I remember well when I was eight that she decided to go to college two nights a week to hopefully be able to get a better job. She'd take all her class notes on index cards and then Scotch-tape them on all the kitchen cabinets so she could study while she cooked. This went on for eight years! Whenever there was an important issue to be decided in the family, the power was with my mom. We might discuss it with Dad, but everyone knew that what Mom said went. I'm sure that my father's inability to share with my mother the household and child-rearing tasks made him feel even more depressed and inadequate than his aborted career made him feel. Actually, the power balance was so skewed that he was treated like one of the kids. My mom would always say, "I have six sponges wringing me dry." In a way she was right, but in a more important way I think she helped put my father out of the picture. The few times I thought of asking my father for help, he always came through. In fact, one of my most cherished memories is when I was in ninth grade and was going to a big dance. My cousin had given me a beautiful dress she had outgrown, but it needed a hem. My mom said she didn't have time to hem it so I asked my dad. He pinned it and sewed it for me. I was so proud of how it came out I was bursting. My mom made a few derogatory comments about it being uneven and the stitches showing through. I don't think she liked the fact that he had done "her" job. I think she was jealous in a way too. In retrospect, the inequality between my parents was the basis for nearly all the strain and tension between them.

I knew by age ten that my marriage was going to be different than my mother's. I wanted a fifty-fifty partner. I've succeeded—in a sense. My husband and I married in 1980. We were both teachers but while I loved it, he was bored. After five years, he decided to go to medical school. On his first day of school our daughter, Rose, was born. For the past seven years I've worked full-time or part-time. Still, I expect Don (my husband) to cook, wash vacuum, and do things with the two kids. He has been very busy these past years and sometimes I resent that I'm being forced into my mother's role. But

(continued)

> *(continued)*
>
> then I'll start leaving lists of what he needs to do and when he has time he does it. This way he feels like he's an adult member of the family with equal power. We both know that if he went into private practice, he'd shortchange the family for the next ten years, so he isn't going to do that. In fact, we're both looking forward to sharing more; Don wants to plan the next vacation and I'm thinking of taking a job that requires occasional overnight travel. I guess I feel like the mother who, as her daughter took off on the space shuttle, said, "Thank you, Gloria Steinem."

Therapeutic Roles

One of the most important therapeutic roles any family member can provide for another is to unconditionally accept him or her as a valuable individual despite invariable and unavoidable weaknesses of character and defects in achievement. Indeed, one of the ideals in most modern Western marriages is for each spouse to openly support and express affection for the other.

When both spouses are affectionate and supportive, an invisible bond is created that allows each individual to maintain feelings of self-worth and confidence. But what happens in an inequitable relationship when one spouse is uncaring, critical, or callous? It can be argued that even here, if one spouse is very open in positive love feelings for the other, both spouses should benefit—the giver because he or she feels the freedom to be intimate, the receiver because love disclosures have great reinforcing value and make one feel accepted and important. Precisely because affective disclosures are so important, however, they are viewed as positive only in equitable circumstances. If two romantics are whispering sweet nothings to each other, every day of life is grand. If only one partner verbalizes such involvement, feelings of deprivation or suffocation may sprout like wild mushrooms (Davidson, Balswick, and Halverson, 1983).

DEVELOPING AN EQUITY PATTERN

Each couple must develop a formula that weighs each of these roles and then distributes them evenly. Apparently, families use four major styles of distribution. First, some families choose to achieve equity within each of the goals; that is, each spouse is expected to provide half the child care, housekeeping, money, and so on. If an inequality exists within any one area, these partners get upset.

Second, the equity formula can be based on each spouse's fulfilling those roles that are personally easiest or most enjoyable. For example, the greater contribution of men to the provider role is often viewed as equitable because of the greater contribution women make to housekeeping and child care. In this way equity can be achieved within rigid definitions of role responsibilities.

Third, families may view equity as a process—a long-term goal achieved by different kinds of contributions at different points in the family life cycle. Boszormenyi-Nagy and Spark (1973) consider this type of equity most important for healthy families.

Fourth, the equity of roles may also be calculated entirely in terms of the total amount of time spent satisfying family needs. Whether those hours were spent in paid or unpaid work is not important here. Recent studies, using time as the sole measure of equity, found that when the wife was employed full-time or part-time, husbands and wives had almost equal work days (ten-hour work days). Time equity may indeed be the most valued type of equity for families in the new millenium. In the 1970s, the working woman's day was nearly two hours longer than her husband's. Currently, when the wife is not employed, her work day averages nearly two hours less than the husband's work day (Fox and Nickols, 1983).

Regardless of the distribution system, both partners have certain expectations about what resources and rewards their spouses should give them. Those whose spouses exceed their expectations, fulfilling or helping to fulfill more of their needs than they expected, are very content. By contrast, spouses who are always disappointing their mates, never meeting their expectations, and always leaving them needy will have partners who are very unhappy with their marriage. When both partners feel that they are giving more to the marriage than they are receiving, conflict is inevitable.

Equity theory predicts that "when individuals find themselves participating in inequitable relationships, they will become distressed. The more inequitable the relationship, the more distress individuals will feel" (Walster, Walster, and Berscheid, 1978:6). Equity theory then suggests that when someone in a family receives many more rewards or many less rewards than the other family members, that someone will feel distressed.

When people discover that they are in an inequitable relationship, they try to reduce their distress by restoring equity. The more inequitable the relationship, the more distress exists and the greater the motivation to restore equity. When an inequality exists between the spouses, the over-benefitted person will feel guilty (I don't deserve all this), and the under-benefitted person will feel angry (I'm not appreciated at all. What am I doing it for?). When a spouse is getting many rewards from a relationship (financial support, love, companionship) and contributing very little, he or she is unhappy and discontented. Also, those who perceive themselves as getting no rewards from their partner but as giving a lot to the relationship are very unhappy. Happiness is maximized only when people feel that they are giving and receiving with equal costs and equal benefits (Walster, Walster, and Berscheid, 1978).

Thus, when one partner brings a bevy of socioeconomic resources into the marriage such as a high income, high educational achievement, and occupational prestige, the "lesser" spouse is confronted with the baffling task of executing enough of the other family roles with sufficient competence to gain parity. If the "lesser" spouse fails, which is easy to do because of the enormous value placed on the provider role by most couples, the marriage is going to be strained.

When an inequality persists for a very long time and all efforts to restore equality have failed, couples begin to think about abandoning the relationship. For the dating couple, this is a difficult but fathomable task in most cases. For married couples, breaking up is costly in both emotional and financial terms. Instead of physically abandoning the relationship, many married couples withdraw psychologically from the situation. The withdrawal can be exhibited in many forms. They may become blindly ambitious in their careers, they may become narcissistically involved with sports and their physical well-being, they may become superparents, or they may develop an all-consuming hobby. Such withdrawal is not necessarily bad. The world is very complex, and so is the road each marriage travels through an uncharted wilderness.

Most of us have observed marriages that are not at all equitable but appear not only viable but happy. How can this be? First, many people view marriage as a nonvoluntary relationship; once committed to the venture, such people accept impositions on their rights as unavoidable burdens they "have to" cope with. Second, many people expect marriage to be an inequitable relationship. For example, in much of the Orient and the Arab world, women and men expect that the man will reap more rewards and incur fewer costs in the marriage. Third, the irretrievable investments discussed in Chapter 3 apply here as well; individuals invest so much time, energy, and emotion in a marriage partner that even when the relationship becomes unsatisfying there is enormous hesitancy to admit to unhappiness or feelings of betrayal. The less equitably treated partner begins to rationalize: Because he or she has invested so much in the relationship, it must be a valuable and precious union that will soon prove its worthiness once again.

This triad of total commitment, low expectations, and high investment in the marital partner often allows spouses to endure for years in an inequitable marriage. Outsiders usually feel that the less equitably treated partner is being victimized. Indeed, many feminists have for years tried to explain how millions of American women were buying into this triad without realizing it was not in their best interests.

Since equity is so important in maintaining family stability, it comes as no surprise that stepfamilies need to resolve a number of inherent difficulties before they feel like a "real" family (Nelson and Nelson, 1982). Consider the plight of stepparents. As second spouses enter stepfamilies, there is virtually always an explicit contract that children from the mate's first marriage will join them for certain designated times. When the children arrive, they are usually suspicious and hostile; the stepparent tries very hard to give them lots of attention, friendliness, warmth, and caring. The overcompensating stepparent tends to receive small rewards for these efforts. Not only are the stepchildren unresponsive, but the stepparent's own children often feel jealous and neglected. Such a state of inequity may exist for quite a long time, creating at times an intolerable level of stress for the newly created family unit.

Boszormenyi-Nagy's Relational System

> Duty is a pleasure which we try to make ourselves believe is a hardship.
>
>   Elbert Hubbard, *The Roycroft Dictionary*

Boszormenyi-Nagy and Spark (1973) highlight the importance of equity in family relationships by stressing the importance of concepts such as merit, entitlements, obligations, and ledgers. The relationship between Boszormenyi-Nagy's relational system and equity theory is illustrated by his premise that "it is a universal human tendency to expect fair returns for one's contributions and to owe fair return for benefits received from others" (p. 111). According to this researcher, each individual in the family needs to live up to the family's expectations of him or her. When one is successful in achieving these expectations, one gains "merit"; when one ignores, refuses, or fails to fulfill the expectations set forth, one falls into "debt."

Relational theory stresses creating equity with the most far-reaching existential and ethical relationship exchanges. The most meaningful rewards for which equity must be achieved are trust, loyalty, sacrifice, fairness, dependability, and commitment. Families function best when equity exists in relation to these quintessential rewards. Here, the most significant and rewarding elements of family life are not contained in the mere fulfillment of the family roles but in the spirit and sense of obligation with which these roles are executed.

Obligations are by far the chief regulator for maintaining equity. A husband who takes his wife out to a favorite restaurant for a long-awaited night on the town might be repaid the next day when the wife finally arranges a couples weekend with an old college buddy of her husband's. When obligations are not immediately repaid—and most often they are not—the owed family member has a sense of entitlement ("I am entitled to something. I deserve something from you"). So long as everyone acknowledges the claim, the ledger can stay lopsided for many years.

Balancing the parent/child ledger is considered to be fundamental, and it often does take a lifetime to get straight. The difficulty involved in balancing the parent/child ledger is found in the fact that parents are ethically and emotionally obligated to provide for their children. Parents have caused the child's existence; until the child is self-sufficient, they must be nurturative. But the parameters for judging when one has fulfilled parental obligations are not codified or apparent for many couples. What is enough time? Enough support?

Within certain cultural restraints, each family decides for itself what resources the parents will provide and for how long. The children are also in a quandary over exactly what each parent is entitled to and how long they have to repay the debt. Sometimes parental devotion becomes so overwhelming that a child feels incapable of ever repaying the parent. The child feels forever in the parents' debt. Children need to know the exchange rules. They need to know when repayment of obligations is expected and what the "coin of the realm" will be.

Previous societies required parents to physically and psychologically protect the children only during their most vulnerable stages of development. In return, the child was permanently indebted to respect and obey the parent. Today's variable lifestyles require each family to come to grips with its own unique accounting methods. Many children can never find a way to repay their parents directly. They repay by giving to their own children in as unilateral a way as they had been given to. Others find that as their parents age, they are able to pay them back. Sometimes the debt toward one's parents seems overwhelming, and the anxiety and discomfort of the child steers him or her into pathological forms of loyalty, such as being unable to physically separate or emotionally mature. In other cases, the overwhelming nature of the debt causes the child to withdraw and cut off the relationship.

Sometimes, an individual who has been badly hurt or severely deprived by a parent grows up feeling that someone else has to "pay for" or "make up for" these childhood injuries or lacks. Rarely is one able to settle the slate with the parent directly. Instead, a "revolving slate" begins. The adult tries to achieve balance by making an innocent third party, usually a child, "pay."

The classic example of this occurs in the area of child abuse when children who were abused by their parents settle the score by abusing their own children.

Because virtually all children are less powerful than their parents and receive some care and nurturing from them, obligations to parents are nearly universal. Parental neglect, abuse, and scorn will rarely eradicate a child's loyalty. In those unfortunate cases in which children develop a genuinely low regard for a parent, they feel torn. The mandate to be loyal to one's parent is the most basic way of repaying the parents. But how difficult it is to be loyal to someone who does not win our respect and admiration—let alone someone who has abused our bodies or our trust. The analysis of children who have been forced to testify against a parent who has hurt them or another family member reveals how deeply disturbing it is to turn against a parent. For example, a client who testified against her father as a child because she had seen him murder her mother said, "I hope he's not angry with me. Each night I pray that he will forgive me. I always hated him and thought he was useless and yet not a day goes by when I don't ask for his forgiveness."

The Relationship Between Equity and Power

> *One thing in which the sexes are equal is in thinking that they're not.*
>
> Franklin P. Jones

Many consider the antithesis of equity-based relationships to be power-based relationships. With power-based relationships, behavior is not motivated by attempts to maintain a fair relationship but by attempts to influence or change the behavior of another person in accordance with one's own desires. Within the family structure, the assertion of power is inevitable as each member tries to get others to comply with his or her requests. All of us can probably recall the power successfully exerted by one of our parents to make the family go to a museum or church or a relative's house. Why was that person successful in making everyone comply? The answer is threefold, involving equity (or rather, lack of it), social sanction, and competence.

First, the powerful family member has abilities, possessions, or attributes that make it possible to reward or punish the others. Power is found when equity has not been achieved. When one spouse is capable of providing satisfaction to a disproportionate amount of the family's needs, that spouse wields a lot of power. The lesser spouse concedes and acquiesces on disputed decisions because he or she feels like a "lesser" or "unequal" member. If your mother had a lot of power in the family, refusing to go to a museum or church might mean she could refuse to give you the money for a new CD you had been hoping for. It might mean your brother would not be allowed to go to the skating rink, and your father might have no one to talk to for the rest of the day.

Second, the powerful family member exerts power most successfully when the norms of the social group sanction that authority. In groups in which the father is in a patriarchal role and is expected to make decisions on how to discipline and bring up children, his power is high in that domain. In groups in which the mother is in a matriarchal role, her power is high.

Third, power is also related to competence. If everyone agrees that one person in the family is particularly adept at a specific role, that person will wield a lot of power in executing that role. These three attributes usually make the use of power legitimate and accepted by the rest of the family.

DISTRIBUTION OF POWER
BETWEEN MARITAL PARTNERS

Researchers have assessed the degree of control one partner has over the other by directly asking questions such as, "If your husband (wife) wants you to do something that you don't want to do, how do you respond if it requires a large amount of time and effort on your part?" Suppose a wife says, "I never do it." Her husband has little control over her. If she says she occasionally or usually does it, her spouse has moderate control over her. But if she answers, "I always do it," her husband has a great deal of control over her (Stuart, 1980; Bahr, 1982). The critical factor affecting the marital relationship need not be the amount of control one spouse has over another, however. It might be the frequency with which control is exercised or the specific areas the spouse attempts to control.

It seems likely that family members are most concerned about controlling the general direction of their lives. Those who feel free to shape the "big picture" may be willing to have others influence the details. This theory implies two distinct types of decision making within families. First, there are lifestyle decisions that affect income level, where the family will live, and the amount of leisure time available. Important decisions are not made often, but they "orchestrate" a large portion of family life. Therefore, sharing in the making of these lifestyle decisions is critical for an equitable relationship between couples.

The second type of decision encompasses repetitive, time-consuming decisions that are not critical but must be made for the day-to-day efficiency of the family system—when to visit relatives, what to cook for dinner, what shoes to buy, or which auto repair shop to use are typical second-level decisions. Even these secondary decisions vary in significance between and within families. Power may reside in the number of decisions made, but to assume that this is so may be misleading.

POWER ALLOCATION BETWEEN PARENTS AND CHILDREN

Nearly all currently available studies have focused on investigating power allocation in the couple—husband and wife. Although virtually all marriage partners studied were parents, their children were not generally considered instrumental in determining which parent wielded power. Nor were the children considered sources of power in themselves. The few studies in which children have been questioned generally report egalitarian-democratic decision-making patterns within the family. Both children and parents feel offspring have some power in the family politic (Lips, 1981).

However, neither parents' nor children's perceptions of family power necessarily correspond to reality. Olson and Rabunsky (1972) used both subjective and objective measurements to assess decision making. They found that none of the self-report measures adequately predicted who actually made decisions in real life. Clinicians need to assess the objective power of each family member as well as subjective feelings of powerfulness.

Interesting generational and developmental differences are found in how the family "fairly" distributes its resources. With adults, it appears that the proportional contribution rule runs strong. Wagstaff (1997), using a written scenario paradigm, found that when judging adult twins who worked on a job together, one industriously and the other in a very lackadaisical manner, most parents thought the monetary rewards of the job should be shared according to the relative contribution of each adult or child. If the two different-tempered twins were six years old, however, and their parents had given them twenty comic books, most adults thought they should share in the rewards equally. Children are not judged on the basis of their contributions but more on their status as children. Of course, most good, obedient siblings can tell you that they have long ago figured out this parental quirk and feel it is very unjust that their parents do not differentially reward them in a logical manner! Yet, it is precisely in those families where children are differentially rewarded based on their assets (e.g., intelligence, beauty, athletic prowess, personality), that sibling rivalries are probably the most intense and long lasting.

SELF-EXPLORATION: EQUITY

1. "Distribution of Power" is a list of the eight most common roles in the family: provider, caretaker, child socialization, kinskeeper, recreation

JULIE (marketing specialist, age 35)

My parents have a real traditional marriage; my mom does all the housework and my father has always brought home the paycheck. What is sad to me is that my dad didn't really have anything to do with our development. He got into making money, and when he could do that, he decided to make more money. His life didn't intersect with ours at all, except when we were in need of real discipline. My mother waits on my dad hand and foot. In fact, when I had the baby and she spent two weeks with me, she fretted over how he could survive. Fourteen dinners were frozen and a friend came by to straighten up and do the laundry! One of my strongest images of my father is that on a Saturday or Sunday he would supervise our tasks. I looked at my mother as this poor creature who always had to do the boring, dirty, nitty-gritty jobs while dad did the fun projects, such as finishing the basement.

My dad has a lot of power in the family. Once when I was nine or ten, we were acting up at the dinner table and my dad got furious and shouted for us to "shut up." My mom came to our rescue and said we were only having a little fun. My father got real angry then, shifted his attention to my mom, and screamed, "You shut up, too." I was horrified and ran from the table. My mom sat like a bad girl getting her just punishment and I realized then what it really means to have power in a marriage.

When Dad had his heart attack, I rushed to the hospital. I felt as though Len and I were two Amazons who were to stand guard over this helpless little person, my mother. I took her to the coffee shop and I was shocked to hear her tell me that my father might die and that she would have to go back to work and settle all the finances. I was amazed by the strength she showed and felt even sadder that she had to play the sweet southern belle all her life. Now I realize I should not feel too sorry since my mother thrived on the martyr role. I can remember my dad offering to get a maid, but she adamantly refused. A lot of things like that have come up over the years and my mother always wants to take on the burden.

My first marriage was ill-conceived from the beginning. I married Roy with the idea that I could live with anybody for a few years. Roy and I both worked full-time, but everything else was my responsibility. Originally, we shared money management, but he would never pay the bills. They got ready to turn off the electricity and he rushed down with a $500 check with a note attached that said, "Don't bother me!" After that I took over all the finances. During our marriage, he was finishing his PhD and doing a lot of karate and painting. He never had time to do anything around the house, but I was used to living with my father so it didn't seem too abnormal. But at least my dad would do household repairs, work on the cars, and mow the lawn. Roy didn't do anything. We fought about it a lot and finally resolved it by getting a maid.

Even though I brought in more money and did all the tasks, I can't say that I had more power in the marriage, because there really wasn't much of a marriage. He did his thing and I did mine. I suppose the fact that I brought

(continued)

(continued)

in money didn't allow him to boss me around, but I don't think he would have done that anyway. He was too self-absorbed.

   In my current marriage, Mike does everything. He does more cooking than I do, he cleans, he does the wash, he's the only breadwinner, and he does all the traditional male tasks! I feel sensitive about not working and not having any of my own money. A lot of times, I feel guilty that I don't have to work. Also, although Mike always tells me that he's happy to have me at home, he's always sure to tell me that it is "his" money that is providing our vacation or a new appliance or whatever. That gets to me every once in a while. Overall, though, I think we have equal power in the marriage most of the time. When the scales tip, I have to admit, they always tip in his favor.

role, therapeutic role, sexual role, and housekeeper role (Nye, 1976). If you are unclear about what is involved in each of these roles, they are described in detail in Chapter 15. Write down what your mother and father contributed to each role. Include the contributions of any relative who played a significant part in your day-to-day life while growing up. Was there equity in the division of the family roles?

2. To help you further explore this topic, try to answer the questions in the box "Distribution of Power" that refer to how the power was distributed in the family. In your family, what was the relationship between equity and power?

3. What is the long-term debt you owe to your parents and how do you plan to balance the ledger?

Distribution of Power

Answer each question using the following choices:

   a. mother alone
   b. mother more than father
   c. father alone
   d. father more than mother
   e. mother and father together or mother or father equally often alone

1. If there was a disagreement concerning the teaching and disciplining of the children, who made the final decision?
2. If there was a disagreement concerning the nature, frequency, or extent of interaction with relatives, who made the final decision?
3. If there was a disagreement concerning where to vacation or how to spend a weekend, who made the final decision?

(continued)

Distribution of Power *(continued)*

4. If there was a disagreement concerning where or how to provide baby-sitting or child care for the children, who made the final decision?
5. If there was a disagreement concerning the amount of time spent cleaning the house or whether some maintenance job around the house should be done, who made the final decision?
6. If there was a disagreement concerning how best to soothe a child after a disappointing or frightening experience, who made the final decision?
7. If there was a disagreement over the type of sexual activities to engage in or the occurrence of sexual activities, who made the final decision?
8. When only one parent had a particular role, do you think that parent felt the role was equitably given to him or her, or did he or she feel under-rewarded and burdened?

Source: Adapted in part from Stuart, R. B. 1973. Marital Precounseling Inventory (part G). Champaign, IL: Research Press.

Chapter 20

Reactance

Children in a family are like flowers in a bouquet; there's always one determined to face in an opposite direction from the way the arranger desires.

Marcelene Cox

The theoretical concept of *reactance* was developed by Brehm in 1966. It is based on the premise that every individual will struggle and fight to defend *personal behavioral freedoms*—those behaviors that we consider ourselves competent to perform if we choose to (Worchel and Brehm, 1971; Baer et al., 1980; Strube and Werner, 1984). The issue of perceived competency is crucial. For example, an elderly man may feel free to win a U.S. gold medal in skating, but if he perceives himself as unable to reach that level of competency, his sense of freedom is trivial. But, if he felt competent to win the medal (regardless of his actual competency), his sense of freedom would be very meaningful and tightly defended.

MARY, MARY, QUITE CONTRARY

Whenever a person believes that an existing free behavior is threatened with elimination, reactance is aroused. The person feels compelled to engage in the threatened behavior to reassure self and others that, "Yes, I can act that way if I want!" Usually, when someone reacts to a request or demand to refrain from acting in a certain way by proceeding to flaunt that very behavior, we say that person is being "difficult," "stubborn," or "contrary." By understanding the cause of the behavior, we may be able to identify it as an example of reactance.

Reactance is often counterintuitive. We would expect that asking someone for help would increase the likelihood of getting help from that person; that offering to do a favor would nearly always be positively received, and that restricting someone's unacceptable behaviors would be tolerated.

Most times, these expected interactions do occur. Reactance is likely to emerge unexpectedly, however, when relationships are strained, the issues are very important, and the restraints appear arbitrary. Unfortunately, those three factors are often present as family members interact. Reactance in the family becomes a force to be reckoned with, similar to the forces of individuation.

Reactance in Children

Oppositional behavior is a common event in any family. At some time, every member of the family will struggle and fight against the others to defend personal behavioral freedoms. For example, if a young man feels it necessary to play the drums louder than any other drummer at school and the rest of the family scream for him not to play with such force, the urge to bang out deafening beat after beat can become irresistible. After all, the young man knows how loudly he is capable of playing, and it may be very important to him to be the loudest, toughest drummer in the school. The family's attempt to censor his playing arouses enormous reactance, and he strikes out to keep his behavioral freedom intact. Suppose that playing loudly were not particularly important to this young man. If the family threatened to withhold his allowance each time he got too loud, the forces toward compliance would probably be greater than the reactance forces, and the sound level would be greatly reduced. When loud playing is very important, external reinforcements and coercive threats are going to strike deaf ears.

Reactance theory can indeed explain a lot of the oppositional behavior seen in children (Brehm, 1981). Once a child is past infancy, physical punishment, psychological punishment, or material rewards can instigate oppositional behavior. Often, disciplinary strategies that backfire do so because they pose too great a threat to the child's freedom. The greater the threat, the greater the reactance aroused, and the greater the oppositional behavior that will be observed. Consider a child of eight who constantly wants to do "wheelies" on his bicycle. Parents may try spanking the child (physical punishment), calling him a "reckless idiot" (psychological punishment), or promising to take him to the arcade in two weeks if he does not do wheelies (reward). All of these strategies are likely to arouse reactance. Each robs him of the freedom of showing off on the bike.

When parents use reasoning strategies and take the time to explain why they are prohibiting a certain behavior, the limits of the threat are clearly understood and reactance is less likely. Explanations operate by reducing the importance of the threatened freedoms or by reducing the perceived capriciousness of the directive.

Reactance in Adults

Oppositional behavior in adults is often due to reactance, as well. Tell a smoker that you would prefer him or her not to smoke in the kitchen, and that is the very room to which he or she will seem to gravitate. When a husband complains of his wife's reading in bed, the wife will only burrow down deeper under the covers with book in hand.

Thus, reactance theory suggests that one of the best ways to get people to express certain behavior is, paradoxically, to encourage them to inhibit the behavior. Conversely, reactance theory suggests that pressure to exhibit a behavior should have the paradoxical effect of inhibiting it. For example, if a child is wailing loudly in the supermarket aisle, a mother might encourage the child to cry louder and insist that it not stop crying for ten minutes. The manipulative tears may dry up in a matter of seconds.

Another classic example comes from sexual desire dysfunctions found in older married couples. Often in these cases one spouse repeatedly encourages the other to be the initiator of sexual activity. The more one is asked to initiate, the less frequently one wants to initiate. Reactance squelches all sexual interest in the spouse whose freedom to initiate or not initiate is being threatened.

REACTANCE VERSUS COMPLIANCE

As implied in the foregoing examples, a tendency toward reactance coexists with a tendency toward compliance. Particularly within the family, there are numerous intrinsic and extrinsic rewards for complying with others' requests. Wicklund (1974) presents six well-documented factors that help determine whether a family member will exhibit compliance or reactance in any particular situation. Reactance is reduced if:

1. *The threatened freedom is not particularly important.* For example, if a parent asks an adolescent to turn down the stereo, compliance is likely if the music is uninteresting or incidental to whatever else is going on. Reactance is likely if a favorite group is being played. Similarly, if adolescents are alone, they are more likely to comply than if their peer group is present and their feelings of autonomy are threatened.
2. *Many similar behavioral freedoms remain available.* Hence, telling a child that he may not play with a particular peer may meet little reactance if the child can easily find substitutes. If the forbidden peer is the one and only friend in the neighborhood, parents can expect very strong reactance.

3. *The loss of the freedom seems justified.* For example, children often know when they have trespassed and are willing to accept punishment as their just desserts. When they feel that they have not broken their end of the bargain, they will show very strong reactance.

4. *One likes or respects the person taking away the freedom.* In general, members of cohesive families will exhibit less reactance than members of noncohesive families.

5. *The person feels unsure of successfully expressing the behavioral freedom.* Consider a typical situation in which parents restrict an adolescent from going out on New Year's Eve. An adolescent who had very little chance of going out that night will quietly comply with the parents' restriction. One who imagined having a choice of four or five parties will experience strong reactance.

6. *The person has no expectation of being able to express the behavioral freedom in the foreseeable future.* Thus, restricting a child from playing in the snow during the summer months will engender little reactance. Restricting a child from playing in the snow on the morning of the first winter snowfall will engender strong reactance.

Taken together, these factors suggest that compliance to requests from other family members is most likely to occur when a person perceives the request as reasonable, and attractive substitute behaviors are available. Thus, family members should strive to accurately communicate why they are making a compliance request and should try to provide or generate alternative activities. For example, children show less reactance about "needing" the latest toy or fad if the parents have explained why they feel the item is undesirable or unnecessary and have given the child attractive alternative items they can obtain. Reactance is maximized when parents deliver a single, unequivocal, unelaborated "No."

All too often, family members do not respect one another's sense of behavioral freedom and impulsively demand compliance to their own wishes, giving no thought to the deprivation and loss of pleasure they are imposing on other family members. This insensitivity leads to strong reactance responses instead of compliance. Hence, minimizing reactance and maximizing compliance requires the family to have good communication and problem-solving skills. Unfortunately, reactance is most likely to occur in the families with the poorest skills, exacerbating whatever problems exist.

Reactance and Aggression

Reactance theory postulates that certain emotions should accompany reactance, including the emergence of hostile and aggressive feelings (Brehm,

MICHAEL (psychology intern, age 24)

Reactance was a difficult concept for me to understand, but when I tried to explain my family's past using this concept—wow—did it work! In particular it gave me a whole new way of understanding the relationship between my parents.

My mother was in high school when she got pregnant with me. Although it was only 1974, everyone from my father to all the grandparents were pushing my mother to get an abortion. Although my mother had absolutely no understanding of the psychological or spiritual issues surrounding abortion, she absolutely refused to consider it. No one could understand it. The more they argued with her, the more she was determined to have me. She kept on agreeing that she didn't want a baby but that she wasn't going to have an abortion. Was her stubbornness simply reactance to the combined pressure of all around her?

Once it was clear that it was too late for an abortion, everyone started coming up with adoption agencies and couples and lawyers who could handle me once I was born. Again, no sooner did everyone start clamoring for me to be adopted than my mother absolutely refused to consider it. My father was outraged. He was scheduled to begin at Princeton in September and here he would have an infant son living in his hometown! He couldn't bear it and pleaded with my mother. She continually refused. Again, was this stubbornness primarily an expression of reactance?

Of course, once I was born, everyone immediately fell in love with me and congratulated my mother on her inner wisdom. My mother was bent on not burdening my father. Everyone now started encouraging my father to go to Princeton and forget me and Mom. Even my mom encouraged him. His parents constantly pushed this solution. And you know what he did? He moved in with my mom and her parents and went to the state university that was ten miles from our home. Why did he do this? No one ever understood. Was he simply showing a reactance response? My dad lived in the basement of Granny's house for six years, working part time and going to college. He and mom got along like siblings and they each occasionally dated other people. Everyone took care of me. Naturally, after a year or two, this strange relationship at last seemed stable and everyone pushed for a marriage. Of course, they refused. Once again, it certainly seemed like reactance must have been involved.

Eventually both my mom and dad married different people. I ended up spending vacations and summers with my dad and the rest of the time with my mom. The families get along well, and my life story is a favorite among all of my stepbrothers and stepsisters. I've always tried to find deep, mysterious, analytic motives for explaining why my parents behaved as they did. This explanation fits better than any of the others. Also, I like this explanation because it doesn't make them bad people or confused people. It makes them understandable in a way that I've never been able to understand them before. It's taken away a lot of my anger.

1966). When one person's freedom of choice is threatened by another person, one of the most direct routes to reassertion of freedom will be a direct attack on the restricting agent or upon his or her desires and values. Thus, both aggression and hostility are likely strategies for attempting to restore freedom.

Although aggression and hostility are common methods of reasserting one's freedom, they are ofttimes the most destructive. The family members who are the victims of aggression will usually retaliate with their own increased hostile actions or will emotionally numb themselves and restrict their interactions with the aggressor to a bare minimum. Either way, family interactions can only be further impaired and the demands made upon one another can only be seen as more oppressive. A vicious cycle ensues.

The realization that reactance is often accompanied by aggression helps us understand and treat families struggling with the problems of child abuse and spouse abuse. In the case of child abuse, the reactance/aggression connection is easily demonstrated. The abusing parent is likely to be overwhelmed by the time, energy, and affection demanded by children. The parent feels constrained and trapped most of the time, inadequately prepared to meet the responsibilities of full-time parenthood. The baby's cry or even the baby's presence might so threaten the few behavioral freedoms available to the parent (watching TV, resting, or having a conversation) that such parents, in desperation, try to retain their freedom by striking out violently against the child. They see the child not as a person but as an object standing between them and freedom.

Similarly, a frustrated spouse who feels constrained by job, community, and personal history may believe that whatever few behavioral freedoms he or she has can be expressed only at home. A request for help or an invitation to sit by the TV may be more intrusive than the person can bear at the moment, and he or she violently strikes out. Recognition of clients' strong need to protect their personal behavioral freedom is crucial to helping them develop more adaptive coping mechanisms.

A MATTER OF PROPORTION

Reactance in the family appears directly related to the proportion of freedoms that an individual feels are threatened (Brehm, 1966). If only a very small proportion of freedoms is threatened, the rewards for compliance may win out. When a large proportion of freedoms is threatened, reactance will be much stronger. For example, if a family has traveled all over the United States each summer and the wife decides she does not want to go south of Virginia this year, the husband still has over thirty states to choose from and may not feel much reactance at all. Suppose, however, that the couple habitually goes to either upstate New York or the Virginia shore. If the wife excludes Virginia, effectively all her husband's freedom of choice has been taken away; New York is the only remaining option. Under these circumstances the husband is likely to become very committed to going to Virginia.

Adolescents are notorious for becoming highly upset when parents try to put restrictions on their behavior. Parents are often bewildered by the overreaction of their teenagers. Part of the discrepancy in reactions can be explained by the perceived limitations inherent in the parental restrictions. Suppose a father forbids his teenage daughter to go out on a particular Saturday night. He is likely to feel that he has taken one Saturday night out of the hundreds of past and future Saturday nights in his daughter's teen-age years. The daughter, having typically adolescent tunnel vision and egocentricity, may feel that her whole social life forever hinges on her appearance at one particular party on that particular Saturday night. All future behavioral freedoms seem threatened by this one restriction. This triggers the adolescent's overreaction: "Daddy! You're ruining my life!"

ROLE BOUNDARIES AND COPING STYLES

Within a family, reactance behaviors are also fueled by diffuse role boundaries and piggyback coping mechanisms. When a husband and wife shift their role responsibilities in an unprescribed catch-as-catch-can manner, each partner will feel that he or she has freedoms that are available for the asking. This might be true when one spouse is uninterested in exercising behavioral freedoms in a particular area and the other is interested. But when both spouses take on or abdicate the same role responsibility at the same time, one or both parties will feel deprived of behavioral freedoms and will be likely to show reactance.

Consider what happens when a couple share the responsibility of emptying the garbage. When the husband voluntarily takes it out, the wife may appreciate the act or may let it go unnoticed. The same is true if the wife takes it out. Yet, when one spouse tells the other to take out the garbage, the spouse requesting the task may feel totally justified (after all, the mate is supposed to do it part of the time), while the mate may feel used or put upon (after all, the mate is free to do it or not to do it). In this situation, the mate is likely to show reactance and either refuse to take out the garbage or be angry about taking it out.

Similarly, parents and their adolescent son may have a very unstructured agreement about who is to mow the lawn. Sometimes the parent does it, sometimes the son. If the adolescent informs the parents that he is going to have a busy weekend and won't be able to do the lawn, the parents might become intent on the idea that the child must do the lawn. The child, by limiting the perceived behavioral freedoms of the parents, provokes reactance in the parents. If the role responsibilities were clearer, this problem would not emerge. If the adolescent knew that it was his job to do the lawn every week, failure to do it one week would mean that the parents could let it slide, do it themselves, get someone else to do it, or simply insist that the child do it. The insistence that the child do the lawn would be direct. The parents would not have to adamantly refuse to do it to protect their own freedom.

Piggybacking refers to the tendency of many couples to throw old hurts and unresolved problems into any discussion of any problem, no matter how unrelated. As soon as one delicate issue is opened for discussion the rest rush in.

Reactance often piggybacks on other problems in the following way. A person who is burdened by a load of unresolved marital hurts fiercely guards the freedom to express dissatisfaction. Individuals express this freedom by nurturing the unresolved hurts and "carrying a chip on one's shoulder" that encourages and primes reactance behavior. Whenever one spouse asks another to do something, the urge to comply is outweighed by the urge to assert one's freedom to express dissatisfaction in all situations in which the mate is trying to limit it. Reactance is an indirect way of telling the mate about one's angers, frustrations, and disappointments in the relationship and asserting power when one feels generally powerless.

For example, if the husband does not help discipline the kids during dinner, his request to watch the evening movie is rejected—even if the wife had wanted to watch it. She feels she is free to watch it or not watch it. The husband's suggestion seemingly restricts that freedom. Angry and upset about how the husband reacted during dinner, she wants to distance herself and assert her autonomy. Any infringements on her freedoms, no matter how loving and well-meaning, are at risk for a reactance response. Many couples intuitively realize how this type of reactance works and know how to leave the spouse alone at such times. They sense that positive plans can be killed by bringing them up when the other spouse has this oppositional mind-set. Instead, the spouse grits his or her teeth and holds out until the mate is in a better mood.

In a more general sense, reactance can be viewed as a major method of dealing with inequality in a relationship. The less powerful party exerts power in the relationship indirectly by refusing to accept the limitations imposed by the other.

DONNA (legal secretary, age 30)

When I first read this concept, I didn't think that it had any relevance to me. After a few minutes' thought, though, I came up with three instances of reactance affecting my family life in just this week!

The first example comes from a conflict or power struggle that my husband and I are in over birth control. I want my husband to get a vasectomy. Yet, the more I tell him how important this is to me, the stronger his rejection of the procedure. Similarly, he would like me to get my tubes tied. Initially, he brought it up as a joke when I was pushing the vasectomy. And I initially wasn't too threatened and told him I would consider it. The more he suggested it, though, the more adamant I became about not wanting to do it. Really, we're both showing reactance. The freedom to conceive is irrevocably taken away once you're sterilized. The fact that each of us is concerned about the consequences for ourselves and minimizes the consequences for the other makes each of us view the other's decision as irrational, at best.

I also experience a lot of reactance toward my dad, who still thinks that I am his little girl. Often, when I'm over at the house he'll tell me to do something and I'll fly off the handle and spend a half hour explaining why I can't do it. For example, last weekend, he asked me to go to Sears on Monday and pick up this power tool he had ordered through the catalog. As a teenager, I did a lot of these chores since Mom and Dad worked long hours. Now, I have a family of my own, my own work, and my own responsibilities. I feel like he's using me in a way or at least showing he can still have some authority over me. I hate that and so I show reactance. I told him I couldn't possibly pick it up and gave him about ten reasons. None of the reasons were all that valid and I could have picked it up if I wanted to.

The third instance of reactance comes from my daughter, Gina, who is three years old. She's very willful, and if I tell her to drink her milk all up she'll purposely leave a little in the cup! If I tell her to go to bed, even if she's tired, she'll say no. She's always testing her freedom to go against my dictates.

INTERGENERATIONAL ISSUES

Reactance behavior is commonly observed in intergenerational transactions between adults and their family of origin. Most adults can probably recall many such instances: A dilemma or problem was explained to parents who listened dutifully and offered appropriate and heartfelt advice. Yet, no sooner had the reasonableness of the advice registered than an army of objections marched into the conversation to fight a savage "I'll do anything but" battle. Reactance toward parents lingers because historically they are the people who have most effectively been able to limit our behavioral freedoms. For many years, their control of our behaviors was as potent, if not more potent, than our own control system. Even as adults, we feel impelled to be constantly on guard against their potential to restrict or alter our personally derived decisions. Their influence must be monitored carefully.

Another possible expression of reactance occurs when the threatened individual tries to restore freedom indirectly through behavior that is more costly, dangerous, or taboo than the chosen behavior that was eliminated (Wicklund, 1974). This overreaction implies that the threatened behavior remains an option. A child who has been forbidden to run up the stairs may cavalierly begin hopping or jumping from step to step. The message is clear: "I'll show you how much power I have. I can even do this!"

Overreactions are an everyday event for distressed marital partners who constantly feel that their freedoms are being unjustifiably threatened by a spouse. For example, a wife complains about how late her husband comes home from work each night. He overreacts by staying at the office so late he falls asleep there. Or a husband restricts his wife's use of cash and she overreacts by running up astronomical bills on her credit cards.

When individuals are prevented from doing something, reactance makes them want to do it more than before. When they feel they are being forced to do something, reactance makes them want to do it less than before. Reactance theory thus has striking implications for effective parenting strategies. For example, most parents are concerned that their children grow up with a healthy, respectful, wholesome attitude toward sex. Many parents believe this goal is best achieved by protecting their children from exposure to pornographic literature, R-rated movies, and titillating romance novels. Unfortunately, this strategy can lead to a reactance response in which the grown children seek out these types of sexual materials to demonstrate their behavioral freedom from the parental censor. The urge to protect children from influences the parents consider immoral may indeed have the self-defeating effect of making the condemned behaviors more attractive than they would otherwise be.

Reactance phenomena underscore the fact that neither children nor parents like to be told how they ought to think. Yet parents and children with an intuitive appreciation for reactance can often make this phenomenon work to their advantage. A well-known parental ploy of this type involves telling a young child who might protest about taking a long car ride that he or she might not be allowed to go on the trip. Balking about the trip is averted, and quite often the child begins begging for the privilege of going along. A common marital ploy consists of one spouse continually assuring the other that they cannot afford a particular object, knowing full well that this will increase the mate's desire to obtain it at any cost. These ploys are similar to Tom Sawyer's ingenious solution to having to whitewash his aunt's fence. He convinced his friends it was an enjoyable activity but then refused to let them have part of the fun unless they paid him. Sure enough, being told they could not simply join in made the activity that much more appealing and Tom cashed in on their reactance.

INDIVIDUAL DIFFERENCES AND PSYCHOLOGICAL REACTANCE

Reactance is a universal phenomenon but the quality and intensity of its expression depends on a number of variables. The two most important factors influencing reactance are the personality of the person or child whose freedom is threatened and the public or private nature of the threat.

Children and parents who are low in reactance are generally described as easygoing and adaptable. When a brother says, "Let's eat at Burger King," the low-reactance sister says, "Yeah, great idea." The sister who is high in reactance is more likely to say, "No, I want to go to McDonald's." This oppositional behavior makes such children and adolescents far more stubborn than the average kid. Even in psychiatric inpatient hospitals, adolescents high in reactance stay longer before being discharged (Frank et al., 1998). Carter and Kelly (1997) showed this oppositional effect among a group of college basketball players (male and female) who had varying propensities for reactance. In part of the study, the college athletes were given a paradoxical image to focus on, which essentially suggested to them that the game would be difficult and they would not be in top form. As predicted, highly reactance-prone athletes reported feeling less anxious and more self-confident after this paradoxical image than did less reactance-prone athletes. They apparently said to themselves, "I most certainly am going to be on top of my form, no matter what you say."

REACTANCE AND PARADOXICAL INTERVENTIONS

The use of paradoxical interventions (e.g., telling the family they must do precisely what you do not want them to do) is based on the concept of family reactance. The idea is that if you tell the family to refrain from an interaction (e.g., do not tell one another what happened during the work or school day), then the family members will be reactance-aroused, and will feel an irresistible urge to discuss their day-to-day activities with one another. But does it really work that way? Are paradoxical interventions more effective than straightforward interventions? Besides the deceptive aspect of paradoxical interventions, Hunsley (1997) has concluded after examining the available case studies and controlled comparison studies that there is little evidence to support the use of defiance-based symptom prescription.

RESISTANCE AND REACTANCE IN FAMILY THERAPY

One way of understanding "resistance" in family therapy (the idea that even though people come into therapy saying they want things to change, they immediately become unwilling and obstinate about trying any of the recommended changes) is to think of it as a specialized instance of reactance. Resistance (read: reactance) in therapy is provoked by three factors: predisposing factors, enabling factors, and reinforcing factors (Pruitt, Kline, and Kovaz, 1995).

The *predisposing factors* include all those attitudes and beliefs that each family member has that run contrary to the therapists' suggestions. If the suggestion is that Dad drop his son off at the school instead of Mom so they will have some time together, Dad's predisposing reactance might be, "But I'm already running late in the morning," "My son is so negative in the morning, we will only fight more often," or "I wouldn't know what to say to him." The *enabling factors* that might promote reactance would include such things as the son getting an offer of a ride from one of his friends that week, or the father having to take an overnight business trip. The *reinforcing factors* for therapy-induced resistance might include a grandparent who has labeled the child as a "bad apple" and doesn't believe change is going to occur, co-workers who are negative about the effectiveness of therapy, or peers who rally around the son's refusal to be manipulated.

After proposing a homework assignment or family task, the therapist needs to explore these three possible sources of reactance/resistance by asking each family member three questions:

1. What would be the hardships or downside of doing this task? If you had to convince me that this wouldn't help the family, how could you do that? (predisposing factors)
2. What is likely to happen this week that might prevent you from doing this task? (enabling factors)
3. Who, outside of the people in this room, wouldn't be a big fan of this idea? Who would say, "Man, that is a waste of time"? (reinforcing factors)

Once these additional sources of resistance are identified, try to encourage various family members to talk about the probability of success and how they can fight the forces opposing change.

HELPING OTHERS AND ACCEPTING FAVORS

To be merely free is not much. To be able to do whatever you want to do does not in itself produce a good life or a fine character. All you

*can say is that without freedom, the real problem of a good life cannot
even begin.*

Gilbert Murray

Freedom is the intense claim to obey no one but reason.

Heinrich Mann

The security and cohesiveness of families derive in large part from a
deep-seated sense of familial obligation. Everyone expects that if one person really needs help, the rest of the family will be there. Family members
take a deep sense of satisfaction from their ability to help a family member
out of a jam with no thought of a direct reward. Whether the help consists of
physically pitching in to get a chore done, or lending money, or taking care
of that member through an illness, the giver's satisfaction in being able to
balance ledgers is probably as great as the taker's relief in receiving the
needed support. However, helping behavior is subject to reactance just like
any other behavior.

Helping behavior is most likely to occur when there is a justifiable need
and no one has pressured the potential helper to contribute. Once the family
starts stressing how important it is to help, a person is likely to pull back and
find reasons for not helping. For example, every mother of young children
knows that without parental intrusion, brothers and sisters will continually
seek out each other's company; often they will have a wonderful time
playing together. Yet when the parent asks the older one to play with the
younger, the older will balk, complain, and find the most implausible excuses not to be helpful.

Social psychology studies among college students have demonstrated
this phenomenon of refusing to help when it is most needed. The students
were asked to donate bone marrow to a young woman. Subjects who were
told that the woman was greatly in need of the bone marrow and that their
bone marrow was very likely to match were less willing to donate than
those who were told that the need was only slight or moderate and the
likelihood their bone marrow would match was small (Wicklund, 1974).
The more important it was for them to donate the marrow, the more pressure
they felt and the more reactance they showed.

Although no empirical studies have yet been conducted to confirm that
family members also show reactance when help is requested, the anecdotal
evidence for such a phenomenon is quite strong. For example, a woman told
the author that her mother-in-law was a very solicitous, helpful person; the
only way she could make sure that the woman would not take on a chore or
project was to explicitly ask for her help. The request never failed to arouse

reactance, and the mother-in-law would bow out because she was "too busy" or "too tired."

Just as the potential helper experiences reactance, so does the potential recipient of such help. When one person offers to do a favor for another person, potential freedoms of the recipient become restricted. In particular, the recipient loses the freedom to behave negatively toward the giver. One becomes indebted by accepting favors, and one debt is the obligation to have good will toward one's helper. Brehm (1966:66) specifies the conditions when a favor will arouse reactance:

> It would be fair to say that the normal effect of a favor is to enhance one's impression of the person who performs it. Furthermore, to receive a favor tends to obligate one to return it. For both reasons, we might expect that when a favor does not arouse reactance, it will tend to increase the recipient's tendency to perform a return favor. Thus, when it is of relatively little importance to be free of obligation to another person, a favor from him will arouse little reactance, but will create a tendency to return the favor. However, when it is of relatively great importance to be free of obligation to another person, a favor from him will arouse relatively high reactance and a consequent tendency to avoid doing a return favor, which will tend to counter the direct tendency to return the favor.

Reactance to favors explains the reaction adolescents commonly have to receiving help from their parents. Any favors from the parents pose strong threats to the personal freedoms of the adolescent, who is striving to be independent and unobligated to the parents. Strong reactance is aroused, and the adolescent stubbornly refuses to show even the most obvious return of thoughtfulness.

TRISH (lawyer, age 37)

My sister recently gave birth to twin girls. The plans were that I was going to pick up my mother in Newark and together we were going to drive to the hospital in York (a good hour's drive). Along the way, I got a brilliant idea and went into a party store and got a dozen huge pink helium balloons. They took up the entire car. I couldn't see but through maybe a third of the front window but I was real excited about bringing them. When I picked up my mother, she went crazy. How could I think of such a stupid gift to bring to a hospital! And where was she supposed to sit! And how was I going to see! She wanted me

(continued)

(continued)

to take them out but I refused. Once we started driving, a freak hail storm and fierce rain started. I couldn't see a thing. The more she yelled about getting the balloons out before we were killed, the more adamant I became about making sure those balloons got there. Really, my mom was right. It was treacherous driving under optimum conditions for an accident, and with the balloons it was more prayer than perception that got us there. But my reactance was strong, and every time she complained about it I vowed under my breath to get there with all twelve balloons intact. Luckily, we did make it, but it would have been a lot easier not to fight my mother and to leave some of the balloons at the house.

Another prime example of reactance comes from a long-standing problem between my sister, Elaine, and myself. Elaine is very giving and loving—in fact, overgiving to my children. She immediately gets into things with them whenever she visits and is always giving them exciting, lavish gifts that really are just the things they wanted. She laughs and jokes with them easily and they respond similarly to her. My style is much more subdued. While Elaine is fawning over my children, I'll be sitting on the couch trying to engage my niece or nephew in a conversation about school or soccer. Elaine then gets into this thing where she is telling me what to say to them, what to do with them, how to do it, etc. The more she coaches, the more I pull away from her children entirely. I've got to feel free to relate to them in my own way and my own style. The more she interferes, the only freedom I feel I have left is to withdraw. Last winter, I tried to explain this to her and since then it really has been a lot better.

Of course, with my kids there is always a lot of reactance going on. If I tell my youngest son that he has to eat something nutritious for breakfast, he'll refuse to eat anything at all. I know that if I don't mention anything, he'll at least go downstairs and get himself a bowl of Froot Loops. He is always hungry in the morning, and I know he'll have a much better morning in school if he eats. Still, he apparently needs to be his own boss in the morning, so much so that he'd rather go to school hungry than eat what I tell him to eat. As I'm writing this I can see how self-defeating this morning battle is since he's never going to surrender to my way.

SELF-EXPLORATION: REACTANCE

1. Try to recall and write down three times in the recent past you have gotten angry with each of the family members listed below because they have told you to do something that you did not want to do.

    a. Mother
    b. Father
    c. Sister or brother

    d. Spouse or mate
    e. Children

2. Are any of these situations due to "reactance" on your part? To explore this question, ask yourself:

    a. Are my behavioral freedoms being threatened?
    b. Is this behavior important to me?
    c. Is the other person's request irrational?
    d. Do I distrust the other person?

If your answers to these questions are yes, reactance is a likely cause of your opposition.

3. For the situations in which you might be showing reactance, try to analyze whether you would be better off controlling this response and if it is truly serving an adaptive function.

Chapter 21

Cultural Influences on the Family

Amy Boscov

Nobody has ever before asked the nuclear family to live all by itself in a box the way we do. With no relatives, no support, we've put it in an impossible situation.

Margaret Mead

THE CHANGING EMPHASIS OF PARENTING: FROM DISCIPLINE SKILLS TO SOCIAL ACTIVISM

Family life education has moved from a framework of looking at the effects of the family on the child to a more systemic approach that looks at the effects of the community on the family. We are becoming increasingly aware of how much our culture impinges on our families and our children, and that is why a whole spate of books, such as *Reviving Ophelia* (1994) and *In the Shelter of Each Other* (1996) by Mary Pipher, PhD were on the best-seller lists for so long. What follows is a short overview of some of the significant events in the history of family life education, and then a summary of some of the current thinkers on the effects our culture has on boys and girls separately and together.

Humans have always needed some preparation for their roles in families, and all cultures have had some ways of transmitting that information—through observation, stories, and rituals. As societies have become more complex, with changes in technology and loss of community, the modes of more simple societies have not been adequate. According to Kirkendall (1973, as cited in Arcus, Schvaneveldt, and Moss, 1993a), attempts to strengthen families through the use of outside agencies is a common occurrence in societies that have been disrupted by industrialization and urbanization and are exhibiting higher divorce rates and shifts in family roles. Still, written education for parenthood is at least as old as the ancient Greeks (Schlossman, 1983 as cited in Arcus, Schvaneveldt, and Moss, 1993a). We can assume that informal groups of parents have met in many cultures, the way such groups met as early as 1815 in Portland, Maine, to discuss child rearing (Bridgeman, 1930 as cited in Arcus, Schvaneveldt, and Moss, 1993a). Also, religious institutions for centuries have provided guidance and strictures in the area of family life. This model of acknowledging that family problems affect society at large is also shown in the way that academia attempts to address society's ills by assuaging family problems, and has become a pattern of family life education (Lewis-Rowley et al., 1993 as cited in Arcus, Schvaneveldt, and Moss, 1993a).

During the 1960s and early 1970s research emphasized the effects of parent behavior on child behavior. The landmark studies of Baumrind (1973, 1983 as cited in Arcus, Schvaneveldt, and Moss, 1993b) are still the backbone of parent education models. During the late 1970s and the early 1980s systems theory came to the forefront, and while behavior was no longer seen as unidimensionally determined, problems were still considered family affairs, to be solved within the family. During the 1970s some studies demonstrated a community aspect to problems within families. It is not only that family problems create situations that eventually affect children and the community (American Humane Association, 1978 as cited in Arcus, Schvaneveldt, and Moss, 1993b). Current research shows that insufficient income and inadequate housing, alcohol dependence, and social isolation have major indirect impacts on children by affecting one's ability to parent effectively and consistently. However, many negative cultural influences also impact directly on children (e.g., violent TV). Even when parents are spared environmental stressors, they must monitor, reframe, and buffer children from a plethora of potentially negative cultural influences. Parents are now beginning to recognize this, and are looking for guidance about what they can do to ameliorate the negative effects of our culture on children. They are soaking up books such as *In the Shelter of Each Other* and forming study groups to support one another. Mary Pipher (1994) says that while it used to be the job of parents to help children fit into the dominant culture, now for the first time in history we must protect our children from what comes at them from our culture. Parents need to understand behavioral parenting techniques, systems theory, and child development, but that is not adequate any longer. To guide children, we as parents and therapists must know what we are up against as we struggle to help children cope with culturally promoted violence, loss of self-esteem, isolation, and so on.

The Media As a Potentially Negative Influence on Children

Because we learn from the stories around us all the time, we need to be very careful about what those stories are and to understand the implications clearly. Television is our national storyteller, and often both children and adults are more emotionally involved with actors, actresses, and television characters than with neighbors or other real people in their families, schools, and workplaces. This is where our children learn how people treat one another—whether they learn that the way to solve problems is through violence or they learn the roles that either gender is expected to perform. We need to think about the messages that we all receive through television, movies, books, and advertisements, because they are all potent stories. When repeated over and over, as many themes are, they have a significant effect on how we perceive and behave. If the stories were about strong and caring men and women who expected and dealt with adversity, resolving conflicts without violence, we would all feel better about ourselves. Through stories we learn how to treat each other—to be a tough guy, a smart aleck, or a seductress in our interactions. Few models exist that are wholesome, helpful, enduring, or savory. This is one reason why I am so glad that there are some resources parents can rely on. For example, the *Chinaberry Book Catalogue* gives brief summaries of a fine selection of children's literature. It even has an index in the back, where books are categorized under headings such as: Strong Females; Balanced, Inspiring Males; or Environmental Awareness. Some other good books include *Great Books for Girls, Great Books for Boys,* and *100 Books for Girls to Grow On* (see Suggested Readings for Chapter 21 in the back of the book).

Parental Violence and Its Treatment

Perhaps one of the best examples of the effects of our culture on the individual is in the area of violence. Here the research and discussions of parenting do, in some cases, move beyond the idea that proper parenting can totally control the child's personality and behavior. Although many parent education programs are stuck in that mind-set, there are some pioneers. For example, McInnis-Dittrich (1996) adapted the widely used STEP program teaching parenting skills in an isolated community in the Appalachian mountains where domestic and societal violence is prevalent. Child abuse was conceptualized from an ecological viewpoint, including a combination of individual, family, community, and cultural variables. The treatment focused on parents discussing their own childhoods (ontogenic), what makes a good parent (familial), what the community expects of parents (exosystem), and messages from the culture (macrosystem). From the ontological or individual perspective, people are more likely to abuse their own children if they have been exposed to an aggressive environment, even if they were not personally abused. Thus, the first issue dealt with in the parenting classes is corporal punishment, recalling the time when the parent was on the receiving end. The second session deals with familial issues, specifically what makes a good parent. Once again, the approach is initially personal and historical, but leads to a discussion and understanding of the effects of methods of discipline. Session three addresses the parents' relationship to the community (exosystem) both in terms of the community expectations of them and available resources. With limited economic resources to begin with, community messages about social and socioeconomic status can add to the stresses of raising a child. Families were helped to identify or, if necessary, to develop a support system, including family and friends. A discussion of societal messages about violence (macrosystem) was incorporated into session seven. Here the focus was on the messages about violence in movies and television, and the parents' feelings about what effects these messages had on their own children. This model suggests that there is an interaction between the parent's individual history with familial, community, and cultural variables. That interaction influences the extent to which a parent might adopt violence as an acceptable method of parenting. Therefore, the issue of violence and precursors to violence, whether it be personal history or stresses from economic problems or isolation, must be addressed at each of these levels. Although it is difficult to gauge the success of parenting programs, self-reports were very positive. It is only logical that adapting a program to the beliefs of the audience (e.g., understanding that sometimes what we perceive as excessive harshness is an unquestioned way of life, or that it may be someone's extreme attempt to keep the child safe in a hostile environment) will strengthen or maybe even allow the changes to occur. Most behaviors are to some extent multidetermined, and the more areas we address, the more successful we will be.

Childhood Violence and Parental Interventions

Nancy Carlsson-Paige and Diane Levin have written numerous books and articles helping parents and teachers foster a healthier environment within the current sociopolitical environment. In *Who's Calling the Shots* (1990), they detail how children's play has changed as a consequence of the changes in television. In 1984, under the Reagan administration, the FCC removed restrictions on children's programming. By Christmas of 1985 the ten top-selling toys were linked to TV shows. By 1987, 80 percent of all children's programming was produced by toy manufacturers. Children are essentially watching half-hour commercials. Young children average about four hours a day of television viewing. What Carlsson-Paige and Levin (1990) found was that the type of play that was generated by watching these programs was different from children's previous play patterns. The themes that they incorporate in their play are no longer self-generated, but mimic those of the adult scriptwriters. The play is more violent. There are fewer self-generated solutions. The toy companies' only interest in the shows is to produce more specific characters (toys) that have specific qualities, and must be played with in specific ways. This is no longer a creative process.

Piaget makes a distinction between imitation and play, in that play is creative (Piaget, Hodgson, and Gattegno, 1962). Under the guise of a free market and free speech, children's rights of protection of the children are being violated. Parents can respond to this in a variety of ways: they can limit the time spent in front of the television, they can limit television viewing of young children to the array of good programming available, and they can view with the child and point out marketing schemes. One of the rules in our house is that commercials are to be muted (the sound is turned off). Parents can choose toys that are more generic. It is all right if the children turn Duplo blocks into guns; they will at least be making up their own scripts.

Garbarino (1995) mentions a further hazard of TV violence. The American Psychological Association concluded that TV was responsible for up to 15 percent of youth violence. Garbarino feels that this estimate is low because the APA studies neglected to take into account that, in addition to exposing children to massive doses of violent behavior, TV watching decreases interactions with adults—it isolates people. Without adult influence, these children are being exposed to violence in a vacuum of morality, ethics, attention, or affirmation. Television often presents violence as the American way of life, as a punishment, as a strategy of conflict resolution, and as entertainment.

Pollack (1998) says that watching violence is not enough to make children violent, especially if they are growing up in a loving environment, where they can feel connected and can express their emotions. Television violence, on the other hand, can lead children to expect and prepare for violence, reacting to a situation with more violence than is warranted. This is especially true of angry boys. Viewing violence on television will desensitize children to violence, and make them more likely to tolerate it. It leads boys (and everyone else) to believe that their world is more violent than it actually is in most places.

Pipher (1996) begins to address the issue of violence as entertainment and the confusion of sex with violence. Acts of violence are often portrayed in which women are the victims. TV violence desensitizes us to real violence, increases the likelihood of real violence, and increases our fear levels. (We come to expect violence to occur in the same percentage as we see on TV—a scary thought indeed. And what of the children who cannot yet comprehend the distinction between reality and what they see on TV? And what of our psyches that have violent images imbedded in them?) Pipher makes a very good point about how violence has come to be portrayed without consequences, without an opportunity to understand the ramifications of the actions. She uses *Romeo and Juliet* as an example of violence that makes us share in the consequences of a tragic misunderstanding rather than being a thrill, a solution to frustration, or a proof of manhood.

Parenting Strategies for Teaching Nonviolence

After reviewing traditional parenting programs that seek to reduce violent behavior in families and children, I suggest that therapists include the following thirteen strategies in any such program:

1. Allow children to express feelings and encourage the child to do so in an age-appropriate way.
2. Continue to encourage appropriate expression as they get older. In particular, do not cut off boys from their feelings of affection or sadness; it leaves little but anger.
3. Treat all children as if they are important, that they have something unique to give. Help them to do so, and see it as a responsibility. This is a particularly difficult thing to do for poor, young, black boys, who all too often get the message that there is no place for them in this culture.
4. Interact with children, or make sure that someone can. The isolation of television is as harmful as the violence portrayed.
5. Look at conflict as a way to teach problem solving, for yourself as well as your children.
6. Encourage some rite of passage, so that violence is not the only way of proving manhood.
7. Involve other adults—less violence occurs in mixed-age groups.
8. Spend more time with children; the implicit message is that they have worth.

9. Teach that poverty is not a moral lapse.
10. Reverse the trend that the rich get richer, and the poor get poorer. The middle class is in a definite decline. In 1998 the United Nations Human Development Report looked at what proportion of the world's goods and services are consumed by the rich and the poor. They found that the world's 225 richest people (which includes 60 Americans) have a combined wealth equivalent to the annual income of the poorest 47 percent of the entire world's population. The three richest people have combined assets that exceed the gross domestic product of the 48 least developed countries (Crossette, 1998).
11. Teach values other than material worth.
12. We need community-based child care. The burden is too much for individual parents. Families need to be connected to others. As Margaret Mead says, with no support we have put the family in an impossible position.
13. Limit exposure to media violence.

MARKETING AND MATERIALISM

Canada (1998a) contends that it is important for parents (and, I think, for children too) to know that children are up against more than peer pressure these days to wear name brand clothing. Marketing "campaigns" are expert at manipulating the minds of children and adults, like—that is their job. He sums up the effects of advertising by stating "Boys are a prime target for ruthless marketers' attempts to persuade them that their self-worth, happiness, and even manhood is tied to what they buy" (p. 39).

Girls are given similar messages, from early childhood on, that material goods are of the utmost importance. The messages differ slightly. The brand name is less important, "but more is better" is the theme. Barbie is the ultimate consumer, with a wardrobe that could easily clothe a village. Our supermarket has small carts for children, with a flag saying "customer in training." Styles change with such frequency for girls (and women) that new wardrobes are necessary for image, not just for size. Americans spend $8 billion a year on cosmetics, which is $2 billion more than the estimated annual total needed to provide basic education for everyone in the world. (Crossette, 1998).

While there are minor differences, the message is the same: your self-worth equals your financial worth. Parents are up against pretty stiff competition if they try to dissuade children from this. Pipher (1996:93) writes very cogently on this topic:

Since the 1950s, advertising has increased in amount and in sophistication. Much of what modern psychology knows about suggestion and influence has been usurped to sell products. We have t-groups and marketing polls. The general philosophy of ads—create a feeling of longing about a deeply human need, then suggest a product that will satisfy that yearning—works very well. Wishes are induced with the skill of nightclub hypnosis, then elevated into needs. Your wish is your command. Ads elevate feelings over thinking and impulses over common sense. It's hard for parental calls for prudence to compete. The science of marketing is much more precise and focused than the science of parenting.

Ads manipulate us into being dissatisfied. As businessman B. E. Puckett said "It's our job to make people unhappy with what they have." We are encouraged to feel anxious or sorry for ourselves. Advertising teaches us to live on the level of the pleasure principle. This leads to impulse control problems and feelings of entitlement. "I am the center of the universe and I want what I want now." This thinking creates citizens who are vulnerable to quick fixes. It leads to citizens filled with self-pity, which is the flip side of entitlement.

Advertising teaches that people shouldn't have to suffer, that pain is unnatural and can be cured. They say that effort is bad and convenience is good and that products solve complex human problems. Over and over people hear that their needs for love, security and variety can be met with products. They may reject the message of any particular ad, but over time many buy the big message—buying products is important.

In brief, a number of very important messages are embedded in advertising:

1. If there is a problem, there is a commercial cure.
2. Any suffering or discomfort is bad.
3. I deserve what I want.
4. Want and need are confused, deliberately. As a parent, it becomes very difficult to counter advertising that confuses wants with needs, and products with self-worth.
5. Advertising teaches children to be cynical because they know that adults will lie to them in order to make money.

We need to make an attempt to evaluate the effects of materialism on our lives, is both internally and in relationship to other people. Our culture has become very segregated by how much people own. All the $200,000 houses are in one area, which is separate from the $80,000 or $400,000 houses.

Technology has the power to bring people together in some ways, but is just as likely to isolate them. Without air conditioners or television, people spend more time with one another, with their friends and neighbors. The Internet is a very good example of the paradoxical effect of technology on our lives. While the Internet allows us to keep in closer touch with distant friends and family, it cannot replace the hugs and daily interactions with people who are present. In fact, Robert Kraut and his colleagues at the Carnegie Mellon University Human-Computer Interaction Institute (Sleek, 1988) found that the results of a concentrated study of the social and psychological effects of home use of the Internet were completely contradictory to the expectations of the researchers. They found that people who spend even a few hours a week on the Internet report more depression and loneliness than less frequent users. Part of their surprise had to do with the fact that these were not extreme users. The Internet has been seen as a less passive medium than television, allowing interaction. Participants in the study were using interactive forms of communication on the Net, not just information gathering. Most important, they reported a decline in interactions with family members and a reduction in their circles of friends. This corresponded directly to the amount of time they spent online. The Internet can help users communicate more effectively with people in other parts of the world, but they are not going to babysit for you or bring you chicken soup when you are sick. The fact that this was a surprise points out how complex is the question of how new technological devices will affect our lives. It is difficult to make choices without adequate information. However, it can help to remind us to continually evaluate how we want to use technology. A very funny film called *The Gods Must Be Crazy* illustrates this point. A Coke bottle drops from the sky and totally disrupts the order of a society.

Alan Swope, a professor at the California School of Professional Psychology, teaches a course titled "Psychological Perspectives on Technology." Students are urged to look at the choices technology has given them, and those it has taken away. Swope urges his students to find ways to use technology to make the most of human relationships and to reduce stress. For example, many students found that having beepers and cell phones increased their stress. The pace that new technology allows is a major stress because it assumes that we will be available and will respond rapidly. There is no time to get away and to consider a response (Murray, 1998b).

Once we look at the effects, we can begin to make decisions about how we want to use technology. Sometimes items such as television and beepers become so much a part of our world that we forget what it was like without them. Still, we need to be in charge, to constantly reevaluate, and to make decisions as best we can.

Public Policies That Support Effective Parenting

The 1989 United Nations Convention on the Rights of the Child was ratified by all but two members of the United Nations—the United States being one of the two (Garbarino, 1995). The document basically says that childhood is a time in the human life cycle having a special claim on the community at large. Children are to be protected from adult economic, political, and sexual forces. They have a right to be supported by their families and communities. They have a right to be shielded from violence, and obviously therefore from war, and from adult sexuality. The document specifically states that children have the right to be protected from economic exploitation. Garbarino (1995) adds that this includes the right to be protected from the excesses of the consumer economy. Children's purchases should be kept separate from commercial advertising that exploits their cognitive, emotional, and social limitations. In Scandinavian countries, parent groups, television and commercial concerns, and government worked together to set up guidelines protecting children. In our country every day, on television, billboards, magazines, and for that matter on their very clothing, children are commercial targets. It is a very effective but ultimately dangerous method. We are being shortsighted, putting short-term economic goals above the well-being of our children, and indeed, of our planet.

When Sitting Bull was traveling with Buffalo Bill, he saw both the poverty and the wealth in American cities. His comment was: "The white man knows how to make everything but he doesn't know how to distribute it" (Pipher, 1996:94).

Parenting Techniques to Cope with Materialism

1. Make the marketing strategy explicit; show children what the advertiser is trying to do. This includes informing them about the influence of advertisers and owners of magazines and newspapers and how that influences the information in the periodical.
2. Make children feel valued for who they are rather than what they own or produce. Help them to discover who they can be.
3. Have high expectations. Self-worth has additional meaning when attached to a sense of accomplishment, even if it is the accomplishment of a five-year-old consciously trying to be cooperative or taking turns, or a ten-year-old diligently cleaning the kitchen floor. It doesn't need to be, "You're the best reader in your class."
4. Stay away from comparisons in general. It is who children are that counts, not who someone else is or what someone else has.

5. We need to teach children to evaluate the effect of the product. More is not necessarily better. New is not necessarily better. What effect will it have on our lives, our time? These are complex questions.

DENEE (dentist, age 40)

My son, at almost thirteen, has developed an intense interest in name brands. Our attempts to explain that he is at the mercy of the marketing industry have had little effect. For a while we tried to forbid any clothing that had a logo on it, saying that if he were to be an advertisement that he should get paid for it. We came up against a very real dilemma. When he really needed new clothing we could find nothing without a company or a team name on it in the store. There simply were no alternatives in the stores that we go to buy clothes. We are hoping that repeatedly bringing this up to him will have an influence. I think also we must (and do) give him time and support, acknowledge his worth in many ways . . . find outlets for his abilities and encourage these activities. I require at least one sport and a musical instrument for each of my children. I am lucky that usually we can arrange for one parent to be at games and oversee practice sessions. I simply refuse to buy things that I think are outrageously priced or made under inhumane conditions (if I know about it). I have had to provide outlets for him to earn the money to buy an occasional item that I refuse because I cannot see the need. This is me, doing my best and still feeling utterly frustrated and at the mercy of a marketing industry that has no value but the bottom line. If anyone thought about what is best for us and for the planet (which is ultimately what is best for all of us), they would not try to create a need where there is none.

When I was a child, my grandfather owned a small department store, and used to pay for his grandchildren's clothing. My mother, any time we shopped, would ask me "what do you need," not "what do you want." Today it is an even harder question to answer . . . marketing blurs the line.

Different Parenting Styles for Daughters and Sons

Cultural values and gender have a complex interaction. While girls are robbed of their self-esteem and sense of competence as they get older, boys are removed from their emotions to the extent that they often no longer can even know how they feel.

Olga Silverstein and Beth Rashbaum (of the Ackerman Institute in New York City) in *The Courage to Raise Good Men* (1994) say that we do not need to force male children to be independent from mothers. We do not need to sanction the emotional shutdown that has been demanded cultural- ly. To be whole people, we need connectedness. For a culture such as ours that prizes independence above just about everything else, this is a necessary voice. This is also a central theme in the most recent book about boys, by William Pollack, PhD (1998), titled *Real Boys*. Pollack talks about the "Boy Code," which he likens to wearing a mask. He says that many of the young boys that he sees are living behind a mask of masculine bravado. They hide their genuine selves to conform to society's expectations. They cut themselves off from any feelings that society deems unacceptable for men and boys, such as fear, loneliness, dependency, and uncertainty. This also necessitates that they face their problems alone, which cuts boys off from the people who care about them. Pollack expressed some surprise that even though America has been revising its ideas about boys and girls, the old Boy Code is still very much the norm. He says that "the Boy Code puts boys and men into a gender straightjacket that constrains not only them but everyone else, reducing all as human beings, and eventually making us strangers to ourselves and to one another—or, at least, not as strongly connected to one another as we long to be" (Pollack, 1998:6).

This Boy Code is so ingrained in all of us that it is hard to combat. It is evident in how we handle boys from infancy onward. Although infant boys up to several months old tend to be the more expressive gender, by age five or six this expressiveness has gone underground. How does this happen? Pollack says that research points to two primary causes. The first is the use of shame to toughen up little boys. They are made to feel ashamed of any feelings of weakness or fear or despair. The second cause is the separation process that our society deems necessary, considering it important for boys to separate emotionally from the mother at an unnecessarily early age, generally by the time the boys are six years old, and again in adolescence. Pollack feels very strongly about this issue and echoes Silverstein and Rashbaum.

Pollack (1998:40) contends: "I believe the trauma of separation is one of the earliest and most acute developmental experiences boys endure, an experience that plays a large role in the hardening process through which society shames boys into suppressing their empathic and vulnerable sides. What few people realize is that this shame-based hardening process begins as early as the first months of a little boy's life as a narrowing of emotional expressiveness and then continues during early childhood, following boys right through adolescence and manhood. It is, in other words, a lifelong process."

It is self-defeating to continue to insist on a premature independence. While for many topics, results of studies are ambiguous, this is not the case for independence. Study after study has been consistent in showing that securely attached children who are not forced into a premature independence (called pseudoindependence in the literature) are psychologically healthier and stronger. The more secure they feel, the more they feel able to explore and develop their own independence. It makes intuitive sense that it is easier to leave at your own speed than to be left. Alan Stroufe (as cited in Pollack, 1998) at the University of Minnesota found that those who were securely attached to their mothers as infants were more self-reliant, had lower rates of psychopathology, did better at school, and had higher self-esteem throughout their lives.

Mothers have been placed in an uncomfortable position. They are held responsible for the child's emotional growth and development. They are expected to uphold society's emphasis on independence and to push the male child away, while at the same time helping him express his feelings (even though society will shame him if he tries to express caring or empathy). The mother is caught in the bind of trying to give him the love and attention that he needs and to force him into a premature independence. Pollack says that the mother's confusion is a reflection of our culture's mixed messages about masculinity. He contends that society has to change the message.

As a society, we are beginning to appreciate men who are aware of their emotions, able to express caring and empathy. What better way to begin to revise the old behaviors than by allowing boys to remain close to their mothers, who are often in the best position to teach those skills?

Pollack tells parents to trust their own feelings, and that you can never give a child too much love. "Far from making boys weaker, the love of a mother can and does actually make boys stronger, emotionally and psychologically. Far from making boys dependent, the base of safety a loving mother can create is a connection that her son can rely on all his life. It provides a boy with the courage to explore the outside world. But most important, far from making a boy act in girl-like ways, a loving mother actually plays an integral role in helping a boy develop his masculinity—the self-esteem and strength of character he needs to feel confident in his own masculine self" (Pollack, 1998:81).

Pollack offers suggestions for parents on how to help boys reconnect to their feelings and to others. The list includes: give your boy undivided attention at least once a day; encourage him to express a full range of emotions (happy, sad, tired, disappointed, scared, nervous, excited, etc.) rather than just limiting him to anger; do not tease the child when he does express vulnerability; look beyond the anger displayed to see what it may be concealing; express your love and empathy openly and frequently; and help him to create a broad model of masculinity.

Perhaps the place to begin making changes is in the home. Certainly parents are the earliest influences. But they will need the support of society more and more as the child matures. The image of the "strong, silent type" must be enhanced by other images as well.

Although Mary Pipher (1996) chose originally to write about girls, she also states that we need a new image of manhood that allows equality for women without taking away male pride. Men should not be men at the expense of women. Violent misogyny and objectification of women need to be replaced with more positive messages of what it means to be a man. Boys need a model of manhood that allows them to be both adventurous and gentle.

In the 1970s and 1980s a lot of research was done on mental health and "androgyny," androgyny being defined as a personality that had both masculine and feminine traits. The masculine traits were clustered around the ability to get things done; the feminine traits were more about relating to others. Not surprisingly, the people who scored higher on both of those scales, whether they were male or female, were reportedly more "healthy," more satisfied—they had a larger variety of skills with which to meet the world. The women's movement was and is intended to allow women to be truer to all of who they are, to be capable, to get things done, as well as to be caring and empathic. Some men (and women) were threatened by this, and felt that their area was being encroached upon. What has been less clear is that men also need to be allowed to become more androgynous. We need images that allow us, male or female, to be whole, to be all that we can be, to become capable and caring adults. These are the images and stories that our children need to see and read and hear.

Pipher describes adolescence as a period of great internal development that intersects with a time of massive cultural indoctrination. It makes sense that at a time when youth are trying on new roles and discovering who they might become, they are most subject to the messages of what our culture values. The women's movement has made an attempt to broaden the possibilities for girls, but the pressure has intensified in recent years. Now girls get a very mixed message. Yes, some women have high-powered jobs, but most women work for low wages and then have most of the responsibility for what happens at home. I have yet to meet a mother that is happy with her distribution of time. We are told to take time for ourselves. When and at whose expense? No support or backup exists to make real changes for women possible. Margaret Mead said that the family has never been asked to live all by itself before. Roles for women cannot change until the culture makes some concessions. In many cultures, the extended family has a real role. If the mother must be out working, then the aunt, cousin, grandparent, or someone else who the child knows and who cares for the child can take over. For most women this is an impossibility, and yet we ask them to be comfortable without support, to proceed as if that did not matter. The lip service paid to equality makes the reality all the more confusing.

Girls take a nosedive during adolescence, which has been documented in many arenas. They are very sensitive to society's expectations. This is the time when, as DeBeauvoir says, "Girls stop being and start seeming" (as cited in Pipher, 1994). Adolescent girls experience pressure to be untrue to their authentic selves, and to use only a small part of who they are.

Pipher talks of three factors that contribute to making adolescence a particularly difficult time for girls. First is the developmental process. Their bodies are changing. Their emotions are difficult for them (as well as everyone around them) to handle. Their way of thinking is changing, but is not yet adult. They tend to blame and generalize rather than reason abstractly. And yet they are struggling with the most basic questions: Who am I? What is my place in society? What is the meaning of my existence?

Second, if girls look to the culture for any answers, what do they find? This is the time when they are moving into a broader culture, and that culture is replete with sexism, consumerism, and the message that all that really matters for a woman is how she looks.

Third, our culture expects adolescents to distance themselves from their parents at a time when perhaps they need them more than ever. So as they are subject to more pressures, they have to give up the support and protection of their families. Although in many ways boys' and girls' journeys differ, here is an area that they, and most adults, have in common. As a culture we prize independence to such an extent that we cut ourselves off from supports.

Adolescents face enormous cultural pressure from magazines, music, television, advertisements, and peers to conform to a socially acceptable ideal. In some ways the messages are confusing. The ideal is sexy without being sexual; you can stand up for someone else, but not for yourself; and you should be smart without being smart enough to threaten boys. Parents are often at odds with the culture. Parents resist reducing their teens to sex objects and possible consumers, but parents have limited influence at this juncture.

In 1992, the American Association of University Women released the results of a study, "How Schools Shortchange Girls." They found that boys received more classroom attention and instruction than did girls. Boys were called on more frequently and were asked more open-ended questions. Stories about boys appeared three times as frequently as stories about girls. Girls read biographies of men much more often than biographies of women, at a ration of 6:1. Boys were more likely to be praised for their work, girls for their clothing or rule-abiding behavior. Girls were given the message that what matters is how you look and how you comply, and that failure is due to lack of ability, not lack of effort. Is it any wonder that their confidence is eroded? In many places being smart is unpopular. What kind of a message is that? It is a no-win situation.

Young girls do not have the ability to recognize and sort out cultural messages. Mary Pipher (1994:41) states: "By junior high girls sense their lack of power, but usually cannot say what they sense. They see that mostly men are congressmen, principals, bankers and corporate executives. But they don't focus on the political—their complaints are personal."

If girls (and boys) are shown the messages more explicitly, perhaps we will all fare better. Most girls do not know that we have still not passed an equal rights amendment to the Constitution, which currently states that all MEN are created equal. Girls will not label their schools as sexist, but will say they have been sexually harassed. Most girls probably do not even recognize that their textbooks are about boys. We become so used to gender-exclusive language that we fail to see it, or its insidious effect.

Little girls do notice, long before they can speak, and before they simply accept things. When my older daughter was three, she asked me why all the monsters on *Sesame Street* were boys. When my younger daughter was three and I had sung, "How much is that doggie in the window, I do hope that HE is for sale," she asked me how I knew it was a boy. I was careful to use "it" after that. *Sesame Street* does have Zoë and Rosita now, but these instances are just drops in the bucket of the constant barrage of unspoken messages.

It appears that children are most vulnerable to gender messages around the ages of three and four when they are developing their gender identity, and again in adolescence. Unfortunately, adolescence is a time of bodily changes and self-consciousness anyway. At such a time, to be hit with the message that all that really matters is how you look is devastating. Today, with our large schools and lack of community, these messages are even stronger. So few people know enough about adolescents to make any evaluation based on anything other than their looks. Who do these children relate to? Who knows them? What do they see? The average teen spends more time with television characters than with parents, neighbors, and people who might care about them. And all the women on television are beautiful. This is not a reality check, and it emphasizes that what is important for a woman is how she looks.

Accepting your body is an integral part of accepting who you are. With so little diversity in what is acceptable, and a cultural ideal that is unattainable, the cards are stacked against girls. How can they become confident? No wonder self-esteem plummets at this time.

Bodies that were once seen as useful and fun for running, jumping, dancing, or whatever are now seen as the enemy. In addition to not meeting the standard of perfection, bodies are now cause for worry. Because girls now have breasts, they become targets of unwanted attention. The world becomes a more dangerous place, and girls' wings are clipped by it. At a time when they should be trying those wings, they learn that it is dangerous outside the nest, and sometimes inside as well.

With self-loathing comes anger at mothers and peers. Boys and girls are very tough on each other at this age, shunning anyone that does not fit the cultural stereotype. We are far from "I'm OK, you're OK." At this critical juncture, girls are still asked to deny who they are, who they might become, in order to fit into the feminine ideal.

Adolescents suffer so many losses at this point: loss of childhood, loss of the warm, close parental relationship, and even loss of the self, loss of their authenticity. They must cut themselves off from their wholeness in order to fit in. This sounds remarkably like what boys are asked to do—the major difference being that boys are asked to cut themselves off from their emotions, while girls are asked to cut themselves off from their potential.

I began to write a list of what girls need, and what struck me was that so much of what they need is what all children need:

1. All children need to be valued for who they are and their unique properties. We know now that children come into the world with specific personalities and abilities. Valuing their uniqueness will help keep them in touch with who they are, and increase their chances of remaining more authentic. I cannot overstate the importance of this. That does not mean you cannot impart values and make explicit what behaviors are allowable, but you have to acknowledge and celebrate individuality. That does not mean a lack of discipline, but rather the message that "I love you for all of who you are and I have high expectations for you."

2. All people need a sense of connectedness to people who know and care about them. We need to send a different message beyond independence. Children need to learn how to individuate without the pressure to separate.

3. All children need a safe environment in which to explore. They need skills in how to negotiate, rather than to resort to violence as the only solution. Messages in the media must change in this area.

4. We have to broaden allowable behavior for both genders. Women need to be seen as capable; men need to be able to remain in touch with feelings. Women need to be seen as more than sex objects, and men have to be allowed roles other than that of sexual predator.

5. The media needs stories beyond sex and violence. Children need to hear messages of loyalty, courage, endurance, empathy, and altruism in order to value them. The media should show individuals who are less stereotyped in order to model and allow a larger variety of behaviors.

6. Children need to have friends of both genders who are only friends. They can learn from one another, but they need to be able to do that without the relationship being sexualized by the expectations of others.

7. All children need to be able to look inside, to accept all parts of themselves, even the parts that they will want to modify. They need to learn how to be quiet and reflective, to sit with their pains and acknowledge them.

8. We have to shift the messages of the media, or at least make them explicit. The notion that products solve all ills, that if we buy something we will be happier, sexier, more attractive to others, must to be made explicit if it is to be questioned. Likewise, the strong gender stereotyping in the media needs to be made explicit. Children need to know that they are specific targets of the marketing industry, if they are to be able to make conscious choices.

9. Children spend a lot of time in school, and we need to examine and change some of the messages there.

  a. Schools should be smaller so that children can be known and seen as individuals, and held accountable for their behavior.

  b. Learning needs to be an active process, not a passive experience, so that children know "how" to learn.

  c. The heavy emphasis on grades teaches an external locus of control, and diminishes the joy of learning. To be able to think for themselves and resist doing things for the wrong reasons, they need to have a strong sense of self.

  d. Different learning styles and developmental stages must be acknowledged and addressed. Young boys may not be ready to sit still for long periods of time, or have the fine motor skills for writing tasks, especially as we are making the lower grades more academic, expecting more at an earlier age. Some children may learn better when working with others.

  e. The lack of references to females in all subjects, including history, math, and language, gives both genders the notion that females are less important. For males, this makes it easier to discount girls, and increases the likelihood of violence. For girls it leads to self-loathing, of devaluing the self. For all of us it is a tremendous loss when we need to eliminate a major part of ourselves in order to conform.

f. Interest groups would provide a way of forming relationships based on common passions, leading to more authenticity, and a way to belong that is less capricious than cliques.

10. Children need to know that they are important to the adults in their lives. They deserve protection from early sexualization, from the marketing industry, and from violence. If we were to govern our behavior more by what is good for children than by the market economy, the world would eventually be a better place for all of us. Children need to know that they are valued for who they are, not just for what they can get their parents to buy, and that adults will not lie to them to make money.

11. One of the main hazards of television and computers is that it reduces the time children spend with adults who care about them. The messages are absorbed without parental refutation. While the messages need to change, so does the amount of time spent viewing television or being online.

12. Children need nature. It puts things in perspective. They can be aware of how small they are, but also how they are part of something very big. It teaches interdependence.

13. Children need to learn that they have something to offer. With altruism, they learn connectedness and self-respect.

Gender Benders for Parents

I have two daughters, one five and one ten years old. Four-year-olds tend to be the most sexist and gender-bound creatures as they form their own identities. A few months ago the little one was doing something particularly "girlish"—I can't recall exactly what it was—and the older one said, "She's been watching too much Disney." It might be so. Most stories for our children are formulaic. Even if the girls are strong, they are beautiful, and the stories end with them getting married—as if there is nothing to life after the wedding. They just cease to exist—definitely something to think about. My response was to say it's time for *Dealing with Dragons*. The *Chinaberry Book Catalogue* offers a variety of books, mostly for children. It has descriptions of each of the books and includes an index with various helpful categories, one of the headings being "Strong Females." My older daughter was raised on these books. While she has always had an independent nature and has an older brother that she is very close to, I believe these books had a major impact. She does too. One of these series of books from the catalogue is written by Patricia C. Wrede and features a princess

(continued)

(continued)

who is not interested in etiquette or embroidery, and studies fencing and magic behind her father's back. She decides that being captured by dragons would be better than marrying a prince she disdains and so the journey ensues. *Dealing with Dragons* is the first in this quartet of books. As soon as we began reading this series I noticed a difference in my daughter's imaginary play. The princesses became more interesting. I believe that we learn through stories. I believe that the stories we tell our children are very important. Another series that I happened upon while looking through the Chinaberry catalogue was by Tamora Pierce. Here, the main characters, male and female, were all very capable and caring. The work ethic, love of nature, and sense of community only added to the charm. I think that we need more of these stories, and they should be the types of things that we see on TV and in the movies, because I think those media have a bigger impact on our culture at large. I used to fantasize that if I had enough money I would sponsor competitions for shows that told stories that we should hear, that show determination and fortitude, for example. The media industry cops out by saying that they are only showing us what we want to see, that there are fewer female characters because boys will not watch a show about girls, but that girls will watch a show about guys. My response is that if you let the girls do something interesting, the boys will watch. *Sabrina, the Teenage Witch* and *The Mystery Files of Shelby Woo* are both examples of popular shows that feature female characters that have brains and are not just boy crazy.

TECHNOLOGY AND FAMILY LIFE EDUCATION

I have focused on the dangers of technology and the mass media for the adjustment of children. However, family life educators are mobilizing these resources to be positive forces of change. Dr. Barbara Settles (1993) suggests that in addition to choosing to publish articles in a wider range of publications, scholars will want to add more high-tech parent education products such as videos, computer games, and videotex.

Dr. Alan Hawkins of Brigham Young University uses a novel approach that takes advantage of today's technology. He created a Web site at http://fatherwork.byu.edu where anyone can log on and get a range of information, from ideas for activities to do with children to inspirational stories that encourage fathers to connect with and care for their offspring. For example, one story concerned a father who expressed caring for his grown son by showing up with groceries unasked when his son became unemployed. Hundreds of other new Web pages about families can be found at www.familytrack.com. The Web site approach has some distinct advantages. First, it is a way to reach a group of people who feel more comfortable in front of their computers than coming in to classes about parenting or talking about their feelings with a group of strangers. Second, the use of stories has a lot of power. Whereas a didactic approach can sometimes be threatening, stories invite us in and can be interpreted individually by any listener. Stories allow possibilities and creativity. Stories are remembered more easily than facts. The literature indicates that for lasting and meaningful change in parenting, affective, behavioral, cognitive, and ethical dimensions must be employed (Mahoney, 1991 as cited in Dollahite, Hawkins, and Brotherson, 1996). Stories have been rediscovered in the therapy field in the 1990s—McAdams (1985, as cited in Dollahite, Hawkins, and Brotherson, 1996) found that people think of and change their identity in a "life story" and Palus (1993, as cited in Dollahite, Hawkins, and Brotherson, 1996) found that lasting transformations in adulthood become part of life stories. Since people think of their lives as stories, then using their own and other peoples' stories can be a powerful way to open up areas of possibility and encourage change (White and Epson, 1990 as cited in Dollahite, Hawkins, and Brotherson, 1996). It is a nonthreatening way to learn from other people's experiences.

Another popular Web site is the National Parent Information network, which can be found at www.npin.org or can be accessed by telephone at (800) 583-4135. This project, which is funded by the Federal Department of Education, is housed at the University of Illinois. Staff members are researchers with backgrounds in areas of early childhood, health care, day care, and special education. Their database is the largest educational database in the world, established by the Educational Resources Information Service, which is a federally financed and managed network. When people request information by computer or phone, they are linked with expert advice, either online or through a library or community organization. Questions range from how to get a toddler to sleep to how to request federally financed special education assistance. This is a wonderful use of technology, a way to help people who might not be able to get help in another way.

CONCLUSION

As therapists we can help strengthen and support families, rather than blaming or labeling. We can show that we know how hard families try, and respect that effort when we see it. We can emphasize their strengths rather than their weaknesses. We can make conscious the messages from the culture. While we are embedded in something, it is difficult to have the perspective to see it at all. Sexism and consumerism, for example, may be hard to see, because they are so ingrained that we just accept them. We can help families stay connected, to allow parents to give the support that they want to both boys and girls and to see individuation and separation as different. We can tell stories that are solution oriented, not problem oriented, that allow for the possibility of change. We can tell stories that widen possibilities and promote positive behavior. We can validate the many ways to express caring, bringing family members closer together rather than pitting them against one another. We can promote forgiveness. If we assume that everyone makes mistakes, it will be more possible for all of us to try, making our own mistakes along the way. In fact, love means often having to say you're sorry. While we can help promote forgiveness, we cannot offer absolution or the opportunity to deny responsibility. We can help families to define themselves. What is important to them? What are their values, pleasures, backgrounds, and boundaries? We can help them establish their separateness and affiliation as individuals and as families. We can help tie families to their communities. We encourage wholeness by modeling and acceptance. We can acknowledge that there are not always solutions, but that it feels better to be in it together. We can also foster hope and channel energies into community-oriented solutions. We can help connect people to one another, because we all grow better if we know that there are others around who care about us, and whom we can care for. We can help families define what is important to them, and make choices based on those decisions.

SELF-EXPLORATION:
EFFECTS OF AMERICAN CULTURE ON THE FAMILY

1. Discuss with your children the marketing technique of pairing a product with a human need or value such as trust or sex. Watch some ads with them and discuss what strategy you think the ad creator was trying to use.
2. Imagine together what would be different if there were no advertising on television.
3. Discuss with your children the fact that large companies own magazines, and how the ads or articles are influenced by this.
   a. See if you can find out what companies are owned by a couple of large multinational corporations such as General Motors or Nestlé.
   b. Research who owns various magazines or television channels of your choice.
   c. Look at what companies are advertised in these magazines or television channels.
   d. See if any articles are linked to products these corporations sell.

4. Try to find examples of intelligent, kind, caring, and capable men and women in television shows.
5. Discuss how women are generally portrayed on television.
6. Try to find television shows that routinely show good conflict resolution skills.

Chapter 22

Spirituality

Dominicus So

The modern profession of psychotherapy for children and families has often distanced itself from issues of religion and spirituality. Despite the seminal work of Carl Jung and William James, most psychology writers have chosen not to attend to religious and spiritual issues when treating families with problem children and adolescents. Religion and spirituality indeed appear to have been alienated from many aspects of life, including scientific exploration, academia, public health, and government. Yet, polls have found that at least 40 percent of all Americans attend a place of worship at least weekly, and about 90 percent of all American adults say they pray to God at least occasionally (Gallup, 1993).

The reasons for the alienation of child-centered family therapy from spiritual and religious issues are largely historical, rather than therapeutic. Prest and Keller (1993) have pointed out factors that have contributed to the contextual barriers to addressing spirituality in therapy. They cited reasons such as the mental health professions' rigid conceptions of spirituality and their biases against formal spiritual institutions. Similar to family traditions that are transmitted to the newer generations, the older generations in the mental health professions teach the newer ones not to attend to religious and spiritual issues. As a result, although family therapists are found to be the most religious among four different mental health disciplines (Bergin and Jensen, 1990), the alienation of religion from other aspects of life is prevalent in family therapy in general, and child-centered family therapy in particular. To this day, many practitioners of family therapy and child and adolescent psychotherapy are apprehensive about examining religious and spiritual issues with their clients.

Fortunately, the practice of separating spiritual healing from lasting psychological changes has been challenged by many (Bergin, 1991; Kudlac, 1991; Richards and Bergin, 1997). Although family health care professionals readily look into other ecosystemic influences, such as schools, community, and culture, only recently have family therapists begun to look at the common grounds of religion and psychology (Jones, 1996). Religion and spirituality are gradually being integrated into the training, research, and clinical practice of adult psychotherapy and family therapy by an increasing number of mental health providers (Prest and Keller, 1993; Richards and Bergin, 1997; Shafranske, 1996; Shafranske and Malony, 1996). Multiple books on that topic have recently been published by the American Psychological Association (Richards and Bergin, 1997; Shafranske, 1996).

Two important points need to be made before we examine the subject matter. First, while the discussion is largely drawn from a Judeo-Christian tradition of organized religion and spirituality, I hope that much is applicable to other religious traditions as well. Second, I intend not to make fine distinction among terms such as faith, belief, religion, and spirituality. While I understand the importance of differentiating them in theoretical and empirical work, these various terms are interwoven into a whole in everyday family life. Seldom do clients think of them as distinct entities.

THE IMPORTANCE OF SPIRITUALITY
AND RELIGION IN FAMILY THERAPY
AND CHILD-CENTERED PRESENTING PROBLEMS

Despite the alienation of child-centered family therapy from spirituality, they have many common goals which, in short, are to improve the family's strength and quality of life. Stander and colleagues (1994:29) list the overlapping and interacting roles of spirituality/religion and family therapy:

1. To foster a sense of perspective
2. To give meaning to life
3. To provide rituals that transform and connect
4. To provide social support networks
5. To structure society and set ethical norms
6. To give an identity and heritage to family members
7. To support families
8. To facilitate positive change in individuals
9. To look out for the physical and emotional welfare of family members
10. To educate family members

Possible Benefits and Risks of Organized Religious Institutions in the Life of Families with Children

In examining the use of religious beliefs and practices in helping families, Abbot, Berry, and Meredith (1990) have identified several similar functions and benefits that may be found by incorporating religion/spirituality into child-centered family therapy: enhancement of the family's social support network, sponsorship of family activities and recreation, promotion of supportive family teachings and values, provision of family social and welfare services, and encouragement to seek spiritual assistance with personal and family problems.

Participation and membership in organized religious institutions may provide a social support system for members by creating opportunities for friendships with other families. These families may have similar difficult experiences with children's problems, such as temper tantrums, bed-wetting, drug abuse, or premature sexual activity. By giving access to families with similar problems, the church can provide a basis for helping to keep the family intact. Moral and ethical imperatives may also be influential in preventing undesirable behaviors.

Organized religions also provide support through different organizational activities ranging from summer Bible school for children to youth fellowships and kosher cooking classes. When fellow synagogue/church members provide gifts of food during a crisis or give support to new mothers, for instance, the love and caring that is expressed can help alleviate the family's stress. Family therapists who encourage children to participate in congregational activities often indirectly help parents put their children under adult supervision when the parents are not available for such supervision. Such individual participation by the family members also tends to foster a sense of belonging. That is particularly important when a family is going through hardship and possible breakdown. This common connection with the religious organization also allows the family to remain an open system receptive to extrafamilial interventions when necessary.

Another way in which religious affiliations may benefit families is by encouraging them to participate in activities together. Attending church/synagogue services, children's rites of passage, marriage enrichment retreats, family appreciation days, and other family-oriented activities may strengthen family ties. Family therapists may encourage the family's participation in church/synagogue to help members find common meanings in particular life events, speak their unspoken feeling for one another, and foster family rituals and ceremonies.

According to Abbot, Berry, and Meredith (1990), religion may also provide a family with strength through the belief in divine intervention. In times of crisis, the family may look to God for personal and family assistance. Believing that God has intervened or will intervene on one's behalf can provide individuals with comfort, guidance, and inspiration. Family therapists who work with frustrated but devout parents may bring up this belief to help them endure difficult situations, and to renew their hope and feel empowered. If appropriate, the therapists may invite the family to use prayers and petition God for comfort, help, and guidance outside of the therapy sessions.

In some subcultures, such as the African-American culture in the United States, the inclusion of religion and spirituality in treating families is particularly important (Boyd-Franklin, 1989). It is generally recognized that spirituality is deeply rooted in that culture and many other cultures, including the Latin American and Native American cultures. Many of the treatment techniques advocated for specific cultural groups are probably useful for religious families of other cultures as well.

LAURA AND LEONARD

Laura and Leonard were both PhD-level geologists working for the federal government and were devout agnostics. Laura had been brought up by parents who were Episcopalian, in name only. She had never attended Sunday school or church. Leonard was an only child who had been brought up by parents who were adherents of Maharishi Yuni. He had never been pushed into attending events and simply grew up thinking it was his parents' "thing." He had a very humanistic orientation. Leonard's parents died in the Lockerbie plane crash and Laura's parents retired to Arizona the year she got married.

After five carefree years of marriage, they decided to start their family. Their first child was born with spina bifida, but they were stoic and committed to making a joyous home. When their second child was born eighteen months later with club feet, they felt shocked and strained. Their third child was born delivered stillborn, at which point they both became severely depressed and confused about what they had done to "deserve" such pain. They sought treatment at the advice of Laura's parents, who came to help out for a month and felt the children would not be properly cared for unless one of them could "snap out of it."

The grieving process was facilitated in a series of joint sessions as well as individual sessions. The sessions centered on themes of existential meaningfulness and aloneness as well as responsibility. Through these discussions, they realized that while their love for each other was solid, they were isolated in Washington, DC, without any community. They decided to get involved with the

(continued)

(continued)

parent support group for spina bifida children—a group they had previously avoided because it was too overwhelming. They also decided to volunteer a little time each week to work for Easter Seals, whose offices were near their home. In this way, they would be part of the Kerger solution.

In search of more healing, it was their decision to spend an hour each Wednesday evening reading from some spiritually uplifting piece of literature and discussing it with each other. They found this invaluable in relating their experience to the struggles inherent in the human experience. Each week, it helped them to think about ways to nurture their children and each other. It was during this time that they paused to think about how they could rejoice in what they were grateful to have rather than feeling bad about their burdens. Finding a spiritual path for this couple was an essential part of the treatment process.

Family Processes and Issues Affected by Religion and Spirituality

Spirituality and religion impact on many areas of family life and child-centered family therapy. Religious parents and/or children come into family therapy with a system of values, attitudes, beliefs, and behavior prescribed by their religious orientation. This system includes ideals about family life, marriage, parenthood, family purpose, family size, procreation, the meaning of love and unity, boundary and inclusion, sexuality and intimacy, gender roles, division of labor, power and control, and the methods of raising and disciplining children. Almost all religions involve at least some of these aspects. Almost all the clients, parents or children, either adhere to or resist some of the doctrines their religion teaches. Sperry and Giblin (1996) have studied the impact of religious values on family life in three important domains: (1) family boundaries, (2) issues of control, and (3) intimacy. Each will be explained below with specific examples of how therapists can deal with those issues in child-centered family therapy.

Individual and Family Boundaries

Religious traditions sometimes determine who is inside the family, who is in the "congregation family," and who are the godparents. Family therapists often need to identify key informants outside of the immediate family, but within the perceived family boundary. Including such "extended family" in the therapy process can help therapists gain entry into the family system and learn destructive family secrets.

The structural approach of family therapy, as developed by Minuchin, emphasizes looking at boundary and inclusion issues in families. Child-centered family therapists need to evaluate how the family's religion can complicate boundaries in the family system. For example, religion can dictate whether and to what extent a nonbiological parent may serve as a caretaker (e.g., a grandparent, a stepparent, or a godparent). Sometimes, religion-prescribed parental roles may conflict with parental roles expected by society and the children. Other times, religious traditions can foster patterns of enmeshment and/or distance among family members by age, gender, birth order, generation, or cultural experiences. Consider how many fundamentalist Christian religions promote home schooling to avoid more secular influences in the public school (fostering enmeshment) or how many Orthodox Jewish families shun a person who marries outside of the religion (fostering separation).

Within the family dynamics, many adolescents feel that parents use religious dictates as an excuse to invade the children's and siblings' privacy boundaries and subsystem. Sometimes, though, religion can permit people outside of the family, such as a pastor, a Sunday school teacher, or a fellow churchgoer, to enter the family boundary and intervene in what is going on in the family.

On the positive side, the use of boundary instructions can help many families remain grounded and clear about family roles.

Power and Control

Second, power issues that involve the family's capacity for regulation and control and that guide the quality of parenting and role negotiating can be affected by religious and spiritual orientations. Therapists may need to reinforce or challenge the regulatory pattern prescribed by a family's religious tradition.

It is important to be able to recognize if a family member is manipulating or openly abusing power by imposing his or her religious tradition on other family members. Keep in mind that it is not always the adults, in unison, that are imposing a religious lifestyle on wayward children. Sometimes, one spouse is forcing religion on his or her mate or refusing to let their mate practice his or her preferred religion.

The power issues as prescribed by religious traditions can be very important in determining who will actively pursue and who will distance themselves in a variety of family situations.

Intimacy

Third, the issue of intimacy is manifested in the process of nurturing and caring for one another, appreciating one another's unique qualities, self-disclosing, and offering companionship. Most religions in America foster family intimacy and try to offer activities and occasions that increase intimacy. For religious families who are experiencing feelings of remoteness from one another, therapists may foster the family's participation in rituals together as a way of decreasing distance. If the family already participates in some church/synagogue rituals, the therapist can help deepen emotional intimacy by increasing the intensity of the shared interactions. For example, the use of family prayer can be expanded into prayer sharing. This not only allows the family to share their concerns, but also joins the family together in an authentic encounter with their individual weaknesses and need for one another.

The family therapist also needs to understand how intimacy is manifested and fostered by the family's religious background. Some important questions to ask are: How should intimacy be expressed, physically and emotionally, in their religion or worldview? Is there a congruence between how the religion dictates that intimacy be expressed and whether individuals perceive it in the intended way? Has one member's spiritual orientation caused any other members to feel misunderstood or taken for granted?"

Due to the obvious impact of religion and spirituality on child development and family processes, it is unwise for the therapist not to pay attention to the significance of religious and spiritual issues in the evaluation, treatment, and prevention of family issues.

SUE AND GEORGE

Sue and George were immigrants to the United States during the 1950s. Sue was from Florence, Italy, and George was from the Caribbean island of Grenada. Both had been raised Catholic and, while only occasional churchgoers, felt that they tried to live according to the Church's teachings. Sue came from a family with an alcoholic mother and grandmother and an absent father. George had been brought up in an orphanage. Both felt that their belief systems sustained them through many rough times and were essential to their well-being.

They had five children during the first six years of their marriage: four girls and a boy, the youngest. They did not use any birth control until the Church gave the appropriate edict. Their daughters all attended the local parochial school, but each of them had difficult adolescent stages. Two of them became pregnant within a year before graduation and decided to be single parents. The eldest daughter was heavily involved in drugs and alcohol during high school and for many years afterward.

(continued)

(continued)

As the children ran into difficulties, the Church community was very rejecting of their lifestyles. The community did not come forth to offer comfort, support, help, or, most important, forgiveness. Both Sue and George felt guilty about their children's problems and rejection by their spiritual community. Feeling that they were at an impasse, they entered therapy. George had decided to move to a new community where they would not be shunned, while Sue, who became depressed and anxious about the situation, did not want to leave her home.

Therapy focused on affirming the spiritual strength of both daughters who opted to be single mothers: neither could face an abortion or marriage to young men for whom they were not well suited. Both were strong and took responsibility for their mistakes and their values. The spiritual strength of the daughters was supported in accord with the parents' belief that the girls were "good" and trying to do what God wanted them to do.

Second, the parents were put in touch with a very liberal Catholic parish that was some thirty minutes' drive from their home. The idea was to explore the new community and see whether it would be nice to move and live close to that church.

Third, the parents and therapist spent a few sessions discussing only the role of organized religion in one's life. The need to shape a personal view of "life's purpose" as one became older and more mature was discussed. Both Sue and George felt that the church provided them with needed social outlets, but each agreed that they left theology behind them a long time ago. They just wanted to relax and be restored by the ritual and fellowship offered by church attendance. They wanted affirmation in their work as human beings and as family.

After twenty sessions, the couple had renewed enthusiasm for their future and were eager to try rejoicing in their family triumphs instead of feeling shamed by public failures.

ASSESSMENT

When Are Discussions of Spiritual and Religious Issues Indicated?

In evaluating the problems families bring into therapy, family therapists need to be sensitive to issues framed by the family and its members in spiritual and religious terms. For some very religious parents and their rebellious children, religion could be a major emotional button. These religious parents for years may have been trying to make their children adhere to their religion of origin. They may have coerced their children at an early age to conform, only to find out they can no longer coerce them after a certain age. The family therapist therefore needs to be aware of when and how those issues can be brought up and used to elicit the family's discussion of the impact of such conflict on both children and the parents.

One important dimension that family therapists need to assess is the degree of conservatism or fundamentalism in the family's religion. Sperry and Giblin (1996) suggested that this evaluation is crucial for understanding what the clients expect from therapy, as well as whether the family's religious practices will help them integrate, disintegrate, or stagnate.

Religious conservatism affects one's openness to the therapy process. Sperry and Giblin (1996), for example, found that many fewer Orthodox Jews than contemporary Jews enter treatment. Orthodox Jews seek psychotherapy only as the last resort because they are sensitive to the stigma of mental problems. They rely more on their own resources before seeking psychotherapy and are much more concerned about finding a therapist of their same religious tradition. Denton and Denton (1992) also found that conservative fundamentalist Christian families are much less healthy than nonfundamentalist counterparts on family intimacy issues. Nonfundamentalist families are more likely to display care without smothering, and encourage personal growth and individuation without compromising generational boundaries. They found that nonfundamentalist families are less enmeshed and are more likely than fundamentalist families to encourage family members to take age-appropriate responsibilities, make appropriate judgments, perceive change as nonthreatening, and keep appropriate boundaries between immediate and extended families.

Contraindications

In some situations, explicit inclusion of spiritual and religious strategies is contraindicated, at least in the short term. Obviously, if any family members have indicated that they do not desire the use or discussion of spiritual interventions, a nonspiritual approach must be used. Some family members may be particularly resistant to any religious and spiritual discussion if there was some history of religious abuse. Religious abuse includes an overly punitive approach to religious participation, education, and moral and sexual education. In other situations, some individuals may have aversive emotional reactions, such as fear, anger, or hatred, to the power structure of some religious institutions. Any use and discussion of spiritual interventions may cause such families to be so emotionally charged that they cannot stay focused on the concrete issues at hand. In all of those situations, family therapists need to continuously respect the family's desire and need to avoid any such discussion. Moreover, when a family member is apparently delusional or psychotic, such an approach is contraindicated. The bottom line is that therapists should pursue religious and spiritual goals only when the family shows an interest, and such pursuit is in the child's and family's best interest.

How Should the Family Therapist Look at the Family's Spirituality and Religious Practices?

Pruyser (1976) devised seven categories for "pastoral diagnosis," all of which have significance for family functioning and how individual members relate to each other. All are appropriate areas of inquiry for a secular psychologist who is seeing a family with strong religious identifications. For family assessments, these areas of concern can be explored directly in the following ways or used as guidelines for an implicit evaluation:

1. Awareness of the holy: What is sacred for the person and the family as a whole?
2. Providence: Who and what does the person and the whole family place hope and trust in?
3. Faith: What do the person and the family believe in? What do the person and the whole family commit to?
4. Grace or gratefulness: To what extent and for what is the person thankful? What has each person been given? Is he or she aware of and happy for that? What should the family be thankful for? What have they been thankful for, and what have they not been thankful for?
5. Repentance or sin: How does an individual, and the family as a whole, deal with mistakes, lies, and betrayals? Who has the responsibility? And how is responsibility being distributed and decided?
6. Communion: How do individuals ask for help, receive and give care, and express love? Do individuals feel united with the rest of the family? Does the family feel connected to anyone outside the family?
7. Sense of vocation: What is the family's sense of reason for existence and purpose in their individual work and lives? How satisfied is the family with their purposes?

Summarizing the use of more formal statistically sound assessment tools, Sperry and Giblin (1996) suggested the use of some Likert-scale assessment tools, such as the twenty-item Spiritual Well-Being Scale (SWB; Ellison, 1983) and the thirty-eight-item Spiritual Experience Index (SEI; Genia, 1990, 1991). The SWB gives two subscales: Existential Well-Being (EWB) and Religious Well-Being (RWB), measuring (1) an individual's sense of life purpose and satisfaction and (2) the nature of the relationship with God, respectively. The use of these formal measurement tools will facilitate the discussion of spirituality and religious issues in the family. Interested readers can refer to other more thorough and comprehensive reviews of formal assessment tools on faith and spiritual life (e.g., Fitchett, 1993).

Are Family Members Different in Their Spirituality?

One important distinction to make among family members is their individual religious belief and practice. It is a mistake to assume that they have the same degree of adherence to and participation in their religious organizations even if the entire family belongs to the same religious denomination. Richards and Bergin (1997) suggest that family therapists need to be aware of the individual differences among family members and their degree of comfort with various spiritual and religious interventions. Obviously, some members are more open to spiritual interventions than others.

TREATMENT AND PREVENTION

Secular psychologists wanting to utilize the power of spirituality need to walk a fine line between encouraging the healing and strengthening aspects in a family's spiritual life and exposing and trying to change negative and hurtful aspects of a family's spiritual life. Each treatment strategy discussed below varies in how often it can help a family use spirituality to assimilate stressors and how often spirituality must make room for more effective problem solving and relational patterns. It is the constant weighing of how specific forms of spirituality affect a particular family coping with a specific set of stressors that determines whether it is being a help or hindrance to the family in the current crisis. The secular therapist is in a unique position to maximize the family's ability to use spirituality as a flexible and creative resource in coping with the current crisis. Instead of providing "answers," the secular therapist explores with families all possible ways that their spiritual meaning and practices can hinder or help their situation.

Searching and Affirming the Meanings of the Family Relationship

An important focus in assessing and treating families concerns their search for meaning or the "spirituality of the ordinary" (Sperry and Giblin,

1996:518). Sperry and Giblin (1996) suggested that, compared to discussing theological concepts or religious practices, it is more helpful for therapists to focus on the family members' experience of the meanings in relationships. The therapist's task is to help them experience and verbalize the meaning of love, acceptance, and forgiveness, the value dimension of family life together, and the way they communicate, resolve conflicts, remain committed, and decide according to their religious beliefs and commitment to transcendence. An important spiritual strategy is, for instance, to help the angered parents to forgive their wronged adolescents, or to help the disappointed youth to accept the parents' troubled history.

Conversely, in describing cases of negative relational patterns, family therapy should bring spirituality to bear by making the family focus on the love they share, highlighting the underlying positive connections despite the negative exchanges. For instance, if an adolescent complains about the parents' control and discipline, it is the therapist's task to help the parent verbalize the underlying love, and then to work with the family on an alternative style of discipline agreeable to both the parents and the adolescent. In short, family therapy should highlight the successful incidents of good communication, conflict resolution, and mutual commitment to maintaining loving and transcendence-centered family life. To achieve that, the therapist may frequently praise the parents' and child's loving expressions in the therapy setting, and help them generalize such expressions in their home settings.

Therapeutic Disclosure of Spiritual Self

Any therapeutic relationship is about the sharing of life. Other authors, such as Sperry and Giblin (1996), would agree that the family therapist's own spiritual life is an important therapeutic resource. First of all, it is important that the family therapist creates a climate where the family finds it comfortable to discuss their spiritual issues. Child-centered family therapists who are working with openly religious individuals can pave the way with questions such as, "If you had sufficient strength and faith, how would you try to solve the children's problem?" By doing that, the therapist displays his or her attempt to understand the family's entire worldview, including their spiritual worldview. More important is for the family therapist to have an awareness of and skills to verbalize, when appropriate, his or her own prior struggles in life. Therapists' sharing of their own spiritual challenges may elicit the family's own search for the deeper meanings relating to their own stressful events and children's problems.

Family therapists often wonder what is too personal to disclose to the family. One good yardstick is whether the depth and breadth of the disclosure is crucial to facilitating the achievement of the desired therapeutic goals. Also, it is imperative that the disclosure relates to issues that have long ago seen closure and understanding for the therapist. It is inappropriate to share ongoing confusions or crises. In any event, the family therapist should not disclose anything too personal or confidential that they do not feel comfortable with, since it is sure to violate the therapeutic contract, and clients are not bound by any obligation of confidentiality. Inappropriate self-disclosures are a sign of unresolved countertransference or poor self-control and require the therapist to seek consultation and supervision.

Spiritual Reframing

Church attendance is not always a good indicator of the degree of spirituality in an individual or family. For example, African-American family members may not attend services but tend to remain very spiritual and instill this same spirituality in their children. Spiritually reframing statements such as, "God will hold you and guide you for everything you need to do" and "Let go and let God" may be important for enhancing the working alliance with spiritual but nonchurchgoing families, as they communicate an understanding of the belief systems and resources used by the client (Boyd-Franklin, 1989). As secular therapists, the task is to keep connected with the family on a spiritual-emotional level.

Using a systems approach, Kudlac (1991) defined family as an interacting communications network in which one's responses affect the action of the collective (the family), through the flexible use of a linguistic system composed of signs, symbols, gestures, and words with meanings partly derived from the family's religion and spirituality. According to her, therapists need to work with the family's reality as the family defines it. One method is by matching or mirroring, which means that therapists use the family's own religious metaphors to acknowledge the importance of religious matter for the family and to move the therapeutic process constructively. For instance, if the mother says, "I think God is trying to test if we can go through all this while our son is on drugs," the family therapist may ask, "What is the message God is giving you in his drug abuse?" If the mother continues to talk about God as a punishing God, then it may be more appropriate for the family therapist to ask, "How does the punishing God affect the family and contribute to the son's drug use?" or "How does God affect family adjustment and the problem-resolution process?" than to immediately attack or ignore the family view of a punishing God or the notion of a God.

Prest and Keller (1993) suggest the usefulness of discussing religious/spiritual contexts, or any other particular ideological contexts in which meanings of events, problems, and their solutions are derived. The authors list several therapeutic strategies to use within the more conventional belief systems, such as Catholicism, Judaism, and Protestantism: (1) identifying previously used solutions that have become part of the current issue (e.g., So you believed that prayers alone would improve your children's academic problems?), (2) eliciting the family's basic beliefs that have partially caused the problem (e.g., What is your belief about transcendental intervention and your own actions and responsibilities in easing the present problem?), and (3) discussing the misfit between the family's spiritual map and the present situation. It challenges them to mobilize of alternative resources within their belief system to resolve their problems (e.g., It seems that prayer alone did not work. I wonder what other ways your faith would suggest that you act now to resolve your family's issues).

Challenging Religious Views on Boundaries, Intimacy, and Power Structures

Family therapists will frequently find that they need to help families explore religious concepts that are interfering with healthy family functioning. Using a survey of family professionals' perceptions, Brigman (1984) found numerous religious attitudes that are damaging to family life. According to his finding, rigid religious doctrines that are insensitive to human needs; negative about sexuality, contraception, divorce, and marriage; or narrowly focus on sin, judgment, and guilt are all factors that are detrimental to healthy family life. For that reason, child-centered family therapists need to help the parents understand and the adolescents verbalize the impact that religious rigidity and negativity may have on the adolescent's emotional and social life within the family. Some social skills training in communication and conflict negotiation is indicated to help families discuss the individual concerns related to religious doctrine and practices. Such processes will also empower the parents to help their children grow independently and responsibly, but with adequate and necessary input from the parents.

Practicing Implicitly Spiritual Virtues, Such As Trust, Patience, Repentance, Forgiveness, and Acceptance

The spiritual self tends to highlight the importance of unity, communion, harmony, and similarities, which are what families in conflict need the most. Child-centered family therapists should emphasize these spiritual virtues, such as trusting or forgiving one's children, or accepting the parent's chemical dependency history in order to help the family unite and deal with the child's issues at hand. Despite the virtues of forgiveness and acceptance, it is important for the family therapist not to overlook real problems that require immediate attention, and not to discount any victimization within the family. Therefore, it is as important to acknowledge their pain as it is to help the family members practice these virtues to heal one another's pain. Often, these experiences of trust and forgiveness are very similar to a religious conversion experience, which can be brought up as the family processes their feelings regarding the change.

Implicitly Spiritual Techniques, Such As Guided Imagery, Gestalt Techniques, Empty Chair Technique, Journals, and Letter Writing

I have used these techniques to help clients and families verbalize their incomplete feelings relating to a deceased parent with whom thre are strong unresolved feelings or a noncomplying parent. "What would you have said to your father if he was sitting in that chair?" "What will you as a family write in a letter to _____ [whoever they identify as a higher power] as a family about what is happening in your family?" "If [God] is sitting in front of all of us, what will you ask for your family? And what do each of you think [God] would say to you?" It is important for family therapists to attend to the similar and different perspectives and feelings each family member has. The response clients give as their projection of what [God], the universe, or a deceased parent would say are good not only as a treatment process, but also as an assessment tool to find out what relationship the person has, and how it may be changed.

Utilizing the Family's Religious Network

Child-centered family therapists often need to work outside the therapy sessions, in the family's and the child's multiple systems, including the religious community. Many system-based (Joanides, 1996; Nakhaima and Dicks, 1995; Weaver, Koenig, and Larson, 1997; Weber and Wynn, 1986) and minority-focused (Boyd-Franklin, 1989) mental health professionals have provided us with such an approach. When families experience a crisis due to the children, the church can be a very helpful resource. Churches can often assist a family who has been burned out of their home more quickly than government human services in the form of emotional, financial, and spiritual support.

One way family therapists can utilize the church to aid families is by finding churches and church members that an isolated family can rely on in emergencies or when consistent support is needed. Many families that enter mental health clinics are not in contact with their extended families, leaving them with no readily available support. Under constant stress, these families are usually the most overburdened and dysfunctional. Having a stable church network can be vital to the survival of many at-risk families. Both single parents struggling to raise children and patients with no family members or friends who have recently been released from the hospital can benefit greatly from this type of networking (Boyd-Franklin, 1989).

Using Consultative Models and/or Collaboration with the Clergy

Hand in hand with the last approach, consultation and collaboration require the family therapist to step out of the therapy room and the family system. Many writers, such as Boyd-Franklin (1989), Joanides (1996), Weaver, Koenig, and Larson (1997), and Weber and Wynn (1986), have supported some forms of consultative models for working with religious families. Joanides (1996) advocated a consultation model that assumes the family are experts and uses consultation/reflection teams to facilitate the discussion of difficult issues, or intermittent debriefing sessions to allow the family to review what they liked and disliked about the sessions and how they want to be different in the future.

Other consultative models in working with spiritual families look into utilizing other experts. The clergy are often recommended as persons with whom to consult and collaborate. People, especially religious families, often trust them and feel comfortable talking to them about family and personal issues and problems. For many, the clergy represent an extension of assistance from their church home and God. Often the clergy have become receptive in collaborating with the helping professions.

ETHICAL AND PROFESSIONAL DILEMMAS AND GUIDELINES

Dual/Multiple Relationship

Dual relationships should always be avoided, if possible. If a family therapist attends the same religious congregation as the family, it is often very confusing and frustrating for the family to maintain a dual relationship (religious/social and professional) with the family (Stander et al., 1994). This practice should be avoided because it poses many ethical questions. When are they in a therapist-client relationship and when are they in a fellow-congregation-member relationship? When, whether, and how often should religious issues be considered within the therapy context? After the therapeutic relationship has ended, how long, if ever, must the family therapist and any member of the family wait to enter into other relationships such as godparenthood, cofacilitators of a Bible study group, or teacher in religious education for the child who is the index patient? Many other similar questions often come up in the work of family therapists who have close religious and spiritual links with the family. The situation often gets complicated and out of control when the index patient is young. Youngsters often cannot differentiate the family therapist as a fellow churchgoer and as a professional provider. It is possible that the young ones may embarrass the parents or an older sibling by disclosing private, family, or personal issues publicly in a congregational setting.

Moreover, having a religious and professional dual relationship with someone from one's congregation may increase the family's reluctance to disclose in therapy. Family members may choose not to discuss issues such as sexuality, contraception, abortion, violent episodes, and financial problems for fear of embarrassment and potential discrimination or sanction. In addition, it is likely that some current or future conflict of interest may occur. Issues of payment, availability, accessibility, boundary setting, and documentation will all be compromised when a therapist begins a professional relationship with a family in his or her congregation. Normal friendships, working relationships, and professional relationships will also likely be compromised in the present and the future.

Confidentiality

Along with the issue of dual relationship, confidentiality is also difficult to handle. Should the family therapist bring into therapy information about the family received outside of therapy? How should the therapist handle information received in a therapy session from the family about some common acquaintance, such as a pastor? How should the therapist relate to the congregational leaders and other congregation members who know about the therapeutic relationship, and are enthusiastic to volunteer information and support?

In general, therapists should try not to see members of their church community as clients because of the potential risks. Such arrangements often become unnecessarily burdensome for the therapist, potentially embarrassing for the family, and possibly therapeutically undesirable, due to shared subjectivity. A good way to avoid such arrangements is referral or very clear boundary setting at the very outset of the therapeutic relationship, with the therapist discussing what is acceptable and what is not, and what kind of potential risks the family may face in the long run with such an arrangement.

Informed Consent

Due to the sensitive nature of the dual relationship and possible abuse of authority in the future, the family therapist needs to discuss the potential dangers of beginning a therapy relationship with a family in their own religious congregation.

Avoid Imposing Religious Values on Clients

To enhance change in the family, therapists may choose at times to challenge the family's belief systems. Obviously, psychotherapy and family therapy are not meant for evangelization and proselytizing. When the family is angry or disappointed with God, the family therapist needs to empathically listen to their pain, instead of trying to impose his or her "faith" and hope on the family. It is also important that family therapists are clear about the differences between their own religious beliefs and those of the family they are working with. They not only need to respect the difference, but be on guard for their own tendency to impose on the family their own religious beliefs or ideological tendencies, such as feminism or liberation theology, which are often regarded as against traditional religious organizations.

Awareness of One's Religious/Spiritual Self and Its Limits

Like therapists working with individual clients, family therapists need to establish healthy, therapeutic use of the self. It is important for the family therapist to be aware of the influence of his or her own religious and spiritual orientation, or the lack thereof, on his or her life and psychological being. Religion has very often played a role in forming our beliefs, feelings, and behaviors involving gender, power, self-definitions, fate, self-efficacy, interpersonal relations, and family dynamics.

Some means by which family therapists can evaluate themselves are experiential coursework, existential self-reflection, and supportive supervision. Experiential coursework can include courses covering the importance of spiritual practices for mental health/illness, and drawing one's own family genogram, tracing the religious influences throughout one's history. Existential self-reflection may involve psychotherapy or spiritual direction that will allow introspection about one's faith and spiritual development. Supportive supervision may focus on the personal comfort level one has using spiritual approaches in family therapy, understanding therapists' religious counter-transference, challenging spiritual blind spots, and widening spiritual perspectives.

Respect Clients' Religious Authority

Although the family therapist may have negative feelings about the family's religious organization or leaders, it is imperative that he or she respects them. Showing respect for their spiritual leaders may be as important in establishing and maintaining a working alliance as showing respect for their religious belief.

Observing Work-Setting (Church-State) Boundaries

Many family therapists work with families as state or city employees, or on the site of a public institution, such as a community mental health clinic or a state hospital. It becomes a questionable practice if the family therapist chooses to extensively use spiritual strategies under the auspices of the state, with public physical, financial, and human resources.

Practicing Within the Boundaries of Professional Competence

Family therapists, when using spiritual strategies, should be careful in functioning within their prescribed areas of expertise. Therapists who encourage family members to express their wrongdoings should not give the impression that they have the authority to absolve their "sins." Likewise, ecclesiastical leaders who are not trained as mental health professionals need to be aware of where their professional competencies stop. Both groups should refer the family to other, more appropriate professionals or to consult each other in a collaborative arrangement.

Forgiveness and Reporting of Abuse

Family therapists should be careful not to enable oppression and victimization by fostering forgiveness and encouraging tolerance of pain and oppression. As mental health professionals, they need to be very clear about their professional obligations to report child abuse and neglect, while also being sensitive to family dynamics that maintain oppression.

CONCLUSION

In summary, today's therapist will need to deal with a wide range of spiritual and religious issues. At a minimum, they need to explore the following seven areas:

1. *Strengths and limitations of current belief system:* Is religion or spirituality a positive force in the lives of clients or is it contributing to or limiting their problem-solving abilities? Is this an appropriate area to explore with this particular family?

2. *Role of community:* Is the family using the religious or spiritual community to network and expand their helping community? What are the untapped resources?

3. *Coping rituals:* What are the specific practices and rituals that the family or child uses for successful coping (e.g., prayer, church attendance, keeping a diary, meditating) and could they be used with the presenting problem?

4. *Relationship between morals, values, and therapeutic goals:* Understanding the religious and spiritual nature of the individuals in the family will help the therapist pinpoint appropriate goals and intervention strategies. For example, if the parent's religion dictates "virginity," it is counterproductive to encourage them to teach safe sex to their adolescent daughter.

5. *Acceptance and forgiveness:* Are there behaviors or problems that family members ultimately need to "accept" and not try to change? What humanistic or spiritual writings, arguments, or beliefs will further that acceptance process? Are there people that need to be "forgiven"? Again, how can the therapist creatively use the client's spirituality or religion to help further the forgiveness process?

6. *Boundary violations:* Therapists need to make sure that they keep a professional therapist-client relationship that is not competing with or overshadowed by the relationship of sharing a common religion or spiritual path. To the extent that similarity facilitates a therapeutic alliance, such similarity is useful. To the extent that it creates a dual relationship, it can be very toxic and detrimental.

7. *Countertransference problems:* Therapists need to make sure that they do not proselytize or highlight their own spiritual path as the one that may help the client. Secular psychologists are not religious healers and always need to be alert to that pull.

SELF-EXPLORATION:
DRAW A SPIRITUAL FLOWER

1. Draw a simple daisy with an undesignated number of petals on it.
2. On each petal, write a word or two to indicate the spiritual gifts displayed by various family members, e.g., love, hope, faith, trust, guidance, communion, forgiveness, and so on.
3. Add more petals when necessary.
4. Write your family name in the center of the daisy.
5. Visualize all kinds of nurturance being supplied from whatever source you desire (natural or personal, e.g., sunlight, or a gardener applying fertilizer, a mother watering the soil, a passerby appreciating the daisy).
6. Visualize the uniqueness of the color, smell, shape, size, height, and other physical characteristics of the daisy.
7. Enjoy all the sensory images.
8. Take five minutes to appreciate each of those physical qualities.
9. Take ten minutes to appreciate each of the more abstract qualities written on the petals.

Resources

Chapter 1

Bibliography

Bowen, M. 1976. Theory in the practice of psychotherapy. In Guerin, P.J. (Ed.), *Family therapy and practice* (pp. 42-90). New York: Gardner Press.

Bradt, J.O. 1978. Friendship, kinship and work systems. In Simpkinson, C.H. and Platt, L.J. (Eds.), *1978 synopsis of family therapy practice*. Vienna, VA: Family Therapy Practice Network, Inc.

Bradt, J.O. 1980. The family with young children. Chapter 6. In Carter, E. and McGoldrick, M. (Eds.), *The family life cycle: A framework for family therapy* (pp. 121-146). New York: Gardner Press.

Bumpass, L. and Rindfuss, R. 1975. Children's experience of marital disruption. *American Journal of Sociology, 85:*49-64.

Carter, E. and McGoldrick, M. 1980. The family life cycle and family therapy: An overview. Chapter 1. In Carter, E. and McGoldrick, M. (Eds.), *The family life cycle: A framework for family therapy* (pp. 3-20). New York: Gardner Press.

Colarusso, C.A. and Nemiroff, R.A. 1981. *Adult development: A new dimension in psychodynamic theory and practice.* New York: Plenum Press.

Copeland, A.P. and White, R.B. 1991. *Successful families.* Newbury Park, CA: Sage Publications, Inc.

Cromwell, R.E., Fournier, D.G., and Kvebaek, D.J. 1981. *The Kvebaek Family Structure Technique: A diagnostic and research tool in family therapy.* Jonesboro, TN: Pilgrammage.

Erikson, E.H. 1963. Eight stages of man. In *Childhood and society.* New York: W.W. Norton.

Franklin, C. and Streeter, C. 1993. Validity of the 3-D Circumplex Model for Family Assessment. Special issue: Empirical advances in social work assessment. *Research on Social Work Practice, 3*(3):258-275.

Gerson, R. 1995. The family life cycle: Phases, stages, and crises. In Mikesell, R.H., Lusterman, D., and McDaniel, S. (Eds.), *Integrating family therapy: Handbook of family psychology and systems theory* (pp. 91-111). Washington, DC: American Psychological Association.

Guerin, P.J. and Pendagast, E.G. 1976. Evaluation of family systems and genogram. In Guerin, M.P. (Ed.), *Family therapy.* New York: Gardner Press.

Hovestadt, A.G., Anderson, W.L., Piersy, F.R., Cochran, S.W., and Fine, W. 1985. A family-of-origin scale. *Journal of Marital and Family Therapy, 2*(3):287-297.

Howard, J. 1978. *Families.* New York: Simon and Schuster.

Jacobson, G.F. 1983. *The multiple crises of marital separation and divorce.* New York: Grune and Stratton.

Karpel, M.A. and Strauss, E.S. 1983. *Family evaluation.* New York: Gardner Press.

Kerr, M.E. and Bowen, M. 1988. *Family evaluation: An approach based on Bowen theory.* New York: W.W. Norton.

Lindsey, K. 1981. *Friends As family.* New York: Beacon Press.

Mailick, M.D. and Vigilante, F.W. 1997. The Family Assessment Wheel: A social constructivist perspective. *Families in Society: The Journal of Contemporary Human Services, 78*(4):361-369.

McCubbin, H.I., Olson, D., and Larsen, A. 1996. Family Crisis Oriented Personal Scales (F-COPES). In McCubbin, H.I., Thompson, A.I., and McCubbin, M.A. (Eds.), *Family assessment: Resiliency, coping and adaptation—Inventories for research and practice.* Madison, WI: University of Wisconsin System.

McCubbin, H.I., Patterson, J., and Wilson, L. 1996. Family Inventory of Life Events and Changes (FILE). In McCubbin, H.I., Thompson, A.I., and McCubbin, M.A. (Eds.), *Family assessment: Resiliency, coping and adaptation—Inventories for research and practice.* (pp. 103-178). Madison, WI: University of Wisconsin System.

McCubbin, H.I., Thompson, A.I., and McCubbin, M.A. 1996. *Family Assessment: Resiliency, coping and adaptation—Inventories for research and practice.* Madison, WI: University of Wisconsin System.

McGoldrick, M. 1980. The joining of families through marriage: The new couple. Chapter 5. In Carter, E. and McGoldrick, M. (Eds.), *The family life cycle: A framework for family therapy.* New York: Gardner Press.

McMillen, J. and Groze, V. 1994. Using placement genograms in child welfare practice. *Child Welfare, 73*(4):307-318.

Moon, S.M., Coleman, V.D., McCollum, E.E., and Nelson, T.S. 1993. Using the genogram to facilitate career decisions: A case study. *Journal of Family Psychotherapy, 4*(1):45-56.

Mostwin, D. 1981. Life space ecological model of family treatment. *International Journal of Family Psychiatry, 2*(1 Supp. 2):75-94.

Olson, D.H. 1991. Commentary: Three dimensional (3-D) circumplex model and revised scoring of FACES III. *Family Process, 30*(1):74-79.

Pargament, K. 1997. *The psychology of religion and coping: Theory, research and practice.* New York: Guilford.

Pendagast, E.G. and Sherman, C.O. 1977. A guide to the genogram. *The Family, 5*(2):3-14.

Perosa, L.M. and Perosa, S.L. 1990. The use of a bipolar item format for FACES III: A reconsideration. *Journal of Marital and Family Therapy, 16*(2):187-199.

Schaefer, S. 1972. The family and the educational process. In Hilton, H. (Ed.), *Families of the future.* Ames, IA: College of Home Economics, Iowa State University Press.

Smilkstein, G. 1978. The Family APGAR: A proposal for a family function test and its use by physicians. *Journal of Family Practice, 6*(6):1231-1239.

U.S. Bureau of the Census. 1984a. Section of Households and Families. Washington, DC: U.S. Bureau of the Census.

U.S. Bureau of the Census. 1984b. Special estimate done for Select Committee of Children, Youth and Families, U.S. House of Representatives. Washington, DC: U.S. Bureau of the Census.

Visher, J.S. and Visher, E. 1982. Stepfamilies and stepparenting. In Walsh, N. (Ed.), *Normal family processes* (pp. 331-353). New York: Guilford Press.

Wachtel, E.F. 1982. The family psyche over three generations: The genogram revisited. *Journal of Marital and Family Therapy, 8*(3):335-345.

Suggested Readings

Anderson, J. 1990. *The Single mother's book: A practical guide to managing your children, career, home, finances and everything else.* Atlanta, GA: Peachtree Publishers.

Guerin, P.J. 1972. Study your own family. In Howard, J. 1978. *Families.* New York: Simon and Schuster.

Karpel, M. and Strauss, E. 1983. *Family evaluation.* New York: Gardner Press.

Lindsey, K. 1981. *Friends As family.* New York: Beacon Press.

Mendelsohn, M. and Napier, A. (Eds.), *The book of family therapy.* Boston: Houghton Mifflin.

Starkey, P.J. 1981. Genograms, a guide to understanding one's own family system. *Perspectives on Psychiatric Care, 19*(5-6):164 173.

Literature

Simpson, J. 1976. *The American family: A history in photographs.* New York: Viking Press. A celebration of family life throughout its cycle; a rich and varied collection of images.

Film

7UP. 1965. Directed by Michael Apted. A look at the life, dreams, and fears of seven-year-olds.

35UP. 1993. Directed by Michael Apted. A return to see what happened to the seven-year-olds who were interviewed twenty-eight years ago. It traces their ambitions, failures, loves, tragedies, and challenges.

Tell Me a Riddle. 1980. An elderly couple have sharply differing needs that stir up old bitterness. When the wife becomes ill, they travel across the country visiting each of their grown children and reviewing their family life cycle.

Chapter 2

Bibliography

Anderson, S.A. and Sabatelli, R.M. 1992. The Differentiation in the Family System Scale (DIFS). *The American Journal of Family Therapy, 20*(1):77-89.

Bayen, V. 1991. Parent-child and sibling relationships in later adulthood: Predictors of contact frequency and perceived closeness. Paper presented at the Forty-Fourth Annual Scientific Meeting of the Gerontological Society of America. San Francisco, November 22-26.

Bloomfield, H. 1983. *Making peace with your parents.* New York: Random House.

Boszormenyi-Nagy, I. and Spark, G. 1973. *Invisible loyalties: Reciprocity in intergenerational family therapy.* New York: Harper & Row.

Boszormenyi-Nagy, I. and Ulrich, D. 1981. Contextual family therapy. In A. S. Gurman and D. P. Kniskern (Eds.), *Handbook of family therapy* (pp. 159-186). New York: Brunner/Mazel.

Bowen, M. 1971. The use of family theory in clinical practice. In Haley, J. (Ed.), *Changing families: A family therapy reader* (pp. 159-192). New York: Grune and Stratton.

Bowen, M. 1972. On the differentiation of self. In Framo, I. (Ed.), *Family interaction: A dialogue between family researchers and family therapists.* New York: Springer.

Bowen, M. 1976. Theory in the practice of psychotherapy. In Guerin, P. (Ed.), *Family therapy and practice* (pp. 42-90). New York: Gardner Press.

Bowen, M. 1978. *Family therapy in clinical practice.* New York: Jason Aronson.

Bradley, R.II., Whiteside-Mansell, L., Brisby, J., and Caldwell, B. 1997. Parents' socioemotional investment in children. *Journal of Marriage and the Family, 59*(1):77-90.

Bryson, K. and Casper, L. 1999. *Coresident grandparents and grandchildren. Current population reports.* Washington, DC: U.S. Department of Commerce, U.S. Bureau of the Census.

Cohler, B.J. 1983. Autonomy and interdependence in the family of adulthood: A psychological perspective. *Gerontologist, 23*(1):33-39.

Cohler, B. and Geyer, S. 1982. Psychological autonomy and interdependence within the family. In Froma, W. (Ed.), *Normal family processes* (pp. 196-228). New York: Guilford Press.

Cohler, B. and Grunebaum, H. 1981. *Mothers, grandmothers, and daughters: Personality and child care in three generation families.* New York: John Wiley and Sons.

Cronkite, W. 1983. My wonderful mother. *Good Housekeeping,* November, 153.

Fischer, J. and Fischer, A. 1963. The New Englanders of Orchard Town. In Whiting, B. (Ed.), *Six cultures: Studies of childrearing.* New York: John Wiley and Sons.

Hall, M. 1981. *The Bowen family theory and its uses.* New York: Jason Aronson.

Hanson, J.C. and L'Abate, L. 1982. *Approaches to family therapy.* New York: Macmillan.

Komarovsky, M. 1962. *Blue-collar marriage.* New York: Random House.

Lee, E.B. and Browne, L.A. 1995. Effects of television advertising on African-American teenagers. *Journal of Black Studies, 25*(5):523-536.

Leichter, H. and Mitchell, W. 1967. *Kinship and casework.* New York: Russell Sage Foundation.

Mackey, S. 1996. Nurturance: A neglected dimension in family therapy with adolescents. *Journal of Marital and Family Therapy, 22*(4):489-508.

McDermott, J.F. Jr., Robielord, A.B., Char, W.F., Hu, J., Tsens, W.S., and Ashton, G.D. 1983. Reexamining the concept of adolescence: Differences between adolescent boys and girls in the context of their families. *American Journal of Psychiatry, 140:*1318-1322.

McGoldrick, M. 1988. The joining of families through marriage: The new couple. In Carter, B. and McGoldrick, M. (Eds.), *The changing family life cycle: A framework for family therapy,* Second edition (pp. 212-234). New York: Gardner.

Meyerstein, I. 1996. A systematic approach to in-law dilemmas. *Journal of Marital and Family Therapy, 22*(4):369-480.

Minuchin, S. 1974. *Families and family therapy.* Cambridge, MA: Harvard University Press.

Minuchin, S., Rosman, B., and Baker, L. 1978. *Psychosomatic families: Anorexia nervosa in context.* Cambridge, MA: Harvard University Press.

Morgan, L. 1983. Intergenerational financial support: Retirement-age males, 1971-1975. *The Gerontologist, 23*(2):160-166.

Shanas, E. 1967. Family help patterns and social class in three countries. *Journal of Marriage and the Family, 29*(2):257-266.

Stoller, E. 1983. Parental caregiving by adult children. *Journal of Marriage and the Family, 45*(4):851-858.

Sweetser, D. 1964. Mother-daughter ties between generations in industrial societies. *Family Process, 3*(2):332-343.

Teyber, E. 1983a. Structural family relations: Primary dyadic alliances and adolescent adjustment. *Journal of Marital and Family Therapy, 9:*89-99.

Teyber, E. 1983b. Effects of parental coalition on adolescent emancipation from the family. *Journal of Marital and Family Therapy, 9:*305-310.

Theriault, J. 1997. Assessing family differentiation: Four areas of competence in mother-adolescent relationships. *Journal of Psychology, 131*(5):565-568.

Wilmott, P. and Young, M. 1960. *Family and class in a London suburb.* London: Routledge and Kegan Paul.

Wood, B. and Talmon, M. 1983. Family boundaries in transition: A search for alternatives. *Family Process, 22:*347-357.

Young, M. and Geertz, H. 1961. Old age in London and San Francisco: Some families compared. *British Journal of Sociology, 12:*124-141.

Young, M. and Wilmott, P. 1957. *Family and kinship in East London.* London: Routledge and Kegan Paul.

Suggested Readings

Balmain, M. 1997. *Just us: Adventures and travels of a mother and daughter.* Boston: Faber and Faber.

Bloomfield, H. 1983. *Making peace with your parents.* New York: Random House.

Friday, N. 1978. *My mother/my self.* New York: Telamones Press.

Hall, M. 1981. *The Bowen family theory and its uses.* New York: Jason Aronson.

Lieber, P. and Murphy, G.S. 1995. *Stop treating me like a child (but first, can you lend me some money?):Opening the door to healthy relationships between parents and adult children.* Secaucus, NJ: Carol Publishing Group.

Literature

Arlen, M.G. 1984. *Say goodbye to same.* New York: Farrar, Strauss and Giroux. A fresh and sensitive look at the old predicament of a son in the shadow of the father, grappling for recognition.

Godwin, G. 1974. *The odd woman.* New York: Knopf. A southern woman returns to her hometown to confront her past.

Godwin, G. 1982. *A mother & two daughters.* New York: Viking Press. A wonderful story of three women's quests for individuation.

Sadat, C. 1985. *My father and I.* New York: Macmillan. Anwar Sadat's younger daughter and her search for her father's love and recognition.

Film

A Voyage Round My Father. 1982. Produced by MTV. Portrays a stormy but always loving relationship between father and son.

Breaking Away. 1978. An Indiana teenager seeks to develop an identity as a bike racer.

The Last American Hero. 1973. An endearing film of how a young stock-car racer works to be independent and still maintains a caring, mutually respectful relationship with his parents.

Terms of Endearment. 1983. This film portrays the prickly closeness of a mother and her grown daughter.

What's Eating Gilbert Grape. 1993. Directed by Lasse Hallstrom. Highly acclaimed film about the conflicts between meeting the needs of one's family and meeting one's own needs. Story portrays an adolescent's commitment and love for his troubled family and his need to explore new relationships and opportunities.

Chapter 3

Bibliography

Ambert, A. 1982. Differences in children's behavior toward custodial mothers and custodial fathers. *Journal of Marriage and the Family, 44*(1):73-86.

Arbabanel, A. 1979. Shared parenting after separation and divorce: A study of joint custody. *American Journal of Orthopsychiatry, 49*(2):320-329.

Berg-Cross, L., Berg-Cross, G., and McGeehan, D. 1979. Separation experiences in breast feeding and bottle feeding mothers. *Journal of Psychology of Women Quarterly, 3*(4):344-356.

Berg-Cross, L. and Shiller, V. 1985. Divorce and subsequent custody arrangements. In Bloom, M. (Ed.), *Life span development,* Second edition. New York: Macmillan.

Bowlby, J. 1952. *Maternal care and mental health,* Second edition. Monograph Series, No. 2. Geneva: World Health Organization.

Cohen, K.N. and Clark, J.A. 1984. Transitional object attachments in early childhood and personality characteristics in later life. *Journal of Personality and Social Psychology, 46*(1):106-111.

Daniels, P. and Weingarten, K. 1982. *Sooner or later: The timing of parenthood in adult lives.* New York: W.W. Norton.

Everett, J.E. 1995. Relative foster care: An emerging trend in foster care placement policy and practice. *Smith College Studies in Social Work, 65*(3): 239-254.

Folberg, J. 1984. *Joint and shared parenting.* Washington, DC: The Bureau of National Affairs, Inc.

Friday, N. 1978. *My mother/my self.* New York: Delacorte Press.

Ginott, H. 1969. *Between parent and teenager.* New York: Avon.

Goldstein, J., Freud, A., and Solnit, A.J. 1973. *Beyond the best interests of the child.* New York: The Free Press.

Gregory, S.S. and Aunapu, G. 1998. Split decisions. *People Magazine,* June 29, 93-94.

Guttman, K. and Lazar, A. 1998. Mother's or father's custody: Does it matter for social adjustment? *Educational Psychology, 18*(2):225-234.

Haley, J. 1980. *Leaving home.* New York: McGraw-Hill.

Hetherington, E.M. 1999. *Coping with divorce, single parenting and remarriage: A risk and resiliency perspective.* Mahwah, NJ: Lawrence Erlbaum Associates.

Hetherington, E.M., Cox, M., and Cox, R. 1982. Effects of divorce on parents and children. In Lamb, M.E. (Ed.), *Nontraditional families: Parenting and child development.* Hillside, NJ: Lawrence Erlbaum Associates.

Holahan, C.J., Valentiner, D.P., and Moos, R.H. 1994. Parental support and psychological adjustment during the transition to young adulthood in a college sample. *Journal of Family Psychology, 8*(2):215-223.

Jacobson, D.S. 1978. Marital separation/divorce on children. II. Interparent hostility and child adjustment. *Journal of Divorce, 2*(1):3-19.

Kulka, R.A. and Weingarten, H. 1979. The long-term effects of parental divorce in childhood on adult adjustment. *Journal of Social Issues, 35*(4):50-78.

Kunz, J. and Kunz, P.R. 1995. Parental divorce and academic achievement of college students. *Psychological Reports, 76*(3, Pt. 1): 1025-1026.

Leavitt, K.S., Morrison, J.A., Gradner, S.A., and Gallagher, M.M. 1996. Group play therapy for cumulatively traumatized child survivors of family AIDS. *International Journal of Play Therapy, 5*(1):1-17.

Pett, J.G. 1982. Correlates of children's social adjustment following divorce. *Journal of Divorce, 5*(3):25-39.

Roeder-Esser, C. 1994. Families in transition: A divorce workshop. *Family and Conciliation Courts Review, 32*(1):40-49.

Rutter, M. 1979. Sex differences in children's responses to family stress. In Anthony, E.J. and Koupernik, C. (Eds.), *The child in his family.* Huntington, NY: Kreiger.

Santrok, J.W. and Warshak, R.A. 1979. Father custody and social development in boys and girls. *Journal of Social Issues, 35*(4):112-125.

Sherman, M., Hertzig, M., Austrian, R., and Shapiro, F. 1981. Treasured objects in school-aged children. *Pediatrics, 68*(2):379-386.

Shiller, V.M. 1984. Latency age boys in joint and maternal custody: Factors related to outcome. Unpublished manuscript, University of Delaware.

Steinman, S. 1981. The experience of children in a joint custody arrangement: A report of a study. *American Journal of Orthopsychiatry, 51*(3):403-414.

Sullivan, K. and Sullivan, A. 1980. Adolescent and parent separation. *Developmental Psychology, 16*(2):93-99.

Wallerstein, J.S. and Kelly, J.B. 1980. *Surviving the break-up: How children and parents cope with divorce.* New York: Basic Books.

Weinberger, G. and Reuter, M. 1980. The "life discussion" group as a means of facilitating personal growth and development in late adolescence. *Journal of Clinical Child Psychology, 9*(1):6-12.

Yarrow, L.J. 1964. Separation from parents during early childhood. In Hoffman, M.L. and Hoffman, L.W. (Eds.), *Review of child development research, 1.* New York: Russell Sage.

Suggested Readings

Berg-Cross, L. and Shiller, V. 1985. Divorce and subsequent custody arrangements. In Bloom, M. (Ed.), *Life span development,* Second edition. New York: Macmillan.

Haley, J. 1980. *Leaving home.* New York: McGraw-Hill.

Hoekstra, E.M. 1998. *Keeping your family close: When frequent travel pulls you apart.* Wheaton, IL: Crossway Books.

Jonas, S. and Nissenson, M. 1998. *Friends for life: Enriching the bond between mothers and their adult daughters.* New York: William Morrow and Co.

McCracken, A. and Semel, M. 1998. *A Broken Heart Still Beats: After Your Child Dies.* Center City, MN: Hazelden.

Myers, E.P. 1997. *When parents die: A guide for adults.* New York: Penguin Books.

Pelzer, D. 1997. *The lost boy: A Foster child's search for the love of a family.* Deerfield Beach, FL: Health Communications.

Literature

Kenney, S. 1984. *In another country.* New York: Viking. In six interlocking and overlapping stories, the main character reviews the separations that have affected her life.

Yehoushua, A.B. 1984. *A late divorce.* New York: Doubleday. An unusual novel that illuminates the trauma of divorce from the perspectives of nine family members.

Film

The Accidental Tourist. 1988. Directed by Lawrence Kasdan. With a son who committed suicide and a wife who left him, the main character is confused and depressed. He learns to go on by taking up with an offbeat dog trainer.

Kramer vs. Kramer. 1979. This film shows the pain of separation through divorce.

Summer Wishes, Winter Dreams. 1973. When a middle-aged woman loses her mother she is thrust into mourning for her own life's losses.

Chapter 4

Bibliography

Anspach, D.F. 1976. Kinship and divorce. *Journal of Marriage and the Family, 38*:323-330.

Bane, M.J. 1979. Marital disruption and the lives of children. In Levinger, G. and Moles, O.C. (Eds.), *Divorce and separation: Context, causes and consequences.* New York: Basic Books.

Bowen, M. 1976. Theory in the practice of psychotherapy. In Guerin, P. (Ed.), *Family therapy.* New York: Gardner Press.

Bowen, M. 1978. *Family therapy in clinical practice.* New York: Jason Aronson.

Brennan, T., Huizinga, D., and Elliott, D. 1978. *The social psychology of runaways.* Lexington, MA: D.C. Heath.

Goetting, A. 1979. The normative integration of the former spouse relationship. *Journal of Divorce, 2* (Summer):395-414.

Goldsmith, J. 1980. Relationship between former spouses: Descriptive findings. *Journal of Divorce, 4* (Winter):1-20.

Johnson, M.P. 1983. Social and cognitive features of the dissolution of commitment to relationships. In Duck, S. (Ed.), *Personal relationships. 4: Dissolving personal relationships* (pp. 51-73). New York: Academic Press.

Kerr, M. 1981. Family systems: Theory and therapy. In Burman, A.S. and Kriskern, D.P. (Eds.), *Handbook of family therapy* (pp. 226-264). New York: Brunner/Mazel.

Olsen, L., Liebow, E., Manning, F., and Shore, M. 1980. Runaway children twelve years later. *Journal of Family Issues, 1*(2):165-188.

Rands, M. 1986. Changes in social networks following marital separation and divorce. In Milardo, R.M. (Ed.), *Families and social networks.* Beverly Hills, CA: Sage Publications.

Rands, M., Levinger, G., and Mellinger, G. 1981. Patterns of conflict resolution and marital satisfaction. *Journal of Family Issues, 2*(3):297-321.

Rosenfeld, J. 1979. *Legacy of aging: Inheritance and disinheritance in social perspective.* Norwood, NJ: Ablex Publishing.

Rosenfeld, J. 1980. Benevolent disinheritance. *Psychology Today, 10*(3):48-109.

Suggested Readings

Bloomfield, H.H. 1996. *Making peace with your parents.* New York: Hyperion.

Borhek, M.V. 1994. *Coming out to parents: A two-way survival guide for lesbians and gay men and their parents.* Cleveland, OH: Pilgrim Press.

Bowen, M. 1978. *Family therapy in clinical practice.* New York: Jason Aronson.

Drew, J.M. 1992. *Where were you when I needed you, Dad?: A guide for healing your father wound.* Newport Beach, CA: Tiger Lily Publications.

Goetz, M.A. 1998. *My father, my self: Understanding how Dad Influenced your life, a guide to reconciliation and healing for sons and daughters.* Boston: Element.

Herst, C. and Padwa, L. 1998. *For mothers of difficult daughters: How to enrich and repair the bond in adulthood.* New York: Villard.

Hunt, M. and Hunt, B. 1977. *The divorce experience.* New York: McGraw-Hill.

Neuharth, D. 1998. *If you had controlling parents: How to make peace with your past and take your place in the world.* New York: Cliff Street Books.

Literature

Stolz, M. 1973. *Leap before you look.* New York: Dell. A teenager must learn to forgive her father and come to terms with her remote, withdrawing mother during and after divorce. Written for teens.

Film

Autumn Sonata. 1978. A married woman invites her mother to visit after a long period of being cut off. Parent and adult child struggle with their differing perceptions of the past as they try to become a part of each other's lives.

On Golden Pond. 1981. Directed by Mark Rydell. An only daughter visits her parents after a long cutoff, and eventually breaks through to open up her relationship with her elderly father.

Vagabond. 1985. Directed by Agnes Varda. A haunting psychological insight into a woman who decides to cut off her connection to everyone she knows and later, to everyone she meets. Shows the disintegration of personality without social relationships.

Chapter 5

Bibliography

Bowen, M. 1971. The use of family theory in clinical practice. In Haley, J. (Ed.), *Changing families: A family therapy reader* (pp. 159-192). New York: Grune and Stratton.

Cummings, E.M., Davies, P.T., and Simpson, K.S. 1994. Marital conflict, gender and children's appraisals and coping efficacy as mediators of child adjustment. *Journal of Family Psychology, 8*(2): 141-150.

Easterbrooks, M.A., Cummings, E.M., and Emde, R.N. 1994. Young children's responses to constructive marital disputes. *Journal of Family Psychology, 8*(2):160-170.

Falicov, C. and Brudner-White, L. 1983. The shifting family triangle: The issue of cultural and contextual relativity. In Hansen, G. and Falicov, C. (Eds.), *Cultural perspectives in family therapy.* Rockville, MD: Aspen Publications.

Fincham, F.D., Grych, J.H., and Osborne, L.N. 1994. Does marital conflict cause child maladjustment? Directions and challenges for longitudinal research. *Journal of Family Psychology, 8*(2):128-141.

Friedman, E.H. 1971. Ethnic identification as extended family in Jewish-Christian marriage. In Bradt, J.O. and Moynihan, C.J. (Eds.), *System therapy.* Washington, DC: Council Press.

Gilbert, R., Christensen, A., and Margolin, G. 1984. Patterns of alliances in nondistressed and multiproblem families. *Family Process, 23*(1):75-87.

Held, B. and Winey, K. 1984 (unpublished manuscript). College adjustment and perceptions of structural and multigenerational aspects of the family system. (Available from Barbara Held, Bowdoin College, Brunswick, ME 04011.)

Hoffman, L. 1981. *Foundations of family therapy.* New York: Basic Books.

Holden, G., Geffner, R., and Jouriles, E. 1998. *Children exposed to marital violence: Theory, research, and applied issues.* Washington, DC: American Psychological Association.

Hsu, F.K. 1971. *Kinship and culture.* Chicago: Aldine.

Jenkins, J.M. and Smith, M.A. 1990. Factors protecting children who live in disharmonious homes: Maternal reports. *Journal of the American Academy of Child and Adolescent Psychiatry, 29*(1): 60-69.

Karpman, S.B. 1968. Fairy tales and script drama analysis. *Transactional Analysis Bulletin, 7*(26):39-43.

Minuchin, S., Rosman, B., and Baker, L. 1978. *Psychosomatic families: Anorexia nervosa in context.* Cambridge, MA: Harvard University Press.

Mirkin, M., Raskin, P., and Antognini, F. 1984. Parenting, protecting, preserving: Mission of the adolescent female runaway. *Family Process, 23*(1):63-74.

Rutter, M. 1994. Family discord and conduct disorder: Cause, consequence, or correlate? *Journal of Family Psychology, 8*(2):170-187.

Rynearson, E.K. 1978. Humans and pets and attachment. *British Journal of Psychiatry, 133*:550-555.

Suggested Readings

Bray, J.H. and Kelly, J. 1998. *Stepfamilies: Love, marriage, and parenting in the first ten years—Based on a landmark study.* New York: Broadway Books.

Eckler, J.D. 1993. *Step-by-step parenting: A guide to successful living with a blended family.* Cincinnati, OH: Betterway Books.

Gilbert, R., Christensen, A., and Margolin, G. 1984. Patterns of alliances in nondistressed and multiproblem families. *Family Process, 23*(1):75-87.

Lutz, E. 1998. *The complete idiot's guide to stepparenting.* New York: Alpha Books.

Minuchin, S., Rosman, B., and Baker, L. 1978. *Psychosomatic families: Anorexia nervosa in context.* Cambridge, MA: Harvard University Press.

Literature

Lawrence, D.H. 1962. *Sons and lovers.* New York: Modern Library. A magnificent story of a coal miner father, an unsatisfied, unfulfilled mother, and the triangulated son.

Roth, H. 1963. *Call it sleep.* London: M. Joseph. A classic family triangle is described with unusual clarity and insight.

Chapter 6

Bibliography

Baxter, L.A. and Clark, C.L. 1996. Perceptions of family communication patterns and the enactment of family rituals. *Western Journal of Communication, 60*(3):254-268.

Bell, W. and Vogel, E.F. 1968. *A modern introduction to the family.* New York: Free Press.

Bossard, J.H.S. and Boll, E.S. 1950. *Ritual in family living.* Philadelphia: University of Pennsylvania Press.

Caplow, T. 1968. *Two against one: Coalitions in triads.* New York: Prentice-Hall.

Folklife Archives of the Smithsonian Institute. Collected between 1974 and 1977. Washington, DC: Smithsonian Institute.

Friedman, E. 1980. Systems and ceremonies: A family view of rites of passage. In Carter, E. and McGoldrick, M. (Eds.), *The changing family life cycle: A framework for family therapy,* Second edition (p. 127). Needham, MA: Allyn & Bacon.

Gilbert, R., Christensen, A., and Margolin, G. 1984. Patterns of alliances in nondistressed and multiproblem families. *Family Process, 23*(March):75-87.

Hassia, Y. and Tova, Y. 1997. The family album. *American Journal of Family Therapy, 25*(3):261-269.

Hawkins, C.A. 1997. Disruption of family rituals as a mediator of the relationship between parental drinking and adult adjustment in offspring. *Addictive Behaviors. 22*(2):219-231

Howard, J. 1978. *Families.* New York: Simon and Schuster.

Ilg, F.R., Ames, L., and Baker, S. 1992. *Child behavior: The classic manual from the Gesell Institute of Human Development.* New York: Harper Perennial.

Klapp, O.E. 1959. Ritual and family solidarity. *Social Forces, 37*(3):212-214.

Lieberman, S. 1984. *Let's celebrate: Creating new family traditions.* New York: Perigee Books.

Martin, J. 1984. On the purposeful development of family rituals. *The Washington Post,* May 27, 1G, 7G.

Mirkin, M., Raskin, P., and Antognine, F. 1984. Parenting, protecting, preserving: Mission of the adolescent female runaway. *Family Process, 23*(1):63-74.

Morval, M.V. and Biron. 1993. Family rituals and their functions. *Therapie Familiale, 14*(2):149-167.

Richlin-Klonsky, J. and Begnston, V.L. 1996. Pulling together, drifting apart: A longitudinal case study of a four generation family. *Journal of Aging Studies. 10*(4):255-279.

Schvaneveldt, J. and Lee, T. 1983. The emergence and practice of ritual in the American family. *Family Perspectives, 17*(13):137-143.

Yerushalmi, H. and Yedidya, T. 1997. The family album. *American Journal of Family Therapy. 25*(3):261-269.

Zeitlin, S., Kotkin, A., and Baker, H. 1982. *A celebration of American family folklore: Tales and traditions from the Smithsonian collection.* New York: Pantheon Books.

Suggested Readings

Bossard, J.H.S. and Boll, E.S. 1950. *Ritual in family living.* Philadelphia: University of Pennsylvania Press.

Bria, G. 1998. *The art of family: Rituals, play, and everyday spirituality.* New York: Dell.

Dodson, J. 1996. *Final rounds: A father, a son, the golf journey of a lifetime.* New York: Bantam Books.

Johnson, S. and Carlson, J. 1996. *Grandloving: Making memories with your grandchildren.* Minneapolis, MN: Fairview Press.

Lansky, V. 1993. *101 ways to be a special dad.* Chicago: Contemporary Books.

Leiberman, S. 1984. *Let's celebrate: Creating new family traditions.* New York: Putnam.

Schvaneveldt, J. and Lee, T. 1983. The emergence and practice of ritual in the American family. *Family Perspectives, 17*(13):137-143.

Stein, D. 1990. *Casting the circle: A woman's book of ritual.* Freedom, CA: Crossing Press.

Literature

Stead, C. 1965. *The man who loved children.* New York: Holt. One of the greatest novels on family life; filled with unforgettable rituals.

Film

The Big Chill. 1983. A group of college friends have a reunion weekend, reviving all their old rituals, both positive and negative.
Like Water for Chocolate. 1993. Directed by Alfonso Arau. A compelling story revolving around the role of food in love, family, and a meaningful life.
A Wedding. 1978. The true feelings and relationships between family members surface throughout the ritual of the wedding day.

Chapter 7

Bibliography

Baptiste, D. 1995. Therapy with a lesbian stepfamily and an electively mute child: A case report. *Journal of Family Psychotherapy. 6*(1):1-14.
Berg-Cross, L. and Duval, S. 1998. Children of incarcerated parents: A trauma prevention program. Unpublished manuscript.
Bok, S. 1979. *Lying: Moral choice in public and private life.* New York: Random House.
Cleaver, B. and Cleaver, V. 1970. *Grover.* Philadelphia: J. B. Lippincott.
Grolnick, L. 1983. Ibsen's truth, family secrets, and family therapy. *Family Process, 2*(3):275-288.
Imber-Black, E. 1998. *The secret life of families.* New York: Bantam Books.
Karpel, M. 1980. Family secrets. *Family Process, 19*(3):295-306.
Palazzoli-Selvini, M., Boscolu, L., Cecchin, G.F., and Prata, G. 1974. The treatment of children through brief therapy of their parents. In Palazzoli, M. and Selvini, M. (Eds.), *The work of Mara Selvini Palazzoli* (pp. 121-144). Northvale, NJ: Jason Aronson.
Pincus, L. and Dare, C. 1978. *Secrets in the family.* New York: Pantheon Books.
Tyerman, A. and Humphrey, M. 1983. Life stress, family support, and adolescent disturbance. *Journal of Adolescence, 6*(1):1-12.
Weissberg, M.P. 1983. *Dangerous secrets: Maladaptive responses to stress.* New York: W.W. Norton.

Suggested Readings

Baker, J.M. 1998. *Family secrets: Gay sons—A mother's story.* Binghamton, NY: The Haworth Press.
Bradshaw, J. 1996. *Family secrets: The path to self-acceptance and reunion.* New York: Bantam Books.
Cleaver, B. and Cleaver, V. 1970. *Grover.* Philadelphia: J.B. Lippincott.
Fraustino, L.R. 1998. *Dirty laundry: Stories about family secrets.* New York: Orchard Books.
Friel, J.C. and Friel, L. 1988. *Adult children: The secrets of dysfunctional families.* Pampano Beach, FL: Health Communications.

Pincus, L. and Dare, C. 1978. *Secrets in the family.* New York: Pantheon Books,
Weissberg, M.P. 1983. *Dangerous secrets: Maladaptive responses to stress.* New York: W.W. Norton.

Literature

Faulkner, W. 1951. *Absalom, Absalom!* New York: Modern Library. Three generations of the Sutter family are haunted by a variety of secrets, hidden and disclosed.
Simms, J. 1982. *Unsolicited gift.* New York: Harcourt, Brace, Jovanovich. An incident of brother-sister incest goes on to haunt the brother in adulthood and results in his committing incest with his daughter.

Film

Family Name. 1997. Directed by Macky Atston. A White Southerner pokes through his family's closets in search of the African-American descendants of his slave-owning ancestors.
A Walk in the Clouds. 1997. Directed by Alfonso Arau. A young woman gets pregnant and is afraid to tell her father what happened. Instead, she finds a man who is willing to pose as her husband and continue the secret.

Chapter 8

Bibliography

Bentovim, A., Barnes, G., and Cooklin, A. 1982. *Family therapy: Complementary frameworks of theory and practice.* New York: Academic Press.
Boszormenyi-Nagy, I. and Spark, G. 1973. *Invisible loyalties: Reciprocity in intergenerational family therapy.* New York: Harper & Row.
Boszormenyi-Nagy, I. and Ulrich, D. 1981. Contextual family therapy. In Gutman, A.S. and Kniskern, D.P. (Eds.), *Handbook of Family Therapy* (pp. 159-186). New York: Brunner-Mazel.
Bowen, M. 1971. The use of family theory in clinical practice. In Haley, J. (Ed.), *Changing families: A family therapy reader* (pp. 159-192). New York: Grune and Stratton.
Bowen, M. 1976. Theory in the practice of psychotherapy. In Guerin, P. (Ed.), *Family therapy: Theory and practice* (pp. 42-40). New York: Gardner Press.
Bowen, M. 1978. *Family therapy in clinical practice.* New York: Jason Aronson.
Byng-Hall, J. 1982. Family legends: Their significance for the therapist. In Bentovim, A., Barnes, G., and Cooklin, A. (Eds.), *Family therapy: Complementary frameworks of theory and practice.* New York: Academic Press.
Csikszentmihalyi, M. and Rochberg-Halton, E. 1981. Object lessons. *Psychology Today, 15*(12):79-85.

Dodson, F. 1981. *How to grandparent.* New York: Harper & Row.

Ferriera, A. 1963. Family myths and homeostasis. *Archives of General Psychiatry, 9:*457-463.

Held, B. and Winey, K. 1984 (unpublished manuscript). College adjustment and perceptions of structural and multigenerational aspects of the family system. (Reprints available from Barbara Held, Bowdoin College, Brunswick, ME 04011.)

Kalmuss, C. 1984. The intergenerational transmission of marital aggression. *Journal of Marriage and the Family, 46*(1):11-19.

Lieberman, S. 1979. *Transgenerational family therapy.* London: Croom Helm.

Moore, C.D. 1979. La familia chicana. In Corfman, E. (Ed.), *Families today: A research sampler on families and children.* NIMH Science Monographs, DHEW publication no. (ADM) 79-815. Rockville, MD.

Troll, L. and Bengtson, V. 1979. Generations in the family. In Burr, W.R., Hill, R., Nye, F.I., and Reiss, I.L. (Eds.), *Contemporary theories about the family. 1. Research-based theories* (pp. 127-161). New York: The Free Press.

Suggested Readings

Berman, C.G. 1997. *Caring for yourself while caring for your aging parents: How to help, how to survive.* New York: H. Holt.

Boszormenyi-Nagy, I. and Spark, G. 1973. *Invisible loyalties: Reciprocity in intergenerational family therapy.* New York: Harper & Row.

Dodson, F. 1981. *How to grandparent.* New York: Harper & Row.

Ford, J. 1998. *Wonderful ways to love a grandchild.* Berkeley, CA: Conari Press.

Levin, M.O. 1998. *Grandmother's book.* New York: Galahad Books.

Lieberman, S. 1979. Transgenerational family therapy. London: Croom Helm.

Sunshine, L. 1998. *Our grandmothers: Loving portraits by 74 granddaughters.* New York: Welcome Enterprises.

Westheimer, R.K. 1998. *Grandparenthood.* New York: Routledge.

Literature

Davenport, M. 1978. *The valley of decision.* New York: Popular Library. Three generations of a Pittsburgh steelmaking family kept together—and torn apart—by the values of the founder.

Galsworthy, J. 1922. *The Forsyth saga.* New York: Charles Scribner's Sons. This is a popular three-generation family saga chronicling the evils of acquisitiveness.

Rubens, B. 1983. *Brothers.* New York: Delacorte Press. Traces six generations of a family and the legacy that kept them alive.

Film

The Joy Luck Club. 1993. Directed by Wayne Wang. Familial immigration is the subject of this movie. It portrays the love/hate relationship of the younger generation to tradition and the older generation's problems adjusting to the new ways in a funny, heart-tugging, and often profound manner.

My Family: Mi Familia. 1994. Directed by Gregory Nava. An ambitious, multi-generational saga of a Mexican-American family in East Los Angeles.

The River. 1984. A powerful portrayal of a farm family passing on the values of love and land, courage, and perseverance.

Three Warriors. 1977. A touching story of how a young Indian boy learns the importance of valuing one's own heritage.

Chapter 9

Bibliography

Allan, G. 1983. Informal networks of care: Issues raised by Barclay. *British Journal of Social Work, 13*(4):417-433.

Anderson, C. 1982. The community connection: The impact of social networks on family and individual functioning. In Walsh, F. (Ed.), *Normal family processes.* New York: Guilford Press.

Baldassare, M., Rosenfield, S., and Rook, K. 1984. The types of social relations predicting elderly well-being. *Research on Aging, 6*(4):549-559.

Ball, R. 1983. Family and friends: A supportive network for low income American Black families. *Journal of Comparative Family Studies, 13*(1):51-56.

Berg-Cross, L. and Jackson, J. 1986. Helping the extended family: In-law growth and development training program. *Psychotherapy in Private Practice, 4*(1):33-50.

Boissevain, J. 1974. *Friends of friends: Networks, manipulators and coalitions.* New York: St. Martin's Press.

Bott, E. 1957. *Family and social networks,* Second edition. New York: The Free Press.

Bowen, G.L. 1982. Social network and maternal role satisfaction of formerly married mothers. *Journal of Divorce, 5*(4):77-85.

Butler, K. 1997. The anatomy of resilience. *The Family Networker.* March/April, 22-32.

Carter, B. and McGoldrick, M. 1988. *The changing family life cycle: A framework for family therapy.* New York: Gardner Press.

Cohen, C. and Sokolovsky, J. 1981. Social networks and the elderly: Clinical techniques. *International Journal of Family Therapy, 3*(4):281-294.

Faegen, J.R. 1970. A note on the friendship of Black urbanites. *Social Forces, 49*(2):303-308.

Jackson, J. and Berg-Cross, L. 1988). Helping the extended family: Mother-in-law and daughter-in-law relationships among Black women. *Family Relations, 37*(3):293-297.

Kunz, J. and Kunz, P.R. 1995. Social support during the divorce process: It does make a difference. *Journal of Divorce and Remarriage, 24*(3-4):111-119.

Kurdeck, L.A. and Fine, M.A. 1993. Parent and nonparent residential family members as providers of warmth and supervision to young adults. *Journal of Family Psychology, 7*(2):245-249.

Martineau, W.H. 1977. Informal social ties among urban Black Americans. *Journal of Black Studies, 8*(1):83-104.

McAdoo, H.P. 1978. Factors related to stability in upwardly mobile Black families. *Journal of Marriage and the Family, 40*:761-776.

McCubbin, H., Boss, P., Wilson, L.R., and Lester, G.R. 1980. Developing family invulnerability to stress: Coping patterns and strategies wives employ in managing family separations. In Frost, J. (Ed.), *The family and change* (pp. 89-105). Sweden: International Library Publishing.

Meyerstein, I. 1996. A systemic approach to in-law dilemmas. *Journal of Marriage and Family Therapy, 22*(4):469-480.

Moss, M., Moss, S., and Moles, E. 1985. The quality of relationships between elderly parents and their out of town children. *The Gerontologist, 25*(2):134-137.

Moynihan, D.P. 1965. *The negro family: The case for national action.* Washington, DC: United States Department of Labor, Office of Policy Planning and Research. U.S. Government Printing Office.

Nissel, M. 1984. The family costs of looking after handicapped elderly relatives. *Aging and Society, 4*(2):185-204.

Rook, K. 1994. Promoting social bonding strategies for helping the lonely and socially isolated. *American Psychologist, 39*(12):1389-1407.

Rosenblatt, P., Johnson, P., and Anderson, R. 1981. When out of town relatives visit. *Family Relations, 30*(3):403-409.

Rosenfeld, J. 1980. Benevolent disinheritance. *Psychology Today, 13*(12):48-109.

Rueveni, U. 1979. *Networking families in crisis.* New York: Human Sciences Press.

Samuelson, M. 1995. Children's social networks and their association with behavioral disturbances in single-parent families: A comparison between a clinical group and a control group. *Nordic Journal of Psychiatry, 49*(4):275-284.

Shanas, E. 1979. Social myth as hypothesis: The case of the family relations of old people. *The Gerontologist, 19:*3-9.

Shanas, E. and Streib, G. (Eds). 1965. *Social structure and the family: Generational relations.* Englewood Cliffs, NJ: Prentice-Hall.

Shanas, E. and Sussman, M.B. 1981. The family in later life: Social structure and social policy. In Fogel, R.W., Hatfield, E., Kiesler, S.B., and Shanas, E. (Eds.), *Aging: Stability and change in the family.* New York: Academic Press.

Shanas, E., Townsend, P., Wedderburn, D., Frus, H., Milhoj, P., and Stehower, J. 1968. *Older people in three industrial societies.* New York: Atherton.

Speck, R. and Attneave, C. 1973. *Family networks.* New York: Pantheon.

Stack, C. 1974. *All our kin: Strategies for survival in a Black community.* New York: Harper & Row.

Troll, L.G. 1971. The family of later life: A decade review. *Journal of Marriage and the Family, 33*(2):263-290.

Turner, C. 1967. Conjugal roles and social networks. *Human Relations, 20*(2): 121-130.

U.S. Bureau of the Census. 1999. *Sixty-five plus in the United States.* Statistical Brief. Washington, DC: U.S. Department of Commerce, U.S. Bureau of the Census.

Vivrett, W. 1960. Housing and community settings for older people. In Libbitts, C. (Ed.), *Handbook of social gerontology.* Chicago: University of Chicago Press.

Ward, R., Sherman, S., and LaGory, M. 1984. Subjective network assessments and subjective well-being. *Journal of Gerontology, 39*(1):93-101.

Suggested Readings

Adler, P. and Adler, P. 1998. *Peer power: Preadolescent culture and identity.* New Brunswick, NJ: Rutgers University Press.

Boissevain, J. 1974. *Friends of friends: Networks, manipulatory and coalitions.* New York: St. Martin's Press.

Cotterell, J. 1996. S*ocial networks and social influences in adolescence.* London: Routledge.

Rozakis, L.E. and Snyder, T. 1998. *The complete idiot's guide to dealing with in-laws.* New York: Alpha Books.

Rueveni, U. 1979. *Networking families in crisis.* New York: Human Sciences Press.

Shanas, E. and Sussman, M.B. 1981. The family in later life: Social structure and social policy. In Fogel, R.W., Hatfield, E., Kiesler, S.B., and Shanas, E. (Eds.), *Aging: Stability and change in the family.* New York: Academic Press.

Stack, C. 1974. *All our kin: Strategies for survival in a black community.* New York: Harper & Row.

Literature

Faulkner, W. *The Snopes trilogy. Hamlet,* 1940. *Town,* 1957. *Sanctuary,* 1962. New York: Random House. An intensive study of how one family networks itself into the entire community.

Keillor, G. 1985. *Lake Wobegon days.* New York: Viking. Networks are described at their very best in this delightful book.

Film

Antonia's Line. 1995. Directed by Marleen Gorres. The most uplifting and gripping story of how a woman, at age fifty, returns to her birthplace to create a new community and psychological family.

The Birch Interval. 1978. An eleven-year-old girl spends several months with her extended family. Despite severe problems, she experiences a deep sense of family closeness and affection.

Country. 1984. An emotionally gripping film about a farm family who are saved by a supportive network of neighbors.

Driving Miss Daisy. 1989. Directed by Bruce Beresford. The "psychological family" that evolves as a white woman grows in a relationship with her African-American chauffeur.

Grand Canyon. 1991. Directed by Lawrence Kasdan. This film successfully recreates the random, haphazard ways in which individual lives intersect, and captures the sense of menace and disintegration that permeate contemporary urban life.

It's My Turn. 1980. Focuses on how network members shape the fate and romantic involvements of a brilliant mathematics professor.

Chapter 10

Bibliography

Azar, S.T. 1996. Cognitive restructuring of professionals' schema regarding women parenting in poverty. *Women and Therapy, 18*(3-4):149-163.

Becvar, R.J., Ray, W.A., and Becvar, D.S. 1996. A modest/immodest proposal: Reciprocal foster families. *Contemporary Family Therapy, 18*(2):257-265.

Berg, I.K. 1994. *Family based services: A solution-focused approach.* New York: W.W. Norton and Company, Inc.

Bradley, R.H., Whiteside, L., Mundfrom, D.J., Casey, P.H., Kelleher, K.J., and Pope, S.K. 1994. Early indications of resilience and their relation to experiences in the home environments of low birthweight, premature children living in poverty. *Child Development, 65*(2):346-360.

Brickman, P., Rabinowitz, V.C., Karuza, J., Coates, D., Cohn, E., and Kidder, L. 1982. Models of helping and coping. *American Psychologist, 37*(4):368-384.

Caputo, R.K. 1997. Family poverty and public dependency. *Families in Society: The Journal of Contemporary Human Services, 78*(1):13-25.

Caputo, R.K. 1998. Economic well-being in a youth cohort. *Families in Society: The Journal of Contemporary Human Services, 79*(1):83-92.

Drake, B. and Pandey, S. 1996. Understanding the relationship between neighborhood poverty and specific types of child maltreatment. *Child Abuse and Neglect, 20:*1003-1018.

Ensminger, M.E., Lamkin, R.P., and Jacobson, N. 1996. School leaving: A longitudinal perspective including neighborhood effects. *Child Development, 67*(5): 2400-2416.

Garmezy, N. 1993. Children in poverty: Resilience despite risk. *Psychiatry, 56*(1): 127-136.

Germain, C.B. and Gitterman, A. 1980. *The life model of social work practice.* New York: Columbia University Press.

Greene, G.J., Lee, M.Y., Mentzer, R.A., Pinnell, S.R., and Niles, D. 1998. Miracles, dreams, and empowerment: A brief therapy practice note. *Families in Society: The Journal of Contemporary Human Services, 79*(4):395-399.

Halpern, R. 1993. Poverty and infant development. In C.H. Zeanah (Ed.), *Handbook of infant mental health* (pp. 73-86). New York: Guilford.

Hawley, D.R. and DeHaan, L. 1996. Toward a definition of family resilience: Integrating life-span and family perspectives. *Family Process, 35*(3):283-298.

Jarrett, R.B. 1996. Welfare stigma among low-income, African American single mothers. *Family Relations, 45*(4):368-374.

Kaplan, C.P., Turner, S., Norman, E., and Stillson, K. 1996. Promoting resilience strategies: A modified consultation model. *Social Work in Education, 18*(3): 158-168.

McCubbin, M. and McCubbin, H. 1988. Family systems assessment. In Karoly, P. (Ed.), *Handbook of child health assessment: Biopsychosocial perspectives* (pp. 227-261). Wiley Series on Health Psychology/Behavorial Medicine. New York: John Wiley and Sons.

McLeod, J.D. and Shanahan, M.J. 1996. Trajectories of poverty and children's mental health. *Journal of Health and Social Behavior, 37*(3):207-220.

Parker, S., Greer, S., and Zuckerman, B. 1988. Double jeopardy: The impact of poverty of early child development. *Pediatric Clinics of North America, 35*(3): 1127-1241.

Pollitt, E. 1994. Poverty and child development: Relevance of research in developing countries to the United States. *Child Development, 65*(2):1325-1376.

Rutter, M. 1993. Resilience: Some conceptual considerations. *Journal of Adolescent Health, 14*(8):626-631.

U.S. Census Bureau. 1997. *Statistical abstract of the United States* (117th Edition). Washington, DC: U.S. Government Printing Office.

Walsh, F. 1996. The concept of family resilience: Crisis and challenge. *Family Process, 35*(13):261-281.

Weinger, S. 1998. Children living in poverty: Their perception of career opportunities. *Families in Society: The Journal of Contemporary Human Services, 79*(3):320 -331.

Wise, P.H. and Meyers, A. 1988. Poverty and child health. *Pediatric Clinics of North America, 35*:1169-1186.

Zeanah, C.H., Boris, N.W., and Larrieu, J.A. 1997. Infant development and development risk: A review of the past 10 years. *Journal of the American Academy of Child and Adolescent Psychiatry, 36*(2):165-178.

Suggested Readings

Araoz, D.L. and Carrese, M.A. 1996. *Solution-oriented brief therapy for adjustment disorders: A guide for providers under managed care (Mental health practice under managed care, 3).* New York: Brunner/Mazel.

Hetherington, E.M. and Blechman, E.A. 1996. *Stress, coping, and resiliency in children and families (advances in family research).* Mahwah, NJ: Lawrence Erlbaum Associates.

McBride, J. 1997. *The color of water: A black man's tribute to his white mother.* New York: Riverhead Books.

McCoy, K. and Wibbelsman, C. 1995. *Life happens: A teenager's guide to friends, failure, sexuality, love, rejection, addiction, peer pressure, families, loss, depres-*

sion, change and other challenges of living. New York: Berkley Publishing Group.

McCubbin, H.I. and Thompson, E.A. 1998. *Resiliency in African-American families (Resiliency in families, Vol. 3).* Thousand Oaks, CA: Sage Publications.

McCubbin, H.I. 1998. *Resiliency in Native American and immigrant families (Resiliency in families, Vol. 2).* Thousand Oaks, CA.: Sage Press.

Minuchin, P., Colapinto, J., and Minuchin, S. 1998. *Working with families of the poor.* New York: Guilford.

O'Hanlon, W.H. and Bertolino, B. 1998. *Even from a broken web: Brief, respectful solution-oriented therapy for sexual abuse and trauma.* New York: John Wiley.

Scott, S. 1997. *Peer pressure reversal: An adult guide to developing a responsible child.* Amherst, MA: Human Resource Development Press.

Teolis, B. 1997. *Ready-to-use self-esteem and conflict solving activities for grades 4-8.* West Nyack, NY: Center for Applied Research in Education.

Vosler, N.R. 1996. *New approaches to family practice: Confronting economic stress.* Thousand Oaks, CA: Sage.

Film

An Angel at My Table. 1991. Directed by Jane Campion. The true story of how a woman from New Zealand who underwent rejection as a child and unbelievable tortures as a misunderstood adult triumphs due to her own spirit and the help of her family.

A Bronx Tale. 1993. Directed by Robert DeNiro. A story about how boys grow up to be men and the decisions that they have to make between self-respect and group support.

The Color Purple. 1985. Directed by Stephen Spielberg. A most dramatic story about how resiliency can take one from familial and personal tragedy to personal triumph throughout the course of a lifetime.

Chapter 11

Bibliography

Andersson, N. and Wold, B. 1992. Parental and peer influences on leisure-time physical activity. *Research Quarterly for Exercise and Sport, 63*(4):341-348.

Andrew, G., Oldridge, N., and Parker, J. 1981. Reasons for dropout from exercise programs in post-coronary patients. *Medicine and Science in Sports and Exercise, 13*(2):164-168.

Bauman, K., Foshee, V., Linzer, M., and Koch, G. 1990. Effect of parental smoking classification on the association between parental and adolescent smoking. *Addictive Reports, 15*(5):413-422.

Belar, C. 1997. Clinical health psychology: A specialty for the twenty-first century. *Health Psychology, 16*(5):411-416.

Bennett, D. 1994. Depression among children with chronic medical problems: A meta-analysis. *Journal of Pediatric Psychology, 19*(2):149-169.

Biegel, D., Sales, E., and Schulz, R. 1991. *Family caregiving in chronic illness.* Newbury Park, CA: Sage.

Boss, P. 1987. Family stress: Perception and context. In Sussman, M., and Steinmetz, S. (Eds.), *Handbook of marriage and the family,* (pp. 695-723). New York: Plenum.

Boss, P. 1993. The reconstruction of family life with Alzheimer's disease: Generating theory to lower family stress from ambiguous loss. In Boss, P., Doherty, W., LaRossa R., Schumm, W., and Steinmetz, S. (Eds.), *Sourcebook of family theories and methods: A contextual approach* (pp. 3-30). New York: Plenum.

Brand, A., Johnson, J., and Johnson, S. 1986. Life stress and diabetic control in children and adolescents with insulin-dependent diabetes. *Journal of Pediatric Psychology, 11*(4):481-495.

Burg, M. and Seeman, T. 1994. Families and health: The negative side of social ties. *Annals of Behavioral Medicine, 16*(2):109-115.

Cadman, D., Boyle, M., and Offord, D. 1988. The Ontario Child Health Study: Social adjustment and mental health of siblings of children with chronic health problems. *Journal of Developmental and Behavioral Pediatrics, 9*(3):117-121.

Cadman, D., Boyle, M., Szatmari, P., and Offord, D. 1987. Chronic illness, disability, and mental and social well being: Findings of the Ontario Child Health Study. *Pediatrics, 79*(5):805-813.

Campbell, T. 1993. Research reports: Impact of family factors on childhood illness. *Family Systems Medicine, 11*(4), 433-440.

Campbell, T. 1995. Research reports: Families and chronic illness reconsidered. *Family Systems Medicine, 13*(1):109-117.

Canning, R., Harris, E., and Kelleher, K. 1996. Factors predicting distress among caregivers to children with chronic medical conditions. *Journal of Pediatric Psychology, 21*(5):735-749.

Carmody, T. 1989. Affect regulation, nicotine addiction and smoking cessation. *Journal of Psychoactive Drugs, 21*(3):331-342.

Chassin, L., Presson, C., Sherman, S., and Edwards, D. 1992. Parent educational attainment and adolescent cigarette smoking. *Journal of Substance Abuse, 4*(3):219-234.

Chesler, M. and Barbarin, O. 1984. Difficulties of providing help in a crisis: Relationships between parents of children with cancer and their friends. *Journal of Social Issues, 40*(4):113-134.

Clemmey, P. and Nicassio, P. 1997. Illness self-schemas in depressed and nondepressed rheumatoid arthritis patients. *Journal of Behavioral Medicine, 20*(3): 273-289.

Cole, R. and Reiss, D. 1993. *How do families cope with illness?* Hillsdale, NJ: Lawrence Erlbaum Associates.

Crisp, J., Ungerer, J., and Goodnow, J. 1996. The impact of experience on children's understanding of illness. *Journal of Pediatric Psychology, 21*(1):57-72.

Daniels, D., Moo, R., Billings, A., and Miller, J. 1987. Psychosocial risk and resistance factors among children with chronic illness, healthy siblings and healthy controls. *Journal of Abnormal Child Psychology, 15*(2):295-308.

DeVet, K. and Ireys, H. 1998. Psychometric properties of the maternal worry scale for children with chronic illness. *Journal of Pediatric Psychology, 23*(4):257-266.

Doherty, W., Schrott, H., Metcalf, L., and Iasiello-Vailas, L. 1983. Effect of spouse support and health beliefs on medication adherence. *Journal of Family Practice, 17*(5):837-841.

Drotar, D. 1992. Integrating theory and practice in psychological intervention with families of children with chronic illness. In Akamatsu, T. J., Stephens, M., Hobfall, S., and Crowther, J. (Eds.), *Family health psychology* (pp. 175-192). Washington, DC: Hemisphere.

Drotar, D. 1997. Relating parent and family functioning to the psychological adjustment of children with chronic health conditions: What have we learned? What do we need to know? *Journal of Pediatric Psychology, 22*(2):149-165.

Dusenbury, L., Kerner, J., and Baker, E. 1992. Predictors of smoking prevalence among New York Latino youth. *American Journal of Public Health, 82*:55-58.

Eiser, J., Morgan, M., Gammage, P., and Gray E. 1989. Adolescent smoking: Attitudes, norms and parental influence. *British Journal of Social Psychology, 28*(Pt. 3): 193-202.

Engstrom, I. 1991. Parental distress and social interaction in families with children with inflammatory bowel disease. *Journal of the American Academy of Child and Adolescent Psychiatry, 30*(6):904-912.

Fiese, B. 1997. Family context in pediatric psychology from a transactional perspective: Family rituals and stories as examples. *Journal of Pediatric Psychology, 22*(2):183-196.

Fischer, L., Heinrich, R., Davis, T., Peek, C., and Lucas, S. 1997. Mental health and primary care in an HMO. *Family Systems and Health, 1*(4):379-391.

Freedson, P. and Evenson, S. 1992. Familial aggregation in physical activity. *Research Quarterly for Exercise and Sport, 62*:384-389.

Goldberg, S., Janus, M., Washington, J., Simmons, R., MacLusky, L., and Fowler, R. 1997. Prediction of preschool behavioral problems in healthy and pediatric samples. *Journal of Developmental and Behavioral Pediatrics, 18*(5):304-313.

Gonzales, S., Steinglass, P., and Reiss, D. 1989. Putting the illness in its place: Discussion groups for families with chronic medical illnesses. *Family Process, 28*(1):69-87.

Gortman, S., Walker, D., Weitzman, M., and Sobol, A. 1990. Chronic conditions, socioeconomic risks, and behavioral problems in children and adolescents. *Pediatrics, 85*(3):267-276.

Gustafsson, P., Bjorksten, B., and Kjellman, N. 1994. Family dysfunction in asthma: A prospective study of illness development. *Journal of Pediatrics, 125*(3):493-498.

Hamlett, K., Pellegrini, D., and Katz, K. 1992. Childhood chronic illness as a family stressor. *Journal of Pediatric Psychology, 17*(1):33-47.

Harvey, D., Curry, C., and Bray, J. 1991. Individuation and intimacy in intergenerational relationships and health: Patterns across two generations. *Journal of Family Psychology, 5*(2):204-236.

Hauenstein, E. 1990. The experience of distress in parents of chronically ill children: Potential or likely outcome? *Journal of Clinical Child Psychology, 19*(4):356-364.

Holden, E., Chmielewski, D., Nelson, C., Kager, V., and Foltz, L. 1997. Controlling for general and disease-specific effects in child and family adjustment to chronic childhood illness. *Journal of Pediatric Psychology, 22*(1):15-27.

Holmbeck, G., Gorey-Ferguson, L., Hudson, T., Seefeldt, T., Shapera, W., Turner, T., and Uhler, J. 1997. Maternal, paternal and marital functioning in famiies of preadolescents with spina bifida. *Journal of Pediatric Psychology, 22:*167-181.

Ievers, C. and Drotar, D. 1996. Family and parental functioning in cystic fibrosis. *Journal of Developmental and Behavioral Pediatrics, 17*(1):48-55.

Institute for Health and Disability Newsletter. 1998. 5(1). <http://www.peds.umn.edu/centers/inh/>

Ireys, H. and Silver, E. 1996. Perception of the impact of a child's chronic illness: Does it predict maternal mental health? *Journal of Developmental and Behavioral Pediatrics, 17*(2):77-83.

Ireys, H., Werthamer-Larsson, L., Kolodner, K., and Gross, S. 1994. Mental health of young adults with chronic illness: The mediating effect of perceived impact. *Journal of Pediatric Psychology, 19*(2):205-222.

Kager, V. and Holden, E. 1992. Preliminary investigation of the direct and moderating effects of family and individual variables on the adjustment of children and adolescents with diabetes. *Journal of Pediatric Psychology, 17*(4):491-502.

Kazak, A. 1997. A contextual family/systems approach to pediatric psychology: Introduction to the special issue on families. *Journal of Pediatric Psychology, 22*(2):141-148.

Kiecolt-Glaser, J., Fisher, L., and Ogrocki, P. 1987. Marital quality, marital disruption and immune function. *Psychosomatic Medicine, 49*(1):13-34.

Kiecolt-Glaser, J., Kennedy, S., and Malkoff, S. 1988. Marital discord and immunity in males. *Psychosomatic Medicine, 50*(3):213-229.

Klesges, R., Meyers, A., Winders, S., and French, S. 1989. Determining the reasons for weight gain following smoking cessation: Current findings, methodological issues, and futue directions for research. *Annals of Behavioral Medicine, 11*(4):134-143.

Klonoff, E. and Landrine, H. 1993. Cognitive representations of bodily parts and products: Implications for health behavior. *Journal of Behavioral Medicine, 16*(5):497-508.

Klonoff, E. and Landrine, H. 1994. Culture and gender diversity in commonsense beliefs about the causes of six illnesses. *Journal of Behavioral Medicine, 17*(4):407-417.

Lavigne, J. and Faier-Routman, J. 1992. Psychological adjustment to pediatric physical disorders: A meta-analytic review. *Journal of Pediatric Psychology, 17*(2):133-157.

Lavigne, J. and Faier-Routman, J. 1993. Correlates of psychological adjustment to pediatric physical disorders: A meta-analytic review and comparison with existing models. *Journal of Developmental and Behavioral Pediatrics, 14*(2):117-123.

Lazarus, R. and Folkman, S. 1984. *Stress, appraisal and coping.* New York: Springer.

McCubbin, H., McCubbin, M., and Patterson, J. 1983. CHIP—Coping health inventory for parents: An assessment of parental coping patterns in the care of the chronically ill child. *Journal of Marriage and the Family, 45*(2):359-370

McDaniel, S. Campbell, T., and Seaburn, D. 1995. Principles in collaboration between health and mental health providers in primary care. *Family Systems Medicine, 13*(3-4):283-298.

McDaniel, S., Hepworth, J., and Doherty, W. 1992. *Medical family therapy.* New York: Harper Collins.

McGoldrick, M., Giordano, J., and Pearce, J. 1996. *Ethnicity and family therapy.* New York: Guilford Press.

McHale, S. and Pawletko, T. 1992. Differential treatment of siblings in two family contexts. *Child Development, 63*(1):68-81.

McKenzie, T., Sallis, J., Nader, P., Broyles, S., and Nelson, II. 1992. Anglo and Mexican American preschoolers at home and at recess: Activity patterns and environmental influences. *Journal of Developmental and Behavioral Pediatrics, 13*(3):173-180.

McMahon, M., Miller, P., Wikoff, R., Garret, M., and Ringel, K. 1986. Life situations, health beliefs and medical regimen adherence of patients with myocardial infarction. *Heart and Lung, 15*(1):8-85.

Mengel, M., Lawler, M., and Volk, R. 1992. Parental stress response within a family context: Association with diabetic control in adolescents with IDDM. *Family Systems Medicine, 10*(4): 395-404.

Millar, W. and Hunter, L. 1990. Relationship between socioeconomic status and household smoking patterns in Canada. *American Journal of Health Promotion, 5*(1, September-October):36-43.

Miller, B. 1995. Promoting healthy function and development in chronically ill children: A primary care approach. *Family Systems Medicine, 13*(2):187-200.

Miller, P., Wikoff, R., and McMahan, M. 1989. Personal adjustments and regimen compliance one year after myocardial infarction. *Heart and Lung, 18*(4):339-345.

Minuchin, S., Baker, L., and Rosman, B. 1975. A conceptual model of psychosomatic illness in children: Family organization and family therapy. *Archives of General Psychiatry, 32*(8):1031-1038.

Moore, L., Lombardi, D., and White, M. 1991. Influence of parents' physical activity levels on activity levels of young children. *Journal of Pediatrics, 118*(2):215-219.

Mrazek, D. and Klinnert, M. 1991. Early identification of asthma subtypes. *Psychosomatic Medicine, 53*(5):233.

Parker, M. 1996. Families caring for chronically ill children with tuberous sclerosis complex. *Family and Community Health, 19*(3):73-84.

Patterson, J., Budd, J., Goetz, D., and Warwick, W. 1993. Family correlates of a ten-year pulmonary health trend in cystic fibrosis. *Pediatrics, 91*(2):383-389.

Patterson, J. and Garwick, A. 1994. The impact of chronic illness on families: A family systems perspective. *Annals of Behavioral Medicine, 16*(2):131-142.

Patterson, J. and Garwick, A. 1998. Theoretical linkages: Family meanings and a sense of coherence. In McCubbin, H. and Thompson, A. (Eds.), *Stress, coping, and health in families: Sense of coherence and resiliency* (pp. 71-89). Thousand Oaks, CA: Sage.

Patterson, J., Garwick, A., Bennett, F., and Blum, R. 1997. Social support in families of children with chronic conditions: Supportive and nonsupportive behaviors. *Journal of Developmental and Behavioral Pediatrics, 18*(6):383-391.

Patterson, J. and Leonard, B. 1994. Caregiving and children. In Kahana E., Biegel, D., and Wykel, M. (Eds.), *Family caregiving across the lifespan* (pp. 133-158). Newbury Park, CA: Sage.

Patterson, J., McCubbin, H., and Warwick, W. 1990. The impact of family functioning on health changes in children with cystic fibrosis. *Social Science and Medicine, 31*(2):159-164.

Pearlin, L. 1989. The sociological study of stress. *Journal of Health and Social Behavior, 30*(3):241-256.

Pearlin, L., Mullan, J., Semple, S., and Skaff, M. 1990. Caregiving and the stress process: An overview of concepts and their measures. *Gerontologist, 30*(5): 583-594.

Perrin, E., Ayoub, C., and Willett, J. 1993. In the eyes of the beholder: Family and maternal influences on perceptions of adjustment of children with a chronic illness. *Journal of Developmental and Behavioral Pediatrics, 14*(2):94-105.

Peshkin, M. 1930. Asthma in children: IX. Role of environment in the treatment of a selected group of cases: A plea for a "home" as a restorative measure. *American Journal of Diseases of Children, 39*(2):744-779.

Pianta, R. and Marvin, S. 1992. The reaction to diagnosis interview. Unpublished materials, University of Virginia, Charlottesville, VA.

Pless, I. and Nolan, T. 1989. Risks for maladjustment associated with chronic illness in adolescence and childhood. In Shaffer, D., Philips, I., and Enzer, N. (Eds.), *Prevention of mental disorders, abuse of alcohol and other drug use in children and adolescents* (pp. 191-224). Rockville, MD: Office for Substance Abuse Prevention.

Quittner, A., Espelage, D., Opipari, L., Carter B., Eid, N., and Eigen, H. 1998. Role strain in couples with and without a child with chronic illness: Associations with marital satisfaction, intimacy, and daily mood. *Health Psychology, 17*(2):112-124.

Quittner, A. and Opipari, L. 1994. Differential treatment of siblings: Interview and diary analyses comparing two family contexts. *Child Development, 65*(3): 800-814.

Quittner, A., Opipari, L., Michel, M., and Eigen, H. 1992. Parental response to CF: A contextual analysis of the diagnosis phase. *Journal of Pediatric Psychology, 17*(6):683-704.

Quittner, A., Opipari, L., Regoli, M., Jacobsen, J., and Eigen, H. 1992. The impact of caregiving and role strain on family life. Comparisons between mothers with CF children and matched controls. *Rehabilitation Psychology, 37*(4):289-304.

Quittner, A., Tolbert, V., Regoli, M., Orenstein, D., Hollingsworth, J., and Eigen, H. 1996. Development of the role-play inventory of situations and coping strategies for parents of children with cystic fibrosis. *Journal of Pediatric Psychology, 21*(2):209-235.

Reiss, D. 1989. The practicing and representing family. In Ameroff, A.J. and Emde, R. (Eds.), *Relationship disturbances in early childhood* (pp. 191-220). New York: Basic Books.

Reiss, D., Steinglass, P., and Howe, G. 1993. The family's organization around the illness. In Cole, R. and Reiss, D. (Eds.), *How do families cope with chronic illness?* (pp. 173-213). Hillsdale, NJ: Lawrence Erlbaum.

Roberts, M. and Wallander, J. 1992. Family issues in pediatric psychology: An overview. In Roberts, M. and Wallander, J. (Eds.), *Family issues in pediatric psychology* (pp. 5-10). Hillsdale, NJ: Lawrence Erlbaum.

Rolland, J. 1984. Toward a psychosocial typology of chronic and life-threatening illness. *Family Systems Medicine, 2*(3):245-263.

Rolland, J. 1993. Mastering family challenges in serious illness and disability. In Walsh, F. (Ed.), *Normal family processes,* Second edition (pp. 444-473). New York: Guilford.

Rolland, J. 1994. *Families, illness and disability: An integrative treatment model.* New York: Basic Books.

Rolland, J. 1998. Beliefs and collaboration in illness: Evolution over time. *Families, Systems and Health, 16*(1-2):7-25.

Schiaffino, K., Shawaryn, M., and Blum, D. 1998. Examining the impact of illness representations on psychological adjustment to chronic illnesses. *Health Psychology, 17*(3):262-268.

Schilson, E., Braun, K., and Hudson, A. 1993. Use of genograms in family medicine: A family physician/family therapist collaboration. *Family Systems Medicine, 11*(2):201-208.

Sheeran, T., Marvin, R., and Pianta, R. 1997. Mother's resolution of their child's diagnosis and self-reported measures of parenting stress, marital relations, and social support. *Journal of Pediatric Psychology, 22*(2):197-212.

Sherman, R., Oresky, P., and Rountree, Y. 1991. *Solving problems in couples and family therapy.* New York: Brunner/Mazel.

Silver, E., Bauman, L., and Ireys, H. 1995. Relationships of self-esteem and efficacy to psychological distress in mothers of children with chronic physical illnesses. *Health Psychology, 14*(4): 1-8.

Silver, E., Westbrook, L., and Stein, R. 1998. Relationship of parental psychological distress to consequences of chronic health conditions in children. *Journal of Pediatric Psychology, 23*(1):5-15.

Simms, S. 1995. A protocol for seriously ill children with severe psychosocial symptoms: Avoiding potential disasters. *Pediatric Hematology and Oncology, 13*(2):245-257.

Stein, M. 1997. The use of family drawings by children in pediatric practice. *Journal of Developmental and Behavioral Pediatrics, 18*(5):334-339.

Stein, R., Bauman, L., Westbrook, L., Coupey, S., and Ireys, H. 1993. Framework for identifying children who have chronic conditions: The case for a new definition. *Journal of Pediatrics, 122*(3):342-347.

Stein, R. and Jessop, D. 1985. *Tables documenting the psychometric properties of a measure of the impact of chronic illness on a family.* Bronx, NY: Bronx Municipal Hospital Center. Report available from Dr. Ruth Stein, Jacobi Medical Center, Room 817, Pelham Parkway and Eastchester Road, Bronx, NY 10461.

Stein, R. and Riessman, C. 1980. The development of an impact on family scale: Preliminary findings. *Medical Care, 18*(1):465-472.

Stein, R., Westbrook, L., and Bauman, L. 1997. The questionnaire for identifying children with chronic conditions (QuICCC):A measure based on a noncategorical approach. *Pediatrics, 99*(4):513-521.

Steinglass, P. 1998. Multiple family discussion groups for patients with chronic medical illness. *Families, Systems & Health, 16*(1-2):55-70.

Tayor, C., Bandura, A., Ewart, C., Miller, N., and DeBusk, R. 1985. Exercise testing to enhance wives' confidence in their husband's cardiac capacity soon after uncomplicated acute myocardial infarction. *American Journal of Cardiology, 55*(6):635-638.

Thompson, R., Gil, K., Gustafson, K., George, L., Keith, B., Spock, A., and Kinney, T. 1994. Stability and change in the psychological adjustment of mothers of children and adolescents with cystic fibrosis and sickle cell disease. *Journal of Pediatric Psychology, 19*(2):171-188.

Timko, C., Stovel, K., and Moos, R. 1992. Functioning among mothers and fathers of children with juvenile rheumatic disease: A longitudinal study. *Journal of Pediatric Psychology, 17*(6):705-724.

Tritt, S. and Esses, L. 1988. Psychosocial adaptation of siblings of children with chronic medical illness. *American Journal of Orthopsychiatry, 58*(2):211-220.

Varni, J. and Setoguchi, Y. 1991. Correlates of perceived physical appearance in children with congenital/acquired limb deficiencies. *Journal of Developmental and Behavioral Pediatrics, 12*(3):171-176.

Varni, J., Wilcox, K., and Hanson, V. 1988. Mediating effects of family social support on child psychological adjustment in juvenile rheumatoid arthritis. *Health Psychology, 7*(5):421-431.

Wachtel, E. 1982. The family psyche over three generations: The genogram revisited. *Journal of Marital and Family Therapy, 8*(3):335-343.

Walker, L. and Preski, S. 1995. Are maternal health behaviors related to preschool children's adjustment? A preliminary report. *Journal of Developmental and Behavioral Pediatrics, 16*(5):345-349.

Wallander, J. and Thompson, R. 1995. Psychosocial adjustment of children with chronic physical conditions. In Roberts, M. (Ed.), *Handbook of pediatric psychology* (pp. 124-141). New York: Guilford.

Wallander, J. and Varni, J. 1989. Social support and adjustment in chronically ill and handicapped children. *American Journal of Community Psychology, 17*(2): 185-201.

Wamboldt, M. and Levin, L. 1995. Utility of multifamily psychoeducational groups for medically ill children and adolescents. *Family Systems Medicine, 13*(2):151-161.

Wamboldt, M., Weintraub, P., Krafchick, D., Berce, N., and Wamboldt, F. 1995. Links between parental trauma and the medical and psychological outcome of asthmatic children. *Family Systems Medicine, 13*(2):129-149.

Watson, S., Henggeler, S., and Whelan, J. 1990. Family functioning and the social adaptation of hearing-impaired youths. *Journal of Abnormal Child Psychology, 18*:143-163.

Weinstein, A., Faust, D., McKee, L., and Padman, R. 1992. Outcomes and short-term hospitalization for children with severe asthma. *Journal of Allergy and Clinical Immunology, 90*:66-75.

Wood, B. 1994. A developmental biobehavioral systems approach to the treatment of chronic illness in children. In Mikesell, R., Lusterman, D., and McDaniel, S. (Eds.), *Family psychology and systems therapy: A handbook* (pp. 50-69). Washington, DC: American Psychological Association.

Wynne, L., Shields, C., and Sirkin, M. 1992. Illness, family theory and family therapy: I. Conceptual issues. *Family Process, 31*:3-18.

Suggested Readings

Appleton, M. and Henschell, T. 1995. *At home with terminal illness: A family guide to hospice in the home.* Englewood Cliffs, NJ: Prentice-Hall Career and Technology.

Atkinson, J.M. 1995. *Families coping with schizophrenia: A practitioner's guide to family groups.* Chichester, NY: John Wiley and Sons.

Gustafson, K.E. and Thompson, R.J. 1996. *Adaptation to chronic childhood illness.* Washington, DC: American Psychological Association.

Miklowitz, D.J. and Goldstein, M.J. 1997. *Bipolar disorder: A family-focused treatment approach.* New York: Guilford Press.

Wright, L.M., Bell, J., and Watson, W. 1996. *Beliefs: The heart of healing in families and illness.* New York: Basic Books.

Film

Lorenzo's Oil. 1992. Directed by George Miller. There is no more compelling story about how extraordinary parents can resourcefully deal with illness in the family. It is a film all parents can learn from.

Shine. 1996. Directed by Scott Hicks. Another true story about how supportive parents, faced with a "different" child, capitalize on the child's strengths and make life better for all.

Chapter 12

Bibliography

Alexander, R. and Curtis, C.M. 1996. A review of empirical research involving the transracial adoption of African American children. *Journal of Black Psychology,* 22(2):223-235.

Anderson, S., Piantanida, and Anderson, C. 1993. Normal family processes in adoptive families. In Walsh, F. (Ed.), *Normal family processes,* Second edition. (pp. 254-281). New York: Guilford Press.

Bartholet, E. 1993. *Family bonds: Adoption and the politics of parenting.* Boston: Houghton Mifflin.

Benson, P.L., Sharma, A.R., and Roehlkepartain, E.C. 1994. *Growing up adopted: A portrait of adolescents and their families.* Minneapolis, MN: Search Institute.

Boykin, W. 1986. The triple quandary and the schooling of Afro-American children. In V. Neisser (Ed.), *The school achievement of minority children* (pp. 57-92). Hillsdale, NJ: Lawrence Erlbaum.

Brodzinsky, D.M. 1990. A stress and coping model of adoption adjustment. In Brodzinsky, D.M. and Schechter, M.D. (Eds.), *The psychology of adoption* (pp. 3-24). New York: Oxford University Press.

Brodzinsky, D. 1998. Infertility and adoption adjustment: Considerations and clinical issues. In Leiblum, S. (Ed.), *Infertility: Psychological issues and counseling strategies* (pp. 246-262). New York: John Wiley and Sons.

Brodzinsky, D., Schechter, M.D., and Henig, R.M. 1992. *Being adopted: The lifelong search for self.* New York: Anchor Books.

Devor, N. 1994. Pastoral care for infertile couples. *The Journal of Pastoral Care,* 48:355-360.

Grotevant, H. 1997. Coming to terms with adoption: The construction of identity from adolescence to adulthood. *Adoption Quarterly,* 1(1):3-27.

Grotevant, H., McRoy, R.G., Eled, C.L., and Fravel, D.L. 1994. Adoptive family system dynamics: Variations by level of openness in the adoption. *Family Process,* 33(2):125-146.

Haugaard, J.J. 1998. Is adoption a risk factor for the development of adjustment problems? *Clinical Psychology Review,* 18(1):47-69.

Hollingsworth, L.D. 1997. Effect of transracial/transethnic adoption on children's racial and ethnic identity and self-esteem: A meta-analytic review. *Marriage and Family Process,* 25(1-2):99-130.

Hollingsworth, L.D. 1998. Promoting same-race adoption for children of color. *Social Work,* 43(2):104-116.

Johnston, P.L. 1992. *Adopting after infertility.* Indianapolis, In Perspectives Press.

Kirk, H.D. 1964. *Shared fate: A theory of adoption and mental health.* London: Free Press of Glencoe.

Melina, L. 1989. *Making sense of adoption: A parents' guide.* New York: Harper & Row.

Molock S.D. 1995. Adoption barriers for African American families. *Adoptive Families,* 28(2):14-16.

Molock, S.D. In press. Race, culture, and religion in infertility counseling. In Hammer Burns, L. and Covington, S. (Eds.), *Counseling in infertility.* New York: Pergamon Press.

Meyers, M., Weinstel, M., Scharf, C., Kezer, D., Diamond, R., and Rait, D. 1995. An infertility primer for family therapists: II. Working with couples who struggle with infertility. *Family Process, 34*(2):231-240.

Myers, L.B. and Wark, L. 1996. Psychotherapy for infertility: A cognitive behavioral approach for couples. *American Journal of Family Therapy, 24*(1):9-20.

Penn, M.L. and Coverdale, C. 1996. Transracial adoption: A human rights perspective. *Journal of Black Psychology, 22*(2):240-245.

Sandelowski, M., Harris, B.G., and Holditch-Davis, D. 1989. Mazing: Infertile couples and the quest for a child. *IMAGE: Journal of Nursing Scholarship, 21*(4):220-226.

Schooler, J. 1993. *The whole life adoption book.* Colorado Springs, CO: Pinon Press.

Van Gulden, H. and Bartels-Rabb, L.M. 1993. *Real parents, real children: Parenting the adopted child.* New York: Crossroad.

Wierzbicki, M. 1993. Psychological adjustment of adoptees: A meta-analysis. *Journal of Child Clinical Psychology. 22*(4):447-454.

Adoption Resources

Bothun, L. 1994. *Dialogues about adoption.* Chevy Chase, MD: Swan Publications.

Brodzinsky, D., Schecter, M., and Henig, R.M. 1992. *Being adopted: The lifelong search for self.* New York: Doubleday.

Caplan, L. 1990. *An open adoption.* New York: Farrar, Straus and Giroux.

Glazer, E.S. 1990. *The long awaited stork: A guide to parenting after infertility.* New York: Lexington Books.

Krementz, J. 1992. *How it feels to be adopted.* New York: Alfred Knopf Publishers.

Mason, M.M. 1995. *Out of the shadows: Birthfathers' stories.* West Monroe, LA: Howard Publishing.

Melina, L. 1986. *Raising adopted children.* Moscow, ID: Solstice Press.

van Gulden, H. and Bartels-Rabb, L.M. 1993. *Real parents, real children: Parenting the adopted child.* New York: Crossroads Publishers.

Wadia-Ells, S. (Ed.). 1995. *The adoption reader: Birth mothers, adoptive mothers and adopted daughters tell their stories.* Seattle, WA: Seal Press.

Suggested Reading

Peck, C., Wilkinson, W., and Garber, H.K. 1998. *Parents at last: Celebrating adoption and the new pathways to parenthood.* New York: Clarkson Potter.

Saffian, S. 1998. *Ithaka: A daughter's memoir of being found.* New York: Basic Books.

Verrier, N.N. 1997. *The primal wound: Understanding the adopted child.* Baltimore: Gateway Press.

Film

Annie 1981. Directed by John Huston. A universally understood story about the child, Annie, who escapes from an orphanage, returns, and is then selected to spend a short time with a billionaire who grows to love her.

Chapter 13

Bibliography

Baumrind, D. 1973. The development of instrumental competence through socialization. In Pick, A. (Ed.), *Minnesota symposium on child psychology, 7.* Minneapolis, MN: University of Minnesota Press.

Baumrind, D. 1983. Socialization and instrumental competence in young children. In Damon, W. (Ed.), *Social and personality development.* New York: W.W. Norton.

Blehar, M. 1979. Family styles of interacting. In Corfman, E. (Ed.), *Families today, 1-a, Research Sampler on Families and Children* (pp. 71-85). Washington, DC: U.S. Department of Health, Education and Welfare.

Cherlin, A.J. and Furstenberg, F.F. 1994. Stepfamilies in the United States: A reconsideration. *Annual Review of Sociology, 20*:359-381.

Crawford, C., Stark, A., and Renner, C. 1998. The meaning of Ms.: Social assimilation of a gender concept. *Psychology of Women Quarterly, 22*:197-208.

Damon, W. 1983. *Social and personality development.* New York: W.W. Norton.

Doherty, W.J. 1981. Cognitive processes in intimate conflict, efficacy and learned helplessness. *American Journal of Family Therapy, 9*:35-44.

Duhl, F. and Duhl, B. 1979. Structured spontaneity: The thoughtful art of integrative family therapy. *Journal of Marital and Family Therapy, 5*(3):59-75.

Dyer, W.J. 1975. *Creating closer families: Principles of positive family interaction.* Provo, UT: Brigham Press.

Foster, S., Prinz, R., and O'Leary, K. 1983. Impact of problem solving communication training and generalization procedures on family conflict. *Child and Family Behavior Therapy, 5*(1):1-23.

Gottman, J. 1986. Assessing the role of emotion in marriage. *Behavioral Assessment, 8*(1, Winter):31-48.

Gottman J. 1998. Psychology and the study of marital processes. *Annual Review of Psychology, 49*:167-197.

Gottman, J., Coan, J., Carrere, S., and Swanson, C. 1998. Predicting marital happiness and stability from newlywed interactions. *Journal of Marriage and the Family, 60*(1):5-22.

Gottman, J., Notarius, C., Gonso, J., and Markman, H. 1976. *A couple's guide to communication.* Champaign, IL: Research Press.

L'Abate, L. 1976. *Understanding and helping the individual in the family.* New York: Grune and Stratton.

L'Abate, L. 1981. Skill training programs for couples and families. Chapter 17. In Gurman, A. and Kriskern, D. (Eds.), *Handbook of family therapy.* New York: Brunner-Mazel.

Lichtman, H. 1984. Parental communication of holocaust experiences and personality characteristics among second generation survivors. *Journal of Clinical Psychology, 40*(4):914-924.

Markman, R. 1984. The longitudinal study of couples' interactions: Implications for understanding and predicting the development of marital distress. In Hahlweg, K. and Jacobson, N. (Eds.), *Marital interaction analysis and modification.* New York: Guilford Press.

Metcoff, J. and Whitaker, C. 1980. Family microevents: Communication patterns for problem solving. Chapter 10. In Walsh, N. (Ed.), *Normal family processes.* New York: Guilford Press.

Miller, S. 1975. *Marriages and families: Enrichment through communication.* Beverly Hills, CA: Sage.

Miller, S., Nunnally, E.W., and Wachman, D. 1976. A communication training program for couples. *Social Casework, 57*(1):9-18.

Moos, R.H. and Moos, B.S. 1976. A typology of family social environments. *Family Process, 15*:357-371.

Oliveri, M.E. and Reiss, D. 1981. A theory based empirical classification of family problem solving behavior. *Family Process, 20*:409-418.

Olson, D.H., Spenkle, D.H., and Russell, C.S. 1979. Circumplex model of marital and family systems. I: Cohesion and adaptability dimensions, family types and clinical applications. *Family Process, 18*:3-28.

Otto, H.A. 1976. *Marriage and family enrichment: New perspectives and programs.* Nashville, TN: Abington.

Reiss, D. 1971. Varieties of consensual experience. II: Dimensions of a family's experience of its enviroment. *Family Process, 10*:28-35.

Reiss, D., Costell, R., Berkman, H., and Jones, C. 1980. How one family perceives another: The relationship between social constructions and problem solving competence. *Family Process, 19*:239-256.

Rogers, C.R. 1951. *Client-centered therapy.* Boston: Houghton-Mifflin.

Satir, V. 1967. *Conjoint family therapy.* Palo Alto, CA: Science and Behavior Books.

Satir, V. 1991. *The Satir model: Family therapy and beyond.* Palo Alto, CA: Science and Behavior Books

Satir, V., Taschman, H., and Stackowiak, J. 1975. *Helping families to change.* New York: Jason Aronson.

Van der Veen, F., Huebner, B., Jorgens, B., and Neja, P. Jr. 1964. Relationships between the parent's concept of the family and family adjustment. *American Journal of Orthopsychiatry, 34*:45-55.

Waring, E.M., McElrath, D., Lefcoe, D., and Weiss, G. 1981. Dimensions of intimacy in marriage. *Journal of Psychiatry, 44*:169-175.

Waring, E.M. and Reddon, J.R. 1983. The measurement of intimacy in marriage: The Waring intimacy questionnaire. *Journal of Clinical Psychology, 39*(1):53-57.

Yahraes, H. 1979. Parents as leaders: The role of control and discipline. In Corfman, E. (Ed.), *Families today: Research sampler on families and children.* Washington, DC: U.S. Department of Health, Education and Welfare.

Yalom, M., Estler, S., and Brewster, W. 1982. Changes in female sexuality: A study of mother/daughter communication and generational differences. *Psychology of Women Quarterly, 7*(2):141-154.

Suggested Readings

Barnett, D. 1997. *Twenty advanced communication tips for couples: A 90-minute investment in a better relationship.* New York: Three Rivers Press.

Gray, J. 1997. *Mars and Venus on a date: A guide for navigating the 5 stages of dating to create a loving and lasting relationship.* New York: HarperCollins Publishers.

L'Abate, L. 1976. *Understanding and helping the individual in the family.* New York: Grune and Stratton.

Morecal, L. 1984. *Where's my happy ending? Women and the myth of having it all.* Reading, MA: Addison-Wesley.

Ricker, A. and Crowder, C. 1998. *Backtalk: 4 steps to ending rude behavior in your kids.* New York: Simon and Schuster.

Robinson, J. 1997. *Communication miracles for couples: Easy and effective tools to create more love and less conflict.* Berkeley, CA: Conari Press.

Satir, V., Taschman, H., and Stackowiak, J. 1975. *Helping families to change.* New York: Jason Aronson.

Literature

Brown, R. 1994. *Civil wars.* New York: Knopf. A couple in the midst of a marital crisis are forced by family disaster to take into their home a young boy and girl. There are lots of communication problems and successes here.

O'Neill, E. 1956. *Long day's journey into night.* New Haven, CT: Yale University Press. A four-act play that shows poor communication at its best.

Film

Le Chat. 1975. A middle-aged couple whose marriage has grown sour live together unable to communicate. Eventually, they stop speaking altogether but are still unable to physically separate.

The Stone Boy. 1984. The story of what happens after a twelve-year-old Montana farm boy accidentally shoots and kills his nineteen-year-old brother. When he doesn't cry or talk about it, the family thinks he doesn't realize the import of what he's done and doesn't feel remorse. The subsequent failure of communication creates double tragedy.

Chapter 14

Bibliography

Adler, A. 1924. *The practice and theory of individual psychology.* New York: Harcourt, Brace and Company.

Bach, G. and Wyden, F. 1969. *The intimate enemy: How to fight fair in love and marriage.* New York: William Morrow & Co.

Barrett, P.M., Rapee, R.M., Dadds, M.M., and Ryan, S.M. 1996. Family enhancement of cognitive style in anxious and aggressive children. *Journal of Abnormal Child Psychology. 24*(2):187-203.

Chafetz, J.S. 1980. Conflict resolution in marriage: Toward a theory of spousal strategies and marital dissolution rates. *Journal of Family Issues, 1*:397-421.

Creighton, J. 1998. *How loving couples fight: Twelve essential tools for working through the hurt.* New York: Asian Publications.

Douglas, S. and Wind, Y. 1978. Examining family role and authority patterns: Two methodical issues. *Journal of Marriage and the Family, 40*(1):35-47.

Dreikurs, R., Gould, S., and Corsini, J.P. 1974. *Family council.* Chicago: Regnery.

Easterbrooks, M.A., Cummings, E.M., and Emde, R.N. 1994. Young children's responses to constructive marital disputes. *Journal of Family Psychology. 8*(2):160-169.

Fawl, C.L. 1962. A developmental analysis of the frequency and causal types of disturbance experienced by children. *Merrill-Palmer Quarterly, 8*(1):13-18.

Gordon, T. 1975. *Parent effectiveness training: The tested new way to raise responsible children.* New York: Plume.

Gottman, J., Markman, H., Notarius, C., and Gonso, J. 1976. *The couples guide to communication.* Champaign, IL: Research Press.

Harlow, II. 1971. *Learning to love.* San Francisco: Albion.

Harrell, J. and Guerney, B.G. Jr. 1976. Training married couples in conflict negotiation skills. In Olson, D.H.L. (Ed.), *Treating relationships.* Lake Mills, IA: Graphic Publishing.

Jackson, D. and Lederer, W. 1968. *The mirages of marriage.* New York: W. W. Norton.

Jacobson, N. 1981. Behavioral marital therapy. In Gurman, A. and Kriskern, D. (Eds.), *Handbook of family therapy.* New York: Brunner/Mazel.

Kieren, D., Henton, J., and Marotz, R. 1975. *Her and his: The problem-solving approach to marriage.* Hinsdale, IL: Dryden Press.

Klein, D.M. and Hill, R. 1979. Determinants of family problem-solving effectiveness. In Burr, W.R., Hill, R., Nye, F.I., and Reiss, I.L. (Eds.), *Contemporary theories about the family: 1. Research Based Theories.* New York: Free Press.

Kline, P.M. 1995. An exploratory investigation of family functioning for child inpatients: Implications for practice. *Child and Adolescent Social Work Journal, 12*(6):423-434.

Levenson, R. and Gottman, J. 1983. Marital interaction: Physiological linkage and affective exchange. *Journal of Personality and Social Psychology, 45*:587-597.

Powers, S.W. and Roberts, M.W. 1995. Simulation training with parents of oppositional children: Preliminary findings. *Journal of Clinical Child Psychology, 24*(1):89-97.

Prinz, R.J., Foster, S., Kent, R., and O'Leary, D.K. 1979. Multivariate assessment of conflict in distressed and nondistressed mother-adolescent dyads. *Journal of Applied Behavior Analysis, 12*:691-700.

Rands, M., Levinger, G., and Mellinger, G. 1981. Patterns of conflict resolution and marital satisfaction. *Journal of Family Issues, 3*:297-321.

Rueter, M.A. and Conger, R.D. 1995. Interaction style, problem-solving behavior, and family problem solving effectiveness. *Child Development, 66*:98-115.

Rutter, M. 1994. Family discord and conduct disorder: Cause, consequence, or correlate? *Journal of Family Psychology, 8*(2):170-186.

Stohs, J.H. 1991. "Doing gender" and conflicts over the household division of labor. Paper presented at the Forty-Fourth Annual Scientific Meeting of the Gerontological Society of America. San Francisco, November 22-26.

Stuart, R.B. 1973. *Scale of marital precounseling inventory: Behavior change systems.* Champaign, IL: Research Press.

Stuart, R.B. 1980. *Helping couples change: A social learning approach to marital therapy.* New York: Guilford Press.

Vuchinich, S., Angelelli, J., and Gatherum, A. 1996. Context and development in family problem solving with preadolescent children. *Child Development, 67*:1276-1288.

Vuchinich, S., Wood, B., and Vuchinich, M.A. 1994. Coalitions and family problem solving with preadolescents in referred, at risk and comparison families. *Family Process, 33:*409-424.

Winkler, I. and Doherty, W.G. 1983. Communication styles and marital satisfaction in Israeli and American couples. *Family Process, 22*(2):221-228.

Suggested Readings

Bach, G. and Wyden, F. 1969. *The intimate enemy: How to fight fair in love and marriage.* New York: William Morrow & Co.

Gottman, J., Markman, H., Notarius, C., and Gonso, J. 1976. *The couples guide to communication.* Champaign, IL: Research Press.

Kieren, D., Henton, J., and Marotz, R. 1975. *Her and his: The problem-solving approach to marriage.* Hinsdale, IL: Dryden Press.

Kreider, R.S. and Goossen, R.W. 1988. *When good people quarrel: Studies of conflict resolution.* Scottsdale, PA: Herald Press.

Madison, L. 1998. *Parenting with purpose: Progressive discipline in the toddler years.* Kansas City: Andrews & McMal.

Markman, H., Stanley, S., Blumberg, S.L., and Edell, D.S. 1996. *Fighting for your marriage: Positive steps for preventing divorce and preserving a lasting love.* San Francisco: Jossey-Bass.

Nelsen, J. and Erwin, C. 1998. *Positive discipline: The first three years, from infant to toddler—laying the foundation for raising capable, confident children.* Rocklin, CA: Prime Publications.

Samalin, N. and Jablow, M.M. 1998. *Loving your child is not enough: Positive discipline that works.* New York: Penguin Books.

Stuart, R.B. 1980. *Helping couples change—A social learning approach to marital therapy.* New York: Guilford Press.

Literature

Lucas, J.A. 1985. *Common ground.* New York: Knopf. The story of three Boston families trying to solve societal and family problems during the 1960s school-desegregation era.

Film

Night Crossing. 1981. Dramatic true story about two families who work together to escape from East Germany in a hot air balloon.

Stuart Saves His Family. 1994. Directed by Harold Ramis. The main character struggles with family dysfunction and the perpetually precarious state of his own psyche.

Chapter 15

Bibliography

Ables, B. and Brandsma, J. 1977. *Therapy for couples.* San Francisco: Jossey Bass.

Aldous, J. 1981. The consequences of intergenerational continuity. *Journal of Marriage and the Family, 27*(4):462-468.

Anderson, D. 1974. The family growth group: Guidelines for an emerging means of strengthening families. *The Family Coordinator, 23*(1):7-13.

Bee, H.L., Van Egeren, L.F., Streissguth, A.P., Nyman, B.A., and Leckie, M.S. 1969. Social class differences in maternal teaching strategies and speech patterns. *Developmental Psychology, 1*(6, Pt. 1):726-734.

Bell, R. and Bell, P. 1972. Sexual satisfaction among married women. *Medical Aspects of Human Sexuality, 6*(12):140-143.

Berne, E. 1970. *Sex in human loving.* New York: Simon and Schuster.

Blumstein, P. and Schwartz, P. 1983. *American couples: Money, work, sex.* New York: William Morrow.

Brecher, E.M. 1984. *Love, sex, and aging: A Consumers Union report.* Boston: Little, Brown and Company.

Butler, R.N. 1975. Sex after 65. In Brown, L. E. and Ellis, G.O. (Eds.), *Quality of life: The later years.* Acton, MA: Publishing Sciences Group.

Carlson, J. 1976. The sexual role. In Nye, F.I. (Ed.), *Role structure and analysis of the family.* London: Sage.

Carlson, J.E. 1979. The family and recreation: Toward a theoretical development. In Burr, W., Hill, R., Nye, F., and Reiss, I. (Eds.), *Contemporary theories about the family. Vol. 1, Research-based theories.* New York: The Free Press.

Coreil, J. and Parcel, G.S. 1985. Sociocultural determinants of parental involvement in sex education. *Journal of Sex Education and Therapy, 11*:22-25.

Crouchman, R. 1982. Family recreation: A new dynamic in family life. *Journal of Leisurability, 9*:4-8.

Cuber, J.F. 1974. Sex in the upper middle class. *Medical Aspects of Human Sexuality, 8*:8-34.

DiPrima, D. 1975. *Selected poems 1956-1975.* Plainsfield, VT: North Atlantic Books.

Dyer, W.G. 1975. *Creating closer families: Principles of positive family interaction.* Provo, UT: Brigham Young University Press.

Elkind, D. 1981. *The hurried child: Growing up too fast too soon.* Reading, MA: Addison-Wesley.

Fabes, R.A. and Strouse, J. 1985. Youth's perceptions of models of sexuality: Implications for sex education. *Journal of Sex Education & Therapy, 11*:33-37.

Fichten, C. 1984. See it from my point of view: Videotape and attributions in happy and distressed couples. *Journal of Social and Clinical Psychology, 2*(2):125-142.

Fox, K. and Nickols, S. 1983. The time crunch: Wife's employment and family work. *Journal of Family Issues, 4*(1):61-82.

Frost, J. 1980. *The family in change.* Vastards: The International Library.

Ganovetter, M.S. 1973. The strength of weak ties. *American Journal of Sociology, 76*:1360-1380.

Gelles, R.J. 1976. Abused wives: Why do they stay? *Journal of Marriage and the Family, 38*:659-668.

Gilbert, L. and Hanson, G. 1983. Perceptions of parental role responsibilities among working people: Development of a comprehensive measure. *Journal of Marriage and the Family, 45*(1):203-212.

Gilford, R. 1984. Contrasts in marital satisfaction throughout old age: An exchange theory analysis. *Journal of Gerontology, 39*(3):325-333.

Goldman, J. and Goldman, R. 1983. Children's perceptions of parents and their roles: A cross-national study in Australia, England, North America, and Sweden. *Sex Roles, 9*(7):791-812.

Greendorfer, S. and Lewko, J. 1978. Role of family members in sport socialization of children. *Research Quarterly, 49*:146-152.

Gurewitsch, E. 1983. Gymnastics. *Aging,* January/February: 2-7.

Haas, L. 1980. Domestic role sharing in Sweden. Revision of paper presented at the 75th Annual Meeting of the American Sociological Association, August 27-31. New York: American Sociological Association.

Hill, R., Foote, N., Adores, T., Carlson, R., and MacDonald, R. 1970. *Family development in three generations.* Cambridge, MA: Schenkman.

Hite, S. 1976. *The Hite report: A nationwide study on female sexuality.* New York: Macmillan.

Janus, S. and Janus C. 1993. *The Janus report on sexual behavior.* New York: John Wiley & Sons.

Kamerman, S.B. and Kahn, A.J. 1978. *Family policy: Government and families in fourteen countries.* New York: Columbia University Press.

Korn, S., Chess, S., and Fernandez, P. 1978. The impact of children's physical handicaps on marital quality and family interaction. In Levner, R.M. and Spanier, G. (Eds.), *Child influences on marital and family interaction: A life span perspective.* New York: Academic Press.

Land, H. and Parker, R. 1978. United Kingdom. In Kamerman, S.B. and Kahn, A.J. (Eds.), *Family policy: Government and families in fourteen countries.* New York: Columbia University Press.

Laumann, E., Gagnon, J., Michael, R., and Michaels, S. 1994. *The social organization of sexuality: Sexual practices in the United States.* Chicago: University of Chicago Press.

Lawrence, F.C. 1984. Children's participation in housework. *Medical Aspects of Human Sexuality, 18*(1):55.

Lewis, M. and Weinraub, M. 1976. The father's role in the child's social network. In Lamb, M. (Ed.), *The role of the father in child development.* New York: John Wiley & Sons.

Lindsey, K. 1981. *Friends as family.* Boston: Beacon Press.

Mancini, J.A. and Mancini, S.B. 1985. The family's role in sex education: Implications for educators. *Journal of Sex Education & Therapy, 11*:16-21.

Masters, W.H. and Johnson, V.E. 1966. *Human sexual response.* Boston: Little, Brown and Co.

Mayer, N. 1978. *The male mid-life crisis—fresh starts after 40.* New York: Doubleday.

McElroy, M. 1983. Parent-child relations and orientations toward sport. *Sex Roles, 9*:997-1004.

Moore, D. and Hotch, D. 1983. The importance of different home-leaving strategies to late adolescents. *Adolescence, 18*(70):413-416, Summer.

Murphy, J.F. 1981. *Concepts of leisure,* Second edition. Englewood Cliffs, NJ: Prentice-Hall.

Nichols, S. and Meltzen, E. 1982. Impact of wife's employment upon husband's housework. *Journal of Family Issues, 3*:199-216.

Nye, F. 1976. Ambivalence in the family: Rewards and costs in group membership. *Family Coordinator, 25*(1):21-31.

Orthner, D.K. 1976. Patterns of leisure and marital interaction. *Journal of Leisure Research, 8*:98-111.

Parelman, A. 1983. *Emotional intimacy in marriage: A sex-roles perspective.* Ann Arbor, MI: UMI Press.

Pogrebin, L. 1983. *Family politics.* New York: McGraw-Hill.

Questiaux, N. and Fournier, J. 1978. France. In Kamerman, S.B. and Kahn, A.J. (Eds.), *Family policy: Government and families in fourteen countries.* New York: Columbia University Press.

Sanua, V.D. 1978. The contemporary Jewish family: A review of the social science literature. In Babis, G. (Ed.), *Serving the Jewish family.* New York: KTAV.

Satir, V. 1972. *Peoplemaking.* Palo Alto, CA: Science and Behavior Books.

Smith, G. 1982. A senior citizen Olympic. *Aging,* July/August: 30-35.

Stone, C.L. 1963. Family recreation: A parental dilemma. *Family Life Coordinator, 12*:85-87.

U.S. Bureau of the Census. 1998. *Census facts for Mother's Day.* Current Population Survey, Survey of Income and Program Participation. CB98-FF.06, May 5. Washington, DC: U.S. Census Bureau's Public Information Office.

Waring, E.M. and Reddon, J.R. 1983. The measurement of intimacy in marriage: The Waring intimacy questionnaire. *Journal of Clinical Psychology, 39*(1):53-57.

Waring, E.M., Reddon, J.R., Corvinelli, M., Chalmers, W., and Laan, R.V. 1983. Marital intimacy and mood states in a nonclinical sample. *Journal of Psychology, 115*:263-274.

Westley, W.A. and Epstein, N.B. 1969. *The silent majority: Families of emotionally healthy college students.* San Francisco: Jossey Bass.

Suggested Readings

Blumstein, P. and Schwartz, P. 1983. *American couples: Money, work, sex.* New York: William Morrow.

Brecher, E.M. 1984. *Love, sex, and aging: A Consumers Union report.* Boston: Little, Brown and Company.

Dyer, W.G. 1975. *Creating closer families: Principles of positive family interaction.* Provo, UT: Brigham Young University Press.

Elkind, D. 1981. *The hurried child: Growing up too fast too soon.* Reading, MA: Addison-Wesley.

Loomis, C. 1998. *Fodor's Family Adventures.* New York: Fodor's Travel Publications.

Loomis, C. 1998. *Simplify family travel.* Pleasantville, NY: Reader's Digest Association.

Literature

Gilbreth, F. 1948. *Cheaper by the dozen.* New York: Grosset. This is family productivity at its very best.

Film

The Children of Sanchez. 1979. Moving story based on a classic study by sociologist Oscar Lewis of a poor Mexican family. It portrays how the family patriarch tries to meet his family's needs.

*Recommended Books on the Techniques
of Family Therapy*

Anderson, C. and Stewart, S. 1983. *Mastering resistance: A practical guide to family therapy.* New York: Guilford Press.

Arnold, E.L. (Ed.), 1978. *Helping parents help their children.* New York: Brunner-Mazel.

Bandler, R., Grinder, J., and Satir, V. 1976. *Changing with families.* Palo Alto, CA: Science and Behavior Press.

Bloch, D.A. (Ed.), 1973. *Techniques of family psychotherapy: A primer.* Orlando, FL: Grune.

Broderick, C.B. 1983. *The therapeutic triangle: A sourcebook on marital therapy.* Beverly Hills, CA: Sage.

Cromwell, R. et al. 1980. *The Kveback family sculpture technique: A diagnostic and research tool in family therapy.* Cincinnati, OH: Pilgrimage, Inc.

Forehand, R.L. and McMahon, R.J. 1981. *Helping the non-compliant child: A clinician's guide to parent training.* New York: Guilford Press.

Haley, J. and Hoffman, L. 1969. *Techniques of family therapy.* New York: Basic Books.

Hansen, J.C. and Rosenthal, D. 1981. *Strategies and techniques in family therapy.* Springfield, IL: C.C. Thomas.

Minuchin, S. and Fishman, H.C. 1981. *Family therapy techniques.* Cambridge, MA: Harvard University Press.

Patterson, G.R. 1975. *Families: Applications of social learning theory to family life* (Second edition). Champaign, IL: Research Press.

Rueveni, U. 1979. *Networking families in crisis.* New York: Human Science Press.

Sager, C.J., Brown, H.S., Crohn, H., Engel, T., Rodstein, E., and Walker, L. 1983. *Treating the remarried family.* New York: Brunner-Mazel.

Satir, V., Stachowiak, J., and Taschman, H. 1976. *Helping families to change.* Highmount, NY: Aronson.

Schaefer, C.E. et al. 1983. *Family therapy techniques for problem behaviors of children and teenagers.* San Francisco: Social and Behavioral Sciences Service, Jossey-Bass.

Stanton, M.D. 1982. *Family therapy of drug abuse and addiction.* New York: Guilford Press.

Stierlin, H. and Rucker-Embden, I. 1980. *The first interview with the family.* New York: Brunner-Mazel.

Visher, E.B. and Visher, J.S. 1979. *Stepfamilies: A guide to working with stepparents and stepchildren.* New York: Brunner-Mazel.

Zuk, G.H. 1981. *Family therapy: A triadic based approach,* (Revised edtion). New York: Human Science Press.

Chapter 16

Bibliography

Adler, A. 1946. *Understanding human nature.* New York: Greenberg Press.

Altus, W.D. 1966. Birth order and its sequelae. *Science, 151*:44-49.

Borland, J. 1998. *USDA report on the cost of raising a child, 1998.* Release no. 0127.98 Internet report. Washington, DC: U.S. Department of Agriculture.

Bossard, J. and Boll, E. 1975. *The large-family system: An original study in the sociology of family behavior.* Westport, CT: Greenwood Press.

Brink, T.L. and Matlock, F. 1982. Nightmares and birth order: An empirical study. *Journal of Individual Psychology, 38*(1):47-49.

Davis, D., Cahan, S., and Bashi, J. 1977. Birth order and intellectual development: The confluence model in the light of cross cultural evidence. *Science, 196*: 1470-1472.

DeJong, G.F., Stokes, S., and Hanson, S.L. 1980. Long-term consequences of childlessness and one child on labor force participation. In *Mobility, aspirations, and occupational attainment of married women.* Third Progress Report, NICMH and HD, Contract No. N1-HD-92807. Washington, DC: National Institute for Child Mental Health and Human Development.

Ernst, C. and Angst, J. 1983. *Birth order: Its influence on personality.* New York: Springer.

Espenshade, T. 1984. *Investing in children: New estimates of parental expenditures.* Washington, DC: Urban Institute Press.

Falbo, T. 1978. Sibling tutoring and other explanations for intelligence discontinuances of only and last borns. *Journal of Population, 1*:349-363.

Falbo, T. 1982. Only children in America. In Lamb, M. and Sutton-Smith, B. (Eds.), *Sibling relationships: Their nature and significance across the life span.* Hillsdale, NJ: Lawrence Erlbaum Associates.

Harris, I. 1964. *The promised seed: A comparative study of eminent first and later sons.* London: Free Press of Glencoe.

Harris, I.D. 1976. The psychologies of presidents. *Journal of Psychohistory, 3*:337-350.

Hoffman, G. and Leyber, L. 1979. Some relationships between sibling age spacing and personality. *Merrill Palmer Quarterly, 5*(1):77-80.

Mendlesohn, P., Linden, W.L., Green, T.S., and Curran, B. 1974. Heterosexual pairing and sibling configuration. *Journal of Individual Psychology, 30*(2):202-210.

Mott, F.L. and Haurin, R.J. 1982. Being an only child: Effects on educational progression and career orientation. *Journal of Family Issues, 3*(4):575-593.

Pines, M. 1981. Only isn't lonely (or spoiled or selfish. *Psychology Today, 15*(3):15-19.

Steelman, L. and Powell, B. 1985. The social and academic consequences of birth order: Real, artifactual or both? *Journal of Marriage and the Family, 47*(1): 117-124.

Sutton-Smith, B. 1982. Birth order and sibling status effects. In Lamb, M. and Sutton-Smith, B. (Eds.), *Sibling relationships: Their nature and significance across the life span.* Hillsdale, NJ: Lawrence Erlbaum Associates.

Sutton-Smith, B. and Rosenberg, B.G. 1970. *The sibling.* New York: Holt, Rinehart & Winston.

Toman, W. 1976. *Family constellation: Its effects on personality and social behavior.* New York: Springer.

Zajonc, R.B. 1976. Family configuration and intelligence. *Science, 192*:227-236.

Zajonc, R.B. and Markus, G.B. 1975. Birth order and intellectual development. *Psychological Review, 82*:74-88.

Suggested Readings

Ernst, C. and Angst, J. 1983. *Birth order: Its influence on personality.* New York: Springer.

Ganz, D. and Tresmowski, A. 1998. *The book of twins: A celebration in words and pictures.* New York: Delacorte Press.

Sulloway, F.J. 1997. *The born to rebel: Birth order, family dynamics, & creative lives.* New York: Pantheon Books.

Sutton-Smith, B. and Rosenberg, B.G. 1970. *The sibling.* New York: Holt, Rinehart & Winston.

Literature

McCullers, C. 1946. *The member of the wedding.* Boston: Houghton. The youngest child yearns to join her brother and his bride on their honeymoon.

Film

First Born. 1984. Generational boundaries are crossed as the firstborn son fulfills his role and tries to save his mother from a no-good lover.

Welcome to the Dollhouse. 1995. Directed by Todd Solondz. A geeky seventh-grader tries to cope with school and home as a middle child. Winner of the Sundance Film Festival.

Chapter 17

Bibliography

Adams, B.N. 1968. *Kinship in an urban setting.* Chicago: Markham.

Adams, V. 1981. The sibling bond: A lifelong love/hate dialectic. *Psychology Today, 15*(6):32-47.

Adler, A. 1959. *Understanding human nature.* New York: Premier Books.

Bank, S.P. and Kahn, M.D. 1982a. *The sibling bond.* New York: Basic Books.

Bank, S.P. and Kahn, M.D. 1982b. Intense sibling loyalties. In Lamb, M. and Sutton-Smith, B. (Eds.), *Sibling Relationships: Their nature and significance across the life span.* Hillsdale, NJ: Lawrence Erlbaum Associates.

Baran, A., Sorosky, A., and Pannor, R. 1975. The dilemma of our adoptees. *Psychology Today, 9*(1):38.

Begun, A. 1995. Sibling relationships and foster care placements for young children. Special issue: Social work practice with children. *Early Child Development and Care, 106*(1):237-250.

Boer, F., Westenberg, P., McHale, S.M., Updengraff, K.A., and Stocker, C.M. 1997. The factorial structure of the Sibling Relationship Inventory (SRI) in American and Dutch samples. *Journal of Social and Personal Relationships, 14*(6):851-859.

Bossard, J.H.S. and Bell, E.S. 1960. *The sociology of child development.* New York: Harper.

Bryant, B. Sibling relationships in middle childhood. In Lamb, M. and Sutton-Smith, B. 1982. (Eds.), *Sibling relationships: Their nature and significance across the life span.* Hillsdale, NJ: Lawrence Erlbaum Associates.

Bryant, B. and Crockenberg, S. 1980. Correlates and dimensions of prosocial behavior: A study of female siblings with their mothers. *Child Development, 51*:529-544.

Cicirelli, V.G. 1980a. A comparison of college women's feelings towards their siblings and parents. *Journal of Marriage and the Family, 42*(1):95-102.

Cicirelli, V.G. 1980b. *Adult children's views on providing services for elderly parents.* Report to NRTA-AARP, Andrus Foundation.

Cicirelli, V.G. 1982. Sibling influence throughout the life span. In Lamb, M. and Sutton-Smith, B. (Eds.), *Sibling relationships: Their nature and significance across the life span.* Hillsdale, NJ: Lawrence Erlbaum Associates.

Deal, S.N. and MacLean, W.E. 1995. Disrupted lives: Siblings of disturbed adolescents. *American Journal of Orthopsychiatry, 65*(2):274-281.

Freud, A. and Dann, S. 1951. An experiment in group upbringing. In Eisler, R., Freud, A., Hartman, H., and Kris, E. (Eds.), *The psychoanalytic study of the child, 6.* New York: International Universities Press.

Graham, B.S. and Cutler, S.E. 1994. The Brother-Sister Questionnaire: Psychometric assessment and discrimination of well functioning from dysfunctional relationships. *Journal of Family Psychology, 8*(2):224-238.

Hames, A. 1998. Do the younger siblings of learning-disabled children see them as similar or different? *Child Care, Health and Development, 24*(2):157-168.

Kier, C.H. and Lewis, C. 1998. Preschool sibling interaction in separated and married families: Are same-sex pairs or older sisters more sociable? *Journal of Child Psychiatry and Allied Disciplines, 39*(2):191-201.

Koch, H.L. 1956. Sissiness and tomboyishness in relation to sibling characteristics. *Journal of Genetic Psychology, 88*:221-244.

Lasko, J.K. 1954. Parent behavior toward first and second children. *Genetic Psychology Monograph, 49*:99-137.

Martin, J.L. and Ross, H.D. 1995. The development of aggression within sibling conflict. Special Issue: Conflict resolution in early social development. *Early Education and Development, 6*(4):335-358.

McGuire, S., McÓale, S.M., and Updegraff, K. 1996. Children's perceptions of the sibling relationship in middle childhood: Connections within and between family relationships. *Personal Relationships, 3*(3):229-239.

Milgram, J.I. and Ross, H.G. 1982. Effects of fame in adult sibling relationships. *Journal of Individual Psychology, 38*(1):72-79.

Roeder, E.C. 1994. Families in transition: A divorce workshop. *Family and Conciliation Courts Review, 32*(1):40-49.

Ross, H.G. and Milgram, J.I. 1982. Important variables in adult sibling relationships: A qualitative study. In Lamb, M.E. and Sutton-Smith, B. (Eds.), *Sibling relationships: Their nature and significance across the life span.* Hillsdale, NJ: Lawrence Erlbaum Associates.

Schacter, F.F. 1982. Sibling deidentification and split-parent identification: A family tetrad. In Lamb, M. and Sutton-Smith, B. (Eds.), *Sibling relationships: Their nature and significance across the life span.* Hillsdale, NJ: Lawrence Erlbaum Associates.

Senekjian, E. and Trad, P.V. 1994. Applying principles of individual, group and family therapy to the treatment of twins. *Journal of Child & Adolescent Group Therapy, 4*(1):3-26.

Slomkowski, C., Cohen, P., and Brook, J. 1997. The sibling relationships of adolescents with antisocial and comorbid mental disorders: An epidemiological investigation. *Criminal Behavior and Mental Health, 7*(4):353-368.

Slote, W.H. 1992. Oedipal ties and the issue of separation-individuation in traditional Confucian societies. *Journal of the American Academy of Psychoanalysis, 20*(3):435-453.

Stormshak, E.A., Bellanti, C.J., and Bierman, K.L. 1996. The quality of sibling relationships and the development of social competence and behavioral control in aggressive children. *Developmental Psychology, 32*(1):79-89.

Troll, L.E. 1975. *Early and middle adulthood.* Monterey, CA: Brooks/Cole.

Tucker, C.J., Barber, B.L., and Eccles, J.S. 1997. Advice about life plans and personal problems in late adolescent sibling relationships. *Journal of Youth & Adolescence, 26*(1):63-76.

Widmer, E.D. 1997. Influence of older siblings on the initiation of sexual intercourse. *Journal of Marriage and the Family, 59*(4):928-238.

Zuk, G. 1972. *Family therapy: A triadic-based approach.* New York: Behavioral Publications.

Suggested Readings

Bank, S.P. and Kahn, M.D. 1982a. *The sibling bond.* New York: Basic Books.

Bank, S.P. and Kahn, M.D. 1982b. Intense sibling loyalties. In Lamb, M. and Sutton-Smith, B. (Eds.), *Sibling Relationships: Their nature and significance across the life span.* Hillsdale, NJ: Lawrence Erlbaum Associates.

Coursen, V. 1995. *My sister: A treasury of companionship.* Philadelphia: Running Press Books.

Faber, A. and Mazlish, E. 1998. *Siblings without rivalry: How to help your children live together so you can live too.* New York: Norton.

Samalin, N. and Whitney, C. 1996. *Loving each one best: A caring practical approach to raising siblings.* New York: Bantam Books.

Literature

Dostoevski, F. 1977, originally published 1880. *The brothers Karamazov.* Franklin Center, PA: Franklin Library. A complex and profound tale of four brothers who become involved in the brutal murder of their father.
Lawrence, D.H. 1979, originally published 1920. *Women in love.* Franklin Center, PA: Franklin Library. A powerful novel that examines the relationship of two sisters and that of their lovers.
Salinger, J.D. 1962. *Franny and Zooey.* New York: V. S. Pritchett. A brother helps in his sister's recovery from a nervous breakdown.

Film

American Flyers. 1985. Two estranged brothers team up for a bicycle race in the Rockies, but the real challenge is the family reconciliation.
I Sent a Letter to My Love. 1981. Wonderful story about a middle-aged woman who grows cranky caring for her invalid brother. Her brother responds to a romantic ad she placed in the paper under a false name. The correspondence infuses them both with energy and purpose.
Ordinary People. 1980. An intensely moving story of the grief and guilt a sibling feels over surviving the death of his brother in a sailing accident.
Siblings. 1996. A heartwarming story of two immigrant brothers who, with the bonds of love and determination, try to save their struggling restaurant.

Chapter 18

Bibliography

Anderson, H. and Goolishian, H.A. 1988. Human systems as linguistic systems. *Family Process. 27*(4):371-393.
Compas, B.G., Adelman, H.S., Freundl, P.C., Nelson, P., and Taylor, L. 1982. Parent and child causal attributions during clinical interviews. *Journal of Abnormal Psychology, 10*(1):77-94.
Compas, B.G., Friedland-Bandes, R., Bastien, R., and Adelman, H.S. 1981. Parent and child causal attributions related to the child's clinical problem. *Journal of Abnormal Psychology, 9*(3):389-397.
Cooper, J., Holman, J., and Braithwaite, V. 1983. Self esteem and family cohesion: The child's perspective and adjustment. *Journal of Marriage and the Family, 45*(1):153-159.
Doherty, W.J. 1981. Cognitive processes in intimate conflict: I. Extending attribution theory. *American Journal of Family Therapy, 9*(1):3-13.

Doherty, W.J. 1982. Attributional style and negative problem solving. *Family Relations, 31*(2):201-205.

Epston, D. and White, M. 1992. *Experience, contradiction, narrative, and imagination: Selected papers of David Epston and Michael White, 1989-1991*. Adelaide, South Australia: Dulwich Centre Publications.

Fichten, C.E. 1984. See it from my point of view: Videotape and attributions in happy and distressed couples. *Journal of Social and Clinical Psychology, 2*(2):125-142.

Heider, F. 1958. *The psychology of interpersonal relations*. New York: John Wiley & Sons.

Holloway, S. and Fuller, B. 1983. Situational working mothers. *Social Psychology Quarterly, 46*:131-140.

Jones, E.E. and Nisbett, R.E. 1972. The actor and the observer: Divergent perceptions of the causes of behavior. In Jones, E., Kanouse, D., Kelley, H., Nisbett, R., Valins, S., and Weiner, B. (Eds.), *Attribution: Perceiving the causes of behavior*. Morristown, NJ: General Learning Press.

Kanouse, D. and Hanson, L.R. 1972. Negativity in evaluations in attribution: Perceiving the causes of behavior. In Jones, E., Kanouse, D., Kelley, H., Nisbett, R., Valins, S., and Weiner, B. (Eds.), *Attribution: Perceiving the causes of behavior*. Morristown, NJ: General Learning Press.

Kelly, H.H. 1967. Attribution theory in social psychology. In Levine, D. (Ed.), *Nebraska Symposium on Motivation, 15*. Lincoln, NE: University of Nebraska Press.

Kuhn, R.S. 1962. *The structure of revolutions*. Chicago: University of Chicago Press.

Kuhn, T.S. 1980. Theory choice. In Klemke, E.D., Hollinger, R., and Kline, A.D. (Eds.), *Introductory readings and the philosophy of science*. New York: Prometheus Books.

Metcalf, L. 1997. *Parenting toward solutions: How parents can use skills they already have to raise responsible, loving kids*. Englewood Cliffs, NJ: Prentice-Hall.

Mischel, W. 1968. *Personality and assessment*. New York: John Wiley & Sons.

Mischel, W. 1976. *Introduction to personality*, Second edition. New York: Holt, Rinehart and Winston.

Parish, T. 1981. Young adults' evaluations of themselves and their parents as a function of family structure and disposition. *Journal of Youth and Adolescence, 10*(2):173-178.

Passer, M.W., Kelley, H.H., and Michela, J.L. 1978. Multidimensional scaling of the causes for negative interpersonal behavior. *Journal of Personality and Social Psychology, 36*(9):961-962.

Prevett, M.J., Spence, R., and Chaknis, M. 1981. Attribution of causality by children with alcoholic parents. *International Journal of Addiction, 16*(1):367-370.

Smith, C. and Nylund, D. 1997. *Narrative therapies with children and adolescents*. New York: Guilford Press.

Walster, E. 1966. Assignment of responsibility for an accident. *Journal of Personality and Social Psychology, 3*:73-79.

Suggested Reading

Heider, F. 1958. *The psychology of interpersonal relations.* New York: John Wiley & Sons.

Fiction

O'Hehir, D. 1984. *I wish this war were over.* New York: Atheneum Publishers. The book's narrator embarks on a trip to rescue her beautiful, alcoholic mother.
O'Neill, E. 1956. *Long day's journey into night.* New Haven, CT: Yale University Press. An excellent study in how family relationships are affected by the attribution process.

Film

Back to the Future. 1985. A young man comes to understand his parents' present by going back into his past. As the son's attributions change, he experiences a new fondness and protectiveness toward his parents.
The Family Nobody Wanted. 1979. A minister and his loving wife adopt a brood of interracial children. The role of attributions in family life is nicely illustrated throughout the film.

Chapter 19

Bibliography

Bahr, S. 1982. Exchange and control in married life. In Nye, F.I. (Ed.), *Family relationships.* Beverly Hills, CA: Sage Publications, Sage Focus Editions, 46.
Berscheid, E. and Walster, E.H. 1978. *Interpersonal attraction,* Second edition. Reading, MA: Addison-Wesley.
Blumstein, P. and Schwartz, P. 1983. *American couples.* New York: William Morrow.
Boszormenyi-Nagy, I. and Spark, G.M. 1973. *Invisible loyalties.* New York: Harper & Row.
Cavan, R.S. 1973. Speculations on innovations to conventional marriage in old age. *Gerontologist, 13*(4):409-411.
Davidson, B., Balswick, J., and Halverson, C. 1983. Affective self disclosure and marital adjustment: A test of equity theory. *Journal of Marriage and the Family, 45*(1):93-107.
Dreikurs, R. and Soltz, V. 1967. *Children: The challenge.* Chicago: Alfred Adler Institute.
Fox, K. and Nickols, S. 1983. The time crunch: Wife's employment and family work. *Journal of Family Issues, 4*(1):61-82.
Gottman, J.M. 1979. *Marital interaction: Experimental investigations.* New York: Academic Press.

Haas, L. 1980. Domestic role sharing in Sweden. Revision of paper presented at the 75th Annual Meeting of the American Sociological Association, August 27-31. New York, NY.

Hatfield, E., Greenberger, D., Traupmann, J., and Lambert, P. 1982. Equity and sexual satisfaction in recently married couples. *Journal of Sex Research, 18*(1):18-32.

Hatfield, E. and Traupmann, J. 1981. Intimate relationships and equity theory. In Duck, S. and Gilmour, R. (Eds.), *Personal relationships.* New York: Academic Press.

Hoffman, L.W. and Nye, F.L. 1974. Concluding remarks. In Hoffman, L.W. and Nye, F.L. (Eds.), *Working mothers.* San Francisco: Jossey-Bass.

Kelley, H.H. 1979. *Personal relationships: Their structure and processes.* Hillsdale, NJ: Laurence Erlbaum Associates.

Komarovsky, M. 1940. *The unemployed man and his family.* New York: Dryden Press.

Leadbeater, B. and Farber, B. 1983. The limits of reciprocity in behavioral marriage therapy. *Family Process, 22*(2):229-237.

Lips, H.M. 1981. *Women, men, and the psychology of power.* Englewood Cliffs, NJ: Prentice-Hall.

Masnick, G. and Bane, M. 1980. *The nation's families 1960-1990.* Cambridge, MA: Joint Center for Urban Studies of MIT and Harvard University.

Nelson, M. and Nelson, G. 1982. Problems of equity in the reconstituted family: A social exchange analysis. *Family Relations, 31*:223-231.

Nye, F.I. 1976. *Role structure and analysis of the family.* Beverly Hills, CA: Sage.

Nye, F.I. 1980. Family mini theories as special instances of choice and exchange theory. *Journal of Marriage and the Family, 42*:479-489.

Olson, D.H. and Rabunsky, D. 1972. Validity of four measures of family power. *Journal of Marriage and the Family, 34*:224-234.

Osmond, M.W. and Martin, P.Y. 1978. A contingency model of marital organization in low income families. *Journal of Marriage and the Family, 40*(2):315-329.

Pogrebin, L.C. 1984. *Family politics: Love and power on an intimate frontier.* New York: McGraw-Hill.

Rawling, S. 1978. Perspectives on American husbands and wives. In *Current Population Reports Series, No. 77.* Washington, DC: U.S. Department of Commerce, Bureau of the Census.

Stuart, R.B. 1973. *Marital Precounseling inventory (part G).* Champaign, IL: Research Press.

Stuart, R.B. 1980. *Helping couples change: A social learning approach to marital therapy.* New York: Guilford Press.

Traupmann, J. and Hatfield, E. 1983. How important is marital fairness over the lifespan? *International Journal of Aging and Human Development, 17*(2):89-101.

Traupmann, J., Hatfield, E., and Wexler, P. 1982. Equity and sexual satisfaction in dating couples. *Journal of Sex Research, 18*(1):18-32.

U.S. Bureau of the Census. 1998. *MC1. Married couples by labor force status of spouses: 1986 to present.* Washington, DC: U.S. Bureau of the Census. <www.census.gov>

Wagstaff, G. 1997. Equity vs. equality in allocations to adults and children. *Journal of Social Psychology, 137*(4):445-448.

Walster, E. and Walster, G.W. 1969. The matching hypothesis. *Journal of Personality and Social Psychology, 6*:248-253.

Walster, E., Walster, G.W., and Berscheid, E. 1978. *Equity theory and research.* Boston: Allyn and Bacon.

Suggested Readings

Boszormenyi-Nagy, L. and Spark, G.M. 1973. *Invisible loyalties.* New York: Harper & Row.

Horner, B. and Horner, J. 1993. *Resolving conflict in your marriage.* Dallas: Word Publications.

Pogrebin, L.C. 1984. *Family politics: Love and power on an intimate frontier.* New York: McGraw-Hill.

Literature

Lurie, A. 1974. *The war between the Tates.* London: Heinemann. The problems in searching for equity in a problem-ridden marriage.

Schwartz, L.S. 1980. *Rough strife.* New York: Harper & Row. An excellent novel about a trapped wife told with compassion and wit.

Film

Best Friends. 1982. The equity of a long-term relationship collapses under the new obligations and expectations of marriage.

The Two Worlds of Angelita. 1983. An immigrant Puerto Rican family copes with a wife's increasing self-assurance and power as her husband loses both his traditional role in the family and self-respect.

Chapter 20

Bibliography

Baer, R., Hinkle, S., Smith, K., and Fenton, M. 1980. Reactance as function of actual vs. projected autonomy. *Journal of Personality and Social Psychology, 38*:416-422.

Brehm, J. 1966. *A theory of psychological reactance.* New York: Academic Press.

Brehm, S. 1981. Oppositional behavior in children: A reactance theory approach. In Brehm, S., Kassin, S., and Gibbons, F. (Eds.), *Developmental social psychology theory and research.* Oxford, UK: Oxford University Press.

Buller, D.B., Borland, R., and Burgoon, M. 1998. Impact of behavioral intention on effectiveness of message features: Evidence from the Family Sun Safety Project. *Human Communication Research, 24*(3):433-453.

Bushman, B. 1998. Effects of warning and information labels on consumption of full fat, reduced-fat, and no-fat products. *Journal of Applied Psychology, 83*(1):97-101.

Carter, J.E. and Kelly, A. 1997. Using traditional and paradoxical imagery interventions with reactant intramural athletes. *Sport Psychologist, 11*(2):175-189.

Cavan, R.S. 1973. Speculations on innovations to conventional marriage in old age. *Gerontologist, 13*(4):409-411.

Fogarty, J.S. 1997. Reactance theory and patient noncompliance. *Social Science and Medicine, 45*(8):1277-1288.

Frank, S.J., Jackson-Walker, S., Marks, M., Van-Egren, L.A., Loop, K., and Kristen, O. 1998. From the laboratory to the hospital, adults to adolescents, and disorders to personality: The case of psychological reactance. *Journal of Clinical Psychology, 54*(3):361-381.

Hong, S.M. and Faedda, S. 1996. Refinement of the Hong Psychological Reactance Scale. *Educational and Psychological Measurement, 56*(1):173-182.

Hunsley, J. 1997. Defiance-based symptom prescription and psychological reactance: A critical evaluation. *Professional Psychology: Practice and Research, 28*(1):36-43.

Joubert, C. 1995. Associations of social personality factors with personal habits. *Psychological Reports, 76*(3, Part 2), Special Issue: 1315-1321.

Kelly, A.E. and Nauta, M.M. 1997. Reactance and thought suppression. *Personality and Social Psychology Bulletin, 23*(11):1123-1132.

Kremar, M. and Cantor, J. 1997. The role of television advisories and ratings in parent-child discussion of television viewing habits. *Journal of Broadcasting and Electronic Media, 41*(3):393-411.

Mulry, G., Fleming, R., and Gottschalk, A.C. 1994. Psychological reactance and brief treatment of academic procrastination. *Journal of Student Psychotherapy, 9*(1):41-56.

Nail, P.R., Van Leeuwen, M.D., and Powell, A.B. 1996. The effectance versus the self-presentational view of reactance: Are important ratings influenced by anticipated surveillance? *Journal of Social Behavior and Personality, 11*(3):573-584.

Pruitt, R.H., Kline, P.M., and Kovaz, R.B. 1995. Perceived barriers to childhood immunization among rural populations. *Journal of Community Health Nursing, 12*(2):65-72.

Strube, M. and Werner, C. 1984. Psychological reactance and the relinquishment of control. *Personality and Social Psychology Bulletin, 10*(2):225-234.

Wicklund, R. 1974. *Freedom and reactance.* Potomac, MD: Lawrence Erlbaum Associates.

Worchel, S. and Brehm, J.W. 1971. Direct and implied social restoration of freedom. *Journal of Personality and Social Psychology, 18*:294-304.

Suggested Readings

Barkley, R.A. and Benton, C. 1998. *Your defiant child: 8 steps to better behavior.* New York: Guilford Press.

Brehm, J. 1966. *A theory of psychological reactance.* New York: Academic Press.

Riley, D. 1997. *The defiant child: A parent's guide to oppositional defiant disorder.* Dallas, TX: Taylor Publications.

Sutton, J.D. 1997. *If my kid's so nice . . . Why's he driving me crazy?: Straight talk about the "good kid" disorder.* Pleasanton, TX: Friendly Oaks Publications.

Windell, J. 1997. *Children who say no when you want them to say yes: Failsafe discipline strategies for stubborn and oppositional children and teens.* New York: Macmillan General Reference.

Literature

Berger, T. Rheinhart Quartet. *Crazy in Berlin.* 1982, c. 1958. New York: Dell. *Vital parts.* 1982, c. 1970. New York: Dell. *Rheinhart's women.* 1982, c. 1981. New York: Dell. *Rheinhart in love.* 1982, c. 1962. New York: Dell. An excellent study in contrary and one-upsmanship motives.

Twain, M. 1981. *Huckleberry Finn.* New York: Regents. Huck's orneriness can now be viewed in an entirely new light—he's the prototype of a reactance-bent child.

Chapter 21

Bibliography

American Association of University Women. 1992. *How schools shortchange girls.* AAUW Report, Wessley Center. College for Research on Women. New York: Marlow and Company.

Arcus, M., Schvaneveldt, J., and Moss, J. (Eds.), 1993a. *Handbook of family life education, Vol. 1.* Newberry Park, CA: Sage Publications.

Arcus, M., Schvaneveldt, J., and Moss, J. (Eds.), 1993b. *Handbook of family life education, Vol. 2.* Newberry Park, CA: Sage Publications.

Bateson, M.C. 1990. *Composing a life.* New York: Penguin Books.

Benasich, A. and Brooks-Gunn, J. 1996. Maternal attitudes and knowledge of child rearing: Associations with family and child outcomes. *Child Development,* 67:1186-1205.

Canada, G. 1995. *Fist stick knife gun.* Boston: Beacon Press.

Canada, G. 1996. The karate master's method for unlearning violence. *World,* 10(1):12-51.

Canada, G. 1998a. *Reaching up for manhood.* Boston: Beacon Press.

Canada, G. 1998b. Self-worth. *World,* 12 (January/February): 35-39.

Carlsson-Paige, N. and Levin, D. 1990. *Who's calling the shots.* Philadelphia: New Society Publishers.

Crossette, B. 1998. Kofi Annan's astonishing facts, *The New York Times,* September 27. 16.

Dodge, K., Pettit, G., and Bates, J. 1994. Socialization mediators of the relation between socioeconomic status and child conduct problems. *Child Development, 65*:649-665.

Dollahite, D., Hawkins, A., and Brotherson, S. 1996. Narrative accounts, generative fathering, and family life education. *Marriage and Family Review, 24*(3/4):349-368.

Garbarino, J. 1995. *Raising children in a socially toxic environment.* San Francisco: Jossey-Bass Publishers.

Gladwell, M. 1998. Do parents matter? *The New Yorker, 74* (24, August 17): 54-64.

Gurian, M. 1998. *A fine young man.* New York: Penguin Putnam, Inc.

Haiman, P. 1997. Cooperation will make it happen: A proposed alliance on behalf of children and families. *The Journal of Psychohistory, 24*(4):370-376.

Kantrowitz, B. and Kalb, C. 1998. How to build a better boy. *Newsweek,* (May 11):55-60.

Klass, T. 1998. One child, many influences, *The New York Times,* September 9.

Kurcinka, M. 1991. *Raising your spirited child.* New York: HarperCollins Publishers.

Mansfield, H. 1997. Hawaii's Hana like home visitor program, a healthy start program. *The Journal of Psychohistory, 24*(4):333-338.

McFarland, R. and Fanton, J. 1997. Moving towards utopia: prevention of child abuse. *The Journal of Psychohistory, 24*(4):320-331.

McInnis-Dittrich, K. 1996. Violence prevention: An ecological adaptation of systematic training for effective parenting. *Families in Society: The Journal of Contemporary Human Services,* (September): 414-422.

Murray, B. 1998a. Communities "fighting back" to quash neighborhood crime. *American Psychological Association Monitor, 29*(July): 35-36.

Murray, B. 1998b. Exploring the virtues and vices of technology. *American Psychological Association Monitor, 29*(August): 42.

Murray, B. 1998c. Shaping children's thinking so they learn to be nonviolent. *American Psychological Association Monitor, 29*(July).

Murray, B. 1998d. What works in violence prevention. *American Psychological Association Monitor, 29*(July): 36.

Piaget, J., Hodgson, F.M., and Gattegno, C. 1962. *Play, dreams, and imitation in childhood.* New York: W.W. Norton.

Pipher, M. 1994. *Reviving Ophelia.* New York: Ballantine Books.

Pipher, M. 1996. *In the Shelter of each other.* New York: Ballantine Books.

Pipher, M. 1998. Surviving toxic media: How the church can help. *World, 12* (January/February): 18-25.

Pollack, W. 1998. *Real boys.* New York: Random House.

Settles, B. 1993. Finding multiple publication outlets for family science research and development: A case study of project dissemination. *Marriage and Family Review, 18:*183-199.

Silverstein, O. and Rashbaum, B. 1994. *The courage to raise good men.* New York: Penguin Books.

Sleek, S. 1998. Isolation increases with Internet use. *APA Monitor, 29*(9):1.

Suggested Readings

Canada, G. 1998. *Reaching up for manhood.* Boston: Beacon Press.

Chinaberry Book Catalog. (800) 776-2242. This catalog specializes in children's books, which are categorized by level of difficulty, and annotated. A very helpful subject index in the back lists books by categories such as Strong Females and Balanced, Inspiring Males.

Dodson, S. 1998. *100 books for girls to grow on.* New York: HarperCollins Publishers.

Educators for Social Responsibility. 23 Garden Street, Cambridge, Massachusetts 02138. (617) 492-1764. ESR provides support, networking, and resources for teachers and parents. They have an array of materials for teaching about conflict resolution, diversity, and responsible participation.

Family Pastimes. PR4, Perth, Ontario, Canada K7H 3C6. They make a variety of cooperative games for different ages, and have an illustrated catalog. There are many wonderful games that require strategy and cooperation.

Garbarino, J. 1993. *Let's talk about living in a world with violence: An activity book for school-age children.* San Francisco: Jossey-Bass.

Garbarino, J. 1995. *Raising children in a socially toxic environment.* San Francisco: Jossey-Bass, Inc. Garbarino provides an extensive list of resources and ways we can take action (from A to Z).

Institute for Mental Health Initiatives (IMHI). 4545 42nd Street N.W., Suite 311, Washington, DC 20016. They provide materials for areas of focus such as self-esteem, anger management, and other mental health issues.

Johnson, C. and Shaw, M.D. 1995. *Celebrating the Great Mother: A handbook of earth-honoring activities for parents and children.* Rochester, VT: Destiny Books.

Odean, K. 1997. *Great books for boys.* New York: Ballantine Books.

Odean, K. 1997. *Great books for girls.* New York: Ballantine Books.

Pipher, M. 1996. In *The shelter of each other.* New York: Ballantine Books.

Pollack, W. 1998. *Real boys.* New York: Random House.

Self-Esteem Shop Online: www.selfesteemshop.com. Offers such titles as *Parents as therapeutic partners, 101 ways to be a special mom,* and *Cutting losses: Why women who end their marriages do so well.*

Web sites: many Web sites dealing with family issues can be found at: www.familytrack.com. Also, help with parenting issues can be found at the National Parent Information Network, www.npin.org or (800) 583-4135.

Literature

Many good books for children of all ages can be found in the books and catalog listed under Suggested Readings. Perhaps it is telling that I cannot think of any adult fiction that exemplifies good problem-solving skills, or characters that are caring and capable. However, many inspirational autobiographies and biographies can be found.

Film

Apollo 13. 1995. A true story that recounts the ingenuity and cooperative problem-solving skills that were required to bring the astronauts of Apollo 13 safely back to earth.
Fly Away Home. 1996. A caring father and a feisty thirteen-year-old girl have quite an adventure when they adopt an orphaned flock of geese and teach them to migrate.
The Gods Must Be Crazy. 1984. A comic look at the effects of material goods from the outside world on a tribal culture.
Mrs. Doubtfire. 1993. A caring male crosses gender stereotypes in order to be a more effective parent.

Chapter 22

Bibliography

Abbott, D.A., Berry, M., and Meredith, W.H. 1990. Religious belief and practice: A potential asset in helping families. *Family Relations*, *39*(3):443-448.
Bergin, A. 1991. Values and religious issues in psychotherapy and mental health. *American Psychologist*, *46*:394-403.
Bergin, A.E. and Jensen, J.P. 1990. Religiosity of psychotherapists: A national survey. *Psychotherapy*, *27*:2-7.
Boyd-Franklin, N. 1989. Religion, spirituality, and the treatment of black families. In Boyd-Franklin, N. (Ed.), *Black families in therapy: A multisystems approach* (pp. 78-91). New York: Guilford.
Brigman, K. 1984. Churches helping families: A study of the effects of religion on families and how churches can help strengthen families. *Family Perspectives*, *18*:77-84.
Denton, R.T. and Denton, M.J. 1992. Therapists' ratings of fundamentalist and nonfundamentalist families in therapy: An empirical comparison. *Family Process*, *31*(2):175-185.
Ellison, C. 1983. Spiritual well-being: Conceptualization and measurement. *Journal of Psychology and Theology*, *11*:330-340.
Fitchett, G. 1993. *Spiritual assessment in pastoral care: A guide to selected resources*. Decatur, GA: Journal of Pastoral Care Publications.
Gallup, G.H. 1993. *Religion in America: 1992-1993*. Princeton, NJ: The Gallup Organization.
Genia, V. 1990. Religious development: A synthesis and reformulation. *Journal of Religion and Health*, *29*:85-99.

Genia, V. 1991. The Spiritual Experience Index: A measure of spiritual maturity. *Journal of Religion and Health, 30*:337-347.

Giblin, P. 1993. Marital conflict and marital spirituality. In Wicks, R. and Parsons, R. (Eds.), *Clinical handbook of pastoral counseling: Vol. 2* (pp. 237-241). New York: Paulist Press.

Joanides, C.J. 1996. Collaborative family therapy with religious family systems. *Journal of Family Psychotherapy, 7*(4):19-35.

Jones, S.L. 1996. A constructive relationship for religion with the science and profession of psychology: Perhaps the boldest model yet. In Shafranske, E.P. (Ed.), *Religion and the clinical practice of psychology* (pp. 113-147. Washington, DC: American Psychological Association.

Kudlac, K.E. 1991. Including God in the conversation: The influence of religious beliefs on the problem-organized system. *Family Therapy, 18*(3):277-285.

Nakhaima, J.M. and Dicks, B.H. 1995. Social work practice with religious families. *Families in Society: The Journal of Contemporary Human Services, 76*(6):360-368.

Prest, L.A. and Keller, J.F. 1993. Spirituality and family therapy: Spiritual beliefs, myths, and metaphors. *Journal of Marital and Family Therapy, 19*(2):137-148.

Pruyser, P. 1976. *The minister as diagnostician.* Philadelphia: Westminster Press.

Richards, P.S. and Bergin, A.E. 1997. *A spiritual strategy for counseling and psychotherapy.* Washington, DC: American Psychological Association.

Shafranske, E.P. (Ed.). 1996. *Religion and the clinical practice of psychology.* Washington, DC: American Psychological Association.

Shafranske, E.P. and Malony, H.N. 1996. Religion and the clinical practice of psychology: A case of inclusion. In Shafranske, E.P. (Ed.), *Religion and the clinical practice of psychology* (pp. 561-586). Washington, DC: American Psychological Association.

Sperry, L. and Giblin, P. 1996. Marital and family therapy with religious persons. In Shafranske, E.P. (Ed.), *Religion and the clinical practice of psychology* (pp. 511-532). Washington, DC: American Psychological Association.

Stander, V., Piercy, F., MacKinnon, D., and Helmeke, K. 1994. Spirituality, religion and family therapy: Competing or complementary worlds? *American Journal of Family Therapy, 22*(1):27-41.

Weaver, A.J., Koenig, H.G., and Larson, D.B. 1997. Marriage and family therapists and the clergy: A need for clinical collaboration, training, and research. *Journal of Marital and Family Therapy, 23*(1):13-25.

Weber, T.T. and Wynn, J.C. 1986. Consultation with the clergy: A systems approach. In Wynn, L.C., McDaniel, S.H., and Weber, T.T. (Eds.), *Systems consultations: A new perspective for family therapy* (pp. 320-341). New York: Guilford.

Suggested Readings

Daleo, M.S. 1996. *Curriculum of love: Cultivating the Spiritual nature of children.* Charlottesville, VA: Grace Publishing and Communications.

Hopkins, E., Woods, Z., Kelley, R., Bentley, K., and Murphy, J. 1996. *Working with groups on spiritual themes: Structured exercises in healing, Volume 2.* Duluth, MN: Whole Person Associates.

Rozman, D.A. 1994. *Meditating with children: The art of concentration and centering: A workbook on new educational methods using meditation.* Boulder Creek, CA: Planetary Publications.

Schnarch, D. 1997. *Passionate marriage: Love, sex, and intimacy in emotionally committed relationships.* New York: W.W. Norton.

Walch, M.D. and Walch, M.F. 1998. *Ten principles for spiritual parenting: Nurturing your child's soul.* New York: Harper Perennial.

Film

Breaking the Waves. 1996. Directed by Lars Von Trier. A young Calvinist woman prays for her husband to return home from sea, and then feels responsible for the offshore accident that paralyzes him. Consumed with guilt and wanting to repent, her subsequent sexual odyssey, directed by her husband for his vicarious pleasure, shows us the many mechanations of religious fanaticism.

Carrington. 1995. Directed by Christopher Hampton. A true story about the spiritual love between a woman and her homosexual husband. Good for pondering the meaning of love in a marriage.

Partner Yoga. 1997. Demonstrates the basics of partner yoga and how the use of a partner allows one to benefit more physically and spiritually from yoga. Guides viewers through a series of gentle (yet challenging) poses that will build flexibility and promote deeper breathing. Yoga is generally a spiritually and physically healthy activity for a couple to engage in.

Soul Food. 1997. Directed by George Tillman, Jr. A heartfelt drama about a middle-class African-American family's struggle for harmony, love, and tradition. Movie centers on Mother Joe's mouthwatering Sunday dinner of soul food, and the family's adjustment to the usual rivalries among siblings, cheating, and betrayal.

Author Index

Subject Index

Page numbers followed by the letter "f" indicate figures; those followed by the letter "t" indicate tables.

Order Your Own Copy of
This Important Book for Your Personal Library!

BASIC CONCEPTS IN FAMILY THERAPY
An Introductory Text, Second Edition

_____ in hardbound at $89.95 (ISBN: 0-7890-0646-4)

_____ in softbound at $59.95 (ISBN: 0-7890-0941-2)

COST OF BOOKS_____

OUTSIDE USA/CANADA/
MEXICO: ADD 20%_____

POSTAGE & HANDLING_____
(US: $3.00 for first book & $1.25
for each additional book)
Outside US: $4.75 for first book
& $1.75 for each additional book)

SUBTOTAL_____

IN CANADA: ADD 7% GST_____

STATE TAX_____
(NY, OH & MN residents, please
add appropriate local sales tax)

FINAL TOTAL_____
(If paying in Canadian funds,
convert using the current
exchange rate. UNESCO
coupons welcome.)

☐ **BILL ME LATER:** ($5 service charge will be added)
(Bill-me option is good on US/Canada/Mexico orders only;
not good to jobbers, wholesalers, or subscription agencies.)

☐ Check here if billing address is different from
shipping address and attach purchase order and
billing address information.

Signature_____

☐ **PAYMENT ENCLOSED: $**_____

☐ **PLEASE CHARGE TO MY CREDIT CARD.**

☐ Visa   ☐ MasterCard   ☐ AmEx   ☐ Discover
☐ Diners Club
Account #_____

Exp. Date_____

Signature_____

Prices in US dollars and subject to change without notice.

NAME_____

INSTITUTION_____

ADDRESS_____

CITY_____

STATE/ZIP_____

COUNTRY_____ COUNTY (NY residents only)_____

TEL_____ FAX_____

E-MAIL_____
May we use your e-mail address for confirmations and other types of information? ☐ Yes   ☐ No

Order From Your Local Bookstore or Directly From
The Haworth Press, Inc.
10 Alice Street, Binghamton, New York 13904-1580 • USA
TELEPHONE: 1-800-HAWORTH (1-800-429-6784) / Outside US/Canada: (607) 722-5857
FAX: 1-800-895-0582 / Outside US/Canada: (607) 772-6362
E-mail: getinfo@haworthpressinc.com
PLEASE PHOTOCOPY THIS FORM FOR YOUR PERSONAL USE.

BOF96